Schooler's Sagacity and Senility

Homilies

Year B

Schooler's Sagacity and Senility

Homilies

Year B

William C. Schooler

To the people of the parishes I have served.

In a special way, I am grateful to
Kevin Demetroff and John LaMaster
who have given me feedback and great criticisms
over the years in writing these homilies.

Contents

I	Advent

II   Christmas

III   Ordinary Time

IV   Lent

VII Feasts & Solemnities

VIII   Index

Preface

When I was ordained a deacon, the Bishop gave me a book of the Gospels and instructed me to study the Word of God, proclaim it faithfully, and put it into practice in my life. Over the years, I have tried to follow this command in my own halting and various ways. In many instances, you will find my words directed primarily at my own personal need for conversion.

William C. Schooler
June 3, 2020

Advent

1. 1st Sunday of Advent

Readings

Isaiah 63:16–17, 19; 64:2–7
1 Corinthians 1:3–9
Mark 13:33–37

1.1 November 28, 1999

Earlier this week, a member of our parish was describing her feelings about Advent. She had come to Saint Jude as a Candidate for Full Communion. She said that joining us at the Table of God's Word and growing in faith with us was a good experience. But when she came to this time of the year, she expected that the liturgy would be filled with lights, cheerful music, and sounds of "the Season." Instead, she was surprised by the quiet, subdued atmosphere of the First Sunday of Advent – the mood we encountered today when we gathered for Mass. But as time went on, she began to appreciate the sounds, the colors, and the very fabric of this Season. She knows that the best way to keep Christ in Christmas is to keep Advent.

There is no way to ignore the way our culture celebrates "the Season" that began last Thursday and generally ends on Christmas Day! Nor should we ignore it, because we share an incarnational faith. The lights can brighten our hearts at a dark time of the year. Shopping trips can be genuine adventures to find a fitting expression of love for someone else. Parties can be opportunities for people to celebrate the gift of life.

But during Advent, we gather here to focus on one reality – the coming of the Lord. The Lord has come already, born in poverty at a time people least expected him. We prepare to celebrate that coming at Christmas – the Season that begins on Christmas Eve and ends with the Lord's Baptism. We look for Jesus to come again – at the end of time. So, we watch and remain alert, as the Gospel urges us. And right between these two comings, we look for the Lord to come in ways that can be recognized only by faith. We look for him in the Word, in the Sacraments, and in the encounters of daily life.

We gather in darkness and quiet, because bright lights and blaring music can easily distract us from the ways the Lord comes in painful and difficult moments in our lives. We gather without the pressure of a culture saturated with consumerism, because we do not trust that expensive gifts can in themselves convey true love for others. We gather, not in a penitential or mournful way, but in a quiet mood, because we trust that the liturgies of Christmas will more than express our joy at as we mark the 2000th anniversary of the Lord's First Coming.

On the first Sunday of Advent in 1943, Dietrich Bonhoeffer, the German theologian and pastor, marked his seventh month in a Nazi prison in Berlin. He wrote the following words in a letter to his parents: "I like to think of your sitting with the children and keeping Advent with them, just as you used to years ago with us. Only we do everything more intensely now, as we don't know how much longer we have." That same day, he shared the following in a letter to a friend: "Life in a prison cell may well be compared to Advent. One waits, hopes and does this, that or the other – things that are of no consequence. The door is shut and can be opened only *from the outsi◆e.*"

We are waiting for the Lord to come from the outside and open the door to eternity for us. We have no idea when or how that will happen. But we do know the pattern of his coming, both from his first coming and his comings in our daily lives. Firmly rooted in those comings, we must watch, wait, hope and do everything more intensely now, because we do not know how much longer we have. Advent can teach us these lessons, if we only pause long enough to listen!

1.2   December 1, 2002

Jim Brandenburg is a professional photojournalist who normally takes hundreds of pictures each day. A few years ago, he spent three months in northern Minnesota, searching for the soul of his work. He made a pact with himself that he would take only one photograph a day. Each morning – from the fall equinox to the winter solstice – he got up early and walked through the woods, by rivers and lakes, looking for the day's one perfect image. One day in late October, he found himself at 4:30 p.m. without a picture. It had been raining all day, and he was tired and wet. Suddenly, he came upon a small pond, and there was the day's picture: a fallen red maple leaf floating on top of the water.

Our waiting for the Lord is like Jim Brandenburg waiting for that perfect image each day. Like Jim, we need the spiritual discipline to be poised and ready for his coming, because we cannot know when that will be. Advent reminds us of the three ways in which we wait for the Lord's coming. We wait to celebrate the first coming of the Lord at Christmas. We wait for the Second Coming of the Lord at the end of time. Caught between those two comings, today's Scriptures invite us to be alert and watchful for all the ways that the Lord comes to us in our daily live.

That kind of waiting can be difficult, because we sometimes feel Isaiah's impatience, wanting the Lord to rend the heavens and make his coming a little more evident and a little more dramatic. But that is not the Lord's pattern. His first coming was in a quiet backwater town in the Judean wilderness. Only those who had developed a pattern of contemplative silence and reflection noticed it. Advent invites us to practice that contemplative spirit as we remain alert for the coming of the Lord.

A contemporary spiritual author writes that there are three conditions present in our world that work against developing this contemplative spirit – Narcissism, pragmatism, and an "unbridled restlessness." As we begin this Season of waiting, it might not be a bad idea to take a look at each one.

Narcissism is characterized by an unhealthy self-absorption. If we are too busy worrying about our own comforts, our own fulfillment, and our own interests, we cannot notice the ways that the Lord comes in the form of those in need. That is why Advent is a good time for projects like the Giving Tree. They invite us to look beyond our own needs to recognize the Lord coming in the needs of others.

We Americans are pragmatic, because we are practical and get things done. But pragmatism works against a contemplative spirit when we look at people only in terms of how much they can produce. Advent is a good time to spend time with people who cannot repay us for our kindness. With a contemplative spirit, we might catch a glimpse of the Lord's coming in a visit to a nursing home. Or we might be open to the Lord's coming, when we sit with someone who usually eats alone in the cafeteria at school.

If there is any season of the year that encourages an "unbridled restlessness," it is this time between Thanksgiving and Christmas. So many things in our culture tell us to get out and enjoy the "Season," entering as many different experiences as possible. Advent invites us to slow down and spend some time in silence.

Through this new Season of Advent, the Lord is extending to each of us a personal invitation to become a bit more contemplative in our lives, knowing that we can count on God's faithfulness, even when we have not been faithful in return. Seeking this contemplative stance is really not more difficult than what Jim Brandenburg did with his camera – slowing down, walking more slowly, and paying attention to what lies in the path of our lives.

1.3   November 27, 2005

The prophet Isaiah speaks for his people when he tells God everything that has gone wrong. He laments their suffering in exile. He laments the death and destruction all around him. He laments the sins that caused the downfall of Jerusalem. In his lament, he begs God to rend the heavens and come down to fix things.

Isaiah also speaks for us. We have no problem listing all those things that need fixing in our world, our community, and our lives. However, there is one huge difference between the contemporaries of Isaiah and us. God **has** rent the heavens, and God **has** come down to "fix things". That is why we observe this Season of Advent. We wait to celebrate the Lord's first coming in the Mystery of the Incarnation at Christmas. In the person of Jesus Christ, God has come down to us and made his dwelling among us. In a culture that goes into overdrive at this time of the year, Advent gives us space to prepare to celebrate that first coming so that the Mystery can better penetrate our hearts.

Advent also carves out for us a time to wait for the second coming of Christ, when the Lord will come for us at the end of our lives or at the end of the ages. Because we can never know the time of that coming, Jesus insists that we remain watchful and alert, not in fear and trembling, but in confident faith, hope, and love.

In the colonial times of our country, a state assembly was meeting in New England when an eclipse of the sun plunged the gathering into darkness. Some legislators panicked, fearing that it was the end of the world. Others moved to adjourn. But one of them said, "Mr. Speaker, if it is not the end of the world and we adjourn, we shall appear to be fools. If it is the end of the world, I choose to be found doing my duty. I move that candles be brought."

We celebrate Advent at this darkest time of the year. Taking a cue from that legislator, we lit the first candle on the Advent Wreath at the beginning of this Mass. Rather than jumping into the distractions of the "Holiday Season," we are invited to sit in the darkness for a while and reflect on the light of the Lord's presence in our lives, situated between his First Coming at Christmas and his Second Coming at the end of time. God has already rent the heavens and come down in the person of Jesus Christ. We wait in a watchful and alert way, doing our duty, confident that the Lord comes daily through our efforts to serve him. No matter what dark or difficult situations may confront us, Paul reminds us that God is faithful, and that he will strengthen us to the end.

We hear many pleas to keep Christ in Christmas. The best way to keep Christ in Christmas is to keep Advent. Allow the Advent Liturgies to set a tone for these next four weeks. A week from next Sunday, we offer the communal anointing of the sick for the first time in our parish. Bring those who are struggling with the darkness of illness to the healing light of Christ's presence. Come to Lessons and Carols next Sunday evening after the 5:30 Mass. Make it a priority to celebrate the Sacrament of Reconciliation – either at the Communal Advent Penance Service or individually before Christmas. God has rent the heavens and come down. Advent invites us to believe that mystery and make it a more integral part of our lives.

1.4 November 30, 2008

The first readers of Mark's Gospel lived in dangerous times. They had accepted the Good News of Jesus Christ and had been formed into the community of faith through baptism. Instead of bringing them peace and security, their faith brought them persecution and hardship. In recording these words of Jesus, Mark urges his readers to remain watchful and alert. In the midst of the dangers facing them, the Lord would return again, as he had promised.

We too live in dangerous times. The terrorist attacks in Mumbai, India, remind us that we remain vulnerable to random acts of violence. Our economy remains uncertain. Some of you close to retirement have lost almost everything in your retirement accounts. Others cannot afford to pay their next house payment. We watch and wait to see which company will go under next and local jobs with them. We understand the words of the prophet Isaiah, who also lived in uncertain times. With him, we want to ask the Lord to "... rend the heavens and come down."

As the seasonal change of limited daylight at this time of the year matches our mood, we light this first candle of the Advent Wreath to express our desire for the Lord to rend the heavens and come down. In doing that, we are reminded that the Lord has in fact already done that. The Lord rent the heavens and came down as a tiny child born in a stable in Bethlehem. Advent prepares us to celebrate that First Coming and to understand the pattern of that first coming – when the Lord came in poverty, humility, and gentleness.

At the same time, Advent prepares us for his Second Coming – at the end of our lives and at the end of time.

Strictly speaking, Advent is not a penitential season, in the same way as Lent is a penitential season. We wear purple during Advent and show restraint in the liturgy as a way of preparing ourselves, being watchful for that day when the Lord comes to us. However, in making those preparations, we know that there are those changes we must make in our lives if the Lord would come back now to find us watching and waiting.

The best strategy for making the necessary changes is to take Advent seriously. We need to allow the texture of our Sunday liturgies to sink into our hearts. You are welcome to join us on the Tuesday evenings of Advent for the special communal prayers, and to bring those who are sick with you next Sunday to the Communal Anointing of the Sick. Take advantage of the Sacrament of Reconciliation, either at the Advent Penance Service two weeks from Tuesday night, or at one of the individual times which we will offer more frequently before Christmas. If you have not done so already, take a tag from the Giving Tree and participate in bringing Christ's presence to the poor. Take an Advent *Magnifcat* (located at all the doors) for your daily prayer, and use the bulletin inserts as ways of incorporating Advent into your home.

I would be wasting my time and breath in saying that we should avoid all "holiday" events at this time of the year. Those "holiday" events are part of our culture, and we cannot escape them. However, in the midst of the "holiday season," we can incorporate Advent into our lives and homes. When we take Advent seriously – in preparing for the Second Coming of the Lord and for celebrating his First Coming at Christmas – we open ourselves to the third way that the Lord comes to us. Being alert and watchful keeps our eyes and ears open to the many ways in which he comes to us now in our daily lives. He comes to us in this Word, and he will come to us in the Eucharist. Fed by those comings during Advent, we might just be surprised at the many unexpected ways he comes to us now, in the people we encounter, in the situations we find ourselves, and even in the dark quiet of this time of the year.

1.5 November 27, 2011

On this first day of the Liturgical Year, Jesus invites us to consider where we are on our pilgrimage of life. As God's people, we are traveling together on a journey that will ultimately lead us to fullness of his presence in the New and Eternal Jerusalem. At some point in our pilgrimage, the Lord will come to call us home, at the end of our individual lives, and at the end of the world. Because none of us knows that time, Jesus calls us to be alert and watchful.

Martin Sheen recently made a movie about a pilgrimage. He plays a widowed eye doctor at odds with his son, Daniel. He is strongly disappointed when his son abandons his graduate studies to travel the world. When Daniel is killed in a freak accident in the Pyrenees, he goes to a small town in France to claim his body. He discovers that his son was beginning the ancient pilgrimage route to Santiago de Compostela in Spain. On an impulse, he decides to walk the 800 kilometers with his son's ashes to the church where the bones of Saint James are buried.

On the way, the grumpy guy meets three other people. A bitter Canadian divorcee is making the pilgrimage to quit smoking. A Dutch man intends to lose weight. An Irishman wants to write a new novel. On the way, all three are gradually transformed. The divorcee finds forgiveness and acceptance. The Dutchman discovers the kindness and joy within him. The Irishman recovers his lost faith. The eye doctor gains a new appreciation of his dead son. Each one, in very different ways, learns from the journey how to surrender to those forces beyond their control. It is the same lesson we learned four years ago when some of us made that same pilgrimage as a parish group.

That is what Advent can do for us. Advent invites us to take another look at our pilgrimage, and learn the lessons taught by Isaiah. Isaiah reminds us that we are like clay in the hands of our potter. God, the potter, is forming us into the persons he created. Advent invites us to take another look at what is happening on our pilgrimage and surrender to the ways God uses the events in our lives to form us. We watch and wait for the coming of the Lord at the end of our pilgrimage. We watch and wait to celebrate the first coming of the Lord at Christmas. In watching and waiting, we recognize the Lord present in our pilgrimage now, slowly, gradually transforming us, to the extent to which we allow God to do that.

Our culture calls this time of the year "the Holiday Season." The Holiday Season invites us to get up in the middle of the night on Thanksgiving to find fulfillment in Black Friday deals. The Holiday Season tells us that we can cover up the darkness and cold of this time of the year by stringing up lights, surrounding ourselves with "holiday" music, and occupying our time with "holiday" parties. The "Holiday Season" tries to convince us that we can carefully plan and manipulate the "end" of the Holiday Season on December 25.

Advent's message is very different. Advent invites us to dwell in the darkness and cold, humbling acknowledging our sins and failures. Advent invites us to recognize that God can speak to us even in the darkest of the events of our lives. Advent reminds us that there is only one Light that can possibly satisfy our deepest long-ings – the Light of Christ manifested during the Christmas Season, which begins on December 25 and lasts through the Baptism of the Lord.

Advent has much to offer us as fellow pilgrims. We can embrace the spirit of our Advent Liturgies. We can benefit from the Tuesday night Advent liturgies. We can acknowledge our sins and receive the Lord's mercy in the Sacrament of Reconciliation. We can learn to wait in joyful hope, surrendering ourselves to the God who walks each step with us on our pilgrimage which ends not in Santiago, but in the New and Eternal Jerusalem.

1.6   November 30, 2014

The prophet Isaiah gives voice to the frustrations of his people. Living some 600 years before Christ, They had seen the Babylonians destroy Jerusalem, demolish their sacred temple, and murder their king. Worse, they had been in exile in Babylon for almost fifty years. They had come to realize that the prophet Jeremiah had been correct in telling them to turn back to their Covenant with God and had seen their exile as God's punishment for not listening. Now, completely dispirited, they beg God to rend the heavens and come down and save them.

As we begin this new Liturgical Year, we enter into the Season of Advent to consider how God saves us. God answered the prayers of the exiles in Babylon by rending the heavens with a pagan King, Cyrus of Persia, who issued a decree allowing the refugees to return home. In a few weeks, we will celebrate the Christmas, when the Father sent his only begotten Son to rend the heavens and come down to save us as a tiny child born into poverty. This Season of Advent has the potential to teach us valuable lessons about how we can prepare for the ways that God rends the heavens to come down to save us.

The first lesson is countercultural. We live in a culture of immediate results. In our world of instant communication, we can be in touch with everyone at the tap of the "send" button. That means that we can send angry and hurtful emotions without looking into the face of the one who receives our messages. One of my nieces assumed that we are all against her when she got married last summer and "unfriended" all of us, even those of us who do not have a clue about using Facebook. Our culture has been observing the "Holiday Season" since the first of November, and the voice of consumerism promises instant gratification to those who shop.

In contrast, Advent invites us to wait. Advent tells us that there is value in backing off from the glare of lights and holiday gatherings to spend time in prayer and contemplation. In prayer and contemplation, we can hear the ways in which we have not listened to the authentic prophets of our day and have strayed from the Lord's Covenant of love. The more contemplative style of our Advent liturgies sets the tone for the season. Take one of the resources at the doors of church to help in daily prayer and contemplation at home. Come to the devotional prayers on Tuesday nights during Advent, including the communal Penance Service on the last Tuesday before Christmas. We will offer many opportunities for the Sacrament of Reconciliation, allowing us to look at the ways in which we have ignored the Lord's presence and to begin again.

The second lesson comes from today's Gospel. As we prepare to celebrate the way the Lord has rent the heavens and come down to save us a child, we are aware that he will rend the heavens at the end of time to bring to completion his work of salvation. None of us knows when the Lord will rend the heavens to come to us at the moment of our death or at the end of the world. For that reason, we are to be watchful and alert. Prayer and contemplation can help us understand that being watchful and alert does not mean that we cower in fear, worrying that we will be caught doing something wrong. It means that we are actively engaged in living our Baptismal promises, being awake to the ways in which we connect with other people to make our world a more welcoming place for the coming of the Lord.

Finally, when we combine prayer and contemplation with watching and being alert, we will be much more conscious of the ways that the Lord rends the heavens and comes to us now. To use Isaiah's image, we are the clay, and the Lord is the potter who is forming us. The Lord does that in the sacramental life of the Church. With our eyes, ears, hearts, and minds opened by these real encounters, we become more aware of the ways in which he is forming us now.

1.7   December 3, 2017

In this new Liturgical Year, we hear from the Gospel according to Saint Mark. His audience would have been very interested in the subject of the Second Coming of the Lord. Even more, they wanted to know when he would come again. In response, Mark records this parable of the gatekeeper. The master who has traveled abroad is Jesus himself. The servants whom he left in charge are his disciples. No one knows the time when the Lord will come again. Instead of knowing the time of the Second Coming, the disciples need to be alert and watchful.

Jesus tells this parable just before the Passover which will begin his passion. The master who left on the journey gives each of the servants a task to be accomplished, according to each one's abilities. The gatekeeper is to be watchful for his return, alert that he may return during the non-working hours: dinner, midnight, pre-dawn, and early morning. Ironically, these are the precise hours when the important events of Jesus' passion would take place. Just a few days later, he would share a final meal with his disciples and give himself to them in the form of bread and wine. At midnight, he would ask Peter, James, and John to watch and pray during his agony. Instead of being alert, they will fall asleep. When Jesus would be betrayed by one of his closest friends in the garden, most of them would run away in fear. At cockcrow, Peter would abandon any idea of being alert to Jesus and deny knowing him three times. In the morning, Jesus would be handed over to Pontius Pilate to be condemned to death. Instead of being alert to these crucial moments in their master's passion, they would be hiding.

We are the servants whom the Lord has put in charge. He has given each of us talents to be invested in his Kingdom. We do not know the time of his Second Coming, either at the end of time or at the end of our lives. But he will come again, and he tells us that we must be alert and watchful, especially at those times when we want to run away from the implications of his passion. We listen to him and feast on his Body and Blood at this Eucharist, the Memorial of the Last Supper. We are sent from this Eucharist to be watchful, especially in those dark moments when we share in Christ's agony and passion. We must remain alert, even when we deny knowing Christ by our sinful actions. We remain alert when we are handed over to carry some heavy cross that seems to crush us.

This is why the Church gives us the Season of Advent. It is easy to fall into a spiritual stupor and become so self-indulgent that we do not consider the Lord's presence in our daily lives. Advent reminds us that the Lord will come again, and that we need to be alert and watchful. Being alert and watchful does not mean that we lock ourselves up and huddle together in fear, worrying that some crazy person will break in and start shooting at us. Instead, we need to be attentive to one another during those darkest times of our lives.

This Advent is the shortest possible Season with only 22 days. The Fourth Sunday of Advent falls on Christmas Eve. Ironically, we can miss the opportunities to become more alert and watchful with our frantic efforts to prepare to celebrate the Lord's first coming at Christmas. Please take advantage of Advent. Take one of the books we offer for private prayer. Come to Lessons and Carols on Tuesday night. Go to the Sacrament of Reconciliation sometime during this Season to confess those times we have fallen into a spiritual stupor and focused only on ourselves. The Lord is coming again at some time which we do not know. We need to be alert and watchful, not living in fear and dread, but giving ourselves in prayer and humble service. Even those who hid experienced another morning – the morning of the Lord's resurrection.

2. 2nd Sunday of Advent

Readings

Isaiah 40:1–5, 9–11
2 Peter 3:8–14
Mark 1:1–8

2.1   December 5, 1999

When doctors informed Cardinal Bernardin of Chicago that he had
terminal liver and pancreatic cancer, they told him that he probably had less than six months to live. He responded to the news by
expressing gratitude that he had been given time to prepare himself to meet the Lord. In his book, *Gift of Peace*, Cardinal Bernardin
said, "Many people have asked me why I'm at peace . First of all,
you have to put yourself totally in the hands of the Lord. Secondly,
you have to begin seeing death not so much as an enemy but as a
friend . Thirdly, you have to begin letting go."

The earliest Christians fully expected Jesus to come again
within their lifetimes. As they began to ask why the second coming
was being delayed, the author of the second letter of Peter gives an
interesting answer. He argues that God's sense of time is different
from ours. For God, one day is as a thousand years, and a thousand
years as a day. He tells his listeners (including us!) that we should
not worry about the exact timing of the Lord's second coming –
either in terms of our own death or the end of the world. Instead,
like Cardinal Bernardin, we need to see time as a gift from God so
we can "make every effort to be found without stain or defilement
and at peace in God's sight."

Advent invites us to use that gift of time in preparing for the Lord's coming. We use some of it preparing to celebrate the first coming of the Lord at Christmas. But we need to invest much more time preparing for the Lord's second coming. None of us can be found without stain or defilement at this moment! We have erected mountains out of our pride that block the Lord's coming into our lives each day. Those mountains support the illusion that we are in control and that we can determine our own destiny. We have developed deep ruts of bad habits that swallow up God's initiatives. Among those habits is a tendency to blame everyone else for our problems. When we shift the blame, we can gossip by finding delight in the faults of other people.

A great way to use the gift of time is to take advantage of the Sacrament of Reconciliation in Advent. We sometimes avoid the sacrament, because we know that exposing our mountains and ruts to the purifying fire of God's love is painful. But taking the time to deal with our mountains and ruts pays off in the end. There are several communal Reconciliation Services scheduled in the area, beginning next Sunday. Father Bob and I have set aside more times for individual Reconciliation, as we get closer to Christmas. Those times are listed in this week's bulletin.

Someone sent me a wonderful saying last week: "Live your life in such a way that you feel free enough to sell the family parrot to the town gossip." We don't need to sell our family parrots or bear our souls to the parish! You young people do not need to stand up in the middle of school and tell all your faults. But in the light of the second coming of Jesus, when all our sins will be revealed, this is a good time now to confront them! We can do that in a confidential and grace-filled sacrament designed to give the gift of peace when we bring our sins to the purifying fire of God's love.

2.2   December 8, 2002

A middle-aged school teacher invested her life savings in a business enterprise that looked like it would make her rich. A swindler had talked her into the elaborate and convincing plan. When her investment collapsed and she saw her dreams of becoming a wealthy woman disappear into thin air, she went to the office of the Better Business Bureau. The bureau staff listened to her story with great sympathy, but also with great amazement. "Why on earth didn't you come to us first? This could have been prevented! Didn't you know about the Better Business Bureau?" "Oh yes, I did," said the woman sadly. "I've always known about you. But I didn't call, because I was afraid you'd tell me not to do it."

Every Advent, we hear the same message from John the Baptist, demanding that we embrace the spirit and meaning of our baptism

– to become more compassionate, more forgiving, more just, and less selfish. Like the swindled schoolteacher, we know that John's message is true. But, like the school teacher, we ignore his message. We are so accustomed to walking our crooked roads, trying to find our own way to happiness, that we ignore John's call to make a straight path into our lives for the Lord. We prefer to keep rushing around, leaving little time for prayer or reflection. We become short with those we love – our families and coworkers. We continue to lie to our parents, because we know that if they knew the truth, we would have to change our lifestyle. Behaviors like these are the mountains and valleys in our lives – those obstacles that keep God far away from us. We want to ignore them and continue to live our lives as we please.

This Second Sunday of Advent gives us a new chance to listen to John again. Dressed in camel hair and speaking from the Judean Wilderness, John has the credentials of a prophet. He speaks for God. Even his food has a message. In the Ancient Middle East, vast swarms of locusts (or grasshoppers) would consume an entire seasonal crop. The prophets saw these destructions as instruments of God's judgment. Honey, on the other hand, signified peace and plenty. The Israelites returning from their slavery in Egypt saw honey as an expression of God's comfort and care.

In eating locusts, John challenges us to take a hard look at our lives and make a judgment about what is destroying us, what is tearing us apart, and what peaks and valleys keep God at arm's length. In the second reading, Peter reminds us that God will make that judgment when the Lord comes again in glory. He argues that we might as well face the truth about our lives right now, before it is too late!

In eating honey, John tells us that God will provide comfort and care to those who repent. In the first reading, our translation instructs the prophet to speak "tenderly" to the people, telling them that their punishment is at an end. A better translation of the original Hebrew says that the prophet should speak "to the heart" of the people. Ancient people regarded the heart as the seat of the intellect and the will. God speaks to us, appealing to our minds and memories. God wants us to think seriously about the need for real change in our lives. God wants us to remember those times when we experienced the sweet honey of comfort and care when we made some important changes in our lives.

The best way to deal with locusts is in the Sacrament of Reconciliation. You can either choose the Advent Penance Service a week from Monday. Or, you can come during the individual times just before Christmas. The Sacrament is an excellent tool to open our spiritual lives what locusts did to fields – stripping them of all that blocks us from God. Once stripped, the honey of God's comfort and care is abundant. Like the swindled school teacher, we know how to open ourselves to the God who comes to save us. Advent encourages us to do it now!

2.3 December 4, 2005

People do not go into a desert to maintain their status quo. The Book of Exodus says that a group of slaves left Egypt and went into the desert to learn how to become free people. Isaiah tells his people that they will be freed from their captivity in Babylon and enter the rough terrain of the desert to return home to Jerusalem. John the Baptist entered the desert, wore distinctive clothing, ate desert food, and pointed to a completely new reality – the coming of the Messiah and the Son of God.

As we light the second candle of our Advent Wreath, the Baptist urges us to enter more deeply into the spirit of the Advent desert to see how our lives need to be changed. In the light of the Second Coming of Christ, which the letter of Peter says is certain, and in the light of the First Coming of Christ, which we are waiting to celebrate in three weeks, the Baptist calls us to repentance, to look for ways to change our lives.

A friend of Father Dan's is pastor of an Italian parish in the Bronx. Father Eddie Whalen has already provided ample homiletic material for Father Dan from his colorful parish, and he did so again last week via e-mail. Some parishioners had heard that a piece of the tablecloth from the Last Supper was included in the Fra Angelico exhibit at the Metropolitan Museum of Art. So, four busses took them to Manhattan, laden with huge amounts of food to sustain them for such a lengthy journey. When they arrived, they immediately destroyed any sense of decorum at the Met, rushed to the exhibit hall, and began screaming the rosary in front of the paintings. The "cultured people" of the art world were horrified. As Father Eddie apologized to various people for their behavior, a docent referred to them as "quaintly folkloric." In Father Eddie's own words, "they terrorized the museum today – and had a great time." Instead of quietly viewing an exhibit of Italian art, they overturned the expectations of the museum by responding in their own way to Fra Angelico's original intention in creating the pictures – to bring people to prayer after reflecting on the sacred images portrayed on canvas.

I am not suggesting that we load ourselves on busses and disrupt the Fra Angelico exhibit when it comes to Chicago. Instead, we might reflect on changes that need to be made in our lives that might upset the status quo of our society or the expectations of other people. Those of you who are in high school know that your behavior will not change if you remain with the same group of friends that support your bad choices. You need to enter the desert of finding a new group of friends. Those who have gone through a twelve-step program know that it is impossible to remain sober if you keep hanging out with the guys at the bar. Staying sober requires the desert of changing those habits. If we find ourselves trapped in the temptation to view pornography on the Internet, we know that change will only happen in the desert of putting restrictions on the computer.

Advent calls us to behave differently, to enter into a desert of change in order to prepare ourselves to celebrate the First Coming of Christ and to be ready for his Second Coming. Come to the Advent Penance Service a week from Monday. Christ comes in that Sacrament to free us of the baggage to start over. If you are discouraged by chronic illness, come to the Communal Anointing next Sunday. The Coming of Christ in that Sacrament can strengthen you to face your illness with greater hope and trust. Christ is coming for us. In the light of the ways in which he comes, Advent provides a desert where changes can be made, so he will recognize us, when he comes.

2.4 December 7, 2008

During this Season, we are busy running around, looking for the perfect gift to give to those whom we love. We know that a perfect gift is not measured by how much it costs, but by how it expresses our love for that person. The perfect gift is a reflection of the ultimate gift given to us at Christmas – the gift of God himself carefully wrapped in the form of a child born into poverty. As we search for those gifts for others, the Second Letter of Saint Peter tells us of another gift that God has given to us. He reminds us of the certainty of the Second Coming of Jesus Christ – at the end of our lives and at the end of the ages. He tells us that the Lord has delayed that second coming to give us a gift: the gift of time to get our act together.

When we take Advent seriously, we accept the gift of time and pay attention to the words of John the Baptist – repent and change your ways! God's gift of time gives us a chance to take a good, honest, and courageous look at our lives and make some changes, before he comes at a time when we least expect him and finds us unprepared. It takes a certain amount of courage and honesty to use God's gift of time. It is much easier to identify the mountains that block relationships and the valleys that become barriers to love in the lives of other people, especially in the lives of the people with whom we live or work. Even when we take the time to consider our own mountains and valleys, we are tempted to be very general and speak of being nicer or have vague thoughts of changing our priorities. Real change happens only when we deal with the specific mountains and valleys that block the coming of Christ in our own lives.

That is why we are given another gift at this time of the year – the Sacrament of Reconciliation (or Confession or Penance or whatever you want to call it). When we encounter the Lord for whom we wait in this Sacrament, we must be specific about those mountains and valleys in our lives. In examining our conscience and speaking our sins, we are giving back to God what he wants most from us. When we honestly and courageously speak our sins, we are taking all the trash, all the garbage, and all that smells really bad in our lives and carefully wrapping it up in a beautiful package and giving it back to God. A certain pastor of a neighboring parish (Queen of Peace) suggested this image at his Penance Service last week, and it has stayed with me ever since. He is correct. When we have the courage to be very specific about our sins and say them, it really is like wrapping the trash as a gift and giving it to God. We are submitting all that trash to the locusts of God's judgment. Those locusts consume the gift we give and give us back the honey of God's mercy and love.

I can tell that more of you of you have truly heard our consistent pleas to take Advent seriously, because so many of you are teasing me about being the "Grinch" that is stealing the holiday season. I gleefully accept that charge, because it separates all the noise and glitter and busyness of a secular "Holiday Season" from the more hopeful and profound message of the Season of Advent. Advent enables us to accept God's gift of time to get our act together, as we prepare for the Second Coming of Christ lives. The Sacrament of Reconciliation opens our hearts and minds to Christ coming into our lives, as we have the honesty and courage to identify exactly what needs to change. More than anything else, Advent becomes the straight path that allows us to celebrate Christ's First Coming at Christmas in a way that will truly bring us peace. In the desert of frightening economic news, job losses, and terrorism, the gift of internal peace at Christmas is the best gift we can possibly receive from the God who took flesh in our world.

2.5   December 4, 2011

The Second Letter of Saint Peter is addressed to a community wondering about the final aspect of the Paschal Mystery. They believed that the Lord had died, been raised from the dead, ascended into heaven, and sent the Holy Spirit to the Church. But, he had not come again in glory yet, and some were teaching that he would not return again. Peter's letter insists that his coming is certain, even if it has been delayed. The letter argues that the Lord looks on time differently than we do. Whether his day lasts 24 hours or a thousand years, he will come again. In the light of that sure fact, the letter invites us to consider the patience of God and accept it into our lives, as we patiently prepare ourselves for the coming of the Lord at the end.

If we are honest with ourselves, we have more in common with the community of Peter than we care to admit. Because the Lord has delayed his coming for over two thousand years now, we seldom give a second thought to this part of the Mystery of Faith. We carry on with our lives as if there will be no end point.

That is why we need to hear these Scriptures from Advent so much. John the Baptist dresses in camel's hair to remind us of the power of Elijah to renew God's Covenant with us. He eats locusts as a sign of God's judgment and honey as a sign of God's mercy. Echoing the Prophet Isaiah, he tells us to clear the path for the coming of our God. In the ancient world, hundreds of workers would descend on a road to prepare it for a king to travel on it. They would clear all obstacles and fill all potholes, so that the king could ride in his carriage or on his royal animal more smoothly.

Given the certainty of the Lord's coming, both at the end of our individual lives and at the end of the world, the Scriptures invite us to use the time God has given us now to make a clear path for the coming of the Lord. Instead of being paralyzed by fear, we can take an honest look at ourselves, applying the locusts of God's judgment to our lives now. Taking a look will reveal bad habits that have become obstacles that make God's coming into our lives more difficult. It is always easier to see the bad habits developed by others. For example, I find myself becoming more annoyed by the bad habit of those who leave Mass right after Communion. But, focusing on the bad habits of others can keep me from noticing the bad habits in my own life. We might be in the bad habit of not telling the truth, leading us to lie, even when we don't have to. Or we can easily slip into habits of talking about others behind their backs, or judging those who are different from us, or being lazy, or many other obstacles that block the Lord's coming.

Clearing our lives of bad habits is not an easy task. We can get an insight from the changes in the translation of the Mass. Consider how difficult it has been to make those changes. We have been so accustomed to responding "and also with you" that it is going to take a long time to get into the habit of responding "and with your spirit." With effort, time, and God's grace, we will make these adjustments, until we form the new habits of liturgical speech.

The same is true with the obstacles in our lives. We can bring our bad habits to the locusts of God's judgment in the Sacrament of Reconciliation. The honey of God's mercy will give us another chance to put in a little more effort, take some more time, and work with God's grace to replace the bad habits with good habits. The honey of God's mercy will prepare us to celebrate the First Coming of the Lord at Christmas. Even more, the honey of God's mercy will open our eyes to the ways in which the Lord comes to us every day.

2.6 December 7, 2014

By the time the Second Letter of Saint Peter was written, it was clear that the Lord Jesus would not be coming back any time soon. As a result, some began preaching that the Lord would not come again and that there would be no final judgment. To that error, the author, writing in the name of the Apostle, responded that the Lord would definitely come again. He has not delayed his promise. Instead, he has delayed his second coming.

Using the metaphor that one day with the Lord is a thousand years; it has been two "days" since the Paschal Mystery. In our day, we are also tempted to live as if the Lord will not come again and as if there will be no judgment at the end of time. For that reason, we need to hear the author telling us to be vigilant, a lesson we learned two times on our Pilgrimage last summer. Had we been more vigilant in Lucca, our bicycles would not have been stolen. Had we been more vigilant in Rome, thieves would not have taken all the rest of our belongings. If we could go back in time, we would have behaved differently. We would have walked our bikes through the streets of Lucca and taken turns sitting with the bikes while visiting local churches. We would have unloaded our luggage first in Rome and then gone to Saint Peter's Square to celebrate our arrival after 1,200 miles. But, we cannot go back in time. We can only learn from those lessons and do things differently if we ever do something like this again.

The author of the Second Letter of Saint Peter knows that we cannot go back in time. Instead, he provides a reason for the Lord delaying his second coming. By delaying his second coming, the Lord is providing us valuable time to look back on ways we have not been vigilant and to use the time remaining as a gift to change our ways. To use the image of the Prophet Isaiah, the Season of Advent gives us time to make straight the way of the Lord, so that he can come directly into our lives. We can remove the mountains that have become obstacles and fill in the valleys that have become pitfalls for the Lord to come to us in an intimate way.

John the Baptist provides ways of using the time in this Season of Advent. John's father was a priest in the Temple of Jerusalem. He helped people to prepare the paschal lambs for sacrifice to ask God for reconciliation. That is not where John speaks in today's Gospel. John has gone to the wilderness, to the quiet of the desert, where his ancestors had found God in their Exodus from Egypt. From that barren place, he points to the coming of God's only begotten Son, who will become the real Lamb of God sacrificed, not in a sacred Temple, but on a hill where criminals were executed outside the city walls. That sacrifice will become the perfect sacrifice that reconciles us with the Father. As recipients of that sacrifice, we are formed into a living Temple guided by the gift of the Holy Spirit given to us when we were baptized.

John the Baptist eats locusts, which speak of God's judgment, and honey that speaks of God's mercy. John invites us to take some time from the craziness of our culture's holiday season to use Advent as a time to look back on ways in which we have not been vigilant and aware of the Lord's presence and change those patterns of behavior in the time given to us by the Lord. One very real way of using this gift of time is to make a good confession. Come to the Advent Penance Service a week from Tuesday. There will be 17 priests. Together, we hear the Word of God that can open our eyes to God's judgment on our failures. Individually, we encounter the Lord's mercy in the Sacrament. As we wait for others to do the same, we sit in the quiet to be with the Lord. Through the Sacrament of Reconciliation, the fire of the Lord's love burns away our sins. In experiencing the fire of that love, we can face the fire of the Lord's Second Coming with vigilance and without fear.

2.7 December 10, 2017

The words of the Prophet Isaiah are addressed to a people who are suffering greatly. Those few remaining children of Abraham had witnessed the execution of their leaders, the complete destruction of Jerusalem, and the dismantling of their Temple. Now they are languishing in exile in Babylon. Isaiah is honest with them. They have brought this destruction upon themselves. But he also tells them that God has not abandoned them. With tenderness, he tells them that their time of suffering is about to end. He promises that God will lead them through the wilderness back to their own land. Just as God had filled in the valleys and leveled the hills for their ancestors in the desert between Egypt and the Promised Land, God would now accompany them in their return to Jerusalem. In the desert, God is giving them a new beginning.

Saint Mark remembers those words as he sits down to write his Gospel, which literally means "the proclamation of joyful tidings."

Mark echoes the words of the Book of Genesis: In the beginning, God created the heavens and the earth. In the person of Jesus Christ, the Son of God, God is beginning something new. John the Baptist is not proclaiming these joyful tidings in the sacred Temple, where his father serves as a priest. He proclaims them in the desert, in that barren wilderness where God walks with his people and calls them to pursue new beginnings. He is not wearing the sacred vestments that were his as a member of the tribe of Levi. He is wearing the rough garments of Elijah the prophet, who called his people to repent of walking away from God. He is not eating the rich foods in Jerusalem. He is eating the locusts and honey consumed by his ancestors in their 40 day journey through the desert to the Promised Land.

John the Baptist speaks to us in the darkness of our world. We live at a time where there are so many deep divisions between groups of people. Not only are there dangerous tensions between nations, but there are steep mountains of arrogance and deep valleys of distrust dividing so many in our country. If we are to embrace his glad tidings of a new beginning, we must enter the desert. We must repent. The Greek word for repentance is metanoia, which implies a complete change of mind and heart. In other words, we need to take a good look at the ways in which we have dug valleys that separate us from people we don't like or don't agree with. We need to admit that we have built up mountains of pride that focus our attention on ourselves and our own needs, forgetting the needs of those around us. It is the Holy Spirit who can help us to fill in these valleys and level these mountains – the same Spirit who raised Jesus from the dead an in whom we have been baptized. Then the glory of the Lord will be revealed!

This Second Sunday of Advent is surrounded by two feasts honoring Mary, the Mother of God. On Friday, we celebrated the Solemnity of the Immaculate Conception. We recalled that the Virgin Mary became the new Eve by recognizing that she was truly free when she trusted the Word of the angel and agreed to do God's will. On Tuesday, we will celebrate the Feast of Our Lady of Guadalupe, a feast central to the experience of so many of our brothers and sisters in our sister parish of Saint Adalbert. Our Lady had entered into the culture of Saint Juan Diego, and she remains in the mess of our culture as the Patroness of the Americas, pointing to her Son.

These main figures of the Advent Season speak to us. The Prophets Isaiah and John the Baptist call us to look for a new beginning, as Mary had the courage to do. Take some time to listen to these figures. Retreat for a few moments from the noise and sounds of the "Holiday Season and spend some time alone in the desert which is known as Advent.   Make a really good Confession sometime before Christmas.   The Lord invites us to travel through repentance to meet him, not only as a child born in a stable, but as the Lord who returns to set us free.

3. 3rd Sunday of Advent

Readings
Isaiah 61:1–2a, 10–11
1 Thessalonians 5:16–24
John 1:6–8, 19–28

3.1 December 12, 1999

Saint Paul knew the difference between being *happy* and being *joyful*. There were plenty of occasions in his life when pleasant circumstances caused happiness. At this time of the year, you children are look forward to Christmas with a lot of happiness. Merchants are certainly happy as they ring up sales. We can be happy as we enjoy a party with friends. But Paul also knew some pretty tough times in his life – when he was run out of town, or when he was shipwrecked on one of his journeys, or when he was held in prison at the end of his life. Even at those times when life was not exactly *happy*, Paul could encourage other to rejoice – to know the "joy" of a heart filled with faith.

The people who lived in Jerusalem during the 6th Century before Christ had few reasons to be *happy*. They had returned from a fifty-year exile to find that their homes and businesses and fields had been destroyed. The Temple no longer existed. Even worse, the physical destruction symbolized the loss of the spiritual status with God that had been destroyed by sin. So, moved by God's spirit, the prophet Isaiah announced the glad tidings that God was granting them a year of favor. All their debts were being wiped out. God was giving them another chance. God would be present to bring about a joy that had little to do with their physical surroundings.

In that same spirit, Pope John Paul II has announced that our Jubilee Year will begin on Christmas Eve. Like the Biblical year of favor, the year 2000 will be a new beginning. It will not be a time to fear the end of the world or worry about whatever disasters we might bring upon ourselves. The Jubilee Year is intended as a time of joy, when we are invited to see how God works in our lives. Like the ancient Hebrews, we will be invited to forgive old debts, to free those we have held in any kind of slavery, and to allow our hearts to be softened.

It is my hope that in this coming Jubilee Year, we can see more clearly how the Holy Spirit works with us. Taking Paul's advice, we cannot quench the Spirit, who constantly renews us with new members, new ideas, and new ways to celebrate God's presence. There will be plenty of opportunities – in retreat programs like Christ Renews His Parish, in the Celebration of Confirmation at the Coliseum next spring, in the Eucharistic Day at Notre Dame in August, or in our Parish Mission next October.

But we must also take Paul's advice to "test everything" in evaluating what the Holy Spirit may be saying. Many of you young people will fall in love with someone. That can be the work of the Spirit. But, the *happiness* you feel must be tested to make sure that your relationship is built on a solid foundation. Those of you who will experience any kind of spiritual renewal might feel the *happiness* of a spiritual high. You must test those feelings to allow the Spirit to lead you to a firm commitment in faith that involves joy. New ideas have been introduced about the way we distribute the parish subsidy for school tuition. Along with those ideas have come a lot of informal discussion and plenty of fears and apprehensions. There is no need to be afraid, because we will make no hasty decisions! The Jubilee Year gives us a chance to expose any new ideas to testing, to gather information, and to prayerfully discern together where the Spirit might be leading us. That will take time, and lots of it!

Happiness comes and goes. As we prepare to celebrate the first coming of the Lord at Christmas, there should be happy times for all of us. *Joy*, on the other hand, is an inner calm that is born of a confidence that God is an integral part of our lives. In the Jubilee Year, we may not always be happy as we test everything to retain what is good. But we can rejoice, because the one who calls us is faithful and will not abandon us!

3.2   December 15, 2002

Saint Paul knew the difference between being *happy* and being *joyful*. His letters reveal those times when he was happy – when the leaders of the Jerusalem Church accepted him, when Timothy stood by his side, and when people responded positively to his message. But, they also reveal when he was unhappy – when he was shipwrecked, when an angry crowd in Ephesus beat him, and during the many times he was stuck in prison. And yet, Paul clearly tells the Thessalonians – and us – that whether or not we are happy, we need to rejoice always.

Isaiah did not find much reason to be happy. He was like residents of a trailer park being interviewed after a tornado, standing where they used to live. The prophet was standing where the Temple had been. The Babylonians had destroyed it, along with all the houses and shops of Jerusalem. And yet, in the midst of ruins, prophet boldly proclaimed that he "rejoices heartily in the Lord." He was joyful, because he recognized his people's return from exile as a sign of God's forgiveness. He looked to the future, confident that God would be with them in their job of rebuilding.

This distinction between being happy and being joyful is important for us during Advent. Everywhere we go, our culture literally screams at us to be happy! With all the bright lights, music, parties, and shopping going on, the constant message is that we need to do everything possible to make Christmas a happy time. But, we know from our own experience that happiness is not always possible at this time of the year. In fact, our expectations can be raised so high that we set ourselves up for failure!

Ten years ago, my family did not look forward to Christmas with much happiness, because my Mom had died three months earlier. In fact, one of her traditions made it worse. She always insisted that I celebrate Mass on Christmas afternoon with the family – the last thing I wanted to do after all those Christmas Masses! Like a typical mother, there was a method in her madness. She was concerned that one of my brothers no longer went to Mass. She figured that she would get him there at least once a year! Without her, that Mass was the most difficult I have ever celebrated. It was awful as we stumbled through all the tears, and we agreed to end the custom that year. But, reflecting more deeply upon that painful experience, I understood better what John is telling us in the Gospel. There is one among us whom we do not recognize. Overwhelmed by sadness, we could better appreciate why God took on human flesh in the first place. We understood better the Mystery of that birth in poverty and difficulty.

During these final two weeks of Advent, we continue to wait in joyful hope for the coming of the Lord. We need to be grateful for those times we are happy. But, we also need to rejoice heartily in the Lord, even when we are not happy. If you are grieving the loss of a family member or friend, you can rejoice in the Lord's promise of eternal life for your loved one and consolation for you. If your boyfriend has just dumped you, you can rejoice in the lessons you have learned from that relationship and look for a new and unexpected relationship. If your company has downsized and dumped you, you can find joy in the Lord's promise that he will not abandon you.

There is a difference between being *happy* and being *joyful*. John the Baptist invites us to find reasons for rejoicing in hope, even as we wait. Like him, we look for the one whom we struggle to recognize in faith.

3.3   December 11, 2005

Last Sunday, St. Mark introduced us to John the Baptist, telling us what he wore (camel's hair and a leather belt around his waist) and what he ate (locusts and wild honey). Quoting the prophet Isaiah, Mark begins his Gospel with John as the voice crying out in the desert, calling people to recognize God's judgment about their sins and God's mercy. This Sunday, St. John begins his Gospel by introducing the Baptist to us as one who gives testimony. After stating that the Baptist is not the light, John introduces us to the religious establishment of the day, who begin to cross-examine the star witness for Jesus Christ. To their questions, the Baptist declares who he is not. "I am not the Christ. I am not Elijah. I am not the Prophet." Using the same quote from Isaiah, the Baptist points to the One who comes after him as the true light.

With the Baptist as the first witness to the truth, the author of the fourth Gospel presents many more witnesses to the identity of Jesus. Echoing the answer given to Moses (I am who am), Jesus refers to himself as, "I am." "I am the Good Shepherd. I am the Way, the Truth, and the Life." As he slowly reveals his identity, he invites us to recognize him, as the Baptist had given reliable testimony to him as Christ and Savior.

In these last two weeks of Advent, the Baptist invites us to take a good look at ourselves and honestly acknowledge what we are not. I am not always loving. I am not always faithful. I am not always light to a darkened world. Once we honestly admit the reality of who we are not, then Paul's words in the second reading make more sense. He tells us not to quench the Holy Spirit. In being honest with ourselves about who we are not, the Spirit can prompt us to consider ways in which we can point to Christ, ways in which we can be witnesses to Christ, as John was. Paul tells us to bring those promptings to prayer and our daily experience, as a way of testing them. Those of you who are struggling to discern a vocation must do that – taking what you think the Spirit is telling you and test it. We do this frequently in the workings of this parish. People bring new ideas of how we might do things all the time. We must consider those ideas, and then test them before making them a part of the spiritual life of this parish. We have been going through a similar process in our building project. Beginning last summer, we submitted what we believed were promptings of the Spirit to Diocesan scrutiny – and more importantly, a Diocesan loan! After months of testing, we received good news, and it looks like our project will move on.

Paul tells that there is reason for rejoicing. We can rejoice, only when we are honest about who we are not. That is why the Sacrament of Reconciliation can be so helpful at this time of the year. As we wait to celebrate the first coming of Christ in a stable, and as we wait for his second coming at the end, we submit the truth about ourselves to his real coming in mercy in this Sacrament. The Sacrament becomes an important tool in discerning the promptings of the Spirit and helps us test what we think is important against what we learn about the Lord's priorities for us. The Spirit of the Lord is definitely upon us, when we admit who we are not, and when we point to the One who is coming.

3.4   December 14, 2008

Saint Paul tells us that we should rejoice always. We might wonder about the timing of this advice! How can we rejoice, when we do not know where the economy is going? How can we rejoice, if our salaries are cut and we worry about a job in the New Year? How can we rejoice, when our pensions have disappeared?

I found the answer to that question on – of all places – the bumper sticker of a car. The bumper sticker read: THERE IS A GOD … AND IT IS NOT YOU! We can rejoice, because God has taken on human flesh and become one of us. Isaiah could tell his people to rejoice heartily, because God had brought them back from their Babylonian captivity. They may have found the Temple destroyed and Jerusalem in absolute ruins. But, Isaiah tells them that there is a God who acts like a faithful bridegroom and bedecks, Jerusalem, his bride, with her jewels.

Trusting in this God, we wear the hopeful vestments of rose today. We wait to celebrate his First Coming at Christmas, and we wait for God to come like a faithful bridegroom or us, his Church, at the end of our lives and at the end of time. But, we rejoice now that God comes to us in Word and Sacrament. We can rejoice that God walks as one of us in our darkness, because Jesus Christ knew pain and disappointment and loss. Our rejoicing is not some feeling that is comes and goes with cheerful lights and holiday music. Neither is our rejoicing some attempt to distract us from our real pain. On Friday, I was amused when I visited one of our nursing homes to realize that they had changed its name to "Golden Living," as if that silly euphemism would somehow cover over the pain of being confined and depending on others for care. Our rejoicing involves a profound sense of hope and joy in Christ that Paul recommends to his beloved Thessalonians, even as they were being persecuted for embracing Paul's faith.

There is another cause for rejoicing. God is neither you nor me! We set ourselves up for a deep sadness when we think that we are God, when we think that we know what is best for our future, or when we think we are in control of life. We make ourselves into a god when we think that we are the center of the universe, and that everything revolves around us and our needs. That is why John the Baptist provides such a powerful message on Gaudete Sunday. John was extremely popular and drew huge crowds to the waters of the Jordan. That popularity could have easily gone to his head, and he could have presumed that all the fuss was about him. But, he resisted that temptation and clearly pointed to the One who is coming, the One whose sandal strap he was not worthy to untie.

John the Baptist teaches us an important lesson. Like John, we are invited to point the way to Christ. When we do that, we become like these candles at the Altar. As the candles produce the light that pierces the darkness, they give of themselves, so the light can shine. When we find ourselves consumed with our own problems and overwhelmed with our own darkness, the best thing to do is to get involved in serving the needs of others, especially those who have far less than we do. In putting ourselves in humble service, we direct the attention away from ourselves and point to the Light coming into the world. Then we can truly rejoice, because there is a God, one who walks among us, and it is not us. We rejoice at this message, and neither any person nor any circumstance can take this kid of joy away from us.

3.5 December 11, 2011

On this *Gau ete* (Latin for rejoice) Sunday, both the prophet Isaiah and the apostle Paul tell us to rejoice. In telling us to rejoice, neither the prophet nor the apostle is looking at life through rose colored glasses. Each knew that his respective community was struggling with many things that bring unhappiness. Isaiah's community had just returned from their fifty-year exile in Babylon. Jerusalem had been destroyed, and the prospect of rebuilding the ruined city was more difficult than the returning exiles had imagined. Six centuries later, the Thessalonians had their own share of difficulties. They were being torn apart internally by people who were placing doubts in their minds about the second coming of Jesus Christ. They were being persecuted externally by authorities who saw their faith as a threat to civil order.

Both Isaiah and Paul know the difference between being happy and being joyful. Happiness is a temporary response to individual circumstances in our lives. Joy, on the other hand, is a keen awareness of the presence of God. Truly joyful people can face the wonderful and terrible events of their lives, because they know that God is near, in the midst of loss, pain, struggle, or fear. John the Baptist is a truly joyful person. He may be wearing unusual clothing, and his diet may be a little odd. He does his share of ranting and raving about turning away from sin. He even falls into doubt about the role of the Messiah when he is waiting for execution in Herod's prison. But, during the course of his life, he has learned to trust in God's presence in his life, maintaining a joyful hope that no one could take away from him.

In one of his homilies, Saint Augustine helps us to understand John's role in the coming of our God. He makes a distinction between John being the voice and Jesus being the Word. John's voice announces the Word and invites us to prepare ourselves to receive the Word. The Word lives deep within as thought, feeling, and experience, even before the voice announces it. Long after the voice has been silenced, the Word continues to live in the minds and hearts of those who hear and accept it. As the voice, John carefully tells us who he is not. He is not the promised Messiah. He is not Elijah. He is not the prophet. But Jesus, the Word who has taken on human flesh, is the Way, the Truth, and the Life. He is the Good Shepherd who will lay down his life for his sheep. He is the Bread of Life. He is all of those identifications with God that we will find as we read the Gospel of John.

As we light this rose candle and wear rose vestments, we have many reasons to rejoice. There may be all kinds of reasons to be unhappy these days. The economy is not doing so well. We experience turmoil and division at many levels of our lives. We are keenly aware of wars, insurrections, poverty, hunger, and all kinds of insults against the dignity of human persons. Each of us can describe those dark parts of our lives which make us unhappy. But we can learn how to be joyful people, precisely because of the Mystery we will celebrate in two weeks.

Jesus Christ is the Word become flesh. We hear John's voice pointing to that Word, and we join our voices today in anticipation of celebrating Christ's First Coming at Christmas. In these next two weeks, we can do what the Baptist urges us to do. We can go to the Sacrament of Reconciliation and make a straight path for the coming of the Lord into our lives. You are welcome to our communal celebration of the Sacrament on Tuesday night. There will be plenty of other opportunities for individual reconciliation in the next two weeks. The Sacrament allows us to empty ourselves of our sins and clear the way for the coming of God into our lives. Then, we will begin to understand what it means to be people who live in joyful hope for the coming of our God.

3.6 December 14, 2014

The words of Isaiah the prophet are filled with hope and promise. Standing on the ruins of Jerusalem after the return of his people from their fifty-year captivity in Babylon, he is filled with the spirit of the Lord and makes some bold promises to save his people. 500 years later, when expectations for the coming of the Savior were very high, many people identified John the Baptist as the one who would fulfill these promises. He fits Isaiah's job description well. The spirit of God is definitely upon him. He announces glad tidings to the poor. His words heal the brokenhearted, and all the other duties assigned by Isaiah. His bold words in the desert raise the question about who is the Messiah – John or Jesus. Both proclaimed the Kingdom of God. Because John came first and baptized Jesus, some thought that Jesus was a disciple of John.

But John the Baptist is very secure in his identity and in his role. When the religious authorities start grilling him, he defines himself in terms of who he is not. He is not the Christ. He is not Elijah come back again. He is not the prophet described by Moses. He is the one who points to the one who identifies himself as "I am" in the rest of John's Gospel. Jesus uses that term, "I am," to identify himself with God who revealed himself to Moses in the burning bush. Jesus is the Good Shepherd. He is the vine. He is the Light of the world. He is the way, the truth, and the life. John's role is to point to him and tell people the truth about him.

In knowing his true identity and mission, John displays true humility. He is in sharp contrast to the frog in one of Aesop's Tales. The frog is tired of the muddy pond where he spends his life. He wants to see the world. So, he talks a stork into allowing him to hold onto his leg to fly above the earth's beauty and diversity. But the frog's small hands are too small and slimy. Every time the stork takes off, the frog loses his grip and falls back into the water. Finally, the frog decides to attach himself with his mouth. It works. As the stork flies high with the frog attached to his leg, some bird watchers marvel at the incredible sight of these two creatures working so well together. They say, "How ingenious these two animals are! I wonder which of them came up with this idea." Swelling with pride at their compliments and wanting to take credit for his cleverness, the frog blurted out, "I did." And he fell to his death.

It is with the humility of John the Baptist that we enter into these final two weeks to prepare to celebrate the first coming of Christ at Christmas. Instead of pointing to himself and giving in to the adulation of the crowds, John keeps his gaze fixed on Jesus Christ. He invites us to do the same. We may be preparing to celebrate his first coming and waiting for him to come again, but he is already in our midst. He invites us to keep our gaze fixed on Jesus, who tells us over and over again that we can recognize him in the least among us. Formed by our contact with him in the Sacramental life of the Church, we humbly recognize him in our Latino brothers and sisters of our sister parish of Saint Adalbert and in the poor served by the Giving Tree. We humbly dedicate ourselves to serving others, without worrying whether or not we get credit or whether or not people give us credit for our good work. We recognize him in those people who annoy us most in our lives with a humility that reminds us of the ways we are probably annoying them also.

With the humility of John the Baptist, we can also be honest about the ways in which we have not shown the face of Jesus Christ in our words and actions or recognized him in others. Come to the Advent Penance Service. There, we can be honest about our failures to imitate the example of John the Baptist. There God's mercy will allow that light to shine through us in a world filled with too much darkness, as these rose vestments shine in the purple of Advent.

3.7 December 17, 2017

The son of Zechariah and Elizabeth was attracting a lot of attention in his day. We met him last Sunday when we heard the beginning of the Gospel of Saint Mark. Instead of preaching in the Temple, he is drawing crowds to the desert. Instead of wearing the priestly vestments of his father, he is clothed in the camel's hair garment of the Prophet Elijah. Instead of eating fine food at the table with the other priests in Jerusalem, he easts locusts and honey, the food eaten by his ancestors as they left Egypt for the Promised Land. He attracts so much attention that the authorities in Jerusalem send priests and Levites to find out who does he think he is!

He responds by saying who he is not. At a time of heightened expectations of the coming of the messiah, he insists that he is not the Christ. He is not Elijah, the prophet who returned to God in a fiery chariot. He is not the Prophet who would equal Moses. Instead, he defines himself in the words of Isaiah the Prophet: "I am the voice of one crying out in the desert, make straight the way of the Lord." Responding to the Pharisees, the lay leaders of the people, he explains why he baptizes. He is inviting people to immerse themselves in a river of repentance to make a straight path for the true Messiah, Jesus Christ.

The Gospel of Saint John clarifies his identity. While the priests and Levites were sent by the religious authorities in Jerusalem, John was sent from God. The Greek word for "sent" comes from the root word for "apostle." John knows exactly who he is: the first Apostle whose role is to point the way to the light. He is to give testimony to the true Messiah, because he is a witness who is not worthy to untie the sandal strap of the light that has come into the world.

John the Baptist invites us to be witnesses to the light of Christ dispelling the darkness of our world. Each of us knows who we are not. We may not have the loving kindness of a Mother Teresa. We may not have the moral courage of a Nelson Mandela. We may not have the preaching skills of Martin Luther King. But, like John the Baptist, each of us has a calling from God. Each of us is called to make people aware of God's love. Each of us is called to live a life that points to God's amazing grace.

As we prepare to celebrate the Lord's First Coming in the Flesh, all three Scripture readings call us to be authentic witnesses of the power of God's love in the world. Isaiah says that authentic witnesses are mindful of the needs of the brokenhearted, captives, and those imprisoned in any way. Saint Paul insists that authentic witnesses must have the ability to test what appears to be the will of God. Once we have done that, then we must embrace it fully to make us blameless for the coming of our Lord Jesus Christ. Paul understands from his own experience when as Saul of Tarsus he was breathing murderous threats against the Christian community. He did not see himself as evil. He saw himself as right, only to discern later that he was dead wrong. John the Baptist shows that authentic witnesses do not point to themselves and boast about their accomplishments. They point beyond themselves.

On this Gaudete Sunday, we can sense a real joyful spirit in all of these readings from the Word of God. In particular, Saint Paul tells us to rejoice always. He is not talking about a feeling of happiness or of pleasure rooted in our senses. It is impossible to have a feeling of happiness or pleasure all the time. In fact, there are times when we have feelings of great sadness, grief, or disappointment. Instead, he is talking about a state of our souls. The Incarnation of Jesus Christ which we celebrate at Christmas and his death and resurrection which we celebrate at Easter display the power of God's love to give meaning to everything in our life. So, rejoice always! Pray without ceasing! In all circumstances, give thanks!

4. 4th Sunday of Advent

Readings
2 Samuel 7:1–5, 8–11, 16
Romans 16:25–27
Luke 1:26–38

4.1 December 19, 1999

There is a Chinese saying that a good question is like beating a bell. It interrupts the silence and makes us listen. God's question to David – "Should you build me a house to dwell in?" – got the King's attention. Delivered through the prophet Nathan, God's question shows that David did not understand the Lord at all. David had taken care of his own needs. He had conquered his enemies, established peace, and built himself a very nice house out of cedar. Only after he was comfortable in the lap of luxury did he think of God. God, for King David, was an afterthought.

So, God's question shatters David's illusions. God reminds the king of his humble origins as a shepherd. God raised him to be commander of the people. God guided David's victories and gave him peace. And God will continue to be with the king and his people. God would dwell with his people not in a building made with human hands, but in the "house of David" made of human beings. Eventually, God's goodness would surpass whatever David or anyone else could imagine.

Centuries later, another of God's questions rang out like a bell and shattered the silence of a young woman. Mary was just as puzzled by this question – delivered this time through an angel – as King David had been. The question may have upset her. But

Mary had none of the advantages of King David. She had won no victories. Nor did she live in the comfort of a King's house. She knew that everything she had was a gift from God. God was no afterthought. In responding with faith and humility, she became the handmaid through whom God could take on human flesh in a way that no one could ever have imagined.

At most Masses during Advent, we have been called to worship by a bell shattering the silence. That bell has set the tone for the questions posed by the Scripture readings of Advent. Are we alert to the second coming of the Lord at a time we cannot know? Are we prepared to celebrate the first coming of the Lord next Saturday? Are we awake to the ways the Lord comes to us – not only here in Word and Sacrament – but in the events of our daily lives?

If we rely on our own abilities and think of our successes as our own making, then these questions may not make much sense. Then we are like King David, thinking of God only after we have been assured of our own comfort and security. But if we realize how much God has blessed us, if we acknowledge that God is the source of all we are and have, we can be more attentive to the ways God comes to us. Then we are like Mary, opening our hearts to allow Jesus entrance into our flesh and blood in our time and place.

Advent asks good questions. Like bells, these questions interrupt the silence and make us listen. If we listen with the attitude of Mary, then we will come to know the answers in the silence of our hearts. We will not be fearful of the Lord's second coming. We will understand Saturday's Feast as a Mystery that continues to unfold in our lives. Most importantly, we will more readily recognize all those other comings in the confusion of our daily lives!

4.2   December 22, 2002

David had some very reasonable expectations. Once he had settled into his own palace, he expected that he would build for God a proper dwelling place. But, through the prophet Nathan, God told David not to build a physical house. Rather, God would dwell in David's House, in the flesh and blood of his descendents. God exceeded David's expectations in ways that David could never have anticipated.

Mary probably had her own expectations. Like her contemporaries, she remembered God's promise to David. She was about to marry a man who was from the House of David. She expected that someday God would save his people through one of those descendents. Her expectations were exceeded when Gabriel visited her in her humble house in Nazareth. In saying, "Yes," Mary opened her own body to be the house in which the Word-Made-Flesh would dwell. By making herself vulnerable and open to this unexpected request, she opened the door for God to dwell with the human race in a way that could never have been imagined.

As we wait, holding our breath, to celebrate the Mystery of the Incarnation this week, all of us have our own expectations of what Christmas should be like. Like David, we are conditioned by so many expectations of our culture. We expect Christmas to be a very happy time when families gather to share their warmth and love. We anticipate that giving and receiving expensive gifts will make our holidays. We want this time to be a time of peace, good will, and good cheer.

But, all too often, our expectations are unrealistic. All families have their issues, and gathering at Christmas can cause smoldering problems to boil over. My family will descend on our house on Wednesday, and we'll see how we do together this year! My one brother is already threatening to break family tradition and go to Las Vegas for Christmas next year. Many times, the presents we have worked so hard to buy and wrap are thrown to the side, and we cannot even remember what we got last year. And no matter how hard we try to be cheerful, we cannot keep the realities of death or sickness or fear away from our homes at any time, much less this time of the year.

By her very attitude and by her response, Mary shows us how to be open to the ways in which God will dwell with us that exceed our expectations. When she was surprised by the Angel's questions, she asked how this could happen to her. She did not put the word "I" into the question, as her cousin Zechariah had done when the angel visited him in the Temple to announce that he and Elizabeth would be the parents of John the Baptist. Instead, she simply accepted the angel's words and trusted that God would work in and through her in unexpected ways.

We need that same trust as we approach Christmas. God can dwell in midst, even when our families are dysfunctional and our lives are a mess. God can dwell in our midst, especially when we begin to understand that we give gifts as external signs of an internal act of the will. God can dwell with us even when our hearts are broken, our bodies weary, and our minds filled with fear of war. God always exceeds our expectations. With Mary, be open to the ways God will surprise you this Christmas. With Mary, stay attuned to God dwelling in our midst, exceeding every expectation.

4.3   December 18, 2005

King David had some very definite expectations. Now that he was living in an upscale neighborhood, he expected to build a proper home for the Lord. At first, the prophet Nathan, who spoke for God, told him to go for it! The Lord is with you, he said, indicating that David enjoyed God's favor. After all, he had gone from being an insignificant shepherd to the commander of his people. He had been successful in defeating his enemies and had become a celebrity. However, upon reflection, Nathan came back to tell David that his expectations of building a beautiful Temple would not happen. Instead, Nathan told him that his house – those who would succeed him – would become a permanent dwelling place for the Lord. Based on the Lord's role in his past success, Nathan invited David to trust that God would exceed his expectations in the future in ways in which he could not imagine.

We have no idea what expectations Mary might have had. We can only guess that she expected to live a normal life with her husband in Nazareth, and that God would bless her with children. Those likely expectations were completely shattered when the Angel called on her. Using the same words Nathan used for David, the Angel assured her that the Lord was with her, that she enjoyed God's favor. Saying nothing about any of her accomplishments, the Angel invited Mary to trust that the promises made centuries before to David would be fulfilled in her. Overshadowed by the Most High, her womb would become the Temple of God made flesh. Having expressed her human fear, and not understanding what this would mean, she trusted that God could do the impossible and declared herself the handmaid of the Lord. With an openness that defies all logic, she trusted that it would be done according to the Lord's word.

All of us have our own expectations, both spoken and unspoken. Odds are good that we expect to enjoy a good Christmas next weekend. Odds are good that we have worked hard to accomplish those expectations. We have shopped, prepared, cleaned, wrapped, cooked, and written greetings. At a very basic level, there is nothing wrong with our expectations and with the work we have put in to realize them. But, in this final week before Christmas, Mary invites us to trust that God can exceed our expectations in ways that we cannot imagine. She invites us to trust that God will provide, even when our expectations are dashed, and when we are filled with fear.

We often set ourselves up for failure at Christmas, precisely because our expectations are not realistic. Many people struggle with loneliness throughout the year, while others have suffered tragic losses. They look toward Christmas with a certain dread and fear. We expect that our families will look like the Hallmark expectations of Christmas. We become disappointed when our families look more like that family in the movie, *The Christmas Story*, which runs non-stop on TNT all day on Christmas. They remain the same old families – with red neck brother in laws smelling up the garage with cigarette smoke, pagan brothers complaining already how long the Easter Vigil will be, and children fighting an hour after they open their presents.

We need Mary's attitude in this final week of Advent. We need to back off and spend some time in silence and reflection. If you have not already done so, you might take advantage of the Sacrament of Reconciliation. We are more like David than Mary. While Mary may have been sinless from the moment of her conception, David was great, precisely because he repented of his great sins. We need to develop a deep-seated trust that God can and does exceed our expectations, if we only watch and wait quietly. The Lord took flesh in a cold, dark, smelly stable. He can take flesh in our smelly, messy, and often dysfunctional families, and exceed our expectations every time.

4.4   December 21, 2008

Jim Collins is a business guru and writer. He wrote a best-selling book (*Goo* *To Great*) which some of you may have read. His book tracks some qualities in businesses that are good, and then examines those qualities in other businesses that have made them great. If you are still looking for a Christmas gift for people interested in business, you might think of this book to help them understand the difference between good and great. But Saint Luke is not interested in business. He tells the story of a young Jewish woman who was willing to move from "good to great," to exchange a good plan for a great plan. Her name, of course, is Mary.

This young maiden from a modest Jewish family in Nazareth probably had a good plan: she would fall in love with Joseph, enter into marriage with him, have children by him, raise their children, and live a quiet life. There is nothing wrong with this good plan. But, God has a greater plan for her, and the Angel Gabriel proposes it. Mary is shocked and afraid and wonders how such a plan could work. But, she is completely open to God's plan, and she agrees that God's will would be done, changing a good plan into a great plan and opening the way for the coming of the Savior. Because of Mary's openness, Luke gives her to us as the model disciple, hearing God's word, pondering these things in her heart, and then acting on them.

You and I have all kinds of good plans for our lives, and that is fine. But, God has a way of offering us ways to change good plans into great ones. Few of us have been visited by an Angel. But, we are visited by unexpected changes in our lives, by unforeseen difficulties, and by circumstances we could never have anticipated.

Mary invites us to be open to God working in our lives at these times, trusting that God can change our good plans into great ones.

So many times, we make plans like King David did. He was embarrassed that he was living in a fine mansion, while the Lord was still housed in a tent. God spoke through Nathan the prophet and told him that God would turn his good plans into much greater ones. Instead of constructing a physical house for the Lord, God would make of his own house, his physical descendants, a house that would bring forth a Savior and last forever.

We need to listen to Nathan as we make our good plans for Christmas. If we are open to God's great plans, our celebration of Christmas this year may open new great avenues of faith for us. I see that happening in our family plans for Christmas. As you know, I often talk about my family in my homilies. When my Dad died last February, and people came to pay their respects, I was busted! Many of you came through the line and asked my brothers and sister about specific things I had said. At first, they seemed upset that I had been telling stories about them. But, they began to appreciate the fact that they have served as homily material for many years. In the end, they seemed to like the idea that stories about our family would help other families connect with the ways in which God works in ordinary circumstances.

This year, we have to alter some of our plans for our Christmas. It will be the first Christmas since our Dad's death. Two of my nephews recently became engaged, and they will bring their fiancs to the rectory later in the week. Most amazingly of all, my attitudes toward my redneck brother-in-law have changed in the past year. He has emphysema and is on oxygen all the time, and his disease has shown him that people truly care about him, and that he is a member of our family. His attitude is significantly changed. Ponder your own family dynamics in your heart as you make your good plans for Christmas. Be open to events which are out of your control. Trust, like Mary did, that your good plans can be turned into a great encounter with the mystery of God taking on human flesh in ways you could never have anticipated.

4.5 December 18, 2011

We are familiar with Saint Luke's account of this annunciation from the Angel Gabriel to the humble virgin of Nazareth. For that reason, we need to take another look at the story. In taking a careful look, we might draw some lessons for our own faith.

There are at least five words that help us to make this connection. First, Mary is **surprised** by the Angel's announcement. Her cousins Zechariah and Elizabeth might have wanted a child for years. But, God's invitation to become the Mother of God came completely out of the blue. Second, Mary gives **permission** for this Mystery to occur, even if she does not totally understand its implications. The Angel does not force Mary to agree to be the Mother of God. He clearly gives her a choice, and her choice permits the Mystery to happen. Third, Mary is **curious**. She wants to know how this child can take flesh in her womb, since she has had no relations with any man. Fourth, Mary immediately becomes aware of God's **grace**. The Angel promises that God will do most of the heavy lifting for Mary, because "the Holy Spirit will come upon you and the power of the Most High will overshadow you." Finally, Mary shows an incredible **acceptance**. She does not shrug her shoulders, as if to say, "Okay, if that is the way it has to be." Instead, she boldly declares, "let it be done according to your will." She is the handmaid of the Lord.

These five words can guide us in this final week before we celebrate the first coming of the Lord at Christmas. I am convinced that we set ourselves up for failure each year, because we have the perfect Christmas worked out in our heads. But, the perfect Christmas never happens, because our plans hardly ever work out the way we want them to. For that reason, we need to be open to surprises this week. God may have something in mind for us. If we keep our eyes and hearts open to what happens to us this week, we might catch a glimpse of what he has in mind through events that surprise us. When a surprise happens, we can give permission for it to occur, instead of stewing over it or trying to control the situation. There is nothing wrong with being curious about the surprises in life. We can bring our curiosity to prayer in the darkness of these final days and try to make sense of what is happening in our lives. In doing that, we can count on God's grace to get us through. If we can imitate Mary, the Mother of God and our mother, than the acceptance of situations beyond our control can bring a deep and abiding peace, which no manner of frantic preparation can bring into our lives.

During the past couple of days, you may have seen or heard the commercial spots being sponsored by our Diocese. Bishop Rhoades has initiated this campaign to invite Catholics to come home. He is counting on us to help in this effort. He invites us to identify with both characters in the Gospel. Like Mary, we reflect on our role of being open to the way God might surprise us. Like the Angel Gabriel, we can announce the Good News to those who no longer practice their faith. Maybe someone in your neighborhood might be moved by the commercials. If they see one of the yard signs you put up in your yard, they might take strength that someone else is practicing their faith. We can make sure that visitors will find one of these cards in the pew when they join us for Christmas. We can go out of our way to welcome those who join us at Christmas, instead of snarling at them for taking our family's pew.

We ask for the intercession of Mary, the Mother of God, as we open our eyes, our hearts, and our ears for the ways God might surprise us this week. Perhaps we can even be the angel of surprise to our neighbors who are attracted by the commercials. We welcome them with open hearts, as Mary welcomed the message of the Angel.

4.6   December 21, 2014

King David was a powerful man with ambitious plans. He had united the tribes of Israel into a stable nation and established Jerusalem as its capital. He had defeated the enemies and brought peace. He had built himself a nice house. Now he wanted to build a proper house for the Lord who had given him his success. At first, Nathan the prophet agreed. But the Lord spoke through Nathan and told David to scrap his plans. God had greater plan than a physical temple, which would be built by David's son, Solomon. God told David to trust that he would build of his line of descendants a house that would endure forever.

One thousand years later, we meet a teenage girl living in a remote village 90 miles north of Jerusalem. We have no idea of what Mary was planning, because she had none of the fame or power of King David. We can only speculate that she was planning to settle down with her betrothed, Joseph, have children, and raise a family. However, the Angel Gabriel startles her to announce that the promises made to David would be fulfilled in her. Like the Spirit of God hovering over the void at the time of creation, the Holy Spirit would come upon her. Her body would become the Ark of the New Covenant, bearing God's only begotten Son.

When the 15th century artist, Fra Angelico, painted this scene, he used a device to help us understand what the Angel's message did to Mary's plans. In his painting, Gabriel is leaning in toward Mary. The artist linked them by writing the words of their conversation between them. The Angel's declaration that the Holy Spirit will come upon her is straight forward. But Mary's response, "Behold, I am the handmaid of the Lord. May it be done to me according to your word" is written upside down and backward. By doing this, Fra Angelico shows us that Mary's plans are reversed, and her world is turned upside down. In agreeing to be the handmaid of the Lord, Mary enters into a certain darkness that comes with uncertainty and unexpected change.

Today is the darkest day of the year. Not only do we experience a short period of light today, but also cloud cover around here makes this time of the year gloomier. This darkness is a sign of the deeper darkness that is experienced by those who have had their worlds turned upside down and their plans reversed. Those who have lost loved ones to death and are facing their first Christmas without them know the darkness of having their world turned upside down. The same is true of those who are suffering from any kind of illness or depression or even the flu. Others bring the darkness of broken relationships and dysfunctional family dynamics to this week. Many dwell in the darkness of being alone.

When we find ourselves in any kind of darkness, we are tempted to believe that God is distant from us. But, in fact, the opposite is true. God's presence is much more profound than an emotional feeling of warmth or happiness. When our world gets turned upside down and our plans are reversed, God keeps his promise to us, just as certainly as God kept his promise to King David and to Mary, the Mother of God. It took 1,000 years before God's promise to David was fulfilled in Mary's response. Mary continued to ponder all these things in her heart as she faced the darkness of her new and unexpected condition. Mary trusted that the Lord's promise to her would be fulfilled, even when the village gossiped about her pregnancy, even when the child was born in a stable, even when they were exiled in Egypt, and even as her Son hung on the cross.

It is Mary's faith that sustains us in these final days before Christmas. Of course, we need to do the work of preparing for our celebration. But, if we prepare in a way that allows God to surprise us, even in turning our lives upside down and backwards, then we can also say with Mary, "Let it be done to me according to your word."

4.7 December 24, 2017

King David has a pretty good idea. With Jerusalem at peace, he lives comfortably in a house of cedar. The ark of God, which had preceded his ancestors in the desert, is housed in a tent. He wants to build the Lord a proper temple. Nathan the prophet also thinks that it is a pretty good idea. However, Nathan discovers in a dream that God's plan is different. God does not want David to do something for him. Instead, God is going to do something for David. God reminds David of what he has already done for him – lifting him from caring for sheep in Bethlehem to leading a nation. Instead of David building a house for God, God will establish a house for David. God promises that he will remain with the house of David and make his house forever. This is one of the Covenants portrayed in mosaic in the main aisle of our church.

The kingly line of David lasted for over 400 years, until the Babylonians ended the dynasty with exile. When the people of Israel returned from exile, they were not successful in restoring the

Dynasty of David. Instead, they kept track of all who had been born into the same tribe that David had been born into. They never lost hope in the covenant made with David.

In today's Gospel, we see the Covenant with David fulfilled in a way that no one could ever have expected. The angel Gabriel approaches an insignificant teenager betrothed to an insignificant carpenter from David's tribe in the insignificant village of Nazareth. The Angel asks Mary to become the mother of the Messiah promised to David. Even though Mary does not understand, she trusts the Angel's assurance that the Holy Spirit would overshadow her, as the spirit of God had overshadowed creation in the beginning. She would become the Ark of the Covenant, carrying the promised Messiah who is also the Son of God.

When Mary says "yes," she is responding to an invitation to enter into an infinite union with an infinite God. She has three important attitudes that opened her to enter into this union. First, she is detached. She is willing to be detached from the gossip of the neighbors and even the possibility of being stoned to death because of her perceived adultery. She trusts completely in God. She has become the handmaid of the Lord. Second, she knows that she cannot do this on her own. She trusts that all things are possible with God. That trust enables her to say, "Be it done to me according to your word." Third, she counts on God to help her through her upcoming ordeal, even to standing at the foot of the cross when he is crucified. She trusts the Angel's promise that the Lord is with her and will not abandon her.

Those three attitudes can serve us well as we prepare to celebrate Christmas tomorrow. Christmas invites each one of us to an infinite union with an infinite God in the person of Jesus Christ. If we can detach ourselves from so many of our concerns and worries, we can trust that our encounter with then newborn Christ can have the power to change us in ways we might not expect. If we are humble enough to admit that we cannot create the spirit of Christmas on our own, we open ourselves to trusting that God will grace us with a love we can never earn. If we can count on God to help us in celebrating the birth of his Son, we can grow in confidence that God will be with us well beyond Christmas and throughout the New Year.

Saint Paul speaks of the Mystery of the Incarnation in his Letter to the Romans. He tells them that the best response to this Mystery is to be obedient. The root meaning of the word "obedience" is "to listen." Mary listened carefully, detached herself, counted on God to help her, and trusted that God is with her. Listen carefully to the Christmas Mystery that we celebrate and imitate Mary's example.

Christmas

5. The Nativity of the Lord

Readings

Vigil Mass
Isaiah 62:1–5
Acts 13:16–17, 22–25
Matthew 1:18–25

Mass at Midnight
Isaiah 9:1–6
Titus 2:11–14
Luke 2:1–14

Mass at Dawn
Isaiah 62:11–12
Titus 3:4–7
Luke 2:15–20

Mass During the Day
Isaiah 52:7–10
Hebrews 1:1–6
John 1:1–18

5.1 December 25, 1999

If we played word association games with our experience of Christmas, the words "giving" and "getting" would probably be among the most frequently mentioned. For the past few weeks, many of us have been rushing around searching for the right gifts to give family and friends as expressions of our love. For the same past few weeks, you children have been fantasizing about what you will get today! And not a few adults!

Clearly, giving and getting are at the heart of the Feast we celebrate today. The Scripture readings make it very clear that God has taken the initiative in giving the gift of his Son. God is the "giver," and we are the "getter." Tonight, our task is to search for the proper way to accept the gift coming to us from above.

We adults sometimes struggle with this giving and getting stuff. We worry whether the gift we have given is appropriate. Then we fret about whether the gift we have gotten is of equal value. We also look for reactions to the gifts we give. Have you ever given anyone a really valuable gift, only to be disappointed when the getter did not recognize its value? When you searched everywhere for the perfect gift, you expect the getter to hold it, look at it for a time, and comment on how much it means. It hurts when the person indifferently says, "Thanks for the Rolex. It's nice. Am I getting anything else?"

So, there is a simple question we Christians need to ask ourselves tonight as we celebrate the coming of our Savior. Do we – even vaguely – appreciate the worth of what we have been given? Our being here at this Mass is one indicator! Jesus' birth obviously has some meaning for us. But do we really know what we are getting? Have we any idea that the Divine Giver has very different expectations in gift giving? Do we understand that God's gift is an absolute emptying out without conditions? What, precisely, does it mean that God gives us his Son?

Perhaps these might be the questions we ponder during this Jubilee Year – this Year of Favor from God. Because of the Mystery of the Incarnation – of God taking on human flesh – life has been changed. Because of God's gift of self, everything in God's creation has the potential for redemption. We can find hope not only in our triumphs and joys and happiness, but we can also find God in our sorrows, our tragedies, and our burdens. The Mystery of the Incarnation opens the way for us to find hope even in the midst of our sins, because it opens the way for the Mystery of our Redemption.

How do we express our gratitude for this gift of ours? We are on a roll already by gathering at this Eucharist. We can continue by carrying this expression of our gratitude out of this church to our homes and families, to our jobs and schools, even into the streets. We can extend it by opening our hearts to a love that is incarnated in every moment of the new Jubilee Year.

Merry Christmas!

5.2 December 25, 2002

One of the wonderful things about the stories surrounding the birth of Jesus is that they allow us to fill in the blanks with our imagination. For example, Saint Luke tells us "there was no room in the Inn for them." Although he does not say one word about the innkeeper, most Christmas plays, stories, and movies usually feature such a person, and occasionally his wife joins him. Sometimes, he is grumpy and dismisses them with harsh words. At other times, he is an efficient businessman who is too busy to deal with this poor couple from Nazareth. Every once in a while, he is a kindly man who feels sorry for the expectant mother and provides a space for them in his stable. No matter how the innkeeper is pictured, the bottom line is that he did not recognize the Mystery and failed to make room for him in the Inn.

As we gather today to celebrate the Mystery of the Incarnation, we are invited to reflect again on what it means for our God to take on human flesh. We are invited to renew our faith that God became one of us, so that we can become like God. More specifically, we are invited to reverse the mistake of the Innkeeper and make room for the Incarnate Word Made Flesh to dwell in our midst.

What does it mean to make room for him? We make room for him when we recognize the Incarnation as a total gift from God. We did not earn this gift, nor did we deserve it. God gave us the gift of himself purely and simply out of a total love for us. As we look at this gift, wrapped in the form of a vulnerable infant, we sense that it is best to carefully unwrap it and reflect on it, as we unwrap the presents we receive on this day as tokens of love. In the process of understanding it, we can renew our intention to give of ourselves more generously outside of the Christmas Season.

We make room for him when we take this time to be fully present to our families gathered together. Right in the middle of a bleak and dark winter, Christmas gives us a break from our normal routine. Like Mary, we have a chance to step back a bit and ponder our lives from the perspective of time almost standing still. When it is time to dive back into the regular rhythms of our daily lives, we might be a little more attuned to the dwelling of the Incarnate Word in the ordinary events of our lives. Unlike the innkeeper who did not see anything special in a homeless couple about to give birth, we can look with renewed eyes of faith for signs of Jesus Christ dwelling in our midst.

We make room for him when we gather here on a weekly basis. Some of you have joined us as guests, because you are visiting friends and families. Others of you come because it is Christmas. We are delighted that you are here, and we hope to avoid the mistake of the innkeeper and welcome you. However, please give some consideration to joining us on a regular, weekly basis. The Lord whose birth we celebrate is truly present in the Word proclaimed, and he is truly present in the bread and wine transformed into his Body and Blood. As we reflect on that infant, lying in Bethlehem (literally the house of bread) in a manger (from which animals are fed), we trust that he speaks to us and nourishes us every Sunday se we can better recognize the pattern of his coming into our daily lives.

There is no need to berate or lament the mistakes of that innkeeper twenty centuries ago. The Mystery of the Incarnation happened, even without his help. We have a chance to welcome the newly born Lord today, and allow him to be born through us.

5.3 December 25, 2005

For centuries, pilgrims have walked across northern Spain on the ancient Camino de Santiago ("Way of Saint James") to the city of Santiago on the western coast, because they believed in miracles. They believed that the body of Saint James the Apostle had been transported to the western shores of Spain from Jerusalem after his martyrdom. They believed that the Moors had been expelled through his intercession. Confident that the invisible spiritual world does manifest itself in various ways in their ordinary lives, they made the journey expecting to see miracles – signs of God's hand in their lives.

When our group of bicyclists embarked on that same pilgrimage last summer, we had a somewhat more skeptical view of miracles. We live in a more secular age, which is not as open to manifestations of the divine. So, we initially scoffed at the stories of some of those miracles told in villages all along the Camino, especially the ones that stretched the imagination. We smiled when we heard of a boy who had been wrongly hanged in the Village of Santo Domingo de la Calzada, only to be kept alive on the gallows by the hand of Saint James until his parents returned. We wondered how a body could be transported by boat from Jerusalem and remain buried for eight hundred years before a monk discovered it in a dream. We took pictures of the many images of Saint James riding on the back of a horse killing the Moors, so people would believe us at home.

However, our perspective began to change as we began to travel together, when we gathered each day to pray Morning Prayer, celebrate the Eucharist, and as we got to know each other better. We began to recognize our own miracles – the ways in which the Divine was breaking through our experiences. We reveled in the gentle rain that cooled us as we struggled to climb the steep grade of a mountain. We marveled at the genuine concern of every pilgrim who passed us when one of our members had a bad fall. We had our breath taken away when the sacristan of the Cathedral allowed us to celebrate Mass in the cramped chapel where the bones of Saint James were kept. At a final meal near the Cathedral, we recounted the many miracles we had seen on the way to Santiago.

As we gather today, we pause on our pilgrimage through life to reflect on the first great Miracle of our faith. The God who has no beginning is conceived in the womb of a Virgin. The God who created the heavens and the earth is wrapped in swaddling clothes and laid in a manger. The God who formed us from the clay of the ground becomes flesh himself. Christmas establishes the pattern for the rest of the miracles we experience in our lives. If the Word Made Flesh could be born in a cold, dark, smelly stable, then he can be born daily into our lives, our families, and our parish – even in the most difficult of situations. By celebrating this Miracle today, we are invited to keep our eyes open for all those ways the Lord is manifested throughout the rest of the year.

Just as we did not end our pilgrimage in any of the villages in which we stopped on the way to Santiago, so we do not end our pilgrimage at Bethlehem today. Having taken flesh in our midst, the Lord Jesus invites us to continue walking with him to Jerusalem, where the wood of the manger will become the wood of the Cross, and where the swaddling clothes will be replaced with a burial shroud. Jesus knows how difficult it is to walk this pilgrimage from Bethlehem to Jerusalem alone. So, he invites us to gather with this community every Sunday to hear his Word. When we hear that Word every Sunday, we begin to know its power to form us and help us to distinguish those miracles that truly show us the face of God from those illusions that confuse us. Having fed us with his Word, he invites us to feed on his Body and Blood, to nourish us and form us into his Body as we walk with him.

Bethlehem is only seven miles from Jerusalem – not a long physical distance. But that journey represents our individual pilgrimages and the Lord's desire for us to recognize him walking with him. Once we decide to walk with him all the way to Jerusalem, we will recognize the second and even greater miracle – the resurrection of Jesus Christ from the dead. Having known the power of that miracle, we will also know the end of our pilgrimage – in the heavenly Jerusalem, our true and lasting home.

5.4 December 25, 2008

Christmas is a Feast for children. God became a child, and children know best how to celebrate this feast. Children teach us to develop a trusting attitude toward those responsible for their care, and they invite us to snuggle up to God who has become one of us, as they snuggle up with those they trust. Children joyfully forget about yesterday and don't worry much about tomorrow. Children could care less about the things that cause us to fret so much. Children have a gift for focusing on what is most personal.

Celebrating Christmas as a child is not as easy as it sounds, because we sometimes confuse childlike faith with childish behavior. We exhibit childish behavior when we pout or throw tantrums to get our own way, or when we consider ourselves to be the center of the universe. Learning to celebrate Christmas with childlike faith takes a lifetime, because learning that faith requires traveling from

Bethlehem to Jerusalem. The physical distance between Bethlehem and Jerusalem is only seven miles. However, the real journey takes a lifetime.

When the earliest followers of Jesus traveled that way with him, he gave them a number of names. He called them apostles and disciples. He named them friends and servants. He called Peter "Satan" once, and referred to another as the devil. But only in the very last chapter of John's Gospel does he call them "children." In their journey with him from Bethlehem to Jerusalem, they had experienced failures, trials, humiliations, and all kinds of shocks to faith and hope. There were times when they were plunged into desolation and could not pray. They experienced a great deal of weariness. They had witnessed his death. Only after all these difficult experiences could they muster the childlike faith to recognize him standing on the shore of the Sea of Galilee as the One raised from the dead, rewarding their faith by calling them "children."

There is a beautiful Icon of the birth of Christ that expresses this journey from Bethlehem to Jerusalem, from Christmas to Easter. The artist understood well the geography of Bethlehem and placed the stable in a cave. The darkness of the cave matches the darkness of the tomb. The hill above the open cave clearly reminds us of Calvary, situated just beyond the walls of Jerusalem. The wood of the manger points to the wood of the cross, and the swaddling clothes of the infant will become the shroud that wrapped the Lord's body. Yet, shining in the darkness of that cave is the bright and shining infant, surrounded by Mary, Joseph, shepherds, Magi, animals, and angels.

At Christmas, we focus on those bright and hopeful images in the Icon, trying to see them as children do. With childlike faith, we ponder the implications of the Mystery of God taking human flesh in our midst, giving us a new sense of joy as we continue our journey from Bethlehem to Jerusalem. Christmas is the first of the Christian Mysteries. Easter is the second. With our faith renewed at Bethlehem, the Lord invites us to listen every Sunday to his Word, teaching us how to have the faith of children, as he taught his first disciples. Every Sunday, he feeds us with his Body and Blood to strengthen us to face the challenges of life and the threats to our faith. As we move from Bethlehem ("the House of Bread") to Jerusalem, we too encounter the pain, suffering, and disappointment of Calvary. But Calvary is just outside Jerusalem, where the Lord was raised from the dead. With childlike Christmas faith, it is easier to recognize his risen presence in our midst, walking with us to the New and Eternal Jerusalem.

5.5   December 25, 2011

There is a French legend that at midnight on Christmas Eve, a mysterious spirit of peace prevails throughout the world. It is a spirit so powerful and all-encompassing that even the cattle in the stables and the deer in the forest fall to their knees in adoration. William Shakespeare refers to this mysterious Christmas peace in *Hamlet* (act 1, scene 1):

> Some say that whenever that season comes
> Wherein our Savior's birth is celebrated
> The bird of dawn sings all night long;
> They say that no spirit can walk abroad,
> No planet strikes,
> No fairy takes,
> No witch has power to charm,
> So hallowed and gracious is this time.

We know that this Christmas night is both hallowed and gracious. In gathering for Mass and in spending time with our families, we take a break from the regular rhythm of our daily lives to adore the Lord who takes on our human flesh and dwells with us. And he dwells with us, no matter what is happening in our families. Some of you are grieving the loss of a loved one. Others are struggling with some kind of dysfunction which causes great pain. Many families are torn apart by divisions and anger that defy healing. Some of you might even be experiencing a graced year of peace.

If Christ could be born in a smelly stable with less than ideal circumstances, then we can trust that Christ can be born into our homes and into our hearts tonight. He was laid in a manger where cattle fed. Tonight, he is laid upon this Altar and becomes the Bread of Life for us. The first witnesses are outcasts and those not trusted by society – shepherds who wandered with their flocks and had a reputation for dishonesty. In expressing their wonder at his birth and in spreading the good news, they demonstrate the power of this Mystery to change people. In the same way, he entrusts us with this incredible message that has the power to transform us and sends us out to tell others about it.

And that is the real power of the Mystery of the Incarnation. This day may be hallowed and gracious in so many ways. But this day passes, and the world resumes its normal stormy circumstances. God came down to take flesh in the fullness of time, so that we can be changed by this Mystery in the time in which we live our daily lives. God became one of us, so that we may become one with God.

Mary wrapped the tiny, vulnerable child, and placed him in the wood of the manger. As that child grew and became aware of the will of his Father, his journey of obedience ultimately took him to Calvary, the place of execution outside the city walls of Jerusalem. There, only a few miles north of Bethlehem, he would take on his shoulders the wood of the Cross. There he would give his life for us, trusting that the Father would raise him from the dead.

The Lord Jesus invites us to make this same journey with him. We leave this hallowed and gracious night to walk with him, to allow him to mold us as he molded those outcast and lowly shepherds, and to join him at the foot of the Cross at Calvary. Emboldened by this hallowed and gracious night, we too can allow him who took on our human flesh to transform us into the Divinity in whose image we were originally created.

5.6   December 25, 2014

Imagine the "breaking news stories" on this day if the ancient had our technology and our twenty-four-hour news cycle. The leading stories would feature the complaints of so many citizens that they have to return to their home towns to be counted. Everyone knew that the government was counting them only to get more taxes out of them. News from Rome would feature the problems caused by unending deployment of troops, along with problems caused by insurgents in the Middle East. Local news would feature the continued reconstruction of the Temple in Jerusalem under King Herod, a real tyrant with ties too close to Rome, but a pretty good builder.

The news would certainly not include the reason why we are here tonight. The birth of Jesus Christ would not have been featured at all. There had been no royal caravans heading to a magnificent palace for the birth of an important person. Instead, two peasants had walked from Nazareth and had no choice but to give birth in a stable. The angelic chorus had chosen to announce this birth to a bunch of shepherds. Today, we tend to romanticize the shepherds. But in that day, they lived on the fringes of society. When I was pastor of Saint Paul of the Cross in Columbia City, I learned how shepherds would have been regarded. In that small town, no one ever locked their doors, except when the carnival came to town at the end of every summer. The locals did not trust the traveling carnival workers and considered them criminal, just as the residents of Bethlehem would have regarded the transient shepherds as thieves who would steal from them and move to the next town as soon as possible.

The birth of Jesus was completely unnoticed by most of the culture of the time. Even today, the twenty-four-hour news cycle is interested in other stories. However, the Mystery we celebrate tonight is just as present now as it was 2,000 years ago. God has taken on human flesh and dwells in our midst. God continues to announce this Mystery through the lowly and the insignificant. The Lord speaks especially through our little children, who can hardly contain themselves with joy and expectation at Christmas. He speaks the news of this Mystery with ordinary human words just proclaimed in the Scriptures. He humbles himself by identifying himself with ordinary bread and wine and feeds us with his very Body, as his physical body had lain in a manger in Bethlehem (which means "House of Bread"). Formed by our encounter with him in these sacramental signs, we more easily recognize the ways in which he dwells with us in our families gathered for Christmas. We look beyond whatever family conflicts and dysfunctions may be present to see him present in the mess of our family gatherings. We open our eyes to recognize him in the homeless, the poor, the stranger, and those who live on the margins of our society.

When we leave Mass tonight, we will return to a world that really has not changed much. But we leave with changed minds and transformed hearts. We leave more convinced than ever that God so loved the world that he sent his only Begotten Son. That Son dwells in the midst of our messy world. He has shared in our humanity, so that we can share in his divinity. There is no better news that that!

5.7 December 25, 2017

In the northern hemisphere, Christmas comes at a dark time of the year. Even though we suffered through the shortest and darkest day of the year last Thursday, it is still cold and dark. And it remains dark under our "perma-cloud" here. Worse, we live in a world filled with darkness. Far too often, nations and groups resort to violence, hatred, and racism to resolve their disputes. In our country, we live in a time of deep polarizations. Instead of listening to each other, we shout at each other and label our opponents as evil. We also bring with us the darkness of our lives: the darkness of our sins and failures, the darkness of failing health and sickness, the darkness of grief and loss, and the darkness of so much pain outside of our control.

When we come to celebrate Christmas, we cannot pretend that all of this darkness disappears in the "Christmas spirit." Instead, we dare to celebrate this incredible mystery in the midst of darkness. The infinite God has decided to reveal himself not as a powerful ruler born in a royal palace. Instead, God has taken flesh as a tiny, naked, helpless baby born in a stable. Saint Francis of Assisi was so moved by this epiphany of God that he decided to make the mystery more tangible to the people who came to celebrate Christmas with his community. He built a stable and placed an ox and a donkey in it. Then one of the friars set up an Altar and began Mass. Francis sang the Gospel as a deacon with great emotion. They held the real presence of the Lord in their hands, as Mary had cradled him in her arms, and were nourished with the Eucharist. Saint Francis created the first nativity set, a practice that continues. Be sure to visit our new nativity set in the Parish Life Center to begin to understand why Saint Francis called Christmas the "feast of feasts." He was not drawing attention away from Easter, when the Lord emerged triumphant from the tomb to change everything. Rather, he was pointing out that the Paschal Mystery could not have taken place without the Mystery of the Incarnation. Francis understood that we have to approach this Mystery with great simplicity and humility.

Those who visit the Church of the Nativity of the Lord in Bethlehem do that in a very real way. To enter the Church where tradition says that Christ was born, pilgrims must line up in a single file and bend down to go through a very small and narrow entrance. The original massive entrance has been blocked off to prevent soldiers from riding their horses into church! (Don't get on your horse and try to ride through those doors!)

That is the attitude we need as we approach our newborn Savior. We need to get off our horses of pride and arrogance in order to approach the Lord's Table with simplicity and humility. We need to imitate the examples of children who love to build forts out of all kinds of materials and bend down to enter. We need to let go of so many passing trappings of Christmas that can easily distract us from the real Mystery hidden in a tiny child lying in the manger. Only then can we embrace the true meaning of Christmas. Once we approach the manger with humility and simplicity, we reinforce our faith that this tiny child will eventually dispel all darkness, in our world and in our lives. The birth of Jesus Christ reveals that God does not want darkness to prevail. In the person of Jesus Christ, God shines with hope.

Christmas reminds us that God emptied himself of the privilege of divinity in the person of Jesus Christ and took on our humanity to transform us into divinity. If we embrace the Christmas miracle, we will understand that God's love, revealed by a tiny child born in a stable, has the power to transform us throughout the years. But it takes time. The Incarnate Lord will continue to reveal himself in the Sacramental life of the Church and in our daily experiences. But we have to be alert to his transforming love. Light will prevail. Christmas promises that.

6. Feast of the Holy Family

Readings
Sirach 3:2–6,12–14
Colossians 3:12–21
Luke 2:22–40

6.1 December 26, 1999

A mother of seven children went to Reconciliation and confessed that she was often impatient and angry with her children. The confessor gave a pious speech (as only a *celibate* priest can give!) and closed by saying, "Now try and imitate our Blessed Mother, who is a model of patience and long-suffering for us all." As the woman left the Room, she was overheard muttering to herself, "O sure, Mary with her one!"

Like that mother, many of us have an unreal picture of the Holy Family. It is true that they were a unique family – a divine Son, a virgin mother, and a husband who was not the child's biological father. There have not been many families like this one! But that family had more in common with our families than we think.

The Gospel writers record three incidents that should open our eyes to the common ground we share with the Holy Family. Luke tells the story of Mary and Joseph losing the twelve-year-old Jesus for three days. When they finally found him, Mary asked him, "Why have you done this to us? See how worried your father and I have been, looking for you?" The response of the pre-teenager was hardly comforting: "Why were you looking for me? Did you not know that I must be busy with my Father's affairs?" Parents, how would you accept this response?

John tells the story of poor planning at a wedding feast in Cana. When the hosts ran out of wine, Mary knew her Son could solve the problem. His response to her was puzzling: "Woman, why turn to me? My hour has not yet come." Mothers, would these words put you at ease? And on a third occasion, Matthew, Mark, and Luke report another incident when the mother of Jesus came looking for him, and Jesus replies: "Who are my mother and my brothers?" Mothers, wouldn't you be tempted to throw up your hands?

It is not too difficult to read between the lines of these stories to understand what human qualities our families have in common with the Holy Family of Nazareth. These types of situations raise all kinds of uncomfortable emotions in our families. And feeling these emotions is not sinful! But they can also become opportunities for growing in holiness. Our families share that common call with the Holy Family to grow in holiness.

Authors sometimes refer to the family as the "domestic church" – a community of people living together in a home. Our parish church – this community of people gathered for worship and service – is as strong as the domestic churches that make up this parish of Saint Jude. As a church, we can respond to tough situations and grow together in holiness, to the extent that this dynamic happens in our domestic churches.

As we continue to celebrate the mystery of the Incarnation – God's total gift of self to us – we need to remind ourselves that the Christ born into a human family can also take flesh in our domestic churches. That can happen in households with two parents and children, in single parent homes, in divorced and separated homes, and even in homes torn apart by huge problems. Let's face it. If the Word could take Flesh in a stable full of manure, then he can be present in the midst of those same qualities present in all our families.

6.2 December 29, 2002

The custom of sending and receiving Christmas cards is a wonderful way to keep in touch with friends whom we do not see much. Reading those long letters about what the family did in the last year can get a little tedious. Looking at the family pictures that people include in their cards is much more interesting. Many times, the children are dressed up in matching outfits, with colors that coordinate, and with bright and happy smiles on everyone's faces. These pictures are intended to present this particular family in the most ideal of all situations.

When my family gathered for Christmas, we did not have one of those family pictures taken, because we could never have agreed on a matching outfit! We know that we are not the ideal family.

There were the usual tensions, the underlying problems that we do not talk about, and the heartbreak of knowing that some situations just cannot be fixed. During our three days together, my family clogged up the toilets, destroyed the house, violated poor Father Dan's privacy, and my brother-in-law insisted on smoking in our garage. I'm trying to figure out how to connect a garden hose with a barrel of Fabrese. But, at the same time, we had a great time together. We laughed, made fun of each other, played lots of games, ate together, and my nephews increased their college education fund when they took all my loose change in our annual poker game.

Saint Paul was not interested in taking a group shot of the Colossians either. However, he reminds them (and us) in today's second reading that they (and we) have been formed into a unique family through baptism. He tells us that God had chosen us to be holy and beloved. Instead of recommending that we wear matching outfits for a group picture, he describes the types of garments we should be wearing – reminiscent of the white garments we donned as we emerged from the waters of baptism. He tells us to put on heartfelt compassion, kindness, humility, gentleness, and patience. Wearing that kind of clothing makes us look like the family we really are.

In celebrating the Feast of the Holy Family, we are given a model of what a holy and beloved family looks like, especially from the mouth of an old man who predicts pain and sorrow for this family. However, the holy family of Nazareth does not want us to leave this Church feeling defeated because we do not measure up to them. Rather, the holy family shows that God has come down from heaven to dwell in our midst to give us glimpses of the divine in each of our families, no matter what our problems may be.

Today, we give thanks for our individual families, for this parish family united in baptism, and for the entire human family touched by God's love. Today is a day to change our clothes. If I wear heartfelt compassion, then I will not be so critical of my chain-smoking redneck brother-in-law. If children can wear kindness, humility, and gentleness, then we might be so jealous of what another brother or sister got for Christmas. If we – as a parish community – can wear patience a little more prominently, bearing with one another and forgiving each other more quickly – then residents in Granger will notice that we are holy, despite our faults and failures. If more people see the common bond we share with all humanity loved and redeemed by God, perhaps peace will have a chance in the New Year.

6.3 December 28, 2008

The New Testament Scriptures introduce us to a wide variety of characters at Christmas. We meet Joseph and Mary, as well as an Inn Keeper who has no room for the family in his Inn. We meet angels and shepherds, not to mention mysterious visitors from the East. We are told stories of a murderous king who wants to get rid of the child. In the midst of all these characters we find a number of old people (which warms my heart!). We meet Zechariah and Elizabeth, who conceive a child in their old age, and we meet Anna, an eighty-four-year-old widow who has spent most of her time hanging out in the Temple.

Along with Anna, we meet Simeon, a righteous and devout man who had waited his entire life to behold the Mystery he is now holding in his arms. We automatically assume that Simeon is also an old man, because God had promised him that he would not die before seeing the Messiah. We pray his "Nunc Dimittis" (Now, Lord, you can dismiss your servant in peace...) every night at night prayer before, and we sometimes sing this song before we take the bodies of our loved ones out of church for burial. But, Luke does not tell us that he is old. There is nothing in the text to indicate his age.

For that reason, please allow me to indulge your imaginations for a moment. Let's say that Simeon is a young man, or a middle-aged man. After singing his canticle that he could now leave the Temple in peace, he did not go out to die. Instead, he left the Temple that day jumping for joy, so that he could really, really live in a spirit of joy and hope. Even though Simeon himself prophesized that this child would be the downfall of many in Israel, even though he told Mary that a sword would pierce her soul, he left the Temple to live with the hope that he had seen. God came to save his people. He recognized that salvation in a tiny child. Now it was time for him to live that hope and joy, no matter what would happen in his life.

We gather today as a people of all ages. We are young, middle aged, and old (like me!). With Simeon, we have worshipped the Lord born in a manger. Reflecting his joy, we continue to sing Christmas carols and wrap ourselves in the trappings of Christmas, because we too have seen our salvation, prepared for us in the sight of all the peoples.

We also gather as human families and members of this parish family. At the end of this Mass, and at the end of every Mass, we are dismissed (like Simeon) and told to go in peace. That means that we are sent to take the faith, joy, and hope that we celebrate here into the places where we live our daily lives – in the communities of our families, our schools, our work places, and our neighborhoods. There were times when I was younger when I would leave the beautiful Christmas Masses to join my family for our Christmas celebration, and I would wonder if there was really any connection between the two. But, over the years, the distance between my two families began to narrow. As I would become more an integral part of our parish family, I recognized in our parish family many of the same traits as I encountered in my human family – good, joyful, happy, bad, painful, ugly, and all the elements we share in common. The true Christmas miracle became much clearer in my mind and heart. The same Lord whom we behold here dwells in the midst of all of families, because that Lord was not born into privilege or special circumstances, but in the messiness of human existence.

With Simeon, we behold the Mystery here and worship the Lord with great beauty, splendor, pomp, and circumstances. Having held him in our hands and received him into our bodies, we too are dismissed: not to die, but to really and truly live with hope and joy at the presence of the Word Made Flesh.

6.4 December 28, 2014

When we celebrate this Feast of the Holy Family, we might be tempted to become discouraged. How can any of our families compete with this family? Here is a family where the child is the only begotten Son of God, the mother is an immaculate virgin without any sin, and the father learns all kinds of incredible things when he is dreaming! Other than what we hear today and what we read later in Saint Luke's Gospel about Jesus being lost in the Temple at the age of 12, we know nothing about the details of their family dynamics.

There is no way to keep up with this family. That is why I have always been more than willing to share stories about my own family gatherings at the rectory at Christmas. To be honest, it was a pretty uneventful Christmas for us this year, and I have no stories to tell. The reason we celebrate this Feast is to learn lessons from the Holy Family to apply to our own. In the light of our celebration of the Eternal Word of God taking flesh and dwelling in the midst of our families and their messes, the characters of today's Gospel can give us some helpful hints.

The first lesson comes from the parents of Jesus. Saint Luke is careful to tell us that they are following the law of the Lord in presenting their first-born child in the Temple. Because they are dirt poor, they can only afford a pair of turtle doves as a sacrifice. But this ritual is more than a demand of the law. They use it to thank God for the gift of a healthy son and commend him to the Lord's service. Parents today can learn from this lesson. Parents keep the promises they made when they had their children baptized by bringing them to Mass, teaching them to pray at home, and helping them to understand the ways they can love God and neighbor.

The second lesson comes from Simeon. He trusted the Lord's promise that he would not die before seeing the savior. His trust is rewarded when he recognizes the Christ and proclaims the canticle which we pray every night at Compline, or Night Prayer. Simeon teaches us how to find joy in each of our families. In sharing his joy, Simeon is also very realistic. He does not promise that everything will always be rosy and sweet for this family. He talks about the sword that will pierce Mary's heart and the suffering that would be endured by her Son. He reminds us that God's faithfulness and promise will not keep our families from tragedies or even divisions that will tear us apart. In fact, he realistically states that practicing our faith may get us into more trouble. But, he also promises that God will be as faithful to us as God had been to him.

We know the least about Anna. She is a daughter of Phanuel of the tribe of Asher, which was the smallest and least significant of the twelve tribes of Israel. We know that she had only seven years of marriage before her husband died, and she lived as a widow till the age of 84. Instead of dwelling in the past and becoming bitter about the difficulties of her life, she lived in the present and praised God for this family and the child she encountered. Her lesson is important. It is easy to become angry and bitter over the ways in which life might have battered us around. But Anna teaches us to let go of all that bitterness, to live in the present moment, and to look for ways in which God is revealing himself now.

No matter what might be happening right now in each of our families, Christmas reminds us that the Lord has taken on human flesh and lives in our human families and lives in this parish family that gathers to celebrate his presence every Sunday. With Mary and Joseph, we commit ourselves to sharing the riches of our faith as much as possible. With Simeon, we recognize the Lord's presence in our midst and share the joy, trusting that the Lord will be faithful to us, no matter what difficulties we will endure. With Anna, we let go of any bitterness we might be holding to give praise for the ways in which God works in and through us now.

6.5   December 31, 2017

As we continue to celebrate the Incarnation on this sixth day of the Octave of Christmas, our Scripture readings invite us to consider the ways in which the Word Made Flesh is present in our families. As observant children of Abraham, Joseph and Mary do not consider themselves merely "spiritual" because they are caring for the infant Messiah and Son of God. They are also deeply "religious." They observe the religious demands of the Law of Moses for women giving birth to a first-born son and travel to Jerusalem. In the Temple, they meet two other children of Abraham. Both ancient of days, Simeon rejoices that he could hold the Messiah in his arms before he dies. Prompted by the Holy Spirit, he sings a canticle describing the child's identity and warns of the dangers of his mission. Anna too rejoices that God had kept his promise, as he had kept his promise centuries before to Abraham and Sarah.

Saint Luke recounts this incident to consider the implications of the Lord's Nativity. Even though Jesus Christ is the Second Person of the Trinity and was present at the creation of the world, he has also taken on the fullness of our humanity. He is a tiny, vulnerable baby who needs the care of parents, as any baby does. As he grows up, he learns the truth not from angels giving him beatific visions, but from parents sharing their faith through the religious customs they cherish. In cultivating their love, they prepare him for the mission which Simeon describes.

The incarnate Lord is present in each one of our families. He is not present physically as he was to Joseph and Mary. But, because of the Mystery of the Incarnation, of God taking on human flesh, he dwells in our families, no matter what they look like. Some of you will go home to a family with two committed parents and children. Others will go home to a family broken by death or divorce. Some of you will go home to a dysfunctional family. Some of you are like Anna the widow, with no one waiting for you. None of our families are like the Holy Family of Nazareth. That is the reason I talk about my own family on this feast. With the death of my very colorful brother in law, my stories are not as dramatic. But, as we gathered in the rectory at Christmas, we had our own "issues." One of my nieces till refuses to come to family gatherings, because she thinks we hate her. One of my brothers was so sick that he lost his desire to join us for our annual outing to the casino on Wednesday. One of my nephews and his wife brought their two little children. They are adorable and precious. But they also got tired quickly and threw some pretty nice fits (making me more grateful for my gift of celibacy!).

Be sure to look for aspects of holiness in your family. Pope Francis says that there are three marks that make a family holy. They spend time in payer. They keep the faith. They experience joy. Look for these marks, even if they might be marginal. Be open to conversion – to ways in which the Holy Spirit can help you to change in the New Year.

We also belong to a larger family – our family constituted by baptism and gathering here on Sunday. We pray together. We work to keep the faith, to bring our "spiritual" experiences to this "religious" setting. We hear God's word and are nourished by the Eucharist to be formed into a spiritual temple. We experience joy at parish gatherings. The Lord challenges us to recognize these marks of holiness and continue to turn more completely to him. Abraham and Sarah trusted that God would keep his promises. But it took time, and they had to be patient. That is why we put the Covenant with Abraham (showing the stars in the sky and the sands on the shore). Simeon and Anna waited in hope. So did Joseph and Mary. Their examples encourage us to look for marks of holiness already present in our families and to trust that God always keeps his promises.

7. Mary, Mother of God

Readings
Numbers 6:22–27
Galatians 4:4–7
Luke 2:16–21

7.1 January 1, 2000

For the past couple of weeks, the media has inundated us with statistics about the 20th Century. We could probably argue for hours about what are the most significant changes we have seen in the past 100 years, in fact the last 1000 years! But I have center stage, and here is my opinion! I find the changes in communication to be among the most amazing developments. From the telephone and radio of 1900, we have moved to the Internet, e-mail, television, networking, and cellular phones. These innovations have provided us with fantastic and ways to communicate with each other.

But like all advances, there have been bad effects among the good effects. A sense of privacy has been lost. Not too long ago, a funeral in this church was interrupted by someone's cell phone ringing. Last year when we were skiing, a woman ordered me to shut up on the chair lift, because she as closing a stock deal in San Francisco. We cannot go anywhere without pagers beeping! Sometimes, cars go past the church on State Street with their car radios booming so loud that we can hear the bass "boom, boom, boom" in here! We seem to have lost a sense of solitude and silence in our technological world.

In stark contrast to the noise of our world is the situation of Mary, the Mother of God. Luke tells us that Mary was so moved by the birth of Jesus and all the events surrounding it, that she needed time to ponder them and what they meant. "And Mary kept all these things, reflecting on them in her heart."

We need silence and solitude for two reasons. First, we need silence in order to hear the Spirit of God speaking to us. Just as we miss the beauty of creation when we drive 65 miles and hour along an Expressway as we talk on our cell phones, so we miss the many ways God speaks to us when we allow no time for silence. Second, we need silence as a way of reflecting on the many ways God speaks to us. Only in the silence of our hearts can we make sense of so many of life's mysteries.

So, I have a suggestion as we enter this New Year, this new century, this new millennium. Let's enter it in silence! More importantly, let's ask Mary to help us. She must have spent a lot of time alone in Nazareth pondering the events of Bethlehem. How else could she have been so open to what was happening? It is she who can help make us into lovers of silence in an extraordinarily noisy world!

7.2 January 1, 2003

It is customary for the media to look back on this last year and to give a list of the most compelling stories of the year. Among many other issues, Bethlehem has been in the news this past year. Bethlehem has been robbed of its tourism since the Intifadah broke out two years ago, and its economy is in tatters. Bethlehem is an occupied town, with Israeli soldiers enforcing a very strict curfew. During this past spring, Palestinian militants took refuge in the Church of the Nativity, the only Byzantine-era church still standing in the Holy Land. The siege lasted for thirty-nine days, and both Muslim and Christian Arabs suffered from it.

The reality of Bethlehem as it appears in the news today seems to be in stark contrast to the little town of Bethlehem of our Christmas stories and carols. However, a closer look will reveal that today's Bethlehem has much more in common with the first century Bethlehem than we might think. At the time of Jesus, Bethlehem was an occupied town, with Roman soldiers patrolling the streets. Occupation forces always bring with them tensions, and the crowds coming to town for the census forced Mary and Joseph into one of the many caves in the hilly area to give birth to the child. In fact, Jesus was born into a world not much different from ours today – a world filled with tensions, fears, and threats of war.

This Feast of Mary, the Mother of God, invites us to do what Mary did. Like Mary, we are invited to turn over the events of the past year in our hearts. We are invited to look with hope on her newborn child and enter this New Year with hope. Like Mary, we are invited to develop a contemplative spirit that steps back to evaluate what is happening in our lives, always trying to recognize the Prince of Peace in everything.

We may not live in a city occupied by enemy forces. But, as Saint Paul notes in his letter to the Galatians, we have been freed from slavery to sin and have become sons and daughters through the Mysteries of the life, death, and resurrection of Mary's Son. No matter what happens in this New Year, we belong to God.

7.3   January 1, 2006

Four years ago, Mishawaka made national news when a surveillance camera at Kohl's caught a woman apparently beating her child in her car in the parking lot. As the tape was played back repeatedly, the press reported that this woman was part of a group known as the Irish Travelers. Based on Texas, they come to our area in the summer looking for work. With more press coverage, the public identified the group with shady deals, stealing, and swindling. However, Father Dan and I saw another side to the Irish travelers, because they came every Sunday to the 12:15 Mass. Father Dan had baptized one of their babies. When the Feast of the Birth of Mary fell on Sunday that year, most of us forgot. But, the Irish travelers did not. They placed balloons and flowers and before the image of our Lady. The group that no one trusted had a child-like faith.

The shepherds in the Christmas story were like those Irish travelers. In the barren landscape, shepherds had to keep moving their flocks to find grass and water. Local people never trusted these shady groups of shepherds who owned nothing but their flocks, and they got the reputation for being thieves and swindlers. Yet, angels announced to the shepherds that the Savior had been born. They went to Bethlehem to see what they had been told. In their child-like simplicity, they believed. This unlikely group of people became the first evangelists by telling others about the Good News.

The shepherds can teach us a valuable lesson. Like them, we continue to come here to see for ourselves the Good News of the birth of Jesus Christ. Today, we look around and ask where are all those other people who were here last weekend. We are tempted to congratulate ourselves for being more faithful, better people than those "Christmas and Easter folks." And the shepherds tell us not to do that. The shepherds invite us to look at our own faults, our own sins, and our own ways of betraying the trust of others. With a humility that causes us to look at ourselves as we really are, we can use a child-like faith and become evangelists to carry the Good News of Christmas to our homes, our work places, and our schools.

Mary can also teach us a valuable lesson. We honor Mary as the Mother of God and our Mother, because she came to know the will of God in her life and followed it faithfully. In today's Gospel, Luke indicates that Mary did not immediately know and understand God's will. Instead, she kept all these things, reflecting on them in her heart. Instead of reacting impulsively to the mysterious events swirling around her, she took them to prayer, reflected on them as both joyful and painful events in her life unfolded, and she trusted God's mysterious will slowly and gradually revealed to her.

In this New Year, Mary invites us to seek to know God's will in our lives, a task that is even more difficult in an age of instant communication. The cable news networks put banners across the bottom of the TV screens announcing breaking news. As a helicopter hovers over a burning building or over a house where someone is holding someone else captive, neighbors tell us exactly what is happening. Two hours later, it turns out that nothing happened at all. Or a major figure gives a speech, and the talking heads tell us what is significant. Or a TV advertisement promises us the coolest toy in the world. We beg our parents to give it to us, and it breaks the day after Christmas. Our age encourages us to seek immediate answers and immediate results.

In sharp contrast, Mary invites us to step back, bring the confusing events of our lives to prayer, speak about it with mature people we trust, and be patient as God manifests himself in our daily lives. Christmas tells us that God has truly manifested himself in a child wrapped in swaddling clothes and placed in a manger. Mary tells us to be patient as we come to understand the mystery of how this child will take flesh in our lives and in our world in this New Year.

7.4 January 1, 2012

On this first day of the new calendar year, the Church concludes the Octave of Christmas by celebrating the oldest solemnity in honor of Mary, the Mother of God. It is through her experience that we continue to reflect on the Christmas Mystery. This young maiden from the backwater town of Nazareth has gone through an incredible nine months. She was startled by the Angel Gabriel when he announced to her that she had been chosen to be the mother of God. She had traveled south to the hill country north of Jerusalem to be with her cousin Elizabeth, who had conceived a child in her old age. At the end of her nine months, she and Joseph made what must have been a very difficult journey to be counted in Bethlehem, where her child was born in a smelly stable surrounded by animals. The angels had announced the good news to the least likely people – transient shepherds who had the reputation of being dishonest. When those shepherds returned, transformed by the Mystery they had encountered, Mary's head must have been swirling!

Saint Luke describes what Mary does with all of these events. He tells us that she kept all these things, reflecting on them in her heart. Literally translated, the Greek word means "to toss things together in one's heart." By tossing all these things together in her heart, Mary quietly begins to make sense of all that has happened. As a result, she begins to understand what it means for the Word Made Flesh to dwell in her midst. Because she tosses these events around in her heart, she can maintain her faithfulness, even when she sees her son rejected by so many, executed as a common criminal, and buried in a tomb. With her son's resurrection, ascension, and sending of the Holy Spirit at Pentecost, she understands the Mysteries that began with Gabriel's annunciation.

The best resolution we can make in this New Year is to imitate Mary's example. We live in an age of instant communication, which gives us many benefits. But our age can rob us of the time needed to recognize the Mystery of the Incarnate Lord dwelling in our midst. Instead of keeping our eyes glued on the latest "breaking news" in the 24-hour cable news cycle, we might resolve to turn off the television and spend some time to reflect on the events of our day, recognizing God's presence. When we are angry about something, we might resolve to work through the emotions first before sending a biting tirade, ending with the words, "have a nice day." If we toss the situation around in our hearts for a while, we can still communicate the truth with love, rather than with angry words. Young people who are trying to discern how God is calling you to live your baptismal promises might bring those decisions to prayer and toss them around in your hearts in front of the Blessed Sacrament. That is a wonderful practice for any of us struggling to make the best decisions that affect the lives of our families.

Mary understood that the greatest gift ever given to the human race was wrapped in swaddling clothes and laid in a manger. As she slowly and prayerfully unwrapped that gift by tossing all these events in her heart, she became a model for the rest of us. In this New Year, we will encounter many events over which we will have no control. But, if we resolve to imitate Mary's example, we can recognize the presence of the Mystery of the Word Made Flesh in our families, in this parish, in our school, and in the places where we work. Spending more time in prayer will not protect us from the messes and confusions of our lives this year. But, it will help us see how the Lord truly blesses us and keeps us, how the Lord lets his face shine on us and is gracious to us, and how the Lord looks upon us kindly and gives us peace. Those gifts are present in the Mystery of the newborn Christ, dwelling in our midst.

8. The Epiphany of the Lord

Readings
Isaiah 60:1–6
Ephesians 3:2–3a, 5–6
Matthew 2:1–12

8.1 January 2, 2000

The word *Epiphany* is a Greek word that means, "to manifest," or "to reveal." Since Christmas Eve, we have been celebrating God manifested (revealed) in human flesh. A theologian calls what we have been doing "epiphany business," and he compares it to a stone dropped into a pool of quiet water. Just as the stone produces concentric ripples that grow larger and larger until the entire surface is witness to the stone being dropped into it, so it is with the "epiphany business" we have been observing. It began with a private annunciation by an angel messenger to Mary. Then it spread to Joseph, to Zechariah and Elizabeth, to the shepherds, and finally to the mysterious Magi who traveled from the East. By telling this wonderful story, Matthew makes it clear that the concentric circles of this Mystery will eventually reach the entire world. Today's Feast of the Epiphany is both a celebration and a challenge. It is a celebration, because we continue to mark the birth of Jesus Christ, manifested as light and life for the world. It is a challenge, because we are invited to live lives that manifest light and life. When we do this, we become part of the ever-widening concentric circles of "epiphany business" that continue to spread in our world today. We must be willing to see, hear, touch, and attend to the presence of God not only in so many predictable people and places in our lives, but also in those people and places where we least expect to find God! The Magi traveled a long and difficult distance to become part of this "epiphany business." Being part of the ever-widening concentric circles requires each of us to make our own internal journey toward that same light as well. The poet Edward Hayes expresses the difficulty of this journey in one of his prayers:

> Oh God, how lonely it is to be the light of the world, to be your justice and love in a world devoid of them, to be kindness and compassion in a world of competition. Yes, I find it lonely being luminous. As all alone as our solitary sun, at times, that's how I feel, Radiant God. How hard to be the light of the world, to hold a glowing warmth in a world so cold. So, forgive me, Beloved, for being just a momentary shooting star in the darkness of my world.

Lonely or not, this is the challenge of Epiphany for all of us, as it was for Jesus himself. In this new Jubilee Year, we have a unique opportunity to be more than momentary shooting stars in a cold world. Our observance of Christmas is much more than observing an anniversary of a birth that happened 2000 years ago. It is an invitation to be part of "epiphany business," called to renew our resolve to be like Jesus, a sun that lights the world despite the loneliness and the struggle.

8.2 January 5, 2003

For centuries, people have made pilgrimages to Chartres Cathedral in France. As soon as they enter the magnificent Church, they see a huge star with a pattern of torques and curves around it on the stone floor. It is a labyrinth, inviting the pilgrims to trace the path from the outside of the labyrinth to the circle in the center. Whether the pilgrims have walked the 60 miles from Paris or 1,000 miles from surrounding countries, the labyrinth reminds them of why they began their journey in the first place – to find Christ.

That is the lesson of the Magi. We know nothing about these mysterious astrologers from the East. They must have had a difficult journey, as they crossed the very deserts our troops are threatening to invade today. In addition to the inherent difficulties of such a physical trip, they had to endure their own doubts and the complaints of those with whom they traveled. Matthew tells us that they had to face the intrigues of a local king who was threatened by the birth of the Child they sought. But, despite all their difficulties, the star led them to Jesus Christ, the newborn king of the Jews. They expressed their faith in Him with their gifts – gold (for a king), frankincense (for a priest who bridged the gap between God and humanity), and myrrh (to anoint his body after he had been crucified). Having successfully maneuvered their complex labyrinth, they returned home changed by the Mystery they encountered.

The Magi's journey is our journey today. Once again this year, we have been celebrating the Mystery of the Incarnation – God taking human flesh and dwelling among us (pitching his tent, as John puts it so colorfully). Having renewed our faith in this Mystery, our task is now that of the Magi's. We need to maneuver the labyrinth of our own lives and find the One who dwells in each of our lives. Like the journey of the Magi, our journey can be difficult and twisting. We encounter challenges in the form of doubts and confusion. We sometimes run into the roadblocks set up by our own selfishness and hard-heartedness. We find ourselves lost when we confront injury or disease or death. The Magi urge us to keep in mind the inner circle of that labyrinth – the Lord Jesus, the Light of the world, the one revealed at Christmas.

Over the course of history, people have handled their own labyrinth journeys in different ways. Some have reacted like Herod and refused to enter into the journey at all. Others have followed the pattern of Herod's advisors, the Scribes and High Priests, who were so preoccupied with the events of their daily lives that they did not care whether they journeyed or not. And some, like the Magi, have persisted in their search and found Jesus Christ. It has been through these people that the Light of the world has shined. The choice is ours. Like the Magi, we are invited to follow the star in this New Year and find the Christ who truly dwells in our midst.

8.3 January 8, 2006

When Matthew tells us of the mysterious Magi arriving in Jerusalem inquiring about a newborn King of the Jews, he tells us nothing about their homes, their lives, how they became interested in the birth of the Messiah, or the journey. They simply arrived on the scene. At Saint Pius, we give the same impression, because our images of the Magi have been lurking in the sacristy since Christmas Eve. Today, they appear in the crche to join the shepherds, along with the gray-haired pastor seated before the stable and the younger associate roller blading down the hill.

We can only imagine the difficulties encountered by the Magi on their way from the East. Unlike the shepherds, who were told directly by angels, the Magi had to figure it out on their own. Their journey had to be difficult, crossing barren deserts, facing thieves and murderers who preyed on travelers, and putting up with all the negativity and infighting that accompany large groups of people who travel together. They surely got lost and had to ask for directions many times along the way. When they finally arrived in Jerusalem to ask for their final set of directions, they encountered a king who tried to manipulate them for his own murderous intentions. What a trip they must have had!

Matthew tells us this story to invite us to make our own journey to find the Christ today. Like the Magi, we too have looked to the stars and determined that there is more to life than what we can see around us on earth. Like them, we have spent our lives searching for Christ. Our journeys are not always easy. We've had to endure the complaining and negativity of those who travel with us. We have gotten lost countless times. Some of us might feel lost at this moment. We've had to ask for directions. And we have all encountered our own versions of King Herod, trying to manipulate us.

But, like the Magi, we have heard the same Word told to Herod by the high priests and scribes. Like the Magi, we too have found the newborn Christ here in Bethlehem, the House of Bread. In encountering his real presence at this Eucharist, we acknowledge the gold of his kingship, the frankincense of his divinity, and the myrrh of his suffering and death.

There is an ancient tradition of proclaiming the calendar dates that are most important to us in this New Year. As soon as I am done babbling, Jeremy will proclaim that calendar in song. As we listen to it and look ahead to these coming dates, we need to trust that the light of Christ will shine, even when there are thick clouds of darkness in our lives. The Magi teach us to continue on our journey – to listen to the Word of God, to come to the Bethlehem of the Eucharist every Sunday, and to ask for directions when we lose our ways. When the Magi learned the truth about Herod, they returned to their homes by another route. That change of route was much more than geographical. Their encounter with the Child profoundly changed them and set their lives on a new course. Our encounter with the Child in this New Year has the power to change us profoundly and set us on a new course as we continue our journey together to the Heavenly Jerusalem.

8.4   January 4, 2009

Saint Matthew tells about mysterious visitors coming from the East to pay homage to the new born King to make a very important point. God took on human flesh and is manifested not only to the Jewish shepherds. God became a child and is manifested to Gentiles, who had no connection with God's chosen people. In telling this wonderful story of God's intention to offer salvation to everyone, Matthew sparks our imaginations and invites us to reflect on the ways we experience God manifested in this Season in our lives.

Many creative people have wondered what changes the Magi made in their lives after their encounter with the Child. Matthew implies that their pilgrimage had a positive effect, because they go home by another route. But we can never know how their lives were changed. We can only use our imaginations and reflect on our own pilgrimage of faith.

Like the Magi, a group of us from Saint Pius in 2007 embarked on a pilgrimage that changed our lives. Like them, we headed west toward Santiago de Compostela to pray at the bones of Saint James. Some of us began our journey at the French border, with others starting 100 kilometers from Santiago. We found the journey more difficult than expected, with two of our pilgrims suffering serious injuries the first day. Some had not prepared themselves well enough, while others encountered difficulties we had never imagined. Along the way, we had to learn how to live together as a community, to handle strange situations, and adjust our expectations to the present reality. When we finally reached the Cathedral for the noon pilgrim's Mass, we rejoiced in our destination and recognized the Lord's presence in that huge cathedral with so many other pilgrims we had met along the way. That must have been the experience of the Magi. Like them, we too had to leave that sacred place and return home.

We have reflected on the pilgrimage and are convinced that it has brought significant changes in our lives. Our pilgrimage forged bonds of friendship that had not existed, as well as memories of the kindness of strangers who manifested the face of God to us. We have been able to put the difficulties and pain into better perspective. To this day, when life gets tough, I simply remember what we did every morning: we put one foot in front of the other and headed west. I will never forget my gratitude at the Pilgrim's Mass that God had protected us from any truly serious injury or harm. The pilgrimage made us more conscious of God's blessings.

We can do this same kind of reflecting as we continue our pilgrimage of faith together, as we head west (to the place of the setting sun) and pause during the Christmas Season to reflect on the implications of God taking on human flesh. In this final week of Christmas, we ask the question: how has our encounter with this Wonderful Mystery changed us this year? We answer that question when we reflect on the common bonds of friendship and family we share in this Season. We remember unexpected acts of kindness and gifts we had not expected from others. We put the pain and dysfunction of our families into better perspective, and we remember that we take so many things for granted, calling us to a deeper sense of gratitude.

In reflecting on what is happening in our journey at this Season, we have two choices. We can look through the lens of fear, as did Herod, who regarded Jesus as a political threat, even in the form of an infant. Looking through the lens of fear paralyzes us and keeps us from making those changes necessary to embrace God dwelling right in our midst. Or we can look through the eyes of the Magi and see Jesus as a King (gold), Priest (incense), and Sacrifice (myrrh). When we do this, Christmas is not just a memory of the "Holidays" which occur each year, but as a life changing experience in our common Pilgrimage of Faith.

8.5   January 8, 2012

Over the centuries, artists, poets, musicians, story tellers, and painters have used their imaginations to reflect on Saint Matthew's account of the visit of the magi. In time, three names were given to the magi, because there were three gifts for the newborn King. Balthazar became the youngest, Caspar the middle, and Melchior the oldest. According to one legend, each of the magi enters separately into the cave to encounter no one but a man of his own age. When all three take their gifts together, they find inside only a 13-day-old infant.

If we consider this legend, we can use our own imaginations to explore the conversation each one might have shared. Perhaps the young Balthazar met a young prophet who shared his thoughts on promise and reform. Caspar met a middle-aged man who talked passionately about leadership and responsibility. When Melchior entered, he met an old man like himself, with whom he felt at ease. Together they shared memories of days gone by.

We too are invited to use our imaginations to reflect on the epiphany of the Lord. The root meaning of this Greek word means "to manifest." The gifts of the magi tell us that in this tiny child, the Lord has manifested himself as King (gold), as God (frankincense), and as one who would suffer and give his life for the salvation of his people (myrrh). This manifestation, this epiphany, is not given for a few select people who share a wonderful secret, but to everyone. That is why Saint Matthew tells this story of gentile astrologers who follow the natural stars to make the journey to a people who had been chosen by God to receive his direct revelation.

It makes no difference how old or young we are. It makes no difference what we do for a living or where we come from. Christmas speaks of the Lord's wonderful manifestation to us and reminds us that the Word has indeed taken flesh, dwelling with us on a permanent basis. We leave the Christmas Season tomorrow when we celebrate the Feast of the Baptism of the Lord, manifested in the waters of the Jordan. In the next few weeks, we will hear Saint Mark tell us about the ways in which the Lord manifests himself through his miracles and teaching. As we are fed with his real manifestation in the common elements of bread and wine, we can explore ways in which the Lord manifests himself to us in the events of our daily lives.

There is an ancient custom of proclaiming the Solemnities of the Lord's Paschal Mystery on the Epiphany. Jeremy will do that as soon as I stop babbling on here. As we hear the dates of these liturgical observances which will mark our daily lives this year, we need to pay attention to a specific detail in today's Gospel. Saint Matthew tells us that the magi changed their direction, and took a different route home, because of the threats of King Herod. That change of direction indicates that they had been profoundly changed by their encounter with the newborn King, even in the face of the murderous intents of the insecure king. We too can be changed by our encounter with this King who dwells in our midst. His presence provides us with the courage to continue our journey of faith in this New Year, no matter what threats we might encounter.

8.6 January 4, 2015

The magi used their own human reason and the science of astrology to search for the newborn King. Imagine if they had today's technology. After checking out a variety of philosophies and spiritual exercises, they would have connected their GPS system onto the backs of their camels and began their journey. Once the GPS had guided them into Jerusalem, it would have told them: "turn right at the next intersection, and then take the 3rd exit on the roundabout. Herod's Palace is the second palace on your left." And then they would have lost their signal, because the latest technology and a variety of spiritual practices could only lead them so far. Even King Herod, with his massive ego and insecurities, knew that. He had to turn to the chief priests and the scribes for directions. They knew that God had continually revealed himself through the Scriptures. So, they quoted the prophet Micah and told the magi to go to Bethlehem.

Many people in our own day are honestly seeking for the truth. A recent poll reported that there is a large percentage of Americans today who consider themselves "spiritual," but not "religious." I have sensed this in our own parish. Many young people are honestly searching for the truth, exploring many different paths and looking at a variety of philosophies or spiritual practices to find God. At a certain level, there is nothing wrong with this searching. But in itself, this searching only goes so far. This human searching looks for a God who will fit into comfortable categories and preconceived notions of who God is.

We gather here today, because we have learned that our spiritual searching can only lead us so far. That is what the Magi learned. In their search for God, they found the One who had been searching for them. We know the truth about the Incarnate Word of God, lying as a tiny child in a manger, through the gifts given by the Magi. The gold speaks of his being the King of kings. The frankincense reveals that he is God. The myrrh points to his role as Suffering Servant. He is born, so that he will eventually die, have his dead body anointed with myrrh, and be raised from the dead to share that rising with us.

An ancient legend gives names and ages to the three magi. Caspar was very young. Balthazar was middle-aged. Melchior was a senior citizen. When they arrived at Bethlehem, each entered one at a time. Melchior met an old man his age, and they spoke of memory and gratitude. Balthazar encountered a middle-aged teacher, and they spoke passionately of leadership and responsibility. Caspar met a young prophet, and they talked about reform and promise. After that, they entered together to meet an infant with his mother. They began to understand that the Savior speaks to each of us at every stage of life. The elderly hear the call to integrity and wisdom. The middle-aged hear the call to generosity and responsibility. The young hear the call to authenticity and intimacy.

That is why we gather in this church every Sunday to practice our religion. We hear the Word of God speaking to each of us in our own specific situations, much as the Lord Jesus spoke to Saul of Tarsus on the road to Damascus and revealed the mystery to him. We encounter his real presence in the Eucharist, much as the magi encountered him when they entered that stable. We continue to reflect on the mysterious ways in which the Lord dwells in our midst. We leave this church changed by our encounter with the Lord, just as the magi took another route home, signifying that their encounter with the newborn King changed their lives forever. As we reflect on the mystery of the Word Made Flesh dwelling in our midst and practice our religion, we too can be a light to the nations, giving direction to those who pursue their spiritual searching. The Lord can use us as instruments, guiding honest seekers to the truth that we explore.

8.7   January 7, 2018

The Magi had set out on a journey to discover God. In their search, they were using all the tools at their disposal – their knowledge of the stars, their study, their wealth, and their natural intelligence. These tools had led them to Jerusalem, the capital city where a proper Jewish king should have been born. But that was as far as they got. To find this king, they have to ask questions of the Jewish religious leaders. The chief priests and scribes quote the words of the prophet Micah and tell them that the promised Messiah would be born in Bethlehem, the city of King David's birth. These Gentile visitors need the truth of revealed religion to complete their journey to Bethlehem, where they encounter the newborn king of the Jews. In searching for God, they find that God had been searching for them and reveals himself through his Word that had been entrusted to the people of a particular religion.

Today, many people, especially young people, are honestly and sincerely searching for God, just as the Magi were searching. They use the tools at their disposal – philosophy, science, spiritual writings, the beauty of nature, and the study of world religions. But, like the Magi, they need the help of our living religious tradition to realize that God is searching for them. Through Word and Sacrament, the Lord reveals himself as he is, and not as we create him to be.

There is an interesting analogy to this search in the many dating services found on line these days. There is a Catholic dating site. The searcher is told that the match will be a practicing Catholic and provides all kinds of information about that person. But, in order to form a real relationship, the searcher has to meet the other person. In the course of dating, the desired person gradually reveals herself or himself. In the course of that self-revelation, the searcher discovers the truth about the other and can enter into a loving relationship (or not!).

In the ancient world, astrologers regarded the stars as gods who determined the fate of human beings. The Magi used God's creation in their search and eventually encountered the truth that the God who had created the stars was incarnate in a tiny child in Bethlehem. Saint Matthew uses their gifts of gold, frankincense, and myrrh to express the truth about the child. He is a king. He is the Son of God. He is the Suffering Servant who will give his life for everyone.

As we continue to celebrate the Mystery of God taking on human flesh, this Feast of the Epiphany reminds us that the Lord has revealed himself as a tiny child for everyone, and not just for us. That is why we need to do everything we can to allow the light of Christ to shine through us. We need to be patient and hospitable to those who are truly seeking. We who hear God's Word and celebrate the Lord's presence in the sacramental life of the Church must be bold in sharing the joy of the Gospel. The evangelist, Saint Matthew, tells the story of the Magi to help the Church at his time understand the same point which Saint Paul, the Apostle to the Gentiles, makes to the Ephesians. It was the Lord's intention all

along to draw everyone to himself, and to invite everyone to encounter the Lord, who has been searching for them all along.

This task is not always easy, and it requires a profound faith
in the Christmas Mystery. When the prophet Isaiah proclaimed to
his people many centuries before Christ's birth that the glory of the
Lord was shining upon them, they were struggling in the darkness
to rebuild the ruined temple and city of Jerusalem. As the Magi
prostrated themselves in the presence of the Lord, Herod was plotting to kill him. The Feast of Epiphany invites us to trust in the
glory of the Lord, even in the midst of darkness of our world. When
Saint Matthew tells us that the Magi returned home by another way,
he implies that they have been transformed by their encounter. We
too are transformed by our encounter with the Incarnate Lord, and
we need to share it.

9. The Baptism of the Lord

Readings
Isaiah 42:1–4, 6–7
Acts 10:34–38
Mark 1:7–11

9.1 January 9, 2000

For many people in our society, "Christmas" is being used in the past tense. Retailers are talking about how good their Christmas sales were. Amazon.com has learned from last Christmas how to handle returns better. Most of us have taken down our Christmas decorations and packed them away. But not here at Saint Jude! We still sing Christmas carols, and our church is still beautifully decorated! Last Sunday (Epiphany), we reflected on the way God was manifested (showed) as a tiny child. On this last Sunday of the Christmas Season, we reflect on how the Son of God is manifested as the adult Jesus in the waters of the Jordan River.

As we return to Ordinary Time beginning next Sunday, the Gospels will become vehicles through which this adult Jesus will speak to us. But not today! Instead, we hear God the Father's voice speaking to the Son: "You are my beloved Son; with you I am well pleased."

These awesome words are significant for the life and ministry of Jesus. The Father is well pleased not because of anything the Son has done. At this point in his life, Jesus had just left the security of his home. He had not done anything yet. He had chosen no apostles, healed no blind people or lepers, given no sermons, handed out no bread or fish to the crowds, not even met any opposition. The

Father was well pleased with the Son because of who he was. Those few words must have rang in Jesus' ears for the rest of his ministry. They became the secret of his strength, the source of his dedication, the motivating force for everything he said and did.

Those same words are significant for the life and ministry of each one of us. We have become God's adopted children (and Jesus' brothers and sisters) through the waters of baptism. Even if we were baptized as infants, God spoke these words to us: "You are my beloved son/daughter; with you I am well pleased." As baptized members of God's People, we do not earn his favor or win our inheritance! We have it already. Once we really understand these words, then they can become the secret of our strength, the source of our dedication, and the motivating force for everything we say or do.

What we have been doing as a church since Christmas Eve is much more than observing the 2000th anniversary of the birth of a great man. We have been reflecting on a Mystery that continues to take flesh in our lives in this New Year and new century. It does not make any difference where you might be in life right now – whether you are in grade school or high school. You might be a young adult or a newly married couple. You might be struggling to raise a family, moving into middle age, or going toward retirement. If you have been baptized, you must know God is well pleased in you!

We must take that confidence out of this church and into our families, work places, schools, and streets. Our job is to look for ways that God is taking flesh in those places. More importantly, we need to allow the security of God's love given at Baptism to take our baptismal promises seriously and permit the mystery of God's love to be manifested through what we say and do.

9.2 January 11, 2009

When Jesus emerges from the waters of the Jordan, Mark provides some interesting details. He tells us that the heavens are torn open, that the Spirit, like a dove, descends on him, and that the voice from the heavens declares, "You are my beloved Son; with you I am well pleased." With these details, Mark moves us from the Christmas Season in which we reflect on God dwelling among us to continue our journey of faith knowing the identity of Jesus: the Son of God, the suffering servant in whom the Spirit dwells, and in whom a new age has dawned."

We sometimes forget the critical role that baptism plays in each of our lives. Through Baptism, we are identified with Jesus Christ, the Son of God, and we become God's beloved sons and daughters who are given a generous share of the Holy Spirit. With our identity closely tied with Jesus Christ, we can bear our share of the sufferings that come from being his disciples. We are invited to give people a glimpse of the new age by the way we conduct ourselves once we are dismissed from this assembly.

When we speak of "vocations," we need to remember that our common vocation is the live the identity of Jesus Christ given to us at Baptism. The way in which we live our unique identity depends on the particular vocation to which each of us has been called. Most of you in this assembly live out your baptismal identity through your marriage vows. Some of you have embraced the single life. Others, like Father Bob or me or the vowed religious Sisters of our parish, live out our baptismal identity through the distinct ways in which we serve the Church. We have been blessed during this Christmas Season with the services of Jacob Meyer, who has been bossing the servers around with great gusto and who returns this weekend to resume his preparations for the priesthood.

During these past few weeks, we have suffered an unusually high number of deaths at Saint Pius. In responding to the pain, grief, and doubt caused by death to people, we can clearly see how our different vocations work together. Diane Schlatterbeck and her team meet with the family, plan out the service, and make all the arrangements. Jeremy Hoy and our musicians provide the liturgical music. Deacon Tug and the other liturgical ministers make sure that the liturgy goes smoothly. Allison Bossler and her workers provide a meal for the mourners, and many of you drop off food for them to serve. The maintenance workers set up and tear down, and the school children do their share by eating lunch in the atrium of the Education Center. Father Bob and I provide the preaching and sacramental ministry. Working in our own unique ways through our own unique vocations, we reflect the identity of Jesus Christ to those who are vulnerable and hurting, even in our own failings and sinfulness. We evangelize those who have been away from the Church for a long time, making sure they know that we care about them.

Much is written these days about the lack of vocations to the priesthood and religious life. I am convinced that when we work at living out the identity we receive at our baptisms, (each in our own unique ways); we will attract the attention of young people trying to discern how God wants them to live out their baptismal identity. In moving from Christmas back to Ordinary Time, this Feast of the Baptism of the Lord invites us to consider our celebration of Christmas this year as more than a memory. It becomes a vivid reminder of the ways in which Christ dwells in our midst, calling us to be faithful to the identity given at baptism, and inviting us to live our individual vocations faithfully, giving good examples to the young people of our parish.

9.3 January 11, 2015

In the ancient world, a person's identity was determined by membership in a family. When Jesus leaves his family in Nazareth, he in effect sacrifices his identity. However, he does not go to the Temple in Jerusalem to establish his true identity. He goes to the wilderness, to the periphery where God had created a Chosen People from a group of escaping slaves. In accepting the baptism of John the Baptist, he allows his Father to confirm his true identity and membership in God's family: "You are my beloved Son, with you I am well pleased." With his identity as God's beloved Son clearly established, Jesus leaves the wilderness and goes to the places where people dwell to overturn their expectations of the identity of the Messiah. Filled with the Spirit, he sets out to win the ultimate battle over Satan, sin, and death.

All of us have received our identities from the families of our origins. But, it was on the day of our baptism that we received our true identity as members of the Body of Christ. On that day, our identity was firmly established in Jesus Christ. Although some of us may remember that day as children, or teens, or adults, most of us were baptized as infants. More often than not, Catholics do not know the date of their baptism until they are required to obtain a recent copy of their baptismal certificate for the Sacrament of Marriage.

After infants are baptized, we smear Sacred Chrism on their heads. The word Chrism comes from the Greek word, Christos, meaning the anointed one. The Chrism speaks of our new identity as priests, prophets, and kings, the titles identified with Christ, the anointed one of Isaiah. As we conclude the Christmas Season today, we recall the identity we received on the day we became one with Christ in baptism. Reflecting on our identity as priests, prophets, and kings can cause us to make some significant resolutions in this New Year.

We all share a common priesthood through Baptism. Father Terry and I have been ordained into a ministerial priesthood, charged to offer sacrifice and to pray as mediators. As priests, all baptized people are called to offer sacrifice and pray. All baptized people are called to make sacrifices, putting ourselves in humble service of others. In this New Year, we might ask ourselves whether we spend enough time in prayer, praying with and for our parish families and our human families. Our ultimate prayer occurs here, when we become full, active, and conscious participants at this Eucharist.

Prophets are people who speak for God. Throughout the Old Testament and culminating in John the Baptist, prophets spoke the truth, whether it was convenient or not. All too often, authentic prophets got into trouble for speaking the truth. How courageous are we in speaking the truth about our faith? We do not need to wear our faith on our sleeves. But, we can be a bit more courageous in speaking up for the truth and let people know through our actions that we are Catholics, and that our faith means something to us. We can make even greater strides when we resolve to avoid the gossip and slander that tear apart the fabric of truth.

Kings were in charge of managing things. In this New Year, we can ask ourselves how well we are doing as managers. Parents in particular are called to manage their households with a loving firmness. In a culture where we are pulled in a thousand directions, we are called to manage our daily schedule in a way that puts proper priorities to the time allotted to us.

Jesus Christ, God's faithful servant and God's Anointed One, is the perfect and ultimate priest, prophet, and king. During this Christmas Season, we have reflected on the Mystery of his dwelling in our midst. This New Year gives us a wonderful opportunity to make that Mystery more evident, by living our Baptismal promises as priests, prophets, and kings.

Ordinary Time

10. 2nd Sunday in Ordinary Time

Readings
1 Samuel 3:3–10, 19
1 Corinthians 6:13–15, 17–20
John 1:35–42

10.1 January 16, 2000

A car skidded on wet pavement and slammed into a pole. Several bystanders ran over to help the driver. A woman was the first to reach the victim. But a man rushed in and pushed her aside. "Step aside, lady," he barked, "I've taken a course in first aid!" The woman stood there for a few minutes. Then she tapped his shoulder. "Pardon me," she said, "but when you get to the part about calling a doctor, I'm right here!"

Like that doctor, God also is in the midst of our lives, calling us to "come and see" his presence in ways that may surprise us. Samuel's mother placed him in the service of the priest, Eli, because she was convinced that God wanted that. God had other ideas and called him in the middle of the night to "come and see" in a new and unexpected way. Samuel did and became one of the greatest prophets of ancient Israel. Andrew thought he was responding to God's call when he became a disciple of John the Baptist. In the meantime, he came upon Jesus of Nazareth and saw the messiah for whom Israel had been waiting. Not only did he become one of the twelve apostles, but he also dragged his brother Simon, who eventually became the leader of the apostles.

This is a great Sunday for those of us who are adults to reflect on how we have gotten to where we are today. Odds are pretty good that who we are today, where we are today, and even what we are doing today might be very different from the expectations we had when we were growing up. The Scriptures invite us to look into the twisting and turnings of our lives, even to look at the effects of our sins and bad choices, and see God calling us.

Once we begin to reflect on our own responses, then we might be in a better position to guide our children. Every one of you young people is being called by God to come and see what God wants for you in life. Many of you are probably being called to come and see God by entering the sacrament of marriage. Some of you are being called to be lay ministers in the church. God is calling some of you to the priesthood or vowed religious life. You might be confused about that call at first, as Samuel was. He thought it was Eli speaking to him. But God keeps repeating that call at any time, at any place, and during any human activity – even in the middle of the night. Just as Samuel relied on the help of Eli to discern God's call, so you need to come to us and ask for advice. And you can rely on the power of God's grace as you respond, just as surely as Peter and Andrew did during the confusing days when they were trying to sort out exactly what it meant for them to follow Jesus Christ. It is vitally important that you remain part of this believing community, because we want to be part of the ways God calls you.

The story is told of Ludwig van Beethoven being awakened in the middle of the night by someone banging on a neighbor's door. Those four taps (tap, tap, tap, tap) repeated over and over again became the inspiration for one of his most famous concertos. The concerto begins with four soft taps of the drum, and those four taps are repeated countless times during the course of the concerto to create a wonderful and impressive effect. God's call is like that. God keeps knocking and knocking on our hearts, no matter how old or young we are. With the support of this believing community and with some time to reflect, we eventually will respond by coming and seeing the way God takes flesh in our lives.

10.2 January 15, 2012

Samuel's mother had made a promise to the Lord. In her old age, Hannah promised that if the Lord would give her a son, she would dedicate him to the service in the Temple. When she bore a son, she named him Samuel, which means "the Lord hears." In the first reading, the young Samuel is sleeping in the Temple. Scripture scholars suggest that he was in charge of keeping an eye on the vigil light, which must continue to burn around the clock. I think that Eli had been talking too long, as preachers sometimes do, and Samuel is dozing off. In any case, something extraordinary happens to Samuel. He does not understand, and he turns to his trusted mentor, Eli, who eventually figures out that the Lord is calling his young charge. With Samuel listening and Eli guiding him, Samuel figures out that his vocation is not to serve in the Temple. Instead, he realizes that he is being called to a prophetic vocation. As prophet, Samuel becomes instrumental in establishing the monarchy, which will guide Israel for many centuries.

All of us have been called to follow Jesus Christ, through our baptisms, just as Andrew and Peter were called. We would not be present at this Mass if we were not aware of that call. In living out our baptismal calls, we can learn a great deal from Eli and Samuel. Young people, you can be open to the way in which the Lord is calling you to live. Be sure to seek out a wise and experienced disciple. Like Eli, he or she can guide you in discerning the Lord's call for you. Those of us who have already discerned our calling can be like Eli to young people. Like him, we can share our experience and guide the Samuels of our time to know what the Lord is calling them to do.

That is what Paul did for the Church of Corinth. As an Eli, he had founded the community and guided them in their development. The pagan culture of the time did not value the human body. If anything, they regarded the body as trapping the soul. Because of this thinking, they felt that it did not matter what people did with their bodies. Paul, as Eli, argues that our bodies are created by God, and that they are temples of the Holy Spirit. He argues that we need to care for our bodies in every way. Sexual sins are not private affairs. Instead, they affect the Body of Christ, the community of believers.

One thing is clear, whether we are mentors like Eli, or students like Samuel. If we are serious about our call to be disciples, we will be changed! Andrew has already been changed by his encounter with Jesus Christ. When he tells his brother Simon about the one who drew him away from John the Baptist, he no longer refers to him as Rabbi, or teacher, but Christ, or Messiah. We know the significance of Jesus changing Simon's name to Peter. He is no longer a fisherman, but the Rock on which Jesus builds his Church. The same can happen to each of us, as we live out our callings in Christ.

10.3   January 14, 2018

When we encounter Samuel in today's first reading, he is a young child sleeping in the Temple of the Lord in Shiloh. His mother, Hannah, had come to this same Temple in absolute anguish. She and her husband had not been able to conceive a child. When the priest Eli heard her crying out her pain to the Lord, he thought she was drunk. When he finally understood what was happening, he sent her home with the confidence that she and her husband would conceive a child. On her way home, she made a promise. If the Lord would bless them with a child, she would dedicate him to the Lord. Hannah kept her promise and brought him to live at the Temple, trusting that Eli would form him and help him understand his role in life.

In a sense, Hannah becomes a model for all parents. In gratitude for the gift of a child, parents bring that child to the waters of Baptism. In return, parents promise to do what Eli had done for Samuel – to raise their child in the ways of faith and to teach the child to listen carefully to the ways in which the Lord is calling them. As parents quickly learn, the process of teaching children in the ways of faith is not always easy. It took Eli three times before he understood that the Lord was calling Samuel to become one of the greatest prophets of his people. In the Gospel, John the Baptist clearly points out the identity of Jesus as the Lamb of God. However, it takes the rest of the Gospel for Andrew and Simon Peter to understand what that means. Eventually, they will learn that Jesus is the gentle lamb led to slaughter. They will see him as the suffering servant of Isaiah. They will understand that this lamb will destroy evil and the power of death.

That is why it is so important that we gather here every Sunday to listen to the Word of God. The Lord speaks to us just as surely as he spoke to Samuel, or just as surely as Jesus spoke to his first disciples and invited them to stay with him. We stay with him and abide with him as he feeds us with his Body and Blood at this Mass. He is calling every single one of us to live a life of holiness, a life that will eventually make us saints. As we listen, we guide our children to listen carefully also. In time, with our guidance, they will respond.

Boys and girls, you are never too young to listen to the Lord as he calls you in specific ways to live your baptism. My guess is that most of you will respond by entering the vocation of marriage. Some of you will dedicate yourselves to serving the Lord in the single life. Some of you are being called to serve the Lord as priests or religious. Our parish is blessed with two young men who are pursuing the vocation of priesthood and have returned to the seminary to continue to listen. Two young women are being formed into the religious life with the Sisters of Saint Francis in the convent across from Marian High School.

The Lord will definitely continue to speak to us through his Word every Sunday in our journey through Ordinary Time. As we respond, there are several ways in which our parish can help us to listen carefully. One of those is the weekend retreat, Christ Renews His Parish. The women's retreat is scheduled for the first weekend in February, and the men's will be the next weekend. Over the years, many members of our parish have benefitted from this retreat, which brings them closer to Jesus Christ, connects them in a more intimate way with other members of the parish, and helps them to renew the parish in some remarkable ways. Members of this retreat would love to talk to you after Mass. Like the original disciples of Jesus who remember exactly the time (4:00) when they encountered the Lord, these ordinary men and women remember how the retreat touched them. Come and see! Talk to them. You too can be changed in ways that might surprise you!

11. 3rd Sunday in Ordinary Time

Readings
Jonah 3:1–5, 10
1 Corinthians 7:29–31
Mark 1:14–20

11.1 January 26, 2003

Our Diocesan Vocation Office hosts a series of *An•rew Dinners* each year. Priests bring young men who might be interested in the Priesthood to these dinners, much as Andrew brought his brother, Simon, to meet the Lord. The young men get a chance to meet the Bishop, the food is pretty good, and usually the Bishop invites a young priest to tell his story of how he was called. I have been impressed with many of these stories, especially Father Dan's. He tells of going to Notre Dame for college, taking a few years to do post graduate study, and teaching at Saint Joseph's High School. During this time, he began discerning the Lord's call. With a great deal of maturity and reflection, he responded. And we know the rest of the story.

At one of these dinners, the Bishop asked me to tell my story. When I was finished, he leaned over to me, thanked me, and informed me that he would probably return to asking the younger priests to talk! My story is a little different. I entered the seminary at a very young age (probably for mixed reasons), and I coasted through the system without a lot of serious reflection. My story is more like Jonah's, who tried to escape on a ship to avoid responding to God's call to preach to the Babylonians, who were the bitter enemies of the people of Israel. I had very little clue about what I was getting myself into at ordination. Like Jonah, I found myself in the belly of a whale more than once. But, over time, I have become convinced that God has called me to be a priest. When good friends left the priesthood, I would retreat into the whale's belly and ask why I am staying. When I would get transferred and have to start all over again, I would count on God's grace from the belly of another whale to get me through the process of dying to the old assignment to rise to the challenges of a new one. Eventually, the whale would spit me up, and here I am!

In today's Gospel, Mark does not bother with the intimate details of how the two sets of brothers heard and responded to the call of Jesus to be his followers. Instead, he gives us the end result – they left everything (including their father in the boat) to follow him. By virtue of our baptism, Jesus continues to call each of us to follow him in some unique way. Through the Living Word, he invites us to respond.

For those of you who have already responded and are living your vocation, take a moment to thank God for your call. Take a few moments to reflect on the ways God may have worked in strange and confusing ways in your life. Those of you who are married need to remember that God called you in mysterious ways to love each other as God has always loved us. All of you evangelize in your places of work and in your homes in ways that neither Father Dan nor I could possibly do.

For those of you who are still discerning your call, make every attempt to remain open. God certainly calls in mysterious and twisting ways sometimes. God is probably calling many of you to marriage. Be open to the Lord calling you to the priesthood, religious life, and the many ways in which lay people can serve the Church in unique ways these days.

Some people respond directly, as did Andrew and Simon, James and John, Father Dan and some of the younger priests. Other people respond in ways that might be confusing and twisting, as did Jonah and yours truly! Paul reminds us that the time is running out. God is waiting for our response in faith.

11.2 January 22, 2006

As the second reading from Paul was being proclaimed, it was interesting to watch the glances shared by married couples when Paul gave the advice that husbands should live as if they had no wives. Those glances seemed to say, "You can tell Paul was never married!" As I read the same reading last week and heard Paul telling me that I should not rejoice, I thought, "You can tell Paul was never a skier!" How could we not rejoice? We had the best snow we have ever seen in twenty years. It snowed every night. The skiing was fantastic. We renewed our friendships. All the people who share the same condo still think that a group of priests living down the hall is weird, but they were glad to see us. We did plenty of rejoicing.

But then it occurred to me that Paul's Letter to the Corinthians was one of the first he had written. In the early stages of his ministry, he was convinced that the Lord would come again soon. As a result, there is a definite urgency in his advice. Two thousand years later, we are still waiting for the Lord to come, and it is easy to dismiss these words. They don't apply to us, we think.

However, that would be a mistake. Even though Paul's calculations about the Second Coming may have been a bit off, he still makes a very good point. As a good Jew and Christian, Paul knew the goodness of family life. Within that context, he is not advising husbands to leave your wives. He also knew that God's gifts were meant for our use. He is not telling us to avoid rejoicing over the gifts we have received. Rather, Paul continues to tell us through the living Word of God that our first priority must be our relationship to Jesus Christ. As important as spouses and families may be, we cannot define ourselves completely in terms of marriage, or status, or possessions, or even pleasant memories of a great skiing trip. Because this world is passing away, and because all of us eventually will lose even what is most valuable to us, our ultimate hope lies in defining ourselves as followers of Jesus Christ, who announced that his kingdom is at hand. That is what Simon and Andrew did. That is what James and John did. They clearly saw the kingdom of God and left all that had been important to them to associate themselves with Jesus Christ.

Their repentance, their wholehearted change of heart continues to be a model for us. None of us are completely grounded in Jesus Christ, no matter where we are in our journeys of faith. We need to repent. In responding to the call of Jesus Christ, our repentance sometimes requires drastic changes. Sometimes we are like the people of Nineveh. Through unlikely people like Jonah, and the Word of God breaks through our experience opens our eyes to allow us to see that we have defined ourselves in ways that will never sustain us. Repentance in those situations involves making drastic changes. More often than not, repentance is a slow process in which we turn gradually to the Lord and our relationship with him. Repentance involves letting go of habits or patterns of behavior that do not destroy our relationship with Christ, but slowly get us off course.

Being serious about improving our relationship with Christ will always involve making changes in our lives. Ironically, being serious about that primary relationship will enhance all those other

relationships and activities that truly enhance our lives. With the
world in its present form passing away, putting Christ first will
open our eyes to the kingdom of God, which is still at hand.

11.3   January 22, 2012

At the time that Saint Paul wrote his second letter to the Church in
Corinth, many in that community were expecting the Lord's Second Coming to occur during their lifetimes. That is why he writes
to urge them to reconsider their priorities and put the Lord Jesus
first. He reminds them that the world in its present form is passing
away.

If you watch the History Channel on television or have seen the
movie, *2012*, Paul's words might seem to support all of the attention
given to the predictions that something dreadful will happen on December 21, 2012, at 11:11 p.m. At that moment, the Mayan Long
Count calendar finishes the last of its 5,125 years. At the same moment, the ecliptic of our sun will be crossing the plane of the Milky
Way galaxy. According to the History Channel and the movie *2012*,
this will cause unpredictable disasters, most likely ending human
life on the planet.

In our times, we have lived through many failed predictions of
the end of the world, and the world as we know it continues to go
on. More than likely, that pattern will continue after December 21,
just as all the Corinthians went to meet the Lord before his Second
Coming. But Paul's words have the same significance for us in the
year 2012, as they had for the Corinthian community in the year
57. Given the certainty of the end, we need to look at what must
be changed in our lives to put the Lord Jesus first.

That is what happened to the two pairs of brothers in today's
Gospel. Andrew and Simon, and James and John were doing fine
in their lives. They were part of the family fishing businesses on
the Sea of Galilee. But they heard the Lord's call and completely re-
ordered their priorities. They gave up what was comfortable and familiar to take the risk of becoming followers of Jesus Christ. Their
change of careers not only completely refashioned their lives, but it
also laid the foundation for the Church as we know it today.

Bob Buford wrote a very popular book called *Halftime*. The
book tells of his change of career in midlife. Having enjoyed a very
successful career as a Texas businessman, he invested the second
half of his career in giving himself in service to others. In our own
community, we see retired people giving their time volunteering in
the hospital or giving more of their time and talent to their families
and to the parish. They understand what the two sets of brothers
understood. It can be life giving to take a risk and invest in a second
career centering on service.

The Lord does not limit his call to those who have been successful. Jonah had been very unsuccessful. He had run away from the Lord's call to preach repentance to his sworn enemies, the Ninevites. Spending three days in the belly of the fish did not completely change his heart. But it did change the direction of his feet, and he preached repentance to people who responded.

It does not matter whether we are encountering successes or failures in our lives at this time. It does not matter whether we are doing well or badly at the moment. No matter what our situation, the Lord invites us to take another look at the way in which we are living our call to follow Jesus Christ, received at our baptism. Saint Paul is correct. The world as we know it is passing away. Now is the time to take a look at our priorities and make any changes necessary to focus more completely on those things which will not end – our relationship to Jesus Christ, and through him, to each other.

11.4   January 25, 2015

In hearing from Saint Paul's letter to the Corinthians, it might seem like he is an alarmist, trying to frighten his listeners into behaving themselves. He seems to be saying that the end of the world is near. But, in fact, Saint Paul is making a practical application to the Gospel we just heard from Saint Mark. He believes what Jesus is saying, that he proclaims the Gospel of God. The Greek word for Gospel means "Good News." Not only does Jesus speak the good news that the time of fulfillment is near. He is the Good News, the Incarnate Word of God who ushers in the Kingdom of God.

When Saint Paul encountered the risen Christ on the road to Damascus, he understood that the Kingdom of God was not some vague place in the distant future. Jesus Christ had transformed his life and the way in which he looked at reality. Like Peter and Andrew, James and John, Paul completely abandoned his old way of living and saw everything from the perspective of his relationship with Jesus Christ. His advice to the Corinthians applies equally to us. We have encountered the Lord Jesus on the day we were baptized. Saint Paul advises us to view reality from the perspective of that relationship. In living the reality of the Kingdom of God, we can recognize the Lord Jesus in whatever situation we find ourselves in, whether we are married or celibate, rejoicing or weeping, buying or not owning, using the world fully or not.

As the two sets of brothers learned more about the Good News of Jesus Christ in following him over the next three years, they also came to understand that the Good News of the Kingdom would sometimes involve some very bad news. They would learn about betrayal, suffering, and the death of the Lord on the cross. But in the midst of all that bad news, they learned to see reality through the experience of the death of the Lord and embrace the incredibly good news of the Resurrection. Like Saint Paul, they would learn to persevere in faith both in the good times and in the bad.

I was thinking of Saint Paul's advice last week. My time away on my annual skiing trip was great. Through the generosity of friends, we rent a condo at a reduced rate. We ski for five hours every day, enjoying the fresh air, the views, and the physical challenges of skiing. Despite my best efforts, I failed again this year to do bodily harm to myself. And yet, the world of skiing can totally ignore the reality of the Kingdom of God. Everything is geared to the pleasure of the moment, to the best conditions, and the best ski runs. Having developed a pattern of reading the obituaries in the South Bend Tribune, I read the obituaries in the Vail Daily. Not once was there any mention of a funeral liturgy. Every service was listed as a "celebration of life," indicating that nothing else exists except for the past life of the deceased.

Like the two sets of brothers and Saint Paul, we are invited to abandon whatever does not last and focus our vision from the perspective of the Good News of Jesus Christ. In the midst of God's Kingdom, we experience good times, bad times, and very difficult moments when the cross of Jesus Christ dominates our lives. As much as I love the sport of skiing, I have learned that the friendships we have made over the years are what really matter. Graced by these friendships, I return to my day job with renewed energy. That energy is present for each and every one of us, as we learn to embrace our relationship with Jesus Christ and view our lives from that perspective. The time of fulfillment in now, and the Kingdom of God is in our midst.

12. 4th Sunday in Ordinary Time

Readings
Deuteronomy 18:15–20
1 Corinthians 7:32–35
Mark 1:21–28

12.1 January 29, 2006

The Psalmist tells us that if we have heard God's voice today, then we should not harden our hearts. The people of Israel had heard God's voice many times as they wandered across the Sinai Desert from slavery in Egypt to freedom in the Promised Land. They heard God's voice as the angel of death passed over their homes in the final plague. They heard it when the Sea swallowed up Pharaoh's army. They heard it at Mount Sinai through Moses when God made the covenant with them and gave the terms of that unconditional love in the commandments. And yet, they did harden their hearts, for a number of reasons. They were hungry, and thirsty, and lost, and hot, and afraid, and faced those things that happen in people's journeys through life. They had so hardened their hearts at Massah and Meribah that they asked if God was in their midst or not.

Those people who gathered in that synagogue at Capernaum on that Sabbath not only heard God's voice. They also experienced God's Word in the person of Jesus and were astonished by his teaching. The unclean spirit immediately recognized his voice and asked the question, "What have you to do with us, Jesus of Nazareth? Have you come to destroy us?" And the unqualified answer is, "YES!" Mark uses the rest of his Gospel to explain how Jesus has come to destroy the power of the evil one. Just as Jesus names the unclean spirit and drives him out of that man, so he will confront the power of evil and name it at every step of his ministry. Mark will tell us how the power of evil will appear to win a huge victory at the cross, when Jesus was convulsed by death, our ultimate enemy. But, he will also tell us how Jesus finally defeated that power by his resurrection and ascension to the right hand of the Father.

We too have just heard his voice. In response, we are asked to not harden our hearts as we reflect on the voice of God and apply it to our lives. As we listen to God's voice in the coming weeks, God's voice sometimes will heal hearts that have been broken or burdened. At other times, God's voice will shake us up and call us to name whatever unclean spirit may be interfering with our lives and our relationships with God, with other people, and with ourselves. Sometimes, God's voice will reveal unclean spirits that we have not noticed.

In the ancient world, many diseases and conditions which people could neither understand nor control were lumped under the heading of "unclean spirits." We may be more sophisticated and advanced in our modern scientific world. But, we still struggled with demons – with unclean spirits. Those spirits take many forms: greed or jealousy or lust or anger or laziness or a host of nasty habits. They can appear in the form of addictions and obsessions. The demons of the Gospel are still very much with us today.

Mark tells us that Jesus taught with authority, and not like the religious teachers of his day. His authority comes directly from his union with the Father, and Mark invites us to trust that authority, that power. In the ancient world, the demons were controlled when they were named. In our day, the voice of Jesus invites us to soften our hearts and have the courage to name our demons. In naming them and acknowledging their power over us, we might be shaken up and convulsed violently. But, in naming them, we give them over to the power of the One who defeated the Prince of Demons by his life giving death and resurrection. We have heard his voice today. We cannot harden our hearts.

12.2   February 1, 2009

Saint Paul seems to be telling those of you who are married that non-married people are closer to the Lord. He tells the Corinthians that unmarried men and women are more anxious about the things of the Lord, while married men and women are more anxious about the things of this world. Over the centuries, too many people have read his words and concluded that those of us who are called to be celibates are more authentically holy than those of you who respond to the call to marriage.

However, that is not what Paul is saying. In writing to the Corinthians, Saint Paul is convinced that the Second Coming of the Lord is near. Those who receive his letter have the same conviction, because they had just heard that the Romans had completely destroyed the city of Jerusalem, and that they had demolished the Temple. In the light of this sudden and violent ending of an old order, they concluded that Jesus would keep his promise and end the entire world soon, coming for them.

It is within this context that we can understand what Paul is saying. Paul advises his listeners to keep their focus squarely on the Lord Jesus. In giving his advice to married and unmarried people, he urges them not to make sudden changes that would distract them. Rather, he says, keep your eyes focused on the risen Lord, the one whom you hear in the Word, recognize in the breaking of Bread, and see in the assembly of the faithful. It is this Lord who will come again, and he will not abandon you.

We celebrate the Jubilee Year of Saint Paul this year, observing his birth and the impact he has made on our faith. It has been almost 2,000 years since Paul wrote these words, and we are still waiting for the Lord to come again. Since the Second Vatican Council, we have learned that our fundamental call to holiness is rooted in our baptism. God calls us to live authentic holy lives, whether God has called us to live our baptismal call as married couples or as celibate priests or religious.

Paul's words have a special urgency for us in our situation today. We may not be expecting the Lord to come again soon in our lifetimes. But, we face an uncertain future in terms of our economy and the Recession that frightens all of us. In our community, too many people have already lost their jobs, and we do not know when that trend will end. Retirement accounts and savings have been depleted. As the father of this parish family, I share many of the same worries that burden you parents as you wonder what will happen to our ability to function. Paul gives us the same advice which he gives to the Corinthians. In a time of uncertainty, in a time of fear and anxiety, he tells us not to panic and made radical changes in our lives. Rather, he says, we need to keep our ears attuned to his Word, and our eyes fixed to the Eucharist we share and the assembly in which we gather.

Mark tells us that Jesus rebukes an unclean spirit and speaks with authority. That expelled unclean spirit clearly recognizes the truth about him – that he is the Holy One of God. The Lord Jesus continues to speak with authority to us, and he has the power to drive out the demons of fear, anxiety, and lack of trust. With our attention focused on him, we too can use the present situation to sort out what is central to our lives and what is peripheral. Focused on Jesus Christ, the Holy One of God, we can continue our journeys of faith with confidence, no matter what the future holds for us.

12.3   January 29, 2012

When Saint Paul wrote to the Christian Community of Corinth, there was a general consensus that the Second Coming of Jesus Christ would be very soon. That is why he writes with such urgency. He advises his readers to live in this world in a way that will not allow any other attachment to keep their focus from Jesus Christ. Paul is a celibate. He is convinced that not being married is the best way for him to keep Christ at the center of his life and to remain free of anxieties in the light of the Lord coming again soon. And he urges other unmarried men and women to remain celibate. But, he also tells married men and women to continue to take care of one another in their marriages. That will happen, he says, if they keep the Lord first in their marital responsibilities.

Two thousand years later, the Lord has not come again. Without this same sense of urgency, how are we to understand to Paul's advice? There are two ways. First, Paul's words help us to look to the future with hope. Our salvation does not depend on our own success in restructuring the world. Instead, our salvation depends on the gracious mercies of God.

Saint Mark makes that point very clear in today's Gospel. On the Sabbath, a sacred time, he enters into a synagogue, a sacred space, to confront an unclean spirit. That unclean spirit clearly knows the identity of Jesus of Nazareth. He is the Holy One of God who has come to destroy the powers of sin, death, and evil. The unclean spirit tries to dominate Jesus by shouting out to him. But Jesus drives the spirit out of the man, revealing through this miracle what he will do by his own suffering, death, and resurrection – destroy the power of sin and death completely.

Those in that synagogue in Capernaum recognize that Jesus is teaching with authority, and not like their scribes. Saint Mark invites us to recognize that authority here in this Church of Saint Pius X in Granger. Because of the death and resurrection of Jesus Christ, we can continue to live with the confidence that all those unclean spirits in our world and in our lives will not prevail. Not only in the future, but his presence in the Sacramental life of the Church can help us deal with those demons now. Through this Eucharist, we are strengthened to face whatever demons might be convulsing our lives now. Those demons might include addictions or any crosses me may be carrying at this time. Through the Sacrament of Reconciliation, the Lord frees us from the demons of our sins and bad choices. Through the Sacrament of the Anointing of the Sick, the

Lord heals at such a deep level that we do not lose heart. Through the grace of the Sacrament of Matrimony, married couples gain the strength to continue to put the Lord first in their marriage, enabling them to take care of one without anxiety.

There is a second benefit to heeding Paul's words. If we are serious about finding our true identity in Christ, then we will not be determined by the roles which our society assigns us. We will not be categorized as privileged residents of Granger, or less affluent members of Saint Adalbert's in South Bend. We will not be classified by all those stereotypes that tend to polarize our society today. We won't be Democrats or Republicans. We won't be single, married, divorced, or widowed. No matter how the culture ways may divide us, we belong to Christ. No unclean spirit has the power to change that!

12.4 February 1, 2015

In the first sentence of his Gospel, Saint Mark lets us in on a great truth: Jesus is God's Son! He writes the rest of his Gospel showing us how people respond when Jesus reveals that truth to them. Today, Jesus enters a sacred space (the synagogue) on a sacred day (the Sabbath) and teaches. We are not told what he teaches, but how he teaches. Jesus teaches as one having authority. There is no need for him to quote experts of the law and prophets, as the scribes would teach. He is the prophet promised from the time of Moses.

However, the unclean spirit knows exactly who he is – the Holy One of God. The evil spirit knows his mission – he will destroy the power of evil. In fact, the means of his destroying the power of evil is established already in this early part of Mark's Gospel. Jesus has invaded the sacred space of the scribes. He has identified himself as Lord of the Sabbath. Eventually, those who claim these sacred spaces as their own will have Jesus executed. His death on the cross will be the final defeat of the power of sin and evil. It will be at the side of the cross that the Roman soldier will say the same thing we already know: Truly this is the Son of God!

It is significant that the mission of Jesus begins to take shape in a synagogue. In the ancient world, synagogues were places where people worshipped and were taught. These two realities are exactly what we are addressing in our capital campaign, "Behold, I Make All Things New." We need a bigger beautiful church for worship. We need more space in our facilities for teaching. Our physical buildings (our synagogue) provide opportunities for people to encounter Jesus Christ and come to know him as God's Only Begotten Son. In the course of the year in which we have been running our campaign, we have raised 11.7 million dollars in gifts and pledges. I thank you from the bottom of my heart. I thank God for what he is doing through you to ensure that our "synagogue" will provide worship to God and service through the parish community for many years. Be sure to join us after Mass for the second annual "We are Saint Pius" celebration in the auxiliary gym. What has happened is nothing short of remarkable.

As much as we need to express gratitude and celebrate, we cannot rest on our laurels. We are involved in a marathon, not a sprint. As we prepare for Bishop Rhoades to preside over our ground breaking for the new church on April 19, we cannot forget our educational needs. We cannot forget what remains to be funded after this first phase is completed in two years. We need adequate space for Catechesis of the Good Shepherd. We need a multipurpose room for a school cafeteria, and youth ministry, and after school care. With those needs taken care of, we can use the gyms for athletic events, and grade school students won't be practicing after they should be in bed. We also need more bathrooms, classrooms, and space for all day preschool.

When Saint Paul wrote this passage to the Corinthians, he was responding to a question they had asked of him. In the midst of a pagan culture that regarded the body simply as a container for the soul, most members of Corinth did what they wanted with their bodies. Saint Paul responds to the question asked by the Christian community from the perspective of the second coming of Jesus Christ. He urges believers not to have divided loyalties. To those who are unmarried, he encourages them to focus on the Lord. To those who are married, he affirms the sacred bond of marriage and the mutual love given to each other. He urges the community to be a beacon in a darkened and confused world. That is our task. We can continue to be a beacon of hope in a darkened world. We will worship the Lord in a beautiful church and learn the ways of the Gospel in a more adequate Education Center. As living stones, we too can be a beacon of hope, celebrating the victory of Christ over evil, and living that mystery for years to come.

12.5　January 28, 2018

Moses was the greatest figure in the Old Testament. As a prophet, he spoke God's Word directly to his people. Long before Israel had priests or kings, he sacrificed himself for the good of his people and led them from slavery in Egypt to freedom in the Promised Land. But, as great as he was, he tells his people today that God would raise up a prophet like him from among his kin who will speak in God's name.

Throughout the history of Israel, Rabbis would remember that promise. When they taught, they would cite Rabbis who had gone before them, much as lawyers today base their arguments on legal arguments that preceded them. Ultimately, any Rabbi would trace his teaching back to Moses, the greatest teacher. However, that is not what Jesus does when he teaches in the synagogue in Capernaum. He does not cite previous authorities. He speaks on his own authority. His teaching astonishes those listening to him. Ironically, it is the unclean spirit who knows exactly who Jesus is. He is the one promised by Moses. He does not cite any authority, because he speaks the truth in his own name as the Son of God.

It will take the rest of Mark's Gospel for the disciples to understand who Jesus truly is and what he accomplishes through his death and resurrection. It is the new reality that Paul explains to the Corinthians, a new turning toward Christ that will take priority over everything else in our lives, even the many blessings of married life.

During this liturgical year, we will hear the words and actions of Jesus Christ on most Sundays from the Gospel of Mark. Through this Gospel, Jesus will invite us to deepen our understanding of him and make a new commitment to be his faithful disciples. He will invite us to hear his voice and to let go of our hardened hearts. He will invite us to trust that he has power over unclean spirits. And we all have our demons: whether they are addictions, habits that rob us of true freedom to embrace the person of Jesus Christ, or hearts so hardened that we cannot recognize Christ in the people around us. In our contemporary culture, there are demons lurking in all kinds of instant communication: email, Instagram, twitter, Facebook, and on and on. Recently, Pope Francis proposed a prayer modeled after the prayer of Saint Francis of Assisi:

> Lord, make us instruments of your peace.
> Help us to recognize the evil latent in a
>   communication that does not build communion.
> Help us to remove the venom from our judgments.
> Help us to speak about others as our brothers
>   and sisters.
> You are faithful and trustworthy; may our words be
>   seeds of goodness for the world:
> Where there is shouting, let us practice listening;
> Where there is confusion, let us inspire harmony;
> Where there is ambiguity, let us bring clarity;
> Where there is exclusion, let us offer solidarity;
> Where there is sensationalism, let us use sobriety;
> Where there is superficiality, let us raise
>   real questions;
> Where there is prejudice, let us awaken trust;

Where there is hostility, let us bring respect;
Where there is falsehood, let us bring truth. Amen.

The internet did not exist in that synagogue in Capernaum. But, faced with its reality today, both good and bad, the Pope's prayer might help us to recognize the truth about Jesus Christ and learn to respond better as faithful disciples.

13. 5th Sunday in Ordinary Time

Readings

Job 7:1–4, 6–7
1 Corinthians 9:16–19, 22–23
Mark 1:29–39

13.1 February 6, 2000

A woman was the mother of ten kids – the wildest kids you could imagine. To make matters worse, her husband traveled frequently for his work. For all practical purposes, she raised her children on her own. The poor woman's life was unbearable. A sister from the local parish heard about her plight and visited her. She saw her small house and was struck by the behavior of the children. Her heart went out for the mother and volunteered to provide what little support and help she could.

She offered the woman a playpen someone had donated to the church. Even though the woman had never heard of a playpen, she was so distracted that she said, yes. Some time later, the sister met the mother at church. With tears in her eyes, she thanked her for the gift. "That playpen has saved my life!' she said. "It's marvelous. Every afternoon at 3:00, I jump into the playpen with a book, and the children can't get to me!"

Jesus may not have had ten children. But he had a hectic schedule! During the past few Sundays, the Gospel of Mark has given us glimpses into a "typical day" in the life of Jesus of Nazareth. Last Sunday, he preached and expelled demons. Today, he restores Simon Peter's mother-in-law to health, heals all kinds of sick people, and drives out even more demons! No wonder Christian art has portrayed the Gospel of Mark as a lion! In Mark's Gospel, Jesus roars through life at breakneck speed.

In the midst of that hectic schedule, Mark is careful to tell us that Jesus had his own playpen. Mark says that he withdrew to a deserted place and prayed there. That time spent in the early morning of a "typical day" gave him a chance to communicate with his Father. He reflected on his identity. In quiet, he put this early popularity with the crowds into a proper perspective that allowed him to keep a clear vision of his true mission. He spent as much time as he could in his sandy playpen, before Peter and the others pursued him and dragged him to the next activity.

We can identify with Jesus' schedule. Young people run from school to the next activity. Parents return home from work exhausted, only to face the demands of attending to a family and keeping up the home. Those of you who are involved in any kind of ministry at Saint Jude know the hectic pace we keep as we rush from one activity to another meeting. Our lives are lived in the lion's den – the fast lane.

Each of us desperately needs to find playpen time, no matter how old or young we may be! It takes effort and planning to find one. Finding the proper playpen varies with each of us. For some of us, getting up early in the morning before the rest of the house wakes up is a good time. For others, it might be a brief visit to the church at lunch, or a little time in the Perpetual Adoration Chapel after work. It might be the last few minutes each evening before going to bed. I always know when I have not given myself enough time for quiet prayer and reflection. My homilies get longer and out of focus. I get crabby and start throwing myself a "pity party."

If things are going reasonably well for you, now is a good time to carve out some playpen time. Sooner or later, things will fall apart in our lives, as they did for Job, or as they did for Peter's mother-in-law. At those low points, we can easily lose our faith without the focus we receive from spending time in the playpen. Take a cue from what we do here every Sunday. By its very nature, the Eucharist is an action that invites us to become full, active, and conscious participants. But even in the midst of this action, we always take time to be quiet and reflect. When we leave this church, we resume lives that require full, active, and conscious participation. Give yourself a gift and find quiet time. Like Peter, others will pursue us and drag us to the next activity. But like his mother-in-law, who experienced God's loving kindness in such a powerful way, spending time in the playpen will give us the focus to pick ourselves up and serve the needs of others.

13.2 **February 9, 2003**

If you have ever been part of a Bible Study Group, you know how
the Biblical text can come alive when the members bring their own
experiences to the text. You also know that members can also bring
their preconceptions of what they think the text should be saying.
Once, I joined a group of women studying today's Gospel text from
Mark. One woman, who was receiving very little support from
her husband at the time, began complaining loudly about Peter's
mother-in-law. "Isn't that just like a man," she asked, "to expect
that poor woman to get off her sick bed and feed him?"

After talking about men who fail to appreciate the hard work of
women in their lives, we got down to the business of interpreting
what Mark really meant. Mark tells us that Peter's mother-in-law
experienced the presence of Jesus Christ in her life. Not only did she
receive the Gospel from the Incarnate Word of God, but she also
received the gift of healing. Grateful for those gifts, she became the
model of how all followers of Jesus should respond to his gracious
gift. She gave herself in humble service.

That is what Paul explains to the Corinthians. When they tried
to pay him a consulter's fee for preaching the Gospel to them, he refused. He insisted that because God had given him this incredible
gift in the first place, he was responding by giving it to others, without expecting any kind of recompense.

As we introduce Stewardship to Saint Pius, we bring our own
expectations and preconceptions. I certainly did. I knew very little
about Stewardship when I introduced it to my last parish. We chose
it, because it seemed to be the least expensive option to addressing
a crisis. We did not have enough income to pay our employees!
But, as I began to preach and reflect on it, I came to understand
that Stewardship is not about money. Rather, Stewardship is a way
of life.

Christian Stewardship opens our eyes and our hearts to the
truth that everything we possess is a gift from a gracious and
loving God. Even when we have built careers with hard work, we
realize that the fundamental building blocks – intelligence, health,
and good breaks – are ultimately gifts from God.

When we truly believe this, then it makes more sense to share
a generous portion with others. Like Peter's mother-in-law, I become much more willing to sacrifice some of my precious time to
serve others. Giving a portion of my time and talent to Saint Pius is
not something I do if I have some time left over from my busy schedule. Instead, I make that time a priority, along with a willingness to
be trained in giving my gift. And Stewardship is not just for adults.
Eighth graders are required to give some time in service in order

to receive the Sacrament of Confirmation. If you see yourselves as stewards, then that requirement becomes a small opportunity to give back a portion of what you have so graciously been given by God. Like Paul, I am more likely to give a first portion of my treasure to this community and to the poor, because I realize that my treasure is a gift from God.

Mark tells us that Jesus withdrew from his hectic schedule to spend time in prayer. That is what we are asking you to do in the next few weeks. Next weekend, Father Dan will preach on the stewardship of time and talent. Bill and Diane Schlatterbeck will speak of their experience in giving time and talent. We invite all of you to come to the Ministry Fair in the gym after each Mass. On the following Sunday, I will preach on the stewardship of treasure, and A.J. Bellia will give his reflection. For now, simply listen, read what we send to your home, and bring those things, along with your own life experience, to prayer. God has been incredibly generous to us. What will be our response?

13.3   **February 5, 2006**

We are fond of using stereotypes to describe people, because they allow us to put complex individuals into neat little boxes. Those who had stereotyped our present Pope as an inquisitor were surprised when he published his first encyclical last week not blasting the dictatorship of relativism but proclaiming the love of God. He is not so easy to put into a neat little box as many had thought.

Saint Mark does something similar in today's Gospel. It is easy to read our own cultural expectations into the story of Jesus healing Peter's mother in law. As soon as she gets off her sick bed, some might complain, she assumes the subservient role of women and waits on the men. But, it is not that simple. In describing the healing of Peter's mother in law, Mark invites us to see the true identify of Jesus Christ. Jesus heals her and others not to make a name for himself, but to give a sign of his true identity. Jesus has come to offer salvation – complete healing for everyone caught in a variety of evils, most notably sin and death. Peter's mother in law understands that gift when he grasps her by the hand and helps her up, because she sees in that gesture the act of being raised from the dead. Having experienced that salvation, she responds in gratitude by giving herself in humble service. Those words "she waited on them" are also used to describe ministry in the early Church. She becomes a model of humble service in a church admittedly dominated by men.

That is what Paul tells the Corinthians. He too had experienced the fullness of the Lord's healing gift of salvation on that road to Damascus. Overwhelmed by this gift, he responded by dedicating the rest of his life to preaching that Good News. In giving that gift free of charge to others, he refused a salary from the Corinthian community. As a result, some accused him of not being an authentic Apostle. His response is the same as Peter's mother in law – I give back to you what I received, because I am convinced of the Lord's gift of salvation. He wants to be a good steward.

That is what God is calling each of us to do. Like Peter's mother in law, like Paul, we too have received the gift of salvation and know that our blessings come from God. In response, we are called to respond by giving a portion back. Being a good steward is truly a way of life – not a fundraiser nor a gimmick to get people more involved in the parish. First and foremost, it is a fundamental sense of gratitude in the face of God's gifts. It is an invitation to give back a portion of what God has given us. When faithful Catholics truly understand and believe this, then of course the parish, their families, and their community will benefit. But that benefit is only secondary.

Next weekend, we will begin our annual stewardship renewal by preaching on the stewardship of time and talent, and we will offer the Ministry Fair after Mass. On the following weekend, we will speak on the stewardship of treasure. Father Dan and I have decided that we will continue to allow you to continue to pay us the big bucks we receive for preaching the Gospel. But we invite you to begin reflecting on a disciple's response to the Lord's gift of salvation. Life is not always easy. Sometimes, we identify with Job in crying out in pain and wondering why life can be so cruel. But, as good stewards, we put our pain and sorrows within the same context of God's gracious gift of salvation. Throughout the good and bad things of our lives, we remain good stewards and respond with humble gratitude.

13.4 February 8, 2009

Job is not shy about putting into words what it feels like to suffer. Job has lost everything – his wealth, his home, his children, his wife, and even his health. When three friends try to comfort him, they make things worse, because they mouth pious sayings that offer too simple a solution. So, Job complains that his life is a drudgery, that his days feel like those of a hireling. He speaks of months of misery and troubled nights that drag on. In doing so, he speaks for lots of people in today's Gospel. He speaks for Peter's mother-in-law when she lay sick with a fever. He speaks for those who have a variety of illnesses and who are possessed by demons.

Jesus enters into the lives of these suffering people and gives them hope. He restores Peter's mother-in-law to health. In doing so, he gives her a glimpse of his ultimate power to save her from death. In saying that he "helped her up," Mark uses the same words to denote Jesus' ultimate power in the resurrection to "raise up" those who die. When she realizes his power in her life, she waits on him. In other words, she responds to God's saving action in her life by giving herself in humble service to other people. As Jesus continues healing people and driving out demons, he gives them hope and signs of his saving power, which will eventually save them from sin and death.

Job also speaks for us. With Job, we know what it feels like to lose loved ones or to suffer financial ruin. Too many of you know the drudgery of losing your job and worrying about your family. With those in the Gospel, we know the pain of sickness and demons in various mental illnesses and addictions. Mark tells us these stories of Jesus' healing power to give us hope and to remind us of his saving presence in our lives.

Mark tells us that Jesus rises very early before dawn and goes to a deserted place to pray. In spending time in prayer with his Heavenly Father, Jesus remains focused on his ultimate mission to bring salvation. As he makes this important connection, Peter and the other disciples do not quite "get it." They want him to work more wonders in their home town, and they come to drag him back to the same village to heal more people. Jesus gently reminds them that he has not come to win the esteem of everyone. He has come to give signs to draw people to the deeper truth about him. Having shown those signs in Peter's home village, it is now time to move to the next village, speaking his message of salvation and providing signs to draw more people to deeper faith.

We often speak of the patience of Job. If you read the Book of Job, you will see that Job had no patience whatsoever. He is not quiet about his suffering. And that is good, because he gives us permission to voice our pain in our suffering. However, Job is passionate and never loses faith in God. Jesus invites us to face our own pain and suffering in the same way and to draw hope from the signs of his saving presence in our lives. We hear of that presence in the Scriptures and are fed with the most profound sign of his presence in bread and wine transformed into his Body and Blood. Fed by the Eucharist, we are sent forth to keep our eyes and ears open to the signs of his presence in our daily lives. We can confront all those realities that have the power to turn our lives into drudgery and pain, because the Lord gives us hope of salvation. When we respond to his saving actions with humble service, we too spread the Good News and, in effect, take the message to our neighboring villages.

13.5 **February 5, 2012**

Job speaks words which all of us can understand at one time or another. Job finds life drudgery. He has lost everything. His children had been killed. His property and wealth had been destroyed. He has completely lost his health. His wife tells him to "curse God and die" before she walks away from him. His three friends tell him that his suffering is a result of being punished for some great sin. In trying to help, they make things worse for Job. Even though Job knows that this is not true, he cries out in pain and asks why all of this has happened.

The Book of Job never gives an answer to the reasons for human suffering. It concludes that God gives good things that we take for granted, and allows suffering for reasons we will not understand. But God does answer the question about human suffering by sending his only Son to bring salvation to us. In today's Gospel, Saint Mark describes the work he does. Jesus leaves the synagogue to heal Peter's mother-in-law. He cures the sick with various diseases and drives out demons. He moves on to the nearby villages to proclaim the message of salvation.

Saint Mark is not just giving us a glimpse into the average day of Jesus of Nazareth. He describes how Jesus reveals his ultimate defeat of all that causes disease and death. When he says that Jesus grasps the mother-in-law by the hand and helps her up, he uses the same words that we will hear at the end of the Gospel when Jesus is raised up from the dead. Her response is not that she goes to the kitchen and waits on him like women of his day. Rather, the term for "waiting on him" refers to being involved in the ministry of the early Church. People responded to the saving power of Christ in their lives by giving themselves in humble service. The demons are not allowed to speak, because they have no power over him. All that Jesus does on this day points to his ultimate victory over sin, death, and evil through his saving death and resurrection.

Saint Mark invites us to look at our lives to recognize his saving power, given to us in the waters of baptism. We have just heard him speaking to us in the Word. We are about to be fed by his Body and Blood. Then, he sends us out to give ourselves in humble service, as Peter's mother-in-law did. He invites us to endure diseases and sufferings with hope. He strengthens us to face those demons that drag us down, trusting that they will not have the last word in our lives.

But he also invites us to imitate one other detail in the daily life of Jesus. Exhausted by his work, he gets up early the next morning and goes to a deserted place. Like his ancestors who had encountered God in the barren desert of the Sinai Peninsula, he encounters his Father in quiet prayer. We can do well to imitate his example. We can get so caught up in our daily activities and in the constant noise of our culture that we can miss God's presence in our lives. We can easily forget his great blessings in those happy moments of our lives. We can even more easily miss his presence in the difficult and painful situations.

When we see someone who has the virtue of patience, we sometimes speak of the "patience of Job." In fact, Job had no patience whatsoever (a characteristic which I admire greatly, lacking that same virtue myself!). He constantly cried out in pain to the Lord and asked him why this had happened to him. We also can cry out in pain and ask questions in our prayer. But we can also imitate Job's perseverance. He never gave up on God. We ask for the grace of that same perseverance, so that we never give up on the power of the Lord's saving death and resurrection in our lives.

13.6   **February 8, 2015**

Today we hear Job crying out in pain, because he does not understand why he is suffering so much. He has lost everything – his possessions, his entire family, and even his health. His wife has abandoned him, telling him to curse God and die. His "friends" try to comfort him, but only make things worse. Convinced that suffering is the direct punishment from God for sin, they try to talk Job into confessing that he is a terrible sinner. Their narrow perspective and easy solutions cause him more doubt and discouragement. Throughout the entire Book, Job continues to ask God why he is suffering so much. However, no matter how much Job complains and asks questions, he never loses faith. In the end, God poses a series of rhetorical questions asking Job if he understands the good things of life that he has taken for granted. When he answers "no," God responds that suffering is also a mystery, something we can never understand.

In the Gospel today, many people who share the sufferings of Job seek out Jesus. In response, Jesus shows compassion, heals some of them, and drives demons out of others. Jesus does not explain the mystery of human suffering. Throughout the New Testament, he does not provide any further explanation than did the Book of Job. Instead, he embraced our human condition in every way except for sin. In the course of his ministry, he endured the pain of criticism and rejection. Eventually, he would suffer greatly and enter into a terrible death. As the Eternal Word of God, he would show that suffering could be redemptive. By his suffering, we are redeemed and freed from the grip of sin, the devil, and death. When we find ourselves in Job's shoes, we can place our suffering within the suffering of Jesus Christ and trust that our suffering can also have a transforming power, especially in ways we would never expect.

When Jesus heals Peter's mother-in-law, he gives some insights into how this mystery affects us. She is sick with a fever, which not only causes physical pain, but which also isolates her from the community. Jesus touches her and raises her up, just as the Father would raise him up from the dead. Not only is the pain gone. But she is also restored to her family and friends. Having recognized the Lord's saving power, she waits on them. Saint Mark uses those words to speak of official ministry in the Church. She provides an example of a proper response to the healing power of Jesus Christ. Those who have experienced that saving power respond by giving themselves in humble service to the Body of Christ, the Church.

Suffering is a part of the human condition, and faith in God does not protect us from suffering. If anything, faithfulness to the Gospel can open us to more intense suffering. Jesus does not give us easy an answer when suffering invades our lives, causes great pain, and separates us from family and friends. But we encounter Jesus Christ in the Sacramental life of the Church, just as surely as Peter's mother-in-law did. He washes away our sins in the waters of Baptism and strengthens us through Sacrament of Confirmation. He heals us with his mercy when we fail to live our baptismal promises, restores us to the community of family and friends, and heals us in the Sacrament of the Anointing of the Sick. He feeds us with his Body and Blood in the Eucharist. He strengthens us to live our permanent commitments in the Sacraments of Matrimony and Holy Orders.

Once we become aware of his healing actions in our lives, we respond as Peter's mother-in-law did. We give ourselves in humble service to the community. That humble service allows us to show the same compassion which Christ has shown us. That humble service renews our faith that he will raise us up with him in the Mystery of the Resurrection.

13.7   February 4, 2018

Last Sunday, we heard that the people in the synagogue at Capernaum were amazed, because they heard Jesus teaching with authority. Unlike other Rabbis, Jesus did not base his teaching on the authority of others. The demon expelled by Jesus knew exactly why Jesus taught in this way. He knew that Jesus was the Son of God who had come to destroy what demons love best: sin and death. Today, Jesus expresses that authority again by grasping the hand of Peter's mother-in-law. During this flu season, many of us know how a fever can turn us into ourselves. So Jesus helps her up. Saint Mark uses the same Greek verb to describe the Father raising Jesus from the dead. Peter's mother-in-law has already experienced a foretaste of the mystery of the Lord's dying and rising in her healing. His healing power frees her from concern for her welfare to the welfare of others. Saint Mark will use that same word two more times to speak of the humble service embraced by followers of Jesus, who came not to be served, but to serve.

When the risen Christ reached out to Saul on the road to Damascus, he helped him up from his narrow focus on the Law and himself. Completely changed by that experience, the Apostle Paul did the same thing that Peter's mother-in-law did. He died to himself and gave himself in humble service to proclaim the Good News to anyone who would listen. In a culture where a majority of its citizens found themselves as slaves, Saint Paul proudly announces that he has made himself a slave to all. He did not become a slave by having his home town invaded. Nor did he become a slave because his parents could not pay their bills. He freely enslaved himself to the mission of telling the Gospel to as many people as possible. His Jewish brothers and sisters had heard stories of people speaking for God and bringing glad tidings. His glad tidings centered on Jesus Christ, the fulfillment of glad tidings. The Gentiles had often heard the glad tidings of a military victory won by the armies of the emperor. Paul gives them the glad tidings that Jesus Christ has won the ultimate victory over sin and death.

In just a couple of weeks, we will enter into Lent and spend forty days preparing to renew our faith in the Mystery of the death and resurrection of Jesus Christ in a special way at the Sacred Paschal Triduum. We celebrate that Mystery at this Mass and we are sent out to live the Mystery we have encountered in our daily lives.

Saint Mark is one of the four Evangelists who proclaimed the glad tidings some forty years after the death and resurrection of Jesus Christ. But evangelizing did not stop with the writing of the Gospels. We too are called to evangelize, to tell everyone about the glad tidings which we have received and experienced. We do that by our example – by the way we welcome strangers, or forgive those who have hurt us, or respond to the needs of the poor, dying to ourselves out of love for those who depend on us. We also need to talk about our faith. That is exactly what is happening this weekend with the men who are participating in the Christ Renews His Parish Retreat. They are learning to talk about their faith in the ways that Saint Paul talks about. In becoming all things to all, he entered into the lives of those who listened to him. He did not beat them over the head with the truth, but spoke boldly and kindly to anyone who would listen. All of us need to learn how to speak boldly and kindly about our faith.

We live in a world that knows the pain and suffering described in the first reading from the Book of Job. Jesus Christ did not take away that pain or explain that suffering. He entered into it and gave us hope. That is certainly glad tidings, and we cannot keep those tidings to ourselves!

14. 6th Sunday in Ordinary Time

Readings

Leviticus 13:1–2, 44–46
1 Corinthians 10:31, 11:1
Mark 1:40–45

14.1 February 13, 2000

The old saying, "cleanliness is next to godliness," is not just a modern phrase invented by parents to get their children to wash their hands or take a bath occasionally. Rather, we can thank our spiritual ancestors, the Jewish people, for putting such a high priority on being clean. They had spent 40 years in the desert anticipating a land flowing with milk and honey – and hopefully, water! Once they reached the Promised Land, they shook the sand out of their clothes, soaked their sweaty bodies, and made every effort to keep themselves clean!

We can see that compulsion for cleanliness in today's first reading and Gospel. In ancient Israel, leprosy was not just a contagious disease that kept lepers separated from the general population. Rather, the word "leprosy" was used to describe a variety of repulsive skin diseases. It became an image for being unclean –a word used six times in the reading from Leviticus. Lepers were considered *unclean* until the priest made a determination otherwise. In the Gospel, the operative word is *clean*. Jesus makes the man *clean* and restored him to the community.

What do these ancient biblical concerns about being clean have to do with us today? Plenty! We have been washed *clean* through the waters of baptism. As baptized members of Christ's Body, we want to keep ourselves clean and develop an aversion to dirt. We try to stay away from whatever is *irty* – reading dirty books, finding the dirt on other people, giving dirty looks to others, doing dirt to someone else.

But there is another way of using the word *irty* that is completely unacceptable and contrary to anything Jesus represents. This happens when we apply that term to certain people or any group of people. In the 1930's, powerful people in Europe took advantage of a feeling that the Jewish people were dirty. As a result, six million Jews were murdered. The Tutsis and Hutus of Rwanda consider one another dirty, and thousands were slaughtered in the last decade. We read every day about the murderous outcome when Serbs and Romanians regard each other as dirty.

When Jesus healed the leper, he made him clean and removed anything that made him dirty! His healing action affects every single one of us today. Because he made that man clean, we can never consider anyone else dirty. Young people, Jesus' action is a direct challenge to you to go to school on Monday and take another look at the kid your group might consider *irty*. You can make Jesus' miracle present by reaching out to that person. All of us can look again at a group in the parish we might regard as *irty*. We don't have to travel to a shrine to look for a miracle. The miracle happens when we look through eyes of faith, sit with them at the next potluck supper, and extend a hand.

By curing the leper, Jesus invites us to be honest about individuals or groups whom we consider to be *irty*. Then we can listen carefully to the Prayer over the Gifts at today's Mass: "Lord, we make this offering in obedience to your word. *Cleanse* and renew us, and lead us to our eternal reward." Yes, Lord. Reach out your holy hand of compassion and cleanse our minds and hearts of our deep-down discrimination against those who are different from us. Empowered with the Spirit of your Son, give us the courage to cure the lepers in our midst today!

14.2 February 12, 2006

Leprosy was a terrible scourge in the ancient world. The disease caused more than great physical pain and disfigured people. Much worse, the disease caused the sick person to be separated from the rest of the community. In listening to the reading from the Book of Leviticus, we can sense the fear coming from the healthy members of the community who feared that contact with a leper would infect them.

Mark tells us that Jesus was moved with pity when a leper approached him. The Greek words are the English equivalent of Jesus "having his gut wrenched" at the sight. But instead of drawing back in horror at the sight, he stretched out his hand, touched the infected man, and healed him, restoring him to his rightful place in the community.

We do not encounter many people afflicted with Hansen's disease – the modern term for leprosy – in our First World existence. However, there are plenty of situations where people are isolated from the community. People can be isolated by almost anything – illness, grief, depression, shame, hurt, or many other situations. In response, many rightly say that the Church should reach out to those who are isolated and do something. And they are absolutely correct. We are Christ's Body, and our baptism pushes us to reach out as Christ did to the leper. We must reach out our hands to those who are isolated, and especially those who are new to us, even when we fear that contact with them might change us.

That is why we speak so often about stewardship of time and talent. Saint Pius X can reach out to those who are isolated only if parishioners step forward and give back a portion of the precious time and talent they have received from God. Jocie Antonelli found herself isolated from this community, and she will tell you how this community reached out and was instrumental in her healing. Please listen carefully to her story, and hear in her words the Lord's invitation to step forward and touch the lives of other people, as Christ did.

14.3 February 15, 2009

The laws about the treatment of lepers in Leviticus were not intended to punish those with skin disease. Rather, they were given for the safety of the community. Skin diseases were highly contagious, and there were no known cures for those illnesses that caused terrible pain and disfigurement to those who suffered them. Lepers were forced to dwell apart, making their abodes outside the camp as a way of keeping the dreaded disease from infecting everyone. By excluding the few who suffered from the disease, these laws protected the common good.

By the time of Jesus, many of his contemporaries used these laws to make judgments on those who suffered from leprosy. Their external disfigurements were seen as revealing their internal sins, and their exclusion was seen as a punishment from God. As a result, lepers were abandoned to suffer lives of loneliness and separation, with most people forgetting the part of the Law of Moses which required them to be attentive to the needs of the poor and the most vulnerable. Even if there would be some kind of cure, lepers were forced to approach the priests to certify that they were deemed worthy to come back into the community.

That is not the attitude of Jesus to this leper. Looking beyond the open sores of the leper's body, Jesus sees a faith in him that others lack. Even though Jesus is not a priest, he dares to do something no one would ever do. He reaches across that divide of pain and suffering and touches the leper. He tells him to fulfill the Law of Moses by showing himself to a priest, so he could be returned to the community. He does not want him to tell anyone about this healing, because Jesus is not interested in people chasing after him for his wondrous powers. Rather, he is more interested in using these signs as a way of helping people see the truth about him.

The truth about Jesus is that he is the Son of God without any blemish of sin whatsoever. But, he has become one of us and has reached across that divide between God and us, a divide which we created by our bad choices (sin), and he has reconciled us. To use the words of Saint Paul, he who is without sin has become sin for us, to reconcile us to the Father.

Because we recognize Jesus as the Son of God who touches us, Jesus invites us to have the courage to reach across lines of division and offer his reconciling love to the lepers of today. Leprosy, known as Hanson's Disease, is virtually eradicated in First World countries. Yet, we tend to isolate people today as if they were lepers. This happens in our grade schools and high schools. Certain individuals are isolated, and most kids refuse to reach out to them, because they are afraid that they will "catch" their isolation. We adults are more sophisticated. We tend to avoid those with whom we disagree, or those who are different in any way from us, keeping them as far away as possible. In our fear, we become too paralyzed to respond to their needs.

Jesus sends the healed leper to the priests, who will make a judgment on whether or not the man's sores and blemishes are gone. As Jesus continues to reveal himself through such signs, the priests and members of the religious establishment are so busy making judgments on the wounds of those who respond to Jesus that they fail to see their own blemishes and sores. We must avoid their mistake. As members of Christ's Body, we need to continue to reach out and touch those who need healing. That includes our partnership with Saint Adalbert's and our efforts to serve the needs of the poor who come to us. It is easy to make judgments about their "worthiness," and we are sometimes accused of aiding "illegal immigrants," those who break the law. We too have our own blemishes and sores. In reaching out to those in need, we rely on the healing and reconciling love of Jesus Christ, which we extend to others.

14.4   February 12, 2012

In this healing story, Saint Mark provides an interesting detail. After the healing, Jesus warns the leper sternly and dismisses him. Jesus shows great pity for the leper as a human being. But, he is angry at the condition that had placed him in a living hell, for three reasons. First, the leper suffered terrible physical pain, as the nerves were deadened and his flesh rotted. Second, the leper was separated from his community. The Book of Leviticus clearly legislated that lepers must live on the outer fringes of society. It was a way of protecting the health of the community from a contagious disease without a cure. Third, everyone presumed that the man became a leper because he was being punished by God for some terrible sin he had committed.

Suffering physical pain, banned from the community, and assumed to be abandoned by God, this man ignores the law and approaches Jesus. In his desperation, he trusts that Jesus can heal him. Jesus also breaks the law and physically touches the man. Through this miracle, he heals the man's horrible pain, reconnects him to the community, and assures him that he is loved by God and valued as a human person. Having put the leper's needs for healing ahead of any concern for his own health and welfare, Jesus withdraws from the community and goes to the fringes of the community. He knows that it will be only after his resurrection that his followers will understand his power to heal and save.

Modern science may have found the cure for leprosy, known today as Hanson's Disease. And yet, people continue to suffer from a different form of leprosy today. Just ask any teenager. They can tell you about the pain associated with being pushed to the fringes of society. Others are afraid to touch these modern lepers, for fear that they will be associated with those outcasts. To be honest, we adults are just smoother at the ways in which we isolate people and push them to the fringes. The Lord Jesus invites us to take risks, to stretch out our hands, to touch those on the fringes, and draw them into the community that nourishes them.

We have a word which describes the condition of the leper in the Gospel. We call it "sin"! Serious sin infects each of us just as surely as leprosy infected the man who approached Jesus. It causes deep pain and isolates us from the community, pushing us to the fringes. It also separates us from the love of God. The Lord Jesus touches us in the Sacrament of Reconciliation and heals us, just as effectively as he healed that man. We come to understand the Lord's deep compassion and pity for us, just as we know that he is angry at the sin that is so destructive in our lives and in our community.

In just a week and a half, we will enter into the Season of Lent. Lent gives us an opportunity to address our sin, which causes pain, isolation, and separation from the Lord. Be sure to pick up your Lenten packet on the back table. The packets give specific suggestions on how we can use this Season of grace to confront the sin that infests each one of us. Through acts of penance – prayer, fasting, and almsgiving – we can acknowledge our sins and the damage they do. We can open ourselves to the healing power of the Lord in our lives. But, most importantly, Lent prepares us to celebrate the Paschal Mystery at the Great Easter Triduum. The Lord no longer has to retreat to the fringes of our society. He is front and center, the victor over sin, death, and evil. He is the one who will heal us at depths we can only imagine!

14.5 February 15, 2015

The laws in the Book of Leviticus seem very harsh to our 21st century ears. When anyone had any kind of skin disease that "appears to be the sore of leprosy," that person was banned from the community. Not only did the person suffer terrible physical pain, but also banishment from family, friends, and any kind of a supportive community. As tough as it was for the individual, the real concern was for the common good, the health of the community. In a pre-scientific age that had no cures for skin diseases, excluding the contagious people was the only way to prevent the destruction of the fabric of a closely knit society.

In our culture, the opposite dynamic is true. We so value the rights and freedom of the individual that we sometimes do not consider how our behaviors affect the common good. In our families, having it my own way can have negative effects on the rest of the family. We can become seduced by the message of consumerism so much that we do not see how our greed for things we do not need affect the poor. We can be tempted to become consumers of the good things of our parish and give no thought to those stewards who can burn themselves out by doing all the heavy lifting. We engage in gossip and slander without giving a thought to the damage done to the reputations of those around us. There are many examples of making decisions without giving any thought to their impact on the common good.

That is why we need the Season of Lent. Lent invites us to take a good look at our lives and examine how our choices have harmed the common good, whether in our families, in our local society, or in our parish. Lent invites us to take an honest look at the ways in which we have become lepers and separated ourselves from or damaged the communities in which we live.

All of us are sinners. All of us have known the shame that comes from making bad choices. Like the leper in today's Gospel, we have learned that we can bring our blemishes to the Lord without being condemned. He reaches out, touches us, and reconciles us to the community damaged by our sinful choices. He can also heal those smaller, sometimes habitual actions that tear apart at the fabric of the societies in which we live.

Once we acknowledge how we have made ourselves lepers, the disciplines of Lent have the power to bring us closer to the Lord, whose sacrifice reconciles us to the Father and to each other. Please take home your packet and resolve to enter into some meaningful form of prayer, fasting, and almsgiving. In particular, pay attention to the suggestions for renewing our stewardship of prayer. It is that aspect of stewardship that is most critical, because prayer not only reveals the ways in which we have made ourselves lepers, but it also reminds us that everything is a gift from God who reconciles us.

You would expect me to talk about the importance of prayer. That's my job. Please direct your attention to Mary Colbert, who will speak about the place of prayer in her life.

14.6 February 11, 2018

The laws concerning skin diseases in the Book of Leviticus were designed to protect the community. Because leprosy and other skin diseases were contagious, lepers were forced to rend their garments, declare that they were unclean, and stay away from contact with the community. While these laws may have protected the community, they had terrible effects on the poor people suffering these ailments. The leper who approaches Jesus not only suffers terrible physical pain, but he is completely alone. Even worse, he is considered spiritually unclean.

He breaks the Law of Moses by throwing himself at the feet of Jesus, because he trusts in the power of Jesus to heal him. Seeing his faith and having pity on him, Jesus also breaks the Law of Moses and touches the leper. Restored to health and intimacy with his family, the man spreads the good news of his healing to anyone he meets.

On this last Sunday before Lent, the Scriptures invite us to reflect on the way we have made ourselves lepers. We become lepers when we fail to live our Baptismal Promises, when we separate ourselves from God or other people through our sins. By embracing the disciplines of prayer, fasting, and almsgiving, we throw ourselves at the feet of Jesus and ask for healing. That is why Lent provides a perfect opportunity to renew our stewardship of prayer, the most important of the three dynamics of stewardship. Please listen carefully to Stephanie Allen, as she shares the ways in which prayer has transformed her life.

15. 7th Sunday in Ordinary Time

Readings
Isaiah 43:18–19, 21–22, 24b–25
2 Corinthians 1:18-22
Mark 2:1–12

15.1 February 20, 2000

Father Gary Smith wrote an article in a Catholic paper about a friend who was stricken with multiple sclerosis. At first, his friend experienced embarrassing falls and awkward inconveniences. But as the disease progressed, he found himself flat on his back. So, a group of his friends came to his aid. He called them "the roofers," alluding to those resourceful friends in today's Gospel who removed the tiles of the roof to get their friend to Jesus. "The roofers" included lawyers, physicians, teachers, architects, blue-collar workers, psychologists, and priests – all people who had come to know him from his brief stint in the Jesuits and through his career. "The roofers" took turns taking him to the doctor, attending to his needs, and helping him meet his financial obligations.

When the man died, one of "the roofers" – a priest – preached the homily. "We were indeed the people of the Gospel: packing him on his litter, down the alleys, cross the river, up the stairs, to the very roof. We pulled off the tiles. We hardly had a choice. He was yanking on us to do so. It really wasn't hard. He was pretty light, after all. He didn't complain. His spirits were pretty good most of the time. He used to say, 'My vocation, during this part of my life, is to lead people to God by their taking care of me.' It worked. Our hearts opened. He showed us faith; he showed us caring; he showed us forgiveness; he showed us kindness. He led the way to God. Our job was easy. All we did was carry him."

In today's Gospel, Mark tells us nothing about the faith of the paralyzed man! Instead, he describes the faith of his friends (the original "roofers"). They too were concerned about the plight of their friend. They went through all the effort and even embarrassment of getting him to Jesus. They believed that Jesus could make a difference in his life. And the faith of "the roofers" paid off! Not only did Jesus free their friend from his physical inability to move out toward others. But he also freed him from a much deeper paralysis – the spiritual inability to move toward others that results from sinning.

Today's Gospel story has tremendous implications for all of us at Saint Jude. We belong to this parish, because God calls us to be "roofers" – people broken open by our acts of love. As "roofers," we focus on our wounded brothers and sisters and learn from selfless service what it means to extend Jesus' healing hand of truth and compassion. We do not participate in this parish because we want people to notice how nice we are. We are here to nourish a faith that caused the original "roofers" to bring their friend to Jesus.

If you are a young person thinking that you no longer fit into this community of people on Sunday mornings, take another look! You need to be part of this community as you explore how the faith given you by your parents will fit into your own life. And we desperately need you! If you have lost someone in death, you need to be here every Sunday, no matter how painful that may be! We need to carry you through your grief to the consolation promised by the Gospel. And if you are hurt or confused by conflicts in this very human group of people, you need to hang in there and stay with us! Faith lived in isolation can easily lead to self-pity, anger, and deeper paralysis.

Evelyn Underhill once described faith as "consecration in overalls." Faith is much more than saying we believe in God. "The roofers" in Mark's put on their overalls and consecrated their paralyzed friend to the healing power of Jesus Christ. As members of this parish, we put on our own overalls and carry others, consecrating them to that same healing power. At other times, we must allow ourselves to be carried to Jesus by others. Wearing our overalls, we "roofers" learn that faith is a lived response to the reality of God in our midst. And that faith grows best in the hard work of friendship and communal caring.

15.2 February 23, 2003

The paralyzed man had some good friends. They believed the Good News being proclaimed by Jesus of Nazareth, and they trusted that an encounter with Jesus could change their friend. They were so anxious to be part of the assembly gathered around Jesus that they went to the trouble of removing the tiles of the roof and lowered him down. Jesus did not disappoint them. Touched by their faith, he relieved the paralytic of what most burdened him – his sins. To silence his critics, he healed him of his paralysis, permitting him to walk away from that encounter a changed person.

Like those friends, we also go out of our way to gather here each Sunday, because we trust that every encounter with the Lord present in his Word and in the Eucharist will change us. In this Eucharistic Sacrifice, we express our gratitude for all God has given us, and we express our trust that God will continue to provide for what we need.

Gathering here as friends has tremendous implications for our stewardship of treasure. Just as we can give back a first portion of our time and talent, so we can give back a first portion of our treasure – possessions that are ultimately gifts from God. This giving back of a first portion of our treasure involves a different attitude than giving something as an afterthought. This style of giving is called "sacrificial giving," because it joins our sacrifice with the perfect Sacrifice of Jesus Christ.

All of us have varying amounts of treasure. Because of that, the Biblical standard of giving back a percentage makes sense. Sacred Scripture speaks of tithing – giving a first 10% back. (*Bring up basket of apples*) If these ten apples represent all my treasure, the first one is given as an expression of my gratitude. 5% goes to this Eucharistic Assembly – Saint Pius. Moved by the Spirit, the other 5% can go to the Cancer Society, Women's Care Center, Bishop's Appeal, the extra envelopes in our packets, or to any charity that the Spirit might move us to support. The other nine are for our personal use.

That is why the use of envelopes becomes so important. Once we have made a prayerful decision about the amount of our sacrificial gift, using the envelope helps to keep our intention consistent. I have gotten into the habit of writing a check every Saturday night and putting it into the envelope, much as I would carefully wrap a gift to show another person a sign of my love. Using the envelope is a powerful way of making sure that the gift is a first portion, and not an afterthought when the bills are paid.

To be perfectly honest, none of this made any sense to me when I was first ordained. I had given my entire life to the Church and wondered what more they could take from me! But, over the years, encountering Jesus Christ with a lot of friends has changed me. The Word of God has changed my attitude – especially hearing the many times Jesus warns about the danger of greed. The Eucharist has opened my heart to the depths of the sacrificial love of Jesus Christ. Visiting Fr. Tom McDermott in Africa forced me to see how rich I actually am, compared to the way that most of the world lives. It took me fifteen years to reach the point of giving 10% of my income. And that is what I urge you to do – take one step at a time. When I came to Saint Pius and saw that we normally take in more than we need each week, I began to wonder if my money should go somewhere else. But, as I began to understand what will be required to meet the growing needs of this parish, my thanksgiving sacrifice becomes foundational in investing in the future of our parish.

You may expect me to say these things, because I am the pastor. But, please give your attention to A. J. Bellia, whose job is not to preach on Stewardship, but to tell you his own experience. A. J. is "normal," and you will find his story interesting.

15.3 February 22, 2009

As Jesus is preaching, he is interrupted by four men ripping off the roof of the house. (Our roof may leak sometimes. But no one has removed it while we were preaching – yet!) As he is being distracted, Jesus notices two things. First, he clearly sees the faith of the four men carrying their friend on the mat. Mark uses a word for faith that also implies loyalty. They are so loyal to the plight of their friend that they go to the trouble of removing the roof as a way of getting their friend to Jesus. Second, Jesus sees that there is a worse paralysis than not being able to walk. So, he heals the man of the paralysis of his sins, those actions or failures to act that have separated him from this closely knit bond of family and community.

Mark tells us this story, inviting us to believe what the scribes could not believe: that Jesus Christ is the Son of God, who can reconcile us and heal whatever separates or weakens our ties to our families and communities. Knowing their lack of faith, he tells the man to pick up his mat and walk home, giving a sign of his more significant power to heal the spiritual wounds that paralyze people and keep them apart.

On Wednesday, Jesus gives us another sign of that power to heal the wounds that divide us. He marks us with ashes to remind us of our own spiritual paralysis. For those preparing for Baptism at the Easter Vigil, the ashes will be a sign of their final forty days of preparation for their union with Christ and with the Communion of the Church through the waters of Baptism. For those of us who are baptized, those ashes will be a sign that these forty days will be a time to examine ways in which we have not kept our baptismal promises and damaged or broken the bonds established with Christ and the rest of the community.

In giving us this sign of ashes, Jesus sees our common faith. Like the four men carrying the paralytic, we walk together through these forty days. We carry one another to the Lord, and we trust that all the efforts that go into an observance of Lent are worth it. We do not need to tear apart this roof to get to the healing power of Jesus. We can open the mailing from the parish to see the opportunities available during this season. Be sure to review the various ways we can enter into penance: through prayer, fasting, and almsgiving. Use the commitment card as a way of making a commitment to remove any roofing that stands in the way of getting to the Lord.

We often use the word "stewardship" at Saint Pius. We find the most basic form of stewardship when we enter into a spirit of prayer. It is through prayer that we see what the scribes could not see: that Jesus is the Son of God who has the power to save us and provide all that we need. Lent provides the structure for tearing off whatever roofing is keeping us from that contact with God. As you make your commitment to deepen your prayer life, please give your attention to Tim Fulnecky. Tim will briefly talk about his own commitment to prayer, not to brag, but to speak of the way prayer has opened his heart to God.

15.4 February 19, 2012

Jesus has a way of looking beyond the physical and seeing something much deeper. Last week, he looked beyond the appearance of the leper and saw the man's pain, his complete isolation from the community, and his presumption that God did not love him. He reached out and touched the leper, healing his physical pain, reconciling him with the community, and proclaiming that he was a child beloved of God.

Today, he sees the care of four friends bringing a paralytic to be healed. He looks beyond their destruction of the roof and sees their deep faith in him and loyalty to their friend. He looks beyond the physical pain of paralysis and sees the greater paralysis caused by sin. So he forgives the spiritual paralysis. He heals the physical paralysis and tells the man to pick up his mat and go home, only to demonstrate that he possesses the power to release people from sin.

We have much in common with the leper. Through our bad choices, we cause much pain to ourselves, isolate ourselves from our community, and separate ourselves from the God who loves us. Ask any family torn apart by infidelity, and they can tell you. Ask a young person being bullied or isolated from the crowd. We also have much in common with the paralytic. We can get so caught up in our grudges, anger, and resentment that we cannot move beyond ourselves. Gandhi once said, "To carry anger and resentment rather than forgiveness is like taking poison thinking that it will kill the one you resent."

Jesus invites us to admit our leprosy and paralysis and seek his healing. He invites us to face these realities beginning on Ash Wednesday, and to find acts of penance that open our hearts to the truth about ourselves and seek his healing mercy. Be sure to read the materials we have prepared in your stewardship of prayer packet. But, for now, please give your attention to Gwen O'Brien. Gwen will tell her story of how she and her family faced their own leprosy and paralysis and opened themselves to the Lord's healing through a growing appreciation of prayer in their lives. As you listen to her, remember that we do not enter into this Season alone. We carry one another, much as the four friends carried the paralytic to Jesus.

16. 8th Sunday in Ordinary Time

Readings

Hosea 2:16b, 17b, 21–22
2 Corinthians 3:1b–6
Mark 2:18–22

16.1 February 27, 2000

Have you ever tried to re-live a situation in life that you once enjoyed? We try to go back to places where we lived before, or gone to school, or worked, or even to a place where we had that perfect vacation. Odds are pretty good that we will be disappointed. We have changed, and those places and situations have changed.

That is what Jesus implies in saying that we cannot sew pieces of unshrunken cloth to an old cloak, or pour new wine into old wineskins. Once we have accepted the new, fresh, and different perspective of the gospel, we cannot go back to old ways.

That is true of the gospel message of stewardship. Those of you who have embraced it as a way of life know that there is no going back. Kirk and Karen Dunkelberger understand that, and they have agreed to tell their story of coming to believe in stewardship as a way of life. Listen to what they have to say.

It does not matter where you are in terms of stewardship. If it has become a way of life for you, or if you have taken some initial steps, it is time to renew your commitment for another year. If you have taken no steps at all, their story might touch your heart.

16.2   March 2, 2003

Hosea lived at a time of prosperity and peace. However, in the midst of wealth and comfort, the prophet noticed that greed was causing many people to ignore the needs of the poor. Their worship of God was becoming haphazard. Their commitment to the Covenant was weakening. Speaking in God's name, Hosea used marital imagery to charge that Israel – the bride – had been unfaithful to God – the bridegroom. Out of love, the Bridegroom would lead his bride back into the desert – to that place where their original "marriage" took place at Mount Sinai. In the starkness of that desert, there were few distractions. Facing God alone, they could reorder their priorities and return to what was important – their Covenant relationship with God.

On Wednesday, we – God's people and the Bride of Christ – will enter into the desert of Lent. This desert is not fashioned out of sand, but carved by a disciplined commitment to enter into some serious self-denial. In that desert, we reflect on our own covenant relationship sealed by the Blood of Jesus Christ. This desert of self-denial can open our eyes to ways we have been unfaithful. The desert of Lent invites us to face God with fewer distractions and reorder priorities in our lives.

Official Church regulations for Lent are very minimal. They require fasting and abstaining (refrain from eating between meals and from meat) on Ash Wednesday and Good Friday. They require abstaining from meat on the Fridays of Lent. Without strict and specific Church laws, we have the freedom to use the ancient disciplines of fasting, prayer, and almsgiving to form a desert experience that fits our individual situations. Now is the time to decide what kind of fasting fits best – from food, snacks, drink, television, gossiping, or complaining. Now is the time to plan for extra prayer – participating in any of the extra Masses scheduled during Lent, or praying the Stations of the Cross on Friday nights, or joining a Disciples In Mission group. Although any almsgiving project can work, you might consider Operation Rice Bowl, an almsgiving project we have used at Saint Pius for years.

Because of the growing conflict in the Middle East, the Muslim month of Ramadan made headlines this year. A visitor to a Muslim country immediately knows that it is Ramadan – the month in which faithful Muslims fast from sunup to sundown. But, we live in a secular society, and there is no cultural support for our fasting during Lent. Rather, the focus is on March Madness, Spring Break, and garden shows. That is why it is so important for this parish to go through Lent together. Be sure to check the bulletin for some options. For example, on Tuesday evenings, you can participate in prayer by coming to Mass at 6:30, share a simple fasting meal of soup, bread, and water in the gym, and give alms to Operation Rice Bowl. Some of the Disciples in Mission groups will meet that night.

At the time of Jesus, most people did not have bottles or earthen vessels large enough to hold wine. So, they poured their new wine into animal skins. Because wine continues to expel gasses as it ferments, new wineskins worked better. Old wineskins did not have the elasticity of new skins, and they could easily burst as the wine continued to ferment. The same is true for us. God wants to transform us with his love into a bride more faithful to our bridegroom. Entering the desert of Lent provides new wineskins for us. We become more pliable. We can become new wine.

16.3 February 26, 2006

Those who fasted at the time of Jesus did so as a form of self-humiliation. Everyone fasted on the Day of Atonement. The priests and scribes who worked in the Temple fasted during their two-week time of service. The Pharisees – a lay group – extended the practice of fasting beyond the temple precincts into the ordinary lives of people by fasting on Mondays and Thursdays. The disciples of John the Baptist fasted as a way of underlying their call to repentance. All of them made a big deal out of their fasting – by wearing special clothing and announcing to everyone their fasting.

When Jesus is asked why his disciples do not fast, he identifies himself with God, the husband described by Hosea, who led his unfaithful people back into the desert to renew their marital contract. Jesus is the new Bridegroom. People do not fast when they are feasting with the Bridegroom at his wedding feast. When the Bridegroom is taken away, then they will fast.

On Good Friday, the Bridegroom was taken away. Ever since, his followers have observed Friday as a day of fasting. This Wednesday, our catechumens will begin their fast. For them, the fasting of Lent will prepare them to be united with the Bridegroom through the Sacraments of Initiation at the Easter Vigil. The rest of us are invited to join them in this time of fasting. Like the ancient Israelites, we have not been faithful to our baptismal promises, and we have turned away from the Bridegroom in our lives.

Our fasting is a way of expressing our deep sorrow for those times we have been unfaithful. Our fasting gives us an opportunity to make a break with the sins of our past. Just as it is impossible to pour new wine into old wineskins, so it is impossible to change our ways without beginning again. Young people cannot turn themselves around if they insist on hanging around with the same crowd that got them into trouble in the first place. Spouses who have become emotionally involved in someone else cannot focus on working on their marriage without letting go of that attachment. I cannot break any of my bad habits without making a dramatic gesture, expressed by fasting.

Like the contemporaries of Jesus, the ashes on our heads this Wednesday will proclaim our fast. However, on Thursday, our society loses interest in Lent and turns its attention to Saint Patrick's Day and Spring Break. Our Church no longer has stringent laws about fasting. We are required to fast on Ash Wednesday and Good Friday, and abstain from meat on the Fridays of Lent. Other than that, we are on our own.

That is why we provide the commitment cards. These cards provide practical suggestions along the three ancient traditions of doing penance – prayer, fasting, and almsgiving. Take a card from the pew and look at the suggestions. In particular, look at the ways in which we can do penance together – the Tuesday night Lenten series, Friday evening Stations of the Cross, the Lenten Penance Service, daily Mass, or the Fish Fries offered by the Knights of Columbus. Penance is easier when we do it together.

Make a commitment, sign your name if you like, and fold the card in half. Put it in the collection basket when it comes around. We will place these cards in front of the Crucifix during Lent and burn them in the fire at the Easter Vigil. Lent is often called the springtime of the Spirit – a time of spiritual spring housecleaning. We fast now as we reflect on the ultimate gift of the Bridegroom on the Cross, fully aware that we will feast with the risen Lord at Easter.

17. 9th Sunday in Ordinary Time

Readings

Deuteronomy 5:12–15
2 Corinthians 4:6–11
Mark 2:23–3:6

17.1 March 5, 2000

A chain of discount department stores in the southeastern section of the United States posts a sign on its doors that reads: "Closed Sundays: The Day is Worth More than the Dollar." We do not see many signs like that these days, because making a dollar has become the first priority for so many people. In our fast-paced culture, there is no built-in allowance for a day of rest. Not much pauses in our service-based economy. Those who observe the Sabbath today must choose to make it a priority and set aside the first day of the week (or the last day for Jewish people). We gather here this morning, because we acknowledge that God has given us everything. Our presence expresses our need to take a day of rest, as God took a day of rest in the work of creation.

The same is true for the message of Stewardship. Stewardship is not a fund raising activity or a get rich scheme. It is spirituality, a way of life. We live in a world that puts a high value on hard work and achievement. Those who embrace Stewardship acknowledge the same point we make when we observe the Sabbath – God is ultimately the source of everything we are and have. For that reason, good stewards set aside a first portion of what God has given us – gifts of time, talent, and treasure. Good stewards make a sacrifice and give a first portion back to God as a way of expressing our gratitude. Good stewards take time each year to examine where we are. Guided by prayer, we carefully plan how those gifts will be given. We do not wait until we take care of everything else before making a decision.

Because God has not given everyone equal amounts of time, talent, and treasure, good stewards give proportionately. That is why Jesus praises the widow in Luke's Gospel. The tiny amount of money she gave could never compete with what the Scribes and Pharisees placed into the treasury. Their large gifts were safe – from their abundance. Her gift was from her substance – a percentage. Her sacrifice was equal in God's eyes! God calls us to equal sacrifice, not equal amounts of gifts.

It is always easy to play games with religious customs and laws. That is what the Pharisees were doing in the Gospel today. They did not care about the essence of the Sabbath. They did not care whether Jesus' disciples were hungry. They used laws against harvesting and processing food on the Sabbath to set a trap for Jesus. They did not care about the man with the withered hand. They used laws against working on the Sabbath to accuse Jesus of disregarding the Sabbath law. They revealed themselves as hypocrites! It did not matter to them that they were engaged in work also – the deadly work of entrapping the Son of Man.

We must be careful about playing similar games with our stewardship of treasure. We recommend the biblical tithe of 10% as a goal. For years, I have suggested that you might allocate 5% of your treasure to Saint Jude and the other 5% to any charity of your choice. That might include the Annual Bishop's Appeal or the Cancer Society. Those of you who sacrifice for Catholic education for your children are often strapped for funds. For that reason, I have suggested that you might consider tuition as part of your second 5% at this time in your life. But these percentages are guidelines intended to help people come to decisions about sacrificial giving. If you are just beginning to respond, start small and gradually increase your percentage as time goes on. Some people exceed the Biblical tithe of 10%. I choose to give the lion's share of my 10% to Saint Jude.

Saint Paul says that God has given us a treasure in the person of Jesus Christ. We hold that treasure in earthen vessels, which by definition are weak and rough and vulnerable. We hold that treasure in the earthen vessel of this parish community, with its many ideas, opinions, feelings and priorities. We hold that treasure in the earthen vessels of our families, with their pressures and difficulties. We hold that treasure in the earthen vessel of our human nature, which is weak and prone to selfishness. If you take a step in faith to return to God a generous portion of your treasure, that treasure is poured into these earthen vessels, with all their faults and weaknesses. But God is present in these vessels, and God invites us to trust that our gift will not be wasted.

18. 10th Sunday in Ordinary Time

Readings

Genesis 3:9–15
2 Corinthians 4:13–5:1
Mark 3:20–35

18.1 June 10, 2018

Being a disciple of Jesus Christ in the first century was difficult for many reasons. Opposition to the belief that Jesus Christ was crucified and raised from the dead came from three sources. The pagan Roman culture regarded that belief as ridiculous. The Roman authorities executed Saint Paul. The Jewish community rejected the followers of Jesus Christ and threw Saint Paul out of many synagogues for preaching the Gospel. Saint Paul also suffered rejection from some of the Christian communities that he founded, because some accused him of not being an authentic Apostle. Despite all of this opposition, Saint Paul never let go of his encounter with Jesus Christ on the road to Damascus and did not lose heart.

To be honest, it is easy to lose heart and waver in our faith. Sometimes we lose heart, because we are fooled by false promises, like Adam and Eve, and suffer the consequences of our bad choices. We blame each other and cause further division. Sometimes life serves up disappointments, failing health, career crises, and all kinds of challenges. In these situations, we might want to ask Saint Paul: how did you do it? How did you not lose heart? He gives us the answers today from his second letter to the members of the Corinthian community.

First, he argues that we do not lose heart, because the foundation of our faith does not come from an idea or a system of beliefs. Our faith is grounded on an encounter with a real person, Jesus Christ, who has been raised from the dead. Because he lives, we live.

Second, we do not lose heart, because we are not alone. We are part of a community of believers. Even though the words of Jesus in today's Gospel might have shocked his family, who are worried that he is out of his mind, his family is much broader, and includes us. We can endure hardships, because we are walking together as members of this parish, supporting one another, praying for one another, and comforting one another when life becomes difficult.

Third, we do not lose heart, because God has only begun his work in us. That is what Saint Paul is saying when he points out that our outer nature is wasting away. No matter what happens to us in our lives, our inner nature is being renewed every day. As long as we do the will of God as members of the Lord's family, nothing can take away that inner sharing in the life of Christ. In fact, Paul argues that these afflictions actually prepare us to share in Christ's glory.

Finally, we do not lose heart, because we trust that even when the earthly tent in which we live is destroyed, we have a building from God, a dwelling not made with hands, eternal in heaven. In other words, we can stare death in the face and trust that death will not have the last word. The last word lies in the resurrection of Jesus Christ and his promise of eternal life.

Over the past ten years, I've had the privilege of going on pilgrimages with other people – usually on bicycles. Twice we've travelled the Camino de Santiago in Spain, and I walked the final 100 kilometers on the second pilgrimage with our youth group. Twice I rode my bicycle on the Via Francigena, once from the Alps to Rome, and the second time from Canterbury to Rome. These pilgrimages have taught me the importance of traveling together – enduring the hardships together, sharing the joys together, and sharing prayer and meals together. Being on the journey has taught me some valuable lessons about our common pilgrimage through life. We need to make the most of our pilgrimage together. But, we also need to remember that we have a final destination, not Santiago or Rome, but the new and Eternal Jerusalem. Jesus warns us that the only obstacle to reaching that destination is when we blaspheme against the Holy Spirit. Saint Paul would argue that this blasphemy involves losing heart and giving up on God. With Paul's advice in our minds, we continue this pilgrimage together.

19. 11th Sunday in Ordinary Time

Readings
Ezekiel 17:22–24
2 Corinthians 5:6–10
Mark 4:26–34

19.1 June 17, 2012

When Ezekiel spoke in God's name, he spoke to a people in dire straits. Israel had once been a strong cedar tree, growing tall and independent from the root of Jesse, David's father. But now that tree had been cut down. Jerusalem was in ruins. The Temple had been destroyed. The king and priests had been killed. All that was left of this majestic cedar was the topmost branches, the people suffering greatly in exile in Babylon. So, Ezekiel says that God will take what is left of his people and transplant them back to the land of Israel. Even though the people had not been faithful and had been responsible for the destruction of the cedar which represented their nation, God would remain faithful to the promises of the Covenant. God has the power to transplant and restore his people.

Six hundred years later, Jesus uses similar images to help his listeners understand the Kingdom of God. Saint Mark records two parables of Jesus to encourage his followers, also discouraged by an apparent lack of success. Jesus compares the Kingdom of God to a farmer who scatters seed on the land. No matter how much effort that farmer might put into weeding, hoeing, or watering his crops, the growth of the grain is ultimately out of his hands. It is God who causes the crop to grow. The same dynamic occurs with those who are disciples of Jesus Christ. Although we must do what we can to show forth God's Kingdom, we must trust that its growth is out of our control and in God's hands.

He makes a similar point with the parable of the mustard seed. That tiny seed eventually becomes a very large bush, allowing birds of the air to dwell in its shade. Just as Ezekiel uses birds resting in the branches of the cedar as an image for God's people dwelling safely under his care, so Jesus assures us that we can trust our ultimate safety in God's Kingdom. Mustard seeds were used for seasoning and for medicinal purposes. Those who embrace God's Kingdom provide flavor and healing for our society.

When Jesus speaks of the mystery of God's Kingdom, he speaks of a present reality. He describes a situation in which God is totally in charge of life. God is in charge when we imitate the death and resurrection of Jesus Christ, trusting that God's life will quietly grow in us, like the seed sown in the field. God is in charge when we live his commands to love God and neighbor, trusting that God will be with us, even when we fail, and even when his presence seems as small as a mustard seed. God is in charge when we develop the virtue of patience, watching for ways that servants become leaders, for suffering to become triumph, and for death to become life.

This is a message which we who are fathers need to hear. Our vocation – whether we are biological fathers or spiritual fathers like Father Terry and me – involves planting seeds. We cooperate with God's Kingdom when we give life and nurture it. When we demonstrate through our actions what life looks like when God is in charge, we allow the Kingdom of God to break through into our world. So, fathers, take heart! God is in charge. We are his stewards, and he can work through us even when we fail. God continues to work in those we give our lives to, even when our weeding, hoeing, and watering seems to be in vain. God is present in our families, even if that presence seems as small as a mustard seed. We must be patient and trust that God, who is our Father, knows what he is doing.

19.2   June 14, 2015

Saint Paul says that we need to be courageous and walk by faith, not by sight. In saying that, he is really telling us to walk through life with the conviction that God is in charge. That is what the prophet Ezekiel had told his people some six hundred years earlier. He was among the 3,000 movers and shakers who had been taken into exile in Babylon. While in Babylon, he and his fellow exiles heard that the Babylonians had completely destroyed Jerusalem, torn down their temple, and murdered their king. That royal tree of David which had grown strong from the root of Jesse had been cut down. In the midst of their grief and despair, Ezekiel assures his people that God is in charge. He tells them that God will take the top part of what is left of that majestic tree and transplant it back on Mount Zion. Because God is in charge, people from every nation will be drawn to the reconstructed Jerusalem and dwell in God's shadow.

We see Ezekiel's prophecy fulfilled in Jesus Christ. Jesus proclaims the Kingdom of God: that God is in charge. In sending out his disciples to proclaim that Kingdom, he instructs them to spread the Word as well as they can, like a farmer sows seed in a field. Once that work is done, disciples need to trust that the Kingdom will grow, because God is in charge.

For those who first heard the Gospel of Saint Mark, the parable of the mustard seed spoke strongly to them. They had chosen to follow a peasant from Galilee who had been murdered like a common criminal outside the walls of Jerusalem. They came to believe that God was in charge, because the Father had raised Jesus from the dead. The initial growth of the Church was as small and insignificant as a tiny mustard seed. But because they believed that God was in charge, they gradually watched as those humble beginnings begin to grow and attract new members, even in the face of persecution by a state that saw this movement as dangerous to the culture. This new Church spread throughout the Mediterranean Sea and took root in Rome.

This has been the way the Church has grown throughout history. This pattern has repeated itself over and over again. In the late 19th century, a group of young men were invited to become pages of a powerful king at a place called Namugongo in Uganda. These young men had recently become Christian. Some were still Catechumens. When they discovered that the king wanted sexual favors from them, they resisted him, under the leadership of Charles Lwanga. In the face of his threats, they trusted that God was in charge. He ruthlessly murdered all of them, and the situation was desperate. It seemed like a mustard seed. But the word of their courage began to spread and brought other people to believe in the Kingdom of God proclaimed by Jesus Christ. We celebrated their Feast Day on June 3. My friend, Father Larry Kanyike, e-mailed me to say that a million people gathered at the Shrine of the Martyrs in Namugongo on that day to celebrate Mass. Christianity has become the fastest growing religion in sub-Saharan Africa and has grown into a very large shrub, attracting many people to dwell in it.

Saint Paul wants us to walk by faith, not by sight, trusting that God is in charge. We must do whatever we can to further the Kingdom of God. We need to practice our faith and teach our children. We need to work for a more just world. We need to share our resources with those in need. We need to pray for those things that we think we desperately need. But, then we need to trust that God is in charge, even when we watch our world descend into violence, and even when it seems like our prayers are not being answered.

It takes courage to walk by faith, not by sight, because our sight alone cannot see the ways that God is in charge. What seems like a mustard seed grows eventually into a very large bush. We may not see that bush now. But it exists. We trust that through faith.

19.3 June 17, 2018

The prophet Ezekiel writes to his people who are in exile in Babylon. Although he is honest with them that their infidelity to the Covenant caused the destruction of their beloved Jerusalem and the Temple, he also wants to encourage them. They have given up and presume that they will never return to their homeland. However, he uses the image of a mighty cedar to give them hope. The mighty cedar represents Zedekiah, the corrupt and powerful king who had dominated the scene before the exile. But he was gone. The Lord has made low the high tree. Now, the Lord will take a tender shoot off the top of the tree, who is Jehoiachin, the king's nephew. The Lord will transplant Jehoiachin and the remnant of his people back to Jerusalem. The Lord will lift high the lowly tree and rebuild his people. God's plan is to restore his people from exile. But it is also God's plan to establish a future messianic kingdom.

We see the fulfillment of this prophecy in Jesus Christ. In today's Gospel, Jesus uses two other images from nature to help us to understand the kingdom of God. The Kingdom of God is not a place. Rather, the kingdom of God is what happens when God is totally in charge of life. The kingdom of God is like a man who scatters seeds and then watches the plants emerge from the ground and are eventually brought to the harvest. The kingdom of God is also like a mustard seed, the smallest of the seeds on the earth, which eventually grows into the largest of plants. In both cases, the growth occurs beyond human control.

The earliest disciples of Jesus needed to hear these parables, because they were becoming discouraged. They had embraced the person of Jesus Christ. But their communities were small and being persecuted. These parables instilled courage in them and gave them hope.

These parables also give us hope. We live in a world filled with violence, hatred, division, injustice, and fear. Our eyes are drawn to the big cedars of our world – the powerful, the wealthy, and the famous. The parables draw our eyes away from them and point to the ways in which God tends to begin small and grown his kingdom gradually. C.S. Lewis said that God took on human flesh in a dusty outpost on the fringes of the Roman Empire. Jesus snuck in behind "enemy lines" and was executed for his efforts. But, because of the resurrection, many other disciples took heart and started small. Saint Francis heard the Lord speaking to him in a tiny chapel in Assisi. He founded the Franciscans, and order that has served the Church for many centuries. Charles Lwanga (on our triumphal arch) refused to give up his faith. For that refusal, he was executed. Those who killed him thought they were done with him. On his feast day last week, a million Africans gathered at the shrine of the martyrs in Uganda to celebrate their faith. Mother Theresa (also pictured on our triumphal arch) began picking up dying people and orphans on the streets of Calcutta. Today, the sisters of her religious order attend to the most desperate people throughout the world. Many people have planted seeds and trusted that God would work through their initial efforts to make the kingdom of God more visible.

Saint Paul was another one of those people who stared small. He encountered the risen Christ on the road to Damascus, and the seed was planted. Through his efforts, the Gospel spread to the gentiles. He reminds us that our efforts will please the Lord while we are at home with our bodies. He encourages us to trust that our smallest acts of kindness and feeble attempts to love will make a difference. Today, we fathers especially need to hear this message. It is easy to get discouraged. It is tempting to think that our sacrifices are in vain. We wonder how we can make a difference in a world full of towering cedars. Keep planting those seeds. Even if you don't see results, even if your children rebel against you, don't lose hope. God will do the rest!

20. 13th Sunday in Ordinary Time

Readings
Wisdom 1:13–15; 2:23–24
2 Corinthians 8:7, 9, 13–15
Mark 5:21–43

20.1 July 2, 2000

There is a prayer to Saint Jude that gets circulated around here from time to time. People receive either a chain letter or a piece of paper left in church instructing them to say certain prayers to Saint Jude for nine days in a row. They are to send the chain letter to five other people. Or they are to leave so many copies of the paper in church. The instructions say that if these directions are followed exactly, whatever intention is being offered will be granted. The letter promises that this prayer has never failed.

Now, I have nothing against praying novenas! Making the same prayer for nine consecutive times is part of the rich prayer tradition of the church. Nor am I against praying through the intercession of Saint Jude. As a pretty hopeless case myself, I have done my own share of pleading through our patron. Nor am I opposed to begging God for a specific need. But there are real problems with this particular prayer to Saint Jude. It is not a prayer prayed with a sense of open trust in God's loving kindness. It is really a superstition, binding God to do what we want by performing the correct formula.

This is how the woman with the hemorrhage approached Jesus! She was a desperate woman. She had been bleeding for twelve years. She had spent all her money on doctors. She had nowhere else to turn. She heard about this traveling preacher, Jesus of Nazareth. By law, her flow of blood prohibited her from mingling with other people. Yet, she defied that law in desperation and joined the crowd surrounding Jesus. She resorted to superstition, "If I but touch his clothes, I shall be cured." In other words, if she performed the correct formula, God might give her what she wanted.

Notice the woman's reaction when power went out of Jesus to stop her flow of blood. She was frightened! She approached him in "fear and trembling." And that is what happens to us, when we approach God presenting with what we want, instead of considering what might be best for us. When we approach God with a superstitious attitude that I must do my prayers in an exact formula, then we too will be afraid.

Instead, we need to approach God the Father through Jesus like the synagogue official did. That man also had a desperate need. He was pleading for the life of his daughter. But he did so with a sense of trust that Jesus would do what was best for him, his family, and his daughter. Even in the face of death, which always brings the greatest fear, Jairus maintained a deep sense of trust in what God could do through Jesus.

When we pray the Lord's Prayer at Mass, we do not cross our arms over our chests with our fists clenched. Rather, we extend our hands and open our palms in an expression of trust that God will always do what is best for us. Today's Scripture readings provide a dramatic choice. We can try to bribe God with our prayers (with arms crossed and hands clenched) and continue to be afraid. Or we can bring our most desperate needs (with arms extended and palms opened) to the Father who loves each of us tenderly. That kind of prayer turns fear into trust!

20.2 June 28, 2009

Only a parent can understand the incredible grief and desolation experienced by Jairus as he watches his twelve year old daughter suffer to the point of death. I caught a glimpse of this parent-child relationship last week. In our family, I have the custom of taking my nieces and nephews on a trip to wherever they choose when they graduate from the eighth grade. My niece Shannon wanted to go to Ireland, because she heard that they named a river after her there. She also wanted her brother, Ben, and her mom, to go with us. In the ten days we spent together, I marveled at the attention and care directed by my sister-in-law on her daughter. Like Jairus, she would do anything to ensure her safety and health of her daughter.

Jesus senses the great pain of Jairus and responds to his pleas. But on the way to his home, he encounters another daughter in great pain. At first glance, these two women seem to have nothing in common. The daughter of Jairus is a pre teen. The one with a hemorrhage is a grown woman. The daughter of Jairus has great support, as crowds gathered around her home. Her father is a respected leader of the local synagogue, highly valued in the community. The grown woman is all alone. Because of the flow of blood, she is supposed to be isolated, separated from the community. Even being in a crowd causes her great fear, because she is not supposed to be there.

However, these two daughters have much in common. The daughter of Jairus is 12 years old, and the adult woman has been suffering from her hemorrhage for 12 years. With his daughter on the verge of death, Jairus is desperate. He is willing to risk his reputation as a respected community leader to beg for help from this traveling preacher who is causing such a stir. The woman is also desperate, having exhausted all of her resources on purchasing cures from doctors. In both cases, three is physical contact. When Jesus enters the room, he knows that touching a dead body would make him ritually impure for a week. But, he takes her by the hand and tells her to get up. The woman has the courage to touch his cloak. Even though Jesus knows that contact with a woman considered unclean because of her flow of blood, he talks about that contact openly and welcomes her back into the fullness of the community.

Jesus has that same love and concern for us, his daughters and sons. It does not matter whether we are young or old. It does not matter whether we are well connected or completely alone. Jesus loves us deeply, knows our needs, and waits for us to take the risk of reaching out to him. He knows that we are reluctant to take the risk of reaching out to him when things are going well. Sometimes, he waits for us to fall into desperate situations, or to exhaust all of our resources in an attempt to solve our own problems.

A week ago, we would have considered the following question as the beginning of a bad joke if someone addressed it to us: What do Ed McMahon, Farah Faucet, and Michael Jackson have in common? Except for all of them being in the spotlight, we would have responded: "nothing." But, today, we know that they have one important fact in common. They all died at the same time. We have that same terrifying reality in common with them, and with all human beings, including Jesus himself. Of all the realities we fear in our lives, death is the one certainty none of us can avoid. No human attempt and no human resources can prevent it.

In healing the two daughters, Jesus reveals the fullness of truth in the Book of Wisdom: "God did not make death, nor does he rejoice in the destruction of the living." Jesus entered into death himself. In his resurrection, he reveals this truth. He loves us and will heal us of all that causes death. All he asks is faith. Like Jairus and the adult woman, we need to trust his love.

20.3 July 1, 2012

When Saint Paul writes to the Church in Corinth, he thanks the people of that community in advance for "this gracious act." "This gracious act" refers to the collection he is taking up for the Church of Jerusalem. Paul is well aware of the tensions between the Jewish members of the Jerusalem Church and the gentile members of the Churches he has founded. The tensions and divisions come from differing interpretations of the Law of Moses. Those who had been raised in that tradition expect the new gentile converts to follow all the purity laws found in the Torah. Paul argues that the Old Law has been replaced by the new law of Jesus Christ. To help bridge that gap, Paul reminds his readers that all had saved by the "gracious act" of our Lord Jesus Christ in his total gift of self to all on the cross and in the power of his resurrection. In the face of that gracious act, he asks the more financially secure Corinthians to share a portion of their material goods with the Church of Jerusalem, who are suffering poverty and persecution.

It is in the light of this gracious act that we hear the two healing stories in Saint Mark's Gospel. Both Jairus and the woman with a hemorrhage show a deep faith in Jesus. Jairus is a prominent figure in the community who risks the criticism of his peers, because he trusts that itinerant preacher can save his dying daughter. The woman comes from the bottom of the social and economic system. Having tried everything, she risks being condemned by the Law for mixing in public with contamination of blood. She has the deep faith to touch the hem of Jesus' garment. Instead of being harshly condemned for breaking the Law, Jesus turns and addresses the woman with the affectionate title of "daughter." When Jesus reaches the home of Jairus, he brings life and hope to the most desperate and hopeless situation. He raises her from the dead.

Saint Mark records these miracles for those who are afraid to take risks in embracing the person of Jesus Christ. That is why the number twelve is so important. The daughter of Jairus is twelve, and the woman has been bleeding for twelve years. Saint Mark invites the fearful to trust that the Church, established on the foundation of the twelve apostles, is the fulfillment of God's work through the twelve tribes of Israel. He urges his readers to approach Jesus, whether they are prominent members of the community or poverty stricken individuals who have tried everything else in vain. Contact with the risen Christ brings healing and eternal life to those who trust enough to enter into relationship with him.

As baptized members of Christ's Body, we too share in the promise of healing and eternal life through the Lord's gracious act. Although Saint Paul did not use this particular word, the message of stewardship provides a wonderful means of living out that gracious act. Through prayer rooted in the Sunday Eucharist, we become more aware of the rich life we have received through Jesus Christ. That is why we can share a generous portion of that life with others. We imitate the healing action of the Lord Jesus by putting ourselves as humble servants of our time and talents to others. That is why we can be like the Corinthians in sharing a portion of our material possessions with those who are not as blessed as we are. The gracious act of Jesus Christ is made present in this Eucharist. As Catholics united by this gracious act and as Americans preparing to celebrate our Independence on Wednesday, we are graced with plenty of opportunities to extend the Lord's gracious act to others with confidence and without fear.

20.4 July 1, 2018

Last week, a 14-year-old parishioner was killed in a senseless accident. He was a well-liked and respected young man connected with many others through our parish and sports. The outpouring of support and love for Nolan's family was incredible. But, his death raised many questions about our trust in God's providence. Many asked the question: was his death part of God's plan? Even if it was not part of God's plan, why did a loving God allow it?

The first reading from the Book of Wisdom gives us some guidance in answering these questions. The Book of Wisdom states very clearly that "God did not make death, nor does he rejoice in the destruction of the living." The author reminds us of the truth found in the Book of Genesis. God created us in his image. God intended us to be imperishable. Death was caused by the envy of the devil and by the disobedience of our first parents. They believed his lies and separated themselves from God. And that is what death is: a separation not caused by God, but by our sinful rejection of God.

The two miracles in today's Gospel reveal God's plan to destroy death in the person of his Incarnate Son, Jesus Christ. Whenever Jesus teaches by the sea in Mark's Gospel, he reveals something about himself to the large crowds gathered to listen. Both miracles involve women. One is a daughter of an upper class and influential synagogue leader. The other is an anonymous woman without resources. In both cases, the number twelve is significant. The daughter of Jairus is twelve years old. The woman has been suffering from hemorrhages for twelve years. Both women represent God's people: the twelve tribes of Israel. In both cases, there is the pain of separation. The twelve-year-old girl is separated from her family by physical death. The woman is separated from society, because the flow of blood makes her ritually impure and excluded from society. In both cases, the situation is hopeless. The daughter has died. The woman has exhausted her finances trying to find a cure.

Jesus marches boldly into both situations, where he encounters a deep faith. Jairus trusts that Jesus can save his daughter by laying his hands on her. The woman trusts that that the one she had heard about can save her. In both situations, Jesus moves beyond the restrictions of the Law of Moses and shows that it has been fulfilled. Jesus risks ritual impurity by touching the woman with hemorrhages and by touching the body of a dead person. In raising the girl from the dead, Jesus prefigures his own victory over death in the resurrection. In healing the woman, he shows the power of his death and resurrection to free us from the separation that comes from sin.

Jesus gives strict orders that no one should know about raising the girl from the dead, because the miracle will only draw attention to himself. The miracle will make sense after his own death and resurrection to those who have come to believe in him. Then he orders them to give her something to eat.

We are among those who have come to believe in him. We will eat and drink at this Mass, where the mystery of his death and resurrection is made present here. Like Jairus and the woman with the hemorrhage, we believe that Jesus Christ has destroyed the power of sin and death. We entered into the dying of Christ in the waters of Baptism. We emerged one with him when we came out of the watery font. We trust that our union with him will not be destroyed by physical death. We trust that our life will be changed at the end of our earthly life, not ended. Our task is to remain connected with the person of Jesus Christ and live our baptismal promises. This is the message that grieving people need to hear. It is the message all of us need to hear, because we all live in the shadow of death.

21. 14th Sunday in Ordinary Time

Readings
Ezekiel 2:2–5
2 Corinthians 12:7–10
Mark 6:1–6

21.1 July 9, 2000

When we know someone well, we tend to take that person for granted. We put him or her into neat categories and expect them to respond according to our expectations. So it was with Jesus of Nazareth. His family and the people of his hometown knew him well. They had put him into some tidy categories. They did not expect him to start talking like a prophet – "one who speaks for God." So, when he told them truths that did not conform to their expectations, they treated him like their ancestors had treated all the true prophets of Israel. They threw him out on his ear!

For thirty years now, we Catholics have been known as people who are "pro-life." We have stood our ground that human life is sacred from the moment of conception until the moment of natural death. Our positions have not always been popular. Nor have many people always understood them.

During this past year, Pope John Paul II has clarified another of our "pro-life" issues in regard to the death penalty. The latest edition of the *New Catholic Catechism* reflects these clarifications. The official Catholic Church' stand on this issue does not fit into neat political categories. No one political party completely reflects our consistent ethic respecting the dignity of human life. Our position was clarified long before capital punishment became an issue in the current presidential campaign.

Please remain after Mass to view a video that explains our position well. Like those in Jesus' native place, it is easy for us to form a quick opinion. It takes time and prayer and discussion to see things clearly from the perspective of the living Word of God, and in light of the teachings of the church. Take that time today!

21.2 July 9, 2006

Saint Paul does not tell us what his "thorn in the flesh" is. His thorn could have been a chronically painful condition. Perhaps it was a speaking impediment that made him a better writer than a speaker. Maybe his thorn was his appearance (a really ugly man) or his manner of dealing with people (he had a way of infuriating a crowd). The thorn could have been some kind of addiction or habit that he could not break. Whatever his thorn, Paul hated it and begged God to get rid of it. But God did not grant his request. After bringing it to prayer, Paul concluded that God had given the thorn to keep him from being too proud and to allow his power to shine through Paul's weakness.

Paul did us a favor by not naming his thorn. Like Paul, each of us has our own "thorn in the flesh." No matter what it is – a physical or mental condition, an addiction or habit or hated quality – we pray that God takes it away from us, and we want it gone. When that prayer goes unanswered, Paul invites us to believe that our thorn in the flesh can allow God's power to shine through our weakness.

Nathaniel Hawthorne is a 19th century American author. Most of us have read *The Scarlet Letter* some time in school. Some are familiar with *The Birthmark*, his story that reveals his Puritanical obsession with perfection in physical appearance. Hawthorne speaks of his thorn in the flesh when he visited an orphanage in Liverpool, England. Admitting his tendency to have "ice in his blood," he tells of a wretched child running up to him. The child was so dirty and such a mess that Hawthorne could not tell whether the child was a boy or a girl. Totally repulsed by that child, he says that it took everything in his being to pick up the child and show affection. Even after he put his "undesirable burden" down, "it" continued to follow him and demand his attention.

Hawthorne's daughter, Rose, remembered this story. She eventually became a Catholic and founded a religious order dedicated to the care of poor people who suffered from cancer in New York City. Her Sisters, the Servants of Relief for Incurable Cancer, established seven free cancer homes throughout the country. They continue to take in victims disfigured in horrible ways by cancer and give them extraordinary care. Rose Hawthorne (aka Mother Alphonsa) said that her father's account of embracing that child in spite of the "ice in his blood" inspired her to do for disfigured and suffering adults and children what her father could do only with the greatest difficulty. His "thorn in the flesh" became an occasion of God's power being made perfect in weakness. What her father could not do is now done in spades many years after his death.

When Jesus came to the area where he grew up, the hometown folks rejected him. They could not look beyond his humble origins or imagine any message beyond the misery that they endured. Jesus accepted this "thorn" of rejection and continued to preach the Kingdom of God. In response, each one of us is invited to be honest about our own "thorn in the flesh," especially when it has become a source of great pain or embarrassment. There is nothing wrong with pleading to God to rid get rid of our thorn. But, we need to believe that it can truly be a source of God's power working through our human weakness. Perhaps we will see that power in our own lifetime. But, because Jesus showed himself to be much more than his hometown folks could imagine, we need to trust that God can take our thorns turn them into grace and strength for people we will never meet.

21.3 July 5, 2009

Our Scripture readings present us with three instances of failure. God calls Ezekiel to be his prophet and instructs him to speak the truth. But he also warns him that he will utterly fail. Because the people are hard of face and obstinate of heart, his words will fall on deaf ears. They will not pay attention to him. Saint Paul speaks of a thorn in the flesh. He does not tell us what that thorn is, whether it is a moral or spiritual failing, or whether it is some physical affliction. But whatever it is, it is getting in the way of his mission, and he has begged God to remove it. His prayer fails, and the thorn remains. Jesus comes home to Nazareth after performing some incredible miracles, including the healing of the woman with the hemorrhage and the raising of the daughter of Jairus from the dead. But, the home town folks know his background and his family. They find him too much for them. He cannot work any miracles in his home town, because of their lack of faith. Some people call it the "Nazareth Syndrome" – an inability to believe beyond their own mediocrity!

We hear these three examples of failure on the weekend when we celebrate our Independence. We Americans are grateful for our gift of freedom, and we thank God for that gift on the 4th of July. However, we sometimes confuse our gift of freedom with the need to be powerful and to succeed. We are the remaining superpower of the world, and we call our president the most powerful man in the world. We sometimes think that we need to be powerful to get what we want. That certainly is the message of our culture. We work hard to achieve positions of power and success. We want those corner offices where we can feel secure that we are in control. We try to keep ourselves in good physical shape, knowing the power of good health. Those of you in grade school and high school are all too familiar with the bullies who will stop at nothing to assert their power. It is easy to confuse freedom with power.

There is nothing wrong with power or success, especially when we use them to serve others. But, the Scripture readings remind us that we are not always powerful or successful. In fact, they tell us that God can work better through us when we are weak and vulnerable. Ezekiel may never have seen any visible success in his preaching as God's prophet. Most of his listeners ignored him or made fun of him. But, because he trusted in the power of the Word he was called to deliver, he learned to trust God in all his apparent failures. That Word has had incredible effects on the world for centuries after he died.

Paul may have pleaded with God to remove his thorn in the flesh. In not receiving what he wants, Paul learns that power is made perfect in weakness. His thorn keeps him from being prideful and boastful about his accomplishments as the Apostle to the Gentiles. We can be glad that Paul did not specify his thorn. We can insert our thorns into his words – a moral or spiritual weakness, a painful physical condition, a personality trait that we hate about ourselves. God can use our thorns to keep us humble and appreciate his grace working in and through us.

Jesus' failure in Nazareth can also be helpful to us. We are embarrassed often by our families, and we sometimes get little recognition for our accomplishments from those who are closest to us. We too know the "Nazareth Syndrome." We remain grateful for the many gifts which God has given us, especially the gift of freedom. But these three instances can teach us valuable lessons about God's presence in our lives. Failing, being vulnerable, and being misunderstood may be painful. But, they can also serve as ways for God to work through us.

21.4 July 5, 2015

The job of a prophet is never easy. God called Ezekiel to speak the truth to his people in exile in Babylon. He had to tell them the reason why they were in captivity. They had rebelled against the Covenant and now were paying the consequences. They certainly did not want to hear this harsh truth. But, in time, they learned that facing the truth would bring them to repent and accept God's gracious mercy, returning them to their homeland and rebuilding their lives.

Jesus has a similar experience when he comes home. His reputation has preceded him, and people had heard of the miracles and healings he had worked. They are astonished when he gets up in the synagogue and gives them his amazing wisdom. But they cannot believe, because he is too ordinary. They had grown up with him. He had no special training and was an ordinary laborer. He had broken ties with his human family and had formed a new family of disciples who traveled with him. In seeing his humanity so fully, they cannot recognize his divinity. They cannot believe that he is the living Word of God.

We have a similar problem in this family that is the Church. We clearly see the humanity of the Church. In the last fifty years, our Church has gone through many changes. It is easy to walk away when those changes make us uncomfortable. We can divide ourselves into certain categories, calling ourselves conservatives or liberals, digging in our heels to avoid those with whom we disagree. We can change parishes, because we do not get along with the new priest or do not agree with the decisions of crazy pastors like me. The scandals of the past decade have shaken the faith of others. In seeing the very human face of the Church, we can become like those people of Jesus' hometown. We have problems recognizing the divinity behind the very human traits of our Church.

When babies are baptized, they are anointed with Chrism, signifying that they have become priests, kings, and prophets. As prophets, we are called to recognize the truth and speak it. We do that best by remaining faithful to God's presence in our Church and trusting that the Lord continues to work in our midst, even when we might be baffled by the very human weaknesses of our Church. We depend on God's grace to remain faithful and be open to the miracles that the Lord continues to work in our midst.

Saint Paul can be very helpful in learning how to be a good prophet. Saint Paul could easily brag about his accomplishments. Scripture scholars estimate that he traveled 15,000 miles to spread the Gospel of Jesus Christ. Paul was responsible for taking a movement within Judaism and making Christianity a worldwide religion. But, instead of bragging about his many accomplishments, he boasts about his weakness. He talks about having a thorn in the flesh. We do not know what that thorn was. It could have been something about his personal appearance. It could have been an annoying quality that he hated about himself. It could have been some habit that he could not break. Whatever it was, he prayed that God would remove his thorn, just as Jesus had prayed three times in the Garden of Gethsemane that his Father would remove the cross. In accepting his thorn, Paul learned the power of God's grace. In accepting his weakness, he learned that he had to depend on God's grace. It was God's grace working through him and not his own gifts that allowed him to be such an effective prophet.

Each one of us has our own thorn in the flesh. There is some kind of defect that we cannot change and that drives us crazy. When I can honestly admit my thorn, then I can more easily look beyond the very human qualities of the Church and allow God's grace to open my eyes to his presence. God's grace is sufficient for me, as it is with the Church he has established.

21.5 July 8, 2018

Biblical prophets have never filled out application forms to get the job of being a prophet. Most were like the prophet Ezekiel, sent to speak the truth in God's name to his own people who had rebelled against him. God frankly admits that those who will hear Ezekiel's word are hard of face and obstinate of heart. They will refuse to listen and reject him. The success of Ezekiel's mission will not be determined by how many people listen and respond. The success will be determined by Ezekiel's faithfulness in speaking the truth in God's name.

Jesus Christ not only speaks the truth in God's name. He is the eternal Word Made Flesh, Incarnate by the power of the Holy Spirit and having taken flesh in the womb of Mary, the Mother of God. Yet, when he returns home after proclaiming the Kingdom of God and bringing back a twelve year old girl from the dead, his homeys reject him! Even though they may be astonished by the words he speaks in their synagogue, he is too ordinary for them to put their faith in him. They know him too well. He is an ordinary carpenter in the same social class as they are. They call him the son of Mary. They may be raising questions about the legitimacy of his birth. Or they may be insulting him in avoiding the custom of calling a man the son of his father. Instead of believing in him as the Son of God, they believe only in their own mediocrity. They cannot imagine God working through this person whom they had known since his birth.

In truth, none of us applies to be a prophet. We think of prophets as weird figures from the Bible or professional Church people today. However, all of us were called to be prophets when we were baptized. When babies emerge from the font, the priest (or deacon) anoints them with Chrism and says: You are now a priest, a prophet, and a king. We share in the priesthood of Jesus Christ, because we are called to pray and offer ourselves as sacrifice out of love. We share in the kingship of Jesus Christ in the kingdom of God. We are prophets, sent to speak the truth in the name of Jesus Christ.

Speaking the truth in the name of Jesus Christ is not easy, because we sometimes have to speak the truth to those who do not want to hear it. Spouses and family members of those trapped in addictions know the angry denials when they try to speak the truth. Parents know rejection when their teenage children do not want to hear the restrictions placed on their freedom. We priests hear negative comments when we say something in the homily that people do not want to hear or when we make decisions that people reject. Prophets understand that success is not measured by whether or not people listen to them. Success is measured by being faithful to the person of Jesus Christ, incarnate in a world that prefers for God to be distant.

However, prophets have to learn how to speak the truth with love, not with arrogance, judgment, or condemnation. Saint Paul learned that lesson as he was rejected by his own people, just as Jesus was rejected by his own family in Nazareth. Saint Paul may have had much to brag about, especially with his extensive travels, his mystical experiences with Jesus Christ, and the many converts he made with Gentiles. But he did not see himself as being superior to any of them. Instead, he boasts of a "thorn in the flesh." We do not know what his "thorn in the flesh" was. It could have been a physical affliction, a moral failing, and even some kind of debilitating condition. Whatever it was, Paul hated it and begged God to remove it. When God did not remove his "thorn in the flesh", he realized that God's power is made perfect in weakness. It kept him humble. Each of us has a "thorn in the flesh." We need to be aware of our "thorn in the flesh" when we speak the truth to someone else. It keeps us humble. It reminds us that God is in charge. It is God working through us, whether we are successful or not.

22. 15th Sunday in Ordinary Time

Readings
Amos 7:12–15
Ephesians 1:3–14
Mark 6:7–13

22.1 July 16, 2000

Imagine that you are sailing on a large ship. The ship runs aground on a reef and starts sinking. Your only chance for survival is to lash together a raft from the broken boards of a sinking ship. You quickly gather together whatever you can salvage from the mother ship – some water, a knife, a length of rope, a blanket or a tarp. Then you launch your tiny raft into the sea in search of safety, and hopefully, home.

This is how philosopher Plato suggested that we look at our lives. He compared our beliefs and values to the raft of a ship-wrecked sailor. Each of us has one of these rafts. It is made out of things snatched from the cabin. We might have a life preserver made out of a psalm or verse of Scripture. The planks are held together by the lessons of our experience. The skills we have learned serve as our tools and provisions. We ride our shaky, leaking raft through the storms and troubles of life, paying attention to the raft we have fashioned and trusting that God will guide us.

Jesus knew what he was talking about when he told the Twelve not to take much with them on their journey. He sent them to preach the Good News to the people of Galilee. That task was so important, that they could not afford to drag too much baggage around with them. Jesus had already formed for each of them the rafts they needed. Any more stuff would just get in the way of what they were sent to do.

As I spent time during the last couple of weeks packing for a four-month journey, my list of *necessary* items was a lot longer than Jesus'. As I spread out my stuff on the floor, I had a lot more than a pair of sandals and a walking stick. You wouldn't believe how much time I wasted too many hours worrying about things over which I have no control! Packing for this trip revealed to me how little I trust in the raft I have been given and in God's guidance in my life.

Our lives all involve journeys, whether we are flying around the world (like someone we all know) or staying right here in Fort Wayne. We have a tendency to accumulate too much stuff. We forget that we proclaim the Good News of Jesus Christ best by the way we live our lives. This is a good Sunday to take a good look at the life raft each of us has fashioned. It is also a good time to give away the stuff we don't need. Today's Gospel has already helped me in my travels. I left behind half of what I thought was necessary!

22.2   July 16, 2006

When Jesus sent the Twelve to proclaim the Kingdom of God, he was very clear about what they should take. He told them to take only their sandals and a walking staff. I have learned from my own experience of traveling that it is not good to get loaded down with too much stuff. Last year when I rode the Camino in Spain, I sacrificed half of my luggage to get up the steep inclines of the Pyrenees. This year, I took a small suitcase and a carry-on bag, dragging them easily onto every mode of transportation we took, including the South Shore. In contrast, they were to take nothing! Jesus was not sending them on a pilgrimage or vacation. He was sending them to do serious work – to do battle against unclean spirits. They must have wondered how they would make it with so little.

They must have recalled other stories of God sending people out to do battle with very little. The Book of Judges tells the story of Gideon, who went to do battle with 32,000 troops against the Midianite army, whose army was enormous, "like sand on the seashore." But, because God considered 32,000 too much, he told Gideon to reduce the number of his troops. When Gideon tells those who are frightened that they can leave, he loses 22,000. God tells him to sift through his men again. Gideon watched as they stopped to drink from a stream. He kept the ones who lapped up the water like dogs. That left him only 300 soldiers. 99% of his troops have gone home, and Gideon is left with next to nothing. What is Gideon to do? He goes into battle, and he wins!

That is the point of the story. The victory clearly belongs to God, and not to Gideon or his troops. And the same is true of those

Twelve sent out (apostolos in Greek) to do battle with unclean spirits. They too are victorious, not because of their own skill or abilities, but because God wants the victory. Through the death and resurrection of Jesus Christ, the unclean spirits are defeated, not through their own means, but only because the victory belongs to God.

You and I are not Apostles in the same sense that the Twelve were. We call our Church "apostolic," because it is built on the foundation of those Apostles. We call our Church "Apostolic," because we are guided by our Bishop, a successor to the Apostles, in union with the Bishop of Rome, a successor of Peter, the head of the Apostles. We are apostles in the sense that we too have experienced the risen Lord. We are apostles in the sense that we too are sent from this church to do battle with unclean spirits.

Like the original Twelve, we cannot proclaim the Kingdom of God if we carry too much baggage. We can define "baggage" as material possessions, which consume us with taking care of all of that. "Baggage" can also weigh us down in the form of fears and hang-ups and insecurities and sins that we carry around. Carrying too much baggage, especially when that baggage involves excuses for not acting, consumes our energy and attention, keeping us from proclaiming by what we say and what we do God's Kingdom.

Jesus tells us that all we need are a walking staff and sandals. We use walking staffs to lean on, and sandals are synonymous with being disciples on the move. Through his death and resurrection, the Lord has given us power over all kinds of unclean spirits. He sends us on the same mission and tells us to leave our baggage at the door, because it will just get in the way of our task. Besides, the victory is certain, not because of anything we carry or do, but because it belongs to God.

22.3   July 12, 2009

In Mark's Gospel last Sunday, Jesus came home to Nazareth, proclaimed his message of repentance and change of heart, and the locals rejected him. He was too ordinary for them. This Sunday, Jesus sends the Twelve to proclaim the same message, and he warns them that what happened to him would likely happen to them. He gives them authority, encourages them to be faithful to the message, and bluntly tells them that they should not measure their success by whether or not their message would be received. He urges them to unload their egos, take nothing with them, and rely on his Father's protection alone. In traveling lightly and depending on the hospitality of others, they could give credit for any success to God. When they failed, they can simply shake the dust from their feet and go to the next town.

This is interesting advice to us, as we are sent out of this church at the end of Mass to carry our faith with us. In contradiction to a culture which urges us to consume more and confuse our wants with our needs, Jesus tells us to get rid of the stuff we do not need. That is why the Saint Vincent de Paul truck is here this weekend. We can give away what we do not need, so that those with greater needs can live. Father Larry Kanyike is a living example of the instructions of Jesus. He arrived last week with almost nothing, and he is depending on our hospitality in his visit here. He is amazed at all the things we have. Uganda and other African countries have been hit harder than we have by the global recession, and he wonders if we can learn some lessons of this downturn in the economy. He points out that more stuff cannot make us happy. In fact, more stuff will just weigh us down on our pilgrimage through life, and we become like travelers stuffing their oversized carry on bags into the bins on airplanes.

But we also carry other baggage that is internal. We hold onto festering old wounds, not because we enjoy being hurt, but because we are afraid to let go. We carry resentments, anger, and all kinds of hatred and prejudices, thinking that these heavy pieces of baggage will protect us from further hurt and injury. Jesus urges us to let go of these things that weigh us down. Take only the sandals of discipleship, he tells us, along with a walking stick to support us. Take the risk, he tells us, of depending on the hospitality and kindness of others. In telling us to travel in pairs, he encourages us to trust the community of believers, the other members of this parish, to support us in living the Gospel values he teaches.

Eight centuries before the birth of Christ, the priest Amaziah yelled at Amos from his national shrine in the northern Kingdom of Israel and told him to go back to his home in the southern kingdom of Judah. Amaziah was threatened by the words of Amos, who bluntly told him that he was part of a system that supported wealth and ignored the needs of the poor. Amos was very much like the Twelve sent out by Jesus, because he carried only the word that God had given him. He was not a professional prophet, and no one paid him for speaking the words God had given him. Amos shook the dust of Amaziah's criticism from his feet and returned home, knowing that he had spoken the truth. His words had a lasting effect on the kingdom of Israel.

In the spirit of Amos, and in the spirit of the Twelve, who form the apostolic foundations of our faith, we are sent out at the end of Mass to proclaim with our lives the message of Jesus Christ. We don't need a lot of material stuff to do that. Nor should we carry the internal baggage that weighs us down. The Lord speaks to us in this Word. He feeds us with his Body and Blood. He sends us, unburdened, to take the risks of giving the faith to others, whether they accept it or not.

22.4 July 15, 2012

Last Sunday, we heard that the family of Jesus and his hometown neighbors rejected him. Even though they had heard about his miracles, they could not believe in him, because he was too familiar. They found it impossible to see in these miracles his power over sin, evil, and death. So today, Jesus turns to his new family, those disciples who remain with him. Even though they do not completely understand yet the implications of his words or his actions, he sends the Twelve out, giving them authority over those same unclean spirits. In giving them some very simple directions, he gives us, his disciples formed into his family through Baptism, our direction also. Even though we do not completely understand the Paschal Mystery, he gives us the same authority through his victory over death which we celebrate at this Mass.

Like them, he does not expect us to live our baptismal promises in isolation. As he sent them out two by two, so he sends us out as a community of believers, united at this Altar through our participation in the Eucharist. A friend of mine told me the story of his young son who ran cross country track for the first time, but was afraid of failing. Even though my friend is not in the best of shape, he ran along with his son to encourage him. His son could never have made it on his own, and my friend was on the verge of collapse. But, they supported each other, just as we support each other in our efforts to live the Gospel message.

Jesus clearly tells the Twelve not to take much with them. They need sandals, because the Gospel of Mark describes the process of discipleship as walking on the way. As we walk on the way, we do not need to take much equipment. The Gospel is best spread by trusting that God is with us in the present moment. Because we live in a consumer society that insists that more things will make us more successful, Jesus reminds us that having too much stuff just gets in the way and slows us down. That is certainly the lesson my fellow travelers and I learned as we lugged our junk around the Celtic Islands last week!

Jesus tells the Twelve to depend on the hospitality of others, so we need to depend on the welcome of those to whom we bring the message of faith. Just as the Larkins family welcomed us with open arms in Scotland, and my priest friend welcomed us into his rectory in Ireland, so people will be more receptive to the message of faith than we think. We don't need to move from place to place, because there is plenty of room for evangelization right here in Granger.

Jesus warns that not everyone will accept the message of the Gospel. In sharing our faith, risk being rejected and mocked. Just as he tells the Twelve to shake the dust from their feet and move on, so he gives us the same message. When we are rejected, we cannot take it personally. We must shake our disappointment off and go on to the next house. If we do not, we risk the danger of carrying the burden of resentment, anger, hate, and rejection. Those burdens will get more in the way of witnessing to our faith than the material possessions that weigh us down.

We do not need to have any special credentials to proclaim the Gospel. Amos was a common shepherd who spoke the truth more plainly than the priest Amaziah. The Twelve certainly had little standing in the culture of their time. We do not need to do anything terribly dramatic, like making signs and banners and standing on the corner of Fir and US 23. We do not need to push our faith on anyone at work, or at school, or in our neighborhood. But, we do need to follow these simple instructions given to the Twelve. Following these instructions opens the way for us to live our faith in a very joyful way in the present moment. In following these simple instructions, we exercise the authority given to us at Baptism, strengthened by Confirmation, and fed at this Altar.

22.5   July 12, 2015

When Saint Paul begins his letter to the Ephesians, he shares his vision of faith. Ephesus was an important port city in the ancient world. With ships bringing in goods from around the Mediterranean Sea, Ephesus had a very diverse culture with many nationalities and languages. Under the authority of Caesar, whom the citizens called "lord," there was an emphasis on learning. By studying the various philosophers and appealing to the correct gods, the Ephesians were searching for what was really important and what would really last. Even today, the faade of the great library still stands in Ephesus.

To this diverse and educated group, Saint Paul clearly states that God, the Father of Jesus Christ, is the ultimate meaning of life. He calls on the Ephesians to let go of whatever they are currently worshipping and give their allegiance to the one God who had revealed himself in history to his Chosen People. He insists that the real Lord is Jesus Christ, not Caesar. Through Jesus Christ and through the Mystery of his death and resurrection, God has chosen us to be holy and without blemish to accomplish his will, drawing everyone to himself.

These words form the beginning of one of Saint Paul's most eloquent letters. They remain more than a nice beginning. They speak to us today. We too live in a diverse culture. We too pride ourselves on being educated people. We live in a culture that emphasizes the individual and stresses the importance of making choices to form our lives. We may not have a pantheon of statues of gods in a temple. But, our culture tells us that the most important values involve living comfortable lives, making money, getting the best jobs, and being happy.

Although these things are not bad in themselves, Paul insists that the source of our ultimate happiness lies in being in union with God. He challenges us to take another look at our lives to see what we worship today. We can easily put all our energies into pursuing those things in life which turn out to be false gods and which cannot last.

Saint Paul encourages us to make sure that Jesus Christ is truly the Lord of our lives, trusting in the Paschal Mystery. If we trust in that Mystery and recognize Jesus as Lord, then we can more easily embrace those crosses that seem to have the power to destroy us. If we are willing to enter into the Mystery of the Lord's dying by giving ourselves in humble service to others, then we can trust that we can share in his rising. We can recognize those sacrifices we make not as burdens that oppress us, but as the means to free us to make better choices.

Just as Paul knew that he had been chosen by Jesus Christ to spread this Good News to the ancient world, he wants us to see that whatever choices we make must be rooted in our awareness that God has chosen us in the first place. Just as God had chosen Amos to speak the truth to the people of the Northern Kingdom of Israel, God has chosen us to be his people and speak the truth in our culture. Just as Jesus sent the Twelve to continue his work of teaching and healing, he sends us to do the same today.

We do not need a lot of stuff to carry on his mission. In fact, too much stuff can get in our way and obscure the presence of God in our midst. But we do need each other. That is why Jesus sends the Twelve out in pairs. In our culture, more and more people are saying that they are spiritual, but not religious. They are implying that they can live and spread the Paschal Mystery on an individual basis. We know that is not true, and that is why we are here today to celebrate the Eucharist. It is true that where two or three are gathered, the Lord is present. As Saint Paul tells us, the promised Holy Spirit guides us as God's Chosen People. The Holy Spirit is the first installment of our inheritance. Together, we trust that installment.

22.6 July 15, 2018

Last Sunday, Saint Mark told us about Jesus returning home to Nazareth. The locals had heard of his success in preaching the kingdom of God. They even knew that he had raised a twelve-year-old girl from the dead. But, they could not believe in him. They knew him too well. They could not see beyond their own mediocrity. The Incarnation made no sense to them.

Instead of fretting over his rejection or plotting to get even with his homeys, Jesus shakes the dust of rejection off his feet and continues his mission. He has already chosen the twelve who are willing to put more faith in him that his human family. They may not understand fully the Incarnation any more than his homeys do. But, he trusts them enough to proclaim the kingdom of God. He sends them out to drive out unclean spirits and cure those who were sick.

We are like the Twelve in more ways than we suspect. Like them, we do not have professional qualifications to confront demons or cure the sick. Except for Simon Peter, James, and John, we know very little about the rest of the Twelve (aside from Judas, of course). Like them, we do not always understand the ways in which Jesus works in our midst. But, he sends us as apostles ("those sent out") from this Church every Sunday to confront the demons of our world and to evangelize the culture in which we live.

Jesus sends the twelve out, not as isolated individuals, but in pairs. Together, they can support one another. They will learn how to live together in community, sharing the positive bonds that hold them together and facing the challenges that might tear them apart. The same is true for us. We gather at this Mass, not as isolated individuals, but as a community of believers. The Lord speaks to us, just as he spoke to the twelve. Through our sharing in the Eucharist, he strengthens our common bonds. In admitting our brokenness and facing our sins that cause conflict and division, we can confront the demons of our culture in humility. We can proclaim the kingdom of God without arrogance or judgment to a broken world that needs healing.

The Lord tells the twelve that they do not need anything for their journey – only a walking stick. They do not need food, a sack, or money in their belts. They need to learn to trust in God and in the basic goodness of people, not on their own resources and resourcefulness. The same is true for us. We don't need to rely on money or power or lots of things. Ironically, those are part of the demons we need to confront. Our culture teaches us that wealth, resources, power, and control over other people are the most important realities in life. Nothing else matters. However, in the last few weeks, we received an insight into what is most important. The attention of the world was on those twelve Thai soccer players and their coach. What mattered most was the effort to save their lives. We mourned the loss of the brave diver who drowned trying to rescue them. The parents forgave the coach for putting their sons at risk. Parents throughout the world hugged their children in appreciation for the gift of their children. We rejoiced when they were saved. Those lives mattered, not wealth and power and control.

Finally, the Lord knows that not everyone will accept his message. He knows that the twelve will suffer the same fate as he would suffer. He tells them to shake the dust from their feet, as he has just done, and continue their mission. The same is true for us. We will not always find a warm welcome and a ready embrace of the message we try to bring. When that happens, we cannot become bitter, angry, and pessimistic. We must move on and trust in the Lord's presence in our efforts to live and proclaim the Gospel. Through God's grace, we have been successful in building this beautiful church. Now, more than ever, the Lord sends us out to be Church, to share the beauty of the kingdom of God with those whose lives we encounter.

23. 16th Sunday in Ordinary Time

Readings

Jeremiah 23:1–6
Ephesians 2:13–18
Mark 6:30–34

23.1 July 20, 2003

The Prophet Jeremiah knew that bad leaders tended to scatter the people they were supposed to lead. He knew that from his own experience. When he warned the people of Judah that their infidelity to God's Covenant would bring them disaster, the religious leaders of his day threw him into a cistern. By the end of his life, he saw the results of the bad leadership from three of Judah's worst kings. As he predicted, the Babylonians destroyed Jerusalem and scattered the people – the direct results of bad decisions by these three kings.

So, it might surprise us when we hear the advice that Jesus gives today to his apostles, the future shepherds of his Church. We would have thought that the one who completely fulfilled Jeremiah's prophecy – the one who literally laid down his own life for the sake of the flock – would tell his shepherds in training that they need to work until they dropped. We would have thought that he wanted them to be on the job 24/7! Instead, he takes them to a deserted place and tells them to rest! He teaches that they cannot shepherd anyone, until they have rested in him and drawn their strength from him.

This is good advice for those of us who are shepherds; especially in the light of all the bad shepherding we have seen in our own day. We have seen how Saddam Hussein took care of himself and his family, with terrible results for the Iraqi people. We have witnessed corporate leaders feathering their own nests, while their accounting practices have destroyed the retirement funds of thousands of people. As a Church, we will know for a long time the results of priests and bishops who spent more time covering up sins, rather than trying to heal those whose trust had been horribly violated.

In telling shepherds to go off, get some rest, and draw strength from him, Jesus is speaking not only to those of us who are the religious leaders of our Church. He is speaking to any of you entrusted with the care of others – parents, teachers, civil servants, or health care workers. He encourages us to go off by ourselves, connect with him, and remind ourselves that we shepherd not in our own names, but in his name.

Last Monday, Father Michael Heintz and I took the Good Shepherd's advice and spent part of the week with the Trappists at the Abbey of Gethsemani in Kentucky. We pretended to be monks – not talking, spending time in prayer, and collecting our wits. We returned on Thursday afternoon, refreshed and ready to handle the demands of our parishes. Father Dan is doing the same somewhere in Europe, and I plan to take a few days during the first week of August with my classmates pretending to be cultured at the Shakespeare Festival in Ontario.

If you have not had a chance to a summer break yet, get away when you can. Even if you are not a leader yet, take some time to rest. Those of you, who are students, take a break from your busy summer activities before school starts. Take some time away from the TV, away from sports, away from the computer. Sit outside by a beautiful tree or flower and tell God how thankful you are for every good thing in your life. Give God a chance to speak to you, by giving yourself some quiet time.

Even if you cannot get away this summer, see in our weekly gatherings here a unique opportunity to rest with the Lord. Just as Jesus taught the crowds when they finally caught up wit them, so he teaches us now in his Word at this Mass. Next Sunday, we will hear the story of Jesus satisfying the hungers of the crowds by feeding them. We will approach this Altar, and he will feed us with his Body and Blood. We take a full hour, rest in his presence, and gather our wits together. Then, fed by Word and Sacrament, the Good Shepherd sends us out again into the chaos of our lives to lay down our lives for those entrusted to his care.

23.2 July 23, 2006

The prophet Jeremiah is not shy about telling the leaders of the people what he thinks of them. Calling them "shepherds who mislead and scatter the flock of the Lord's pasture," he accuses them of attending to their own comfort, while at the same time neglecting the needs of their people. Speaking from the Babylonian Exile seven hundred years before the birth of Christ, he blames them for the way in which the people have been scattered. Speaking to a remnant who have survived the Exile, he promises a shepherd who cares for them, and who will be called "the Lord our justice."

We know this "Lord our justice" as the Good Shepherd who gave his life for us, his flock. Paul reminds us that it was through the shedding of his blood that he has brought those who were once far off to come near. Last Sunday, Saint Mark told us about the training this Good Shepherd gave to those whom he had chosen to be the first shepherds in his name. He sent them off with only walking staffs and sandals to do battle against the unclean spirits. This Sunday, he tells us that they returned from their labors and reported back to him. In response, Jesus commands them to come away by themselves to a deserted place and rest a while.

As followers of that same Good Shepherd, we are responding to his command by gathering here to rest a while with him. Resting a while does not mean that we rush into the church at the last minute, go through Mass as quickly as possible, and dart out after Communion. We rest with the Lord when we give ourselves plenty of time to get here, when listen carefully to his Word and share his Body and Blood, and when we take our time resting in his presence. Hopefully, that resting in the Lord extends to the time we take to enjoy the presence of our family or those closest to us on the Lord's Day.

Hopefully, that resting with the Lord will also involve taking some time away from the hectic pace in which we live. Hopefully, you have either had a chance to get away already this summer, or you are planning to get away sometime before school starts. However, taking time away implies more than going on a vacation. Each of us needs to spend time resting in the Lord by giving ourselves the gift of some type of retreat experience. Canon Law requires that we priests take some time on retreat each year, and the Gospel extends that invitation to all followers of Jesus Christ.

We are offering two parish retreat experiences at the beginning of August. On the first weekend, the women who have been working with the parish retreat program, *Christ Renews His Parish*, will share the gift they have received with other women of our parish. The retreat begins on Saturday morning and ends on Sunday afternoon. The men will do the same on the second weekend of August. We have found these retreats – these opportunities to rest in the Lord – powerful experiences of renewal for those who take the time to be part of them. We trust that Christ will renew our parish through those who have participated. But we also know that these weekends are not the most ideal in most people's schedules. We had no choice about the timing, because we had to go with the availability of Sacred Heart's Parish Center, and we must use that Center until our own Education Center is built. While there are plenty of women signed up for the first weekend, the men's weekend has lots of openings.

Earlier this summer, I observed the letter of Canon Law and participated in the diocesan priests' retreat at Notre Dame. I biked over to hear the talks by the retreat master, and I biked right back again. Rushing back and forth violated the spirit of the Law. I was worried about what people might think, because I had plans to get away for a couple of weeks in June and then another week in the first week of August. "People will think I am not a decent shepherd," I feared and blew that opportunity. Speaking as a man who tends to define my identity in terms of how much I accomplish, I suspect many more men struggle with the same insecurities. Please consider responding to the invitation of Jesus – extended through the men preparing for this retreat – to accept his invitation. Don't make the same mistake I did, worrying about all the things that need to be done or what others might think of you. The men who will give that retreat are at all the doors, and they will be happy to answer any questions and sign you up. Your responsibilities (including that of being a good shepherd to your family) will not be compromised.

Jesus' plans for rest for the Apostles had to be set aside, because so many people needed to hear his Word at that moment. His compassion led him to minister to them, in spite of his exhaustion. Those of us who are shepherds know that the best laid plans to rest with the Lord sometimes get trumped by other people's needs. That is why you men must take a careful look at your calendar now and respond positively, before something else comes up!

23.3 July 22, 2012

The prophet Jeremiah is critical of the religious and political leadership of his day. He compares them to shepherds. Because sheep have no natural defenses against wolves and thieves, sheep need to be cared for. Instead of herding and driving them like cattle, shepherds walk ahead of their sheep, make sure that they have food and water, and protect them from dangers. Jeremiah accused the leadership of his day of putting their own needs ahead of the needs of the people they were supposed to lead. As a result of their lack of care, the city of Jerusalem has been leveled, the Temple has been destroyed, and the remains of those who have survived are in exile in Babylon. Speaking for God, Jeremiah promises that God will raise up a righteous shoot to David and appoint shepherds who truly care about the welfare of their people.

Saint Mark sees this promise fulfilled in Jesus of Nazareth. In healing the sick and driving out demons, Jesus points to his ultimate power over sin and death which will be shown in his death and resurrection. In teaching the crowds, Jesus communicates God's total and unconditional love for them. In sending out the Apostles to do these works in his name, he extends his mission beyond the narrow constraints of his home town. He is the Good Shepherd who will eventually lay down his life for his flock.

Today, the Apostles return from their mission to report what they have done and taught. Jesus invites them to come away by themselves to a deserted place to rest a while. He knows that their work has been exhausting. Like Moses had done in a desert many centuries before, he wants to help to reflect on their experiences and learn more about his mission. But the people would not leave them alone. So Jesus takes his chosen Twelve across the sea to another deserted place, as Moses had taken his people through the Red Sea. The people run to the next deserted place, so hungry for his message that they do not bother to bring food with them. When Jesus sees their need, his heart is moved to pity. The Good Shepherd is so moved by the needs of these people that he puts their needs ahead of his own need to spend time with his Apostles. He feeds them with his words of truth and love.

In this encounter, there are at least two lessons for us. The first lesson is for those called to serve as shepherds. Our mission is the same as that of the Apostles. Jesus calls us to give of ourselves to the multitudes, as he does. And yet, that message is not our own. Its success does not depend on our efforts alone. That is why we must balance our activity, our service, with times of solitude and spiritual refilling. Like the Apostles, we need to go off by ourselves to a deserted place and spend time with the Lord. Like them, we need to rest. But like the Good Shepherd himself, we need to remember that the needs of our people come before our own.

The second lesson is for need of the flock to be fed by the authentic Word of God. Because communication today is immediately accessible, there can be many false shepherds. This is especially true in an election year. We can tune into talk show hosts on both sides of the political spectrum who are more interested in riling people up and increasing their ratings than informing and helping them sort through the real issues. It is easy to find blogs and websites claiming to be official Catholic teaching. That is why we have been so careful to provide information which comes from the United States Conference of Bishops.

Today, Jesus feeds the crowds with his Word. Next Sunday, he will feed the crowds with bread and fish. As we reflect on that feeding in the following Sundays, we realize that the Good Shepherd speaks to us now through his Word and nourishes us at this Altar with his Body and Blood, providing food for our journey though those deserted places in our lives.

23.4 July 19, 2015

Jesus is teaching the apostles how to do healthy ministry. He had sent them out to do the work he had been doing: expelling demons, healing the sick, and proclaiming the message that the Kingdom of God had arrived. When they return, they gather around Jesus to report on all they had done and taught. But the joy generated by their accomplishments is tempered by some very bad news. Herod had executed John the Baptist. The one who had preached repentance, pointed out Jesus as the Lamb of God, and baptized him in the Jordan River, is dead. His death brings sorrow and distress for them. It also brought a sense of gloom that what happened to John the Baptist could happen to any of them, when they choose to speak the truth.

Jesus responds by inviting them to go away by themselves to a deserted place to rest. At that deserted place, they would not only get some much-needed physical rest. In their solitude, Jesus can teach them and help them reflect on everything that had happened and make sense of it all. In this solitude and reflection, they can receive a spiritual refilling. Jesus wants to teach them that healthy ministry involves hard work with multitudes of people. It also involves stepping back and taking time to listen to the Word and be renewed.

However, this spiritual refilling takes a back seat to the needs of people. The people of Galilee had been considered to be of little value to the religious authorities of Jerusalem. They are hungering for direction, like sheep without a shepherd. They crave the teachings of Jesus so much that they rush to the other side of the lake to "cut him off at the pass". Even though Jesus and the apostles are exhausted, Jesus has pity on them. His pity is a compassion that is born out of sorrow for their suffering. So, he sets aside his own needs and the legitimate needs of the apostles to rest, and teaches them.

There are two lessons for all of us who hear God's Word today. The first lesson is for us who are called to minister in the Church. Whether we are ordained, serve as lay ministers on staff, or as lay ministers in any capacity, we are called to serve the needs of the parish. In order to be effective, we must set aside time for solitude and prayer, allowing the Lord to refresh our spirits. However, the needs of the parish come first. We might feel spent after celebrating so many funerals. But, if someone else is near death, we must set aside any problems in our personal lives, and serve their needs. That is why Jeremiah is so critical of the religious leaders of his time. They were so busy taking care of their own needs that they ignored the needs of their people. Like sheep, they were scattered and hauled into exile.

The second lesson is for all who are disciples of the Lord. Rejected by people of his home town, Jesus knows that the vast majority of the people living in the northern part of the Sea of Galilee understand that he can give them direction. They realize that they have needs that only Jesus and his apostles can give. The same is true of us. We do not have all the answers. In gathering here today to hear the Word of God, we are acknowledging that we need guidance and direction. We admit that we are like sheep, not being able to guide ourselves. We need the care of the Good Shepherd, and of those who minister in his name, to refresh our souls.

After Jesus teaches this vast crowd of 5,000 people, he will take five loaves and two fish and feed them all. Beginning next Sunday, we will depart from the Gospel of Mark and listen for five Sundays to the Gospel of John, helping us to understand how the Lord feeds us with his Body and Blood in the Eucharist. But for now, we focus on the Liturgy of the Word. The Lord feeds us with his Word, challenging us to be good and healthy ministers. The Lord feeds us with his Word, especially when we are honest enough to know that we are needy people.

23.5 July 22, 2018

The prophet Jeremiah speaks to his people, who have been scattered when the Babylonians had destroyed Jerusalem. Jeremiah gives the reason for their difficult condition. Those charged with leadership have failed them. Jeremiah calls them shepherds. Instead of watching over their flock, protecting it, keeping it together, and caring for the injured or the sick, they were too taking care of themselves. Knowing his people's discouragement, Jeremiah promises that God himself will gather the remaining members of his people and care for them. Even though the last remaining descendant of King David has been killed by the Babylonians, Jeremiah promises that God will raise up a righteous shoot to David who will govern wisely and do what is just and right in the land.

We see Jeremiah's promises fulfilled in today's Gospel. Jesus is a descendant of David. Those seeking his help often cry out and address him as "the son of David." Jesus is also the only begotten Son of God, revealing his identity through his miracles. As the promised shepherd of Jeremiah, he had sent his apostles on mission to proclaim the good news of God's kingdom. They have returned and are telling Jesus about their successes and failures.

Jesus listens, even though he is mourning the execution of his cousin, John the Baptist. So, he gets into a boat with them and crosses the Sea of Galilee to a deserted place to get some rest. Moses had led their ancestors through the Red Sea to a deserted place, where they rested from years of slavery in Egypt to allow God to teach them how to behave as free people. Now, the Good Shepherd takes his tired apostles to a place where they can rest and learn from him. However, a vast crowd waits for them in that deserted place. Jesus is moved with pity for them, because they are lost and scattered. He sets aside his own grief about the death of his cousin, as well as his own exhaustion from his ministry, and teaches them. The Incarnate Word of God speaks God's word to them. When he realizes that they had not brought any provisions with them, he feeds 5,000 of them with five loaves and two fish.

On this Sabbath day of rest, we have just heard the Lord speaking to us. In just a few minutes, he will feed us with his Body and Blood. Beginning next Sunday, we will switch from the Gospel of Mark to the Gospel of John to hear the "Bread of Life" discourse for the next five Sundays. In listening to the Lord and sharing in the Eucharist, we can reflect on the dynamics of being disciples. We need to trust that the Good Shepherd heals those wounds which cause us to be broken and scattered. We need to work hard to meet the needs of others who depend on us. But, we also need to rest, to take time to spend quality time in intimacy with the Lord.

We too are "apostles," in the sense that we are sent to proclaim the good news of the kingdom of God. Thanks to the writings of our last three popes, we are becoming more aware that each of us has a role in sharing our relationship with Jesus Christ with others. The popes have called our role the "New Evangelization." That is especially true of those of us who are called to be "shepherds." We are shepherds as priests, religious, and parents. We are moved with pity toward so many who are lost or scattered. Without pushing them or putting guilt trips on them, we can make new efforts to reach out to the "nones"– those who respond that they have no religion when asked. As a parish, we are putting together a five year strategic plan to explore ways in which we can be more effective in our role of evangelizing, and especially of reaching those who call themselves "nones" and meet their needs. The Good Shepherd provides a good model for us. We rest on the Sabbath to listen to the Lord and to have him feed us in the Eucharist. Then he sends us beyond these stone walls as living stones formed as Church.

24. 17th Sunday in Ordinary Time

Readings

2 Kings 4:42–44
Ephesians 4:1–6
John 6:1-15

24.1 July 27, 2003

Over the centuries, people have speculated how Jesus fed five thousand people with five barley loaves and two fish. Many have concluded that the Incarnate Word of God simply suspended the laws of nature. Others have speculated that Jesus caused a greater miracle by causing people to share with each other the food they had already been hoarding in their garments. By sharing the little he had been given, he changed the hearts of those who wanted to hang on to the extra they already had.

However, Jesus fed so many people with so little food, the miracle of today's Gospel had a tremendous impact on those who wrote the Gospels. All four Evangelists tell this story, and Matthew and Mark each recorded it twice. Saint John did not include an account of what Jesus did with bread and wine in his account of the Last Supper. However, he describes this miracle in such Eucharistic terms that its connections with what happens here in the liturgy of the Eucharist cannot be mistaken. Earliest Christians used the drawing of a fish to identify Jesus, because the Greek letters for fish spelled out his title – Jesus Christ, Son of God. John describes the same Eucharistic action we will enter into in just a few moments – Jesus took bread, blessed it, broke it, and gave it. He even uses the technical term for the fragments left over from early Christian Eucharistic Celebrations, and notes how they must be respected.

During this current Lectionary Cycle, we normally listen to a continuous reading from the Gospel of Mark. But beginning with John's account of the feeding of the five thousand today, we will depart from Mark's Gospel for the next four weeks to listen to John's discourse on the Eucharist, the Bread of Life. Just as we will never fully understand how Jesus could have fed five thousand people with five barley loaves and two fish, so we will never fully understand how he can feed us with his Body and Blood today. The One who fed the crowd with fish and bread has become the Living Bread, forming us into the full stature of his Body, the Church.

Our readings from the Gospel of John during these next four weeks will give us a chance to reflect on the gift of the Lord's Body and Blood, broken and poured out for us each Sunday. In a sense, we are invited to go on an extended picnic during these final weeks of summer to reflect on how the Lord feeds us with his Body, so that we in turn – as his Body – can feed others. Jesus' words in this extended discourse from John's Gospel can help us understand just a little better this Mystery we share here. We can take some time to make sure that we do not take our Eucharistic gift for granted. Perhaps this might be a good time for us, as a parish, to begin what the General Instruction asks us to do before we take the Body or the Blood of Christ – make a simple bow (show people how to do it).

Earlier this year, we introduced the concept of Stewardship to the parish. Stewardship at its basic level means that we accept gratefully what God has given us, and share a generous portion of that with those who are poor. Barley loaves used to be food for the poor. God worked through Elisha to take what was reserved for poor people to feed a huge crowd. In Jesus, the Incarnate Word, God shows that he continues to nourish his people to continue to feed, clothe, and bring compassion to a suffering world. Both Elisha and Jesus provided for many from provisions intended for a few. Nourished by the Eucharistic Banquet, we are challenged to do the same.

24.2 July 26, 2009

In our daily lives, we are all familiar with leftovers. At the rectory, Father Bob and I thrive on leftovers, using the microwave as our primary source of cooking. A mother announces to her family at least once a week that the meal is a collection of "must goes" – leftovers that must be used up for a meal. We take home carry out packages from restaurants to eat as lunch on the next day. I lived with an elderly priest once who proudly declared that he reached the age of 80 because he never ate leftovers. He did not know that the cook concealed the leftovers in such a clever way that he did not recognize them.

Today's readings speak of two instances in which people feasted on meager resources, with leftovers to spare. 700 years before the birth of Christ, the prophet Elisha received a small offering of grain from a farmer, gave thanks to God, and fed 100 people, with leftovers to spare. Jesus takes five loaves and two fish, gives thanks to his Father, and feeds 5,000 hungry people, with twelve baskets left over.

As we prepare to be fed by the Body and Blood of Christ, the leftovers in today's Word of God teach us a great deal about what we are doing here. First, God welcomes every sacrificial gift. It does not matter how big or small our gift is, God welcomes any gift given out of love. Andrew may have considered the little boy's gift of five loaves and two fish insignificant for such a crowd. But, the little boy did not offer a safe portion of his box lunch. He gave the entire package, without holding back. Jesus gratefully accepted it.

Second, we have much more to give than we think. Last week, a young woman approached me after Father Larry had asked for financial help to build his new church in Uganda. She apologized that she had only six dollars. Those six dollars, given out of love, may be small in terms of what Father Larry needs. But, they are huge, in terms of what she could give. Her big heart was a much bigger and more important gift. We can never underestimate what a smile, or a kind word, or a gesture of support can do to build up another person.

Third, given to God, little becomes much. David picked up a small stone and put it into his slingshot to bring down Goliath. Gideon led a small army against the Philistines. Each of us brings the sacrifices we have made during this week – many of them small and seemingly insignificant. We join those sacrifices, made out of love, to the sacrifice of Jesus Christ. In turn, he gives us completely of himself in the form of bread and wine and nourishes us to be sent back into our daily lives. Those small sacrifices produce much good fruit. That good fruit is produced not so much by our own efforts, but through the Lord himself transforming our efforts and forming us slowly and gradually into his Body, united through one faith and one baptism.

Finally, we need to trust that leftovers abound in God's Kingdom. The twelve disciples doubted if five loaves and two fish could feed 5,000 people. Can you imagine their surprise when all those people were not only completely satisfied, but had twelve baskets of leftovers! The Lord Jesus challenges us to put aside our doubts and trust his power through the Eucharist to recognize the Kingdom of God in our midst. He does not feed all those people to draw attention to himself. In fact, when they try to make him a king, he withdraws and hides from them. He is more concerned about their deeper hungers, and will address those hungers as he explains the Bread of Life in the next four Sundays. He invites us to listen carefully and to open our eyes to see what our world may consider leftovers. If we look closely, we can more clearly see the abundance of God's love and grace in our lives and in our world.

24.3 July 29, 2018

When we hear about this miracle of Jesus feeding 5,000 people with five barley loaves and two fish, our reaction might be: "Wow, what an incredible event that happened over 2,000 years ago! All those hungry people were fortunate to have been fed!" But that is not the reason why Saint John recorded this sign in his Gospel. He wrote it so that we can deepen our faith in Lord's presence at this Mass.

Just as a large crowd gathered around Jesus after he crossed the Sea of Galilee, so he gathers all of us (from east to west, as the Third Eucharistic Prayer proclaims) in this church for this Mass. Just as ancient people saw mountains as places where the divine touched the human, so we encounter the Lord on this "mountain". Teachers in the ancient world spoke from a seated position. Jesus has just spoken to us in his Word. Just as he understood the hunger of all those people for meaning in their lives, he knows that we come to this church with many hungers, and he helps us to understand better what can fulfill those hungers. Through his Word, he warns us against putting all our energies into those passing solutions which will never satisfy our deepest hungers. Just as the Jewish Passover was near, so we are entering into the Memorial of the Lord's Passover from death into life. That is why the Lamb of the New Passover is pictured in the mosaic on the front of our Altar.

When he decides to satisfy the physical hunger of the vast crowd, he asks for help from Phillip and Andrew. Phillip sees it as impossible. Andrew points out a boy who has brought five barley loaves and two fish. But he doubts if the boy's box lunch could make much of a difference with so many hungry people. Jesus invites the vast crowd to recline on the grass. Reclining in the ancient world was a posture for those sharing a meal together. Instead of having them find a seat among thorns and thistles (the result of Adam and Eve's sin and their being expelled from the Garden of Eden), he invites them to sit on grass, a sign of the new Eden he will bring through his new Passover. He takes the five barley loaves and two fish and gives thanks to the Father. Then he distributes the food to satisfy the hunger of everyone who had gathered there. Once they have had their fill, the disciples gather twelve wicker baskets with fragments left over from the five loaves and two fish.

In just a few minutes, people will bring up a gold paten filled with hosts made from unleavened bread, along with some wine. The priest will take those gifts. In the Eucharistic Prayer, he will praise the Father for the sacrifice of Jesus made present as we remember. During the singing of the Lamb of God, we will break the consecrated host and place the rest of the hosts into ciboria. Along with the extraordinary ministers of the Eucharist, we will distribute them to the assembly. We will take the remaining fragments for the sick and homebound, and we will place the rest of the consecrated hosts in the tabernacle.

Those who were fed on that mountain were so impressed that they wanted to make Jesus a king. They did not understand that this physical feeding was a sign of the more profound feeding that would occur at every Mass celebrated throughout the world after the Pascal Mystery had been completed. Jesus withdrew to draw attention away from him. At the end of Mass, he will send us forth to proclaim the Mystery we have received and behave as members of his Body. That is why he feeds us with his Body and Blood. Our reception of this Eucharist increases our trust that he can transform our meager efforts and our limited resources into powerful witnesses to the Kingdom of God. We can make a difference, not because of our own efforts, but because he feeds us with the bread from heaven and the cup of eternal life.

25. 18th Sunday in Ordinary Time

Readings

Exodus 16:2–4, 12–15
Ephesians 4:17, 20–24
John 6:24–35

25.1 August 5, 2012

The people of Israel found themselves in a hostile environment in the Sinai Desert. In their fear, they did what we all do. They complained about not having enough food and blamed it on their leader. They were so consumed with their need that they completely forgot the gift that God had given them: the gift of freedom. So, Moses interceded for them, and God gave them manna and quail for food. Several hundred years later, Jesus finds himself in a similar situation. He had just fed thousands of people with five loaves of bread and two fish. Instead of looking beyond this sign to understand what God is doing in Jesus, they want more free food!

So, Jesus patiently answers their three questions. First, as John had stated at the beginning of the Gospel, he comes from God. He is the eternal word made flesh. Second, the only work they have to do is to believe in him. Third, he can do more than Moses ever did. He is the bread of life, capable of satisfying the deepest hungers and thirsts of the human race.

We can learn a great deal from these two groups of people. Like them, we too face difficulties in our lives. Like them, we can be so focused on our own needs and our own problems that we forget the incredible blessings God has given us. That became very clear last week when I represented the parish at the dedication of Father

Larry Kanyike's new church in Uganda. Looking at life through
the eyes of his African parish community, I could see that we take
so many things for granted. Our homes are large and comfortable,
compared to the shacks most of them inhabit. We enjoy dependable
electricity (most of the time), flush toilets, clean sources of water,
and hundreds of other advantages to which we have become accustomed. We even have the luxury of tithing a portion of our material
wealth, permitting Father Larry to build the second largest church
in his Diocese (and according to him, the most beautiful!).

Yet, despite what these people lack in material possessions, they
make up for it in their joy and obvious love of life. As I concel-
ebrated at the four-hour Mass and sat through the Archbishop's
hour long homily in the native language, I could clearly see the ties
that bind us – our common Baptism celebrated in the Eucharist and
fed with the Bread of Life. From the lens of that Eucharistic bond
of thanksgiving and gratitude, I could see the work accomplished
through our generosity: not only the new church, but the medical
clinic we helped to build in his native village and many more of his
projects presented to parishioners at all five parishes I have served
in this Diocese since we have been ordained. The profoundly deep
gratitude of those people often brought tears to my eyes, and their
gratitude was expressed in some interesting ways. The Sisters who
run the health clinic gave us two live chickens to express their gratitude! Now that is a challenge to put that gift in the overhead bin
of a plane!

Saint Paul tells us that we have learned Christ. We first learned
Christ when we passed through the waters of Baptism. With the
grace given to us in this Sacrament, we continue to "learn Christ."
In other words, we continue to learn how to conform ourselves in
Christ. In conforming ourselves to Christ, we die to our old ways
of selfishness and rise to a new way of living with Christ. When we
live with Christ, we become more grateful for his many blessings
which we take for granted. When we live with Christ, we face the
difficulties of our lives with confidence that the Lord will be with
us. With this confidence, we can readily give ourselves in humble
service to others. We can learn to love others in a way that goes
well beyond our feelings. We can be obedient to the will of God.
And the best news of all is that the Lord feeds us with the Bread of
Life to be the people he has called us to be.

25.2 August 2, 2015

When the children of Israel were slaves in Egypt, they were not
treated as human beings. As a result, they learned to distrust any
authority figure, especially Pharaoh. Slowly, they learned to trust
Moses, as he pointed to the ten plagues as signs that God wanted

them to be his free sons and daughters. But when they ran out of food in the hostile environment of the desert, they slipped back into old patterns, lost trust in Moses, and wanted to return to being slaves in Egypt. So, Moses used signs in the desert to regain their trust. He instructed them to collect the secretions of insects as food before the sun became too hot. They called this food manna. Moses also taught them to gather quails exhausted from flying over the Mediterranean Sea for meat. Moses called the manna "bread from heaven," because it was a sign that they could trust in God as he taught them how to behave as free sons and daughters.

Jesus used a sign to teach the crowds how to behave as God's sons and daughters. He fed 5,000 people with five loaves and two fish as a sign that they could trust his power to free them from whatever enslaves them. But just as their ancestors could not look beyond manna as a sign that they could trust God, the crowds cannot look beyond the loaves and fishes to believe that he is the one sent by God. They need to trust that he can free them from the slavery of sin and death. They want him to give them another free lunch. Like their ancestors, they see God as a Pharaoh who punishes when they are bad, or a Santa Claus who rewards when they are good.

We gather for this Mass today, because we believe that Jesus is the Bread come down from heaven. He feeds us with bread transformed into his Body and wine transformed into his Blood. As partakers of the Mystery of the Eucharist, we are invited to take another step in trusting God. But we cannot trust when we are living in any kind of slavery. We can become slaves to almost anything – from alcohol to drugs to sex or food or bad habits. We can be slaves to consumerism, believing that buying stuff will make us happy. We can be slaves to popular opinion and become what others think we should become. Television reality shows seem to take delight at the ways people can be enslaved and sell them as entertainment.

Jesus invites us to take a closer look at our daily lives to admit the ways in which we might be slaves. He invites us to trust him in our journey through the desert of recovery to learn how to behave as his sons and daughters. Anyone who has gone through a twelve step program knows how difficult that journey can be. The first step is to admit that I am not truly free, because I am enslaved to something. With that honest admission, we take the next steps of learning that we can let go of whatever had enslaved us to a deeper trust in God. Instead of seeing God as a Pharaoh who punishes us when we misbehave or Santa Claus who rewards us when we are good, we develop a faith in God who will always provide us with what we need.

One important way of growing in this deeper faith is to open our eyes to see the signs of God's love already around us. The first sign might be the sun coming up in the morning. In the light of a new day, as we open our eyes to signs of God's love in the embrace of a loved one or the smile of a friend. Kindness from a fellow worker can be a sign of God's love. Special occasions like births or baptisms or weddings can be powerful signs. The sign might be the presence of our friend from Africa, who always lets us know how we can make life better for the people of his parish in Uganda. When we become attentive to these natural signs of God's love, as the ancient Hebrews became attentive to the food they received in the desert, we can approach the ultimate sign of God's love in the Eucharist with a depth of faith that enables us to trust God, no matter what is happening.

26. 19th Sunday in Ordinary Time

Readings
1 Kings 19:4–8
Ephesians 4:30–5:2
John 6:41–51

26.1 August 10, 2003

Three years ago, the Eli Lilly Foundation provided a generous grant to finance my four-month Sabbatical to Ireland and the Middle East. Since then, I have done some work for the Foundation, helping them to pick through hundreds of application forms to reward grants to 30 pastors across the country. So, I did more last week than go to Shakespearean plays, pretending to be cultured. I read 85 applications and graded each one. I read stories about pastors who had worked long and hard, pastors who were discouraged by lack of results, pastors who spoke of being "burned out," and pastors who were trying to convince Lilly to give them $40,000 to go off and renew themselves.

However, none of these stories compared to the story of Elijah in today's First Reading. Ten centuries before the birth of Christ, Elijah was the only surviving prophet of the One God, because the pagan Queen, Jezebel, had run out all the other prophets and priests and installed her own fertility rites. Elijah worked hard for God and won an overwhelming victory over Jezebel's pagan priests on Mount Carmel. Instead of being rewarded for his faithfulness, he was threatened with death. Running away from those who were trying to kill him, he collapsed in the desert and wanted to die. But that was not what God wanted for Elijah. Instead, God fed him with a hearth cake and a jug of wine and told him to keep going – to Mount Horeb (known to the people of Judah as Mount Sinai), where he would encounter God's presence.

All of us can tell our own stories of trying to do the right thing, making ourselves available in service to others, and taking risks. All too often, instead of being thanked and rewarded, we have been criticized or made fun of. All of us have done our share of complaining, as did the people we meet in today's Gospel. For that reason, Jesus wants us to live and continue on our journey of faith. He himself is the Bread of Life. He continues to feed us with his own Body and Blood in this Eucharist. He wants us to believe what the crowds could not believe – that his Eucharistic food will not only get us through the deserts of our discouragement, will also feed us into Eternity.

Last Sunday, my 12 classmates and I did something we rarely do. We went to the tiny Catholic Church in Bayfield, Ontario, for Mass, and sat in the pews. Afterwards, we did something we rarely do – we went out for a leisurely breakfast on Sunday morning. We did our share of criticizing the priest's style of presiding and the lady who started the singing too low. But we also talked about of all the ways we have changed during these past thirty years we have been gathering in Canada on the first week of assignments. All of us have had a number of assignments. Many of us have suffered the deaths of parents. Two of our members have left the active ministry. One has died. We've all had our share of disappointments and frustrations. And we are all getting older. But, in the midst of all of that has been the Eucharist – the Lord's constant presence in Word and Sacrament feeding us to continue our journeys. We simply trust that the Lord will continue to feed us and keep us going, until we meet again next August to evaluate where we will be.

Hopefully, many of you will go out for breakfast after Mass this morning and will have a chance to talk. This might be a good day to reflect on all the changes in your life, on the joys and disappointments you have experienced. It might be a good time to listen to the younger members of the family share their perspective. But, also, pay attention to the ways in which God has fed you to keep going, even when you were ready to give up. I always return from Canada with a renewed intent to do whatever is possible to make our celebrations of the Eucharist as beautiful as we can – to work on preaching, our singing, our active participation, and all that goes into making our Sunday gatherings as pleasant as possible. But at the bottom of all these efforts remains the core of our faith – that Jesus Christ is our Bread of Life, that he feeds us at this Eucharist, and that this food gives us the strength to keep going!

26.2 August 13, 2006

When we celebrated the Feast of the Transfiguration last Sunday, we met Elijah, clothed in glory with Moses and Jesus on Mount Tabor. That moment provided Peter, James, and John with a momentary glimpse of the true glory that belonged to Jesus, who followed in the line of Moses (who mediated the Covenant) and Elijah (who vigorously defended it). We meet Elijah again this weekend, some 700 years earlier. He is on no mountain, and he is in need of more than a glimpse of glory.

When everyone in the Northern Kingdom of Israel had abandoned the terms of the Covenant made between God and his people, Elijah alone had stood firm. He had challenged the prophets of Baal – the false gods of the Phoenicians – to a duel on Mount Carmel. He won that victory, convinced his people to return to the terms of their Covenant with God, and angered Queen Jezebel. Her troops had chased him into the desert, and Elijah was about to give up. Having won a great victory for God, he now felt completely abandoned and wanted to die. But, God sent an angel to get him back on his feet. The angel provided a hearth cake and water and told him to continue his journey. Strengthened by this food and drink, he walked through the Sinai Desert to Mount Horeb (which the southerners called Mount Sinai). Like Moses, who was nourished by manna and water from the rock and who had journeyed through that same desert for forty years, he renewed his faith in the God who had established the Covenant 500 years earlier.

It is easy to understand Elijah's predicament. We too might have thrown ourselves into worthwhile projects, only to be beaten down. Those of you in school might have thrown yourself into try-outs for sports or cheerleading, only to get cut. You might have studied hard for a test and flunked it, while your friend cheated and did well. You might have gone out of your way to be completely honest in your business dealings, only to lose everything and watch your competitor corner the market through shady business deals. You might have given your time and talent to Saint Pius, only to see that no one even noticed your sacrifice. You might have poured out every bit of energy for your children, only to see them walk away from all that is sacred to you. The list goes on and on. We know the discouragement and defeat of Elijah. We know what it feels like to want to give up.

In response, angels do not normally bring us hearth cakes and water and order us to keep walking. But, we do drag ourselves into this church every Sunday, beaten up sometimes by our efforts to be of service during the week. After we have gathered ourselves together, God truly speaks to us through his Word. Then, Jesus feeds us with his Body and Blood. Nourished not by manna or hearth cakes, but by the bread that came down from heaven, he sends us forth ("Go in peace, the Mass is ended") to continue our journey toward the God who will show himself to us.

When Moses led his people from their slavery in Egypt through the desert to their ultimate freedom as God's children, he told them that the manna from heaven and the water from the rock were signs of God's presence in their journey. They still murmured among themselves. After Jesus fed the crowd of 5,000 with the five loaves and two fish, he explained that this food is a sign of God's greater gift – the gift of his Son given as the bread from heaven. This crowd also murmured among themselves and complained, because he was too ordinary for them. As we begin to let go of the lazy days of summer and return to our normal schedules, the Scriptures invite us to take another look at the Eucharist which nourishes us each Sunday. It is not something ordinary that we can take for granted. It is truly the living bread that came down from heaven. It nourishes us on our journey to the heavenly Jerusalem, just as much as the hearth cakes and water nourished Elijah on his difficult journey to God's Holy Mountain.

26.3   August 9, 2009

Elijah was the first of the great prophets of ancient Israel. Of all the people of 8th century Israel, he had been among the few who remained faithful to the Covenant with God. Most of his contemporaries put their faith in the Baals, whom their pagan neighbors saw as agricultural gods. They saw the God of the Covenant as a god who dwells in deserts and looked to the Baals of the fertile fields of northern Israel to help them produce their crops. Elijah had taken on the prophets of the Baals on Mount Carmel. He demonstrated without a doubt that there was no substance to the Baals, and that there is only one God. His victory won his people back to the God of the Covenant, the God whom Moses had encountered on Mount Sinai. But, his victory also enraged Queen Jezebel, who sent her armies to pursue Elijah and kill him.

That is where we meet Elijah today. Jezebel's armies have chased him into the desert, and it seems to him that God has abandoned him. Elijah throws up his arms and wants to die. But, as God had given manna and water from the rock to his ancestors who had traveled in this same desert for forty years, God feeds Elijah with a hearth cake and a jug of water, so that he can walk forty days to that same mountain where Moses had originally mediated the Covenant a few centuries earlier. The message is clear. God is consistent and does not abandon his own people.

The same dynamic happens in today's Gospel. Just as God had led his people out of slavery from Egypt, and just as God had worked though Elijah on Mount Carmel, so Jesus has fed 5,000 people in this deserted place with five loaves and two fish. Now, they complain, because they cannot trust that he is truly the bread that comes down from heaven. They cannot trust that he will feed them with his own flesh and his own blood, and that he will satisfy their deepest hungers and thirsts. Like the Israelites in the desert, and like Elijah after them, they conclude that God has abandoned them.

We too have seen the wonderful works of God in our lives. We recognize the Lord's hand in creation and see the ways in which God is present in our families and friends. Like the Israelites and Elijah, God has shown himself in a variety of ways to us. However, we too have experienced our own disappointments and tragedies. Sometimes it seems like God has abandoned us, and we complain and throw up our hands in despair.

It takes great faith to come here on Sunday to be fed by the Lord. We gather to be fed at the table of the Lord's Word, just as Jesus fed the crowds with his teaching. We gather around this Altar, and recognize in ordinary bread and ordinary wine the actual Body and Blood of the Lord, who feeds us with his very substance, just as he promised the crowds.

Not too long ago, I was talking to a man who had been away from the Catholic Church for many years. He told me how going to Mass was boring for him as he grew up. He left the Church when he left home, because he was getting nothing out of coming to Mass. But, as he grew up and matured, life began battering him around, as it has a habit of doing. After experiencing a great loss, he began coming to Mass again and paid more attention. He opened his ears to what the Lord was saying in the Scripture readings. He opened his heart and his mind to the Lord's real presence in the Eucharist. For the first time in a long time, he was fed here, giving him the strength to continue his own individual journey through his own particular desert.

During these final weeks of summer, it is good for us to hear these readings and to reflect on the absolute gift we have in the Eucharist. It takes great faith and trust to believe that the Lord feeds us. But, that faith feeds us in ways that we too can continue walking through whatever deserts the Lord may be leading us.

26.4   August 12, 2012

The prophet Elijah is not having a good day! He sees himself as a total failure. Even though he had successfully defeated the prophets of Baal on Mount Carmel, that victory has not returned the worship of the one true God to Israel. Instead, the pagan Queen Jezebel has sent her soldiers to kill him. On the run, he sits down under a broom tree in the desert and throws himself a pity party. Like so many people who battle depression, he falls asleep, wanting to die. But the Lord sends an angel to feed him with a hearth cake and a jug of water and encourages him to continue his forty day journey through the desert to Mount Horeb. On that mountain, known as Mount Sinai in the southern kingdom of Judah, he will encounter the God who had entered into a Covenant of Love with Moses and his people. On that mountain, God will show him the ways in which he been successful. Sending him down from that mountain, God uses him as an effective instrument in restoring the ancient Covenant.

All of us can identify with Elijah. At some time in our lives, we have been ready to give up. We may have failed miserably in a sporting event or a contest at school. We may have lost our jobs or disappointed those who had depended on us. We may have become so discouraged that we have found our own version of a broom tree, sat beneath it, and tried to sleep our depression away. In these situations, we often find ourselves isolated from other people.

However, like Elijah, we too are fed by the Lord who encourages us with his Word and urges us to continue our journey, our pilgrimage in faith. He does not feed us with hearth cakes and jugs of water. Instead, he feeds us with his very Body and Blood and invites us to recognize him in the Eucharist we share at this Altar. Especially in our darkest moments, he gives us himself as bread that promises eternal life.

Jesus has just fed thousands of people with five loaves and two fish. In this discourse from Saint John's Gospel, he is inviting them to look beyond these signs to recognize him as the Bread of Life. As we listen to these same words, we reflect on the Mystery of the Eucharist and its central place in our journey of faith. Our seminarian, Bill Meininger, has joined our parish and walked with us during this past year. He has been an integral part of our little dysfunctional community in the rectory. He has served our parish well. On this last Sunday before returning to the seminary, he will share a few words with us, as he prepares to leave us.

26.5   August 9, 2015

As we continue to reflect on the Lord's real presence in the Eucharist, our Scripture readings remind us that God created us with a hunger and thirst that only God can fill. Jesus reminds the crowds that God had offered manna and water from the rock in the desert as a sign of his power to satisfy their real hungers and thirsts. Jesus has been sent from God to fulfill that hunger and thirst at a level that Moses could never have imagined.

Thomas Merton wrote a book that became a *New York Times* best seller soon after World War II. That book, *The Seven Story Mountain*, was the autobiographical account of his conversion. Not only did turning to God bring him to Baptism after living a rather selfish life, but it also led him to become a Trappist Monk at the Abbey of Gethsemani in Kentucky. As Merton continued to reflect on his conversion experience, he wrote about his continuing journey into eternity. He wrote that we find God when we find our true self. At one level, finding our true self is simple: who we are, and always have been, in God. Who we are in God is who we are forever. However, that journey is difficult, because we are tempted to define ourselves in terms of what Merton called the "false self" – our reputations, titles, possessions, and other roles that ultimately pass away. Merton does not define the false self as bad. Rather, if we wrap ourselves with pleasures, experiences, titles, and accomplishments, there will be nothing left of us when we die. We have failed to find God in failing to find our true selves.

Jesus tells us that he is the Bread of life. In believing in him, who feeds us with his own Body and Blood, we slowly and gradually find our true self. We received our true self in Christ on the day when we were baptized. To use Saint Paul's term, we were sealed with the Holy Spirit. In the ancient world, slaves were sealed with their master's insignia, proclaiming that they belonged to someone. Paul tells us that we belong to God, who draws us to find our true selves. When we live our baptismal promises, we can let go of all those things that tend to tear apart at our true selves: all bitterness, fury, anger, shouting, and reviling, along with all malice.

That is why the Eucharist is so critical to our journey of finding our true selves, and ultimately finding the God who created us. Jesus is very clear about it: "I am the Bread of Life. Whoever believes has eternal life. Whoever eats this bread will live forever. The bread that I will give is my flesh for the life of the world." Jesus feeds us with this bread every Sunday (or every day for those who choose to come to daily Mass). He feeds us when life is going well. He feeds us in desperate situations, as God fed Elijah when he was running for us life from Queen Jezebel, who was trying to kill him for speaking the truth about the God of the Covenant.

Sometimes young people tell me that they get away from the habit of regular participation at Sunday Mass, because they don't get anything out of Mass. (Don't worry, I felt the same thing when I was your age, when my parents dragged me to Mass. My Dad would remind us that if we wanted a meal, we had to go to Mass). Do you expect that you will get "something out of Mass" every time you come, especially when the homily is not so good! We continue to set aside this hour and make Mass a part of our weekly routine, because it is easy to get caught up in our false selves, to think that those false selves define who we are, and forget where we are going.

As the Body of Christ, joined to others, we become what we eat. The journey is long and filled with danger. What the angel said to Elijah, he says to us: "Get up and eat, else the journey will be too long for you!" Eating and drinking, we walk on this journey together to the God who created us, gave us our true selves, and wants us to be with him in eternity.

26.6 August 12, 2018

In today's first reading, we find Elijah in a state of deep depression. The last remaining prophet of God, Elijah had defeated the priests of the false gods of the Baal at Mount Carmel. He demonstrated the faithfulness of God and had proven that the leadership of King Ahab had failed the northern kingdom of Israel. But instead of basking in his victory, he is running for his life. Ahab's wife, Jezebel, has sent her armies to kill him. After a day's journey in the desert, Elijah sits under a broom tree and asks for death. Instead of granting Elijah's desperate wish, God sends an angel to feed him with a hearth cake and a jug of water. Still depressed, Elijah lays down again. When the angel feeds him a second time, he obeys the order and walks for forty days and forty nights to Mount Horeb. It was at Mount Horeb (which is the name given to Mount Sinai by the people of the northern kingdom) that Moses had originally mediated the Covenant between God and his people. It is to Mount Horeb, nourished by the hearth cake and water, that Elijah would encounter God and regain his confidence in God's promises.

Like Elijah, we too are walking on this pilgrimage of life. As members of the New Covenant sealed with the blood of the Lamb who gave his life for us, we know the many ways we have experienced God's faithfulness in our lives. But we also know times when the Lord seems distant from us. All of us know that there are times in our lives when depression has a way of paralyzing us. Some battle depression as a chronic condition. Others experience times of depression that rob us of energy, of hope, and of a sense of God's presence in our lives.

For the third Sunday, we continue to reflect on the Bread of Life discourse from the Gospel of John. Just as God fed Elijah with bread and water to strengthen him on his journey, so the Lord feeds us with his body and blood to strengthen us on ours. Those who hear his words for the first time cannot believe his promise to be the bread of life. He is too ordinary for them. They cannot see beyond his ordinary appearance to believe that he is the Eternal Word who has come down from heaven to give them new life. They forget that their ancestors had complained about the manna in their pilgrimage through the desert from slavery to freedom. They do the same thing. They murmur against Jesus and refuse to believe that he will become the new Passover Lamb whose blood will wash away their sins and give eternal life.

At this Mass, we hear those same words that we who eat his bread will live forever. Saint Paul believed that promise and reaffirmed it in his letter to the Ephesians. In writing to the Church of Ephesus two thousand years ago, he might as well have been addressing the conditions of our world today. Like them, we walk in a world filled with bitterness, fury, anger, shouting, and reviling. We know the political divides that polarize us and end up in shouting matches. We know the pain when we are attacked on social media. We know the terrible effects of grief resulting from failure or the death of a loved one. Like Elijah, it is easy to fall into depression and give up. But when we share in the Lord's gift of the Eucharist here, we are nourished to continue our pilgrimage together with a sense of hope and love. Nourished by the Body and Blood of Christ, we can truly be imitators of God as his beloved children and act like God's beloved children in a broken world. Aware of the bonds that bind us, we renew our intentions to be kind to one another, compassionate, and forgiving one another as God has forgiven us in Christ. Nourished by the Eucharist, we can learn to imitate the Lord's kindness not only to those we like or agree with, but also to those with whom we disagree or dislike. That is why we march together to be fed at this Altar. We are Christ's Body, and we can make a difference in our world today by behaving as Christ's Body.

27. 20th Sunday in Ordinary Time

Readings
Proverbs 9:1–16
Ephesians 5:15–20
John 6:51–58

27.1 August 20, 2006 (Feast of St. Pius X)

For one year, we have been praying our Jubilee Prayer at all Masses. This prayer was written by Father Dan. As you might expect, the prayer is clearly a result of prayer and reflection. It displays a remarkable grasp of what a parish celebrating its fifty years should be. As you might not expect from Father Dan, it is very brief! As we conclude our Jubilee Year, we can reflect on this prayer and its implications for our future.

We begin by thanking God for the blessing of fifty years as his parish. Those foundations have truly been a blessing to us, as we discovered when we made our pilgrimage from Saint Joseph Farm last year to our present site. We have been blessed to have had the ministry of the Congregation of the Holy Cross in our growth. We began as a small rural parish, rooted in the earth of Saint Joseph Farm and those farmers who worked the earth. In the course of fifty years, we have become the second biggest parish in our Diocese, with all the joys and growing pains that accompany such incredible growth. Today, we stand on the shoulders of those who have gone before us.

We praise God for the graces we have received in this Jubilee Year. Many of those graces can be seen in what we do every year – educating young people in the faith; reaching out to the poor; bringing infants to baptism, children to the Sacraments, and young people to the Sacrament of Marriage; caring for the sick; and burying the dead. We have celebrated the Mysteries of the Incarnation at Christmas and the Paschal Mysteries at Easter. In this year, there have been extraordinary graces. We celebrated this Feast last year with great solemnity. Some of you went on pilgrimage with Father to the places sacred to our patron, Pius X. We grew through a week-long parish Mission. We enjoyed each other's company at a dance in the middle of winter. We added a lot of activity with our Vacation Bible School this summer. The bidding on our sewage and water extension is a graced moment (believe it or not!), because it opens the way for the breaking of ground next spring for our long-awaited Education Center.

Finally, we glorify God for the future growth of our Holy Communion. In today's Gospel, Jesus reminds us that we share a Holy Communion with him each time we share in the bread that has been transformed into his Body and the blood that has been changed into his Blood. That taking of his flesh and blood also has a radical effect on our Holy Communion with each other. We are truly one family through the waters of Baptism and through the profession of our common Catholic faith. Coming forward to Communion implies a radical unity that allows Christ to slowly, gradually transform us into his Body. As we gather for the picnic, we catch a tiny glimpse into our identity at Christ's Body, situated here in Granger, Indiana.

Now that we have completed our Jubilee Year, we trust that God will continue to sustain our growth in Holy Communion with him and with each other. This Communion is visible, clearly today. Jesus promises that this Communion has such enduring power that even death cannot break it. Sharing in this Holy Communion, we trust that our shared life in God's Spirit of friendship may renew all things in Christ for many years to come. Saint Pius X, pray for us!

27.2 August 16, 2009

A few weeks ago, Saint John tells us that Jesus fed five thousand people in a deserted place on the northern shore of the Sea of Galilee with five loaves and two fish. Jesus did not perform this sign, simply because the people were hungry. Nor did Jesus change water into wine at Cana, just to save the host the embarrassment of running out of wine. Neither did he raise the official's son, nor did he heal the paralytic on the Sabbath simply to draw attention to himself. He performed these signs (miracles) as ways of revealing who he is. He invites those who witness these signs to open their eyes and recognize the truth about him – that he is the Christ, the Son of the Living God.

Today Jesus is very explicit about his identity. The crowd already understands that God fed their ancestors with manna in the desert during their forty year journey to freedom. Jesus tells them that he is the living bread. In other words, he wants them to believe in the Incarnation, the Mystery we celebrate at Christmas. Just as manna had come down from heaven to feed the people, so God has taken human flesh in a stable in Bethlehem (the House of Bread). He is the living bread given not only to feed us on our own journey through life, so that we can never die.

Most of the crowd misses the point of the Incarnation and can only recognize Jesus in his humanity as their relative growing up in Nazareth. So, they ask how he can give his flesh to eat. Their response implies that they think Jesus is inviting them to be cannibals. That is why we need to our attention to the other great Mystery – his own death and resurrection. This discourse about the Bread of Life makes sense only when we embrace the Easter Mysteries and see Jesus as the Paschal Lamb sacrificed for our salvation. In John's Gospel, Good Friday falls on the Preparation Day for the Passover. As the priests prepare the unblemished lambs for the Passover celebration, the real Passover Lamb is being sacrificed on a hill outside the city. Just as the blood of the paschal lambs smeared on the doorposts in Egypt had caused the angel of death to pass over their homes, so the blood of the real Paschal Lamb is poured out to win our victory over sin and death. Just as the bones of those paschal lambs are not broken, neither are the bones of the Paschal Lamb broken on the cross. Nourished by the Passover meal, the Israelites crossed from slavery to freedom. Fed by the Body and Blood of our Paschal Lamb, we can continue our journey in faith toward the Promised Land where sin and death have no more power.

Last spring, we celebrated the Victory of the Lamb during the fifty days of Easter. As the days begin to get shorter and as our children return to school, we begin to look forward to celebrate the Incarnation at Christmas. The Bread of Life discourse invites us to connect these two mysteries. The one who took on human flesh (the living bread that came down from heaven) gave himself in sacrifice and was raised from the dead. The Lord is really and truly present in the bread and wine that feed us. We are not cannibals when we eat his Body and drink his Blood. But, we are united with him and with one another in a radical way each time we accept his presence in the form of bread and wine. We are also strengthened to continue to make our own sacrifices, to face those daily dyings that come from those sacrifices, trusting that the Eucharist we share will give us the courage to face our own deaths in our shared journey to a life that can never end.

27.3   August 19, 2012

Jesus continues to tell the crowd that he is the "Living Bread come down from heaven." He explains that the bread he gives is his flesh for the life of the world. Their response is swift: "How can this man give us his flesh to eat?" They would have been disgusted and horrified at this idea. They were certainly not cannibals! In addition, they were keenly aware of the sacredness of blood taught in their religious tradition. They would never have been allowed to eat of an animal's flesh with its blood. And now, this rabbi is telling them that they would eat his own flesh and drink his blood!

We can understand their reaction. In their defense, the words of Jesus only make sense from the perspective of his death and resurrection. From the perspective of his death and resurrection, his feeding of the thousands with a few loaves and fishes becomes a sign pointing to his own identity. God may have fed his people with manna in the desert. This fourth sign points to Jesus as the "Living Bread come down from heaven." In other words, God took on human flesh in the mystery of the Incarnation and dwells among us.

We have to look at the seventh sign in John's Gospel to put this fourth sign into its proper context. That sign takes place on the cross, and the beloved disciple and the mother of God are at the foot of the cross as reliable witnesses. In this sign, Jesus becomes the Lamb of God, sacrificed without blemish, like the lambs sacrificed at the Passover. He pours out his blood, much as the blood of the paschal lambs was smeared on the doorposts. Blood and water gush forth from his side, giving us spirit and life. In this sign, he passes over from death to the resurrection out of obedience to the Father's will.

Jesus does not back down from the stark realism of his language. As he hangs from the cross which has taken his life, the water flowing from his side symbolizes our baptism, through which we have been joined to the mystical Body of Christ. The blood flowing from his side represents the Eucharist that has the power to transform us every time we partake of it. He invites us to look beyond the appearance of bread to see his Body, given out of love for us. He invites us to look beyond the appearance of wine to see his blood, poured out in obedience for us.

In the Jewish tradition, blood is sacred. Blood is used as an equivalent word for life. In pouring out his blood for us, Jesus pours out his entire life for us. A friend tells me the story of his teenage son who wanted him and his wife to buy him a war video game. Even though it was rated as "Mature," all his friends were allowed to buy the game. He wanted to be cool. So, my friend sat down with his son to take a serious, reflective look at it. He noticed that the graphics were very engaging. There is blood everywhere! Blood splatters on the screen. You pass by dead bodies lying in pools of blood left and right. He could understand how this game would appeal to young warriors. So, he told his son, "Real warriors do not think of spilled blood as if it is nothing. I think that playing this game repeatedly would profoundly affect your experience of what happens every week at Mass. I do not want you to take for granted the Blood that Christ poured out for you." The son stopped bugging his dad for the game for a long time!

The Eucharist that we share is not just a symbol. In praising the Father for the Sacrifice of Jesus through our liturgical remembering, the mystery of his death and resurrection is made present for us. He feeds us with the Eucharist so that we can gradually be changed into our identity – members of his Mystical Body. Manna in the desert may have formed a group of wandering slaves into a free people loved by God. Even more so, the Bread of Life and Cup of Eternal Salvation can transform us as we make our journey together through life.

27.4   August 16, 2015

At the end of our first year of Theology in 1971, one of my classmates talked about a Festival in Stratford, Ontario, which offered quality Shakespearean plays. Since none of us owned cars capable of traveling that distance, one of the guys borrowed his father's big Lincoln, and six of us made the trip for the first time. We stayed in a cheap hotel for the first two years, until we found the Deer Park Lodge on the shores of Lake Huron. For the past 42 years, everyone knows us there as "the American Priests" for a week in early August. Over time, other priests joined our group, bringing its membership to 15.

Last week, the remaining six of us made our annual trek to the Deer Park Lodge in Bayfield. We traveled to Stratford (45 minutes to the east) for two plays on Wednesday and Thursday and enjoyed two dramas on stage: *The Taming of the Shrew* and *The Diary of Anne Frank*. However, the real drama continued to unfold offstage in our cabins. We remembered the three members who have died. We called our two professors who cannot join us because of their health. And we talked about others who have lost interest or left the active ministry. Because we are from different Dioceses, we brought each other up to date on current affairs in our lives. We did most of our talking over the meals we shared. Over the years, we have learned how to cook. In sharing quality food (and pretty cheap wine), we laughed about the hamburger helper we used to make in the early days. Within the context of shared meals, we became more grateful for all the gifts that God has given us over the years, and for all the ways in which God continues to bless us.

The Book of Proverbs personifies God's wisdom as Lady Wisdom. Lady Wisdom has built a house large enough for everyone, and she feeds all who accept her invitation with the best foods and the finest wines. But she makes it very clear that only those humble and open enough to God's Wisdom will be fed. Over the years, my classmates and I have learned that lesson the hard way. We have been humbled by our sins and failures. We have become more grateful to the ways in which God's grace has worked in our lives. Years of experience have taught us that we need God's Wisdom in our lives and in our ministries, because God's wisdom always exceeds any ways in which we might have thought ourselves to be wise.

Jesus makes it clear that he is the Word made Flesh who is dwelling among us. Moses may have been the mediator for God feeding the Israelites in the desert with manna. Jesus is much more than a mediator. He is that bread come down from heaven who feeds us with his own flesh and blood – with his very self. Over the centuries, the Catholic Church has never backed down from the reality of the promise of Jesus in the Eucharist. We may never understand how he can feed us with his real presence. We may never comprehend how eating his flesh and drinking his blood will give us eternal life. But he invites us to trust his promise. Using the words of Saint Paul, we have to be careful about how we live, how we keep our baptismal promises. Eating and drinking from the trough of possessions, experiences, titles, or any other passing reality will not bring eternal life. Only living the life of Jesus Christ can draw what we are doing at this Mass into life that will never end.

When we prayed the psalm today, we stated that we have tasted and seen the goodness of the Lord. Adam and Eve tasted (experienced) the fruit of the forbidden tree. Having tasted (experienced) their own arrogance, pride, and disobedience; they have seen the results of their choice. Our Lord invites us to taste his real presence in the Eucharist, and to see the eternal life he promises, when we approach with humility and openness.

27.5   August 19, 2018

As we continue to reflect on the Bread of Life discourse from the Gospel of Saint John, we must remember that Jesus has fed the crowd of five thousand people with five barley loaves and two fish at the time of the Passover. Those who hear this discourse for the first time understood the importance of the paschal lamb. In their Passover rituals, the people would slaughter the lamb and smear its blood on their doorposts, as their ancestors had done in Egypt to allow the angel of death to pass over their homes. As they ate the paschal lamb, they would share four cups of wine blessing (praising) God for their journey from slavery to freedom. They would speak of the Covenant which God had made with their ancestors at Mount Sinai. In speaking of the manna that fed their ancestors in the desert, they would tell of the ways in which God continues to be faithful to that Covenant.

Jesus makes it clear that he is the new paschal lamb. He will be sacrificed on the cross. Blood and water will flow from his side as he dies on that cross, signifying the water of baptism and the Eucharist in the new Covenant. He insists that he is the living bread come down from heaven. Even though he was present at the creation of the world, he had taken on human flesh in the Incarnation and dwells among us. Through the elements of bread and wine in the Eucharist, his Incarnation is made present in a real way. He promises that those who eat his flesh and drink his blood will live forever. In our journey through the desert of life, eating his flesh and drinking his blood will bring us into an intimate relationship with him that cannot be destroyed by death.

The crowd is horrified. Because they understand blood as a sign of life, they would never consider drinking any blood. They think that Jesus is inviting them to be cannibals, eating the flesh of human beings. They do not understand that the man speaking this message is the only begotten Son of God. The Incarnation makes no sense to them, because Jesus is too ordinary for them. They can only ask, "How can this man give us his flesh to eat?"

Saint John records these words for those who believe in Jesus Christ as the Son of God after the Paschal Mystery has been completed. He invites the readers of this Gospel to reflect on what happened to Jesus Christ. After washing the feet of his disciples at the Last Supper, he had been betrayed and subjected to a fake trial. He had calmly accepted the verdict of Pontius Pilate and had been executed like a common criminal and buried in a tomb. He had been raised from the dead and given the Holy Spirit to his disciples. He had been taken up to heaven, where he intercedes for us at the right hand of the Father. His Incarnation continues to be present every time the Christian Community gathers to celebrate the Eucharist.

That is exactly why we gather here every Sunday. We hear about the Lord's continuing presence in our lives in the Liturgy of the Word. Trusting in that presence, Saint Paul reminds us to live our Baptismal promises. He tells us to make the most of the opportunity. In other words, he tells us that we can redeem the times by our witness to the Gospel. Then, we take bread and wine, bless God the Father for the Sacrifice of Jesus made present as we remember, break the consecrated bread, and give it.

Even though we stand on the shoulders of countless theologians who have developed the theology of the Eucharist over the centuries, we might ask the same question: "How can this man give us his flesh to eat?" We can never fully understand that Mystery. That is why the Lord invites us to renew our faith today in his real presence. He invites us to eat his flesh and drink his blood under the elements of bread and wine. He invites us to trust that we who eat his flesh and drink his blood are members of his Body, and that death cannot destroy that reality.

28. 21st Sunday in Ordinary Time

Readings

Joshua 21:1–2, 15-17, 18
Ephesians 5:21–32
John 6:60–69

28.1 August 24, 2003

When 17th century London playgoers went to see *Taming of the Shrew*, they saw a great deal of humor in William Shakespeare's comedy. They laughed when Hortensio refused to give his younger daughter to anyone in marriage until someone married his older daughter, Kate, the shrew who did not behave like a proper lady. They enjoyed the outrageous behavior of Petruchio, who not only married her, but also tamed her into becoming a submissive wife who obeyed all his commands. But, five hundred years later, contemporary audiences have a little more problem seeing the humor in all of this, especially when Kate refers to Petruchio as "her Lord." Patterns of marriage have changed, and very few women these days call their husbands "lord"!

The same is true of Saint Paul. Almost 2,000 years ago, Paul wrote a letter to the Church of Ephesus. In this letter, he tells wives that they should be subordinate to their husbands. Ever since, husbands have poked their wives every time they hear this passage read in Church, and wives have tended to look disdainfully at their husbands in return! But like *Taming of the Shrew*, we must put Paul's words into their proper context. Just as Shakespeare reflected the marital customs of his day, so Paul was using the household code of ancient Greece as a way of explaining the mystery of Christ's love for his people. Jesus is the faithful bridegroom who gives himself totally and permanently to his bride, the Church. As God's people, our response to his total gift of self is to subordinate ourselves to his love, just as he urged wives to subordinate themselves to their husbands. For those chauvinists who want to exploit those words, don't forget what Paul tells husbands they must do – die for their spouses, as Christ died for his bride. By the end of *Taming of the Shrew*, it is clear that Petruchio and Kate truly love one another. By the end of Paul's Letter to the Ephesians, it is clear that Christian marriage is a Mystery – a radical commitment in which two believers give themselves totally to one another, in imitation of the one who gave himself totally to us.

For the last five weeks, the Gospel of John has given us an insight into another Mystery. In the "Bread of Life" discourse, Jesus has promised to give himself as the new manna, the bread from heaven that leads to eternal life. On this Sunday, at the end of the Discourse, people react strongly to his words. Some think that Jesus is inviting them to become cannibals. Others cannot bear his words. And many decide it is time to leave. They could not believe that he could give himself as food.

The same thing has happened in the history of Christianity. Although the Eucharist is the Sacrament of unity, it has also been the cause of division. Like those who heard the original discourse, there have been a variety of responses. Some have defined the Eucharist as a reminder of what Jesus did. Others have seen it as a sign of the Lord's presence. Many have restricted its celebration to a few times in the year. Our Catholic tradition has been very specific. We trust that every time we take, bless, break, and give bread and wine, the Lord is really and truly present. In obeying the Lord's command, we praise the Father for the sacrifice of his Son, made present to us by our active remembering.

William Shakespeare's plays continue to teach us about human nature. Paul's letters continue to help us understand the mystery of Christian marriage. In a more unique way, this Eucharist makes the Mysteries of our redemption present. We may not completely understand. But, like Peter, we ask, "Lord, to whom shall we go?"

28.2 **August 27, 2006**

Joshua addresses his people at a crucial time. They had escaped their slavery in Egypt and had spent forty years in the Sinai Desert learning how to act like free people. Now that they were ready to settle into the land that had been promised them, they were exposed to the worship of all the pagan gods of their neighbors. It was time to make a choice. Would they choose these new gods who seemed to control the fertility of this new land? Or would they choose the

God who had made a Covenant with them at Mount Sinai; the God who had fed them with manna from heaven and water from the rock; and the God who helped defeat their enemies? Joshua was clear about his family's choice. In choosing to worship the one true God, the people expressed their trust that God would continue to remain faithful to the Covenant he had made with them.

Jesus also addresses his followers at a crucial time. He had fed five thousand of them with five loaves and two fish. With this sign as a starting point, he invited them to trust that he is the living bread come down from heaven. He invites them to believe that eating his flesh and drinking his blood would bring them eternal life. Now, he offers them a choice. Will they choose to believe the truth of what he is saying? Many of them simply could not believe and walked away. Peter speaks for those who stayed, "Master, to whom shall we go? You have the words of eternal life." Even though he may not have understood what Jesus was saying, and even though he struggled with the cross that would become the gate to eternal life, Peter chooses to stay and trust Jesus' promises.

We have been hearing this "Bread of Life" discourse for the past few Sundays. Like Peter, we too have chosen to stay and trust his promises that eating his flesh and drinking his blood will bring us to eternal life. Like Peter, we do not fully understand the full implications of the Eucharist. Like Peter, we may not be thrilled with the prospect of those crosses we must carry and the deaths we must endure. But, like Peter, we stay.

Staying involves making tough choices. Paul speaks of one of those choices when he writes to the Ephesians. In trying to explain Christ's relationship to his Church, he uses the example of the marriage customs of his time. Like a loving bridegroom, he says, Christ has given his entire life for us, his Bride, the Church. In return, Paul argues, we, the Bride, must be subordinate to Christ, as wives are to their husbands.

To be perfectly honest, I was tempted to use the shorter form and avoid the can of worms that this passage opens. For those of you men who think Paul is giving you the license to do whatever you want with your wives, you take this passage out of context. Paul is using the marriage customs of his day to help the Ephesians understand their relation with Christ. And for you women who think Paul might be trying to turn back the clock on any advances you have made, you too take his passage out of context. Even within the context of a culture that identified the husband as "lord of the household," Paul takes his cultural expectations one step further and says that the marital bond implies a mutual love. He may be telling wives to be subordinate. But he is also clearly telling the husbands that they must do what Christ did – die for their spouses and children!

Even when we understand Paul's words correctly and let go of all the cultural baggage, the topic of marriage today is not an easy one. At its very heart, we believe that a marriage between two baptized people is a Sacrament – a sacred sign of a man and a woman choosing to give totally of themselves to each other for the rest of their lives. That is a tough choice, and there are many implications that come from setting the bar much higher than our culture sets for civil marriages.

For that reason, Father Dan and I have will offer an adult education series later this fall on the topic of Christian Marriage. It is impossible to delve any more deeply into this topic and all its ramifications in a ten minute homily. Look in the bulletin next weekend for more specific information. We will offer six sessions, giving people a chance to listen, read, reflect, ask questions, and bring up all kinds of related issues. Father Dan calls these "hot button" issues, and we must face them together.

We have joined Peter in trusting that Jesus has the words of eternal life. We are nourished at the table of his Word and feed on his Body and Blood in the Eucharist every Sunday. That food forms us more perfectly into his Body, his Bride – the Church. That food strengthens us to make choices that are tough, but that ultimately bring life.

28.3 August 23, 2009 (Feast of St. Pius X)

Paul has a knack for getting our attention – especially if you are a wife who has just heard that you are to be subordinate to your husband in everything! But before going off on a tirade, consider that the Ephesians too would have been surprised by Paul's instructions about family life. The Ephesians certainly would have recognized their family structure in his words. They knew that the stability of a family depended on a man who was clearly in charge. The stability also depended on spouses, children, and slaves who followed his instructions. However, they too would have been surprised by the motives Paul gives for following this family structure. He reminds the Ephesians that Christ is the faithful bridegroom who had given his life for them, his bride, the Church. Just as Christ gave himself out of love, so husbands must give themselves to their wives out of love. Even though Paul did not suggest any structural changes to the family unit of his time, he insists that spouses and parents who act out of love can transform the culture in which they lived.

Our family structures may be very different today, and wives can breathe a sigh of relief that they are co-heirs with their spouses in the life of Grace, and that a collaborative relationship in marriage is more than acceptable. Single parents can also know that Paul is supportive of their efforts. Families seldom have slaves any more. Children still need to be respectful and obedient, but with a sense that they will not be beaten for expressing their opinions. However, no matter what our individual family units may look like, Paul invites us to imitate Christ in our dealing with each other. As Christ gave his life for us, his Church, so we are invited to give our lives out of love for each other, trusting that those sacrifices we make out of love will transform the family units and the culture in which we live.

It is especially good to hear Paul's words as we celebrate our patronal feast of Saint Pius X. We too are a family, gathered as one through the waters of baptism. In celebrating our Feast this weekend, we celebrate all that is good and life giving about our parish. In celebrating our Feast, we also acknowledge that we are like any family, with our share of difficulties, conflicts, and challenges. We do not always see eye to eye with each other, and sometimes people feel that the sacrifices they make for the common good are not appreciated. We are an exceptionally large parish, and some people get lost in the numbers.

For the past few weeks, we have been hearing the Bread of Life discourse in the Gospel of John. At the beginning of that discourse, Jesus fed 5,000 people with five loaves and two fish. They were very happy with their free lunch. But as Jesus began to explain the implications of this sign, they became more skeptical. They had difficulty believing that he is the Incarnate Word of God, the manna from heaven. They could not understand how he could give them his flesh to eat and his blood to drink. They refuse to recognize him as the Paschal Lamb, sacrificed for their journey through life into eternity. Today, many of his disciples return to their former way of life, because they find him too much for them.

Peter has much in common with us. Like him, we do not fully understand the Mystery of the Lord's Incarnation, nor his dying and rising. Like him, we can never comprehend how the Lord is truly present in the Eucharist. But, like Peter, we are not walking away, no matter what our difficulties may be, because we trust that Jesus has the words of eternal life. This Sunday Eucharist is the source and summit of all that we do as a parish. The Eucharist nourishes us and feeds us to continue our journey, doing what we can to renew all things in Christ in our culture. In the Eucharist, we trust the Lord's presence to remain as disciples in this parish.

28.4   August 26, 2012 (Feast of St. Pius X)

Saint Paul has a way of getting our attention, especially when he tells wives to be subordinate to their husbands! But once he gets our attention, we have to listen carefully to what he is really saying. We have to remember that the families of first century Ephesus observed a household code of conduct dating back to Aristotle. When family members observed their roles in that code of contact, with the father firmly in charge, there was stability and order. Paul simply accepts the code as the way most people lived. But within that common household code, Paul inserts the person of Jesus Christ. Out of reverence for Christ, the faithful bridegroom who gave his life for his bride, the Church, everyone needs to be subordinate to one. Paul did not change the role of wives. But he dramatically changed the role of husbands. Husbands must act as Christ did. They must die to themselves in loving their wives as Christ loved his Church.

Household codes are much different in our 21st century American world. But Paul's advice still applies to us. Christ gave his life for us. Out of reverence for Christ, we must subordinate ourselves to one another as members of his body, the Church. There is no room for anyone to dominate, manipulate, control, or get their own way if Jesus Christ is part of our families and part of our lives.

Paul's message takes on special meaning as we celebrate our Feast of Saint Pius. As a parish family, we have been hearing Jesus speaking through the Gospel of John since the last Sunday of July. He has been telling us that he is the bread come down from heaven (the mystery of the Incarnation). Because he is the paschal lamb who has given his life for us (the Paschal Mystery), he feeds us with the Bread of Life and the Cup of Salvation to nourish us on our pilgrimage of faith, trusting that allegiance to him will bring life.

In today's Gospel, many walk away, because they cannot accept this message. Like Peter and the Twelve, we remain. In remaining, we make a choice similar to that made by the people in the Book of Joshua. In response to Joshua's demand that they make a choice between the God of the Covenant and the agricultural gods of their neighbors, they choose the God of the Covenant. It was the God of the Covenant who had led them out of slavery in Egypt through their forty year trip through the Sinai Desert. Jesus urges us to do the same. In celebrating our feast day, we become more aware of the many gifts God has given us as a parish family, gifts that could not have been given through the many false gods of our day. Those gods offer many limited gifts: consumerism, or the passing gods of fame or wealth or power. They urge us to harbor resentment and anger instead of offering mercy and forgiveness. They tell us to worry about ourselves without giving any thought to the poor or the most vulnerable in our society.

We are the Body of Christ, situated in Granger as the parish of Saint Pius X. As with any human community, our parish is filled with imperfect people who live in imperfect families. But the Lord dwells with us. The Lord feeds us with the Eucharist. The Lord will continue to guide us as we subordinate ourselves to one another out of reverence for Christ.

28.5 August 23, 2015 (Feast of St. Pius X)

For the last four Sundays, we have been reflecting on the Mystery of the Eucharist. After feeding 5,000 people with five loaves and two fish, Jesus has revealed that he is the Incarnate Word of God, come down from heaven for the life of the world. He promises that his sacrifice on the cross will continue even after he has been raised from the dead and ascended to heaven. Those who eat his flesh and drink his blood will live forever.

Today, he asks for a decision, much as his ancestor, Joshua, had asked centuries earlier. Joshua reminded his people of all that God had done for them in bringing them out of slavery. Would they make a commitment to God, or to the false gods of the pagans? Their response was clear: we will serve the Lord our God. The response to Jesus is not as positive. Many of his disciples (those who had previously committed themselves to him) cannot believe that he is the Incarnate Word of God who can continue his Real Presence under the form of bread and wine. So, they walk away. In turning to the Twelve, he asks if they will leave. Simon Peter speaks for them: Where else can we go? You have the words of eternal life.

As we celebrate the Solemnity of our Patron Saint, Pius X, we look back at all the ways in which God has manifested himself in our lives and in our parish. We may not understand any more than Peter did about how the Lord can be really present under the form of bread and wine. But we believe in his Real Presence. In gathering to celebrate the Lord's Real Presence at this Eucharist, we give thanks for all that we have been given and all that we are.

Like Joshua's community, and like the disciples of Jesus, we are at a crucial time in the history of our parish. After years of study, we have embarked on a bold construction project to ensure that our parish can sustain our community and serve its needs and the needs of the poor for years to come. We see the visible signs of the construction. I remain extremely grateful for the outpouring of generosity so far – $12 million pledged. Those funds have enabled us to begin the first phase of our project: the construction of the new church and the renovation of this church into a gathering space and meeting rooms.

In the next two years, as this construction continues, we cannot forget the other needs outlined in our facilities study. The Parish Education Center expansion will provide six more classrooms, including 3 rooms for our growing parish preschool, more restrooms, a multipurpose room for the school for the school cafeteria and youth ministry programs, and a dedicated space for Catechesis of the Good Shepherd. We will continue to work on raising the $3 million needed to accomplish these goals. I am also grateful to those who have set aside our educational needs to begin this first phase. I am hopeful that all parishioners will take part in these efforts and will commit a sacrificial gift to this important project.

When Saint Paul wrote to the Ephesians, he knew the household code of the Roman Empire that brought order to families. That code established the father as head, and clarified the roles of the rest of the family. That included slaves, who were a part of every family. Within the context of daily life, Paul urged the family to be subordinate to one another out of reverence for Christ. In other words, he tells everyone in the family to treat each other as Christ (the Bridegroom) treats us (the Church): to lay down their lives for each other. Living in this way has the potential to transform ordinary human existence into a living temple.

Saint Paul's words apply equally to us today. Treating each other as Christ would treat us can transform our ordinary lives and allow God to create a new reality. I give thanks to God that you have remained in the parish, and not walked away in the light of our challenge. Keeping the Eucharist as the source and summit of our parish life, we move together to equip this parish with the facilities we need to accomplish the motto of our patron saint: To Renew All Things in Christ.

28.6   August 26, 2018 (Feast of St. Pius X)

For the past five weeks, we have been hearing the Bread of Life Discourse from Saint John's Gospel. The discourse began with Jesus feeding five thousand people with five barley loaves and two fish. It has continued every Sunday (actually as long as the Season of Lent) and concludes today. Jesus has been trying to help people understand the true significance of his sign of that miraculous feeding. He is the Bread come down from heaven. He has taken on human flesh. He will become the sacrificial lamb slain on the cross. After his Resurrection and Ascension into heaven, he will send the Holy Spirit to continue his real presence in the Eucharist. He promises that those who eat his flesh and drink his blood will live forever.

It is good for us to hear the conclusion of this discourse as we celebrate our patronal feast. It reminds us that the Eucharist is at the heart of everything we do as a parish. The vitality of our parish comes from the Eucharist and draws us back again every Sunday.

Unfortunately, we celebrate our patronal feast when the news of the Grand Jury report from Pennsylvania has rocked our Church. It is sickening to know that over 7 decades, 300 priests have been guilty of abusing thousands of children. Even worse, we have learned that too many bishops had turned a blind eye and failed to protect the innocent victims. Just as many of the disciples of Jesus left his company in today's Gospel, people are walking away from the Church today because of these new revelations. At some level, their reaction is understandable. But Jesus turns to us, as he turns to Peter, and asks, "Do you also want to leave?" By our very presence here today, we have already responded with his words, "Master, to whom shall we go? You have the words to eternal life. We have come to believe and are convinced that you are the Holy One of God." I sincerely thank you for that response!

At one level, there is not much we can do about those outright crimes and horrible abuses of power. We can pray for the victims and support them in their healing. That is why Bishop Rhoades is publishing the names of all credibly accused priests of our Diocese, whether living or dead. We hope that other victims will come forward to be healed. We continue to enforce the child protection procedures in place since the clergy abuse scandal broke in 2002. They provide better safeguards for children under our care. We expect that offending bishops will be punished or removed for their failure. We trust that current bishops have learned from the failure of their predecessors and pay close attention to victims of abuse. Because Bishop Rhoades was the Bishop of Harrisburg before coming here, his name has been implicated. Please read his statement printed in the bulletin today. He deserves our trust and support.

No matter how many reforms have been introduced, we know that the humans of our Church, both clerical and lay, are sinners. Jesus entrusted the care of the Church to Peter, whose sins are evident in the New Testament. His worst sin was on the night of the Last Supper when he denied knowing Jesus. He repented from his sins and worked with the Lord's mercy to be a better shepherd. The same is true of us. We are all sinners. If you don't believe that I am a sinner, ask Fr. Eric or any member of the staff. Those who were guilty of abuse committed crimes and abused their power in terrible ways. In effect, they ignored Saint Paul's advice. Rather than making themselves subordinate to Christ and placing their lives in service to others, they made their innocent victims subordinate to their own darker urges. We remain in the Church, not because of any human shepherds, but because we subordinate ourselves to

Christ and trust that Christ will remain with us, forgive our sins, and feed us with his Body and Blood. That is his promise. That is at the heart of our celebration of our patronal feast today.

29. 22nd Sunday in Ordinary Time

Readings

Deuteronomy 4:1–2, 6–8
James 1:17–18, 21–22, 27
Mark 7:1-8, 14–15, 21–23

29.1 August 31, 2003

When Jimmy Carter was president, he admitted that he had "lusted in his heart" after a woman who was not his wife. That admission made him the brunt of jokes for weeks. Print journalists, comedians, and newscasters made light of what was actually a profound statement of faith. After leaving the White House, he wrote a book entitled *Living Faith*, a spiritual autobiography that put his famous comment into context. Agreeing with the Letter of Saint James, Carter insists that faith is a verb. As a doer of the word, and not a hearer only, his faith affects all he says, does, and thinks. That faith allows him to realize that the good things a person does, as well as the evil, originate in the heart. Even though he may never have acted on the lusting in his heart, he realized its potential for evil and confronted it, head on.

That is the point of today's Gospel. Jesus wants us to look into our hearts and admit not only the good we do, but also the evil to which we are drawn. That is why he attacks the Scribes and the Pharisees. They focused so much on the external observance of laws, rituals, and customs, that they separated them from what was going on in their hearts. Once that happens, it is easy to excuse immoral actions, "as long as no one gets hurt." It is easy to justify dishonest behavior, because "everyone else is doing it." It is easy to face the consequences of our immoral actions, only when we have gotten caught.

It is also easy to take the words of Jesus out of context. He may criticize those who substitute laws, rituals, or traditions for taking a good, honest look into their hearts. But, he is not throwing out all laws, rituals, and traditions. Instead, he challenges us to make sure that our laws, rituals, and traditions express what is in our hearts.

Living in the Arab world three years ago helped me understand better how external rituals can support the internal workings of the heart. Like ancient Jews, observant Muslims use a ritual washing as a way to prepare their hearts for prayer. When the call to prayer was blasted from the loud speakers of the Mosques five times a day, people went through an elaborate ritual cleansing of the senses. In fact, we learned quickly to avoid public washrooms at times of prayer, because the men splashed water everywhere. But, the point of the ritual was clear. The ritual washing symbolized the interior desire of the person entering into prayer to be clean and holy.

The same is true of us. We Catholics are known for our laws, rituals, and traditions. Young people accuse us of being boring (which we are), because we repeat the same ritual actions every Sunday at Eucharist. Our rituals and traditions may be repetitive, but they can provide a framework for expressing what is in our hearts. We bless ourselves with holy water to remind ourselves that we are God's baptized people. The priest washes his hands at the Preparation of the Altar and Gifts, as a way of acknowledging his sinfulness and his need for God to cleanse him of his sin. We bow before we take the Eucharist, as an external expression of our faith in the Real Presence.

Jesus challenges us to make sure that these ritual actions express what is in our hearts. Of course, evil exists in all of our hearts. But, God has the power to transform that evil into something beautiful and good. We can squarely face that evil in our hearts, because we hear God's Word here. Having heard, God's grace can use our rituals to change our hearts, so that we can become active doers of that Word.

29.2 September 3, 2006

Moses tells his people that God gave them the law as a gift. Now that God has entered into a permanent love relationship with the people of Israel, God's Law defines how God behaves toward his people, and how they are to respond in they behavior on a day to day basis. God's expectations are clear, and that is a gift.

If there was any group who saw the Law as a God's gift to his people, it would have been the Pharisees. As a lay group working within Judaism, they were anxious to extend the gift of the Law to the average person. The Torah (the first five books of the Old Testament) specified that priests should engage into a ritual washing of their hands before offering sacrifice in the Temple. This ritual washing signified a desire on their part to be pure in approaching God's Altar. The Pharisees took this ritual washing one step further and extended it to all Jews. They developed oral traditions to guide average people in this ritual washing, and the custom spread rapidly. We priests still go through a ritual washing of hands at Mass. I can assure you that I have washed the dirt off my hands with soap and water before Mass. The ritual washing is an extension of the Jewish custom, and the silent prayer is simple, "Lord, wash away my inequities, and cleanse me from my sins." In similar fashion, Moslems in Arab countries go through a ritual washing before kneeling on their prayer mats to pray five times a day.

Jesus' problem with the Pharisees is that they had tended to take these oral customs to an extreme. The rules became so complicated that scribes had to interpret them. The Pharisees were city dwellers, and they forgot that common peasants did not always have access to water, as they did, and that peasants just did not have the time or energy to enter into these elaborate rituals. The Pharisees also did not understand that fishermen regularly came into contact with dead fish in their nets and were unable to do all those ritual offerings. So, looking down their noses from these pious, ritual practices on the peasant followers of Jesus, many of whom were fishermen, they judged them to be lax in their practice of their faith. They looked only at the externals.

Jesus defends his disciples and points out that real defilement does not come from a failure to go through a ritual washing. Instead, it comes from our hearts, just as good intentions come from our hearts. Jesus calls the Pharisees and the scribes "Hypocrites," a Greek word that implies that they are acting. Their external ritual observances could be separated from their intentions and from their hearts.

As Roman Catholics, we too rely heavily on rituals, and that is good. We bless ourselves with Holy Water to remind ourselves of our Baptism. We show signs of reverence for the Blessed Sacrament, and we use medals and scapulars to remind us of our identity as Catholics. All of those things are good. But Jesus challenges us today to take another look at all the ritual actions we do and make sure that they are expressions of our faith. Sometimes we are tempted to look at the external manifestations of other Catholics and judge them to be not as "Catholic" as ours. That was the danger of the Pharisees, and that is the danger we must avoid. Our laws and customs support us as we struggle to respond to God's love in our lives.

But, they are not at the heart of our observance. To recall the advice of Saint James, we must be doers of the Word, and not hearers only.

29.3 August 30, 2009

During the days of Prohibition in the 1920's, it was against the law in this country to buy any kind of alcohol. The only way to get a drink was to buy it from illegal bootleggers. That practice proved to be very dangerous, because there was no regulation or oversight. Bootleggers would tend to sell their products at whatever price they could get, and they would often mix dangerous or poisonous substances to their products, sometimes causing death. There was one bootlegger, however, who was known for the integrity of his product. William McCoy mixed no substances in his alcohol, and word spread that it was safe to buy from this man. As a result, consumers would ask if the product they were buying was "the Real McCoy."

Today's Scripture readings raise the issue: how can we spot the "Real McCoy" in holiness? The Pharisees had their method, which can be described as an "outside in" way of spotting holiness. They valued the Law of Moses as the heart of their efforts to remain close to God so much that they continued to construct an oral tradition of laws which became a "fence" around the law to protect it. They regarded the washing of hands and the purification of pots and kettles and vessels as part of that fence. To be honest, their method is not a bad one. In fact, parents use it all the time with their children. If children get into the habit of brushing their teeth, or in the habit of buckling their seat belts, or in the habit of saying "thank you" when they receive a gift, they may eventually develop attitudes of safety and good behavior.

However, Jesus criticizes this method, because he sees this fence as being a burden, especially on the poor and on those who do not have ready access to water when they eat. He also recognizes that the external observance does not necessarily guarantee an interior holiness. He uses the word "hypocrite," which literally means "to act" or "to put on a mask." He accuses them of acting like they are holy, while ignoring the true realities of growing in holiness – drawing closer to the God and to each other bonded together by the Covenant.

Jesus says that we can recognize "the Real McCoy" of holiness by going from the "inside out". This method is more difficult, because it involves reading the human heart and looking at the efforts of a person to be in a continual process of conversion: turning away from one's self and becoming closer to God and to neighbor. God is the ultimate judge of looking from the inside out, and we have to be very careful not to be fooled by outward expressions of holiness. Sometimes external expressions of holiness can involve acting. Sometimes, they are burdens, especially when people begin to compete in showing external manifestations of holiness.

When Jesus speaks to the Pharisees, he speaks to us. Like them, we have our own traditions of acting holy. We bless ourselves with Holy Water when we enter the Church. We genuflect to the Lord's Real Presence in the Tabernacle and bow to the Altar. We hold our hands in gestures of prayer, and each of us has our own style. We bow before receiving the Body and Blood of Christ. All of these external acts are fine and can be expressions of profound holiness. But the Lord knows "the Real McCoy," and invites us to stop making judgments about the holiness of others. More importantly, the Lord calls us to connect these "outside in" traditions with our "inside out" efforts to grow closer to God and others. As James so bluntly reminds us, we must be doers of the word and not hearers only.

29.4   September 2, 2012

We often think of the Law which Moses brought down from Mount Sinai in terms of the Ten Commandments written on the stone tablets. Those commandments summarize the more entire Law found in the first five books of the Bible – the Torah (Hebrew) or the Pentateuch (Greek). Moses reminds his people that the Law is a great gift from God. The Law provides a very practical way of living their Covenant relationship with God and with each other. Living the Law of God brings them life, the land which they inhabit, wisdom, and a closer relationship with God. In other words, the Law is a practical guide for becoming holy.

To give the Pharisees their due credit, that is exactly what they are trying to do with the Law. In order to protect the Law, they had developed a system of oral teaching to put a fence around the Law to protect it. This oral tradition contained ritual purifications to help them preserve their identity and keep the Law. That is why they needed scribes to record and keep track of their many oral traditions. Those oral traditions were so complicated that only professional scribes could keep track of them. Worse, they became very judgmental of those who were not as observant. Fishermen had trouble with ritual purifications because they handled dead creatures every day in their nets. Illiterate peasants could not sort through these rules, because they were too busy scraping together a living in arid areas where with little water.

When the Pharisees and scribes attack the followers of Jesus for not observing the ritual purification rules, Jesus points out the weakness of their complicated system of laws and regulations. He quotes the Prophet Isaiah to underline the central reason for the Law – growing closer to God and one another. He calls them hyp-

ocrites, using a Greek word which means "to act." Instead of working at becoming more holy, they are acting as if they are holy. Real
evil comes from within, he says, and no manner of ritual washing
will cleanse a person of that evil if there is no interior desire to recognize our own sins and accept the grace of God's mercy to change
our lives.

Jesus speaks directly to us. We Roman Catholics also have a
set of laws, rules, and regulations designed to help us become more
holy, to grow closer to God and other people. The word "religion"
comes from Latin word which means to bind us closer together.
Our religion is the glue which holds things together and keeps us
focused. Just as Jesus called the scribes and Pharisees to look at the
central reasons for laws and traditions, so he calls us today. In this
new school year, we have many opportunities to grow in our understanding of our religion. Our children begin a new year, either
in CCD or in our Parochial School. The Rite of Christian Initiation
of Adults began last Tuesday. We will provide adult education series on hot button topics this fall. All of these sessions are designed
to explore our religion and understand it better.

Saint James is very clear about the purpose of religion. Bound
together by religion, our relationship with God and with others is
best seen in action, in care for the poor and the most vulnerable,
and in growing closer to God and others. As we make the transition
from summer to fall, we can heed his words. Authentic growth in
holiness will make us better doers of the word, and not just hearers!

29.5   August 30, 2015

When Jesus responds to the Pharisees, he also responds to us
Catholics. In our religious observance, we resemble these contemporaries of Jesus in many ways. They regarded the Torah
as the foundation of their faith and allowed a living tradition to
guide them in living it. We too accept the Word of God as the
foundation of all that we believe. We also have a living Tradition
that emerges from the Word and guides us in our faith, with the
teaching authority of the Church interpreting it. The Pharisees
developed 613 laws to serve as day to day practical guides. We
have the *Core of Canon Law* and the *Catechism of the Catholic Church*
to guide us in living our faith. The Pharisees were a lay group who
did not limit holiness to the priests assigned to the Temple. Like
them, we see God's call to holiness applying to everyone. Their
ritual practices helped them to maintain their identity. So do ours.
We bless ourselves with Holy Water when we enter the Church.
We bow to the Altar. We genuflect to the Tabernacle. The ritual
actions we take for granted sometimes baffle those who are just
beginning the RCIA.

Jesus does not criticize the Pharisees for having laws and traditions. He criticizes them, because they have lost sight of the real purpose of the Law that we heard from the Book of Deuteronomy. Moses stressed that the Law as a gift given by God to guide their lives toward greater holiness. Once the Pharisees lose sight of this central purpose, their laws and traditions become so complicated that they need Scribes to interpret them. As urban dwellers, they can more easily follow their laws and traditions. They have better access to the water needed for purifications. The disciples of Jesus are country people and travelers who did not have the same access. They are fishermen who are handling dead fish all the time and cannot perform the purifications needed to make them ritually clean. In his criticisms, Jesus goes to the heart of the matter. The evils that defile us do not come from external sources. They come from within. He calls everyone to repent and accept the Kingdom of God to become holy.

Unlike the Pharisees, we have accepted Jesus Christ and his call to repent and grow in holiness. As the Letter of Saint James explains, we must be doers of the word and not hearers only. Our living Tradition helps to be doers of the word and adjusts religious traditions for our growth in faith. Like the Pharisees, we have traditions regarding the use of food. There has been a long tradition of abstaining from meat on Fridays to remind us of the Lord's death for us on Good Friday. However, after the Second Vatican Council, the Bishops, the living interpreters of Tradition, noticed that Catholics tended to abstain from eating meat only because it was the law. They relaxed the tradition, limiting the law to Fridays in Lent. When I received my First Communion, Catholics were required to fast from all food and drink (even water) from midnight. That tradition caused us to distinguish regular food from the Eucharistic Food. They relaxed the tradition to fasting for one hour before receiving Communion, as a way of encouraging the faithful to receive the Eucharist more frequently.

The Scriptures today remind us of the importance of God's Law and the role of the living teaching authority of the Church to interpret and guide us in living it. They also remind us of the purpose of all laws and teachings: to help us to grow in holiness. As Pope Francis keeps reminding us, that holiness involves care for orphans and widows – those who live on the fringes of society. Guided by the teaching of the Church, we recognize those evils that defile us and turn more completely to the One who saves us in the Paschal Mystery. Our laws and traditions guide us as we imitate that Mystery in our lives.

29.6 September 2, 2018

When the Pharisees and scribes criticize the disciples of Jesus for not washing their hands before eating, they are really accusing Jesus, their teacher, of having no regard for the Law of Moses. But that criticism is not true. Jesus understands the intent Moses words in the first reading from the Book of Deuteronomy. He accepts the Law as a gift from God to guide the people to live a holy life in communion with God. He accuses the Pharisees of doing exactly the opposite. They had introduced many customs intended to become a "fence" around the Law to protect it. Instead, those fences had become rituals putting the emphasis on external piety instead of true internal holiness. Our readings today help us understand true holiness.

We are holy when we are aware of God's presence in our lives. That is why Moses erected a tabernacle in a tent in the midst of the camps of the Israelites in the desert. God was traveling with them. God fed them with manna and water from the rock. God would not abandon them. God will not abandon us either, especially in these dark times.

Saint James reminds us that a holy life is focused on God's call to action. He encourages us to hear God's Word. We hear God's Word at every Mass, only after we have admitted at the beginning of Mass that we are sinners. But Saint James also insists that we must be doers of God's Word. We are dismissed from Mass to put that Word into action. That is why the current crisis in our Church is so shocking. We have learned that bishops and priests who have led us in pious exercises have done horrible things that have caused so much pain.

Once we understand the importance of acting on God's Word, we can understand better the importance of being part of the Church. The recent revelations of sexual misconduct on the part of the clergy have caused many people to give up on the Church. However, we need to remain connected with one another as the Body of Christ even more in this time of crisis. The Lord does not call us to live solitary lives in isolation from one another. The Lord calls us to gather for the Eucharist and to trust that he continues to walk with us, even as God traveled with the Israelites through their worst times in the desert. His presence allows us to trust that our Church is being purified so that we become more truly holy and conformed to the Lord's love.

Like the Pharisees, we Catholics have developed many human customs and traditions intended to draw us into closer communion with the Lord. Before the Second Vatican Council, we observed the Church law of abstaining from meat on all Fridays. Those who were not Catholics saw this as our identity: we were fish eaters! But abstaining from meat was not the heart of our identity. Being the Body of Christ remains our true identity. To be honest, we tended to abstain from meat more out of obligation than out of a desire to become more holy, much as the Pharisees and their scribes were more concerned about purification rituals than about turning more completely toward God. After the Council, the law was changed to require abstinence from meat only on Fridays during Lent. These days, I see more and more Catholics returning to this practice voluntarily, embracing the external practice as a way of doing penance on the day that the Lord died and drawing them more closely into his Passion.

This is the challenge for our Church today. We need external reforms to protect innocent children and address the problem of clerical privilege. We need external reforms to purge the Church in many ways. But we also need to listen to the words of Scripture today. The Lord remains with us. He calls us to act on the Word we hear. We are all sinners who are connected to one another as the Body of Christ, seeking better individual holiness.

30. 23rd Sunday in Ordinary Time

Readings
Isaiah 35:4–7
James 2:1–5
Mark 7:31–37

30.1 September 7, 2003

When Jesus worked the miracle that allowed the man to hear and speak, he uttered an Aramaic word – "*Ephphatha.*" Mark translated that word as "be opened." Today, we continue to hear that word whenever people are baptized. With adults, it is spoken to them on Holy Saturday morning. With infants, it is spoken at the end of the Rite of Infant Baptism. In both cases, the priest touches the person's ears and eyes, and he prays that God may "open your ears that you may hear his Word and your mouth that you may loudly proclaim it!"

That is the real miracle we are invited to accept. We who have been baptized have had our ears opened, and we hear the Word of God proclaimed to us every Sunday. We have had our mouths opened, so that we may leave this Church to loudly proclaim what we have heard.

James gives a specific example of this listening and speaking in the second reading. He addresses an affluent congregation and wonders whether they have opened their ears to the way God has spoken to them through the poor. James asks us, in this assembly, whether we would treat two guests differently. Would we invite the well-dressed and wealthy guest to take a seat of honor, while urging a homeless person to take a seat where he or she would not be noticed? James is not giving us an excuse to avoid dressing up for the Lord's Banquet. Rather, he is asking us if we have truly heard God's Word that people's value comes not from how many possessions or titles they have, but on the value that comes from their being created in God's image.

For almost a year, our Strategic Planning Process has been trying to listen to God's voice to know how we should proceed as a parish in the future. Generously blessed by God, we know that we must listen to God's voice in the poor. We have established a Saint Vincent de Paul Society to serve the immediate needs of the needy in our midst. Some may sneer about being needy in Granger. But, there are many hidden cases of genuine need. We have formed a Social Justice Committee, to coordinate our efforts to serve the poor. We have tithed 2% of our offertory income to Saint Adalbert School, which does not have the financial resources to support itself. Beginning in July, we have committed an additional 2% of our income to distribute to those in need. These are good initial steps. But, God continues to call us to cooperate with the miracle begun at baptism – to open our ears to the cry of the poor and speak – not so much with words – but with the actions proscribed by James in last week's second reading.

We sometimes think that giving to the poor only benefits them. On the contrary, they have much to teach us. When we hear their needs, we learn gratitude for what we have, instead of a greedy yearning for what we do not. When we understand their pain, we learn the joy of being alive, of being able to pray and love and put our talents to the good service of others, rather than dwelling on the pessimism that comes from focusing on the negatives of life. When we give a generous portion of what has been given us, we learn serenity in the knowledge that we are loved by God, not for what we have or don't have, but simply because God has created us in his image. When these lessons are truly learned, then Jesus' words to the deaf and dumb man create a new miracle in our lives today ⬜ *Ephphatha!* We are opened!

30.2   September 10, 2006

Jesus is not afraid to be physical in healing the deaf mute – laying his hands on him, putting his finger in his ears, spitting, and saying "*Ephphatha,*" the Aramaic word for "be opened". A friend of mine tends to be fanatic about germs and carries around a bottle of Purell with him all the time. He could not have handled all that physicality. With those gestures, the man's ears are opened, and he loudly proclaims the power of the one who healed him.

These gestures have been repeated countless times in the last twenty centuries through Christ's Body, the Church. Every time someone comes to the waters of baptism – whether as an adult or as an infant – Jesus Christ works through the one administering the Sacraments. Through the minister, Christ lays hands on them. For many centuries, those preparing for Baptism were invited to spit toward the west, the direction of the setting sun, which the ancients associated with darkness, as a way of reinforcing their triple renunciation of the power of the Evil One. Today, they simply respond "I do" in renouncing Satan three times. On the morning of Holy Saturday for adults, and just after the waters of Baptism for infants, Jesus Christ touches their ears and mouths through the minister and says those same words, "*Ephphatha*," or "be opened!" The newly baptized who has heard God's Word can now confidently proclaim it.

Just as Jesus did not intend for that word, *Ephphatha*, to be uttered only once, so also that word is repeated repeatedly as we grow in faith and struggle to live our baptismal promises. In the second reading, James tells us to "*Ephphatha*", "be opened" to recognize Christ in those who might be different from us. James is not giving us an excuse not to dress up for Sunday Mass. Rather, he is telling us to open our eyes to see beyond wealth, influence, and power to see Christ in the poor or the immigrant or the person who is a different race or ethnic background than we are.

We need to hear that word, *Ephphatha*, frequently if we are to live our baptismal promises in any authentic way. Christ speaks "*Ephphatha*" when we insist on holding onto our tunnel vision, of seeing life through a very narrow lens that makes us feel secure when we are threatened. Christ speaks "*Ephphatha*" when we fall into the habit of making racial slurs and think that those words will not affect a classmate of color who has been stung by the sin of racism. Christ speaks "*Ephphatha*" when someone cares enough about us to challenge us about behavior that is harmful to ourselves or those around us.

Saint Mark tells us that Jesus was traveling in the district of the Decapolis when he worked the miracle of making the deaf mute hear and speak. His intention is not to give us a geography lesson. Because this district is where the pagans lived, he tells us that Jesus intends his mission to extend well beyond the limitations of his own people and his own territory. Jesus continues his Mission with and in us today, as he constantly speaks the word, *Ephphatha*, to invite us to open our eyes and ears, that we may hear and see, in order that we may proclaim the Good News of Salvation.

30.3   September 6, 2009

In April, an unusual event took place during the first round competition of *Britain's Got Talent*. A self admittedly frumpy 47 year old woman presented herself before a panel of judges and a live audience. As she walked to center stage, a rumbling of comments and giggles could be heard from the audience. The judges, who have a reputation for being caustic and critical about contestants, looked both amused and apprehensive. During the interview, the woman announced that she would like to become a professional singer, and her words were drowned out by derisive laughter. But when Susan Boyle opened her mouth and began to sing "I Dreamed a Dream" from *Les Miserables*, the audience grew hushed as they listened to her clear, beautiful voice and jumped to their feet in loud applause at the end. The audience had misjudged Susan Boyle because of her appearance and was proved wrong by her extraordinary performance.

In today's second reading, Saint James warns us against making judgments of people because of their appearance, or based upon how much money they have. In fact, he urges us to look at other people as God does, with no partiality. James knows that the vast majority of Christians at that time were very poor and certainly not in any upper class situations. He points out that God has chosen the poor of this world to be rich in faith and heirs of the Kingdom.

Jesus exhibits this same impartiality as he ventures outside the comfortable confines of Jewish territory to bring his message to the Gentiles, considered unclean by his contemporaries. Instead of launching into a long and complicated explanation of his message of salvation, he says one word to a man who could not hear or speak: "*Ephphatha*," an Aramaic word which literally means "be opened." The man not only hears the message. He also directly disobeys Jesus' commands and tells everyone about it. He demonstrates that the harsh judgment leveled by the Scribes and Pharisees on the Gentiles is wrong.

We use this same word at every Baptismal ceremony. After we baptize infants, we touch the baby's ears to invite the child to hear God's Word and then the mouth to loudly proclaim it. (By the time we have been doing all this fussing, most babies are more than willing to loudly proclaim their displeasure.) On Holy Saturday morning, we use the same gestures with adults, teens, and children waiting for Baptism at the Easter Vigil. We touch their ears, and then their mouths, inviting them to hear God's Word, so they can clearly proclaim it in their daily lives.

Not only does Jesus speak this Aramaic word which we still use in baptisms, but he also uses some dramatic actions. He touches the man with his hand. He puts his fingers into his ears. He spits and touches his tongue. Those external signs point to the truth expressed by his looking up to heaven. He is the beloved Son of the Father, bringing God's power to heal. In much that way, our parish also shows some pretty dramatic signs that we have heard the word of God about not judging others by appearances. We speak by our actions. That is why the Saint Vincent de Paul Society helps those who have emergency needs, using the funds we have provided them and the food we bring this Sunday. That is why we tithe 5% of our income each month to Saint Adalbert's, looking beyond any cultural or political differences which might exist. That is why we set aside another 2% of our monthly income to provide means for the needs of the poor who come to us with needs.

Getting involved in the lives of those who are different from us can become messy and challenging. It is easy to make simple judgments about them and their specific circumstances. Jesus gives an example by the way he looks into the heart of the deaf mute. We are his Body, and we are living our baptismal promises when we respond in the same fashion.

30.4 September 9, 2012

The prophet Isaiah dreams of a time when God will come with vindication to save his people. Isaiah sees his dream happening when the eyes of the blind will be opened, when the ears of the deaf will be cleared, and when the tongue of the mute will sing. This dream gave his people direction and kept them hopeful in the darkest moments of their existence.

The evangelist Mark sees Isaiah's dream fulfilled in Jesus, the itinerant preacher from Nazareth. Saint Mark tells us this story of Jesus healing a deaf man with a speech impediment to open our eyes to the ways in which the saving power of Jesus Christ is present to us. If we look closely at the details of this story, we can recognize at least three ways in which the saving power of Christ can affect our lives.

The first way can be seen in the place where Jesus works this miracle. The district of the Decapolis draws its name from ten cities situated east of the Jordan River, in pagan territory. Observant Jews would have regarded this area as a place where God was absent. Most good Jewish folk would never go into this territory inhabited by unclean pagans. But Jesus does. And he continues to enter our lives today, even into situations where God seems to be absent or where there seems to be no hope.

The second way involves the deaf and mute man's encounter with Jesus. Because of his impediment, he could not come to Jesus. So, his friends grab the initiative and take him there. There are people in our lives who care deeply for us and are willing to lead us to Christ, especially when things are not going so well. That might be why friends keep bugging you to go on a Christ Renews His Parish Weekend, or sign up for ARISE, or to attend the Respect Life Fair this Wednesday evening. So many times, we cannot hear the Lord speaking to us. It takes others to bring us to a closer relationship with Christ.

Finally, Jesus does not draw attention to himself or make a huge spectacle of healing this man. Jesus takes the man aside away from the crowd and works quietly with him. He reveals his relationship to the Father by looking up to heaven and groaning. Then, Jesus becomes very physical. He does not put on a mask and rubber gloves. Instead, he puts his fingers in the man's ears, touches his tongue, and spits! Living in an age of hypersensitivity to germs, we would be looking for a gallon of Purell! But Jesus is demonstrating a sacramental principle in healing this man. He uses very tangible and visible of God's invisible and mysterious love. With his ears open, this unnamed man will continue to hear the words Jesus will speak to him with greater understanding and appreciation. With his mouth freed, he can speak plainly of the love of God which he received in such concrete ways from Jesus Christ.

We too encounter Christ in very tangible ways. Through the waters of Baptism, we were freed from sin and were incorporated into the Body of Christ. At every Baptism, we speak the same words of Jesus as we touch the ears and mouth of the newly baptized child: "Ephphatha, that is be opened, that you may hear the Word of God and loudly proclaim it!" As we are sealed with the Holy Spirit through the symbol of sacred oil and as we are fed with the Body and Blood of Christ through the symbols of bread and wine, we continue to open our ears to hear the Word of God speaking to us now. Once we hear that Word, we loudly proclaim the truth spoken by Saint James in the second reading. God shows no partiality. Rich or poor, well dressed or shabbily dressed, we are all created in the image of God. Isaiah's dream has been fulfilled in Jesus Christ, and he has come to save us!

30.5 September 6, 2015

Jesus has great compassion for this man. The poor guy has no sound, no voice, and no hope. There was always something missing in his life. He could never enter into conversation. As a child, other kids probably made fun of him. As an adult, those who knew him probably are embarrassed for him or because of him. He is like a stroke victim whose voice has been affected. He is in his right mind, but is paralyzed in expressing any of his thoughts.

Saint Mark does not record this miracle so that we can marvel at a first century Helen Keller, as wonderful as coming to hear and speak might be. Mark records this miracle for a spiritual reason. Last Sunday, Jesus confronted the religious leaders of his own people to go beyond external observances and look into people's hearts.

Today, Jesus goes to the Decapolis, the ten cities in pagan territory. He signals that the Kingdom of God is meant for everyone who is willing to listen. That is why he heals a man who cannot hear. Jesus takes the man off by himself, away from the clamor of many voices. He becomes very physical with the man, acting like many of his contemporary healers. He puts his finger into the man's ears, spits, touches his tongue, groans, looks up to heaven, and uses a word that means "be opened." Then he orders the people not tell anyone. Jesus wants this parable of action to speak for itself.

This parable of action is addressed to us. The Word of God has great power. God's Word brought creation into existence. God spoke his word to Abraham, Isaac, and Jacob to form a Chosen People. God continued to speak through prophets like Isaiah, who assured his people that God would never abandon them, even when they refused to listen to his word. Now, the Incarnate Word of God speaks to us. We live in a world filled with many competing voices screaming at us day and night. The confusing crowd of voices tells us that we can be happy if we own certain objects, or if we exclude this particular group of people, or countless other messages that promise happiness. Jesus has taken us away from the crowd into this church. Away from the crowd, he is very physical with us. He speaks to us in the Word. He feeds us with his Body and Blood. He touches us through the Sacramental life of the Church. He opens our ears and speaks his Word to us, inviting us to listen and reflect on his words.

Once we can hear the Lord speaking to us, then we can begin to speak. We often hear of the "New Evangelization," a phrase used by the last three Popes. As Catholics, we scratch our heads and ask what this means for us. The "new" involves modern methods of communicating, especially those methods which are available through so much of social media. To evangelize is not new. Once our ears have been opened to hear the authentic Word of God, then we can speak the truth of our experience of God. We can speak of the word received from the Letter of Saint James that wealth and social status have nothing to do with the way God looks at people. In hearing that Word, we are invited to act on it. We evangelize not only by sharing our gifts with the poor, but also by welcoming them into our midst.

During the fall, we are offering a number of opportunities to open our ears to hear a little more clearly. We are offering two different series on marriage. There will be a series on the Pope's recent Encyclical on the Environment. Take a look at the bulletin and the website for Bible Study sessions, RCIA, and other Adult Education opportunities. They are designed to draw us away from the crowd,

open our ears more attentively to God's voice, and help us to speak
of what we hear, especially to family members, friends, and neighbors. At every Baptism, we touch the baby's ears and mouth and
say, *"Ephphatha,"* be opened. We can open our ears to hear God's
Word, and then accept his grace to loudly proclaim it in a number
of creative ways.

30.6   September 9, 2018

Saint Mark tells us that Jesus has been traveling from the district of
Tyre and passes by Sidon to the Sea of Galilee into the district of
the Decapolis. In other words, Jesus is moving out of the comfort
zone of his Jewish roots and is proclaiming his message about the
Kingdom of God to pagans. Saint Mark is signaling to us that the
Gospel is intended for everyone, and not just the descendants of
Abraham and Moses.

It is in this area that people bring to him a deaf man who had
a speech impediment. Trusting that Jesus has healing powers, they
ask him to lay his hands on him. Jesus takes the man away from
the crowd and becomes very physical with him. He puts his hands
into his ears. Like many healers of his day who regarded spit as a
healing substance, he spits and touches his tongue. He looks up to
heaven, because he wants people to know that his healing power
comes from the Father. Using the Aramaic word, *Ephphatha,* he
commands that the deaf man's ears be opened. Immediately, the
man can hear and is able to speak.

Saint Mark records this story to help us to believe that the
Lord's healing power is in our midst. We gather for Mass, because
we believe in the Paschal Mystery. We believe that Jesus died to
destroy the power of sin and death. We believe that he rose from
the dead and ascended to the right hand of the Father. We believe
that he has sent his Holy Spirit to continue his saving work in our
midst. For us, this is not a story of what Jesus did 2,000 years ago
to help a deaf mute. What Jesus did for that man, he does for us
today.

Truth be told, we have trouble hearing. There are many loud
and competing voices shouting at us today. Posts on social media
encourage us to lash out in anger at those who seem to offend us.
Advertisers try to convince us that their products can save us and
bring ultimate happiness. With the current crisis in the Church,
some argue that the Church is completely corrupt and not deserv-
ing of trust. The Lord takes us aside from all that noise into this
church, as he took the deaf mute aside, and speaks his Word to us.
He continues to use signs that appeal to our senses. We hear the
words from Scripture. He gives himself to us in a very real way
through ordinary bread and wine. We also hear the words from

the Diocese giving us correct information about what is happening with Bishop Rhoades. I will offer a question and answer session a week from Tuesday at 7:30 p.m. in the Parish Life Center. Just as the Liturgy has us say *"Ephphatha"* at the baptism of both adults and children, the Lord invites us to open our ears to hear him.

That is why Jesus tells the crowd not to tell anyone what he had just done. He did not want to draw attention to himself as some kind of wonder worker. Only after he had died and rose from the dead could people understand the full impact of what he was doing. Opening that man's ears and allowing him to speak was only a sign of what he is doing with us today. He invites us to believe that he does all things well today.

Once our ears have been opened, and once we hear what the Lord says to us, then we too can continue to listen through reading the Bible, through reflective prayer, and through adult education series that speak to us. As we come to hear clearly, then we too can speak, as the deaf man began to speak. We can speak the message of Saint James that God loves everyone, and that we cannot discriminate based on what people wear or what race they belong to. We can speak the truth about the special responsibility we have to the poor and the vulnerable. We can also speak of the Lord's presence in our difficult situation. It is the Lord who saves us, because he has already conquered the power of sin and death. It is the Lord who purifies our Church and keeps his promise to Peter that he will remain with us to the end of time, no matter what.

31. 24th Sunday in Ordinary Time

Readings
Isaiah 50:4–9
James 2:14–18
Mark 8:27–35

31.1 September 17, 2006

Jesus chose an interesting place to speak to his disciples about his identity. Caesarea Philippi was the northernmost seat of government for the tetrarch Philip, who named the city after his patron, Caesar. This city was also built on the site of an ancient temple dedicated to Pan, the god of nature. When Jesus asks the question, "Who do you say that I am," Peter knows that he cannot find salvation either in the emperor or in some false god. He quickly replies, "You are the Christ" (the anointed one).

However, as correct as Peter may have been about the true identity of Jesus, he completely misunderstands the nature of the mission of the Christ. Jesus insists that his mission involves suffering, humiliation, and death by execution in the cruelest method devised by the Roman occupiers. Jesus' words to Peter make no sense to him, because losing one's life to save it makes no logical sense to him.

We who gather here to proclaim Jesus as the Christ have the same problem. Like Peter, we struggle with the crosses we must bear. Sometimes, those crosses involve the ordinary tragedies of human life. Sometimes, they involve sacrifices that must be made if we are faithful to the Gospel message. Often, those sacrifices we make seem to make no difference, and we look for easier ways.

At the beginning of Mass this Sunday, we talked about the needs of our parish. I am so certain that we need to build this Education Center that I do not hesitate to ask for sacrifices to build a structure that will serve us better now and in the future. But, as we deny ourselves to meet our own needs, we cannot forget the needs of the poor and those who depend on us for help. Saint James clearly spells out the responsibility of those of us who have received material blessings to share them with the poor.

In our parish, there is a small group of men and women who call themselves the Saint Vincent de Paul Society. They meet on a monthly basis, and they use the resources that we provide in the monthly green envelopes marked for the poor to distribute them to those who need help. They work quietly and behind the scenes to express their faith in works of charity. Our parish conference is part of a larger local conference that brings the Saint Vincent de Paul truck to our parish every month and operates a thrift store on the west side of South Bend. On this weekend, we invite you to consider joining them in their effort to serve the poor in our name. Members of our Saint Vincent De Paul Society will be at the table in the area outside the parish offices. Please take some time to talk to them after Mass, ask questions, and consider being part of our efforts to serve the poor.

Peter eventually understood the role of taking up his own cross and denying himself, as he became the rock on which Christ built his Church. Christ depends on our understanding his message and trusting that our sacrifices will make a difference for our world today.

31.2   September 13, 2009

With school underway for this academic year, Mark presents Jesus as a teacher. Up to this point, Jesus had been teaching his disciples by his actions. He now addresses them directly as disciples, as "those being taught," and asks an easy question. What others are saying about him. All their answers indicate that he is regarded in the line of great spiritual leaders in the past. But, then he asks a more difficult question: Who do you say that I am? Peter raises his hand and gives the correct answer. "You are the Christ," he says. Peter got the right answer based on what he had observed. Jesus had attracted large and enthusiastic crowds. His miracles had demonstrated the power he received from God. Peter had given up a secure job of being a fisherman to get on the bandwagon to reap the benefits of following this teacher whom he came to accept as the Messiah (Hebrew), the Christ (Greek) or the Anointed One.

With Peter's correct answer, Jesus launches into a lesson which those being taught did not expect. Instead of being one of the popular messiahs who promised to usher in the "Good Old Days" of King David and restore the Kingdom of Israel to its greatness, Jesus understands that his role would be more like that of Isaiah's servant. Isaiah's servant had gone into the Babylonian Exile in utter defeat and humiliation. This suffering servant, Isaiah says in the first reading, can give new meaning to human suffering, as well as new meaning to what it means to be redeemed by God. This is the role given to Jesus by his Father, and he intends to be faithful to that role. In putting himself at the service of others, Jesus will anger the religious leaders of his day and give himself over to a humiliating death on the cross.

Peter does not understand this lesson. When Mark tells us that Peter rebukes his teacher, he is using some pretty strong language. Peter not only rejects this teaching, but he is telling Jesus that he is wrong. Jesus responds to his pupil with just as much vehemence. He rebukes Peter in return, as he has been rebuking demons and the raging waters of the Sea of Galilee. He calls him "Satan" and demands that Peter get behind him. Jesus will not allow his students to tell him what his role as Messiah should be.

Many of you are sitting in desks and formal classrooms, learning from teachers who are challenging you to grow, to learn, and to understand what lies ahead of you in life. Whether we are in formal classrooms or not, Jesus Christ is teaching all of us about what it means to be a suffering servant, giving his life for us. He clearly tells us that understanding this identity is critical. When we do accept it, then we too become servants, willing to take up our crosses by putting the needs of others ahead of our own, and following him.

Just as Peter wanted to cling to his own notions of learning to follow Christ, so do we. Like him, we are tempted to define our discipleship, our being schooled in the ways of the Lord, in terms of success, power, prestige, and putting our own needs and comfort as first priorities. Instead, Jesus is teaching us to be humble servants, willing to lose our lives on a daily basis for his sake and the sake of the Gospel. To put it in the terms of the Letter to James, he wants us to make sure that our faith, which is a gift from God, is expressed in our works – in the ways in which we treat others. The crosses which come from this lesson might seem to crush us at times, and we are tempted to ignore them. But in ignoring these crosses, we ignore the real lesson of the Cross which finds its fulfillment in the resurrection. God had justified Isaiah's suffering servant by leading his people from Exile to freedom. The Father would justify Jesus, the Suffering Servant, through the power of the resurrection. Jesus offers us the same lesson. If we continue to die with him, we will also rise with him.

31.3   September 16, 2012

Those who watched the Olympics last month saw extraordinary feats of athletic skills. As we watched on television, we marveled at the performances of athletes in a wide range of sports and celebrated the Olympic spirit. However, we did not see the countless hours of disciplined training that each athlete had to endure each day to reach the games in London.

Jesus speaks of his victory as the Christ today, and tells us that we can share in that victory forever. However, he clearly states that we can only share in that victory if we share in his defeat, in his dying. We must discipline ourselves, much as Olympic athletes, in order to die to ourselves each day, embrace the cross that daily dying might entail, and lose our lives for the sake of the Gospel. In practical terms, this means serving God with all our hearts.

We have as much trouble accepting this message as Peter does. With Peter, we recognize Jesus as the Christ and want to share in his victory over death. With Peter, we find it difficult to embrace the cross of that daily dying to self. Jesus rebukes Peter sharply for trying to find easy ways out and tells him to get behind him. Once Peter gets behind Jesus, he will learn how to follow him, how to be a disciplined disciple and walk the way of the cross.

Stewardship provides a structure for learning how to follow Christ as a disciplined disciple. Good stewards are willing to set aside an hour each Sunday and time during the week to praise God as the giver of all that we have. Good stewards die to themselves by giving a portion of our God given time and talent in humble service. Good stewards set aside a first portion of our treasure to give back to our community and to the poor.

We often emphasize that stewardship is not a fund raiser. It truly is a way of life, a way of learning how to be a disciplined disciple. But our treasure is an important part of what God has given to us, and we are invited to renew our commitment to the stewardship of sacrificial giving today. Jesus Christ gave his entire life for us on the cross. Stewardship of sacrificial giving invites us to set aside a first portion of a percentage of our treasure to return to him in gratitude. That is why we place our sacrificial tithe in a basket before the Altar and trust that our sacrifice, joined with the sacrifice of Jesus Christ, will be acceptable to the Father. We get behind Jesus in denying ourselves each day, so that our sacrificial giving becomes a habit.

As a parish, we have taken steps in faith in setting aside a portion of our treasure. Currently we tithe 8.5% of our income – 5% to our sister parish of Saint Adalbert, and 3.5% to the poor. We will continue to increase our tithe until we reach 10%. Please take a look at your own treasure and consider taking a step of faith. Please pray over your decision for this next year, and please consider setting aside a portion of that gift to the Annual Bishop's Appeal. As you pray over your decision, please listen to the experience of Scott Null.

31.4 September 13, 2015

We accept pollsters these days as part of the fabric of our ordinary American life. Those running for public office rely on their standings in polls to make decisions about their campaigns. But polls are not new. In today's Gospel, Jesus conducts a poll to seek public opinion about him. Professional pollsters call this "an informal survey." His disciples come up with three results: John the Baptist come back to life, Elijah back from heaven, or one of the prophets. Then Jesus turns the polls on them and asks who they think he is. Peter, always one to blurt things out, gets the correct answer: "You are the Christ (Messiah)."

Jesus knows that his disciples accept the common understanding of the messiah as a hero who would free them from oppression. Their ancestors had been slaves in Egypt, and then again in Babylon. As servants of Roman rule, they want the messiah to ransom them from their slavery. They are keenly fearful of the way the Romans use the cruel and humiliating tool of crucifying those who oppose them as warnings to others not to attempt a revolt.

Jesus knows that his Father has not called him to be this popular kind of messiah. Versed in the suffering servant songs of the prophet Isaiah and reinforced by his 40 days in the desert, Jesus has developed an unflinching trust that he can speak the truth about the Kingdom of God, even when the religious authorities oppose him. God will not fail him. He has been revealing this mission by his miracles and healings. Even though the demons understand his true mission, his disciples do not. So, now he openly tells them that he is the Messiah who will become a slave himself, humbling serving others. He will endure the humiliation of the cross and pay the ransom for sin and free them from sin and death.

Peter speaks for the rest of the disciples in telling Jesus that this is crazy! But Jesus rebukes him in the strongest terms, calling Peter a demon and telling him not to tempt him to abandon his mission. Peter and the other disciples would eventually learn the truth. After the resurrection, they would eventually put their faith in Jesus the Christ before their own security. They would deny themselves and embrace the cross with the same unflinching trust in God.

Many Christians are living this message in a very literal way. In the Middle East and in parts of Africa, those who profess their faith in Jesus Christ are losing their lives for the sake of the Gospel.

In areas controlled by the Islamic State, some are taxed heavily, others driven out of their homes, and many put to death. They face these horrors with the unflinching trust that Jesus keeps his promise. Those who share in his dying will share in his rising.

This same message applies to us, who are disciples of the Lord. Every time we keep our baptismal promises, we die to ourselves and trust that we will share in the Lord's rising. Saint James understands this dynamic. He knows that our salvation is a gratuitous gift from Jesus Christ, who died to pay the ransom for our sins. He knows that we cannot purchase our way to heaven with good works. But he also knows that we must do more than talk about our faith. We must become humble servants, die to ourselves, and respond to those in need.

When I am done talking, we will profess our faith and recite together the Nicene Creed. In praying the Creed, we express what we believe in words. But we must translate those words into action. We reaffirm our conviction that being humble servants will not destroy us. Dying to ourselves may be painful and sometimes discouraging. Carrying the cross of pain, rejection, or suffering may frighten us. Watching others without faith get ahead may anger us. But we express our unflinching trust that God will not fail us. This knowledge is not the result of a pollster seeking our opinion. It is the result of the death and resurrection of Jesus Christ.

31.5 September 16, 2018

Jesus asks his disciples, "Who do people say that I am?" They respond that the gossip circles are saying that he might be Elijah, or John the Baptist, or one of the prophets. The expectation is that he will be a powerful leader who will overcome the Romans, their current oppressors. Peter blurts out the correct answer: "You are the Christ." However, Peter has the same expectation about a messiah. He rebukes Jesus when he defines his role in terms of suffering and death. In turn, Jesus rebukes Peter and says to him, "Get behind me, Satan."

Even those Jesus rebukes Peter harshly and says that he is tempting him to disobey his Father's will, he tells Peter to get behind him. In other words, he wants Peter to continue to follow him and to learn the difficult lessons of the cross.

As followers of Jesus Christ, we have also chosen to "get behind" and follow him. Like Peter, we find the message of the cross to be very difficult. That is why I have come to embrace stewardship as a way of life, as a structured way of getting behind Jesus Christ. Good stewards spend generous amounts of time in prayer, with the Eucharist as the source and summit of our lives of faith. Good stewards give themselves in humble service, as our Lord washed the feet of his disciples at the Last Supper. Good stewards share a generous portion of their treasure with the Body of Christ, and not just what is left over. Jesus clearly said that it is by your love for one another that everyone will recognize you as my disciples. Stewardship, simply, is love in action.

We renewed our stewardship of prayer at Lent and our stewardship of service during the Easter Season. This weekend, we invite you to make a commitment to sharing a sacrificial gift with the parish. Please read the information in your stewardship of sacrificial giving packet and pray over your decision. Currently, Saint Pius tithes 5% of our income to Saint Adalbert and another 3.5% to those who come to us in need. Pray over your decision and set aside a portion for the Annual Bishop's Appeal.

You would expect me to say these things. But, please listen to Brian Jacobs, as he tells his story of coming to embrace stewardship as a way of life.

32. 25th Sunday in Ordinary Time

Readings
Wisdom 2:12, 17–20
James 3:16–4:3
Mark 9:30–37

32.1 September 21, 2003

Rodney Dangerfield complains that he never gets much respect. That same complaint is also heard from parents and teachers. Mothers get fed up with picking up dirty clothes from the floor and want to know who made them the slaves of the rest of the family. Fathers get tired of explaining why certain rules are in place and snap back, "Do it because I said so!" – which is another way of saying that children will understand later in life. Teachers reach a point where all the excuses for not doing homework cause them to throw up their hands and wonder if these students will ever learn anything.

If you are an adult in a similar situation, you need to know that Jesus understands your frustration. During Ordinary Time this year, we have been hearing from the Gospel of Mark. We have heard Mark telling stories of Jesus patiently trying to explain to the Apostles what kind of Messiah he was called to be. After telling the parable of the sower and the seed, he realized that they did not understand what he was talking about. When he multiplied the loaves and fishes, he accused them of not "getting it", because their minds were closed. Just before he calmed the waters that almost swamped their boat, he wanted to know why they had such little faith. After explaining for the second time that as Messiah, his role was to suffer, die, and be raised from the dead (and not to chase out the Romans once and for all!), he caught the Apostles arguing about who had the most important positions in his new regime! Peter might have argued that Jesus gave him the keys. Judas may have bragged that he held the money. John might have said that Jesus loved him best. They just didn't get it!

Patient teacher that he was, Jesus sat down. That action of sitting was significant, because teachers in the ancient world sat when they wanted to say something important. He put his arms around a little child – not because the child was cute, but because children were the least significant, the most vulnerable, and the most dependent in his society. Using the child as a lovely prop, he insisted that the greatest in his kingdom would be those who receive this child openly. In other words, their greatness will not be measured in terms of power or position or wealth, but rather in terms of how they put themselves at the end of the line and how well they serve the needs of others.

If you are a parent, a teacher, or someone who knows the frustration of not getting any respect, take some comfort from the words of Jesus Christ today. Your service of those who may not appreciate you is making you great already. Learn a lesson from the master teacher, who never gave up on his Apostles, no matter how slowly they may have learned. His trust in their eventual "getting it" paid off after his death and resurrection. The slow learners became the foundation stones of the Church he founded.

If you are a child or a teenager, you might learn a lesson from today's readings. You might pause for a moment before you react with anger to something your parents or teachers demand of you. Perhaps you may not understand what they are trying to teach you now. But, be open to the possibility that it might make sense later, when you can see the bigger picture. And you who are very young! You can teach us the most valuable lesson. You can teach those of us who are adults, who have responsibility for others, what it looks like to be vulnerable and dependent on the presence of God in our lives. When we learn that lesson, we become better servants!

32.2 September 24, 2006

Mark presents Jesus as the good teacher to his disciples. He patiently tries to correct their notion of what kind of Messiah he would be. Very carefully, he explains that his victory will not be won with swords or horses or chariots. Rather, his victory would come from suffering, the cross, and death. However, they were not paying attention. When he finally asked them what they were arguing about, they fell silent. They were embarrassed and ashamed. Instead of listening, they had been arguing about who was the most important.

The key to understanding their argument lies in the phrase, "on the way." Mark uses that term to state that the disciples had embraced the "way" of Jesus Christ and were walking with him. They had some understanding of the demands of the "way," because they had given up everything to follow him. Sitting on their shoulders, though, is a little devil whispering into their ears, "Look what you have sacrificed! What will you get in return?" Filled with self-pity and self-absorption, they were arguing about the importance of their positions in this new social order. We can almost hear Peter saying, "He gave me the keys;" or Judas arguing, "he entrusts the money to me;" or John saying, "he loves me the most." When caught by Jesus, they lowered their heads and remained silent.

We know why they remained silent, because we have been in their shoes. You and I are also walking with the Lord "on the way." While "on the way," we too can harbor angry or resentful thoughts. The devil sits on your left shoulder and whispers, "your parents love your brother better than they love you," when a younger brother gets away with something for which I had been punished. That same devil whispers, "The parish doesn't really appreciate what you are doing," when you've given enormous amounts of time or talent, and no one seems to notice. We all harbor these temptations and allow them to grow into arguments in our heads about who is the greatest. Instead of embracing the Mysteries of the Lord's dying and rising in our lives, we are too busy replaying those old videos in our heads over and over again. James is correct. Violence and murder come from within us. Look what happened to Pope Benedict! A respected academic gives a lengthy, learned lecture in a university setting. The press, which loves media bites, takes one sentence out of context. That one sentence causes smoldering resentment to boil over in the Islamic world, killing a nun and destroying property.

Jesus confronts us today as he confronts his disciples. With them, we are embarrassed and ashamed to admit what has been playing over and over again in our heads. Jesus invites us to focus on that little child he places in our midst. In the ancient world, children had no social importance at all until they became adults. In fact, the word for *talya* in Greek can be translated either as "child" or "servant." Receiving that child implies a willingness to embrace the role of being a humble servant. In receiving that child, humble servants receive Christ and the Father who sent him.

Jesus remains the good teacher, patiently leading us to embrace the Paschal Mystery that ultimate life comes from death, that rising with him means that we are willing to die with him. Being humble servants is a daily way of living that Mystery. As we walk "the way" with Jesus Christ, it is easy to slip into self pity and a desire for more discernible results of our service. Jesus firmly, but lovingly, invites us to resist those temptations and continue walking with him to the Kingdom.

32.3   September 20, 2009

Saint James urges us to be passionate people. As the head of the Church in Jerusalem in the early years of the Church, James displayed his own passions. He fearlessly proclaimed Jesus Christ crucified as the Messiah. He was part of the Council of Jerusalem and respectfully debated with Paul the role of Jewish laws in the early Church. His passionate leadership got the attention of King Herod, who beheaded him.

However, James tells us that we need to learn how to direct our passions. He warns that investing ourselves only in the standards of this world will bring divisions and conflicts. We can see this warning at work in today's Gospel. Even though Jesus has clearly told his disciples that the Messiah would give his life as a humble servant, they don't listen. Instead, they argue about who is the most important. Jesus reduces them to silence, allowing us to see how the warnings of James can be so true. Their passions for prestige, honor, and power will only bring jealousy, selfish ambition, disorder, and ultimately outright warfare with each other.

James tells us to direct our passions from worrying about our status to loving God. God's love is revealed through his will, something disciples can learn only through persistent and open prayer. Doing God's will brings a peace the world cannot give. In the Gospel, Jesus draws a child into the circle of his disciples to make a point. In the ancient world, children had no social status at all. If we can be like this child, Jesus says, if we can accept a role that does not bring attention to ourselves, then we can be good servants, trusting that those who are last will be first.

At Saint Pius, we often use a word which describes this humble service, this way of being a disciple. We call it "stewardship". I have come to believe in Stewardship, because it gives a specific structure for learning how to be humble servants of the community. It truly is a way of life. Our faithful and persistent prayer – especially here at the Sunday Eucharist – reveals to us that God is the origin of all the goods we enjoy. But there is a danger when we pay attention to the status which our service may or may not bring us. When we worry about whether our service is recognized or appreciated, or when we argue about whose service is more important, then those passions begin to cause jealousy and division. In one of his sermons, Saint Augustine talks about this danger in his life. He had just been named Bishop of Hippo. He says that "the honors I receive are for me an ever present cause of uneasiness. Indeed, it terrifies me to think that I could take more pleasure in the honor attached to my office, which is where its danger lies, than in your salvation, which ought to be its first fruit. This is why being set above you fills me with alarm, whereas being with you gives me comfort. Danger lies in the first; salvation in the second."

Learning the way of discipleship as good stewards does not come without a cost. The just person of the Book of Wisdom becomes obnoxious to those who do find the truth of his service to be a judgment on their way of life. That can easily happen to servants at Saint Pius. Being a humble servant brought the cross to Jesus, and it will bring the cross to us. Next weekend, Father Bob and I will speak about the third component of stewardship – sacrificial giving, or sharing of our treasure. This third component often ruffles feathers and causes some to pull back, because it involves money, and money can easily stir up passions that divide.

Listen carefully to what we have to say next week, and listen especially to Chuck Ball, who will tell his story. Stewardship provides a very practical way of becoming a faithful disciple. If embraced fully, it teaches the lesson of today's Gospel. If understood correctly, it directs our passions to the love of God and the peace that God's love can bring.

32.4   September 23, 2018

When Jesus takes a child into his arms, he tells his disciples that whoever welcomes this child welcomes him. Tragically, we have heard too many horrific reports of priests who have done great harm to children, and by extension, to Christ and to his Church. If you are outraged, scandalized, ashamed, and confused, please know that you are not alone. Bishop Rhoades, Father Eric, I, and our staff share these feelings.

However, we also need to remember that the holiness of the Church relies not on the leaders of the Church, but on the total self-giving love of Jesus Christ. That is what he says to his disciples and us today. He invites us to respond to his total gift of selfless love by imitating him and dying to ourselves. As we rely on his total gift of selfless-love, it is important that we express our feelings. We also need to look to the future and trust that Christ will heal his Church as she is now being purified. Trust is hard, because trust has been lost.

Saint James says that conflicts arise when our passions are disordered. While we need to express our passionate feelings, we have to be careful not to allow our anger and fear to do any further harm to the Body of Christ. We need to remember that under the leadership of both Bishops D'Arcy and Rhoades, successful reforms have been put in place to ensure the safety of our children. As time goes on, we will find ways of dealing with this situation. But, they must be positive ways that bring about healing and renewal.

In just a moment, Bishop Rhoades will explain the good work done in our Diocese through the Annual Bishop's Appeal. Please listen with an open heart and prayerfully consider what is being asked of us. Also, remember that our parish is so accustomed to the generous response of so many that we rely on the funds which come back to us once we go over our goal.

To be honest, those of us on staff questioned whether it is wise to do the Bishop's Appeal video after the names of the credibly accused priests was listed last week. But, it really provides an opportunity for reflection. A good friend told me that he had considered withholding his contribution as a way of sending a message. But he prayed over it and talked to his wife. He was able to let go of his anger and choose love instead, and love changed him. He recognized that he was being tempted by Satan to lose faith in the core of the holiness of the Church: the total self-gift of Jesus Christ. As you will hear from Saint Paul in the video, "The love of Christ urges us on."

33. 26th Sunday in Ordinary Time

Readings
Numbers 11:25–29
James 5:1–6
Mark 9:38–43, 45, 47–48

33.1 September 29, 2003

In *A Christmas Carol*, by Charles Dickens, Ebenezer Scrooge meets the ghost of Christmas Yet-to-Come. The ghost shows Scrooge the misery of those who have died in their wealth. Making their misery worse are the cries of the poor they have systematically robbed of basic necessities.

James makes the same point in the second reading today. He warns those of us who are blessed with material possessions that our wealth, our fine clothes, and even our gold and silver will not bring us happiness. Like the ghost of Christmas Yet-To-Come, he invites us to consider the needs of the poor, as a way of expressing our gratitude for our blessings by sharing with them now.

The Annual Bishop's Appeal provides one opportunity for us to share the blessings we have received with the poor and needy of our Diocese. Please direct your attention to the screen, as Bishop D'Arcy shows how the sharing of our wealth benefits those who have not been so blessed.

33.2 October 1, 2006

During the middle of the Civil War in 1862, one of the northern leaders asked President Lincoln for prayer that God would be on their side. Lincoln responded, "Sir, my concern is not whether

God is on our side; my greatest concern is to be on God's sign." Jesus makes it clear today that being on God's sign does not always involve spectacular works like driving out demons in his name. Rather, he says, doing simple acts of kindness like giving a cup of water to drink because we belong to God are signs that we are on God's sign. These simple acts of kindness participate in his redemption mission, and they are more important than the temple demands for ritual purity that would have excluded someone missing an eye or a hand or a foot.

In last week's Gospel, Jesus taught an important lesson about who is the greatest on his side when he sat a child in the midst of the disciples and told them that whoever welcomes a child welcomes him. Children in the ancient world were completely vulnerable and had not way of repaying any acts of kindness. Today, he takes that statement one step further and warns against scandalizing, or putting stumbling blocks, in the way of faith for those humble servants who are great in his company. To make his point stronger, he tells us that it would be better for a millstone to be put around our necks and thrown into the sea, rather than to put stumbling blocks in the way of faith for these little ones. Millstones were huge pieces of granite that oxen pulled to ground grain, and being tied to a millstone would take us immediately to the bottom of the sea.

For many years now, the Bishops of our country have asked us to pause on this first Sunday of October and reflect on the gift of life, and to use this month – traditionally set aside as the month of the rosary – to pray for the protection of the dignity of human life. Our culture tends to emphasize comfort, wealth, and security as top priorities. In our pursuit of these values, it is easy to overlook those vulnerable in our culture, those who cannot repay acts of kindness to us – the unborn, the handicapped, the disabled, the elderly, those falsely accused, those caught in war zones, and the list goes on.

Jesus' words are harsh. Telling us that it is better to cut off a hand or a foot or an eye rather than allowing ourselves to ignore the needs of those most vulnerable gets our attention. Getting our attention jolts us into paying attention. Our culture lulls us into rushing around with our lives and ignoring issues that relate to the dignity of human life. I see it in my own impatience, when I miss a traffic light that has turned green, because we have to wait for a funeral procession to pass. I noticed it in the last couple of weeks when we changed the drop off and pick up pattern for religious education. Some people were not too happy when we established new patterns that made picking up children more inconvenient, but – in our opinion – safer for the welfare of the children.

Saint James is right. In the light of God's love for us and for God's wonderful gift of human life, wealth and possessions can get in the way of our being on God's side. In focusing this Sunday and the month of October on the dignity of human life, he invites us to reflect on our priorities – on our need to welcome Christ in protecting the life of the most vulnerable. James is not telling us to abandon our wealth or our nice clothing or our treasures. Rather, he is insisting that we put them at the service of building relationships with God and each other.

33.3 September 27, 2009

During these last few Sundays, Saint Mark has been telling stories of Jesus teaching his first followers how to be disciples. He told them that they must carry their cross with him. Last Sunday, he instructed them that being good servants is more important than having positions of honor. Today, he tells them that they cannot put limits on the promptings of the Holy Spirit.

Mark tells these stories, not to give a history lesson of how the first disciples learned to be disciples, but so that all who hear them may learn the same lessons. The community to which Saint James writes struggles with these lessons. Some members of that Christian community were blessed with material wealth. James does not condemn their wealth. He simply warns them of the dangers of relying on the three signs of prosperity in the ancient world (wealth, clothing, and gold and silver). Wealth, he insists, should be used as a means to building up what cannot be destroyed – relationships with God and other people.

We hear these Scripture passages so we can learn how to be disciples. With the first followers, we learn that prayer is central to our role as disciples, especially the Sunday Eucharist. With the first disciples, we learn that giving ourselves in humble service is the way to greatness. With the community to which Saint James wrote, we are grateful for the material blessings which we have been given. With them, we recognize our wealth as a gift from God, best used to build up relationships.

We have a word to describe the way of being disciples: "stewardship." During Lent, we renewed our commitment to stewardship of prayer. During Easter, we renewed our commitment to be servants. Now, it is time to renew our commitment to share a portion of our treasure. This past year has been a difficult year, because we have suffered through the worst Recession since the Great Depression. Too many people have lost their jobs or have had their hours or benefits cut. But, I have been simply amazed and humbled that so many have not abandoned their habit of sacrificial giving. Many have maintained the percentage of their income which they give away. The dollar amount may be smaller. But, their sacrificial giving has remained the same. That is the beauty of deciding on a percentage. That is why Saint Pius has been able to maintain our financial obligations.

Please take some time to pray over your decision for next year. Only you can know your financial situation, and only you can determine which percentage works for you. Even though we encourage people to take a step in faith toward a goal of 10%, only you can make that decision. The same dynamic works for the parish. We had discussed the possibility of increasing our parish tithe to 8% this year. But, given the economic realities, we maintained it at 7%. To help you in your decision, Chuck Ball has agreed to talk about his situation. Chuck is a living example of what it means to be a good steward. Please give him your attention.

33.4 September 30, 2012

When John complains to Jesus that someone outside of their small, approved group is driving out demons, Jesus responds. "Don't prevent him," he says and teaches that anyone who performs an act of kindness bringing health to another person is part of the Kingdom of God. He even goes further to make another point. It does not take a dramatic or extraordinary action to be part of the Kingdom. Even a simplest act of kindness, like giving someone a cup of water to drink, has redemptive value.

This response of Jesus is radical, because it challenges us to look more broadly at the faith which we share. *The Catechism of the Catholic Church* assures us that we are on the right path, and that the fullness of the Church subsists in the Catholic Church. But, we are not alone in trying to live holy lives, and we have no right to judge those who are outside our communion who are bringing health to others. Jesus' radical response warns us against the danger of being "holier than thou." We do not have the corner on holiness. People outside our circle perform many acts of kindness, both big and small. They have redemptive value, because of the sacrifice of Jesus Christ, and we cannot be jealous of them or underestimate their worth.

But just as his response is radical in favor of those who do acts of kindness in his name, so his response to our failure to do acts of kindness is just as radical. Jesus uses some very strong language and some very vivid images to describe that failure. Gehenna was a stinking garbage dump which burned all the time in a small valley just south of Jerusalem. It became a perfect image for what happened to believers who scandalize, or put stumbling blocks, in the way of faith for other believers. In a world which saw physical health and well being as a sign of holiness, Jesus says that it is better to cut off a hand, rather than giving in to stealing. It is better to cut off a foot, rather than run away from responsibility. It is better to pluck out an eye, rather than give into a temptation to cheat on a spouse.

Jesus warns against scandalizing his little ones. The word for scandalize literally means to put a stumbling block in the way. Saint James points out that wealth may become one of those stumbling blocks to holiness. Wealth can make us so comfortable that it might cause us to ignore the plight of the poor. He condemns those landowners who try to increase their wealth by cheating those whom they hire to bring in the harvest. The proceeds from that harvest which cheated workers will not last. But, he insists, the One who harvests will be the ultimate judge of what is rewarded and what is punished.

Our readings from today's Scriptures make it very clear that we have a choice. We can choose to participate in the mission of Jesus Christ, embrace his cross, and participate in acts of kindness, both big and small. Or, we can choose to ignore his invitation and put up stumbling blocks to the path of salvation. Some might find this choice to be absurd, because it is so radical. The word "absurd" comes from the Latin word for "deaf." Those who turn a deaf ear to these words of Jesus choose a path which leads to death. The word "obey" comes from the Latin word for "to hear," or "to listen." If we hear with open ears, we open ourselves to the grace of obeying his words about the way of compassion, righteousness, and ultimately sharing in his cross. Obeying will bring us not death in Gehenna, but life in the Kingdom of God.

34. 27th Sunday in Ordinary Time

Readings
Genesis 2:18–24
Hebrews 2:9–11
Mark 10:2–16

34.1 October 5, 2003

The Pharisees rarely asked Jesus a question because they were interested in his response. Usually, they were trying to trap him, and that is what knew that the Law of Moses allowed divorce. They knew that there were two widely different interpretations of the Law of Moses allowing a man to divorce his wife. Rabbi Shammai insisted that a man could divorce his wife only if in the case of adultery. Rabbi Hillel interpreted the law much broader, allowing men to divorce their wives for any reason – bad cooking, body odors, sloppy housekeeping – you name it!

In response, Jesus acknowledges that the Law of Moses allowed divorce – but only because people hardened their hearts. He avoids the question and insists that the real issue is marriage, not divorce! By quoting Genesis, he says that it has been part of God's plan from the beginning that a man and woman become one flesh. The word for flesh implies much more than two bodies coming together. It implies a unity of body, mind, heart, and spirit that cannot be broken by anything, except for death. For those who believe this, Jesus says that divorce is not an option.

In spite of his words, every one of us is affected in one way or another by the reality of divorce. Spouses struggle with his words when they are abused or manipulated by their partners. Divorced

Catholics struggle with his words when they realize that a civil divorce does not end what we consider to be a valid marriage. But, in struggling with his words, we must avoid the mistake of the Pharisees. We cannot forget the real issue – the nature of the Sacrament of Marriage. In defining marriage as a Sacrament, we take seriously the words of Jesus that when two people bind themselves as one flesh, nothing can separate them except death. It is a clear, but difficult teaching, in a world where there is often very little clarity.

We may be a Church wounded by scandal. But we are also a Church that is clear when we teach about the nature of marriage, and about all areas that define the dignity of human life. During this month of October, we reaffirm our belief that human beings are created in the image of God, and that the dignity of human life must be protected. That is why we take strong stands against abortion, capital punishment, euthanasia, and a number of issues that affect the dignity of human life.

Together, with the mutual support of this community of faith, we must face these difficult issues as they occur to us in our daily lives. It is with the clear teachings of Jesus and with our Church that we have the confidence to handle them.

34.2 October 8, 2006

Jesus knows that the Pharisees are laying a trap for him. Talking about divorce was as much of a controversial topic in the first century as it is in the twenty-first century. In the first century, some rabbis argued that a husband could write a bill of divorce only if the woman committed adultery. Others allowed the husband to divorce his wife for any reason, even if she was a bad cook. However, only the husband had the right to divorce – never the wife. Jesus responds by cutting through all these arguments and appealing to the second chapter of Genesis. When a man and woman join themselves to each other in a radical way as one flesh, he says, God intends for that communion to be unbreakable.

The Church today struggles to be faithful to this vision. Because being faithful to the words of Jesus involves so many complicated issues, we are covering them in the five-week series on Thursday evenings at 7:15 in the gym. Each session can stand on its own, and you can come this week, even if you have been unable to do so before.

After the General Intercessions at Mass, we continue to pray for another holy communion – the communion that results from our baptism and profession of faith. We tend to think of that communion only in terms of what we see – the limits of this parish. But that communion also involves the local Church – the Diocese of Fort Wayne-South Bend – under the leadership of our shepherd,

Bishop D'Arcy. As we prepare for this year's Annual Bishop's Appeal, please direct your attention to the back of the church. Watch and listen as Bishop D'Arcy outlines the needs of our communion – both at Saint Pius and including the broader local Church.

34.3 October 4, 2009

The Biblical story begins with God. The first chapter of Genesis shows God's delight in creation. In the first story, God pronounces the work of creation as "good." *An• it was goo• ...an• Go• saw that it was goo• ...an• Go• saw that it was very goo•*. We hear this refrain repeated at the end of each day. However, when we get to the second creation story in Genesis, there is a jarring interruption to this pattern. In this story, God says that it is **not good** for the man to be alone. The gift of creation may be very good, but his being alone is not. So, God forms a woman from the rib of the man. He does not take the woman from the animals, but from the very substance of the man. This detail tells us that God creates a radical equality of two very different persons. Adam joins God's delight by crying out, "This one at last, is bone of my bones and flesh of my flesh." With this step, God created the beginning of human relationships and pronounced them good.

When the Pharisees approach Jesus in today's Gospel, they are acutely aware of the destructive effects of sin and the ways in which relationships can turn sour. They ask him a question about divorce, not because they are sincerely seeking his opinion, but to try to trap them. Jesus recognizes their trap and tells them that the Law of Moses allowed divorce, only because of people's hardness of hearts. In responding, he is well aware that the laws of divorce were very discriminating against women. Only men could file for divorce, and the rabbis argued about the reasons. Some argued that men could divorce their wives only in cases of infidelity. Others allowed divorce if the husband did not like his wife's cooking.

Rather than getting trapped, Jesus points to Genesis and says that God's intention from the beginning was that man and wife should remain one, and that following God's intentions is the way to maintain human relationships. Jesus calls on those who follow him to know the intentions of the Creator and work to keep this vision of the goodness of human relationships.

We are followers of Jesus Christ. But, we still struggle with the same problems. It is good for us to reflect on these words on this day which has been set aside for many years as "Respect Life Sunday." In a culture which tends to emphasize many other priorities, we are reminded of the centrality of married love. Most of you live out your baptismal promises as married people, and living this Sacrament is the way you are becoming holy. The Church has developed laws to deal with the breakup of marriages. While they may be challenging, they are ways of being faithful to Jesus' command that a valid marriage is indissoluble.

As we reflect on the impact of our culture on human relationships, we also become aware that it does not support the priority of the gift of human life. The laws of our country allow the taking of a human life in the womb of the mother for any reason. With the pornography industry as one of the biggest industries, God's gift of our human sexuality is taken out of context and misused time and time again. The culture tends to look at those who have any disability as not quite useful. Our laws allow capital punishment, even though studies have shown that our safety is not protected by this practice. Some are advocating for euthanasia and pushing this direct killing of a human being at the end of life to be put into law. And the list goes on.

Pope John Paul II called on Catholics to help create a culture of life in order to combat a culture that brings so much death. Today's Scripture readings set the tone for this month. They challenge us to see the goodness of human life and human relationships. They encourage us to do what we can to preserve and hold both sacred.

34.4 October 7, 2012

As Jesus gets nearer to Jerusalem and to his impending death at the hands of the authorities, the opposition to him is mounting. The Pharisees ask this question about divorce, not because they want his honest opinion, but because they want to trap him and draw him into one of the great polarizing debates of the day. Jesus knows their intent and asks them what Scripture says about divorce. The Pharisees quote the Book of Deuteronomy which says that a man could write a bill of divorce and dismiss his wife for a scandalous act. Jesus knows that there is a huge debate about how to interpret this "scandalous act." Rabbi Shammai interprets a scandalous act very narrowly as an act of adultery. Rabbi Hillel, however, defines a scandalous act in much wider terms. According to Hillel, the wife can scandalize in almost any way – with bad cooking or critical talk of her in-laws. In this debate between the two extreme interpretations, Jesus knows that the woman has absolutely no rights. She cannot initiate any legal proceedings, nor can she defend herself in any way.

Instead of getting caught up in endless arguments about the reasons for a man to divorce his wife, Jesus argues that Moses had made the accommodation for divorce because of the hardness of their hearts. Then he quotes from the first book of the Bible. Genesis clearly states what had been God's original intentions in creating man and woman. God created woman from the rib of man, not to allow men to dominate or control women, but to show the radical equality of man and woman, created in his image. God created man and woman to be complementary to one another, Jesus argues. When man and woman are joined as one flesh in marriage, that bond cannot be broken. In speaking of marriage, Genesis uses the term "one flesh" to mean not only the physical union of a couple in the marital act, but also the total spiritual unions of their being.

As we know, divorce continues to be a hotly debated topic in our culture today. It affects all of us. That is why it is good for us to focus on this very direct teaching of Jesus. When couples enter into the Sacrament of Matrimony, the Catholic Church always presumes that this bond is strong enough to last until death. Because of these words of Jesus in the Gospels (and in the letter of Saint Paul), we do not see divorce as ending a valid bond of marriage. Divorce becomes an absolute last resort, when all else has failed.

This month has been set aside as "Respect Life" month. Please take some time and look at the display about our respect life ministries in the back of church. If you can give your time and talent to one of these ministries, you can help further our work to respect the dignity of human life from conception through natural death. But if you are married, you can also further the cause of respecting life by putting new energies into that unbreakable bond between you and your spouse. Healthy bonds of marriage show us in action what the love of God looks like in our parish. If you are having difficulties in your marriage, be humble enough to seek help in healing and strengthening your bond. If you are separated or divorced, don't be afraid to ask for help in healing and learning to move forward.

Jesus balances his tough teaching about the unbreakable bond of marriage with a gentle embrace of children. He becomes impatient with his disciples for trying to dismiss children whom they regard as having no status and whom they regard as unworthy of Jesus attention. He draws them to himself and uses them as an example. Just as children are vulnerable and receive his presence in a simple and uncomplicated way, so he urges us adults to have a similar attitude. If we can maintain the simple and vulnerable attitude of a child, then we can count on the Lord's presence in the ways we live our commitments, both in good times and in bad.

34.5 October 4, 2015

The Pharisees are not interested in hearing the opinion of Jesus about the difficult subject of divorce. They realize that Jesus knows the Scriptures. Moses is clear in Deuteronomy 24:1-4: a husband can divorce his wife. They want to draw Jesus into the current contentious debates about how to interpret this Law. Will Jesus side with the Rabbi Hillel, who is very conservative and limits the reasons for divorce to infidelity? Or will he side with Rabbi Shammai, who is so liberal that he would allow any reason for divorce (like the wife burning toast)? Jesus does not take their bait and enter into their arguments, just as Pope Francis did not take similar baits in his visit to our country. Instead, Jesus cites a higher authority. He quotes the second chapter of Genesis and points out that, from the beginning, God intended that man and woman should be united in one flesh. Formed in one flesh (physically, spiritually, psychologically, and emotionally), Jesus teaches that no one can separate this radical union. In a perfect world, symbolized by the Garden of Eden, Jesus makes God's intention for marriage clear. Marriage is intended for harmony, mutual love, and complementarity between the two sexes.

As we know all too well, we do not live in a perfect world. We live in a world wounded by our own sin and the sin of others. In this fallen world, it becomes much more difficult for couples to maintain this radical union until death. But in this fallen world, we remember that Jesus Christ is the Messiah who has come to save us and to usher in the Kingdom of God. For this reason, the Church has faithfully maintained this difficult teaching in her proclamation of God's Kingdom. The Church has always taught what Jesus teaches today: a valid bond of marriage is indissoluble and ends only with the death of one of the spouses.

You who are married know that this is a difficult teaching. There is no such thing as a perfect marriage. You know that you carry the cross when you open yourselves to the grace of the Sacrament of Marriage and allow the Lord to help transform your love gradually into the reality of remaining together as one flesh. When you face challenges and outright obstacles, it is hard work to maintain your union in one flesh. You need to be humble enough to seek professional help when you cannot work things out on your own. You need to understand that working on your bond of marriage affects a community much wider than the two of you.

Many of you have found that you cannot live this union of one flesh in a fallen world, and you have either separated or divorced. You understand that a civil divorce does not end a valid bond of marriage, precisely because of what Jesus says in the Gospel. That is why the Church has set up the Marriage Tribunal process. Directed by the Bishop's Judicial Vicar, Father Mark Gurtner, the Tribunal is given the task of examining whether that bond of marriage truly existed from the beginning. It is not an easy process. But it is intended to remain faithful to the teaching of Jesus about one flesh and our Catholic understanding that a valid bond of marriage is indissoluble. Do not be afraid of the Tribunal. Bishop Rhoades has eliminated all charges for annulments, and Father Gurtner is working to make our Tribunal more efficient. Pope Francis has recently made changes to streamline the process and make it easier.

The Letter to the Hebrews reminds us that Jesus Christ was made for a little while lower than the angels when he took on human flesh. In his human flesh, Jesus knew suffering and death. Jesus knows the pain of those of you working to remain one flesh, those of you who are separated or divorced, and those of you who are widowed. Take courage! The Lord calls you his brothers and sisters. He will not withhold his grace and mercy in this central and critical vocation in our Church and in our world.

34.6 October 7, 2018

When the Pharisees ask Jesus their question about divorce, they already know the answer. The Law of Moses allowed a husband to divorce his wife. They are trying to trap Jesus into taking sides on the issue of what constitutes the reason for the divorce. Those who interpreted the law strictly argued that infidelity would be the only reason. Those who interpreted the law loosely argued that any reason would suffice. A husband could divorce his wife if he did not like her cooking. Filing for divorce was the husband's right. The wife had absolutely no rights.

Jesus knows the hardness of their hearts and that they are trying to justify their actions by appealing to the law. He appeals to God's original plan in Genesis. God created us in his image. God made us male and female. God intended the union of husband and wife to be a relationship that can only be broken by death. Pictured as the first of the mosaics in the main aisle of our church, this covenant of marriage reflects God's unconditional love for us.

When the disciples find themselves alone with Jesus in the house, they also question him about his teaching. They find it difficult. He rebukes them and invites the children to come to him. Children have a way of being vulnerable and putting their trust in those who love them. We see this type of trust when we offer Penance Services in Advent and Lent to our children. They come rushing to the priests who are seated for the Sacrament of Reconciliation. They display a trust in the Lord who will forgive them. Those who enter the permanent covenant of marriage can have the same trust that the Lord will give them the strength to die to themselves so that they can rise with the Lord and their spouse and children.

We find this teaching as difficult today as the first disciples of Jesus did. In fact, this Gospel is the basis for the Church's teaching on the indissolubility of marriage. We believe that once a couple has entered into a valid bond of marriage, only death can end that bond, and not a legal decree of divorce. Unfortunately, divorce is part of the fabric of our culture, as it was at the time of Jesus. Every one of us has been touched by divorce, in one way or another.

At Saint Pius, we work to help parishioners to uphold this difficult teaching. Our parish team works with couples preparing for marriage. We have developed programs to assist married couples. We have offered "date night" for married couples, giving them a chance to join other couples in reflecting on the Lord's presence in their marriage. Lou and Lori Giovannini are currently offering their seminar, Married in Christ. We provide resources for those in troubled marriages, giving recommendations for professional therapists who believe in marriage. We offer the services of the Marriage Tribunal to those who have experienced the scourge of divorce. Going through the Marriage Tribunal is challenging. It asks the question whether the marriage under study truly had everything needed to be considered a valid bond of marriage that can only be ended by death. We offer a special ministry to those going through the process.

Jesus' teaching on marriage is indeed difficult. Those of you who have made that permanent commitment know the crosses that you must carry to continue to live that Sacrament. But you also need to know the graces that come from your sacrifices. The month of October is dedicated to our conviction that we are made in God's image and that we must safeguard the right to life from conception through natural death. Please visit our website and the display in the Parish Life Center for ways to be involved. But also know that if you are struggling to live the Sacrament of Marriage, you are already involved as you trust in the Lord's presence in your marriage, as children trust those who love them.

35. 28th Sunday in Ordinary Time

Readings
Wisdom 7:7–11
Hebrews 4:12–13
Mark 10:17–30

35.1 October 12, 2003

Bibles seldom come with the warning – "dangerous to your health." But, the Letter to the Hebrews tells us today that the Word of God can be very dangerous. That letter describes the Word as living, effective, and penetrating – a two-edged sword that has the power to lay us bare. The Greek word for "laying bare" can have three meanings, depending on its context. In athletics, it described the way one wrestler held an opponent by the throat so he could not escape. In cooking, it meant the flaying of a piece of meat. In legal terms, it described the practice of putting a dagger with its point upward on the chest of a person being led to execution. The dagger prevented the man from bowing his head. Instead, he had to show his face and accept the dishonor of the onlookers.

That is exactly what happened to the rich man in today's Gospel. Jesus spoke his living and effective word and laid him bare. Held in a chokehold, he looked on the face of the Incarnate Word of God and was invited to face the truth. The truth was tough! His many possessions had become an obstacle to eternal life. However, he could not face the truth and walked away sad. When we gather to celebrate the presence of the Incarnate Word of God here, that same living and effective Word lays bare whatever obstacle keeps us from living the Gospel and inheriting eternal life. There can be

many obstacles in our lives. Power or titles can become obstacles.
For young people, refusing to trust the experience of parents or
teachers can be obstacles. More often than not, wealth can become
an obstacle.

We may not be as wealthy as Bill Gates. But, compared to the
style of living for most people in the world today, every one of us is
wealthy, in terms of material blessings. Jesus looks at us with love
today and asks whether our wealth has become an obstacle. It is an
obstacle when we spend huge amounts of our time and energy worrying about our financial security. It is an obstacle when we ignore
the needs of the poor. It is an obstacle when we North Americans
believe that we have no responsibility for the way the rest of the
world lives.

Last week, I went with our parish stewardship committee to an
annual Stewardship Conference in Chicago. We came back even
more committed to nurturing the growth of this spirituality in our
parish. Christian stewards do not have to feel guilty about the blessings we have received. Rather, Christian stewards see everything
as a wonderful gift from God. With that awareness, Christian stewards become more grateful and are more willing to give a first portion back. From my own personal experience, sacrificing a first
portion of my time, talent, and treasure has been a powerful way
in which God's Word has opened my heart to blessings that I could
never have imagined.

Sometimes we think that Jesus' words about wealth today apply
only to a few – like Anthony of Egypt, or Saint Francis of Assisi,
or Mother Theresa. In fact, Jesus' living and effective words are
meant for all disciples. In speaking to the rich man, Jesus may have
bared him to the truth. But, he also spoke that word to the rich
man "with love." He may have gone away sad. In other words, he
walked away grieving the loss of something he felt he could not
sacrifice. The words of Jesus may lay us bare and expose us to those
obstacles to eternal life. But, he speaks to us with love and promises
that sacrificing our obstacles will be rewarded – not only in eternity,
but here and now. It is a promise he keeps.

35.2 October 15, 2006

Saint Mark takes care to tell us that Jesus loved the young man who
approached him with an honest question – "What do I have to do
to possess eternal life (to be part of the Kingdom of God)?" Jesus
approves of the ways in which he already treats his fellow men and
women in the ways established by the Law of Moses. And yet, he
knows that there is one obstacle standing in the young man's ability
to receive the gift of eternal life. The young man's riches have become a stumbling block, and Jesus asks him to give them away and

follow him on the road to Jerusalem, a request made in a spirit of love, but rejected in an attitude of fear and an ability to trust. The rich young man goes away sad.

Jesus does not mince words this week, any more than he minced words about divorce last Sunday. Jesus looks at us with love and tells us that the blessings of wealth and possessions automatically bring with them dangers to our eternal salvation – stumbling blocks to the Kingdom. He does not condemn wealth or possessions in themselves. He simply calls us to evaluate them honestly and ask ourselves if they can lead us to a greed that consumes us and stands in the way of the needs of the poor.

It is in this spirit that Bishop D'Arcy asks us to share some of our wealth with the local Church through the Annual Bishop's Appeal. Jesus insists that the bonds of communion are more important than wealth. In fact, he promises family connections not just in the life to come, but also in this life. That is precisely what the Annual Bishop's Appeal strives to do – to put our resources at the service of a holy communion. The Annual Bishop's Appeal benefits the communion that is the local Church – the Diocese of Fort Wayne – South Bend. Our goal this year is $189,000, which will benefit the Diocese in ways in which the Bishop himself outlined in the DVD last Sunday. But the Annual Bishop's Appeal also builds up our holy communion in this parish. Once we have exceeded our goal, all donations above that amount stay in the parish. As we prepare to break ground next Sunday for a new Education Center, that portion of our wealth which we share will serve our holy communion for a long time. Instead of becoming a stumbling block, it becomes a service to our Holy Communion.

35.3 October 11, 2009

The rich man is a good man. Mark makes that clear when he tells us that Jesus loved him. But the rich man goes away sad, because he considers his wealth to be an end in itself. Jesus clearly tells him that wealth has no value in itself. It only has value when put at the service of building up relationships. It is only in this spirit that we ever ask for financial support. It is in this spirit that Bishop D'Arcy asks us to consider a commitment to the Annual Bishop's Appeal. Please turn to the back of the church to listen to his request.

35.4 October 14, 2012

The rich man in today's Gospel has two assumptions which are correct. First, he assumes that even though he is wealthy, faithful, and successful, something in missing in his life. Second, he assumes that Jesus can help him. The man does not accidentally bump into Jesus. He **runs** to Jesus and kneels before him, acknowledges his power, and fixes his eyes on him. However, his next assumption is not correct. As a successful person, he has done a many good things and has worked to keep the commandments. So, he assumes that he can do something else to inherit eternal life. But Jesus' answer stuns him. The rich man does not have to do anything, because salvation is a gratuitous gift from God. All he has to do is to give away his wealth, and God will grant him eternal life. The rich man takes his eyes off Jesus and goes away sad.

This incident completely blows the minds of the disciples of Jesus, because they assume that wealth is a reward for a life well lived. But we need to remember that Jesus looks at the young man with love. He truly wants the best for him. He is not making up some new commandment. He is simply pointing out to the rich man that the issue lies with the first two commandments. He may have thought that he loved the Lord his God with his whole heart, his whole mind, and his whole soul. But, there is a problem with the second commandment. The rich man has put false gods ahead of the one and only God. His false god, his security blanket, is his wealth. It has become an obstacle. It blocks his vision of Jesus, and he cannot let go of it.

The response of Jesus might also trouble us. I certainly never thought of myself as "wealthy." But, going to Uganda for the dedication of Father Larry's new church revealed to me that I am very wealthy. I live a very comfortable life and take for granted the comforts that the vast majority of his parishioners do not have. My wealth and comfort can become obstacles to my salvation. They can direct my eyes away from Jesus and focus on those things that do not last. And the same is true of you. We can become consumed with worry about accumulating more stuff. We are tempted to focus all of our energies on climbing the ladder of success and forget that God gave us those gifts in the first place. We can see only what can benefit us and forget about the Lord's invitation to become humble servants of others. Then, we fall into the same trap as the rich man. Wealth can be an obstacle to salvation. And Jesus looks at us with his eyes of love and invites us to invest ourselves in those realities which last.

Those realities involve first and foremost our relationship with God. Through the Father and with the Son and in the Holy Spirit, all of our other relationships have eternal value. Jesus invites us today to keep our eyes fixed on him, serve the needs of others, and trust that he will give us what we need. He loves us, just as much as he loved the rich man. He poured out his entire life on the cross for us, just as he did for the rich man. He does not want us to walk away sad.

35.5 **October 11, 2015**

We know very little about this man who approaches Jesus today. Many Scripture scholars have called him a young man, because he runs to Jesus (unlike old guys with hip replacements!) As the story unfolds, we learn that he has many possessions. And yet, despite the obvious security that comes from his wealth, he senses a desire for more. Like all of us, he senses that only eternal life – life with God – can fully satisfy him. And he comes to the right person. He could have knelt before Caesar, looking for power; or before Herod, looking for more riches; or before the keeper of the royal treasure, looking for more riches. In kneeling before Jesus, he asks what he needs to do to inherit eternal life.

In response, Jesus quotes the Law of Moses and tells him to cut out those things that separate a person from God. He lists a few of the commandments dealing with relationships with other people. He must avoid killing, committing adultery, stealing, bearing false witness, defrauding other people, and disrespecting parents. The man responds that these egregious sins have not been part of his life. Hungering for something more, he wants to take the next step.

Jesus looks at the man with love. He sees this man's desire to take that next step in his spiritual growth. So he tells him the truth: you need to move out of your comfort zone. You need to sell what you have, give it to the poor, and follow me. But the man goes away sad, because he cannot rely on anything for security other than his many possessions. He cannot embrace this cross and put complete trust in the power of Jesus to give him eternal life.

As the disciples of Jesus watch this man walks away sadly, they are blown away. They live in a culture that regards wealth as a sign of God's favor. Jesus is turning the cultural norm upside down, as he has been turning so many other expectations upside down. The Messiah will win the victory through suffering and death. The last will be first. Wealth can be an obstacle to membership in God's Kingdom. Only through the power of God can anyone be saved.

We became disciples of Jesus Christ when we passed through the waters of Baptism. Like the man in today's Gospel, we have a desire for something more – to share in eternal life. We have come to the right place, encountering Jesus Christ in his Word and in his Sacraments. Each of us is at a different place in removing those things that separate us from God. When we have failed, we have received the Lord's mercy, especially in the Sacrament of Reconciliation. Today, Jesus looks at every single one of us with love and invites us to take another step in faith and trust in his power to save us. The Letter to the Hebrews describes that Word well: it can cut through us like a two-edged sword, penetrating into the depths of our being.

For some of us, wealth may be the obstacle. It is tempting to put too much trust in that fancy car or lake house or extra stuff that we do not need. Jesus calls us to loosen our grip and share our blessings. Some may be holding too tightly to their free time. To those, Jesus asks for a sacrifice of time alone and to give more time in humble service to others. Others may trust too much in power or prestige. Jesus calls us to let go of that need to control other people.

We may ask the same question that the disciples asked: what is in it for us if we give up these things? Jesus gives the same answer – a supportive community, and eternal life (along with some possible persecutions). I have been reflecting on his answer during these last three weeks. Years ago, I took a pretty scary step in faith and committed myself to a life of celibacy. In my recovery from surgery, in the absence of a spouse and biological children, I have clearly seen the outpouring of love from this parish family. In humility, I understand better the Lord's promise of eternal life better. Take a step in faith to embrace the Lord's promise in your life!

35.6   October 14, 2018

The young man in today's Gospel was definitely attracted to Jesus. He did not stroll up to greet him. He ran and knelt before him. He has listened to Jesus proclaiming the Kingdom of God and wants to be part of it. He even calls Jesus good, recognizing his share in the goodness of God. The young man is sincere in following a moral life. The commandments were part of his daily life. But, he also senses that something is lacking. Jesus looks at him with love and tells him that is one thing getting into his way, preventing him from becoming an intentional disciple: his wealth. This young man walks away with great sadness, because he cannot bring himself to remove the many possessions keeping him from the Kingdom of God.

The disciples of Jesus had already left everything to follow him. Yet, they are also amazed at his words. In their culture, wealth was seen as a positive sign of God's favor. Peter speaks for the rest when he reminds Jesus that they had already given up everything to follow him. Jesus points out that giving everything away opened them to the richness of God's gifts in ways that they could never imagine. It will not be until after his resurrection that they would understand what Jesus is promising. By proclaiming the death and resurrection of Jesus Christ, these intentional disciples would attract many more people willing to embrace the kingdom of God in their midst. Even more, they would be part of an eternal kingdom without end.

We are like this young man, because we too have approached the Lord Jesus in his real presence at this Mass. We are also doing our best to keep the commandments. When we fail, we have access to the Lord's mercy in the Sacrament of Reconciliation. We who are blessed with many possessions want to be part of the Kingdom of God. We also want eternal life.

The Lord looks at us with love, just as he looked at the young man with love. Without judgment and with love, he speaks the same word to us. He wants us to take the next step in becoming more intentional disciples and invites us to remove whatever is holding us back from becoming more intentional disciples. Could it be that we pray only at Mass on Sunday, without setting aside time during the week with our family? Could it be that we cannot find time in our busy schedules to give ourselves in humble service? Could it be that we cling so tightly to our possessions that we cannot see the need to share a portion of them with others?

Each of us must answer these questions in our own unique way. Over the years, I have found the message of stewardship to be a structured way of becoming a more intentional disciple. If we regard stewardship as a way of life, and not just a fund raiser, we can understand the importance of setting aside time during the week for prayer, becoming more aware that everything is a gift from God. We can take another look at our busy schedules and carve out time for humble service. We offer many opportunities to share, not just within the context of our parish, but also to serve the needs of those who do not have the blessings that we have. We can take another look at our possessions and realize that we can set aside a first and generous portion to give back in gratitude. As a parish, we set aside a first 8.5% of our income to support our sister parish of Saint Adalbert and those who come to us in need. Our new church is a testament to those who have been willing to make financial sacrifices for the good of the community.

When Jesus challenges us in these ways, we can see the truth of the Letter to the Hebrews. God's word is living and effective. It cuts through us like a two-edged sword. Don't be afraid of that sword cutting through us today. Jesus Christ loves us and wants us to become more intentional disciples. He will keep his promise and give back more to us than we can ever give ourselves in terms of prayer, service, and sacrificial giving.

36. 29th Sunday in Ordinary Time

Readings
Isaiah 53:10–11
Hebrews 4:14–16
Mark 10:35–45

36.1 October 19, 2003

We sometimes think that the art of politics invaded the Church in recent years. But, today's Gospel reveals that being political has been with us from the beginning. Even though Jesus has told his closest disciples for the third time that his mission as Messiah was to suffer, die, and be raised from the dead, James and John were more interested in what was in it for them! They took him aside privately and asked him if they could have the best seats in his Kingdom. The others were angry, not because they did not want those best places, but that James and John beat them to the punch!

Jesus tells them that the best seats are not his to give. He can only promise that they will drink of the same cup as he does. Drinking from his cup involves pain, suffering, and death. Humble service will define greatness in his kingdom, he tells them, not blind ambition and politicking for honors.

In Rome today, the Pope marks his 25th anniversary by declaring Mother Teresa blessed. In effect, he is assuring the world that she a very good seat in the Kingdom of Heaven. But, her seat comes not from being political, but from her life of humble service to the poor and forgotten of the streets of Calcutta.

Mother Teresa began her discipleship by teaching girls in a comfortable high school near the slums of Calcutta. On her way to a retreat in 1948, she had a personal encounter with Jesus Christ. That religious experience changed her life. Impelled by that unforgettable moment, she began the process of leaving her order, founding a new one, getting approval from Rome, and changing the entire focus of her ministry.

As she responded to this religious experience, Mother Teresa drank often from the cup Jesus offers to James and John. Her extensive journals reveal that she never again felt this intense, emotional presence of Jesus Christ. In fact, she descended into a dark night of the soul, sometimes doubting whether she was doing what the Lord wanted her to do; and at other times wondering if he was really present. She continued to embrace lepers and give comfort to dying people, not because her service to them made her feel good, but because she believed that she was tending to the needs of Jesus Christ himself. In drinking this difficult cup of doubt and uncertainty, she remained faithful to caring for the poorest of the poor, sometimes in the face of harsh criticism from other people.

Few of us will ever be disciples in the same way as Mother Teresa was – either by joining her order or ministering to the lepers and dying of the streets of Calcutta. But as disciples, we drink form the same cup. Married couples may not always feel like facing issues that divide you. But you work at them, because you believe that being faithful is important. Young people do not always feel like coming to Mass or participating in the life of the parish. But you do it – not just because your parents sometimes drag you here – but because you believe that Christ feeds you to be faithful in the tough areas of your life. You who give of your time and talent to the parish may not feel appreciated. You might feel like others are taking advantage of you. But you give yourselves in humble service, because you believe that the community needs your presence.

At one level, James and John speak for all of us. We want to know what is in it for us in being a disciple. But, like James, John, Mother Teresa, and Pope John Paul II himself, we learn that Jesus does not offer us the best seats. He offers to share his cup – a cup that invites us to be faithful, even when we don't feel like it!

36.2 October 22, 2006

When James and John ask Jesus make their request, they may well have been thinking of Psalm 110: "The Lord says to you, my lord: 'Take your throne at my right hand, while I make your enemies your footstool'." Believing that he was the Messiah promised in the psalms, they wanted the best seats in the Kingdom. They may have been thinking of the best seats at the next Wedding of Cana, or the best spots on the Mount of the Transfiguration. They certainly wanted seats from which they could watch their enemies get what was coming to them. But Jesus had told them three times that his role as the Messiah would involve humiliation, suffering, and death. They had ignored these words and did not understand what he was talking about when he told them that they would have to drink from the same cup as he would.

The other ten became indignant with James and John, not because they had made this request, but because they had beaten them to the punch. In a society which emphasized honor and shame, they all wanted the best seats. And, truth to be told, so do we! We too want the best seats in the Kingdom, although we may not put it exactly like that. In fact, we often pray exactly as they did: "Lord, we want you to do for us whatever we ask of you." A friend of mine has long complained that her husband has spent too much time at work, and she has prayed that they could spend more time together. A couple of months ago, her husband was diagnosed with brain cancer, and he had to quit his job. She spends all of her time with him, taking him to the doctor, and driving him nuts with the way she drives. When I visited them, I was struck by their affection for one another and for the way they truly treasured spending time together. She took me aside and advised me, "Be careful what you pray for!"

James and John eventually learned what they were praying for. After their Lord's dying and rising, they began to figure out that the only way to the best seats in his kingdom was to hang – one on his right, and the other on his left – on the cross that took his life and would eventually take theirs. In their Holy Communion with all the saints in the New Jerusalem, they have been given their seats by the Father, who accepted the perfect sacrifice of his Son. My friends are carrying their own heavy crosses now, and they are now drinking of that cup of which Jesus speaks, just as they drank from that cup when Joni battled breast cancer and their son served in Iraq. That cup comes to all of us sooner or later, either through the crosses thrust upon us by life, or through the consequences of our decision to make the way of Jesus Christ an integral part of our lives. I join my friends in praying for Bob's recovery and healing. But we also join them in praying the Lord's Prayer, in which we say, "Thy kingdom come, thy will be done, on earth, as it is in heaven."

36.3 October 18, 2009

James and John make request we can all understand. They had given up everything to follow Jesus, because they believed that he was ushering in God's Kingdom. They recalled the words of Psalm 110, which promise true believers that they will be seated at the Lord's right hand. They want those best seats in the house. They want recognition, honor, and privileges for the sacrifices they have made to follow him.

But, they have not been listening to Jesus as he describes the true nature of what it means to be the Messiah. They have ignored his talk of suffering and dying. They have been focusing on sharing the cup of joy, mentioned so often in the Scriptures. Jesus rebukes them, because they ignore the cup of suffering, which is also mentioned often in the Scriptures. He is to be baptized into an overwhelming floodwater of pain, suffering, and death. He understands his role, because he has been listening to what the Father wants. The brothers are very clear about what they want. What the Father wants is different. He wants them to follow the way of the Suffering Servant, learning from him what it means to be a humble servant.

You and I have also made our own sacrifices to follow Jesus Christ. More and more members of this parish have embraced stewardship as a way of life. We take seriously the Lord's call to pray, especially to gather here every Sunday for the Eucharist. We give our time and talents in service. We share generous portions of our treasure to support the work of the parish. Like James and John, we too want to be recognized for what we do. We desire the honor and privileges that should come to us as a result of our sacrifices. But in pursuing these desires, we can also cause discord and division. The other ten became indignant at James and John, not because they made the request. They became indignant, because James and John beat them to the question. Those desires caused tensions and divisions within the 12.

Jesus speaks to those of us who are priests and leaders of the Church. Like James and John, we have our own desires to be recognized, honored, and blessed with special privileges. Jesus tells us that our first task is to drink the cup of suffering with him and allow ourselves to be immersed in the baptism of denying ourselves for the good of the flock. It is a good reminder, because the Church has always suffered when her leaders have put their own comfort and desires ahead of the needs of those we were ordained to serve.

Jesus also speaks to all who are trying to be good stewards. Discipleship (a.k.a. Stewardship) has the power to build up the body of Christ, especially when disciples share that baptism of self denial and drink the cup of Christ. But when stewards start worrying about being recognized, or honored, or given privileges, the divisions that affected the 12 will affect us. We can become indignant, bringing on division and hard feelings.

At the 8:45 and 10:30 Masses, we celebrated the Rite of Welcome. We welcomed those who have never been baptized as Catechumens, and those who have been baptized in another denomination as Candidates for Full Communion. The Rite of Welcome is intended to make sure they feel welcomed into this community. But in welcoming them, we were also honest with them. We invite them to walk the same way of discipleship that we are called to walk. We made the sign of the cross over them several times to remind them that following Christ involves sharing in his baptism and drinking his cup. In struggling to know the Father's Will in their lives, they too will open themselves to becoming good servants. As good servants, they will learn to trust that the Father will share with them the Glory of his Son, only after they share in his baptism and in his cup.

36.4 October 21, 2012

James and John enjoyed privileged positions among the followers of Jesus. These two brothers were among the first who responded to the call of Jesus. Along with Peter, they went alone with Jesus to the mountain and witnessed the transfiguration. Jesus took Peter, James, and John with him into the house of Jairus to heal his daughter. It will be Peter, James, and John who would accompany him into the Garden of Gethsemane shortly before his arrest. But the brothers want more. They approach Jesus and ask him for a special share in his glory. Actually, I've studied the text carefully and have discovered what they really want. They want to be named Monsignors! And the other ten become indignant, because they want to wear those cool cassocks too! James and John just beat them to the punch!

This request of James and John is especially outrageous, because Jesus has just told them what kind of Messiah he would be. Instead of going to Jerusalem to kick out the Romans, he will go there to be treated like so many of the prophets and murdered outside the city walls. He will be raised from the dead, but the way to that resurrection must begin with dying a horrible death like a criminal outside the city walls. Those words of Jesus bounce off the disciples' hardened hearts like seeds bouncing off a field of rocks. They just do not listen. They can think only in terms of those glamorous qualities of being associated with the Messiah. They are drawn to his miracles and the ways in which he drew huge crowds. They do not understand that those miracles simply revealed who he really is. They do not understand that his mission was to give his life as a ransom for many.

In the ancient world in which they lived, many people were slaves. They became slaves because their village or town had been conquered by an enemy. Or they were sold into slavery when they could not pay their debts. They could become free people if someone stepped up and paid a ransom for their freedom. This is the image that Jesus uses. He understands our human condition. As the Letter to the Hebrews says, he can sympathize with our weakness, because he took on our human nature. He was tempted in every way that we have been tempted. However, unlike us, he never gave in to those temptations. He never allowed himself to be enslaved by any kind of infidelity or any kind of lack of commitment to God's will. By dying, he will destroy our death and slavery to sin. By rising, he will restore our life

It is easy to judge James and John harshly, because their bold request reveals their stark ambition. But we, too, have our own ambitions. No matter where we are in life, we prefer to share in the gain without enduring the pain. Young people want to succeed in school or athletics, but are reluctant to put long hours into homework or the practice field. Newly married couples want to extend that wonderful feeling of the honeymoon. But it becomes tough to die to old habits in adjusting to a new life together, especially when children come along. We might be drawn to give ourselves in service here at Saint Pius. But, that service becomes frustrating when no one seems to notice the sacrifices that must be made. It is easy to get discouraged when those giving themselves in humble service are carrying the weight for so many who do not invest themselves in any way.

Jesus is clear about what his Church should look like. He is not looking for magenta piping on cassocks, or positions of prestige or honor. He is looking for humble service and a willingness to share in his dying. He is interested in disciples who believe in the redemptive power of his dying, so that they can share the triumph of his rising. He knows that true greatness involves being a true servant.

36.5 October 18, 2015

An avowed atheist visiting Saint Pius would feel vindicated by the first reading. Isaiah the prophet announced that the Lord was pleased to crush his faithful servant in infirmity. The atheist's response would be something like: "See, you crazy people worship a God who acts more like Darth Vader hammering Luke Skywalker with a light saber than a loving Father who loves and cares for each person!" We might also wonder what Isaiah is talking about!

To understand, we need to listen to the other two assigned readings for this Sunday. Through the Scriptures, the Lord is trying to help us to understand the nature of true greatness. The Letter to the Hebrews reminds us that God so loved the world that he emptied himself and took on our human form. The Letter recalls the image of the high priest who entered the Holy of Holies in the ancient

Temple in Jerusalem each year on the Day of Atonement. Our high priest, Jesus Christ, offered the perfect sacrifice to atone for the sins of humanity. He offered himself on the cross, trusting that his loving Father would accept his sacrifice, raise him from the dead, and ascend him to the heavens, the eternal Holy of Holies. Our high priest knows the ways in which life continually crushes us, because he shares the weakness of our human condition.

In the Gospel, Jesus is trying to explain this concept of greatness to his disciples. For the third time, he says that he will conquer the power of sin and death through his sacrifice on the cross. He has been trying to teach that his true greatness will come from suffering and death. But, they are not listening. Instead, James and John want to be named Monsignors and wear their fancy cassocks with cool magenta buttons and sit on either side of the great presider's chair of Jesus in the Kingdom of God. And the other ten don't get it either. They are angry, because James and John beat them in seeking their share of power, honor, wealth, and pleasure.

Jesus is very patient. He asks if they can drink the cup that he will drink. Even though they do not understand that this cup is the cup of suffering, they agree. He asks if they can be baptized. Even though they do not understand that this is a baptism in the floodwaters of pain, torture, and death, they agree again. He tries to explain again that true greatness comes not from the perks of power and control over the lives of other people, but from humble service. Just as a person would pay a financial ransom to free a slave, Jesus will pay the ransom of his own life to free us from our slavery to sin and death.

The disciples will eventually learn this lesson after the death and resurrection of Jesus Christ. Fourteen years after this exchange, Herod would behead James, who would become the head of the Church of Jerusalem, just as he had beheaded John the Baptist. The disciples will learn from the risen Lord the meaning of true greatness. They would see their humble service cause the infant church to grow and expand beyond their wildest dreams.

The Lord is teaching us the meaning of true greatness. Being great does not involve piling up wealth, titles, privileges, and pleasure. Even though these things are not bad in themselves, we can use them in selfish ways. Rather, the Lord is calling us to use them in service of other people. When a gunman murdered nine people at Emmanuel African Methodist Episcopal Church in Charleston earlier this year, the members looked at the painful way in which the Lord seemed to be crushing them in their infirmity. Instead of realizing the gunman's vision of creating a race riot, they publicly forgave him and prayed that God would have mercy on him.

Their example displayed extraordinary humble service that can inspire and motivate us to understand what it means to be great. Our greatness comes from humble service to our brothers and sisters, not from acquiring wealth, titles, privileges, and pleasure for ourselves.

36.6 October 21, 2018

James and John enjoy a privileged position among the Apostles. Jesus has taken them aside many times at critical times in his ministry, along with Peter. They had been with Peter when Jesus had been transformed on Mount Tabor. They had enjoyed a glimpse of his true nature and future glory. They already know that Jesus has given Peter a position of primacy in the Church to be established. So, it is completely understandable that they would approach Jesus and ask for places of power and honor and prestige when Jesus comes into his glory. They are following their natural instincts.

However, their timing is horrible. On the way to Jerusalem, Jesus has been teaching them that as Messiah, he is the suffering servant of Isaiah. When Isaiah said that God was pleased to crush his servant in infirmity, he was not talking about a blood thirsty tyrant who can only be appeased by suffering. The suffering servant willingly takes the place of a guilty Israel to suffer the consequences of their sinfulness in a redemptive way. As the promised suffering servant, Jesus would take upon himself all the effects of human sin, hatred, rejection, and betrayal. For the third time, Jesus clearly tells his apostles that their journey on the road to Jerusalem will result in his sacrificial death on a cross. He will drink the cup that represents the Father's will for him in his mission of salvation. He will pay the ransom for the consequences which humankind deserves for our embrace of sin.

James and John have not been listening to his words. Instead of yelling at them for not paying attention, he asks if they can drink of that cup. They glibly say that they can. But Jesus knows that they have no idea of what they are talking about. In time, they will understand that the crucified Lord is surrounded by two thieves on as he dies on the cross on Mount Calvary. He gives himself as a humble servant. After the resurrection, they too will understand that their privileged leadership in the Christian community will involve humble service, and not power and honor and prestige. In being humble servants, they will eventually drink of that same cup and show the world a different style of leadership. They too will share in the redemptive suffering of the one who has taken upon himself the sins of the world.

If we study the history of our Church over the past 2,000 years, we can see many examples of privileged leaders who have understood their roles as humble servants. When leaders have shared in the redemptive suffering of Jesus Christ, the Church has flourished. But, when privileged leaders have repeated the mistake of James and John and have put their desires for power and honor and prestige ahead of the needs of the faithful, the Church has suffered. We are living in such a time now. We see the incredible damage done when certain priests and bishops have put their own pleasure and interests ahead of the people they should have been serving as humble servants. They have done great damage to the Body of Christ.

Jesus speaks directly to us who have the privileged position of being leaders. He reminds us that we are called to be humble servants, putting the needs of the people ahead of our own desires and needs for recognition. He reminds all of us who have become his disciples to imitate his example and trust in his redemptive suffering to triumph over the power of sin and death.

Bishop Rhoades has asked us to pray the Prayer of Saint Michael the Archangel at the end of all Masses. The enemies of the Church are having a field day over our current situation. We will ask for the intercession of Saint Michael the Archangel to aid us in our battle with Satan. In praying this prayer, we will also express our trust that the Lord's redemptive suffering will guide us out of this time and triumph over the powers of hell.

37. 30th Sunday in Ordinary Time

Readings

Jeremiah 31:7–9
Hebrews 5:1–6
Mark 10:46–52

37.1 October 26, 2003

For the last few weeks, Mark has introduced us to some interesting characters – all of whom had good physical sight. However, all of them had difficulty seeing Jesus as he was revealing himself to them. The apostles could not see his true mission as messiah, because they were busy arguing about which of them was the greatest. The rich young man could not see the generous offer of salvation, because he was blinded by his wealth. James and John could not see him serving the needs of others, because they had their eyes set on the best seats in his Kingdom.

Today, Mark introduces us to Bartimaeus, a man who had no physical sight. And yet, this blind man saw the truth more clearly about Jesus of Nazareth than any of the others. Unlike the apostles, he saw what kind of Messiah Jesus was. He called him "the son of David" and asked for pity, not dominance over the Roman occupiers. Unlike the rich man, Bartimaeus saw that his possessions were not important. In fact, Bartimaeus trusted Jesus so much that he threw aside his cloak to come to him – a foolish action for someone who needed that cloak for protection against the cold of the night. Unlike James and John, he was not looking for rewards. He saw Jesus as the Suffering Servant who could teach him how to serve.

Odds are pretty good that most of us have pretty good vision. Even those of us who have to use reading glasses can see well enough to get around. And yet, as we gather to celebrate the Lord's real presence, we all have our own areas of spiritual blindness, much like those who walked with Jesus on his way to Jerusalem. Bartimaeus challenges us to examine our eyes of faith and admit the ways in which we are truly blind. Maybe we are blind like the Apostles – worrying about our reputations and titles too much. Maybe we are blind like the rich young man – tied too much to our possessions. Maybe we are blind like James and John – so worried about rewards that we are fear investing our time and talent. Over the years, the Lord Jesus has opened my eyes in countless situations to the ways in which I had been blind. By spending time in the Third World, my eyes have been opened to how blessed I am with material goods. By serving as pastor, my eyes have been opened to the importance of considering the common good in making decisions. By hearing Confessions, my eyes have been opened to my own sinfulness and stubbornness of heart. By working with a variety of parishes, my eyes have been opened to those prejudices of mine that have placed people different from me into neat and tidy categories.

With his clear eyes of faith, Bartimaeus trusted that Jesus of Nazareth had the power to give him physical sight. He had learned how to be dependent as he sat on the outskirts of Jericho begging for the generosity of pilgrims on their way to Jerusalem. Mark tells that with the gift of physical sight, Bartimaeus stood up and followed Jesus on his way to Jerusalem. In other words, he joined the apostles, including James and John, who ultimately had their eyes opened in Jerusalem when their Master was betrayed, crucified, and raised from the dead. Jesus can do the same for us. He can cure our spiritual blindness, if we only admit the ways in which we are blind. Then we, too, can continue to follow him to Jerusalem.

37.2 October 29, 2006

For most Sundays in this current liturgical year, Saint Mark has been taking us along "the way" with Jesus. Jesus began his "way" to Jerusalem by healing a blind man, setting the theme for the journey. On the way, Jesus works to open the eyes of his disciples to the true meaning of his mission as Messiah, and to the central role of his suffering and death in that mission. On the way, we have met some interesting characters who have been having difficulties seeing that truth and accepting it.

A few weeks ago, we met a sincere young man who respected the Law of Moses. Jesus affirmed his fidelity to the commandments and looked at him with love. However, this young man could not see that his many possessions were an obstacle to follow Jesus on the "way." Like the camel who could not get through the eye of the needle, he went away sad, carrying the burden of his wealth with him.

Last week, Mark told us about a request made by James and John. Filled with blind ambition, they could not see that their request for the best seats in the Kingdom totally violated the spirit of humble service and the complete giving of self required of those who would drink the same cup as Jesus. James and John may have continued on the "way," but they remained pretty clueless.

This week, we meet another man who is physically blind. Like so many destitute people, Bartimaeus knew that the best place to receive alms from pious pilgrims on their way to the Temple in Jerusalem was to camp outside of Jericho, where the pilgrims began their climb from the depths of the Dead Sea to the heights of Mount Zion. This man may not be able to see anything with his eyes. But, the gift of faith he had received enabled him to see the truth about Jesus. He identified Jesus as the Messiah, the Son of David. Unlike James and John, who wanted positions of privilege, he humbly asked for physical sight and mercy. Unlike the young rich man, who could not see the barriers established by his wealth, he willingly lets go of his only possession – his cloak – to come toward Jesus. His letting go of that precious possession shows the risk he takes. Had he not been healed, there was a good chance he may have lost his protection in the cold of the night. But, his faith in Jesus as the Messiah became his salvation. He joins Jesus on his "way" to Jerusalem, and in the very next chapter of Mark's Gospel, walks with him as he enters into Jerusalem in triumph, only to be betrayed, crucified, and raised from the dead.

Mark introduces these characters to us, because he wants us to see those things in our lives which blind us and keep us from walking the "way" with him. Like the rich young man or James and John, we are often the last people to recognize our own blindness. Greed and blind ambition are only two possibilities of many that can keep us from following Jesus Christ on the "way." For that reason, Mark invites us to listen even more carefully next month during the final week of the liturgical year. The readings will open our eyes to the reality of death – not only the deaths of our loved ones, but also the inevitability of our own deaths. The November Scripture readings are not intended to frighten us, but to open our eyes to the truth about our lives and our priorities. Does wealth or the desire for wealth blind us to the more important relationships around us? Does ambition blind us from the Holy Communion we are meant to share with each other? The Scriptures of November become like

Bartimaeus inviting us to accept the gift of faith, let go of our security blankets, and trust the power of Jesus to save us.

37.3 October 28, 2012

During the past few Sundays, Saint Mark has been telling us about the encounters between Jesus and prospective disciples on his way to Jerusalem. He encountered a rich man who wanted to share eternal life. When Jesus told him to give away his wealth to the poor, the man went away sad. His possessions meant too much to him. Last Sunday, James and John asked him for places of honor when he would come into his glory. They had completely misunderstood that his identity had been tied to the role of the suffering servant. He told them to become humble servants without caring about positions of honor.

Today, Jesus encounters a blind man on the outskirts of Jericho. Like so many beggars shouting to pilgrims as they began their final 15 mile climb to Jerusalem, Bartimaeus is used to asking for alms to meet his daily needs. But today, he asks for more than coins. He shouts to Jesus and calls him by his messianic title: Son of David. The crowd tries to silence him, much as Jesus had tried to silence those who used that title in the first part of Mark's Gospel. But he keeps shouting. So, Jesus tells people to call him over. Unlike the rich man who could not part with his many possessions, Bartimaeus readily throws aside his only possession – the cloak that provides warmth at night – and rushes toward Jesus. Jesus addresses him with the same words that he had used with James and John, "What do you want me to do for you?" Instead of asking to be named a Monsignor, Bartimaeus reveals his deep faith in Jesus and asks to be able to see. When Jesus restores his sight, he tells him to go his way. Instead, Bartimaeus chooses to follow the way with Jesus. He goes up to Jerusalem with Jesus to participate in his triumphal entry into the city, to share in his passion and death, and to have a portion of his resurrection.

Jesus invites us to reflect deeply on these encounters and to take another look at what might be obstacles to becoming better disciples. These encounters teach us to share our wealth with those in need, instead of allowing it to become an obstacle. These encounters teach us to share in his role as a humble servant without worrying about reward or recognition. Today, he calls us from those times in our lives when difficulties blind us to God's presence in our lives. The other disciples urge Bartimaeus to take courage and approach Jesus. The root word for courage is to take heart. In taking heart, we know the love of God, and we allow the love of Jesus Christ to empower us and to throw away those things that hold us back.

At the 8:45 and 10:30 Masses, a good number of children, adults, and teens are doing just that. They have been inquiring into the Catholic faith for months. Today, they take their first step in the Rite of Christian Initiation. Those who have never been baptized are being accepted as Catechumens. Those who have been baptized in another Christian denomination are being welcomed as Candidates for Full Communion. As Catechumens and Candidates, they will join us for the Liturgy of the Word and be dismissed after the homily to enter more deeply into the Word of God. Supported by their sponsors, they will continue to open their eyes to Jesus Christ and his teachings on Tuesday nights. As their faith grows, they will see more clearly the presence of Christ in our community.

For our part, we can support them and pray for them. Perhaps our best gift to them is to deepen our own faith. We have to admit that sometimes the darkness of life comes from the bad choices we make, from the sins that cloud our vision. Jesus invites us to come to him, to allow him to open our eyes to his wonderful mercy, and then to follow him on the way to the New and Eternal Jerusalem.

37.4   October 28, 2018

For the past few Sundays in the Gospel of Saint Mark, Jesus has been walking with his disciples on the way to Jerusalem. On the way, he has called people to follow him. One young man responded with enthusiasm and asked what he needed to do to belong to the Kingdom. Jesus looked at him with love. But, when Jesus told him to give away all his wealth, the young man went away sad. He could not see the benefits of giving his wealth away and trusting the spiritual riches open to him through Jesus Christ.

Those disciples who had left everything continued to follow Jesus. On the way, he has been teaching them that the promised Messiah would not be a conquering hero bringing great honor and prestige and power. Instead, he is the Suffering Servant promised by the Prophet Isaiah. Once they reach Jerusalem, he would be rejected, betrayed, and crucified like a criminal. The disciples could not hear this message. In fact, James and John displayed their blind ambition by asking him to sit on his right and left in the Kingdom

Today, Jesus and his disciples reach Jericho to begin their ascent to the Holy City of Jerusalem. As they leave town, a blind beggar starts yelling. He has obviously heard of Jesus, because he calls him the son of David, a title indicating his true nature. He asks for mercy, much as we asked the Lord for mercy at the beginning of Mass. Just as the disciples had tried to silence the children who were drawn to Jesus, they try to silence Bartimaeus. Just as Jesus had called the children and used them as examples of how to trust, he calls Bartimaeus and asks what he wants. Unlike James and John,

Bartimaeus does not want power and prestige and honor. He just wants to see. Unlike the wealthy young man, he trusts so much in the Son of David that he leaves his only possession, the cloak which kept him warm at night, to run toward Jesus. Bartimaeus becomes a true disciple and follows Jesus on the way to Jerusalem.

Bartimaeus has much to teach us about being intentional disciples of Jesus Christ. We may not be physically blind, but we all have plenty of blind spots. The divisions in our Church and our country can close our eyes to the person of Jesus Christ in the pain of other people, in those most vulnerable members of our society, or even in those who drive us crazy. We may not be in the 1% of the nation's wealthy people, but we tend to cling tightly to our possessions and status. Bartimaeus teaches us to acknowledge that we cannot save ourselves. We need to cry out to the Son of David for mercy. He teaches us that we can see more clearly with the eyes of faith. He teaches us to let go of what we think will save and protect us and follow him on the way.

At the 10:00 Mass this morning, we celebrate the Rite of Acceptance for a number of people who have never been baptized and the Rite of Welcome for those who have been baptized in another Christian community and want to be in full communion with the Catholic Church. Each person has heard the Lord Jesus calling them. Each of them has let go of their free time on Tuesday evenings to join us for prayer, catechesis, and formation. Today, they take the first formal step toward encountering Jesus Christ in the Sacraments of Initiation at the Easter Vigil. We pray for them, support them, and join them in learning the lessons of Bartimaeus. He followed Jesus to the cross and experienced the resurrection. Together with our Catechumens and Candidates for Full Communion, we continue to walk the way of discipleship through our crosses to share in the resurrection of Jesus Christ.

38. 31st Sunday in Ordinary Time

Readings

Deuteronomy 6:2–6
Hebrews 7:23–28
Mark 12:28b–34

38.1 November 5, 2006

The scribe is not asking Jesus an innocent question with an easy answer: "Which is the first of all the commandments?" Closely connected with the Pharisees, who saw the Law of Moses as the key to living their Covenant with God, he knows that there are 613 laws. As a scribe who knows all the laws, he helps ordinary people, who had other things to worry about in life, to navigate through these 613 laws and apply them to daily life. In fact, his question is impossible, and he knows it.

Jesus responds by quoting Scripture. He quotes the Book of Deuteronomy, with the familiar words of the "Shema Israel," prayed every day by faithful Jews: "Hear, O Israel! The Lord our God is Lord alone! You shall love the Lord your God with all your heart, with all your soul, with all your mind, and with all your strength." Then, he quotes the Book of Leviticus: "You shall love your neighbor as yourself." By joining these two commands – love of God and neighbor – he tells us that loving God and loving neighbor cannot be separated or prioritized. We love God by loving our neighbor, and we love our neighbor by loving God. They cannot be separated.

We began November by celebrating the Solemnity of All Saints. The Feast of All Saints is a perfect example of the response Jesus gives to the scribe. Those countless men and women who surround the Throne of God in the Heavenly Jerusalem are completely and totally united with God and with one another. The saints are in absolute and full communion with God, and they are in absolute and full communion with one another. Nothing separates them, as the two commandments cannot be separated.

That is why we make special efforts this month to pray for those who have died. God wants our loved ones to be joined to that great Communion of Saints as much as we do. In praying for our deceased loved ones, we commend them to God, trusting that his love and mercy will burn away whatever remains an obstacle to that full communion. We call this process "Purgatory," which we sometimes translate into a place where people spend time. Neither time nor space exists in eternity. When our loved ones opened their eyes in eternity, they completely and totally saw the truth about their relationships with God and neighbor. In the light of eternity, they can see what separates them from full communion with God, and what separates them from full communion with each other. In seeing and knowing the pain that comes from lying or spreading gossip or telling lies or being unfaithful, they are also fully exposed to the fiery love of God, which burns away those obstacles, not to punish them and make them miserable, but to heal them and make them totally one with the Communion of Saints.

As we pray for our deceased loved ones who see completely in the light of eternity, we can open our eyes to those things that damage or destroy our holy communion here. Even though the scribe may have asked a confrontational question, Jesus noticed that he responded with understanding to the radical way in which he joined the two great commandments. The scribe was taking a first step on the road of conversion to the kingdom of God. Jesus invites us to look squarely at the reality of our own deaths, to see more clearly the ways in which we need to repair damages to holy communion with God and neighbor, and to take another step ourselves toward that kingdom of God. We trust in God's healing love, here and in eternity.

38.2 November 4, 2018

When the scribe asks Jesus about which is the greatest of the commandments, the question is much more difficult and complicated than we might think. At the time, there were 614 Commandments just in the first five books of the Bible – the Torah. And for each of these commands, scribes and teachers would develop ways to interpret each of the commandments. For example, there were 39 different categories of work that must be avoided just on the third commandment to observe the Lord's Day! Despite these well intentioned efforts to help people follow the law, law-abiding Jews were crushed under the burden of laws and interpretations.

Jesus responds by quoting from the Book of Deuteronomy: you shall love the Lord your God with every fiber of your being. This commandment is at the heart of both the Old and New Testaments. If we love God, then God will come before anything else we might hope for: power, wealth, success, security, comfort, prosperity, control, or prestige. Then he quotes a second passage from the Book of Leviticus: you shall love your neighbor as yourself. Jesus so radically combines these two commandments that they cannot be separated. We cannot love our neighbor if we do not love God. We cannot love God if we do not love our neighbor.

This love has little to do with emotions or warm feelings. Jesus has already shown the depth of God's love by taking on human flesh and identifying with us in every way except sin, as the Letter to the Hebrews insists. In just a few days after this exchange with the scribe, he will demonstrate his love for neighbor by offering himself as a sacrifice on the cross. This love has no limits, and this love cannot be defined by rules or laws. We live the Great Commandment when we imitate the love of Jesus Christ – placing God above every other reality and giving ourselves in humble service to others.

The Gospels also make it clear that Jesus defines the word "neighbor" in a much wider context than would the scribe. A neighbor is not just someone in my clan or class or tribe or race. A neighbor (as we learn from the parable of the Good Samaritan) is anyone we encounter who is in need. We show our love in many diverse and challenging ways.

That is why the Diocesan Office of the Propagation of the Faith assigns a mission preacher to each parish every year. That office connects one mission from a struggling area to a parish in our Diocese, giving us a chance to share our resources with our neighbors. Most mission speakers stand up here to present the needs of their missions. This year, the office has allowed us to respond to the needs of someone we know very well. Father Larry Kanyike has been to Saint Pius often to present the needs of his people. Through our response, he has been able to build a health clinic, a new church, and most recently a new school. Now he is asking for our help in furnishing a convent to house the sisters who teach in his school. He emailed me last week, saying that the Archbishop of Kampala is celebrating Mass in his parish this Sunday to celebrate the tenth anniversary of the founding of his parish. Remembering his hour-long homily at the dedication of the new church, I wonder how long he is talking today!

The mission preachers in the past have asked us to trust their word about their needs. I have been to Father Larry's parish and have seen their needs myself. Since his "day job" keeps him at his parish this weekend, I am asking for your help in his name. The image of Saint Charles Lwanga, one of the Ugandan martyrs on our triumphant arch underscores our connection with Father Larry and his parish. You will find pictures of the church and the school in today's bulletin. You can place your donation in one of the envelopes in the pew. I can assure you that Father Larry puts our gifts at the service of his people, who are most grateful for our help.

39. 32nd Sunday in Ordinary Time

Readings

1 Kings 17:10–16
Hebrews 9:24–28
Mark 12:38–44

39.1 November 12, 2006

When people think of generosity, they sometimes cite Bill and Melinda Gates as an example. Bill and Melinda distribute a staggering 1 billion dollars a year to aid children in Africa. In traveling to that developing continent, they can see with their own eyes how their extreme generosity benefits so many children. But they also can "afford" to be generous. They retain 50 billion for their own use and the use of their business.

In much the same way, Jesus watches the wealthy of his day make large donations needed for the upkeep of the Temple of Jerusalem. Those generous paid for the operating expenses of the Temple, and they could see the benefits of their generosity as their dropped their many coins into one of the thirteen upright metal trumpets that funneled their donations into the treasury below. However, the loud noise of those large coins does not attract his attention. What he does notice are the two tiny coins put into one of those trumpets by a poor widow – half pennies that would hardly have made any noise at all and which contributed little to the upkeep of the Temple. He notices her, because she gives of her substance, of what she needs to survive, unlike those who gave large amounts and kept a sizeable amount back for their own welfare. He notices her, because he is about to give us the total gift of his life on a hill of execution outside the city walls.

When we talk of stewardship around here, I fear that too many associate that term with raising money. Stewardship really begins with prayer. If we truly spend significant time in a prayerful reflection on the Word of God, we will better understand what the widow of the first reading did. In a sense, Elijah was the prophet most people blamed for the drought that was causing her so much suffering. He had been God's messenger to tell the people that the drought was a result of their infidelity to the Covenant. Instead of seeing him as an enemy, she trusted the Word of God which he spoke and served him a portion of the last bit of flour and oil she had saved for their needs.

To try to make that point, we plan to invite the parish to enter into a deeper spirit of prayer during Lent next year. We will depart from our custom of taking the two Sundays before Lent to speak of Stewardship. Sometime during the Easter Season, we will sponsor a ministry fair, inviting people to understand better how they might serve the parish community. We will simply trust that the fruit of prayer during Lent will open our hearts to make a gift of some kind of humble service to the parish, recognizing all the other ways in which we respond to God's Word by giving service.

I have come to trust that parishioners will share a portion of their resources once they get involved in the parish and see for themselves how those resources are used to provide better service to the community. The widow who got the attention of Jesus saw the fiscal needs of the Temple, even though the Scribes who were running it had a tendency to exploit poor people like her. Hoping that I am a better steward of parish resources than they were, we will not talk about the sharing of resources until the fall.

Stewardship is not a gimmick to raise money, but it truly is a way of life that involves sacrifice. At this Mass, we celebrate the total gift of Jesus in the sacrifice on Calvary, a gift that gives us the fullness of life. Our two widows provide good examples, because both responded to the Word of God and gave a generous portion of themselves. Both the prophet Elijah and the Incarnate Word of God noticed those gifts, seen as insignificant in the eyes of the world, but eternal in God's eyes.

39.2   November 8, 2009

In the ancient world, widows lived precarious lives. In a society which depended on men alone, women without connections with men had no safety net. The Law of Moses may have urged faithful sons and daughters of Abraham to provide special care for widows, orphans, aliens, and strangers. But, they lived in abject poverty, depending on the kindness of others. In living this kind of life, they also learned important lessons in how to trust.

The widow of Zarephath is a good example. She lived in the home town of Queen Jezebel 800 years before Christ. She had talked her husband, Ahab, into replacing worship of the God of the Covenant with devotion to the Baals. As a result of this lack of faith, the prophet Elijah had announced that God would withhold rain as a punishment for infidelity.

The widow of Zarephath suffered from this drought. She was collecting a few sticks so she could prepare what little flour and oil she had left as a final meal for herself and her son. In walks Elijah, the spokesperson of the God who caused the drought! He asks for a drink of water. The widow, aware of the demands of hospitality, gives it to him. Then, he makes an outrageous request. He asks her to make him a cake out of her remaining flour and oil, trusting his word that she and her son would not starve to death. Amazingly, she trusted him. Because she gave of her substance, she received enough flour and oil to last until the rains came.

The widow in the Gospel is cut from the same cloth. She places in the Treasury of the Temple not one, but two small coins. Jesus notices her gift and praises her for it. She too has learned how to depend on the kindness of others. She displays the same trust as the other widow. He points her out as an example of what he will do in just a few days. Like the widow who gives from her poverty, Jesus will give of his entire life as he is crucified on a cross outside the city.

In noticing her, he warns two other groups. He does not condemn the Scribes for wearing their robes of scholarly office or for taking their rightful places in the synagogues. Rather, he warns of the outward dangers of external piety. Like the Scribes, we priests and religious leaders can easily assume that our external expressions of piety are sufficient for leading people to God. He warns us that they can all too easily become substitutes for authentic faith. We too can be tempted to use our positions as trustees of the estates of the widows to benefit ourselves. He gives a similar warning to those blessed with material wealth. Like the rich of Jesus' day, we can make the same mistake and confuse the size of our gifts with the intentions of our hearts. He warns that the amount means very little. What matters is the intentional gift of ourselves.

Both widows remind us that learning lessons of trust and giving of ourselves is a lifelong process which begins with taking small steps. You children learn that lesson when you respond to your Mom's request to watch your little brother or sister while she runs an errand, without complaining or making excuses. We guys may want to take a break after supper. But we learn to give of ourselves when our spouses ask us to help with the dishes. We come to understand, like the Little Flower, that learning how to trust and give of ourselves begins with the little things in life and grows into a habit of generosity and trust. As we develop that habit, we bring our gifts of self, both big and small, to this Altar every Sunday. We join our sacrifices with the sacrifice of Christ. Then we simply trust that those sacrifices have eternal value.

39.3   November 11, 2012

The Prophet Elijah displays an amazing trust in God when he obeys God's word and goes to Zarephath. That region is "enemy territory" for him! The cult of the Baals thrives here, and the pagan followers of the gods of fertility blame Elijah for the drought which has gripped the area. God does not send him into enemy territory to a wealthy benefactor who can supply all his needs. He sends him to a poor widow with no social safety net whatsoever.

In turn, this widow displays an amazing trust in Elijah's word. Knowing that she has enough flour and oil to provide only one more meal for herself and her son, she trusts the prophet's words that she should not be afraid. She gives to him what would have been the final bit of food for herself and her son. Only after giving that incredible gift does she receive the gift of the flour and oil for a year's supply of food. We can only presume that she will eventually come to understand that in trusting the prophet's word, she was actually trusting in God's word, in contrast to the fertility gods whose words had been empty.

We meet another widow in the Gospel. Widows were the most vulnerable people in the ancient world, because they had no male to provide for them. In contrast to the religious leaders who show off the visible signs of their religion, this nameless widow quietly approaches the collection basket of her day. The scribes are in better financial situations, and can afford to throw large amounts into the Treasury without affecting their lifestyle. Their contribution will definitely help the bottom line of the Temple expenses. In contrast, the widow throws in two small coins which will not buy too many bricks. But Jesus notices her sacrifice, because she gives from her needs. Like the widow of Zarephath, she trusts the word of God without fear.

These two unnamed widows teach us a great deal about faith. They teach us that God's Word can be trusted. As we go forward from the elections of last week, the widows remind us that our ultimate salvation and well-being do not rest with candidates or political parties. God's Word will guide us as we continue to walk together on our pilgrimage to the New and Eternal Jerusalem. God will provide for our needs, just as God provided for the needs of the widows.

They also teach us the true meaning of sacrifice. The Lord invites us to see sacrifices as an integral part of our faith. The word "sacrifice" comes from two Latin words, *sacrum* (holy) and *facere* (to make). We are made holy when we make sacrifices out of love. During this last week, God has noticed every sacrifice we have made, no matter how big or small. God has noticed the decision of a teenager sacrificing time to hang out with friends to spend time with family. God has noticed the sacrifice of parents getting up in the middle of the night to take care of a sick child. God has noticed the sacrifice of a parishioner bringing a dish for a funeral dinner. We bring all of these sacrifices, along with the sacrifice of our financial tithe, and place them before the Altar. We ask that the Father accept these sacrifices, joined with the ultimate sacrifice of Jesus Christ, the great high priest. The Father does not consider the quantitative amount. The Father accepts the depth of the sacrifice.

That is exactly Saint Mark's point when he tells us this story about the widow in the Gospel. Her sacrifice points to the sacrifice that will be made a few days later on Calvary outside the walls of the city. As the widow gives of her substance, Jesus will give of his very life, trusting the Father's promise of resurrection. As the Letter to the Hebrews reminds us, Christ's sacrifice has already reconciled us with the Father. In gratitude and love, we continue to offer our sacrifices as we eagerly await him in his second coming. In making those sacrifices, we are guided by God's Word and fed by the Eucharist, which will never run dry.

39.4   November 8, 2015

The Scripture readings today offer two unlikely teachers in the ways of faith. We have no idea of their names. Both are widows. Both lived in poverty at the bottom of society. In a male dominated society, life was difficult for a woman not attached to a man providing for his family. There was no safety net in ancient Israel. Psalm 146 (the appointed psalm today) mentions widows as those who are in special need of God's help.

The widow of Zarephath is not even Jewish. In fact, she would regard Elijah as her enemy. Elijah was blamed for the extreme famine that hit the northern kingdom. He had spoken strongly against King Ahab and his pagan wife Jezebel, because they had turned against the God of the Covenant and built shrines to gods whom they claimed could bring fertility. Instead, the God of the Covenant brought drought. In a desert like atmosphere, Elijah asks the widow for a cup of water. Even though he may have been her enemy, she offers the water, as she would to any stranger entering her village. Then he asks for some food. Even though she is about to use up her last bit of food supplies, she responds to the request of this man who speaks for his God. She makes him a cake first and trusts his word that God would provide food for her and her son. Her trust is rewarded, and she has enough for all three to eat for an entire year.

The widow in the Temple is Jewish. Like the scribes who have important positions in the magnificent Temple being rebuilt by Herod, she understands the importance of the Temple as the dwelling place of God and the center of prayer. Like the wealthy scribes who deposit coins into the thirteen trumpet shaped containers for the restoration and upkeep of the Temple, she also deposits coins. Unlike the wealthy scribes whose large coins attract lots of attention, she deposits two tiny coins that most people would not even notice.

But Jesus does. He has just entered into Jerusalem to the shouts of "Hosanna to the Son of David," the title used by blind Bartimaeus in Jericho. He uses the example of this poor widow to teach his disciples how the Son of David should behave. The Son of David will not draw attention to himself with long robes, seats of honor, and the fancy titles of the scribes. Instead, the Son of David will be stripped of his robes, nailed to a horrible instrument of death, and mocked by those who pass by. Using the language of the Letter to the Hebrews, he will give himself as a sacrifice once for all. He will give us life by losing his.

This is the paradox that both widows teach us about faith, and especially about being good stewards. Like the widows, we believe that all that we have is a gift from God. Like the widows, we can continue to keep giving of ourselves and not be afraid that we will run dry. God cannot be outdone in generosity. God does not measure the amount of time, talent, or treasure that we give away. God measures our willingness. That is why we have decided not to list specific names in our current capital campaign. Of course, we cannot build this new church without large gifts, and we are grateful for them. We are not asking for equal gifts, but for equal sacrifice. As we sign the beam that will be part of a physical structure of a church built of stone, we know that God is forming us as living stones into a remarkable temple to reflect his glory.

Because of their poverty, the widows also teach us how to trust when things go badly for us. They are both at the bottom of their worlds. When we hit bottom, we too can look for an Elijah to tell us not to be afraid and to trust that God will provide what we need. We can trust that Jesus notices our dilemma and gives us strength to see that in our lowliness, we are worthy in the sight of God. It is this trust that enables us to live the Paschal Mystery that we celebrate at every Mass. In losing ourselves, we gain the fullness of life beyond our imagining.

39.5   November 11, 2018

Widows in the Ancient Near East lived at the bottom of society. Without any social safety net in a world where men earned their living, widows were extremely vulnerable. This would have been especially true of the widow of Zarephath in the first reading. Her situation was even worse, because she lived in an area where there had been a severe drought for years.

Into her life walks Elijah. The widow would regard him as the enemy. He was the one who announced the drought as a punishment for the sins of King Ahab and his wife Jezebel. Yet, the widow still offers him hospitality – a small cupful of water. Amazingly, she trusts his word that his God would provide for her and her son when she makes a small cake out of the little oil and water that she has left. She puts herself into the flow of God's giving by giving the little she has. God rewards her trust by providing food for her and her son for an entire year.

Centuries later, Jesus encounters another widow in the Temple. Like the widow of Zarephath, she too is at the bottom. Jesus criticizes the learned theologians who are at the top. They enjoy the benefits of their positions: their long robes, their seats of honor in synagogues, and the best places at banquets. They are the ones who serve as trustees for impoverished widows, keeping too much from their meager resources in payment for their services. In sharp contrast, Jesus points out the poor widow who puts two small coins into the Temple treasury. Unlike the large coins that would have made a lot of noise going down the trumpet shaped containers, her small coins would not have been noticed. But Jesus notices her. She gives of her substance, trusting the God will give back more than she could have given herself.

These two widows have much to teach us as we advance in the spiritual life. When we become too comfortable and accustomed to relying on our own resources, we tend to fill our lives with more stuff. Those who have gone through twelve step programs know this truth. It is only when they have hit rock bottom that they can begin to trust that God will provide what they need to confront their addictions. Those who adopt the attitude of the widows can actually grow in trusting that God will provide. That is why so many in our parish have embraced stewardship as a way of life. Stewardship teaches the lessons that the widows already knew – that God gives back more than we give. Good stewards set aside a first and generous time for personal prayer, especially the hour at

Mass on Sunday when we give thanks to God for all God has given. Good stewards set aside a first portion of their busy schedule to give time in humble service. Good stewards sacrifice a first portion of their treasure, instead of tossing in whatever is left over.

Jesus notices this widow in the Temple just days before he is stripped of everything and gives his life completely for us on the cross. The widow points to what he will do. He will contribute all that he has for our salvation. His trust in the Father will be returned when he will be raised from the dead and share that resurrection with those who die with him.

It takes a lot of courage to take those first steps in embracing stewardship as a way of life, because we fear that we will not have enough. But those who have taken that first step begin to experience the reality that they receive much more back than they ever give. As we pray for the courage to embrace the faith of those two widows, we also pray for our bishops, who will meet this week to confront the damage done by certain religious leaders of our time have used their positions to enrich themselves to the detriment of Christ's Body, the Church. We pray that they will have the courage to listen carefully to the promptings of the Holy Spirit to introduce reforms to the Church and healing to those who have been harmed. Our prayer is based on the experience of the widows that God will always give back more than we can ever offer.

40. 33rd Sunday in Ordinary Time

Readings
Daniel 12:1–3
Hebrews 10:11–14, 18
Mark 13:24–32

40.1 November 19, 2000

Mitch Albom wrote a book called *Tues♦ays With Morrie*. A writer for the sports page of a Detroit paper, Mitch discovered that his old friend and professor, Morrie, was dying. So, he began to visit him on Tuesdays. His book records their conversations. At one point, the dying man made this statement to his former student, "Once you learn how to die, you learn how to live." I'm going to say it again. "Once you learn how to die, you learn how to live." Everybody knows they are going to die, but nobody believes it. Most of us walk around as if we're sleepwalking. We really don't experience the world fully, because we're half asleep, doing things we automatically think we have to do. Facing death changes all of that. You strip away all that stuff and you focus on the essentials. "When you realize you are going to die, you see everything differently."

That is why November is so important for us Catholics. Our Scripture readings remind us that all of us will die, and that our world will eventually die. This focus on death is not meant to frighten us, but to remind us that we need to see things differently. They do not predict when the death of the world will come. Nor do they give us any insight into how and when each of us will die. Instead, our November liturgies call us to remember that our actions and choices have consequences. Believing that I will die gives me the opportunity to begin making changes when my actions and choices are destructive and hurtful to others and myself. If we truly believe that we will die, then we will realize that what we do now is critical. We can look at the essentials of our lives, make better choices, and see things differently.

Being away for four months has given me a unique opportunity to see things differently in my own life. I appreciated your prayers and concern, especially after the violence erupted in September. The political situation in the Middle East is complex, and we cannot make judgments too quickly. But there was something striking in the attitude of the young Palestinians in the West Bank, where we lived. Those young people had trouble looking into the future. All they could see was continued military occupation, unemployment, and lack of opportunities. As a result, they tended to live intensely in the present. They went into the streets after school and picked up rocks, knowing that they could be killed. By living in the present moment, they believed that what they were doing now had consequences for others. They believed that being part of a new Intifadah would make a difference for their people, even if they became "martyrs" themselves.

We do not need to pick up stones or put ourselves in unnecessary danger. We certainly do not need to fret and worry about when and how we will die! But we do need to believe that we will die! Once we believe that, we can live more intensely in the present and focus on the essentials. What we are doing now does make a difference, either for good or for bad. What we do now has eternal consequences!

40.2 November 16, 2003

Those who work with the Liturgy use a book entitled *The Or*o. The right side of *The Or*o gives information about the liturgical life of the Church for that day. It tells us what readings are assigned, whose feast it is (if there is a special feast), what prayers should be said, what color should be worn, etc. The left side of *The Or*o provides another useful bit of information. The left side lists the name of each priest who has died on that day from all of the five Dioceses in Indiana. This information is helpful also, because it invites us to remember those who have gone before us and to pray for them.

*The Or*o for 2004 arrived last week. As I was looking through it, I noticed that more of those names on the left side are becoming increasingly more familiar! It suddenly occurred to me that one of these years; my name would be listed on the left side of *The Or*o! That became the source for a great deal of reflection and thought!

At this time of the year, when the leaves have been completely stripped from the trees, when most of the crops planted in the spring have been harvested, and when the weather is turning a little more nasty, the Scripture readings invite us to reflect on the fact that life as we know it will not last forever. Jesus uses standard Old Testament Apocalyptic imagery to say that the world, as we know it, will come to an end. Odds are pretty good that even if we do not see that event ourselves, each of us will have our names marked in someone's Ordo sooner or later.

The Scripture readings of November are not intended to depress or scare us. Rather, they invite us to examine our lives from the perspective of death – a death that we can never avoid. Being reminded that we will eventually die is not a bad thing, because it affects the way we live. If we know that we will meet the Lord at some unknown time in the future, we will renew our efforts to recognize his presence in our midst now. If we know that we will meet the Lord, we can begin changing now those behaviors or actions that tend to alienate us from the Lord and those in communion with him.

In Mark's Gospel, Jesus makes these statements about the death of the world as he prepares for his own death. In the next chapter, he enters in triumph into Jerusalem and puts into motion all those events that lead him to be betrayed, condemned, and executed. Not only did death come to the Son of God as he hung upon the cross, but resurrection also came three days later. That central mystery of our faith is at the heart of why we can face death without fear. To the extent that we die with Christ, we will realize his promise that we will rise with him.

The obvious question is always, "When will this happen?" Jesus adamantly insists that no one can predict the end of the world, any more than anyone can predict the time or circumstance of his or her own death. But we can learn from that fig tree. Earlier in the Gospel of Mark, Jesus curses a fig tree, because it did not produce fruit. In today's Gospel passage, he uses the fig tree as a sign of hope. The cursed fig tree represents the Temple of Jerusalem, where sacrifices of animals were offered daily in the hope of achieving union with God. The fig tree that sprouts leaves represents his ultimate sacrifice on the cross, which has accomplished that union with God. The mystery of his death and resurrection provides us with the sure hope that we can continue to walk confidently in faith, being prepared for that day when our names will be one the left side of *The Ordo!*

40.3 November 19, 2006

When the Book of Daniel was written 200 years before the birth of Christ, the descendents of Abraham were living in a dangerous world. Their Greek occupiers had defined peace as uniformity in religion and culture (namely theirs!). With the Temple turned into a gymnasium, faithful Jews knew that they could be tortured or killed at any time. When the Gospel of Mark was written some thirty years after the Lord's death and resurrection, the followers of Jesus were living in an equally dangerous world. Those in Rome were being persecuted by the emperor Nero. Those who remained in and around Jerusalem lived in the midst of dangerous preparations for a revolt against the Roman occupation, which would end in the destruction of the Temple and the city.

To address these dangerous times, both Daniel and Mark turned to a style of writing known as "apocalyptic," which means "to reveal" in Greek. Apocalyptic writing uses frightening images, symbolic numbers, and visions to convey to those living in dangerous times that God will not abandon them. Daniel tells his people that the cruelty of the Greek occupiers will not prevail and promises resurrection to those who had become martyrs to justice. In Mark's Gospel, Jesus speaks of the lesson of the fig tree, which had always symbolized the messianic age for those who kept faith. In the midst of all the dangers and tribulations, his saving death and resurrection have ushered in that Messianic Age which promises hope, even in the midst of death and destruction. He tells his followers that they can wait in hope for his second coming, when he will gather his elect from every conceivable place to which they have been scattered.

We, too, live in dangerous times. Since September 11, 2001, we have become keenly aware of the dangers of our world and the darkness that surrounds us. We know the dangers of terrorism. We are horrified by suicide bombers who care little about their own lives as they take the lives of as many innocent people as possible. We tremble as we watch leaders of nations who have this same attitude develop nuclear weapons that could cause untold death and injury. We face the horrors of those ways our individual lives can be turned into darkness by the death of a loved one, by an accident or illness that will change our lives forever, or by the betrayal of those we thought we could trust.

Our Scripture readings use apocalyptic images to comfort us in our dangerous world, rather than frighten us. Christians have been living in dangerous times for the last 2000 years since the dawning of the Messianic Age. God's Word does not predict when the world will end. Jesus clearly tells us that no one knows that day. Instead, he uses it to urge us to remain faithful to his Word, especially in the midst of chaos. Nor does God's Word protect us from the dangers that surround us, especially those realities in life which we can never control, with death being the ultimate. Jesus teaches us the lesson of the fig tree. Facing the dangerous world in which we live with faith, he invites us to trust in his risen presence and the power of the Holy Spirit. Even if we lose everything else (which we ultimately will!), conforming ourselves more closely to his dying promises a full share in his resurrection. We end this liturgical year next Sunday with the Feast of Christ the King. But we begin a new year of celebrating the Mysteries of the Messianic Age on the First Sunday of Advent, when we can start all over not in fear, but in realistic hope – not just here in church, but in our daily lives.

40.4 November 15, 2009

About 150 years before the birth of Christ, the Seleucid King, Antiochus IV Epiphanes, decided that the residences of Israel should be Hellenized. He turned the Temple of Jerusalem into a gymnasium and persecuted those who refused to let go of their faith in the God of the Covenant. In response, the Book of Daniel was written to encourage the people during a terrible time. The author uses a special kind of writing called apocalyptic to tell stories about Daniel and his companions surviving persecution in Babylon some 400 years earlier. Using coded language, symbolic numbers, and visions, the author assures them that God is with them now also.

About thirty years after the Lord's death and resurrection, Christians faced an equally difficult situation in Jerusalem. The Roman commander Vespasian had abandoned his siege on Jerusalem and returned home to deal with Nero's death. The Zealot party saw his withdrawal as an opportunity to defeat the Romans, as their ancestors had defeated the Seleucids. They put pressure on the Christians to support them. That pressure included threats of execution. It is at this time that Mark records the words of Jesus just before his death. As Titus returns to finish the job of attacking Jerusalem and destroying the Temple for good, Mark records the words of Jesus and uses apocalyptic imagery to convey the need to trust in the Kingdom established by his death and resurrection and not resort to acts of violence. Just as his life is coming to an end, so will the life of the world come to an end. He will not abandon them. Just as his resurrection will transform his life, so will his coming at the end of time usher in the new and eternal Jerusalem.

As disciples of Jesus Christ, we also ponder these apocalyptic images as we come to the end of another liturgical year, and as nature prepares for the death of winter. There are always signs of our world and our personal lives falling apart. Our economy has failed, and too many people remain out of work. We fear for our safety from terrorists and their attacks. Our country is deeply divided on the best way to respond to terrorists and on domestic issues. Yesterday, we met our new Bishop. As a sure sign of the End Times, Bishop D'Arcy named me a Monsignor!

In the midst of confusing times, we too can take comfort in the words of Jesus recorded in the apocalyptic images found in Mark's Gospel today. Jesus acknowledges that things will fall apart in our lives and in our society. He confirms that there will be an end for our lives and the life of the world. He does not tell us these things to make us worry about when or how these things will happen. Only the Father knows when the end will be, and not the people who made the current movie predicting that the world will end in 2010.

But he wants us to trust his promise that those who die with him will rise with him. He wants us to learn the lesson of dying – not in some dramatic and overblown fashion, but in the small ways we learn to die to ourselves every day. He wants children to learn to die to your refusal to trust that your parents might just know what is best for you. He wants spouses to learn to die to your own desires. Quoting the Letter to the Hebrews, he wants all of us to see that our daily sacrifices can be joined with his one perfect sacrifice to bring us to resurrection with him.

Once we become more aware of the realities of the end of our lives and the end of our world, we can use God's gift of time to learn how to die better. Not only can we learn the lesson of dying, but we can also trust that God continues to teach that lesson to those who have already died in a physical and final way. That is why we write their names in the Book of the Names of the Dead and pray for them at every Mass in November. We express our confidence that God does not give up on us. He continues to teach us how to die, whether in this life or the next, with the sure and certain hope that our dying with him will bring us to rise with him.

40.5   November 18, 2012

By the time these words of Jesus were recorded by Saint Mark, Christians living in Jerusalem were living in a very difficult situation. Their fellow Jews had begun a revolt against Roman occupation. Surprisingly, the rebel forces had driven the Romans out of the city and toward the Sea. A couple of years later, the Roman general Vespasian attacked again. However, he withdrew his forces and returned to Rome when the Emperor Nero died. The insurgents put tremendous pressure on the small Christian community, reminding them of their own roots in Judaism and insisting that armed resistance would return the glorious kingdom of King David. As Saint Mark records in another part of his Gospel, families were being divided and people were being dragged into the streets, as tensions were raised to a fever pitch.

Into this dangerous and uncertain situation, Saint Mark records the words of Jesus, spoken some thirty years earlier. Jesus says that there will be huge tribulations, much like the tribulations experienced by the Babylonian captivity at the time of Daniel. As we know from history, the Roman General Titus brought his troops to Jerusalem not long after the words of this Gospel were written. His army completely destroyed the Temple and utterly devastated Jerusalem. Using the apocalyptic language of the Book of Daniel, their world utterly collapsed, with their sun and moon being darkened, with their stars falling from the sky. The powers of heaven seemed defeated when the Temple, God's dwelling place, was destroyed forever. For the believers of Jesus Christ however, the Son of Man continued to be present to them in his risen form. Even though everything they had known passed away, his words did not pass away.

We hear this Gospel proclaimed, not because we need a history lesson, but we need to hear the living Word of God addressed to us today. We too live in dangerous and uncertain times. We too are pulled in a number of directions. There are some who are arguing that the end of the world is very near. Jesus Christ speaks to us very directly and tells us that no matter what happens, we can trust his Word, because it will not pass away. We can trust in his risen presence in the Sacramental life of the Church, feeding us on our pilgrimage journey. As the Letter to the Hebrews reminds us, he has already made his one perfect sacrifice for our salvation. No matter what happens to us, that sacrifice remains effective.

We hear these readings in the middle of November, when we learn the lesson of the fig tree. The farmers are finishing their work of harvesting, and nature is preparing for the death of winter. During November, we have been praying in a special way for those who have already been gathered by the harvest of death. We hear these readings near the end of this Liturgical Year, because we know that there will be an end to each of our lives, just as the end had come for all those who names are written in our Book of the Names of the Dead.

We are reminded of all these realities, not to be frightened or to live in a depressive state of dread, but to be alert. We know neither the day nor the hour of the end of the world. The Church has been living in the end times for two thousand years so far. Nor do we know the day or the hour of our own individual deaths. But knowing that these things will happen can be a grace for the way we live our daily lives. With this knowledge, we can increase our efforts to live our baptismal promises, to increase our efforts to follow the way of Jesus Christ by dying to ourselves and letting go of those realities which cannot last. When we do this, we realize that physical death is not the end of our pilgrimage of life. Instead, it is the final door opened through the one Sacrifice of Jesus Christ to the New and Eternal Jerusalem.

40.6   November 18, 2018

Those who have children know their questions when they travel with the family by car. It is the same question I asked my Dad when he drove the family to holidays at his parents' home in Lebanon, Indiana, "When we will get there?" My Dad's stock answer was always, "It is just around the corner." When he retired and joined my brother's family and me on a hiking trip, I got even with him. He wanted to get to the end of the hike. Hearing the same response from me, he was not amused! Today, parents can use their GPS devices to give accurate information. Since little children do not understand those terms, parents still say, "It is just around the corner."

In a sense, this is the response Jesus gives to his disciples. He has already told them that the magnificent temple, which had been under restoration for 40 years, would be destroyed. He is trying to prepare them for his own death, when the sun will be darkened. He tells them that the world as we know it will pass away, and that he will come again in glory to gather his elect to himself. Like children in their parents' car, they want to know when these things will happen. Because he himself does not know that time, and because his disciples cannot understand God's time, he uses the same kind of apocalyptic language used in the Book of Daniel to say, "It is just around the corner."

Throughout this month of November, we have been praying for those whom God has harvested through death. With the Solemnity of Christ the King next Sunday, we will come to the end this liturgical year. So, naturally, with our prayers for our deceased loved ones and our focus on the end, we ask when the world as we know it will end. Jesus gives the same response to us that he gave to his first disciples: "It is just around the corner."

He speaks this truth to us, not to make us anxious or to cause us to be consumed with worry about death. He speaks this truth to reinforce our faith. As the Letter to the Hebrews tells us, Jesus Christ has already made the perfect sacrifice on the cross to defeat the power of the enemy. He has been raised from the dead and has ascended to the right hand of the Father. We live in that time between his victory and his return in glory.

But, the enemy, the devil continues to prowl about the world seeking the ruin of our souls. We live in this in-between time, when we are stretched between Christ's victory and his return in glory.

The forces of sin and evil are very much in evidence, and we experience them in our own lives and in the images of war and terror from around the world. Last year, I traveled with Margaret and Joseph Derbiszewski to Poland, where we visited the Nazi concentration and extermination camps of Auschwitz and Birkenau. It was a stark and powerful reminder of the existence of sin and evil in our world. But as moving as it was, we went to lunch afterward. We did not smell the horrible smells or see the horrific sights of the camps when they were in operation. The visit caused me to see the importance of confronting my own sins and the damage we do by the sinful choices we make that affect ourselves and others.

In this in-between time, God remains in charge. Knowing that our lives and the life of the world will come to an end, we can take great hope in the Lord's presence, not only in the sacramental life of the Church, but also in our daily efforts to die to ourselves and turn more completely to Christ. The Scriptures remind us of our mortality not to oppress us and make us fearful, but to encourage us to hope. The Letter to the Hebrews makes one final point. Having won the victory with his sacrifice on the cross, Jesus now is seated at the right hand of God and waits until his enemies are made his footstool. That will happen when the Lord comes again. For now, God is the parent driving the car. Our destination is just around the corner.

IV Lent

41. Ash Wednesday

Readings
Joel 2:12–18
2 Corinthians 5:20–6:2
Matthew 6:1–6, 16–18

41.1 February 22, 2012

The Heart Attack Grill in Las Vegas makes money by poking fun at death. In this grill, customers are known as "patients" and waitresses are called "nurses." The menu boasts of food not good for overall health. Patients can order "Bypass burgers," "flatliner" fries, buttermilk shakes, and free meals for folks who weigh over 350 pounds. A couple of weeks ago, a forty-year-old man who was eating a Triple Bypass burger suffered a heart attack. As he was being carried out, people were laughing, because they thought it was another stunt to attract business. But it was no stunt, and the owner scrambled to make sense of it. He argued in a television interview that he was sorry that the man had a heart attack. But, he argued that was doing that man a favor, giving him the right to exercise his freedom to do what he wanted.

We do not take the reality of death lightly on Ash Wednesday. The ashes which we bless and trace on our foreheads are sober reminders that all of us were created from dust, and that all of us will return to dust. We cannot avoid the stark reality of death. In the light of that certain reality, Ash Wednesday invites us to question how well we use our freedom. The owner of the Heart Attack Grill is correct. We are free to make all kinds of choices. We can choose to eat food which is bad for our health. We are also free to cut corners in our spiritual lives. We are free to cheat on tests, to lie to friends, to treat people badly, and to make all kinds of choices which bring death in many painful ways. We can be free to ignore bad habits and addictive tendencies, telling ourselves that they do not hurt anyone else. The ashes traced on our foreheads call us to do some kind of penance as a way of learning how to exercise our freedom responsibly. They remind us that true freedom lies in knowing and doing God's will.

The Ashes on our foreheads will be gone by tomorrow. But for forty days, the Lord invites us to embrace some kind of meaningful prayer, some kind of serious fasting, and some kind of generous almsgiving as a way of learning how to make choices that bring life and not death. We cannot avoid our ultimate deaths. But we can change our ways and avoid the death that comes from our sinful choices. By embracing these disciplines, we will learn the truth about the Gospel of Jesus Christ. In dying to ourselves and our own selfish wants, we learn to rise with Christ. Lent prepares us for that ultimate victory which we celebrate at the Sacred Paschal Mystery. We can face death with courage and faith, because Jesus faced his death and conquered it with his resurrection.

42. 1st Sunday of Lent

Readings
Genesis 9:8–15
1 Peter 3:18–22
Mark 1:12–15

42.1   March 12, 2000

Most parents would agree that this (a pacifier) is one of the best inventions ever! This little round piece of soft plastic is remarkable. When the baby keeps crying and all else fails, you just place the pacifier in the baby's mouth. Instant contentment!

As we grow older, we outgrow many objects associated with being a baby. But we never seem to outgrow our need for some kind of pacifier. If we start feeling empty inside; or if we are disappointed with the way things are going; or if we sense that something is missing in our lives; we stick our pacifier into our mouths and suck on it for all we are worth. There are all kinds of pacifiers – eating, shopping, working, blaming someone else, taking care of other people, or trying to control someone else. Whatever we use, our pacifier seems to give us momentary relief when we are missing love or hope or justice or mercy in our lives. That pacifier does not nourish us. It plugs the hole we are feeling at the moment.

On this first Sunday of Lent, we send eighteen catechumens to the Cathedral for the Rite of Election. These people truly thirst for the waters of Baptism. Through their participation in the Liturgy of the Word here each Sunday, through prayer, and through instruction, they have identified their pacifiers and are prepared to discard them. Since ancient times, Lent has been set aside as a time to purify them of their lingering need for pacifiers and to enlighten them to their need for God. At the Easter Vigil, they will renounce Satan and all temptations to believe that pacifiers can satisfy them. They will profess their faith that only God can deliver them from the watery chaos of life.

However, Lent is not just for these people! You and I may have been baptized. We have all used our pacifiers. If we enter into Lent to encounter God, then we must leave our pacifiers behind. That is why we might fast from a favorite food or television show. That is why we might set aside some alms for the poor. That is why we surrender some valuable time to deepen our prayer lives. Whatever we choose to do, Jesus invites us to join him in his desert experience in the depths of our hearts, to that special place within us that belongs to God alone. Nothing on earth can fill that place, despite our best efforts to try.

So, take Lent seriously! The disciplines of fasting, prayer, and almsgiving are exercises in learning to live without all those pacifiers. Allow this season to be a time when all of us finally grow up and throw away our pacifiers. Only then will we honestly say that God is at the center of our lives.

42.2 March 9, 2003

A stained-glass window in our Church pictures our patron, Pope Pius X, with a dove perched on his shoulder. That image portrays the Holy Spirit breathing gentle wisdom into his ear. It is a familiar image. There is also an Irish tradition of picturing the Holy Spirit as a wild goose. Wild geese honk and hiss at anyone perceived as threatening them. One day, while I was jogging, three of them literally chased me, honking at me, and nipping at my legs.

This is the image of the Holy Spirit in today's Gospel. Mark tells us that the Spirit **drove** Jesus into the desert – chasing after him, honking at him like a wild goose. Driven by that Spirit, Jesus learned in the desert that he must depend on his Father alone to guide him in understanding his mission. It was the same lesson that God tried to teach the Israelites as they were driven into the desert to learn how to act like free people.

Mark says very little about what happened to Jesus in those forty days. But two interesting details can fill in the blanks. First, he says that Jesus was among wild beasts. We know that dangerous animals lived in the Negev Desert – leopards, bears, wild boars, and jackals. By saying that Jesus was among them, he signals that the Messianic Age had already begun. He recalls Isaiah's prophecies that the fullness of God's Kingdom would be recognized in natural enemies living in peace with one another. Secondly, Mark says that Jesus battled Satan. In the Old Testament, *Satan* had at least three meanings. Satan is the adversary, who opposed the coming of God's Kingdom. Satan is the one who pleads a case against a person, as he argued against Job to God. Satan is the slanderer, who lied to people and made empty promises.

The Old Testament gives many details about the forty years that the Israelites spent in the desert. Time and time again, the people allowed themselves to be fooled by Satan's lies, refused to believe that God would be faithful to them, and opposed the authentic leadership of Moses. In contrast, Mark tells us that Jesus resisted the lies of his adversary. There was no argument with his Father. After forty days, he emerged from that desert even more determined to proclaim the very Kingdom that Satan opposed.

Like a honking goose, the Spirit has driven us into this desert of Lent. We are not here to win the victory over Satan. Jesus Christ has already won that victory with his death and resurrection. The Spirit has driven us into the desert to reflect on the ways we have allowed ourselves to be fooled by the Adversary – Satan – and believed in his empty promises, rather than trusting that Jesus will be faithful to us. Through our fasting, we become more aware of the ways we have followed our passions, rather than trusting in the steadfast love given us by Jesus Christ. Through our almsgiving, we realize the ways in which greed and selfishness have choked our spirits and hardened our hearts. Through our prayer, we are united with those we have alienated, taken advantage of, or ignored.

At the Easter Vigil, the Catechumens will renounce Satan and all his empty promises and profess their faith in the God who keeps his promises before they are baptized. Like the waters of the great flood in Genesis, those waters will wash away their sins and join them completely with Jesus Christ. Lent for them is a time of final preparation. Lent for the rest of us is a time to consider how Satan has fooled us and trust in God's mercy to bring us back to him.

42.3 March 5, 2006

When the Christians of Rome buried their dead in the Catacombs, they decorated the walls and ceilings with art that described their faith. Surprisingly, images of Noah and the Ark appear frequently. That story from Genesis sparked their imaginations. It also spoke of what they believed about their deceased loved ones, especially if they had been martyred. The waters of the Flood had washed away the sin on the earth and passed Noah, his family, and all the animals through the waters of the chaos to new life. In the same way, the waters of Baptism had washed away all the sins of their deceased loved ones. They had passed through the waters to new life in Jesus Christ. Now that their loved ones had passed through the chaos of death, they trusted that they would live forever with Christ.

The second reading from Peter makes the same point and sets the tone for Lent. Lent is about preparing for Baptism. That is why we send our Catechumens to the Rite of Election at Saint Matthew this afternoon. At that Rite, Bishop D'Arcy will call (elect) them for the Easter Sacraments. At the Easter Vigil, they will pass through the waters of Baptism with all their sins forgiven and emerge completely one with Jesus Christ.

We also send our Candidates for Full Communion to the Cathedral, where Bishop D'Arcy will call them to reflect on their baptism and prepare to be received into full Communion with the Catholic Church at the Easter Vigil. At the Vigil, they will also receive the other two Sacraments of Initiation – Confirmation and Eucharist.

Mark tells us that the Spirit drove Jesus into the desert, where he remained for forty days and was tempted by Satan. In the same way, the Spirit drives the Elect into the desert of Lent – to fast, to pray, and to abstain as a way of making their final preparations for the saving waters of Baptism. In this intense time, they struggle with temptations. The Spirit drives the rest of us who have been baptized into this same desert. We have to be driven, because who would choose on our own to fast from those things that we really enjoy? We have slipped back into chaos through the bad choices we have made, even though we have been delivered through those saving waters. As we do penance for our own sins, we can provide powerful support for those preparing for the Easter Sacraments. They have been meeting on Tuesday nights for several months. Now, the Spirit drives us to join them on the Tuesdays of Lent. Mass begins at 6:00 on Tuesday, followed by a simple fasting meal of soup, bread, and water in the gym. Baskets will be available for almsgiving that goes to Operation Rice Bowl, sponsored by Catholic Relief Services. At 7:30, we will gather in Church for the Lenten speaker. This Tuesday, I will speak about the words of Jesus from the Cross –"Behold your Mother."

The desert for Jesus was a physical one, where there was nothing more than the bare necessities of life. We create our own desert by the fasting we choose. In that desert, we are also tempted. I gave into temptation on the day after Ash Wednesday, using the excuse that it would be rude to refuse the beer offered me. In this desert, we can support those preparing for Baptism at the Easter Vigil. In this desert, the Kingdom of God becomes more visible as we acknowledge our sins, and we depend on God's mercy.

42.4   February 22, 2009

It seems that the reading from Genesis is in direct contradiction to the Gospel. Genesis tells us about Noah and his sons emerging from the Ark after everything was flooded on the earth. Mark tells us that the Spirit drove Jesus into the desert, that dry and desolate landscape that had tested his ancestors as they made their way from slavery in Egypt. There seems to be no connection between a world with too much water and a desert with hardly enough to sustain life.

The First Letter of Saint Peter provides the connection. Scholars believe that the portion we hear today is an early Christian baptismal hymn. The hymn encourages us to trust that Jesus, who emerges from his own baptism in the waters of the Jordan, is the Son of God who came to save us. Tested in the desert, he resisted those same temptations that drew his ancestors away from God and caused them to lose faith. Tested in the desert, his first words demand that we repent and believe in the Good News he proclaims.

Saint Peter reminds us that we are incorporated into the Mystery of Jesus Christ and his saving death and resurrection through the waters of baptism. Just as the flood destroyed a creation that had been corrupted by human sin, so baptism washes away all sins that separate a person from God. Given courage by the rainbow that speaks of God's Covenant, his promise to be faithful, Noah and his descendants became part of recreating the earth. Strengthened by the Covenant made through the blood of Jesus Christ, the newly baptized are recreated in God's image and are sent forth to be signs of Christ's Kingdom that is already present now.

When we understand the connection between the flood and the desert, we understand that Lent is all about Baptism. The Spirit drives us into the desert of Lent, just as much as the Spirit drove Jesus into the desert of Judea. The Spirit drives our Catechumens into this desert, so that Lent will become for them a time of "Purification and Enlightenment." Their desire for the waters of baptism will be purified through their self-denial, and their acts of penance will enlighten their efforts. The Spirit drives the rest of us baptized, including our Candidates for Full Communion, into the desert, so that our penance may express our sorrow at breaking our baptismal promises and prepare us to renew them at Easter. We may go kicking and screaming into this desert. But, we willingly embrace some kind of self-denial. In this desert, we pray more. We have seen clear evidence of that commitment in the large numbers of people at the Lenten Masses and services. In this desert, we fast in a way that connects us with so many who are hungry in our world. In this desert, we give alms and give away those items of clothing or toys which we do not need.

In this desert, we too are tested. Already, I feel the effects of fasting from coffee and wonder if maybe for the sake of my schedule I should get that extra boost of energy. No one will know, the devil whispers into my ears, if you have just a little caffeine here and there! You will find yourself attracted even more to whatever it is you have decided to fast from. Our resolve to use penance as a means to growing closer to God will be tested over and over again. The Israelites failed that test over and over again in their desert journey. Odds are pretty good that we will fail too. But Jesus did not fail the test, and he will walk with us throughout these forty days of Lent. We continue our journey in this desert to the saving waters of Baptism; which will wash away the sins of the Catechumens and make them new Creation; and which will recreate in the rest of us a new determination to live that new life given to us at Baptism.

42.5   February 26, 2012

At the very beginning of his Gospel, Saint Mark describes the baptism of Jesus by John the Baptist in the waters of the Jordan. As Jesus emerges from the water, he sees the sky rent in two and the Spirit descending on him like a dove. Then a voice comes from heaven saying, "You are my beloved Son. On you my favor rests." Now that same Spirit drives the Beloved Son into the desert. He is tested in that barren wilderness for forty days, much as his ancestors had been tested in their journey from slavery in Egypt to freedom in the Promised Land. Unlike the Gospels of Matthew and Luke, Mark gives us no details of that testing. He leaves the details to our imagination. However, Jesus passes the period of testing and emerges from the desert clearly as God's Beloved Son. With John the Baptist removed from the scene by Herod, God's Beloved Son begins his ministry and proclaims that the Kingdom of God is at hand. He invites everyone to become part of that Kingdom by repenting and believing in the Gospel.

We became God's beloved sons and daughters when we were baptized, and that same Holy Spirit was given to us. The Letter of Saint Peter helps us to understand the implications of our Baptism. He remarks that we can regard our baptism as a removal of dirt from our bodies, much as we washed away the ashes from our foreheads last Wednesday. Or, we can consider our baptism like the Flood which washed away the sins of the earth from God's creation. If we have been living our baptismal promises, we are appealing through our lives to God for a clear conscience and acting like God's beloved sons and daughters.

That is why the Spirit has to drive us into this forty-day desert we call Lent. We have not been living our baptismal promises, and we have not been acting like God's sons and daughters. Our period of testing is not spent in a barren wilderness filled with sand and wild animals. We enter into a desert of our own creation, defined by definite acts of penance.

Official Church laws require fasting and abstinence on Ash Wednesday and Good Friday, along with abstinence on all the Fridays of Lent. They are minimal for a reason. The Spirit wants us to design our own Lenten testing that is suited to our particular lives. We can choose from a wide variety of ways to improve our prayer life, either by coming to the Lenten Series on Tuesday, or the Stations on Friday, or an extra Mass during the week. We can fast from almost anything – food or drink, television or video games, or even bad habits we have developed. Lent has a way of opening our eyes to bad habits, like leaving Mass early. Fasting from that bad habit can open us to receive the final blessing at the end of Mass and actually spend some time talking with other parishioners. We have lots of opportunities to give alms. We can donate to Operation Rice Bowl or bring extra food for the poor next weekend. We can give those items in our closets which we no longer wear to Saint Vincent de Paul.

During this Season of Lent, our Catechumens use this time of testing as a final period of purification and enlightenment, as they prepare to make their baptismal promises at the Easter Vigil, renouncing Satan and professing faith in God. When they pass through the waters of Baptism, they will become God's sons and daughters, be sealed with the Holy Spirit, and fed with the Body and Blood of Christ. We who are already baptized join them in this time of testing, to clarify our status as God's beloved sons and daughters, and renew our baptismal promises at Easter.

42.6 February 22, 2015

The Book of Genesis is about beginnings. In the very first verse, God breaks through the chaos and imparts order by creating the world and making everything very good. Beginning with the sin of Adam and Eve, human sin affects the goodness of creation and introduces chaos into the beauty of God's creation. That chaos culminates with the destruction of the world through the flood. As we heard in the first reading, God uses the chaos of the flood to wash away sin and recreates everything. He enters into a covenant, promising a faithful love that will ultimately defeat chaos with order and beauty.

The Gospel of Mark is also about beginnings. Jesus begins his public ministry when he emerges from the waters of baptism in the Jordan River, with the Holy Spirit hovering over him and the voice proclaiming that he is God's Beloved Son. Immediately, that same Spirit drives Jesus into the chaos of the desert. It was in that desert that his ancestors had been tested about their identity as God's Chosen People. Time and time again, they failed the test. Jesus is also tested by the devil, who specializes in chaos, in tearing things apart. Even in the midst of wild beasts, Jesus remains faithful to his true identity and mission. He emerges from that place of testing to proclaim the Gospel of God. He will continue to battle the forces of the devil and all who thrive on chaos, until he finally defeats them with his death on the cross.

The Letter of Saint Peter uses the flood to help us understand our baptism. Just as the flood washed away the chaos that resulted from sin, so the waters of baptism washed away our sins and made us one with Christ. That is why the Elect (those preparing for Baptism) are so important in Lent. As Jesus was tested in his forty day stay in the desert, so our Elect will be tested in this forty-day season of Lent, as they prepare for the waters of baptism to wash away their sins and as they emerge one with Christ. During this season, most of the Rites of the Christian Initiation of Adults will focus on them, as we take them through the three Scrutinies and present the Lord's Prayer and the Creed to them. We will also anoint them with the Oil of the Catechumens to strengthen them in their battle with the evil one, just as angels ministered to Jesus in the desert.

We who are baptized pray for them. As we walk with them to the waters of baptism at the Easter Vigil, we humbly admit that we have not always kept our baptismal promises. Having been saved from the chaos of the evil one, we have made choices that introduce new chaos into our lives, affecting ourselves and those around us. We use these forty days to do penance – through prayer, fasting, and almsgiving. We embrace these disciplines so that we can draw near more closely to the Lord Jesus, who has already won the victory for us. Even though our Lenten penances can become like wild beasts sometimes, threatening to tear us apart, we can keep our eyes open to those angels who will minister to us and sustain us.

This Season of Lent has the potential to bring us closer to Christ as individuals. The Lord's merciful love restores order, no matter how many times our bad choices cause chaos. But, we are not alone in Lent. The Letter of Saint Peter reminds us that the ark became the safe haven for Noah, his family, and all the animals, carrying them through the chaos of the flood. We also have an ark. We often refer to the Church as the "Bark of Peter," carrying us through the chaos of this world. The Letter of Peter reminds us that we are secure remaining in the Church, in that ark. There is no doubt that there is incredible chaos in our world, over which we have not control. As we allow Christ to help us deal with the chaos of our individual lives, we trust that he will remain with us all in the ark that is his Church.

42.7 February 18, 2018

In the passage preceding today's Gospel, Jesus emerges from the waters of the Jordan, and a voice is heard from the heavens: "you are my beloved Son. On you my favor rests." Then, the Spirit drives Jesus out into the desert. The desert is that barren wilderness home to wild beasts. The desert is that place where the ancestors of Jesus had followed Moses for forty years to pass from slavery to freedom. For them, the desert was a place of encounter with God, who formed the Covenant with them. But the desert was also a place of testing, and they had flunked the test many times, not trusting in God and his promises. It was through the desert that the Prophet Elijah traveled for forty days to renew the Covenant that had been abandoned.

Saint Mark tells us very little about the forty days Jesus spent in the desert. He only says that Satan tempted him. We can use our imaginations about the specific ways in which Satan tempted him. We can be sure that he tested him to see if he really acts as God's beloved Son, the Messiah who will conquer the power of Satan not by force or power, but by entering into death. Because he is completely alone in the desert, no one is watching. With no one watching, he could have taken care of his comfort with his divine powers. But, he chose to remain faithful to his identity and to his mission by trusting the will of his Father.

The Spirit has also driven us into the desert of Lent. In this desert, we too are tested. Are we faithful followers of Jesus Christ or not? How do we behave when no one else is watching? Do we display signs of God's love that make the Kingdom of God a little more evident in our world? Pope Francis lists a number of attitudes that keep us from manifesting the Kingdom more clearly: selfishness and spiritual sloth, sterile pessimism, the temptation to self-absorption, constant warring among ourselves, and the worldly mentality that makes us concerned only for appearances, and thus lessens our missionary zeal.

When we embrace acts of prayer, fasting, and almsgiving in this desert, we are making a commitment to free ourselves from these kinds of attitudes. If we are serious, then we can expect a battle with Satan. The devil, who is the father of lies and prince of darkness, wants us to be selfish and lazy. He wants us to be pessimistic and absorbed with ourselves. He loves it when we fight with each other and worry only about our appearance. That is why the focus of Lent is so clearly on baptism, on being incorporated into the Body of Christ. We anoint those preparing for Baptism with the Oil of the Catechumens every week. We will use the readings from Cycle A for the Third, Fourth, and Fifth Sundays of Lent, as we pray the Scrutinies over our Elect. Those Rites for the Elect reveal the ways in which we have not been living our Baptismal promises and have turned away from an authentic encounter with Jesus Christ.

In his letter, Saint Peter reminds us of the centrality of Baptism in this Season of Lent. He reminds us that Baptism is not a removal of dirt, but a complete washing away of sin, just as the flood washed away the disintegrating effects of sin from the earth. Those who will be baptized at the Easter Vigil will renounce Satan and all his empty promises. They will emerge from the Baptismal Font completely one with Jesus Christ, with their sins washed away. Then the rest of us, who have been baptized, will renew our Baptismal Promises.

Just as no one knew what Jesus was doing in the desert, no one really knows what each of us is doing with our own Lenten exercises. We can freely choose to use the Lenten disciplines to practice dying to our own concerns and comforts, trusting that we will share in the transforming life of Jesus Christ. The Kingdom of God is definitely in our midst. Lent opens our eyes to see how we have obscured that Kingdom. Lent prepares us to renew our trust at Easter.

43. 2nd Sunday of Lent

Readings
Genesis 22:1–2, 9–13, 15–18
Romans 8:31–34
Mark 9:2–10

43.1 March 19, 2000

A little boy was walking in the woods when he stumbled upon a cocoon of a monarch butterfly. For a long time, he watched the butterfly struggle to force its way through the tiny hole in the cocoon's casing. Then it stopped making progress. It looked like the butterfly was stuck.

So the boy decided to help. He took his pocketknife and carefully cut away the rest of the cocoon. The butterfly easily emerged from the cocoon. But its body was swollen and small. Its wings were all shriveled. The boy watched for the wings to enlarge, so the butterfly could take flight. But it never happened.

The boy did not understand that the butterfly's struggle through the restricted cocoon would have forced fluid from the body into the wings. That fluid would have given the wings enough stability and strength to sustain flight. The boy did not understand that the butterfly's freedom and flight were possible only after much struggle and hardship.

That was Peter's problem. He was so overcome by his momentary glimpse into the glory of the risen Jesus that he wanted to pitch some tents and stay there. Like the boy, he wanted to be helpful by offering a shortcut to glory. Like the boy, he did not understand Jesus could be transformed only through suffering and death.

And that is our problem. We want a full share in the risen life of Jesus Christ. But we want it without pain, without stress, and without trauma. We forget that we learn through failure. We forget that we find healing through suffering. I forget that the cross burdening me at this moment is the path to the resurrection.

We can learn a great deal from Abraham. If you listen carefully to that first reading, you could almost feel the anguish and pain he experienced in taking his only son to sacrifice him. In his willingness to sacrifice literally everything, Abraham learned some valuable lessons. He learned that God regards human life as the ultimate gift, and that we are not to take it lightly. He learned that he could trust God to keep promises. He learned that God would provide more than he could have ever earned on his own.

We learn that lesson during Lent. If you have embraced some kind of Lenten penance, you are opening yourself to the lessons of sacrifice. Our personal Lenten commitments – either fasting between meals, or giving some extra treasure to Operation Rice Bowl, or spending an additional ten minutes in prayer each day – are not empty gestures. They are ways of disciplining ourselves, ways to learning how to make us holy (*sacrum facere*: the two Latin words that mean "to make holy").

The little boy meant well when he tried to give the butterfly as shortcut out of the cocoon. So did Peter. And so do we! The Father took no shortcuts when he allowed his only Son to be sacrificed. Our Lenten disciplines remind us that there are no shortcuts for us. We are practicing how to empty ourselves in sacrifice, as Jesus emptied himself. Our sacrifices do not earn us God's love. But they have a way of opening our hearts as we keep our eyes fixed on the resurrected glory awaiting those who are willing to face their daily crucifixions.

43.2 **March 16, 2003**

The prospect of a father taking his only son to the top of a mountain so that he can run a sword through him is more than we can bear! Scripture scholars give us some comfort when they explain the context of the story. In the Ancient Middle East, pagans regularly sacrificed what was most valuable to them – their oldest sons – to appease angry gods out to harm them. This story from Genesis makes it clear that God is not an angry god out to get Abraham, and that God does not want human sacrifice.

However, the point of the story is still disturbing. Complete trust in God's love and goodness always requires some kind of sacrifice. When we hear this story, we sense that it really does connect with our daily lives in difficult ways. Those who value quality family time sometimes find themselves sacrificing that promotion or salary increase, because they have put their family first. Those who are willing to speak the truth – even in love – find themselves sacrificing their desire to be well regarded by everyone. Those of you in school know all too well that your promise to remain drug or alcohol-free causes you to sacrifice a certain popularity that goes with partying.

We celebrate at this Mass the perfect sacrifice of Jesus Christ – his offering of his very life in obedience to the Father's will. At the very center of our celebration of the Paschal Mystery during the Triduum is Good Friday, when the Father's only Son was taken to the top of a hill outside Jerusalem and sacrificed. As we prepare to celebrate that Mystery, our Lenten prayer, fasting, and almsgiving can expose all those times when we have done what the pagans regularly did – sacrifice the wrong things. How many times have parents sacrificed quality family time for other values – a nice house, more prestige, or better benefits? How many times have I sacrificed my responsibility to speak the whole truth for other values – being seen as a nice, friendly, easy-going guy? How many times have students sacrificed your integrity or the trust of your parents for values that seem important – running with the in crowd, or being accepted by the in-group?

Making a decision to sacrifice the right thing is a tough decision, much like Abraham's decision to sacrifice what was most important to him. That is why we always hear the story of the Transfiguration on the Second Sunday of Lent. Jesus wants to give us a glimpse of what sacrifice brings – a sharing in the transfiguring love of the Father. Just as Peter, James, and John got a momentary glimpse of what could become of them if they trusted Jesus' promise that those who died with him would rise with him, so God gives us glimpses of what our sacrifices can bring.

We need to keep our eyes open for such glimpses this week. Maybe you parents can catch that glimpse in a momentary expression of trust on the part of one of your kids. Maybe you students might see it in the respect given by a teacher or true friend. Maybe we can examine past times when we were honest, and that honesty brought true growth. Savor those glimpses, as did Peter, James, and John. Most importantly, trust that our sacrifices – no matter how large or small – ultimately make sense within the context of the ultimate Sacrifice of Jesus Christ on the cross.

43.3 March 12, 2006

When Jesus took us into the desert of Lent, he asked a response from us through our stomachs, our hands, and our hearts. He urged us to restrict what we take into our stomachs through fasting, so we can identify with the hungry of our world. He asked us to open our hands in almsgiving, to share with the poor. He implored us to empty our hearts in prayer, to better know the will of the Father in our journey through life.

Today, he appeals to two other senses. First, he urges us to consider our eyes. He takes us with Peter, James, and John to the top of the mountain to see what they saw: his glory shining through his human body. Like Peter, James, and John, we too have caught glimpses of that glory in our lives. For some of us, it may be the first time we fell in love. For others, it might have been the day you were married or had your first child. For some, that transfiguring moment may have happened on a retreat or in the middle of a fiftieth wedding anniversary celebration. From the tops of those mountains, life seemed to make sense, and we could clearly see God's love. Like Peter, we may have wanted to pitch a few tents and stayed in that place forever.

That is what is promised at Easter – the glory of the Lord shining through the light of Christ's resurrection from the dead. At Saint Pius, we have a unique opportunity to participate in the way Christ's light will be shed at Easter. Adam Redjinski is the artist who has carved our Easter candle for the past two years. She is with us this week and will carve our candle here. She also invites parishioners to join her, study the history and significance of the Easter Candle, and learn her art. As we prepare to celebrate the light of the risen Christ at Easter, her sessions will give us a unique perspective. Details are on the special sheet in the bulletin.

Today, God also appeals to our ears. Having seen the glory of his beloved Son, the Father tells us to listen to him. Peter, James, and John had to go down from the top of that mountain and continue to walk with Jesus toward Jerusalem and his death. Those three companions who had marveled at his glory on the top of the mountain could not stay awake with him in the dark valley of the Garden of Gethsemane. They had not listened, and they ran away when their Master was betrayed by one of their own. They had no desire to build tents and stay in that difficult place for very long.

We who have caught glimpses of the Lord's glory also walk through some pretty dark valleys. When we do not see that glory, we have only our ears to hear his voice. He speaks to us through his Word, as our stomachs growl, as our hands remain extended to the poor, and as our hearts remain open to the Will of the Father. He tells us to remain faithful disciples, not only when it is easy and clear, but most especially when it is difficult and dark. With them, we come down from the mountain to continue our journey through Lent, as we question what rising from the dead really means in our lives.

43.4   **March 8, 2009**

Today, we hear the stories of two fathers, both of whom love their only sons very much. Father Abraham dearly loves Isaac. Abraham and Sarah are well beyond their nineties when they have Isaac, clearly a miracle baby! Because there is no concept of life after death, Abraham especially cherishes this son, who can carry his name and his blood line down through history.

On Mount Tabor, we see how much the Father loves his Son. When the disciples of Jesus are discouraged by lack of results and Jesus' talk about suffering and dying, the Father surrounds his Son with the hero saints of old. He makes his clothing dazzle brilliantly. And he plainly declares, "This is my beloved Son. Listen to him."

If these two fathers loved their sons so intensely, then what is this craziness of offering them over to death? We cannot listen to the story of Abraham taking Isaac to slaughter him on an altar of sacrifice without shuttering. What was the old man thinking? We would have called Child Protective Services immediately! But, in truth, Abraham was simply responding to the tenth test that God had given him. Through all of the other tests, Abraham had learned to trust that God would not abandon him. And God did not. Abraham sacrificed a ram in the thicket instead of his son. God blessed his faith with descendants beyond his wildest imaginations.

When we understand the faith of Abraham, then we can begin to understand the Father's love for us in sacrificing his only Son. On Mount Calvary, Jesus was surrounded by criminals, and his clothing was torn from his body in disgrace. Unlike Isaac, whose life was spared by the ram, Jesus actually suffered the horrors of death. But the Father proved his love for his Son by raising him from the dead. The Father did not abandon Jesus.

Because of the Father's willingness to sacrifice his own Son for us, we are blessed in ways that we can never imagine. When we pass through the waters of baptism, those blessings become ours. Every time we keep our baptismal promises, we realize the promise of Jesus that we share in his rising when we enter into his dying. That is what Lent is about. In embracing some kind of personal sacrifice during Lent, we listen to the voice of the beloved Son, who invites us to trust that the Father's way of sacrificial loving is the fullest way of loving.

By the time we get to this Sunday, we begin to wonder if all of this Lenten discipline is worth it. In the middle of Lent, the Father's way of loving may seem crazy. We may be sacrificing our favorite item for 40 days. But we begin to wonder what difference our Lenten sacrifice is making. Fasting from coffee just makes me crankier. I have less energy to do the things I'm supposed to be do-

ing. Besides, what difference does 40 days without coffee do for a
world so hopelessly messed up anyway?

It takes discipline to be authentic disciples. Being faithful in
small matters does make a difference, precisely because it opens
our hearts to the love of the Father who sacrificed his only Son for
us. With more open hearts, we have a better chance to make those
bigger sacrifices that express our love. As disciplined disciples, we
might be more-ready to sacrifice our pride and anger to reach out to
someone who has betrayed us. As disciplined disciples, young people can sacrifice their popularity to reach out to the kid who eats
alone at lunch. As disciplined disciples, we might be more able to
sacrifice our comfort for the sake of the common good. These two
fathers teach us the lasting effects of sacrificial love. Peter, James,
and John understood the importance of dying to self as a way of rising to Christ only after Jesus had been sacrificed on Mount Calvary.
In the same way, our sacrifices will make more sense in the bright
light of Easter glory. When our Lenten sacrifices discipline us to
deepen our commitment to make the sacrifices that really matter,
we too will understand what it means to "rise from the dead."

43.5   March 4, 2012

Peter, James, and John see incredible things today. On that high
mountain in Galilee, they see what the Father had seen in Jesus
when he emerged from the waters of the Jordan at his baptism.
They see that he is God's beloved Son. They see him transfigured
in such a way that their eyes must have been burning. Not only do
they see his true nature, but they also see the two greatest figures
of their faith: Moses who mediated the Covenant, and Elijah who
saved it some three hundred years later. It is a feast for the eyes!

However, it is not what they see that really matters. It is what
they hear. They hear a voice from the heavens telling them clearly
that this is the Father's Beloved Son. They hear that voice tell them
very clearly to listen to him. As they descend that mountain and
walk with Jesus to the Mount of Calvary outside the city walls of
Jerusalem, they will need to listen to him. Losing sight of their vision on the mountain, they will listen to him trying to teach them
that they must die to themselves to truly live with him. They will
hear him speak of his suffering and death. Once they get to Calvary, they will not see him praised for his true nature. They will
see him betrayed and humiliated. They will not see him transfigured. They will see him stripped and dying a horrible death. They
will not see him surrounded by two heroes of old. They will see
him surrounded by two criminals.

Abraham, their father in faith, had to learn the same lesson.
He heard the Lord call him to sacrifice his only son, Isaac, and he

obeyed. Abraham saw in Isaac the fidelity that God had given him. It did not make any more sense to Abraham to sacrifice his most precious possession than it does to us. But he obeyed and took his son to Mount Moriah. Then he listened to God again. This time, God told him to spare his son and substitute the ram caught in the thicket. In listening to God, Abraham came to understand that God does not demand human sacrifice, as the gods of the pagans seemed to demand. He came to understand that God would not go back on his promises. In listening, Abraham became a pattern of faith for all of us.

Unlike Abraham, the Father did not spare his only Son. Saint Paul reminds us of the implications of the sacrifice of Jesus. In allowing him to be sacrificed on the wood of the cross, the Father reconciles us to himself and shows his incredible love for us. For that reason, he will also give us everything else along with him. As Peter will eventually learn from listening, Jesus is not just another great hero like Moses or Elijah who can share similar tents. Peter will learn that Jesus, raised from the dead, will share his risen life with those who die with him.

As the Father's beloved sons and daughters, we too must listen. As we continue our journey through Lent, our fasting, praying, and almsgiving can open our ears to listen in a new way to the lessons of discipleship. Like Peter, James, and John, we catch a glimpse of the Lord's transfiguring presence every once in a while. But, most of the time, we are confronted with the cross, with suffering, and with so many circumstances beyond our control. If we listen carefully to the Word of God proclaimed here, we can hear of the Father's faithfulness in our lives. We can hear that our daily dying to self will eventually lead us to share in the rising of Jesus Christ. We can hear the truth of Paul's words: "If God is for us, who can be against us?"

43.6 March 1, 2015

In the ancient world, mountains were considered border zones between heaven and earth. They were places where people encountered the divine. God tested Abraham on Mount Moriah. God manifested himself to Moses on Mount Sinai and initiated the Covenant. Centuries later, Elijah went to that same mountain to renew the Covenant broken by his people's infidelity.

In the first sentence of his Gospel, Saint Mark tells us the identity of Jesus. He is the Son of God. However, his contemporaries question his identity at every step. Even his disciples, who recognize him as the messiah, do not understand. They cannot see or hear beyond his human appearance. So, Jesus takes Peter, James, and John to Mount Tabor. On that mountain in Galilee, they are given a transfiguring vision. In this moment, they see the truth about Jesus. He is conversing with Moses and Elijah. He is the fulfillment of the Law and the Prophets. They hear the voice clearly telling them that this is God's beloved Son. They are told to listen to him.

Peter's response is understandable. He does not want this moment to end. We can identify with him, especially when we think of those transfiguring moments in our lives. That moment can happen on a retreat, or on a wedding day, or in a moment of triumph on the athletic field. In those transfiguring moments, we can see beyond the ordinary appearances of daily life and glimpse the truth about what we are doing. Like, Peter, we do not want that moment to end.

But there is another level to Peter's request. In wanting to build three tents, Peter is referring to the Feast of Booths, or the Feast of Tabernacles. That feast is celebrated in the fall, during the harvest season. To this day in Israel, Jewish people erect tents in the fields, reminding themselves of the tents their ancestors used in the desert on their forty-year journey from slavery to freedom. In doing that, they also remembered the tent of the Tabernacle, where the stones containing the Ten Commandments were kept, representing God's presence in their midst. The Feast of Tabernacles anticipated the final coming of the Messiah at the end of the ages.

Peter finally gets it! Jesus is the promised Messiah who has come at the end of the age to usher in the Kingdom of God. He wants to build those tents to accommodate that Kingdom. What Peter does not get is that the Kingdom will not be established without the suffering and death of Jesus Christ. Jesus leads them down Mount Tabor to Mount Calvary. Mount Calvary is outside the sacred Temple on Mount Zion, where tradition says that Solomon built the first temple on Mount Moriah. On that mountain, Abraham learned that God does not want human sacrifice. Abraham offered the first sacrifice centuries before the building of the Temple, the place of animal sacrifice. Abraham's sacrifice prefigured the Sacrifice of Jesus on the mount outside the confines of the sacred Temple. On that mountain, Jesus will not be clothed in glory. He will be not be accompanied by two religious figures. He will be crucified between two thieves. The Father will accept this Sacrifice to defeat the powers of sin and death.

Just as Peter, James, and John were given a glimpse of the resurrection, we know the end of the story. We know that we will celebrate Easter when these Forty Days are over. However, we need to learn the lessons of Lent before we can gorge ourselves with whatever we are fasting from on Easter. Lent reminds us that we too must share in the suffering and death of Christ if we are to share in his rising. Lent teaches us how to deny ourselves in small ways, so that we can deny ourselves in so many real ways to identify with Christ. Dying to self is not an easy lesson. The Devil keeps telling us to take care of ourselves first. Christ tells us just the opposite. Trust in God's love for us. Put others first. Recognize in our sufferings a share in the redemptive suffering of Jesus Christ. Trust his victory over death, and keep slogging through Lent!

43.7 February 25, 2018

This story of Abraham about to sacrifice his son is horrifying. The ancient author rushes through this story with sparse details. Our modern minds cannot conceive of a situation in which a mentally stable father would think about sacrificing his only son. (Can you imagine Abraham saying to Isaac later that year, "Isaac, let's go on a father-son camping trip?" No thanks, Dad, I'll pass!) Even worse, we wonder what kind of God would demand such a sacrifice!

Our modern instincts miss the real point. This passage is really about an all knowing and all loving God, and about a man who places his entire trust in God. It is about a man who trusted that God would keep his promise to give him his own land. It is about a man who trusted that God would make his descendants as numerous as the stars of the sky and the sands on the shore of the sea, even when he asks for the sacrifice of the son who is the link to that promise.

Saint Paul takes this dynamic and turns it on its head. He describes a Father who loves us so much that he has sacrificed his Son for our sakes. The Father proves his love by allowing his beloved Son to suffer a horrible and humiliating death for us. Saint Paul writes these words to encourage the Roman Church to put their trust in Jesus Christ, even when they are being persecuted and killed for their faith in his death and resurrection.

Saint Mark has a similar intent in telling the story of the Transfiguration to disciples struggling with the cross. After Jesus tells his disciples that they must share in his suffering, cross, and death, he takes them up a high mountain. On that mountain, he is changed in appearance. Surrounded by the two great heroes of the Old Testament, his clothes became so white that they are nearly blinded. Peter wants to build three tents. And then they hear a voice from the cloud affirming, "This is my beloved Son. Listen to him."

The three disciples are given a mystical experience. And that is what the Transfiguration is – an experience of spiritual things within the ordinary, using classic symbols to describe an experience that is impossible to describe in human language. Mystical experiences place us on a mountain, where we have a clearer vision of how everything fits together. Mystical experiences provide clarity of light – the ability to see beyond the ordinary. Mystical experiences create a need for worship. That is why Peter wants to build three tents. His suggestion connects with the Jewish feast of Tabernacles – when they camped out in tents or tabernacles, like the Israelites had had camped out in tents in the desert and housed the tablets of the law in a Tabernacle. The voice confirms that this is a very personal connection with God.

Many of us have had mystical experiences at one time or another. Today's Gospel invites us to reflect on one of those times when we could not put what happened to us into words. At the Mass when I was ordained a deacon, I had one of these experiences. After the Archbishop of Cincinnati laid hands on me and a priest friend vested me, I was on a mountain. Everything made sense. I could see clearly. After months of struggle, I had made the right decision. Even though that feeling stayed with me for days, I could not put it into words. God was with me!

Be sure to reflect on a transfiguring moment in your life. It may have allowed you to perceive the spiritual within ordinary appearances. It may have called you to worship, to thank God. You may have instinctively known that God loves you personally. These mystical experiences convince us that the spiritual reality is greater and more beautiful than ordinary experiences. We need to hold these mystical experiences in our hearts, because we too must carry the cross and die to ourselves. As we continue our journey through Lent, these mystical experiences convince us that death is not the end. The end is in resurrection!

44. 3rd Sunday of Lent

Readings

Cycle B
Exodus 20:1–17
1 Corinthians 1:22–25
John 2:13–25

Cycle A, Scrutinies
Exodus 17:3–7
Romans 5:1–2, 5–8
John 4:5–42

44.1 March 26, 2000

Those of you who read the daily paper may recognize the comic strip, *For Better or For Worse*. Not too long ago, the strip followed the story of a pretty cranky Grandpa preparing to sell his small house. His wife had died the year before, and he decided to move in with his daughter and her family. His seven-year-old granddaughter, April, is ecstatic. "Honest, Grandpa? You're really coming to live with us?" "Yes, but I'll have to sell my house first," Grandpa explains. And then he reflects on what he must do.

"Oh my⬜ Now that I think about it, this is an awfully big decision. I'll have to get rid of some things! But when you're my age, that's what you do, April. You give up things that aren't so important anymore. All I really need to have with me are a few special treasures," Grandpa says. Then he picks up April and says, "and you're one of those treasures."

In our journey through this life, we are constantly trying to figure out what is an authentic treasure, and what needs to be discarded. The slaves who escaped into the desert could not take much with them. The Book of Exodus unfolds their search in the desert for the treasure that would satisfy their thirsting. They did plenty of complaining, and they expressed their lack of confidence in their leader. In giving them water from the rock, Moses provides the answer to their question: "Is God in our midst or not?" Yes, the God who gives this life saving water is in our midst! Only in the experience of God did they find a treasure that satisfied their thirsting.

The woman at the well may not have walked forty years in the desert. But her internal, spiritual journey was just as far! She had also looked in different places for a treasure, for what would ultimately satisfy her thirst. We do not know much about that woman. But we are told that she was on her sixth husband. And that should tell us something about the dead ends she encountered in trying to satisfy her thirsting. When she encountered Jesus, she began the last leg of her journey. First, she was just curious about a Jewish male who would talk to a Samaritan woman. Then she wanted the living water he promised. Then she saw him as a prophet. Finally, she acknowledged him as the Messiah (Christ) who could satisfy her deepest thirst for meaning in life. With that statement of faith, her journey came to an end.

We are all on the same journey. We have entered the desert of Lent to strip ourselves of small things – food between meals, candy or a favorite TV show, or precious time on a Tuesday evening, or some of our treasure to give to the poor. At the 9:00 Mass, we call forward the elect (those thirsting for baptism) and pray over them. We pray that God will "free them from the slavery of sin, take away Satan's crushing burden, and bless them with the gentle power of Jesus." In other words, we pray that they will have the courage to leave behind whatever cannot satisfy their thirst. We pray that they will open their hearts to the Holy Spirit and come to know the Father in true faith, expressed in love.

Let's face it. We all need that prayer, whether we are baptized or not! We have all spent time and energy pursuing treasures that could never satisfy our spirits, treasures that really were dead ends. We all want things that ultimately are not good for us. By praying, fasting, and almsgiving, we can see more clearly what needs to be stripped away from our lives so that we can recognize the real joys and meaning of life. Our Lenten journey has the power to restore a deeper awareness of God's presence in every moment of our lives.

"Is God in our midst or not?" God certainly is! Let's clear the junk, so we can see God more clearly!

44.2 **March 23, 2003**

Most Samaritan women drew water from wells in the early morning or evening, when it was cool. No one faced the blistering sun at noon – unless they had a reason. As we quickly learn in this Gospel, the Samaritan woman at Jacob's Well had good reasons. She carried much shame with her. Drawing water at noon did not shield her from the blazing sun. But it did protect her from the other women who knew her situation and surely make it more embarrassing and hurtful with their judgments.

She probably expected the same treatment from the Jewish stranger who had asked her for a drink. And yet, she took the risk of telling him the entire truth about herself. She did not deny that she had been through five husbands. Nor did she deny that this sixth man with whom she was living was not her husband. She sensed that this Jewish stranger would continue to be kind to her, even if he knew the total truth.

There is a Biblical tradition that assigns the number 7 to perfection. God created the world in 7 days, and the Gospel of John records 7 miracles. In contrast, the number 6 stands for incompletion. Jesus is the seventh man who comes into the life of the Samaritan woman. Jesus shows that he completely loves her, even though he knows the truth about her. He shows that there is nothing wrong with her desire to be loved. Her sin was in settling for much less, constantly opening herself to manipulation and hurt. Aware of her sin, she began gradually to see the truth about him. First, she saw Jesus as a good leader. Then she recognized him as a prophet who knows the truth. Finally, she came to believe in him as the Christ, the only one who could satisfy her thirst for love.

Those of us who have been working with the RCIA have seen a similar growth in those preparing for baptism. The Elect came to us for a variety of reasons. As they have gone through the process, they have gradually come to believe that Jesus is the Christ, the one for whom they have been thirsting. Today, they go through the First Scrutiny. Like the Samaritan woman at the well, they bare their souls to the one for whom they have been thirsting, admitting that they have settled for far less in their thirst to be loved. In opening themselves to the Lord who loves them, no matter what they have done, they acknowledge their need for salvation as they prepare for the waters of baptism.

These good people do not kneel before us, so that we can judge them, as her neighbors judged the Samaritan woman. They become reminders to the rest of us who have also settled for far less in our thirst to be loved, even though we have encountered Christ through our own baptism. They call us to repentance.

As we scrutinize the Elect for these next two Sundays, we are offered a Sacrament closely connected with Baptism. We bare our souls in the Sacrament of Reconciliation, because we encounter the Lord who loves us, even when he knows everything about us. Come to the Lenten Penance Service a week from Monday, or look at the many times the Sacrament is offered individually throughout the rest of Lent.

The Samaritan woman became the first evangelist when she told everyone in her village that Jesus loved her, even when he knew everything she had ever done. We become evangelists in Granger, when we acknowledge all those times we have settled for far less, and then known in a powerful way the love of the one who completely satisfies our thirst. Then, we provide the answer to the question from Exodus: Is the Lord in our midst or not? Yes, he certainly is!

44.3   March 19, 2006

The Samaritan woman at the well has a great deal to teach anyone who is thirsting for meaning, truth, and love in their lives. In fact, she speaks directly to three distinct groups at Saint Pius this weekend.

She speaks to the eighth graders who spent all afternoon yesterday participating in a retreat. They did fine. However, it was pretty clear that given a real choice, they probably would have been doing other things! On the Second Sunday of Easter, Bishop D'Arcy will confirm them and complete the Christian Initiation begun at their baptism. The Samaritan woman at the well warns them of the dangers of trying to satisfy their thirsts in the wrong places. In her thirst, six different husbands used her, disappointed her, and ultimately fooled her. Her experience teaches these young people that faith is a journey. She slowly grows in an awareness of Jesus Christ. First, she sees him as a kind Jewish man who would talk to a Samaritan and a woman. Then, she recognizes him as a prophet who speaks the truth to her with love. Finally, she sees him as the Christ, the seventh man who will truly become the Bridegroom for which she had been thirsting.

She speaks to our Elect. They have been clear in their choice to participate in the Rite of Christian Initiation of Adults. Having dedicated hours to this process in the last year, they have come to see Jesus as the Christ and Bridegroom, and they are thirsting for the waters of Baptism. Today, they celebrate the first Scrutiny. That word "Scrutiny" can confuse us. We might think that we are dragging these good people in front of the assembly to examine closely their lives. However, to use the words of the Rite, the Scrutinies are intended to "...heal what is weak, defective, and sinful to protect the elect from temptation and heal them in Christ." In celebrating this First Scrutiny, we assure the Elect that they are not alone in their thirst for Christ, and that we know from our own experience how easy it is to chase after false promises.

She speaks to the men who are participating in the Christ Renews His Parish Retreat. Like the Elect, they have committed themselves to an entire weekend during March Madness to get to know Christ better. Like the woman at the well, they have seen Christ in the noonday sun, benefited by the fullness of revelation through the Scriptures and Tradition of the Church. As they continue their retreat, they are willing to expose their lives and their faith to the brilliance of that noonday sun, as a way of knowing better the Bridegroom who gave his life for us, his Bride, the Church.

She speaks to all of us. With Saint Paul, she reminds us that faith is a gift from God, given not because we have deserved it or earned it, but because God looks into our hearts and offers it to us. As we continue our journey of faith, our hearts can become as hardened as the hearts of the Israelites traveling through the Sinai Desert. We too can ask if the Lord is in our midst or not. The woman at the well invites us to soften our hearts and take risks. Convinced that she had seen the Lord in her midst, she left her water bucket at the well to spread the Good News. She invites us to recognize the Lord in our midst and continue our prayer, fasting, and almsgiving as a dramatic way of turning more decidedly to the Bridegroom. She invites us to trust that our penance can affect us so much that others may come and see for themselves what we have seen and come to believe.

44.4   March 15, 2009

On this Third Sunday of Lent, we celebrate the Rite of the First Scrutiny with the Elect (those preparing for Baptism, Confirmation, and Eucharist) at the 8:45 and 10:30 Masses. Most people do not understand the significance of this Rite, because the English word "scrutiny" throws us off. When we hear that word, we think of being dragged before an accusing prosecutor or a judgmental group of people who will grill and interrogate us. The Elect have these thoughts in their minds as they look to this Sunday with some degree of hesitation and fear.

However, that is not the intention of the Scrutinies. They are intended to lay bare whatever is weak in the Elect, so that they can be strengthened through God's power. Jesus himself shows us the true nature of scrutinizing in the Gospel when he encounters the Samaritan woman at the well. He approaches this woman with kindness and asks for a drink of water from the ancient well where Jacob met his future wife, Rachael. Jews would not do that, because she is a hated Samaritan. Her fellow villagers would avoid her, because she is more than likely the talk of the town, because of her marital situation. Looking at her with love, he invites her to recognize in him the living waters that will ultimately satisfy her thirst.

He gently but honestly draws the truth out of her about her troubled past and how so many men have used her. He lays bare those weaknesses, not to condemn her, but to heal her. As she gradually recognizes the truth about Jesus, her basic goodness emerges. In the light of his love for her, we can clearly see her honesty and desire to know the truth. In fact, she becomes the first evangelist when she leaves her jar at the well and spreads the good news about Jesus Christ to the people of her town.

Through the First Scrutiny, Jesus does the same with our elect. As they kneel before the assembly in prayer, and as we lay our hands on them in support, the elect can more easily face what is weak in them, not to be judged or condemned, but to be healed and prepared for their sins to be washed away in the waters of Baptism at the Easter Vigil. In facing the truth about themselves, they open themselves to the same love of Jesus Christ which treated the woman at the well with so much care and respect.

We have 26 elect preparing for the Easter Sacraments at the Easter Vigil. However, the Scrutinies are not just for them. They are for all of us. They do not prepare for the Easter Sacraments in isolation, but in the midst of our parish. That is why for the next two Sundays, we will hear these readings from John's Gospel, which have been used from the earliest days of the Church to prepare people for the Sacraments. Those of us who have been baptized reflect on this story of the woman at the well, because the Lord scrutinizes each of us through our Lenten disciplines. If we open our hearts to him, as she did, he lays bare for us what is weak – not to condemn or judge us, but to heal us and help us to see the goodness in each of us.

Like the woman at the well, we too thirst for ultimate meaning in our lives. We have not always kept our baptismal promises, and we have turned to other things to satisfy our thirst, instead of turning to Jesus Christ. We lay bare our sins and weaknesses for the Lord's Scrutiny, so that he can heal us and bring out so many qualities about each of us that are so good. The Samaritan woman invites us to leave our jars at the well, encounter the scrutiny of the Lord Jesus, and expose what needs to be healed in each of us, as we prepare to renew our baptismal promises at Easter.

44.5 March 11, 2012

The woman at the well is very thirsty. Like her ancestors wandering the Desert of Sinai, she thirsts for much more than water. She wonders whether God is in her midst or not. Like her fellow Samaritans, she had tried to satisfy her thirst for meaning in her many marriages. Over the centuries, they had chased after many false gods, resulting in their being excluded by the faithful Jews who worshiped on Mount Zion in Jerusalem. Being both a woman and a Samaritan, she is at the bottom of the social latter. Used and thrown aside by the six men, she is trained by her culture to be regarded as worthless and without hope. She draws water from the well at the hottest time of the day, isolated from the rest of the community.

She doesn't even realize how thirsty she is until she engages in conversation with this kind Jewish man who asks for a drink. Jesus is the seventh man, the faithful Bridegroom who comes to woo this woman and her Samaritan brothers and sisters. As he engages her in conversation, he points out her sins with a directness and gentleness that does not condemn her. Instead, he draws her to a deeper faith. She gradually recognizes him as a prophet and finally professes him as the Messiah for whom she had been waiting. She realizes that the Christ whom she encounters is the one who can satisfy her deepest thirsts. Like all who follow the Lord, she leaves her water jar – her most valuable possession – at the well to become the first evangelist. She spreads the Good News to the townspeople, and they respond to her invitation with enthusiasm and faith. Having been transformed by Christ, she is no longer an isolated target of gossip, but an integral part of the community again.

Today we celebrate the First Scrutiny with the children, teens, and adults who are preparing for the waters of Baptism at the Easter Vigil. Like the woman at the well, each of these people came to realize that they are thirsting for meaning in their lives. As they have gone through the Initiation process, they have gradually grown in their understanding of the place of Jesus Christ in their lives. They now realize that Jesus Christ is the only person who can fulfill that deep thirsting, and they thirst for the waters of Baptism. In this First Scrutiny, we will pray for them, asking the Lord to uncover whatever is weak and sinful in them, so that they may be healed. Then their goodness can shine forth in these final weeks of Lent as they prepare to encounter Jesus Christ in a very real way in the Sacraments of Initiation.

As we pray over these Elect, we have to be honest about our own thirsting. Even though we have been joined to Christ in the waters of Baptism, sealed with the Spirit, and fed by the Body and Blood of Christ, we have pursued other avenues in an attempt to satisfy our thirsts. We have turned away from the Lord when we have chased after money or fame or possessions as ways of taking care of our thirst for meaning. We have allowed ourselves to be fooled by Satan's lies and embraced a way of living that has denied the promises made at our Baptisms. Like the Israelites in the first reading, we have grumbled against the goodness of God and asked the question with our actions. Is the Lord in our midst or not?

Saint Paul argues forcefully that the Lord is indeed in our midst. Christ died for us, even as we were satisfying our thirsts with all kinds of destructive behaviors. For that reason, we join the Elect in doing penance. Instead of going through a Scrutiny, we can encounter the Lord's mercy in the Sacrament of Reconciliation. Joined once again to Christ, we will be ready to renew our Baptismal promises at Easter. In renewing those promises, we will acknowledge him as the only one who can satisfy our deepest thirsting.

44.6   March 8, 2015

In the Gospel of John, Jesus slowly reveals himself. He first reveals himself at a wedding feast at Cana in Galilee. In turning water into wine, he reveals that he can change the ordinary water of our human existence into divine partnership with God. He is the faithful bridegroom seeking a bride, seeking those who will recognize him as the Christ and who will follow him.

Today, the bridegroom travels to seek new followers who will become his bride. At the well, his ancestor Jacob had wooed Rachel and took her for his bride. But that well is located in Samaritan territory. For centuries, Jews and Samaritans had been enemies. At that well, he not only speaks to an enemy, but to a woman, an action that would be forbidden. In his thirst, he asks for a drink, knowing that drinking from a Samaritan woman's bucket would render him ritually impure. Ritually impure, he could not enter the Temple or have contact with others.

The woman is open to how Jesus reveals himself to her. At first, she recognizes him as a kind man who treats her with respect. When she finds that he knows about her former husbands, she sees him as a prophet who speaks the truth without condemning her. Finally, he plainly reveals himself as the Christ, the seventh and most perfect bridegroom who truly loves and can fulfill her deepest thirst for meaning and for love. She leaves her bucket, her most valuable possession and becomes the first evangelist, announcing the good news to the people of the town and bringing them to meet Jesus to recognize for themselves that he is the Christ.

From very early in the Church's history, this Gospel has been used on the Third Sunday of Lent to guide the Elect in their preparation for Baptism. They are invited to reflect on how they have come to know Jesus and how they have gradually come to see him as Christ. No matter how many false bridegrooms they have been chasing to satisfy their thirst for love and meaning, the Bridegroom seeks them out and invites them to the well of the Baptismal Font. Through those life-giving waters, their sins will be washed away.

They will emerge one with Jesus Christ. They will put on the white garment that speaks of their incorporation in Christ.

There are four Elect in our parish preparing for the Sacraments of Initiation at the Easter Vigil. Those of us who have been working with them know that they are not terrible sinners. But, they acknowledge their bad choices and prepare to encounter the bridegroom, who will quench their thirst in the waters of Baptism. As they open their hearts to the truths of today's Gospel, they will go through the first Scrutiny at the 8:45 and 10:30 Masses. We will pray over them and ask the Lord to strengthen them in their journey.

If the Elect resemble the anonymous Samaritan woman, the rest of us are more like the disciples who return and are amazed that Jesus is talking to a Samaritan woman in public. Those disciples have spent time with him and are trying to learn the truth about him. But they still don't get it. We too have come to know Jesus in the waters of our baptism and have listened to him speaking to us in the Word. Like the Israelites in the desert, we too have complained that the Lord does not seem to be in our midst at times. Like the anonymous woman, we too have chased other bridegrooms who could never satisfy us. We have wandered away and tried to find satisfaction in all kinds of things: pleasure, wealth, success, fame, and any number of false gods.

This Season of Lent provides us with an opportunity to prepare to renew our Baptismal promises at Easter. Through prayer, fasting, and almsgiving, we can draw closer to the One who has justified us by his death. In the Sacrament of Reconciliation, we acknowledge the ways we have chased after other bridegrooms. Joined with the Elect, we renew our commitment to the Bridegroom who has given his life of his, his Bride, the Church.

44.7 March 4, 2018

When Jesus encounters the woman at the well, he asks for a drink. She gives him a drink, but receives much more in return from him. As the story unfolds, it becomes obvious that he is the faithful bridegroom. His ancestors had come to this well to woo prospective brides. And that is what he is doing now. In taking a drink from the woman, he defies cultural norms forbidding men to speak to women alone in public. In taking a drink from a Samaritan, he makes himself ritually unclean. He is reaching out to an outcast. Her ancestors had pursued false gods, just as six different husbands had used her. Jesus becomes the seventh, and perfect, bridegroom.

In talking with Jesus, the woman grows in her understanding of his identity. At first, she recognizes him as a very kind man who treats her with respect. Then she sees him as a prophet, someone who knows and speaks the truth about her sordid background. Finally, she recognizes him as the Messiah, the promised Christ who has come at noon as the Light of the World to give eternal life to those who embrace him. Then the woman does something dramatic. She leaves her bucket at the well and becomes the first evangelist, telling everyone in the village about her encounter with the promised Messiah.

For over a year now, we have been working in the Rite of Christian Initiation with ten young people and adults who have come to know Jesus Christ. By joining us every Tuesday night for prayer, catechesis, faith sharing, and fellowship, they have given something very valuable: the gift of their precious time and energy. Now they have entered the Season of Lent as the Elect, chosen by Bishop Rhoades for the Sacraments of Initiation. At the 10:00 Mass today, we prayed the first of the three Scrutinies over them. We prayed that their thirst for the waters of Baptism would draw them closer to Jesus Christ, letting go of any other "water buckets" that might get in the way of a deep and abiding faith in the One who offers eternal life through the living waters of Baptism, the strengthening Chrism of Confirmation, and the abiding real presence of the Lord in the Eucharist. Like the woman at the well, they are reaping much more than they have been sowing, because they look forward to being incorporated into the person of Jesus Christ and his Church and receiving the promise of eternal life.

As we accompany these good people through the journey of Lent, the Lord challenges us to consider what we might be sowing. Most of us have already renounced Satan and all his empty promises and lies. We have already received the fullness of life through the waters of Baptism. As the Scrutinies heal whatever keeps the Elect from growing closer to Christ, they convict us of not living our baptismal promises. We have weakened or separated ourselves from the faithful Bridegroom by our sins. By giving ourselves to the Lenten discipline of prayer, fasting, and almsgiving, we can distinguish a little more clearly those realities which can never fully satisfy our thirsts. Those water buckets might include our thirst for pleasure or financial gain or fame any other reality which cannot last. In leaving these water buckets behind, we can more readily associate ourselves with Jesus Christ, the source of life-giving water.

For us who are baptized, the Sacrament of Reconciliation invites us to bring our water buckets and leave them there with the Lord's mercy. Like the woman at the well, we can join the newly baptized at Easter and become evangelists ourselves, spreading the good news about our faithful bridegroom, Jesus Christ, who offers eternal life to all who believe. When the Good News of Jesus Christ is spread, then the answer to the question asked in the Book of Exodus is clear. Is the Lord in our midst or not? Yes, he definitely is!

45. 4th Sunday of Lent

Readings

45.1 March 30, 2003

We priests learn a lot from riding in the lead cars with funeral directors on the way to the cemetery. Earlier this year, a director pointed out the first of the 2003 license plates and showed how ugly it was. Some years ago, another funeral director complained that people do not read directions when pasting their expiration sticker on the wrong side of the plate. Instead of pasting the sticker on the upper right side of the plate, many paste it on the upper left side. As an example, he directed my gaze to the license plate of the car in front of us (whose driver had failed to follow directions and who had stalled the procession at a traffic signal). Sure enough, the sticker was in the wrong place!

I was in a particularly negative state of mind at the time, frustrated at my parishioners for not following directions or not reading important notices sent home. So I started watching license plates in traffic. It was unbelievable how many people could not follow simple directions and put their stickers on the wrong side of the plate! I kept a running tally of "idiots" in my head. Those negative judgments came to a screeching halt one day when I got something out of my trunk. Guess who put his sticker on the upper left-hand corner of the plate? Talk about opening my eyes!

The man in today's Gospel did not worry about reading directions! He was blind. He wanted Jesus of Nazareth to make him see. Through the mud smeared on his eyes, he not only came to see clearly the physical Jesus. He eventually came to see him as the Son of God who was the light of the world.

Again, this Sunday, we call forward those preparing for Baptism at the 8:45 Mass. These adults, teenagers, and children over the age of 7 have pretty good physical vision. Unlike their pastor, they might even know how to read directions. Yet, we pray over them, "Free these elect from the false things that surround and blind them. Set them firmly in your truth, children of the light forever." We ask that God will "guide them along the paths of right faith, safe from error, doubt and unbelief, so that with open eyes they may come to see you face to face . . .."

As the man born blind came to see with the light of faith, the spiritual leaders of the time closed their eyes to what happened to him and to the light they should have seen in Jesus. That easily happens to us, who are already baptized. The early Church referred to the newly baptized as the *illuminati* – literally, those illumined by Christ's light. As we scrutinize the elect, we need to explore those ways in which we have lost our sight in faith. Like Jesse in the first reading, we judge people too quickly by appearance and put them into neat little categories, so that we do not have to treat them with the respect they deserve. We become blinded to the Light of Christ shining in our midst by our own pride or ambition or greed or lust or envy or laziness.

As our elect prepare to be illumined through the waters of baptism at the Easter Vigil, we can safely expose our fruitless works of darkness to the bright light of God's mercy. Of course, the safest place to do that is in the Sacrament of Reconciliation. Come to the Lenten Penance Service a week from Monday, or come at any of the many times scheduled in the next few weeks. With our eyes opened, we can see Christ more clearly at Easter. And we might even learn to read directions from the Bureau of Motor Vehicles!

45.2   March 26, 2006

The disciples ask a question asked by many people to this day: What caused this man's blindness, Lord? Was it his sin or the sin of his parents? My parents asked that question 42 years ago when the doctor told them that my youngest brother had Downs Syndrome. Lacking very little about Downs Syndrome at that time, the doctors told them either to place him in a state institution or take him home to raise him without support. My parents asked the question: What have we done to deserve this? But, as time went on, they came to understand the answer of Jesus: "Neither he nor his parents sinned; it is so that the works of God might be made visible through him." Gradually, our family came to accept my brother's condition and recognized how God worked through Tom to affect the rest of us. In his own simple way, he taught us what was important in life. When I discovered that he was delighted to receive a roll of toilet paper for Christmas, I saved tons of money in presents. Looking back, I can honestly say that I would not be a priest today without Tom's presence in our family.

Jesus uses the physical condition of the man born blind as a way of making the works of God visible through him. Once Jesus gives him his physical sight, he begins to see the truth about Jesus through faith. Initially, he sees him as the kind man who gave him sight. Then he sees him as a prophet who tells the truth. Finally, he sees him as Lord and worships him. As the man comes to see the full truth about Jesus Christ, the religious authorities who should have been able to see become more blinded and see only Jesus of Nazareth, who must be a sinner, because he heals on the Sabbath.

Our Elect can identify with the man born blind, because their eyes have slowly and gradually been opened to the truth about Jesus Christ through the Rite of Christian Initiation of Adults. As Diane Schlatterbeck and I interviewed them, they told us that they have come to see the truth and want to be baptized. Using the language of the ancient Church, they seek to be illumined by Christ in Baptism. As we call them for the Second Scrutiny at the 8:45 and 10:30 Masses this weekend, they freely admit their spiritual blindness and pray for the grace of Illumination.

Last week, a friend said that he was glad that he was baptized as a baby, because he would not have wanted to endure all these Rites! I smiled and made a remark that cannot be repeated in church. However, his flip comment underscores the truth about this Second Scrutiny for those of us who have been baptized as infants. If the elect are like the man born blind who eventually comes to see the truth about Jesus Christ, then we can be those religious people who become blinder to the truth around us.

Our blindness does involve sin, because we have been illuminated by Christ, who invites us to walk in the light. We can be blind to the image of Christ in a family member or classmate who drives us crazy. We can be blind to the effects of our greed on the lives of the poor. We can be blind to the possibilities of what God can do with and through us in difficult situations. We do not need the second Scrutiny. But, we do need the Lord's mercy, which we encounter in the Sacrament of Reconciliation. Come tomorrow night to the Lenten Penance Service, where there will be twelve priests available for individual confession, penance, and absolution. If you prefer, come to one of the many times we will offer the Sacrament in the next three weeks. The Lord Jesus wants us to see clearly in the light of his truth, and our Elect can open our eyes to that invitation.

45.3 March 22, 2009

The Pharisees expose the man born blind to a blistering set of scrutinies. As the man comes to see the complete truth in Jesus Christ, the Pharisees keep calling him back to try to shake his growing faith and bring him to their conclusions. They are sure that his blindness is the result of serious sin and that Jesus is a sinner, because he broke the Law of Moses and healed him on a Sabbath. They even drag in his parents and scrutinize them. Even though the parents cave in and avoid the issue by telling the Pharisees to talk to their son in person, the man who had been born blind holds his ground and refuses to be bullied. So they throw him out.

When Jesus hears that the man had been expelled, he too scrutinizes him. However, the scrutiny of Jesus is honest, gentle, and loving. He recognizes his gradual growth in faith – from seeing Jesus as "the man who made clay and anointed my eyes" to seeing him as a prophet to seeing him as a man from God. When Jesus tells him that he is the Son of Man, the man believes what he sees, recognizes him as Lord, and worships him. Jesus brings out what is upright, strong, and good in this man accused of being a great sinner by the Pharisees.

That is exactly what Jesus does for the Elect this Sunday at the 8:45 and 10:30 Masses at the Rite of the Second Scrutiny. We call them forth, have them kneel before us, and pray over them. We invite them "to uncover, then heal all that is weak, defective, or sinful in the hearts of the elect; and to bring out, then strengthen all that is upright, strong, and good" (RCIA, #141). As these people have come to see more clearly the light of Christ in their lives, they look back to acknowledge how they had been blind. Through this Scrutiny, Jesus heals them, so that they may see him more clearly at the Easter Vigil.

In scrutinizing them, Jesus also scrutinizes us. Like the Pharisees, we are the ones who should have clear eyes of faith. Like the Pharisees, we can be blinded and not see the Light of the World standing before us. We can be like the Pharisees, and draw similar conclusions about family or neighbors today – that they are steeped in sin, preventing us from seeing anything good in them. We can be like Jesse, who judged by appearance and could not see what the Lord saw in his youngest son. We can be like Saul of Tarsus, and fail to see Christ in another group that seems to threaten our belief system. We sometimes do not see so well.

When Bernie Madoff was convicted and sent to jail, several victims of his Ponzie scam were interviewed. Many victims were not comforted by the fact that this man would spend the rest of his life in prison, and they expressed outrage to the reporters. However, one couple maintained an amazing composure. They told the reporter how they had come to realize what they still **had**, instead of what they had lost. They still had each other, and they still had their ability to enjoy life. The reporter asked, "How could you have such composure?" They replied, "You should have seen us several weeks ago! We changed!" This couple found a complete freedom they never would have known by looking clearly at what was the truth.

Like the man born blind, the couple did nothing to deserve the tragedy that befell them. But, this life changing experience had the power to open their eyes. Such events can open our eyes, and the Lord's gentle scrutiny invites us to look at our lives with honesty and admit our blindness. During this Lent, the national polls are telling us that we live in a time of great darkness and fear. Jesus invites us to open our eyes to his light of truth now. He invites us to see what is really valuable in our lives, especially when we might lose what we thought would make us happy. He invites us to admit the ways in which we are blind, so that he can heal us and make us see better.

45.4 March 18, 2012

Last week, Saint John introduced us to an unnamed woman drawing water from Jacob's well in Samaria. This woman encountered with Jesus Christ, changing her life. Today Saint John introduces us to an unnamed man near the Temple in Jerusalem. He tells us nothing about him, except that he is blind. In this man's encounter with Christ, Jesus spits on the ground, makes clay with his saliva, smears the clay on his eyes and tells him to wash in the pool of Siloam. Once he had followed Jesus' instructions, his blindness is cured. He can see!

Then the questioning begins about this encounter. First, his neighbors cannot believe that he can see, and they argue whether he is the same man. He answers that he is the same person and tells them about his encounter with the man who healed him. Then he gets sent to the Pharisees. They grill him with their questions, and he sticks to his story. Only now, he refers to Jesus as a prophet. Then the authorities (caked "the Jews" in John's Gospel) jump into the cross examination. They interrogate his parents, who refuse to discuss the matter, because they are afraid. When they put the man born blind under oath to tell the truth, he sticks to his story about his encounter with Christ. Despite their attempts to trip him up by arguing that Jesus is a sinner, he quotes a foundational Scriptural truth that God hears the prayers of those who do God's will and are devout. After they throw him out, he sees Jesus for the first time with his eyes and worships him as Lord. His conversion is complete. He has become a disciple.

Today, the Elect celebrate the Second Scrutiny. They too have encountered Jesus Christ – perhaps in the faith of a spouse, or an event in their lives, or through contact with our parish. During the past year, their eyes have been gradually opened, and they have seen more clearly that the Lord himself has called them to faith. So we pray over them and ask the Lord to heal whatever blindness might remain. As they continue to journey through this Season of Purification and Enlightenment, they look forward to receiving the light of Christ as they emerge from the waters of baptism, with all their sins forgiven.

We who pray over them have been enlightened by Christ when we were baptized. But like the neighbors of that unnamed man, like the Pharisees, and like the religious leaders of his day, we too have allowed the light of faith to dim in our eyes. That light is diminished when we judge people by appearances, as Jesse had judged his youngest son, David. It is diminished when we choose "fruitless works of darkness" and lurk in the shadows, avoiding the bright light of Christ which has the power to burn away our sins.

Jesus gave sight to this unnamed man at the Feast of Tabernacles. On that harvest feast, when people celebrated their ancestors' coming to the Promised Land, priests would draw water from the pool of Siloam in giant silver pitchers. As they poured that water over the Altar illuminated by countless torches, they expressed their hope that the messiah would come at the end of time. In healing the unnamed man, Jesus clearly demonstrates that he is that promised Messiah. He is the Light of the World. He has the power to open our eyes to the truth, to burn away our darkness, and prepare us to renew our Baptismal promises at Easter.

45.5 March 15, 2015

In the Prologue of his Gospel, Saint John identifies Jesus as the Word, present from the beginning, who is a light shining in the darkness. He goes on to explain that the Word, the light, became flesh and made his dwelling among us. Today, Saint John explains how Jesus Christ manifests himself as the light of the world in the course of his earthly ministry.

Jesus picks an ideal time. It is the Feast of Tabernacles, a fall festival when faithful Jews pitched their tents in the field as a reminder of their ancestors dwelling in tents in the desert in their deliverance from slavery to freedom. The priests would dip water from the Pool of Siloam with golden pitchers and pour the water over the Altar in the Temple, brilliantly lit by burning torches. As their ancestors looked forward to their arrival into the Promised Land, participants of the Feast of Tabernacles looked for the arrival of the messiah.

Jesus picks a man who has never seen any light to help him in this revelation. He dismisses the popular notion that the man's blindness was a result of sin, smears a mixture of clay and spit on his eyes, and tells him to wash in the Pool of Siloam. For the first time in his life, this man sees light. As he faces the reaction of those around him, he begins to see the real Light of the world in the person of Jesus of Nazareth. At first, he defends Jesus as a good man who has been very kind to him. As the Pharisees accuse Jesus of being a sinner for doing the work of healing on a Sabbath, he identifies Jesus as a prophet. Finally, when he is thrown out of the Synagogue, as many members of the Christian community of Saint John had been thrown out of their Synagogues, he acknowledges Jesus as Lord and worships him.

The early Church used this Gospel on the Fourth Sunday of Lent to help the Elect in their final weeks of preparation for Baptism. The Elect could easily identify with the anonymous man born blind. Like him, their eyes had been opened gradually to the truth about him: that he is the Light of the world, and that the Light given to them in Baptism can dispel the darkness of their lives. This Sunday, the four Elect of our parish hear these same words. At the 8:45 and 10:30 Masses, we pray the Second Scrutiny over them, asking God to remove whatever may still keep them from seeing fully the truth about Jesus Christ. We pray that they prepare for Baptism at the Easter Vigil not because a spouse or parent or friend brought them to the Catholic Church, but because they have truly encountered Jesus Christ, the Light of the world.

The Elect become an invitation for the rest of us to check our own vision of faith. Even though a lit candle was entrusted to us when we were baptized, we must admit that we do not always allow that light to shine through our thoughts, words, and actions. Like Samuel, we sometimes judge other people according to their outward appearance, instead of looking at them as God does. Or like the Ephesians, we can fall back into darkness, instead of basking in the bright light of Jesus Christ and his way of living.

We wear rose on Laetare Sunday to encourage us in the Lenten prayer, fasting, and almsgiving we have undertaken. Those Lenten disciplines have the potential to allow the bright fire of God's love to expose the darkness caused by our bad and sinful choices. The rose color reminds us that we are more than halfway through Lent. Even if we have not been entirely faithful to our Lenten commitments, there are still two and a half weeks left in Lent to give us a chance to pick ourselves up and start over. Lent can continue to open our eyes more fully to Jesus Christ, the Light of the world. When we renew our baptismal promises at Easter, we will understand more fully the truth that the Lord draws us to his bright presence and out of the darkness of our failures to live our baptismal promises.

45.6 March 11, 2018

In writing to the Church in Ephesus, Saint Paul explains how disciples should live in a pagan culture. He reminds the Ephesians that they were once darkness. They were once blind to the person of Jesus Christ and the Gospel which he proclaimed. Then he tells them that they are now light. When they had emerged from the waters of baptism with their sins forgiven, they were united completely with Jesus Christ, the light of the world. In the ancient Church, they were known as the "illuminati," the illuminated ones who carried candles lit from the Easter Candle to represent their new life in Christ.

Saint Paul's advice to them is simple: Don't fall back into darkness. Live as children of the light! The verb which Saint Paul uses is much stronger than simply "to live." The word means "to walk". If they walk as children of the light, it is no temporary activity. It is a way of life. If they live their baptismal promises and walk as children of the light, the light of Christ will shine through them, illuminating a culture often mired in darkness and despair.

Saint Paul then outlines three ways that walking as children of the light will make a difference. First, their light will produce goodness, an intrinsic quality of the heart. That goodness will manifest itself in works of kindness. Second, their light will produce righteousness, sustaining a right relationship not only with Jesus Christ, but also with each other. Third, their light will produce truth, not just words spoken, but also actions that are noticed. Living the truth will make them constant, sincere, and free from falsehood. Unlike the darkness of deceit and lies, the truth is trustworthy. These three effects are direct gifts from God, graces given to those who walk as children of the light by living their baptismal promises.

During this past year, we have been working with ten people in the Rite of Christian Initiation of Adults. Like the man born blind, they have grown in their understanding of the person of Jesus Christ. Through prayer, study, and fellowship, they have come to see him as more than a teacher, as more than a prophet who speaks the truth, and ultimately as the Christ, the Messiah whose bright light illuminates a darkened world. They were chosen by Bishop Rhoades to spend this season of Lent as a final preparation. We pray the second Scrutiny over these good people at the 10:00 Mass today, asking the Lord to remove any remaining darkness from them as they prepare to be illuminated through the waters of baptism, sealed with the Oil of Confirmation, and fed with the Body and Blood of Christ at the Easter Vigil. Awakened from the waters of Baptism, they will reflect the light of Jesus Christ.

As we pray over them, the Lord scrutinizes us! We may have been illuminated through the waters of Baptism, but we have not always followed Saint Paul's advice. We have not always walked as children of the light. As a result, we have diminished our acts of kindness, making our world even more mean spirited than it already is. We have not always walked in right relationship with Jesus Christ and other people, causing even more polarization and divisions. We have not always been truthful and added to an environment already confused about what is true and what is not. As baptized members of the Body of Christ, we can be restored to our baptismal brilliance through the Sacrament of Reconciliation. We can bring our "deeds of darkness" to that Sacrament and allow the Lord to burn our sins away with the fire of his merciful love. The Lord's mercy will remind us that the light does not originate in us. We can only reflect the true light, who is Christ. Then we will join the newly baptized at Easter in renouncing Satan and all his empty promises and all his lies. Then we can renew our baptismal promises and walk again as children of the light.

46. 5th Sunday of Lent

Readings

Cycle B
Jeremiah 31:31–34
Hebrews 5:7–9
John 12:20–33

Cycle A, Scrutinies
Ezekiel 37:12–14
Romans 8:8–11
John 11:1–45

46.1 April 9, 2000

At the Easter Vigil in 1986, I baptized adults by immersion for the first time. The parish had just completed a new church and had installed a baptismal font with water flowing from an upper basin into a lower pool shaped like a tomb. An 86-year-old man wanted to be the first one to be baptized in this new font. As the newly blessed water poured over Benny Miller from the upper basin as he knelt in the lower font, I understood for the first time what Paul meant when he told the Romans that those who die with Christ in the waters of baptism rise with him to new life. Baptism always involves dying and death, just as much as it always involves rising and life.

At the 9:00 Mass today, we call the elect for the last Scrutiny. At the Easter Vigil, they will go down with Christ into the waters of baptism and die to an old way of living. Then they will emerge soaking wet, with all their sins forgiven, joined completely with Christ and the mystery of his church. So, we pray over them today: "Free these elect from the death-dealing power of the spirit of evil, so that they may bear witness to their new life in the risen Christ."

And we pray, "Do not let the power of death hold them back, for, by their faith, they will share in the triumph of your resurrection."

The elect are powerful signs for the rest of us. Whether we were baptized as infants, or as small children, or as adults, we were baptized into the death of Christ. Every time we keep our baptismal promises, we share in Christ's dying, trusting his promise that those who die with him will rise with him.

Now is the time for the rest of us to reflect on the ways we have failed to keep our baptismal promises. Every time we do not trust God's present in our lives, we put up a barrier between God and us. Every time we allow Satan to fool us with his empty promises, we place another stone over a tomb keeping us from the love of God.

Tombs are terrible places! They are filled with death, decay, stench, and filth. Jesus demonstrated his power over tombs when he called his friend Lazarus out of his tomb. With the body of Lazarus lying in that tomb in a hot climate for four days without being embalmed, there had to be plenty of death, decay, stench, and filth. But Lazarus responded to his command and walked right back into the daylight!

Jesus can do for us what he did for Lazarus, if we only allow him to move away so many stones from our hearts. Our Lenten disciplines can help us identify what kills or weakens our relationships with others. We need to expose the decay of our bad habits to the light of God's mercy. We need to submit the stench of our gossip and false judgments to the open air of God's compassion. We need to trust that God will separate the filth of our dishonesty and greed from the goodness of who we were meant to be.

The elect have done this, and they are ready to pass through the waters of baptism. With less than two weeks of Lent remaining before we celebrate the central mystery of the Lord's dying and rising at the Triduum, we can respond to the Lord's call to be freed from whatever entombs us. That happens in a unique way in the Sacrament of Reconciliation. Through that sacrament, we hear Jesus calling us as he called Lazarus: "Come out of that tomb of yours! Walk back into the daylight of God's love, where you belong!"

46.2 April 6, 2003

Pilgrims to the Holy Land can get an idea of what ancient tombs were like. Visitors to Bethany (the Arab village of Azariyeh today) pay 2 shekels to the owner of the Souvenir Shop across the alley to spend a few claustrophobic moments in the cramped underground tomb of Lazarus. Those who visit the Tombs of the Kings in East Jerusalem can see the heavy round stone that is rolled over the small entrance to a large underground rock quarry. Having crawled through the narrow entrance, they stand in a large area where people brought the bodies of their dead loved ones to be deposited.

Both sites reveal the horror of ancient burial places. Because Jewish custom forbade the embalming of bodies, they were left in the dry heat to return to the dust from which they were made. When I stood in these tombs, I could only imagine what it would have been like to enter these dark places filled with bodies in varying degrees of decay. Modern horror movies could not capture the stench, filth, and decay that would have permeated these tombs.

It was from this horrific place of the dead that Jesus called Lazarus to come out. He did not give Lazarus back to his family just because he was a close friend. At one level, Jesus did not do Lazarus any lasting favors. He had to die again, and his family had to go through the terrible ordeal a second time. Jesus called Lazarus out of that tomb, so Lazarus could be a sign of what would eventually happen to Jesus himself – that he would be raised from the dead. Jesus came out of another stinking and wretched tomb changed – transformed – through the power of the resurrection. He would never die again, and he promised that those who died with him would share in that rising.

Notice that Jesus did not say that he **would be** the resurrection and the life. He says that he **is** the resurrection and the life. He wants us to be free of death and decay now. He calls us to identify whatever is stinking about our lives, whatever is decaying, whatever is filthy, or whatever is dead. Just as he called Lazarus to come out of that stinking place, so he calls us to walk out of our tombs, accept his mercy, and share in his resurrection now. We do not have to wait until we die to share in his resurrection. It can begin to transform our lives now.

Two weeks from today, this church will be absolutely packed with people. And it should be, because Easter is our most important Christian feast. We should welcome those people who come once a year, because we can never underestimate the power of the Lord's resurrection. However, today's Scripture readings invite us to explore more fully what it means to share in Christ's resurrection now. For those of us who come every Sunday (and are unlucky enough to spend Spring Break in Granger rather than in Fort Lauderdale), Jesus extends a specific invitation to make the most of the rest of Lent. We can intensify our prayer, fasting, and almsgiving in this next week and a half. We can use the Sacrament of Reconciliation as a way of recognizing what is dead about our lives. Most importantly, we can set aside the Triduum as a time to enter into the entire Mystery of dying and rising with Jesus. If we join him at his Last Supper, if we stand at the foot of his Cross, and if we watch outside the tomb, then the mystery of the Resurrection will make much more sense to us. We can trust the power of the fifty days of Easter, precisely because we have understood just a bit more the implications of facing the reality of the tombs from which Jesus invites us to emerge.

46.3   April 2, 2006

In the course of pouring out her grief at the loss of her brother, Martha rebukes Jesus in her pain: "Lord, if you had been here, my brother would not have died." Her words may shock us. But, they also reveal such a close relationship with Jesus that she felt free to say anything to him in her pain. Then, she follows her rebukes with words that express her trust in him: "But, even now I know that whatever you ask of God, God will give you." She refers to resurrection as something that happens only after death.

Those of us who have suffered such losses can identify with her rebuke. We too have asked where God was during that terrible time when a loved one died. We too have reaffirmed our faith at the funeral liturgy that our loved one will rise on the last day.

Jesus' response is interesting. He does not tell Martha that he will be the resurrection and the life. He says that he is the resurrection and the life. By raising Lazarus from the dead, Jesus invites us to believe that we share in his resurrection now. That is what the Elect believe. That is why we call them for the last Scrutiny today. In two weeks, they enter the tomb of those baptismal waters and die to their sins and their old selves. They will emerge from those waters, sharing already the life of Jesus Christ raised from the dead.

The same mystery happened to us when we were baptized as babies. Our godparents promised in our name that we would renounce Satan, and all his empty works, and all his empty promises. But, Satan has often fooled us time and time again. We have entered a tomb as confining as that of Lazarus by developing habits or patterns of behavior that are so much a part of us that we cannot break them, even when we have the sincere desire to do so. Those tombs keep us from sharing the risen life of Jesus Christ, available to us now. By raising Lazarus from his tomb, Jesus invites us to take a hard look at our own tombs, and the ways in which they separate us from him.

Charles Lamb, the British essayist, was so precocious that he could read at the age of three. One day, his sister took him on a walk through the cemetery, where he read the inscriptions on the tombstones. He noted that all the tombstones mentioned the positive qualities of the deceased: they all were kind, or loving, or faithful, or other words of high praise. When they got back to the house, he asked his sister where the naughty people were buried.

It is natural for grieving people at funerals to remember the good qualities of the deceased person and to speak about those qualities. However, Lent calls us to be honest with ourselves now. Lent tells us that we should Resurrection is a Mystery we can share now, and that we do not have to wait for it until we die. We cannot depend on loved ones to convince God that we are "worthy of heaven" at our funeral, because eternal life is a gift which we can only lose. Lent invites us to prepare ourselves to renounce Satan, and all his works, and all his empty promises again at Easter. Our penance during Lent can jolt us out of our sinful habits, so we can realize our present share in the resurrection. In raising Lazarus from the dead, Jesus demonstrates his power over death in his own resurrection. In calling us out of those habits that entomb us, he invites us to view our own death not as the end of everything, but as a final step into a risen life with him that will never end.

46.4 March 29, 2009

The 1990 movie, "Awakenings," was based on the life of Dr. Oliver Sacks. Dr. Sacks had worked with a group of mental patients in a New York City hospital. As a result of suffering from encephalitis in the 1920's, they were left in a catatonic state. With the permission of a patient's mother, Doctor Sacks (played in the movie by Robin Williams) administered a drug during the summer of 1969 to him. Astoundingly, Leonard Lowe (played by Robert de Niro) woke up. Several other patients had the same reaction to the drug and began to live again with great enthusiasm. The most striking quality of the movie was the energy and enthusiasm and sense of new life which these patients shared. Sadly, however, the drug's effects were only temporary. Once those effects wore off, the patients returned to their catatonic states.

In a sense, that is what happens to Lazarus. Jesus calls Lazarus out of the tomb and restores him to his family and friends. We can only imagine the energy and enthusiasm of Martha and Mary and the entire village. There is so much enthusiasm that that many people were who witnessed this miracle began to believe in Jesus. Sadly, however, the raising of Lazarus is only temporary. Lazarus must face death a second time. The enthusiasm and energy generated by the raising of Lazarus is soon replaced by the death sentence being planned against Jesus. His gift of life to Lazarus is rewarded by a growing plot to have him executed.

We hear this story of the raising of Lazarus from the perspective of our belief in the Paschal Mystery. Like Lazarus, Jesus is about to die and be buried. Like Lazarus, Jesus will emerge from the tomb to bring new energy and enthusiasm. But unlike Lazarus, Jesus comes forth from his tomb transformed by the resurrection. The risen Christ is changed, and he promises that same transformation to those who are willing to share his dying.

It is from the perspective of the Paschal Mystery that we bring our Elect to the final Scrutiny at the 8:45 and 10:30 Masses. Like the woman at the well, they recognized their initial call to faith in the Lord speaking to them through family or friends. Like the man born blind, they have withstood the challenges to their new vision of faith and see the Lord more clearly now. Like Lazarus, they allow the Lord to heal whatever may be dead within them.

Lazarus invites us to do the same. Paul reminds us that the Spirit of the one who raised Jesus from the dead dwells in us through the waters of Baptism. In these final days of Lent, it is time to allow the Lord to roll away those stones which keep that Spirit from dwelling in those darkest places of our lives. We tend to harbor deep within ourselves those decaying and dead spots that harden our hearts. We carefully protect our hatreds or resentments or jealousies of what other people have. We allow greed to become a driving force in our lives, forgetting how much greed affects the lives of other people. When we stifle the indwelling of the Holy Spirit, we put our spiritual lives in catatonic states that resemble the dark and stinky tomb of Lazarus.

Just as the Elect have experienced healing through the three Scrutinies, so the Church offers the rest of us a powerful means of healing for our spiritual catatonic states. Come to the Communal Penance Service on Tuesday night at 7:30. There will be sixteen priests available for individual confession and absolution. There will be strength in numbers, giving each of us the courage to roll away our protective stones to reveal those dead parts of ourselves. When those stones are removed, we can hear the voice of Jesus calling us out of those tombs and inviting us to remove the bands of death that bind us. Jesus does not say that he will be the resurrection and the life. He **IS** the resurrection and the life, giving us a share of his risen life now that cannot be stopped by death. His healing brings new energy, enthusiasm, and a readiness for Easter.

46.5   March 25, 2012

Jesus loved Martha and Mary and Lazarus very much. The sisters make that clear when they send the message to Jesus that their brother is ill. Saint John reaffirms that love for the family when Jesus receives the news of the illness of Lazarus. When he arrives at the tomb of Lazarus and weeps, the crowd also notices his deep love for Lazarus. However, as much as he clearly loves his friends, Jesus does something very strange. Instead of hurrying to their aid, he stays where he is for two more days. Both Martha and Mary both complain about his delay, saying, "Lord, if you had been here, my brother would not have died."

We can identify with their complaints. We know that the Lord loves us very much. Yet, so many times when things go badly for us in our lives, we ask the same question, "Lord, where are you?" We ask that when accidents occur, when serious illnesses hit, and when loved ones die. We ask that question when marriages fall apart, when friends turn against us, and when we lose our jobs. "Where are you, Lord, when we need you the most?"

Like Martha and Mary, we ask these questions from the perspective of faith. In her complaint, Martha addresses him as "Lord," indicating her belief that he is the Christ. Her faith is stronger than that of the disciples, who continue to refer to him merely as "rabbi," or teacher. Despite her questioning, she has confidence in the Lord. She will come to understand that Jesus has delayed so that her brother's return from the grave will point to the greatest miracle – the death and resurrection of Jesus Christ himself.

Today we celebrate the last Scrutiny with our Elect. Like Martha and Mary, they have come to believe that Jesus is the Lord. As they have grown in faith, they have become more confident that the Lord is present in every situation of their lives, no matter how hopeless that situation may be. They are preparing to enter into the watery tomb of baptism, where they will die to themselves and emerge from those waters one with the risen Christ. We pray over them, asking the Lord to remove whatever remains dead or self-centered in them and heal them.

These good people can teach those of us who have been baptized a powerful lesson. Over the course of the last year, our faith may have weakened, because we may have perceived the Lord's delay in coming to our aid as a lack of love on his part. Or worse, we may have delayed the Lord's presence in our lives by pushing him away with our sins. That is why these last two weeks of Lent can be so important to us. We have veiled our statues and images for a reason. We fast from them as a sign of our inner fasting to strengthen our faith.

At the very depths of authentic faith is the rock-solid conviction that the Lord is present to us, even in the darkest moments of our lives. Martha and Mary had that faith. To use Saint Paul's terms, they were living in the spirit, not in the flesh. Those who live in the flesh have not embraced life in Christ and live only for themselves. Those who live in the spirit have accepted the newness of life in Christ and live selflessly for God and for others. Now that the Elect have finished with their Scrutinies, it is our turn to ask for healing. Come to the Lenten Penance Service on Tuesday. There will be 18 priests, giving us a chance to admit those times when we have delayed the Lord's coming into our lives by slipping back into patterns of living only for ourselves. Strengthened by that mercy, we can continue to walk in faith, even when the Lord seems to be delaying. With this faith, we can keep our eyes of faith fixed on the ultimate Miracle of the Lord's dying and rising, which we will celebrate at the Paschal Triduum.

46.6   March 22, 2015

When the Prophet Ezekiel spoke to his people, they had been in exile in Babylon for over three decades. They had given up any hope of returning home. They had taken the lowly jobs which migrants, immigrants, and strangers would accept. They began to intermarry. There was no home. Jerusalem was in ruins. The Temple had been destroyed. They were permanently buried in the grave of exile. But, Ezekiel speaks for the Lord and promises that they will be raised up and will return home. The Lord could raise up his people from this grave of exile, something no human could ever do.

When Jesus arrives in Bethany, he confronts a similar situation. His friend, Lazarus, has been dead for four days. Most Rabbis would argue that the spirit of a person might hover over a body for three days. By this time, there is no hope! Even the sisters of Lazarus, who are also good friends, chide him: "Lord, if you had been here, our brother would not have died." Jesus even weeps at the tomb of his friend, troubled deep within his gut over the horrible power of death and what death does to people. After praying a prayer of thanksgiving, Jesus confronts the hopeless situation and orders Lazarus to come out of the tomb. He tells them to unbind Lazarus and gives him back to his sisters. Only the Lord can raise up a dead person. No ordinary human could do that.

For centuries, this set of readings has been used in connection with the third and final Scrutiny for the Elect, those preparing for Baptism at the Easter Vigil. At the 8:45 and 10:30 Masses, we pray over the four who are preparing for the Easter Sacraments. We pray that they may let go of whatever might still bind them to the tomb of sin and prepare them to enter into the watery tomb of baptismal water. At the Easter Vigil, we will pray a prayer of thanksgiving over the water and ask the Father to raise up the newly baptized from the waters of Baptism to share with Christ his transforming resurrection.

In less than two weeks, we will celebrate the Sacred Paschal Triduum. These final days of Lent can help us to intensify our preparation for these Mysteries. As the Elect prepare to enter the watery tomb of Baptism, we have to admit that we have not always kept our baptismal promises. To borrow the words of Saint Paul, we were given the indwelling of God's Spirit when we emerged from the waters of our Baptism. In not keeping our Baptismal promises, we have lost our trust in the promise made that we will live with him if we die with him. We have to be honest enough to admit that we have slipped back into the flesh, into giving into our sinful passions and returning to the death filled tombs of our selfishness.

With the Sacred Paschal Triduum in sight, we can renew our Lenten prayer, fasting, and almsgiving as a way of disciplining ourselves to the more difficult task of dying daily to self, of keeping our baptismal promises. Please take advantage of the Sacrament of Reconciliation as an integral part of that preparation process. Confessing our sins and receiving Sacramental Absolution returns us to the innocence of the day of our Baptism. Please come to the Lenten Penance Service on Tuesday evening, when sixteen priests will be present. Father Peter Jarret already knows that his homily has to be very short and to the point. There is strength in numbers! We are not alone in seeking the Lord's mercy and sharing in his risen life. Nor are we alone when we renew our Baptismal promises at Easter with a clear conscience.

46.7 March 18, 2018

When the prophet Ezekiel speaks to his people, they are in an impossible situation. They have been languishing in exile in Babylon for years. The Babylonians had killed their king, destroyed Jerusalem, and tore down the Temple, dashing their hopes of returning home. He speaks to them, telling them that God can deliver them from impossible situations. Walking through a field littered with dead bones, representing their current situation, he reminds them that God will always be faithful to the Covenants – those commitments of love enshrined in the floor of our church and featured in our Lenten Series on Tuesday nights. God will raise up those dead bones of his people, breathe life into them as he had breathed life into clay and formed Adam, and return them to their homeland. Ezekiel insists that God keeps his promises. Their eventual return from exile will remind them of God's faithfulness to his Covenants, even when they had been unfaithful to their end of the deal.

When Jesus approaches the tomb of his friend, Lazarus is in another hopeless condition. He has been dead for four days. There is no chance of him being revived. Martha and Mary yell at Jesus for not coming sooner. (We tend to yell at people close to us!) Jesus marches to the tomb filled with the deepest of emotions, because he hates death as much as Martha and Mary do. He prays a prayer of thanksgiving, showing that his power comes from the

Father, and orders Lazarus to come out of the tomb. Like Lazarus, Jesus himself will die. Like Lazarus, he will emerge from the tomb. Unlike Lazarus, who will eventually die again, Jesus will be transformed through the power of the resurrection and never die again. Jesus has shown his power over the most impossible condition of all: death!

On this Fifth Sunday of Lent, we pray the final scrutiny over the Elect at the 10:00 Mass. At the Easter Vigil, they will renounce Satan and all his empty promises, promise to trust God's presence in their lives, and enter into the waters of our Baptismal font, as Christ entered into the tomb. They will emerge from those waters, sharing fully in his life. In the Scrutiny, we ask the Lord to remove any final doubt in the power of Jesus Christ to bring them to new life.

As we commend them to the Lord's loving scrutiny and support them in their journey to the Sacramental life of the Church, The Lord scrutinizes us who are baptized! We have emerged from the waters of baptism to share in the life of the risen Christ. Every time we have failed to live our baptismal promises, every time we have failed to die to ourselves, we have denied the power of the resurrection. In his discussion with Martha and Mary, Jesus does not promise to be the resurrection at some future time after their death. He promises to be the resurrection and the life NOW! We already share in his resurrection every time we die to our selfish interests, when we choose to be humble, when we let go of our pride, and when we face our fears and trust that he is present in our most impossible situations, including death.

During these last two weeks of Lent, the best way we can prepare to celebrate the Lord's resurrection is to receive the Sacrament of Reconciliation. As the Elect are freed from all sins in the waters of Baptism, we are freed from our sinful failure to live our Baptismal Promises when we bring our sins to the Confessional and trust in the Lord's merciful forgiveness. Come to the Penance Service this Tuesday evening. The Service gives us a chance to reflect together on God's Word, examine our conscience, and spend some time in silence. There will be 21 priests available for individual confession and absolution. Restored to our Baptismal innocence, we will make our own renunciation of sin and renew our baptismal promises at Easter, renewing our trust that Jesus Christ is with us in the most impossible situations.

47. Passion Sunday

Readings
Mark 11:1–10
Isaiah 50:4–7
Philippians 2:6–11
Mark 14:1–15:47

47.1 April 16, 2000

A young boy was consistently late for supper. His parents warned him that he must be on time, or face the consequences. Finally, the boy's father told him that if he were late one more time, he would eat bread and water for supper. The next night, the boy was late. When he sat down at the table, he looked at the one piece of bread on his plate and the glass of water and realized how hungry he was. After the prayer, his father filled the plates of the rest of the family. Once he had filled his own plate with heaping amounts of wonderful food, the father traded plates with the boy being punished.

With a lump in his throat, the boy understood that his father was taking upon himself the punishment that he, the boy, had brought upon himself by his repeated disobedience. When he had grown to maturity, the young man recalled that evening meal and said, "All my life, I have known what God is like, because of what my father did for me that night."

Lent ends this Thursday night when we begin the Mass of the Lord's Supper. For forty days, we have been preparing to celebrate the mystery of God's love, which Mark just eloquently described for us in the Passion. So, bring your children to the Seder Supper on Holy Thursday and stay for the first liturgy of the Sacred

Paschal Triduum (the three holy days) – the Mass of the Lord's Supper. Come to the Celebration of the Lord's Passion on Good Friday. Take part in the paschal fast and the paschal watch around the clock in church. Be part of the Easter Vigil after dark on Holy Saturday or at any of the Masses on Easter Sunday. Check the bulletin for times when we pray the Liturgy of the Hours. Join us as we close the Triduum on Easter Sunday afternoon at 5.

Jesus did not deem equality with God something to be grasped. Beginning Thursday night, we celebrate the mysteries of his emptying himself, becoming obedient to the point of death, and being exalted by God the Father.

47.2 April 14, 2003

The Passion according to Mark is sometimes called the "account of the three Simons." Mark begins his narrative at the house of Simon the Leper in Bethany. At his dinner party, a woman enters and pours expensive perfumed oil on the head of Jesus. Her action points to the anointing of his body for burial. We meet the next Simon in the Garden of Gethsemane. Jesus becomes so frustrated with the inability of Peter, James, and John to stay awake and pray with him after the Last Supper that he reverts to Peter's original name. He asks, "Simon, are you asleep?" Finally, we encounter the third Simon, who is forced to help Jesus carry his cross to Golgotha. Mark says only that he is the father of Alexander and Rufus, and that he lives in Cyrene.

The Season of Lent ends on Thursday night, when this community gathers to celebrate the Mass of the Lord's Supper. That begins the Sacred Paschal Triduum. Like all three Simons, you and I are invited to participate in the liturgies that make present the powerful work of our redemption. At the Holy Thursday Mass, we respond to the Word of God by washing feet and celebrating the Eucharist. At the Good Friday Commemoration of the Lord's Passion, we stand at the foot of the cross and reflect on the price Christ paid for us. At the Easter Vigil on Saturday night, we gather to bless the new fire, carry its flame on the Easter Candle into a darkened church, keep vigil by hearing the Word of God, administer the Sacraments of Baptism and Confirmation, and celebrate the Eucharist. We continue the celebration of the Resurrection through all the Easter Sunday Masses and conclude the Triduum with Vespers on Easter Sunday night.

Mark does not tell us how the first and third Simon was affected by the drama in which they participated. But we know very clearly how those actions affected Simon Peter. He brought his complete humanity to the mystery of what happened to Jesus, and he was changed forever. These mysteries can change us, as they changed

Simon Peter. Be sure to be present for the Triduum Liturgies. Join us for the Liturgy of the Hours. Come to the church at any time to watch and pray. Take part in the paschal fast at home or at work, breaking it with the Eucharist at the Easter Vigil and feasting on Easter Sunday. This week is called "holy" for a specific reason. It is made holy by what the Lord has done for us. Like Simon Peter, we become holy by the way we respond to his saving work.

47.3 April 9, 2006

In Mark's account of the Lord's Passion, those who were the insiders fail him at every turn. Judas, one of the Twelve, betrays him. Peter, James, and John – the inner circle of friends who had witnessed his glory on the Mountain of Transfiguration – cannot stay awake in the Garden to support his agony in the Garden. Peter, named by Jesus as the Rock, denies knowing him three times. All of the insiders run away and are scattered when Jesus is arrested, condemned, and executed.

Ironically, the outsiders recognize the truth. The woman with the alabaster jar anoints him as the Suffering Servant who is also the Christ, the Anointed One. Another outsider, Simon of Cyrene in Northern Africa, assists him to carry his cross. The Roman Centurion, both a gentile and a pagan, makes the ultimate profession of faith in calling him the Son of God after his death. The women who had followed him up to Jerusalem remain near the place of execution. Another outsider, Joseph of Arimathea, a member of the council who condemned Jesus to death, provides a clean linen cloth for his body and a tomb for his burial.

In our day, we are the insiders who put on Christ at Baptism. During Lent, we insiders have humbly admitted that we have betrayed Jesus with our actions. We have enjoyed our faith in those transfiguring moments on the mountain and wavered when we got to the agony in the garden. We have denied knowing him. Like the young man who ran away naked when he abandoned his linen cloth (his baptismal garment), we have abandoned our baptismal promises and known the nakedness of trying to live apart from Christ. During Lent, we have also learned from the outsiders in our midst – the Elect preparing for baptism at the Easter Vigil on Saturday night. They have shown us a new enthusiasm for faith and powerful ways to acknowledge Jesus as Lord.

Together, both insiders and outsiders are about to enter into the central Mystery of our faith. On Thursday night at 7:30, Lent ends when we enter the Sacred Paschal Triduum with the Mass of the Lord's Supper. On Friday at 1:00, we commemorate the Lord's Passion and Death. On Saturday evening at 8:30, we begin the Great Easter Vigil, when we will hear Mark describe that young man dressed in a linen cloth telling the women that the Lord is raised from the dead. Then, our beloved outsiders will become insiders through the Sacraments of Initiation – Baptism, Confirmation, and Eucharist.

Next Sunday, this place will be packed with lots of outsiders. We need to welcome them, because Mark's Gospel today shows God working through unlikely outsiders in the Lord's Passion. As insiders, we need to gather for the major liturgies of the Triduum, because we need to participate fully in these Mysteries. We will better understand the news of the young man dressed in a linen cloth on Easter Sunday when we face the horrors he knew in abandoning that linen cloth on Holy Thursday and Good Friday.

47.4 April 5, 2009

During the three years they had spent together, the disciples had formed a bond that made them a closely-knit family gathered around Jesus. But today, Saint Mark tells us the story of the disintegration of that family. Beginning with a meal which symbolizes unity, Judas betrays the one who loves him. Peter, James, and John cannot stay awake, while Jesus agonizes over his impending death. The young man who had left everything to follow Jesus now leaves everything to get away from him. Three times, Peter denies that he knows him three times while he stands alone in a mock trial. By the time Jesus is tortured and killed on the Romans' cruel instrument of execution, only a few women watch from a distance. Jesus is utterly alone as he faces the ultimate enemy of death. Only nature groans in agony as he dies. A Roman soldier declares the truth that this is truly the Son of God. A secret admirer buries his body.

Of course, we know the end of the story. Through the power of the resurrection, the wounds of this disintegrated family will be healed. With the exception of Judas, this closely-knit family will be gathered together again around the risen Christ. Next Sunday, this church will be jammed with people drawn by the resurrection of Jesus Christ. For us who gather today, it is important that we accompany Jesus in his suffering, passion, and death.

We are his family, closely knit through Baptism. We need to be here on Holy Thursday night at 7:30 to celebrate the Mass of the Lord's Supper and commemorate the institution of the Eucharist. It is important that we gather at 1:00 on Good Friday celebrate the Lord's Passion and venerate the cross that saves us. It is critical that we gather at 8:45 on Holy Saturday night around the fire to enter into the Lord's resurrection and celebrate the Sacraments of Initiation.

Please check the bulletin for the times of all the Liturgies in these last days of Lent and the Triduum Liturgies. Our family of faith also experiences our share of testing and divisions and pain. When we walk together with the One who faced the final enemy of death with courage and unflinching faith in his Father's will, we too will better understand the healing brought by the Lord's rising from the dead on Easter Sunday.

47.5 April 1, 2012

The Romans were experts at cruel and unusual punishment. People who were executed by crucifixion suffered horrible physical pain, made worse by the flogging they received before being nailed to a cross. When we reflect on the horrendous pain suffered by Jesus at his crucifixion, we are moved to gratitude for his suffering such a cruel death for us.

Yet, interestingly, Saint Mark barely mentions physical pain. He says that Jesus is scourged, crowned with thorns, and is crucified. Mark focuses our attention on the spiritual, psychological, and emotional pain suffered by Jesus for us. Despite his total gift of self, one of his best friends betrays him. The one he has entrusted leadership in his Church denies him three times. The rest of his disciples abandon him. One of them, who had given up everything to follow him, gives up everything – including his clothing – to get away from him. He is subjected to an unjust trial before the religious leadership. The crowds who had acclaimed him as king on Sunday demand his execution on Friday, choosing a notorious murderer (son of the father) over him (the only Son of the Father). The Roman governor gives in to the crowd, even though he knows he is innocent. He is stripped and humiliated before all on Calvary, and everyone mocks and taunts him. He dies utterly alone, with only a few women looking on from a distance. Mark's account moves us to reflect on how the Lord teaches us to die.

Not all of us will suffer such terrible physical pain. But, all of us will die. We prepare best for that ultimate death by imitating the way Jesus Christ emptied himself out of love for us, taking on human form, obedient to the point of death. When Lent ends on Thursday evening, we enter into the Sacred Paschal Triduum. As we celebrate his Last Supper on Thursday, his death on Good Friday, and his resting in the tomb on Holy Saturday, he teaches us this lesson of dying in a powerful way. His death and his obedience did not end in the tomb. He was raised from the dead on Easter Sunday, helping us to understand what Saint Paul is saying. Because he emptied himself out of love, he highly exalted, above every other creature.

Please check the bulletin for times of the major Triduum Liturgies, including all of the other times we gather to pray. Come to watch and pray with us. Learn the lessons of dying to ourselves from Jesus Christ, who wants to share with us the joy of rising with him.

47.6 March 29, 2015

Saint Mark begins his Passion with a woman who "wastes" some very expensive perfume pouring it over the head of Jesus. When others criticize her action, Jesus defends her. She is "wasting" the expensive perfume to anoint his body for burial. Throughout his public ministry, he has been "wasting" his life in loving service of others. Now, he will bring that "wasting" to its conclusion by giving himself to the ultimate demon, which is death.

The Passion invites us to evaluate how we "waste" our lives to imitate his example. The Passion portrays people who fail to "waste" themselves, choosing instead to hold on closely to themselves. The Passion gives us some choices. We can be like Judas, who sees the handwriting on the wall and holds on to the thirty pieces of silver to protect himself. We can be like the young man who had previously left everything to follow Christ. Now, he leaves everything to run away from him. We can be like Peter, who holds on to his fear and denies his relationship with Christ. We can be like Pilate, who holds on to popularity instead of standing up for the truth. Or we can be like the religious leaders, who hold tightly to their positions, which are threatened by the example of love and mercy given by Jesus.

But the Passion also gives us some positive examples letting go and "wasting" ourselves out of love. We can be like the owner who opens his fists to the rope of the colt to allow Jesus to ride into Jerusalem. We can be like the man who opens his upper room for the Last Supper. We can be like Simon of Cyrene, who opens his hands to help Jesus carry his cross. Or we can be like the centurion, who opens his eyes to see the truth for which Jesus was condemned to die: that he is the Son of God who enters death, so that we can face death ourselves.

Because the Lord "wasted" his life, he was raised from the dead. We celebrate this central Mystery of our faith when we enter into the Sacred Paschal Triduum on Thursday evening. Please join us for the major Liturgies. The Mass of the Lord's Supper begins at 7:30 on Holy Thursday evening. The Celebration of the Lord's Passion is at 1:00 on Good Friday afternoon. The Easter Vigil begins at 8:45 on Holy Saturday evening. We celebrate the Lord's Resurrection at all Masses on Easter Sunday. Times for the other liturgies are in the bulletin and on our website. The church will be open throughout the Triduum for watching and praying.

In participating in the Triduum liturgies, we can recognize the ways in which we have failed to "waste" ourselves out of love for Christ and others. But we also gain new strength and hope as we open our hearts and our fists to the central Mystery of our faith, which promises that those who waste their lives will be given more than we can ever imagine.

47.7 March 25, 2018

Throughout the Gospels, there is a consistent pattern of Jesus meeting the needs of others. He never asks for anything for himself. However, in today's Gospels from Saint Mark, Jesus needs two things. In the Gospel proclaimed at the blessing of palms, Jesus sends his disciples to bring back a colt. He needs that colt so that he can ride into Jerusalem, not as a conquering king on an Arabian stallion, but as a humble king whose throne will be a cross outside the city walls.

In the Passion, Jesus sends his disciples to find a guest room. He needs that room to celebrate the Passover Meal with his disciples. At that last Passover meal with his disciples, he will give the greatest gift of the New Covenant, the Eucharist which we celebrate now.

Even when Jesus needs something, that need becomes a vehicle for him to give of himself totally to us. That is why he needs us this week. He needs us to enter into the Sacred Paschal Triduum with him to renew our faith in the central Mystery of our faith: the death and resurrection of the Lord. Lent ends on Holy Thursday evening when we begin the Mass of the Lord's Supper at 7:30. Please join us for the major Triduum Liturgies. Be sure to watch and pray in the church. Be sure to carry the fasting into your home. The Lord needs us to be here for the Triduum. He needs for us to renew our faith, so that we can be effective disciples in a world desperately in need of transformation.

V Triduum

48. Holy Thursday

Readings
Exodus 12:1–8, 11–14
1 Corinthians 11:23–26
John 13:1–15

48.1 April 20, 2000

Can you imagine the reaction of your neighbors if you went home from church tonight, slaughtered a lamb in the back yard, and smeared its blood on your doorposts? That is what pagans did in ancient times. They smeared blood on their doorposts, because they believed it would ward off the evil spirits that plagued them. So, smearing the blood of lambs on their lintels came naturally for the Israelites. They were not being superstitious. That blood represented God protecting them from the angel of death passing over the Egyptian houses. That blood reminded them of God guiding their pass over from slavery to freedom. To this day, Jewish people eat the Passover meal to express their faith that God continues to be with them as they pass through life.

At the Last Supper, Jesus gave new meaning to the Passover meal. He was painfully aware that his life was about to come to an end, aware that he was about to pass over from this life to the Father. He told his disciples that a new exodus was at hand. He was to be the lamb whose blood was spilled. Through his blood, he was to accomplish a new deliverance for his people, a deliverance from sin and death.

Like Jesus, each of us is part of a process of passing over – from life to death to eternal life. Like Jesus, we face many mini-Passovers in our lives – from sickness to health, from brokenness to wholeness, hatred to love, disunity to unity, guilt to forgiveness. Passing over is part of the human experience, and we cannot escape it.

Instead of going home and smearing blood on our doorposts to ward off these frightening moments, we have begun the Sacred Paschal Triduum. We enter into this solemn observance not as a group of dramatic actors and actresses intent on reenacting what happened to Jesus. That happened only once in history and cannot be repeated. Rather, we enter into these three days trusting that the Scripture readings, the ritual actions, and the quiet prayer and fasting have the power to make present the Lord's Passover in the ways we pass through our lives today.

It is most appropriate that we begin these three days with the Eucharist – that special Passover moment given by Jesus to strengthen us in our mini-passovers. Fed by the Word of God and the Lord's Body and Blood, we know we cannot stand still during life's Passover moments. Fed by Word and Sacrament, we can best face those moments by putting ourselves at the humble service of other people. As we are busy washing the feet of others, we will not be afraid of the mini-passovers that seem to threaten our security and well-being. God leads us through these moments, because God has literally marked us by the blood of the Lamb.

Most homilies end here. Not tonight! On this night, we are not content to end with mere words. We end with the sacred action of washing one another's feet, confident that such actions translated into our daily lives have power. They ensure that we walk the way of the Lamb who was sacrificed for us.

48.2   April 5, 2012

The people of Israel understood the significance of their ancestors passing over from slavery in Egypt to freedom in the land promised to Abraham. That passing over was the single most important miracle in their Covenant relationship with God. When they gathered to celebrate the Passover meal, they recalled the blood of the lamb applied to the lintels and doorposts of their ancestors' homes. In eating the Passover lamb, along with the unleavened bread and bitter herbs, and in drinking the four blessing cups of wine, faithful Jews did more than simply remember that greatest miracle of their history. They told stories of God guiding their people to freedom in such a way that they came to realize that God was saving them in the present. The Lord may have worked in marvelous ways with their ancestors in the past. Because of his Covenant with them, he continues to work with his people in the present.

As Jesus gathered with his disciples to celebrate the Passover Meal, he knew that God would be doing something extraordinary through him. He is to become the Lamb of God who will be slaughtered. His blood will be poured out in love to set us free from sin and death. He will pass over from life to death, and then through the Resurrection, pass over to a transformed life. This passing over, this sacrifice, will change the history of the world forever. In his Passover, he will initiate a New Covenant sealed with his blood.

In these next three days, we will be drawn into this central Mystery of our faith. And we will do so in some very tangible ways. We will light a new fire on Holy Saturday, carry candles, keep vigil by listening to the Word of God, and celebrate the Sacraments of Initiation, using water, oil, and bread and wine. Tomorrow, we will focus our attention on our Savior's death by kneeling before the Cross and venerating it. Tonight, we take ordinary bread and wine, and praise the Father for the sacrifice of Jesus made present as we remember, break, and give, doing exactly what Saint Paul told the Corinthians to do. Tonight, we who share in the ordained ministerial priesthood of Jesus Christ will kneel to wash the feet of parishioners who share in the common priesthood of Jesus Christ through baptism.

We use these very tangible signs, because God's self-emptying love was made visible in Jesus, the Word Made Flesh. Jesus did not just talk about God's love. He incarnated that love and made it very tangible. He is not an unknowing lamb dragged to the sacrifice, but the Lamb of God who willingly obeyed his Father's will. He does not simply talk about humble service. He puts on an apron, kneels down, and washes the feet of his disciples. He humbles himself to perform a task assigned only to slaves in the ancient world. He shows us by his own dramatic example that real love involves sacrifice – the total gift of self on the Cross. He shows us that real love involves seeing our baptismal garment as our apron of service. We love best by emptying ourselves of our pride and self-absorption. We love best when we realize that there is no task too menial, too degrading, that we can give to one another.

This day is sometimes called "Maundy Thursday," from the Latin word man•atum, meaning "to command." The love which Jesus Christ demonstrates in his Passover is not easy. That is why he does not recommend this style of loving or suggest it for our consideration. He commands us to love in this way. To strengthen us to obey this difficult command to humbly serve, he feeds us with his very Body and Blood. This Eucharistic food is nourishment for foot washing and strength for a life of washing feet.

Most homilies end here, with words. But not tonight! Tonight we invite forward parishioners chosen for their example of humble service. We, the ordained ministers of this parish, will wash their feet to fulfill the Lord's command. In washing their feet, we remind ourselves of our fundamental role as humble servants. In washing their feet, we know that we can return to the Eucharist time after time when we are exhausted from serving. This cycle of serving and being fed was established by the Passover of the Lord. It is that Passover that we remember in this Eucharist, making the New Covenant sealed in the Blood of the Lamb present to us now.

49. Good Friday

Readings
Isaiah 52:13–53:12
Hebrews 4:14–16; 5:7–9
John 18:1–19:42

49.1 April 21, 2000

An article in *America Magazine* caught my attention. Written by Kevin Barry, the article was entitled "The Gift of Cancer." My stomach turned. The *Gift* of cancer! Give me a break! Here is an idealistic writer philosophizing about something he does not understand! Kevin Barry obviously has never experienced the horrors of cancer – the way it affects not only its victims, but also their entire families. He must never have seen what a six-hour surgery does to a cancer patient, not to mention the devastating effects of chemotherapy and radiation. He probably did not keep vigil at the deathbed of a patient who is dying by inches and looks like a skeleton!

Then, I read the article and realized that he had done these things. Kevin had been diagnosed with colon cancer, the same cancer that claimed my mother's life. He knew the roller coaster ride of a cancer patient. He talked about his feelings of depression and emptiness when the cancer returned several years later and invaded his liver. He spoke of the mighty fight he waged, and he described the terrible human costs.

And yet, he still called cancer his *gift* – not because it was a pleasant experience, but because of the way his cancer changed his life. This *gift* opened his eyes to the suffering of other people in the world. It revealed the foolishness of his workaholic schedule.

It forced him to appreciate more those precious moments he spent with his wife and kids. It caused him to trust in God more deeply and live one day at a time. In this context, his cancer was a *gift*.

We gather this afternoon, because we believe that the Cross of Jesus Christ is a gift. On that first Good Friday, the cross certainly did not seem like a *gift* – to his friends who ran away; to the women who remained courageously at the foot of the cross; to his mother who held his dead body in her arms. But, in time, they gradually came to understand the cross as a gift! And so do we. We gather this afternoon to thank God for the gift that has washed us clean in the blood of the Lamb.

If the cross of Jesus is a gift, then the crosses we carry can also be gifts. Crosses come in many different sizes and shapes. For Kevin Barry, that cross was cancer. You might be carrying the cross of alcoholism or drug addiction. Your cross might be mental illness, or heart disease, or bouts with depression. It might be estrangement from family members or friends. It might be a loss of direction; a loss of control over some area of your life; or it might be the aging process catching up with you.

We do not need to look for crosses in our lives. They come readily on their own. Neither do we need to accept everything bad as "God's Will." Like Jesus, or like Kevin Barry, we need to fight to change whatever can be changed. But once we recognize a true cross, something we cannot change, we are invited to embrace it as a gift.

As we bring the needs of the world and the church to the Father in these General Intercessions, think about the cross you carry. Keep that cross clearly in your mind and heart as you come forward to venerate the cross of Christ. By kissing that cross, or bowing to it, or genuflecting to it, or touching it, we make an act of faith. That act of faith tells us that our crosses become gifts, because of the Cross of Christ. They become gifts that mark all of us as being saved by the blood of the Lamb.

49.2   April 18, 2003

The Passion of Jesus Christ is a story of violence, and we catch glimpses of the violent and painful death Jesus suffered when we read the Gospels. In our world, we do not have to look far to catch glimpses of similar violence and pain. During the past few weeks, CNN and Fox News have brought scenes of shock and awe, war, killing, and untold human suffering into our living rooms. Our newspapers have reported the horror imposed on people by a cruel dictator. Our world lives under a constant threat of terrorism, no matter what the official current level of threat indicates.

The Gospels also indicate another type of violence directed against Jesus – a violence that attempted to strip him of his dignity. For reasons we will never know, Judas violated a sacred trust established among a close-knit band of apostles. Out of fear, Peter denied that he ever knew the one he had given his life to follow. The angry crowds and Roman soldiers abused and spit on him, attempting to demean him. To protect himself, Pilate allowed an innocent man to be executed, even though he knew the truth about his guilt. By stripping him of his garments, the enemies of Jesus not only violated the reverence of his body, but they attacked the sacredness, integrity, and privacy of his inner person. They tried to strip him of every shred of human dignity – like human beings today violated by torture or sexual abuse or exploitation. But Jesus knew that his dignity did not depend upon the quality of his clothing or upon the decisions of earthly powers. His dignity depended on the truth about himself – that he is the Son of God. He stood before his persecutors with a dignity and a grandeur that no one can take away.

Whether we want to admit it or not, each of us will be stripped of everything we think is important. Some of us will be stripped of titles or positions or power. Disease or mental illness or failure will strip others of us. Ultimately, death strips all of us of everything. That stripping sometimes happens in an instant. Sometimes it occurs over years. But it happens, and we cannot avoid it.

The Christ we encounter in the Passion according to John teaches us how to handle the violence aimed at us, and the ways in which we might be stripped. Instead of condemning Judas, he looks on him with love. Instead of reacting to violence with violence, he tells Peter to put away his sword. Instead of cowering in the presence of the Sanhedrin, he speaks the truth about his identity. Instead of belittling a second-rate Roman governor in a backwater town, he yields to his judgment, even though he holds the ultimate power of the world. Instead of being ashamed of dying like a criminal on a cruel instrument of execution, he reigns from the cross as king of the world, entrusting us – his sons and daughters – to the care of his Mother. Through these actions, Jesus reveals the truth about himself and graces us with the courage to face the truth about ourselves.

When come forward to venerate the cross, we recognize the intimate connection between the stripping of Jesus and the stripping that is happening or will happen in each of our lives. Each of us venerates in our own way – by bowing, genuflecting, making the sign of the cross, kissing the cross, or simply touching it. That action expresses our conviction that we too have grandeur and a dignity which no one can take away from us. Our dignity has nothing to do with the quality of our clothing or what our status is or what we own. Our dignity depends on the God who was stripped and hung on the cross. Our dignity depends on Christ, who ultimately triumphed over sin and death.

49.3   April 14, 2006

As we heard the Passion according to John, we asked ourselves the question, "Were you there?" At a basic historical level, the answer is, "no, we were not there." We were not there when one of Jesus' closest associates betrayed him. We were not there when another denied knowing him. We were not there when a religious tribunal claiming to speak in God's name accused the Son of God of blasphemy. We were not there when an insignificant governor in one of Rome's remote provinces sentenced the Lord of the Universe to death. We were not there when the eternal Word of God suffered a horrible and humiliating death on a cross. Those events happened only once in history.

However, at a much deeper level, we are there through the Sacramental Life of the Church. At every Mass, we praise the Father for the Sacrifice of Jesus made present to us as we remember. We are there every time we encounter Jesus Christ in the Sacraments. On Good Friday, we are truly there as the Liturgy turns our attention to this most painful and difficult part of the Paschal Mystery – the suffering and death of Jesus Christ. Gathered there, Good Friday invites us to reflect on the reason the Lord suffered and died for us. Clearly that sacrificial death is an expression of absolute love.

C.S. Lewis helps us to understand the sacrificial love of Jesus Christ in the first of his Narnia series: *The Lion, the Witch, an▪ the War▪robe*. When the four children first enter Narnia, Edmund (the second oldest boy) has an attitude problem. Even though he had known the truth about Narnia from his own experience, he accused Lucy of creating Narnia in her imagination. He is jealous and angry with his older brother, Peter, and resented Peter telling him what to do. Edmund meets the white witch, the source of evil in Narnia and the reason why it is always winter and never Christmas. She feeds him Turkish delight and promises more if he betrays his brother and sisters. She sweetens the deal by promising that he will be king and boss his older brother around. Edmund is fooled by these false promises and does betray them, only to find out too late that the witch's promises were all lies, leading only to his death and the death of the others.

The other children plead to Aslan, the Christ figure of the novel, on behalf of their brother. Aslan explains that the white witch now has claim on Edmund. Because of his bad choices, he belongs to her. However, Aslan negotiates with the witch and offers his own life in exchange for Edmund's. As Susan and Lucy watch in horror from a distance, the white witch and her allies brutally murder Aslan at the stone table.

On the next day, Susan and Lucy arrive at the scene to see the stone table broken, with Aslan raised from the dead. The white witch had thought that she had triumphed in her deal to kill Aslan instead of Edmund. But that victory would not last. The reason it could not last lies in the sacrificial love of Aslan. The witch could not understand the motive of pure love. She had no conception of what sacrificial love could look like. For that reason, sacrificial love triumphed over treachery, manipulation, and death.

Every single one of us can identify with Edmund. Like Edmund, we have our own attitude problems. Like Edmund, we have been jealous, or angry, full of self-pity, or resentful. Satan has fooled us with false promises, and we have made some bad choices. We have turned to those things that cannot possibly satisfy us, not realizing until it is too late that they claim our lives. When we fall into sin, Satan has a claim on us just as surely as the white witch had a claim on Edmund. Like the white witch, Satan's claim on us can only bring sorrow and death. But that is exactly what Jesus Christ did for us when he died on the cross. In this great act of perfect love, he has ransomed us from the power of the Evil One, to whom sacrificial love makes no sense at all.

After we have made our Prayers of Intercession, the cross which normally hangs over our Altar will be brought forward from the back of the church. When we venerate this cross in humble gratitude for the sacrificial love of Jesus Christ who has claimed us from sin and death, we can bring with us all those times when we have offered ourselves in sacrifice out of love for someone else. Those sacrifices are acts of love; even they have seemed to be without result. They are acts of love; even when no one noticed. They are acts of love; even if they have been refused. We join our sacrifices – our acts of love – to the sacrifice of Jesus Christ, confident that they have power.

When we venerate the cross, we also bring our own crosses – those situations and conditions in our lives over which we have absolutely no control. We place those crosses within the context of the cross of Jesus Christ. Those crosses may cause pain. They may eventually take our lives. But, we trust that they will not destroy us, just as his cross did not destroy him. We express our faith that those crosses we carry can be an occasion of sacrificial love for someone else.

Last year on Good Friday, Pope John Paul II was unable to participate in the Sacred Triduum, because he was carrying a very heavy cross of illness and impending death. An aide brought a cross to his room, and he venerated it. By embracing his cross, he taught the entire world a lesson about suffering and dying. It is the lesson he learned from the cross of Jesus Christ. It is the lesson we learn again today on this Good Friday.

49.4   April 10, 2009

In listening to John's account of the Passion, we asked a rhetorical question in song over and over again: "Were you there, when they turned away from him? Were you there when they led him off to die? Were you there when they crucified our Lord?" The answer to that question at one level is, no, we were not there on that day. What happened to Jesus Christ on Good Friday happened only one time in all of human history. It happened two thousand years ago. No, we were not there.

However, at a deeper level, at the level of faith, we are there through our celebration of this most painful part of the Paschal Mystery. As we gather to remember the events of that first Good Friday, we are not presenting some kind of drama and acting out what happened. Rather, we are engaged a liturgy which makes present through our liturgical remembering the mystery of the Lord's passion, death, burial, and ultimately resurrection. At the heart of this mystery is the cross of Jesus Christ.

The cross was used by the Romans to execute someone with the most pain and humiliation. It was such a horrendous symbol that it took the Church almost three centuries before she could depict in works of religious art Jesus actually hanging on this crude instrument of death. But, Saint John makes it clear that Jesus willingly embraces the cruelty and horror of the Cross for our sakes. That embrace causes his death.

In reflecting on his incredible gift to us, Jesus invites us to make a connection between his cross and the crosses we carry in our lives. Crosses come in all kinds of sizes and shapes. We do not choose them. They always cause pain and suffering. And they always bring death. Some of us carry the cross of addiction. When we embrace that cross, we die to a certain lifestyle where drugs or alcohol served as a common bond. Some carry a cross of physical or mental suffering. Embracing that cross means dying to a life blessed by good health. Young people sometimes carry the cross of not having the athletic abilities of their friends. Embracing that cross means dying to a dream of being part of a team and participating in sports. Elderly people carry the cross of not being able to live on their own.

Embracing that cross means dying to an old way of being independent and taking care of themselves. The list goes on!

The cross of Jesus Christ gives meaning to these crosses which we carry. After we have prayed the General Intercessions, we will bring forward our cross which hangs above our Altar and invite everyone to come forward to venerate it. We will come from three different sides, as we come forward in procession for Communion. Veneration can be a touch of the part of the cross, or a kiss, or a bow, or a genuflection.

Venerating this cross involves making an act of faith. In that act of faith, we pray for the courage to embrace the death that comes from our cross. In that act of faith, we ask the Lord to remove whatever bitterness or anger comes from a cross that sometimes seems to destroy us. In that act of faith, we express our trust that whatever death comes from that cross will bring new life.

Earlier this week, a five-year-old boy asked his mother why we call today "Good" Friday. He thinks it would be better named "Bad" Friday. Today is good, because it is good for us that the Lord embraced the cruelty of his cross and faced the death it brought. Today is good, because he shows us that the cross is not the end, but the beginning of new life through the power of his resurrection. In this Liturgy, we stand in awe at the love expressed by Jesus in embracing his cross. We are here, as the Lord embraces his Cross. He is here, as we struggle to embrace ours.

49.5 April 3, 2015

During the proclamation of the Passion, we kept asking a rhetorical question in song: "Where you there? Were you there when they turned away from him? Were you there when they led him away? Were you there when they crucified my Lord?" At one basic level, the answer is "no, none of us were there over two thousand years ago in Jerusalem." Had we been there, we would have understood how horrible the cross was. It was a symbol of Roman cruelty. To everyone under Roman dominion, the cross came to say, "If you cross us, we will cross you." The Romans ruled through intimidation and threat. They did this to maintain the upper hand. They imposed their intimidation and threat before someone did it to them. They saw no other way of living. The powers of sin and death shadowed them everywhere.

The cross as a symbol goes beyond Roman domination and control. It is also a powerful symbol of all that is wrong with humanity. We fallen humans tend to cross those who cross us. When someone gets in our way or when we feel slighted, our instincts tell us to strike back, to harm, and to humiliate those with whom we are angry. Our instincts tell us to grab the upper hand, before someone else beats us to it. Even when we have honest disagreements, we cross those who disagree with us and create greater anger, pain, and division.

Jesus Christ has taken that cross and turned it into a very hopeful and life-saving symbol. Instead of using his power as the Son of God to gain the upper hand with those who betrayed, judged, and condemned him to death, he uses the cross to do battle with all that is wrong with humanity. The Passion according to Saint John helps us to understand how he turned the cross into a symbol of self-sacrificing love.

Instead of harboring resentment and anger at a friend who betrays him, Jesus accepts the hurtful kiss and accepts it as the beginning of his role as God's Suffering Servant. He faces the hostility of the Sanhedrin to clarify his true identity as God's Son. He endures the denial of Peter so he can forgive him later. He turns his trial before the Roman governor into a discussion of what truth means. As the priests are preparing the sacrificial lambs for the Passover, Jesus becomes the Lamb of God whose sacrifice enables us to pass from death to life. Instead of focusing on his own agony on the cross, Jesus establishes a relationship between his mother and the beloved disciple, making sure that we, his beloved disciples, understand that his mother is also our mother. After his death, water and blood flow from his side, so that his total gift of self will pass through the life of the Church in the Sacraments of Baptism and the Holy Eucharist.

Artists through the centuries have portrayed the final scene of the crucifixion with the Mother of God holding the dead body of her Son in her arms. We are most familiar with Michelangelo's Pieta in Saint Peter's Basilica in Rome. In the fifteenth century, the Spanish painter, Fernando Gallego, painted his own version of the Pieta. If you have gone to Confession in the past few weeks, you more than likely received a copy of this painting as a penance. In the image, Mary holds the body of her Son under the cross. In the background is the city of Jerusalem. Gallego did not research historical records to understand what Jerusalem looked like at the time of Christ. Instead, he painted the outline of his own city. In an artistic way, he is declaring that he was there when they crucified his Lord. That saving event, which happened only one time in history, is present in his life, in his time, and in his place.

It is in this sense that we are there, when they crucified our Lord. What happened on Good Friday took place only once in history. But, the power of that sacrifice continues today, in our lives, in our time, and in our place. We come forward to venerate the cross today as a sign of its power to save us. In briefly touching it, or kissing it, or bowing before it, we acknowledge our faith that the cross of Christ has become a powerful symbol of Christ's self-sacrificing love, a love that has conquered sin, hatred, revenge and death. By venerating the cross, we reaffirm our efforts to respond to hurt with the same sacrificial, merciful, and courageous love. By venerating the cross, we renew our intentions to embrace those crosses in our lives over which we have no control. It is the cross of Christ that saves us. It is the cross that allows us to refer to this Friday as "Good."

50. Easter Vigil

Readings

Genesis 1:1–2:2
Genesis 22:1–18
Exodus 14:15–15:1
Isaiah 54:5–14
Isaiah 55:1–11
Baruch 3:9–15, 32–4:4
Ezekiel 36:16–17a, 18–28
Romans 6:3–11
Mark 16:1–7

50.1 April 7, 2012

As we have kept Vigil tonight, we have heard some pretty amazing things. We heard the amazing story of God creating everything out of nothing and creating us in his image. We heard the story of Abraham's faith, so amazing that he was willing to sacrifice his son, his most prized possession. We heard the amazing story of God guiding his people through the waters of the Red Sea as he brought them to freedom from slavery. We heard amazing stories from the prophets of God's love for us, even when we walked away from him and denied his Covenant.

In this Gospel, Mark has told us the most amazing story of the history of our salvation. When the women come to the tomb in the early morning darkness and in the darkness of their grief, they find that the stone has been rolled away, and that the tomb is empty. The young man clothed in the white robe tells them something utterly amazing: he has been raised, he is not here. And then, he tells them not to be amazed!

After everything we have heard tonight, those words might strike us as very strange! And yet, when we reflect on the Gospel, Jesus had told his disciples time and time again that he would have to die and be raised from the dead. And then we need to consider the Greek word for being "amazed". "Amazed" in Greek implies being afraid and living in fear. The young man tells the women not to be afraid. This greatest and most amazing miracle in all of history will change their lives forever! They will stand awe of this miracle, but they will not be afraid. The love of Christ in the mystery of the resurrection will bring them only peace and life.

In the light of this mystery, now do something utterly amazing, utterly awesome. Garret, grab that Easter Candle. Servers, light the candles of the faithful in this assembly. The time of grief and darkness is over. It is now time to invite our Elect to pass through the waters of freedom, much as the Israelites passed through the waters of the Red Sea into freedom. Only this passing will be even more awesome, because they will pass through those waters, freeing them of all their sins, and giving them a share in the bright and amazing life he shares with us. Then they will be sealed with the Holy Spirit and fed with the Body and Blood of Christ. Diane, call forth the Elect to celebrate the Sacraments of Initiation!

50.2 April 4, 2015

When people go to graves, they usually go to remember the deceased, to pray for them, and to recall encounters that have been significant. The women go to the grave of Jesus today, because they did not have enough time to prepare properly the body of Jesus before the Sabbath. As they make their way, it is impossible to know their feelings. However, as faithful Jews, they knew the stories we heard as part of our Vigil tonight. They believed that God had created the world and intended it to be good. They understood the faith of Abraham as he responded to the God who began salvation history through him. They were grateful for God leading their ancestors through the Red Sea into slavery. They knew the words of the prophets who had assured their parents that they would be forgiven, no matter how many times they had wandered away from the Covenant. More than likely, they were hoping that God would somehow get them through this terrible loss.

But they were never prepared for what they were about to experience. They never expected to see an empty tomb, with the stone rolled away. They never expected to be told that Jesus had been raised from the dead. It will take them a while to put together the narrative. Only with time and personal encounters with the risen

Christ would they begin to understand that everything we heard tonight would be brought to completion in the resurrection of Jesus Christ.

On Palm Sunday, a young man clothed in a white garment ran away naked in fear, leaving that white garment in the hands of those who were arresting Jesus. He was running away from his baptismal promises. Today, a young man clothed wears a white garment and announces the good news of Christ's resurrection. He ties the experience of Christ's resurrection with the power of Baptism.

In just a few moments, these five Elect will go into the watery grave of the baptismal font with Christ, and emerge with their sins forgiven, completely one with the risen Christ. They will be clothed with a white garment, proclaiming the resurrection to us.

Our Easter Candle proclaims the truth of what is happening to them. Even though we lost the Garden of Eden, we now have access to Paradise through the saving Mysteries of the Lord's death and resurrection. When we renew our baptismal promises, we also renew our openness to allow the resurrection of Jesus Christ to continue to transform us.

50.3   March 31, 2018

A Vigil gives us an opportunity to hear the Word of God proclaimed. For the last hour and a half, that is exactly what we have been doing. We've listened carefully to the Word of God and heard of the incredible surprises of God's love for us. The first surprise was at the beginning. God created the world and made it very good. The next surprise comes to Abraham. Because he trusted in God by being willing to sacrifice his only son, God promised that he would have as many descendants as the stars in the sky and the sands on the shore of the sea. God surprised a group of slaves and led them through the Red Sea to freedom. God surprised his people in their Babylonian Exile and gave them consolation. God surprised others who were guilty of turning their backs on him by forgiving them.

We just heard the greatest surprise of all! The women came on the eighth day, the day after the Sabbath, to do the final acts of kindness to the dead body of their dead Master. Instead of finding his body, a young man dressed in white announced that he had been raised from the dead and went before them to Galilee, where they had started. Out of love, the Father had sacrificed his only Son. Out of love, he raised him from the dead.

Tonight, we renew our faith in this greatest of all of God's surprises. The Elect will stand before us to renounce the power of Satan in their lives. They will profess their faith in the surprising Trinity of Father, Son, and Holy Spirit. Like those women on the eighth day, they will march to our Font, which has 8 sides. They will enter into the watery tomb of that font to share in Christ's dying. They will emerge, completely one with Christ, with all their sins forgiven. Clothed in white, like that young man in the tomb, they will proclaim the resurrection and join in the Sacramental life of the Church, confident that the risen Christ will walk with them in this new creation.

In response, we who have been baptized will renew our baptismal promises. We will renew our faith in the God who always surprises. We will continue to walk with them, never despairing that the God of surprises will always keep his promises.

VI Easter

51. Easter Sunday

Readings

Acts 10:34, 37–43
Colossians 3:1–4 or 1 Corinthians 5:6b–8
John 20:1–9 or Luke 24:13–35

51.1 April 23, 2000

Once, there was a man who sold the best hot dogs in town. His hearing was not very good. So, he did not listen to the radio. His eyes were bad. So, he did not read newspapers or watch television. But he put up a few signs on the highway, rolled out his hot dog stand every day, and yelled at people to buy a hot dog. His hot dogs were so good that he kept increasing his orders for meat and buns. He bought a bigger cooker.

One day, his son came home from college and decided to help him. "Dad," he said, "Haven't you been listening to the radio or reading the papers?" The dollar is losing ground, and there is a recession around the corner. The man figured that his son should know what he was talking about, because he went to college, listened to the radio, and read the newspaper. So, he took his signs down from the highway. He cut down his orders of meat and buns. He did not take his stand out to the street. And sure enough! His son was right! His hot dog sales plummeted to nothing!

We gather today to celebrate our faith that Jesus Christ is raised from the dead. We trust that all who have died in Christ will rise with him. We believe that their lives will be transformed through the power of the resurrection in ways that cannot even be imagined. And we trust that resurrection awaits us when we die.

But we also believe that Christ's rising from the dead affects us now. His rising has the power to transform our lives now. We celebrate the Mystery of the resurrection, knowing that each of us must face a great deal of dying. It does not take faith to recognize those moments – conflicts, suffering, pain, the deaths of those we love, all the terrible times that are part of every human life.

It does take an Easter faith to confront all those dying moments, and see aspects of the resurrection already present in those moments. We can honestly confront conflicts in our relationships, because we trust that our willingness to compromise can bring us to new ways of looking at another person or point of view. We can embrace the suffering that comes from illness, because we trust that God can bring a healing we could never have imagined. We can even face the reality of our own sinfulness, because we trust that God's mercy brings new possibilities for our lives and the lives of those we have wounded.

The hot dog vendor ignored his gut feeling, listened to negative advice, and lost the vitality of his business. The disciples of Jesus peered into an empty tomb and saw the possibilities of resurrection. That is the challenge of Easter for every one of us. Right in the midst of whatever is negative in our lives, there is the power of the resurrection working to transform us. That takes a lot of faith! But that is the faith of Easter Sunday!

51.2 April 20, 2003

Easter is the only time of the year decided by the phases of the moon. We celebrate Easter today, because this is the first Sunday after the first full moon after the spring equinox. The lunar calendar connects Easter with Passover, the time when Jesus died. Fortunately for us in the northern hemisphere, this also means that Easter coincides with spring. Christ is risen, and the entire world springs to life. Saint John of Damascus wrote an ancient hymn that describes Easter as the "spring of seasons bright," after a long winter of our sins. We see new green shoots breaking the surface of the earth. Finches put on their Easter gold. And the smell of lilies fills the air. The connection is helpful, because we see God's creative power.

But that connection between Easter and spring can also be misleading. Spring is natural. We expect it to follow the dark and cold of winter. Resurrection, on the other hand, is not natural. It was not what those first disciples expected to find when they went to the tomb early in the morning, when it was still dark. The darkness of that pre-dawn morning expressed their desolation. Death had robbed them of their hope and of their future. In their shattered world, spring did not matter, much as this spring does not matter to those confronting the harsh reality of death in their lives.

Into that bleak darkness of the first Easter morning burst the glory of the most unnatural event that has ever occurred. To their utter amazement, the resurrection of Jesus Christ shed an unexpected light on the darkness of death, grief, and pain. They sensed that they had witnessed a new creation, a new and final answer to the darkness that had brought them to the tomb.

That is why we gather together this morning. The resurrection of Jesus Christ not only changed those first followers. It has the power to transform us. The resurrection of Jesus Christ invites us to face the darkness of our own world – our sins, the tragedies that befall us, the deaths of our loved ones, war and terrorism – and to trust that the mystery of the resurrection can renew us in ways that we could never expect. We can face death with the sure and certain hope that our life is hidden with Christ in God.

During the next fifty days, this assembly will reflect on the stories of the risen Christ encountering his followers. It would have been natural for Jesus to scold his followers for running away, denying, and abandoning him. It would have been natural for him to shake his finger at them and make them feel ashamed. But, in the unnatural mystery of the resurrection, he never does that. He consistently reaches out in loving compassion, pours out the bright light of his mercy, and invites them to share that profound experience of peace to everyone they meet.

Gerard Manley Hopkins was a Jesuit priest who lived at the end of the 19th Century and who used poetry to convey the Mysteries of the resurrection. In one of his poems, he asks the risen Christ to "easter in us," to "be a dayspring to the dimness of us," to "be a crimson-cresseted east." Of course, we are glad that it is spring! This particular spring brings new life. But we gather today to touch the Mystery that brings permanent change. May the risen Christ truly easter in us, so we can leave here with a renewed intention to forgive those who have hurt us deeply. May the risen Christ be a dayspring that sheds light in the dimmest parts of our lives. May the risen Christ be for each of us a crimson-cresseted east that brings new hope and a lively step.

51.3   April 16, 2006

There is a famous icon of the resurrection that dates back to the earliest days of Christianity. This icon, produced by the Eastern Church (which will celebrate Easter next Sunday) depicts the risen Christ standing on the battered-down doors of hell. He is extending his hands to a man and woman, representing Adam and Eve, who seem to be emerging from their tombs. The two figures look surprised. Locks and chains, symbols of bondage, float mysteriously in a vast black space below the figures.

If you look closely at the icon, it becomes clear that Christ is not just taking Adam and Eve's hands in an affectionate clasp. He has Adam and Eve firmly clenched by the wrists and is forcefully yanking them out of their tombs and into the freedom of the resurrection. But Adam and Eve are not too sure that they want to be freed from their tombs. Their wide iconic eyes suggest not only surprise, but also confusion and anxiety.

We are like those figures in many ways. Like them, we find ourselves in all sorts of tombs, and they smell of death. Some of our tombs are of our own making. We entomb ourselves in resentments and anger and live with divisions and hatred in our families and in our community. We fool ourselves into thinking that mindless consumption of stuff will make us happy, and we bury ourselves in hopeless debt. We look into the face of death, either a loved one is claimed by death or when we are diagnosed with a life-threatening disease, and we sink into the depths of despair and pain. We don't like these tombs any more than Adam and Eve did. But, at least we know their boundaries. We understand their limits. We have figured out how to make life work, even if we remain miserable. There is a certain comfort in the darkness.

Today, on Easter Sunday, the Risen Christ comes along and yanks us from our tombs. He has left behind the linen cloths that had bound his dead body, because they would never combine him to a tomb again. Unlike Lazarus, had needed those linen cloths again, Jesus would never know the confines of death again. He drags us out into the fullness of the light of the resurrection and makes us a promise. He promises that if we die with him, we will rise with him and live forever.

Last night, eighteen people stood before this Assembly and promised that they would die with him. They promised that they would not allow Satan to fool them with his empty promises. They also professed their faith in the Father who created them, in the Son who redeemed them, and in the Spirit who enlivens them. We yanked them into the watery tomb of baptism, and they emerged to embrace the full light of the Risen Christ. Now, we follow their example in faith. We face the Baptismal Font and repeat those promises made when we were baptized. In making those promises, we promise to allow the Lord to yank us out of whatever is a tomb for us and expose us to the brilliance and promise of living the risen life with him.

51.4 April 12, 2009

One of the great hallmarks of Easter is that we dress up in our best clothes and revel in the new life that spring brings. There may not be many Easter bonnets in our assembly today. But you look pretty good. And look at the Easter finery that Father Bob and I wear. Little kids love shiny things and come up to touch our gold vestments.

In his story of the resurrection, Saint Mark also pays attention to Easter finery. He describes a young man dressed in a white garment sitting in the empty tomb. He addresses the startled women who had come to complete the burial procedures for the body of Jesus that he has been raised from the dead. He instructs them to tell the disciples and Peter to go back to Galilee, back to the place where they had spent most of their time with Jesus, because they would see him raised from the dead there.

This is not the first time we have met a young man dressed in white in Mark's Gospel. On Holy Thursday, a disciple following Jesus from a distance after his arrest was covered by a white linen cloth. When the authorities tried to grab him, he left the cloth in their hands and ran away naked. In running away naked, he represented all of the disciples of Jesus who had left everything to follow him now leaving everything to get away from him. The bonds of their family were unraveling. On Good Friday, Mark tells us that Joseph of Arimathea wrapped the body of Jesus in a white cloth and laid him in a new tomb. That white cloth symbolizes the death of a family of disciples who had been bound together around a beloved teacher, rabbi, master, and friend. With the death of Jesus, that family unit was completely dispersed.

That is why the white garment of the young man announcing the resurrection on Easter Sunday is so significant. Only after the disciples had faced the reality of their own cowardice, fear, doubt, and grieving could they possibly understand the mystery of Jesus Christ being raised from the dead. It took Jesus' death and the absolute disintegration of their tightly knit family before they could be gathered again – not just by a teacher or rabbi or master or friend. Their family was transformed by the risen Lord.

Last night, 20 people passed through the waters of baptism at the Easter Vigil. In going into that watery tomb, they died to an old life and rose to a new life in the risen Christ in union with this closely-knit family of the Church. As soon as they emerged from those waters, they were clothed in a white garment and told to live as Christ.

Now, it is our turn. It does not matter when we were baptized – whether as an infant, or in our youth, or as adults. We turn to the waters of baptism and renew those promises made for us. In renewing our promises, we renounce the power of sin and death as forces that tend to unravel and disintegrate the fabric of our families and our lives. In renewing our promises, we state our intentions to better wear those white garments of our baptisms in a more-lively way. In renewing the promises of our baptism which incorporated us into Christ and the Church, we too are told the same thing that they young man told those startled women on the first Easter. He tells us to go – not to Galilee – but to our homes, our schools, and our places of business to proclaim the truth that Jesus is raised from the dead. With clearer Easter faith, we will also see him there.

51.5 April 8, 2012

Easter begins in darkness, always! When Mary Magdalene reaches the tomb, it is dark. That darkness is not only the physical darkness of the time before dawn. The worse darkness is that of her grief. She had come to the tomb to do one last act of kindness to the body of the one who had been taken from her. She is so filled with grief that it had not occurred to her how the heavy stone would be rolled away. It is the same darkness found in as seeds are planted into the cold ground. It is the same darkness found in ashes left from a house destroyed by fire.

If Easter begins in darkness, it ends in light, always! The darkness of Mary's grief is burned away when she recognizes the Lord in the brilliant radiance of his resurrection. She leaves the darkness of her grief behind to become the first evangelist, the first to proclaim the good news to Peter and the beloved disciple that the Lord had been raised. The beloved disciple seems to be more open to the penetrating brilliance of the resurrection burning away the darkness of his grief, and Peter comes to recognize the resurrection a little more slowly. It may have taken him a while, but eventually he allows the bright light of the Resurrection to transform his life. We see that transformation very clearly in his profession of faith given to Cornelius and his family after he had baptized them into this Mystery which he has embraced so completely.

When we entered into the Season of Lent, we were marked with ashes as a stark reminder of the darkness of our death. We who were formed from ashes will return to the ashes from which we were made. When we began planning for our gardens, we stuck those seeds into the dark, cold earth. Those plants are now emerging into the bright light of spring. On this Easter morning, we encounter the brightness of the risen Christ, who has conquered the power of sin and death. We bask in the brilliance of his resurrection, trusting the power of the resurrection to burn away whatever darkness lingers in our lives.

To be honest, we are all like Mary Magdalene when we approach the empty tomb on this Easter Sunday. Like Mary, we all have our share of darkness in our lives. We know the pain of broken relationships and losses of loved ones. We have chosen darkness over light in our failure to die to ourselves by putting our own needs before the needs of other people. We know darkness when we are plagued with doubts that that have the power to eat away at our faith.

That is why it is so important to renew our Baptismal promises on Easter Sunday. Last night nine adults, teens, and children passed through the waters of that font. They faced the darkened west and renounced the ways of Satan, prince of darkness and father of lies. They turned toward the east, the place of the rising sun, to profess their faith in the Father, Son, and Holy Spirit. They marched down the aisle and were baptized into the life of the Triune God, just like Cornelius' family had been baptized. Easter is an incredible source of great light, life, and hope. When we leave Easter to continue our journey through life, which will surely include darkness and difficulties, our Easter faith strengthens us to face them with greater faith. With this bright Easter faith, we can trust that we too can be transformed by Easter faith, to live the promises we made when we were incorporated into the Mystery of God's love through Baptism.

51.6 April 5, 2015

What happened to Jesus on Good Friday was very public. He was betrayed in a garden by one of his friends and dragged before the Sanhedrin and accused of "making himself equal to God." The religious leaders took him to the Roman governor, Pontius Pilate, and incited the large crowd to demand his crucifixion. He suffered humiliation, shame, and horrible pain in front of witnesses on the hill of execution outside the city walls of Jerusalem. Joseph of Arimathea, a member of the Sanhedrin, arranged for his burial with the women who had followed him from Galilee. There were many witnesses to what happened on Good Friday

However, there are no witnesses to what happened to Jesus today. On this day, his followers have to connect what they see with what they believe. Mary Magdalene sees that the tomb is empty and believes that someone has stolen his body. Peter sees that the burial cloths are wrapped up neatly inside the tomb and believes that the tomb is empty. The beloved disciple sees that the tomb is empty, and connects the dots. Having seen Lazarus emerge from the tomb bound in his burial cloths and destined to die again, the beloved disciple believes that Jesus has been freed from the bonds of death. With the gift of faith, he sees and believes in the resurrection of Jesus Christ from the dead.

During these last two days, we too have seen the passion and cross of Jesus Christ in the major Liturgies of the Sacred Paschal Triduum. Those rituals have invited us to connect the sufferings and cross of Jesus Christ with those sufferings and crosses that we carry in our lives. Today, we hear the risen Lord speaking to us in the Word and see his real presence in the Eucharist. On Easter Sunday, he invites us to put ourselves in the shoes of the beloved disciple and believe in the power of the resurrection. He invites us to believe that suffering, the cross, and death itself will not have the final words. He invites us to believe that we too can be transformed by the power of the resurrection.

In his resurrection, Jesus Christ was so transformed that even his closest disciples did not recognize him. As they accepted the gift of faith, his resurrection transformed them also. Look what happened to Peter. During the earthly ministry of Jesus, Peter showed signs of weakness. He hesitated to throw his net on the other side of the boat on when Jesus called him. He tried to talk Jesus out of his role as a suffering servant. He fell asleep in the Garden at Jesus' darkest hour and denied knowing him three times. After believing in the power of the resurrection, Peter is transformed. He guides the infant Church with a firm hand. He breaks Jewish ritual laws and baptizes a pagan, Cornelius, along with his family. He boldly proclaims the truth of Psalm 118 that Jesus is the stone rejected by the builders and has become the cornerstone of a living temple.

Last night at the Easter Vigil, five members of our community renounced the power of Satan in their lives, professed faith in God, entered the watery tomb of Baptism, and emerged one with Jesus Christ with all their sins forgiven. Now, we are invited to renew the promises of our Baptism. In renewing our promises, we trust in the power of the resurrection to transform us. We trust that Easter Sunday will open our eyes to see what the beloved disciple believed: Jesus Christ has been raised from the dead. Because of his resurrection, we can throw out all the old yeast of corruption and wickedness. We can carry on our lives of faith with new vigor and strength. Death has no power over Jesus Christ. And death no longer has power over us!

51.7   April 1, 2018

Mary Magdalene could not go to the tomb of Jesus on the Sabbath, the seventh day of the week. The law forbade her from performing the work of properly anointing his dead body on the day of rest. So she waits in horrible agony until the eighth day, the first day of the week, to approach the tomb in the darkness. That huge stone, the permanent barrier between life and death, had been removed. The tomb is empty. In distress, she runs to Simon Peter and the Beloved Disciple to tell them the news.

It is the Beloved Disciple who makes the connection between what had happened to Lazarus on the Fifth Sunday of Lent and what is happening on Easter Sunday. Jesus had called Lazarus out of the tomb and ordered that his burial cloths be removed. Now, the

Beloved Disciple sees the burial cloths that had bound the dead body of Jesus laid aside carefully. He believes the impossible – that Jesus Christ has been raised from the dead, and that the power of death could never touch him again. Later that day, the risen Christ himself would break through the locked doors and reveal himself, transformed through the resurrection. This eighth day now becomes the first day of the new creation.

Last night at the Easter Vigil, ten people walked to our 8-sided Baptismal Font, as we asked the intercession of the saints. They entered into that watery tomb and died to an old way of living. They emerged from those waters with all their sins forgiven, one with Jesus Christ. Sealed with the Holy Spirit in Confirmation and fed by the Body and Blood of Christ in the Eucharist, they will share in Christ's dying every time they keep their baptismal promises, so they can share in his risen life.

That is what Saint Paul says when he writes to the Colossians. Like those people baptized last night, we too have been buried with Christ in baptism and rose with him to share a new life. He advises us to seek what is above and to think of what is above. He is not telling us to walk around looking up at the sky. Rather, he is telling us that our connection with Christ through Baptism should affect the way we act in our daily lives. If we look at life from the lens of our connection with Christ, we will behave differently. We will be much more willing to forgive and let go of hurts. We will be quicker to avoid judgment and condemnation. We will let go of our own ego, our own insistence on doing things our way, and our own disordered passions.

On this eighth day, the first day of the new creation in Christ, we renew our own baptismal promises. Baptism is always about death, because baptism is about entering into the tomb with Christ. But Baptism is always about life, because Jesus emerged victorious from the tomb. That is why we renew our baptismal promises on Easter Sunday. We renew our promise to die to our selfish interests and desires. We renew our trust that the Lord keeps his promise that those who die with Christ will rise with him. Simon Peter trusted those promises. After encountering the risen Christ and listening to him, Peter has been transformed. He is no longer the bungling Peter who keeps putting his foot into his mouth. He no longer denies knowing Jesus three times out of fear. At the house of Cornelius, he now understands the Scripture that he had to rise from the dead. He speaks with confidence and authority about the power of the risen Christ in his life. The Lord will speak to us during this Easter Season, so that we too can increase our faith in the Mystery of the resurrection. We are the Beloved Disciple. We listen to the Lord, so that we too may be transformed during this Easter Season.

52. 2nd Sunday of Easter

Readings
Acts 4:32–35
1 John 5:1–6
John 20:19–31

52.1 April 30, 2000

Most of the people who worked to build the great cathedrals of Europe during the Middle Ages never saw them completed. It took hundreds of years to complete those magnificent structures. A stonecutter spent his entire life sculpting a huge, beautiful rose. It was all he ever saw. A glassmaker dedicated his life to creating one window for the great church. A laborer worked to shape a few stones that would be hauled into place to create the cathedral's massive walls. Yet, none of them ever entered the completed cathedral. But one day, the cathedral was there.

So, it is with the gift that the risen Christ left for us, his church, on that first Easter night – the gift of peace. His gift of peace is much more than a good feeling. It is much more than the absence of conflict. The peace of Christ is created brick by brick, pane by pane, rose by rose. Strengthened by our Easter faith, we slowly create the great cathedral of Christ's peace every time we perform some small act of kindness, or justice, or mercy.

That is what the earliest followers of Jesus did, so convinced were they of Christ's enduring gift of peace to them. Scholars tell us that Luke painted an overly idealistic picture of the earliest Christian community in today's first reading from the Acts of the Apostles. But even with the conflicts of the early church, Luke's point is clear: gathered around the table of the Lord to celebrate the Paschal Meal, there was a great power in their witness to the resurrection.

How many times have we doubted the Lord's presence in our midst, as Thomas did? Thomas could not believe, because he felt the wounds of Christ so intensely. We get caught up in the wounds of our parish – the power conflicts, the exclusion of certain members, differences of opinion, gossip, and the outright character assassination that is part of any human community. We are like doubting Thomas more than we think, because we allow our experience of those wounds to shake our faith in the Lord's risen presence, and in his gift of peace.

The risen Jesus, present in the Eucharist, is as close to us today as he was to Thomas. He stands in our midst and calls us to believe in his presence, right in the midst of all those wounds of his body, the church. By touching those wounds of our conflicts, problems, and divisions in day-to-day parish life, he invites us to renew our faith during this Easter Season. He invites us to see ways in which our community is united, ways in which we do serve the needs of others, and ways in which we faithfully witness to the power of the resurrection.

Like the builders of the great medieval cathedrals, we may never "enter" the completed structure of Christ's total peace. We may never know that perfect parish we all wished could exist somewhere. But the blessing of Easter gives us the wisdom, the integrity, and the sense of gratitude to carry on our work in building that peace. Once we realize this process, we can fall on our knees like Thomas, and say, "My Lord and my God!"

52.2 April 27, 2003

This Sunday has a number of names. Officially, this is the second Sunday of Easter. More recently, it has been designated as "Mercy Sunday." For centuries, this Sunday has been called "Low Sunday." We do not have to be Church historians to understand where this nickname came from. We only had to be here last Sunday, when we had people everywhere – almost hanging from the rafters! Today, we are back to normal – certainly "low" by comparison.

Why were there so many people in this church last Sunday to hear the story of the resurrection? Why did they not come back again, especially after they had been invited to share a supper with someone who has been raised from the dead and who promises new life to those who eat and drink with him? I wonder if many did not come back, because it is too difficult to believe anything unusual had happened. They might have experienced something nice, maybe even something cheerful and uplifting. But they found it impossible to believe that the resurrection of Jesus Christ changes everything.

Thomas also had his doubts. History has called him the "doubter." But, he was hardly alone. On that first Easter, all the apostles doubted that the resurrection of Jesus Christ could change anything. Otherwise, they would not have locked the doors of the place where they were hiding out of fear – not so much of the authorities – but fear of the one whom they had betrayed and abandoned. Not only did they doubt what the women reported about the empty tomb. They doubted whether their Master would forgive them.

But the risen Christ changed everything. Instead of wagging his finger at them and lecturing them about their infidelity, he shared with them his mercy, his peace, and his Holy Spirit. Isolated from the community's experience of the risen Christ, Thomas simply carried his doubts for a week longer. On that following Sunday, supported by the faith of his fellow apostles and convinced by the wounds of Jesus, Thomas made the most profound profession of faith in the Gospels – "My Lord and My God!"

We gather this Sunday, even though each of us may have our own doubts as we struggle to believe that the resurrection can change everything. To help us to believe, we hear stories from the Acts of the Apostles about how the earliest followers were changed. Today, Luke describes the unity and generosity of the first century Church. Like Thomas, we bring our own pain, confusion, and tragedies to these Eucharistic gatherings. Like his fellow apostles behind locked doors, we wonder whether our parish can become that united and powerful. But the Scriptures of Easter invite us to take another look at our lives and the life of this parish. Change comes very slowly and gradually for us most of the time, and it takes faith to recognize it. Perhaps it comes in our personal lives through the healing of a relationship, or through the gift of peace given in the midst of a struggle to make a decision, or in the forgiveness given by someone we've hurt. Our parish is slowly and gradually changed, as we recognize that we are formed from the wounds of Christ himself, and that any growth comes from his risen presence.

Instead of touching the physical wounds in the hands and side of the risen Christ, we touch his wounds in each other, in his Body, the Church. We trust his risen presence in Word and Sacrament. It is safe to bring our doubts, our fears, and our insecurities here, because our common faith urges us to believe that the resurrection can change everything. With Thomas, we can say with conviction, "My Lord and my God!"

52.3   April 23, 2006

Today is not the first time we have encountered Thomas the Apostle. We met him on the Fifth Sunday of Lent, when the other disciples warned Jesus of the dangers of going to Bethany on behalf
of Lazarus. Thomas assured him that he would go to die with him.
At the Last Supper, Thomas asked a question. When Jesus said
that the disciples knew the way to the Father, Thomas interrupted
him to say that he did know. We meet Thomas again today after
his Master's death. Instead of following Jesus to his death, he had
run away in fear. While the rest of the disciples had locked themselves in a room, he had locked himself further by isolating himself
from the fragile and broken community. That isolation kept him
from believing the other disciples that they had seen the Risen Lord.
Locked with feelings of guilt and grief and despair, he demanded
proof.

We can readily identify with Thomas. We too have been bit-
terly disappointed or crushed with grief. We know how guilt can
isolate us when we betray or disappoint other people. We can understand his despair and confusion. But, like Thomas, we also know
that the Risen Lord breaks through those barriers that we erect
around ourselves and breathes new life and hope into our lives.

That is certainly true of Easter for my family this year. When
the Triduum began on Holy Thursday, my mood and attitude were
far from ideal. There seemed to be no real solution to some of the
problems facing our parish community, and the building project
continued to offer nothing but headaches. Although I was glad that
my 24-year-old nephew was going to be baptized, I worried about
its effect on my brother and sister in law. However, the Easter Vigil
changed all of that. Having reflected on God's Word, I was overcome as each of the Elect entered the waters of Baptism. We who
had walked with them knew their stories and their struggles during
their long journey.

But nothing prepared me for the eighteenth and last baptism.
My Father, supporting himself with his walker, accompanied his
grandson, Adam, to the waters of the font. In baptizing him, I was
overcome with emotions that cannot be put into words, and so they
came out as tears. That experience of the Risen Lord transformed
my brother and sister in law – and all of our family present. Last
week, we even made tremendous advances in redesigning our education center. Easter has caused me to take another, more positive
look at some of our problems, to see that they are not as impossible
as they had seemed. The Risen Christ has broken through those
walled and isolated regions of my heart, and my response has been
a humble "My Lord and my God."

In the Acts of the Apostles, Saint Luke describes a community that knows the effects of the presence of the Risen Christ. Luke says that the risen Lord had broken through their walls of isolation and separation and gave them his peace and mercy. As a result, they lived in harmony, sharing all that they had. Luke is describing our parish. Like that early community, our parish community and our family communities are certainly not perfect. We carry those wounds on the Body of Christ that Thomas insisted on touching. The resurrection opens our eyes to the positive dimensions of our communities and invites us to recognize in those qualities the presence of the Risen Christ. With a renewed Easter faith, we too can recognize the miracles we had missed when we locked our hearts and isolated ourselves. The peace and resulting mercy given to the disciples is now given to us!

52.4 April 19, 2009

The Gospel of John identifies Thomas as "Didymus" (Greek for twin). However, history has known him as Thomas the Doubter. We can sympathize with Thomas for being identified by one of his more embarrassing moments. When my family gets together, especially in the presence of parishioners from Saint Pius, they love to tell stories about Uncle Bill that puts me in less than favorable light! They especially enjoy the story of my trying to lead them in flying kites one Memorial Day. It was much too windy. My kite skills were far too limited. Their enthusiasm was less than I desired. Our family gathering ended in disaster and embarrassment! Even my nephews and nieces who had not been born yet know the story and delight in telling how Uncle Bill made a total fool of himself before the entire neighborhood.

As a family gathered through the waters of baptism to observe the last day of the Octave of Easter, we hear this embarrassing story about Thomas. He had given up everything to be with Jesus for three years, and all his hopes were pinned on his success. He had been devastated by the humiliating execution of his Master. To make matters worse, he had bragged to the rest of the Apostles that he would go with Jesus to die in Judea when they went with him to the tomb of Lazarus in Bethany. Thomas is so filled with guilt, fear, grief, despair, and sadness that he cannot believe the report given to him by the other ten Apostles.

It is good for us to hear this story as a family of faith, because odds are pretty good that we can identify with his experience. Like Thomas, we know the aching pain of disappointment, failure, sin, and death. Like Thomas, we find it difficult to bring ourselves to believe that God will always keep his covenant, and that the risen Christ is present in the midst of our darkness and difficulties. With

Thomas, the risen Christ invites us to be honest about our doubts, not as some kind of sinful denial of the truth, but as honest questions which force us to face the complicated questions of faith and life. Just as the risen Christ is gentle with Thomas the Doubter, so he is gentle with us. He invites us to see doubt not as the opposite of faith, but rather as the other side of the same coin.

Thomas invites us to bring our doubts to this assembly every Sunday. He knows from his own experience that doubting in solitary isolation is dangerous and can lead to despair. That is what happened to Judas when he separated himself from the fellowship of the Apostles, which had been joined by love and now was scattered by sin and denial. Like Thomas, we bring our doubts to this assembly and listen carefully as the Lord speaks to us through the word. Like Thomas, we are fed by the very substance of the Risen One in the Eucharist. Like Thomas, we are likely to know the wounds that are present in this Body of Christ, this assembly of the faithful which has our share of weaknesses, sins, failures, and human limitations. Like Thomas, we are invited to deepen our knowledge of the faith by participating in adult education series offered by the parish and the Diocese.

By facing his doubts squarely and returning to the community of the Apostles, Thomas saw the risen Christ in the flesh and made the ultimate profession of faith, calling him "my Lord and my God." Thomas invites us to face our doubts squarely, bring them to this community of the faithful every Sunday, and recognize the risen Lord in the Word proclaimed and in the Breaking of Bread. In doing this, our faith can actually grow stronger. We are in that number which the risen Lord counts as "blessed" – those who have not seen and have believed.

52.5   April 15, 2012

We can only imagine what the disciples were feeling after Jesus had been crucified. They had left everything to follow him. They had been drawn by his teachings and moved by his miracles. They had puzzled over his talk of the Messiah being a suffering servant. Now, their master and teacher had been executed in a cruel and humiliating way. Even worse, they had run away in fear instead of standing by his side. No wonder they locked themselves in that room! They may have been afraid of the religious authorities. If the women were correct in their report of the resurrection, they were afraid of facing Jesus in their shame at their cowardice.

Thomas the Apostle did something we often do when we faced with disappointment, pain, and guilt. He isolated himself. When Jesus had announced that he was going to Bethany to raise Lazarus from the dead, Thomas had bragged that he would go with Jesus to die with him. At the Last Supper, Thomas demonstrated that he had not understood Jesus' talk of dying and rising when he raised his hand and announced that he did not know the way to the Father. Filled with grief, shame, and disappointment, he removed himself from the rest of that wounded community. He was not present when the risen Lord walked through their locked doors and gave them his mercy for having abandoned him. In his isolation, grief, and guilt, Thomas could not bring himself to believe the news of the resurrection. It was only when he rejoined the community and encountered those wounds on the transformed body of the risen Christ that he could make the most profound profession of faith in the Gospel: "My Lord and my God!"

We gather today in this community of faith to encounter the risen Christ. We just heard his words in the Gospel. As we prepare for the breaking of bread, we are especially aware of our children who will be fed by the Body and Blood of Christ for the first time. When you parents carried them to the waters of Baptism, you joined them to this community of faith. You promised to teach them the ways of faith. You are keeping that promise today by bringing them to this Sacrament of Initiation. This time, they will walk down the aisle on their own to renew the baptismal promises you made for them.

On this joyful day, we can learn a great deal from the community of disciples who locked themselves in the upper room out of fear. Like them, we too have not always kept our promises to teach the ways of faith. We can also learn a great deal from the Apostle, Thomas. Like him, some have isolated themselves from the community for any number of reasons. But the risen Lord speaks to all of us through the faith of these children. He uses their enthusiasm to call us to become more faithful and to trust his mercy as we renew our efforts to keep the promises we made when we brought them to the waters of baptism.

Through those waters, all of us have been recreated into the Body of Christ. As the Body of Christ at Saint Pius, we try to imitate the example of the Church of the Acts of the Apostles by being of one heart and mind. Many in our community try to imitate their example by giving themselves in humble service. But, like that early Church, we too bear our wounds as the Lord's Body. We fail to live these ideals. We sometimes put our own needs ahead of others. But, we trust what the Lord tells Thomas. We trust that we are counted among those who believe without seeing. We trust that by encountering the wounds of the Body of Christ which is Saint Pius today, we are encountering the presence of the risen Christ in our midst. We trust in the Lord's mercy for our failures. We trust that through our faith in the resurrection, we may have life in his name.

52.6 April 12, 2015

The disciples had many reasons for locking themselves in the upper room. Their leader had been executed like a common criminal an extremely cruel and humiliating way. The Roman way of crossing those who crossed them causes fear. They fear that this will happen to them. They fear the scorn heaped on them by the skeptical residents of Jerusalem: "you are in a long line of people duped by fake messiahs." But there is an even greater fear. They know that the tomb is empty and have heard of the claims of Mary Magdalene that Jesus had been raised from the dead. If her report were true, Jesus would certainly be angry with them. Despite their repeated claims of being faithful, they had proven to be cowards and unfaithful.

But the risen Christ breaks through those locked doors. Instead of castigating them and giving them a sermon on being more faithful, he gives them peace. The Hebrew word, shalom, implies forgiveness and the presence of the messianic age promised by the prophets. Now that Jesus has been transformed by the resurrection, he shows them what they would recognize, what caused them to run away: his wounded hands and side. In case they are do not understand, he says again, "peace be with you." Then he gives them the gift of the Holy Spirit and tells them to give this gift of mercy, or peace, to anyone coming to believe in the presence of the risen Lord.

During Holy Week, Father Terry and I spent hours in the Confessional extending this mercy, this incredible peace, to those who were very conscious of their failings and sins. Over and over again, we, who need God's mercy ourselves, became instruments of that same mercy to others. Through the Sacrament of Reconciliation, the Lord does not condemn or yell at us. He forgives us, and gives us the grace to begin again.

And then there is Thomas. We have no idea why he is absent. I suspect that he is locked in his guilt. He had bragged that he would go to the tomb of Lazarus in Bethany with Jesus to die with him. He had told Jesus at the Last Supper that he did not know the way to the Father. Locked in his guilt and self-hatred, he is absent. Locked In his absence, he cannot believe that the Lord had been raised from the dead. He demands proof. He wants to see the wounds that have caused his guilt. And sure enough, the Lord presents those wounds to him on the following Sunday. As a result, Thomas moves from the depths of doubt to the highest expression of faith in Jesus: "my Lord and my God."

We often look negatively at Thomas and call him doubting Thomas. However, he can help us understand our faith. Like Thomas, we are often absent. Through our own sins and human weakness, we distance ourselves from the Lord and sometimes stay away from the believing community. At other times, God appears to us as absent from our lives. Like Thomas, we respond to this absence by wanting tangible proofs of the Lord's risen presence. We look for a personal and real relationship with Jesus Christ, which we eventually find when we touch his real presence in the Sacramental life of the Church and hear him speak in his Word. Then, we too can cry out: "my Lord and my God." We begin to understand that doubt is not the opposite of faith, but rather the path through which we pass to a deeper faith.

Jesus says to Thomas that we are blessed who have not seen and have believed. We have not experienced the risen presence of the Lord in the same way as Thomas or any of the other disciples did. But in our growth in faith from the absence of God to God's intense presence in our lives, we have come to believe. May this Easter Season sustain us in our doubts, carry us through the ways that God may appear absent, and bring us to a deeper faith in the risen presence of our Lord Jesus Christ. Through that faith, we truly have life in his name.

52.7   April 8, 2018

Saint John reminds us that Thomas is called "Didymus," meaning that he has a twin brother or sister. However, Saint John is also reminding us that each one of us is a "twin" to Thomas. Like Thomas, we were not present when the risen Lord broke through those locked doors on Easter Sunday. Like Thomas, we did not hear the words "peace be with you," nor did we see the wounds in his hands and side. That is why Jesus pronounces us "blessed", because we have not seen as Thomas eventually did, and we have not witnessed the physical wounds on the transformed body of the risen Christ, as he did. But we believe.

We are blessed in another very unique way. Today, one of the members of our parish, Father Christopher Brennan CSC, is celebrating his Mass of Thanksgiving. A year ago, he made a commitment to live as a vowed religious in the Congregation of Holy Cross. He has already dedicated himself to doing what the earliest disciples did in the Acts of the Apostles: having everything in common and bearing witness to the resurrection of Jesus Christ by teaching on the authority of the Apostles. Yesterday, he was ordained a priest and received the commission given by the Risen Lord to the Apostles from Bishop Jenky, a successor of the Apostles.

Father Chris, as a "twin" of Saint Thomas the Apostle, you have received the Lord's farewell gift of peace and given a generous share of the Holy Spirit, the Advocate. During your priestly ministry, you will minister many times to the wounds present in our world and in the Body of Christ. In the name of the risen Lord, you will heal the deep wounds caused by sins. You will administer the Sacrament of the Anointing of the Sick to those who are wounded by any kind of sickness. You will release Catechumens from the scourge of their sins when you baptize them. You will prepare couples to enter into the many sacrifices involved in the Sacrament of Matrimony. Having worked with you for a year in this ministry, I am confident that you will prepare them well. Most importantly, you will celebrate the Eucharist, proclaiming the risen Lord's mercy in your preaching of the Word and making the Lord present in bread and wine. You will administer the Eucharist often as food for the journey of many people.

We do not have to look far these days to recognize the many and deep wounds in our world and in our Church. As a Church, we share in both its glories and its blemishes, which is what unites us more than divide us. Touching these wounds, not turning away in horror, you can help the people you serve to live out that shared agape love that we hear in the first reading. Please do not be afraid to touch those wounds, as Jesus often touched the wounds of so many sick people, especially those excluded from society as lepers. Do not be afraid of your own wounds. Jesus never entrusted the Mysteries of the Kingdom of God to perfect people. You know your brother Holy Cross priests and me well enough to recognize our weaknesses, our vulnerabilities, and our sins. Do not allow your wounds to make you fearful.

All of us are "twins" of Saint Thomas the Apostle. We are truly blessed to believe without seeing and to recognize his risen presence in so many wounds. We truly are blessed to celebrate this Mass with you and show our support. You will be a good priest! You come from a parish founded by the Congregation of Holy Cross. Blessed Basil Moreau is looking down on you right now and telling you to serve with zeal "to make God known, loved, and served, and thus save souls." Saint Andre Bessette is standing over there and smiling with pride at you. The Mother of God and the Beloved Disciple are standing on the anchor that is you wear around your neck. Trust the risen Lord to give you the strength to proclaim the Good News of Salvation and bring healing to our wounded world.

53. 3rd Sunday of Easter

Readings

Acts 3:13–15, 17–19
1 John 2:1–51
Luke 24:35–48

53.1 May 7, 2000

A couple of weeks before Easter, Saint John told us the story of
Jesus raising his friend, Lazarus, from the dead. When Lazarus
emerged from that tomb, everyone recognized him. He was the
same Lazarus, brought back to the same life. Today, a couple of
weeks after Easter, Luke tells us a story of Jesus coming back from
the dead. In this case, not even his closest friends recognized him.
They did not know him, because Jesus was not the same. The resurrection had changed him. Only when he revealed himself through
familiar words or actions did they recognize who it was: the Jesus
who ate and drank with them, the Jesus who appeared as "flesh and
bones". It took eyes of faith to recognize Jesus.

This story tells us something about the presence of the risen
Jesus in our lives. The Lord is present and appears to us as "flesh
and bones". But we need eyes of faith to recognize Jesus. We might
see the awkward kid who never gets chosen for a team, and we
want to ignore him. Through eyes of faith, we recognize Christ
inviting us to extend compassion. I might be running to the Parish
Center, late for yet another appointment, and someone demands
my time. Through eyes of faith, I recognize the nail-marked hand
of Jesus. Or, you are reading the paper at the end of another brutal
day. Suddenly, you are interrupted with, "Mom I need help with

my math. Dad, you promised to help me with my scouting project". You look up, and there stands Jesus.

Jesus appears to us time and time again as "flesh and bones." But it takes faith to see beyond the externals and recognize his risen presence. That is why this Eucharist is so critical. We gather every Sunday to praise and thank the Father for all he has given us through his Son and in the power of the Holy Spirit. We recognize the risen Jesus in the breaking of the bread, just as surely as those two disciples recognized him when he broke bread with them at Emmaus. In recognizing him here, our eyes are opened to recognize him as "flesh and bones" when we leave this place.

Each Eucharist has the power to change us, as long as we remain open. Each time we gather here to take bread, bless it, break it, and give it, we are changed a little more. Maybe that is why the disciples were afraid when they first recognized Jesus. They were afraid of the ways they would have to be changed to recognize him as "flesh and bones".

The second graders making their First Communion today have no fears! Their trust in God and their enthusiasm can teach us some powerful lessons. They teach us that we can never take the Eucharist for granted, even though the newness may have worn off years ago. They still have to learn that changes caused by Eucharist can be painfully slow and gradual. But their simple faith can renew our appreciation for this mystery. Our weekly encounters with the risen Lord in this Eucharist can transform us into the full stature of the Body of Christ. That is who we are called to be – the church entrusted today with the task of spreading the Good News.

53.2　May 4, 2003

Those words – "Have you anything here to eat?" – are heard on a daily basis. Mothers hear this question when their children bring half the neighborhood. "Hey, Mom, I'm hungry. Can you get us something to eat?" We hear this question on the street, when a man in ragged clothing thrusts his hand into our face. "Can you spare a couple of bucks for a meal?" We hear this question today from Bishop D'Arcy. "Can you help Catholic Charities provide for the nutritional needs of poor infants in their annual Mother's Day Collection next Sunday?"

When people ask these questions, they are really asking the same question posed by the risen Christ to his disciples in today's Gospel – "Have you anything here to eat?" When the disciples gave the risen Christ a piece of fish, they recognized him not as a ghost, but as the one they had come to know and love. When we respond to people asking us to give them food, we recognize the risen Christ and feed him again when we feed them by meeting their needs – whatever it is for which they hunger or thirst.

Feeding Christ present in those who approach us to satisfy their hungers and thirsts does something else for us. In responding to Christ's needs in the poor and in those whom we serve, we become aware of our own deep-seated hungers and thirsts. Just as the risen Christ completely exceeded the expectations of those two disciples on the road to Emmaus, so he satisfies our deepest hungers and thirsts by giving himself under the form of bread and wine at the Eucharist – at the breaking of bread. Once fed, we can have the strength to feed Christ in others.

This weekend, we invite half of our second graders to share this Eucharist for the first time. They hunger and thirst for uncomplicated things in their lives. Thanks to our patron, Pope Pius X, Christ feeds them at this age with his Body and Blood. Over time, they will gradually open their eyes to understand the ways in which they will feed him in serving the needs of others. Their uncomplicated faith in the risen Lord's presence in the breaking of bread can be a source of inspiration to us, who have shared in the Eucharist often. Their coming to the table reminds us that we need to approach the Eucharist with a deepening awe. But more than anything else, their coming to the table for the first time reminds us of the deep connection between knowing the risen Lord and keeping his commandments. That is the point of the passage from the first Letter of Saint John today. As we get to know him more deeply in the breaking of bread, we understand that our behavior must gradually change to reflect that interchange between the Lord feeding us with his Body and Blood and our feeding him in the poor, the needy, and those who depend on us.

We rejoice with these children today, and with their families. In that rejoicing, we understand that the Lord's commandments to love as he has loved us are not just burdensome laws that must be followed to avoid punishment. Fed by the Lord himself, we wholeheartedly feed him again in our acts of humble service.

53.3 April 30, 2006

The first Letter of John (second reading today) is addressed to a group of people who claimed to know God. Known as "Gnostics," these people insisted that they knew God through secret revelations, and that their knowledge of God was totally unrelated to the way they behaved. The letter tries to correct this impression. John tells the Gnostics that their knowledge of God is closely connected to the way they behave in their lives. The standard for behavior, John says, is no secret. It has been revealed to everyone through the commandments – not only those given through Moses on Mount

Sinai, but also to those given through Jesus Christ that the law and the prophets.

John also writes to us. We know God. We know that the Father has raised Jesus his Son from the dead. We know that, not only from the sermon of Peter in the Acts of the Apostles, but also from our own experiences of the ways in which the Risen Christ shows himself to us. We celebrate this knowledge of the resurrection for fifty days, because it takes at least that much time for it to sink into our hearts and understanding. Like the earliest disciples, we do not always recognize him when he shows himself to us in any number of ways in the ordinary circumstances of our early lives. Like them, we become startled and terrified and wonder whether we are seeing a ghost.

When we become startled and terrified, the worst thing we can is to isolate ourselves from the community. That is what two disciples had done on the first day of the week when they ran away from Jerusalem and headed to Emmaus. The seven miles they traveled were more symbolic than literal, because those miles represented their efforts to separate themselves from what had happened to their Master on Friday. On the road to Emmaus, the Risen Lord walked with them and spoke to them, even though they did not recognize him. When they finally did recognize him in the Breaking of Bread, they returned to the community, which supported their faith when the Lord showed himself in his flesh and bones, wounds and all.

This Sunday, we are inviting half of our second graders to the Eucharistic Table for the first time. In their own uncomplicated way, they might just be leading us to a deeper faith in the Eucharist, in which we recognize the Risen Lord. That is why we celebrate this Sacrament of Initiation during the Easter Season. Some of us gather at this Altar every week. The children remind us not to take this Gift lightly and be more respectful and awed at the Mystery we share. Some of their parents gather here either infrequently or not at all. Their children are calling them to be more faithful to this parish community. Even with all our wounds, we are the Body of Christ, even when we do not always apply the knowledge of our faith to the way in which we behave. The children invite their parents to be more present in this community, to touch our wounds, and to reaffirm their faith in the Lord's presence in this Sacrament.

The First Letter of John has it right! Even though we know the Risen Lord, we do not always keep his commandments. Our behavior belies that knowledge, that faith. The Eucharist has the power to change us every time we approach it. Within the midst of this community, we hear the Lord's Word calling us to repentance.

Fed by his Real Presence, we too are sent from here to preach the Good News of the Resurrection of Jesus Christ.

53.4 April 26, 2009

During this Easter Season, the Scripture Readings help us connect the Mystery of the Resurrection with our daily lives. As we hear the reactions of the earliest followers of Jesus as he reveals himself to them, it is clear that they have trouble recognizing him, despite the fact the three years they had in close contact with him. In today's Gospel, they are startled and terrified when he stands in their midst, just as the two disciples tell them their about their experience of recognizing him in Emmaus. They think they are seeing a ghost. And yet, they recognize him in two ways. He shows them the scars in his hands and his feet. Then, he eats with them. Both of these details are important, because they help us to identify his risen presence in our midst.

Jesus may be transformed through the power of the resurrection. He walks through locked doors. He lives forever. But, he has scars. Those scars are part of the Paschal Mystery. They connect the glory of the resurrection with the pain of the cross. They remind the disciples that the agony of Jesus was real, and that their cowardice, betrayal, and denial are also real. However, those scars speak of the healing of the wounds through power of the Lord's mercy.

As we gather at this Mass, we too have our share of scars. Many of us have physical scars that remind us of surgeries or accidents that have healed. We also have scars that are not so visible. We bear the scars of our own failures and of the ways we have not been faithful. We bear the scars of resentment and anger and grudges we hold against each other. The scars on the body of the risen Lord invite us to believe that he is present among us, scarred as we might be.

Jesus also eats with his disciples. Our Gospel begins with the two disciples returning from Emmaus to tell the others that they had recognized him in the breaking of bread. He now takes a piece of fish, reminiscent of the multiplication of the loaves and fishes, and eats with them. They know that it is really Jesus, because a ghost does not eat food.

We believe in the resurrection because of the witness of those disciples. Unlike them, we have not seen him in the flesh. But, we do recognize him in this breaking of bread and sharing of the cup of salvation. He truly is present in this Eucharist we share, and he invites us to face our scars with hope and confidence, because he feeds us as he heals us and binds us together again.

We who are adults bear many more scars than our second graders who are invited to the Lord's Table for the first time. Life has a way of doing that to us. That is why it is so important for us to be here with them. We share our faith with them, knowing that we all bear our scars. We share our trust that their participation in the Eucharist with us each Sunday will open their eyes to his presence, as they grow up and bear the scars that are part of living in this world.

Boys and girls, you need to know that you are opening our eyes in a new way to the Mysteries we sometimes take for granted, or in some cases, to the Mysteries we have been neglecting. As we struggle with our own scars that come from the painful element of the Paschal Mystery of Jesus Christ, you remind us that the Risen Christ is at the heart of our lives, inviting us to recognize him right in our midst. We carried you to the waters of baptism. Now, you walk back on your own two feet to renew those promises made for you eight years ago. And then, clothed in those white garments that connect you to the waters of Baptism, you walk in procession with us to be fed by the Body and Blood of Christ, scars and all!

53.5   April 22, 2012

When we met Simon Peter on Palm Sunday in the reading of the Passion, he was a coward. Despite his bragging at the Last Supper, he denied knowing Jesus three times out of fear. We met him again in the Gospel on Easter Sunday. He peered into the empty tomb and saw the evidence that Jesus had been raised from the dead, but his faith was not as strong enough to believe in the resurrection. When we meet him today in the Acts of the Apostles, he boldly proclaims the truth about Jesus, knowing that his words would bring the wrath of the Sanhedrin upon him. He speaks the truth with love, giving his audience a chance to change their hearts by telling them that they had acted out of ignorance. What caused such a dramatic change in Peter?

The answer lies in his encounter with the risen Christ. He encountered the risen Lord on the night of the resurrection, when Jesus walked through the locked doors and gave them peace. In his encounter with the risen Christ on the shore of the Sea of Galilee, Jesus asked him three times if he loved him. He repeats the question, not to shame Peter, but to affirm his total forgiveness. Peter's encounters with the risen Christ changed him and transformed him into the rock of faith to which Jesus had called him.

We may not encounter the risen Christ in the same way as the two disciples encountered him on the road to Emmaus. Nor do we encounter him as the disciples do when he shows him his hands and his feet and eats with them. But we encounter him in the same real way in this Eucharist. We recognize him in bread transformed into his Body. We recognize him in wine transformed into his Blood. Every time we encounter the risen Lord in the Eucharist, we give him a chance to transform us into who we became through the waters of baptism – the Body of Christ called to witness to the faith today.

When Saint John wrote his letter to the community of believers, he was addressing a heresy being promoted by a group of people known as Gnostics. This faction believed that good Christians could not sin. They argued that they had been saved through the waters of Baptism, and that there was no connection between their salvation and any ethical living. John points out that there is a strong connection between the faith they profess and the way they live their lives. He knows that no one is a perfect witness, and that we all fail in one way or another to witness to our faith. But when we acknowledge our failures, the same risen Christ forgives us and sends us from Mass to be better witnesses.

Several years ago, a Christian businessman gave a strong presentation at a church on the commandment, "Thou shall not steal." When he boarded a city bus the next day to go to work, he handed a dollar bill to the driver. As he walked back to his seat, he counted his change and noticed that the driver had given him a dime too much. When he walked back and gave the dime back, the driver told him that he had given him too much change on purpose. He had been at the talk the night before and wanted to see if the man lived what he was teaching.

People watch us also, in ways that we sometimes do not understand. In response to God's Word and fed by the Body and Blood of Christ, we go out today to be witnesses of our faith, trusting that the risen Lord will continue to change us in this encounter with him.

53.6 April 19, 2015

Throughout his Gospel, Saint Luke tells us that Jesus often shared meals with people. His biggest meal involved feeding thousands of people with five loaves and two fish. He would eat with sinners and tax collectors, offering them God's fellowship and scandalizing the pious Pharisees. At the Last Supper, he took bread, blessed, broke, and gave it to those who would soon abandon him, making sure that he would be present in a real way to his disciples through the ages in the form of bread and wine. On the day of the resurrection, he walked with two disciples running away from Jerusalem. Even though they did not recognize him, he opened their hearts and minds to the Scriptures that the Christ would suffer and die for them. At Emmaus, he joined them for a meal, taking bread, blessing, breaking, and giving it to them. They recognized him in the breaking of bread.

Today, those same two disciples are back in Jerusalem, back in the same place where their leader had been so cruelly executed, back to the fear from which they had been fleeing. At a meal, the risen Lord appears. Again, they do not recognize him, because he has been transformed through the Resurrection. Again, he gives them his peace, his mercy, his forgiveness for their abandoning him and not believing in him. He invites them to touch his hands and feet. He asks for a piece of fish to eat, showing that he is real, that he is not a ghost or a strong reminder of his former presence among them. In the resurrection, he has redeemed everything that is so wrong with the world, including the betrayal by Judas, the judgment of Pontius Pilate, the hatred of the Sanhedrin, and their own abandoning of him.

We celebrate Easter for fifty days, because it takes that long to sort out the implications of this greatest of our Christian Mysteries. In gathering at this Eucharistic Meal, we hear him speak to us in his Word, inviting us to open our hearts and minds to the ways that our sufferings and pain have redemptive significance because of his suffering and pain. He invites us to face death with the same courage and hope that he did. Then, we recognize his true presence when we take bread, bless the Father for the sacrifice of Jesus made present as we remember, break, and give. Then, he sends us to witness to the power of the resurrection in our world.

When Saint Peter boldly proclaims the power of the resurrection of Jesus Christ, he does not mince any words. He tells it like it is. YOU did not recognize the author of life, he tells the people in the Temple. YOU denied him in front of Pontius Pilate, released a murderer instead, and put him to death. Peter does not say these things out of arrogant condemnation, but out of a realization of his own sins and failures. Like him, they did not know what they were doing, and God's mercy is theirs. He tells them to change their hearts and recognize the truth.

The risen Lord invites us to have this same attitude. In the light of the resurrection, he invites us to look at our behavior. If we really believe in the resurrection, then we need to keep the commandments to love God and neighbor. In the spirit of true repentance, we can address honestly what is wrong and sinful in our own lives and in our world. But, we do so with the spirit of mercy and compassion, the mercy and compassion that comes from the transforming power of the resurrection. We do not gather here to recall the spirit of a great man who taught beautiful lessons and did wonderful things. We gather here to celebrate his real presence in the resurrection, and learn how to be converted, to turn more completely to the One who has the power to save us.

53.7 April 15, 2018

When we meet the disciples in today's Gospel, they are listening to the two disciples who had just returned from Emmaus. These two disciples had told the gathered community what had happened to them. They had been running away from Jerusalem on that first day of the week, because they were devastated by the public execution of the one whom they had thought was the messiah. Since they could not imagine God's messiah being treated in such a horrible way, they had given up all hope and were leaving town. The risen Christ joined them, even though they did not recognize him. He listened to their pain and began to apply the familiar words of Scripture to what happened to him. Those words caused their hearts to burn within them. When he accepted their invitation to stay with them, they recognized him in the breaking of bread. Then, they returned to Jerusalem convinced of the power of the resurrection.

As they are speaking, the risen Christ appears again and greets them with the words, "Peace be with you." We would expect them to be overjoyed. But instead, they are startled and terrified. Those two reactions are important for an understanding of our own Easter faith. Part of their reaction comes from their sense of guilt. They had not been faithful to Jesus when he was betrayed and executed. Instead, they ran away in fear. Despite the consistent greeting of the risen Christ, "Peace be with you," they must have been waiting for the other shoe to drop, for the Lord to chide them for their infidelity.

But another huge part of their reaction has to do with their terrifying experience. Despite Jesus speaking continually of his role as a suffering servant, they could not let go of their expectations that a messiah should be a conquering hero. So jarred by their experience of his horrendous dying, they still had trouble embracing this entirely new concept of rising.

That is why the risen Christ has to assure them that he is truly raised from the dead. He shows them his wounds, not to make them feel guiltier, but to allow them to see the real effects of sin. Instead of feeding them, as he did at the Last Supper, they feed him with a piece of baked fish, proving that he is not a ghost. Then he opens their minds to the words of Scripture, just as he had done for the two disciples on the road to Emmaus. Filled with a deeper understanding of the Paschal Mystery and with joy, they accept his commission to spread the good news.

During this Season of Easter, the risen Lord speaks to us at every Mass, just as surely as he spoke to the two disciples on the road to Emmaus and to the gathered community in today's Gospel. He feeds us with his Body and Blood at every Mass, just as surely as he shared these meals with the original witnesses. But like those disciples, we too can become startled and terrified when we are confronted with those elements of the Paschal Mystery that involved suffering. When we are faced with the death of a loved one, or when we suddenly have a very heavy cross placed on our shoulders, we react in the same way as those disciples did. Like those disciples, we too make some bad choices and are faced with the guilt and weight of our sins. But like those disciples, we can turn to the Lord and receive his peace and divine mercy.

Not only does the risen Christ reveal himself to us here in Word and Sacrament, but he also reveals himself in the graced encounters with other people. In his speech in the Acts of the Apostles, Peter explains that he and John had healed a crippled man, not by their own power, but by the power of the risen Christ. The Easter Season invites us to consider the advice of the First Letter of John and grow in our personal relationship with Jesus Christ. When that happens, we begin to understand the intimate connection between loving him and loving others. Then, we too can experience the joy and amazement of the presence of the risen Lord in our broken world.

54. 4th Sunday of Easter

Readings

Acts 4:8–12
1 John 3:1–2
John 10:11–18

54.1 May 14, 2000

For most of their history, the people of Israel described their leaders in terms of being shepherds. Unfortunately, not all the leaders of ancient Israel were interested in the dynamics of *shepher•ing*. Instead, they resorted to the tactics of *her•ing*. Far too many of them thought only in terms of their own interests, and they herded their people into directions that were not necessarily for the good of the people.

We see examples of herding in our own day. The Nazis herded their enemies into cattle cars during World War II and dumped them into concentration camps. Saddam Hussein herded his enemies into prisons and eliminated those who opposed him. In many places in the orient, mass transit companies hire "professional pushers" to pack a train or bus with the maximum number of people. This custom may be good for company profits and time schedules. But it does not do much for people's comfort or dignity. In this country, Madison Avenue knows how to herd people! Advertisers are careful to hire certain celebrities to promote their product. And then they rely on those endorsements to entice mobs to rush toward their new fashions or fads. How many of us have bought something we do not need, because everyone else (the *her•*) is buying it?

Against this background of herding, Jesus offers us the leadership style of the Good Shepherd. As the Good Shepherd, Jesus is not interested in coercing huge crowds to do what he wants. He knows each of us by name. He never resorts to mob psychology. Instead, he calls each of us to make personal decisions. He does not rely on expediency. He laid down his life that we might have a personal relationship with the Father through him.

With these Scriptural images of leadership in mind, both the pope and our bishop urge us to reflect on our style of shepherding. Enclosed in the bulletin is a booklet with a message from each of them. In the spirit of today's Scripture readings, both challenge those of us who are leaders to reflect on the quality of our shepherding. Parents are challenged to follow the example of the Good Shepherd in setting their children as the top priorities, especially in the face of the incredible demands made on parents (mothers) for their time and energy. Those of us who are vowed religious or priests are urged to resist the temptation to herd our people. With diminishing numbers of priests and sisters and with growing numbers of people in parishes, we are always being tempted to be efficient managers. The Good Shepherd insists that we must be shepherds, paying attention to the individual needs of our flocks.

Shepherding people is much more difficult than herding them. Being a shepherd implies that we lay down our lives in the same way that the Good Shepherd laid down his life for us. But if we are willing to renew our efforts to shepherd those in our care, then we will not have to worry about a shortage of good shepherds in the future. With our example, and with lots of prayer, we trust that our young people will freely respond and choose to become good shepherds themselves.

54.2 May 7, 2006

In the Ancient Near East, kings preferred the image of a shepherd to describe their relationship to their subjects. They noticed that sheep are utterly vulnerable and helpless. Lacking any power of their own, these sheep were at the mercy of self-absorbed shepherds could do anything they wanted with the sheep in their flocks. Kings used this image to justify using their power to do whatever they wanted to serve their own needs.

Jesus refers to such leaders as "hired men." In stark contrast to them, he offers the image of himself as the good shepherd, who does not define his role in terms of power. Instead, he defines it completely in terms of love. Good shepherds herded their sheep into sheepfolds at night, where they could sleep in safety. Because there were no doors to these sheepfolds, shepherds would lay down across the opening, becoming the first defense against a hungry wolf or a greedy thief. Shepherds were known to give up their lives in these instances. Jesus tells us that he lays down his life for us, his sheep, totally out of love for us. In laying down his life for us on the Cross, the Good Shepherd becomes the Lamb of God, given to us as Food.

This Easter Season continues to celebrate his laying down his life for us and the Father raising him up again. On this Sunday, Jesus challenges those of us who serve as shepherds to examine our motives. He holds himself up as a very high bar for those of us who serve as priests and religious. He tells us to let go of any motive of power as we serve our people. Knowing there is only one Good Shepherd, we ask God's mercy for those times we have used our positions for power or personal gain. We humbly trust that even our stumbling attempts to model ourselves after the Good Shepherd will attract the attention of young men and women whom the Lord might be calling. And so, we pray for them today, that they might have the courage to respond to the call of the Good Shepherd. Father Dan and I have made some first steps in identifying some of these young people, and your support of our efforts is critical.

The Lord also speaks to another very important group of shepherds – those of you who live the vocation of being parents. There is no doubt that our parents lay down their lives for their children. Parents work second jobs so they can send their children to a decent college. Parents sacrifice enormous chunks of time and lots of expensive gasoline to be present to their children in their many activities. Parents drag themselves to work, after laying down their sleep for a sick child the night before.

Today, the Good Shepherd raises the bar for parents, challenging them to look beyond the limits of what they can see in this world to the possibilities created by his resurrection. In bringing their children to the waters of Baptism, they have allowed the Good Shepherd to make them children of God. Using the words of the second reading, what they will later be after death can only be imagined. The Good Shepherd speaks through our children coming to their First Communion today to remind their parents to look beyond the limits of their imaginations in this world. Laying down their lives must include bringing them to Mass every Sunday and truly teaching the ways of faith.

The Easter Season celebrates the Life of Christ and his victory over sin and death. The Good Shepherd speaks directly to all of us today to reaffirm our faith in that life by participating more intently on the ways we lay down our lives in love for those sheep entrusted to our care.

54.3   May 3, 2009

From the days of King David, the quality of leadership in ancient Israel was compared to the job of a shepherd. Shepherds spent their entire lives living with and caring for their sheep. They knew their sheep, and the sheep trusted the sound of their voices. At night, shepherds would herd their sheep into a common sheepfold, usually formed out of rocks. Because there was no gate, a shepherd would lie down across the opening and become the gate. Shepherds were known to give up their lives when wild animals or thieves tried to invade. Good leaders had these types of relationships with their people. As the prophet Ezekiel loudly protested, the leaders of his day lacked any of these qualities. He charged them with being more interested in taking care of their own needs, while ignoring the needs of the people entrusted the their care.

Jesus clearly is the Good Shepherd. Jesus knows each of us by name and invites us to trust the sound of his voice. Jesus has laid down his life for us on the cross. Ironically, the shepherd (the leader) has become the Lamb of God sacrificed for our salvation. In the Passion of Saint John, our completely innocent shepherd is taken out to be sacrificed on the Hill of Calvary just as the priests were preparing the unblemished lambs for the Passover celebration in the Temple. At this Mass, we recognize him our Good Shepherd as the Lamb of God who takes away our sins, and he feeds us with his own Body and Blood.

At four of the Masses this weekend, we who are the shepherds of our second graders bring them to this Altar to be fed for the first time by the Lamb of God really present in the Eucharist. As good shepherds, their parents carried them to the waters of baptism, incorporating them into the Mystery of the death and resurrection of the Good Shepherd. Today, they stand prominently in our midst, dressed in the white garments that remind us of their baptism. With our support, they walk on their own two feet to the baptismal font to renew the promises made for them seven or eight years ago. They renew their trust in the Good Shepherd, who knows them by name and who stands with them to feed them as they grow in the knowledge of their faith. Over the years to come, their sharing in this Eucharistic Feast will slowly and gradually form them more completely into Christ's Body, in which they were formed in baptism.

The parents of these children are good shepherds. They literally have laid down their lives for their children. They make countless daily sacrifices for the good of their children. These children hear the voice of the Good Shepherd in the care given by their parents. But the Good Shepherd also speaks through these boys and girls.

Through their open and uncomplicated faith, the Good Shepherd speaks to all of us and reminds us of the incredible gift we receive in the Eucharist. He speaks to us who gather here every Sunday, opening our eyes a bit more to his real presence, which we might take for granted. He speaks to those who come sporadically, gently reminding us to be a little more consistent in making Sunday Mass a higher priority in the ways in which we lay down our lives for our children. He speaks to those who have fallen away from their faith, patiently urging us back into the sheepfold to trust that the strength needed to lay down our lives can be found in this assembly on Sundays.

The Easter Season is a perfect time to celebrate the Sacraments of Initiation. Those who passed through the waters of new life died to an old way of living and rose with Christ to new life at the Easter Vigil. Our eighth graders were sealed with the power of the Holy Spirit on the following Sunday. Our second graders take this step in faith on these last two weekends. We rejoice with all these people, straining to listen to the voice of the Good Shepherd calling every one of us to great fidelity in the Lord's Body.

54.4 April 29, 2012

In ancient Israel, prophets spoke of those in leadership positions using images taken from the occupation of shepherding. It was an image that most of their contemporaries could understand. Shepherds dedicated their entire lives to their flocks, spending all of their time leading them to sources of safe water and green pastures. Because they spent so much time with their flocks, they knew the individual characteristics of each sheep. And each sheep would recognize the voice of their shepherd. When shepherds would lead their sheep into enclosed sheepfolds at night for safety, the shepherds themselves became the gates, lying down at the opening. Should a wild animal or thief try to sneak into the sheepfold, the shepherd would drive them away. More than one shepherd gave his life to protect his sheep.

Jesus is very critical of the religious leaders of his day. Like so many religious leaders who had gone before them, they put themselves, their security, and their prestige and power ahead of the needs of the people entrusted to their care. They shepherded themselves. Jesus sees himself as the Good Shepherd, who would literally lay down his life on the cross for all his sheep. As the Lamb of God sacrificed for our salvation, he feeds us with his very Body and Blood to nourish us and lead us to the green pastures of salvation.

Today, the parish rejoices as these parents bring their children to be fed by the Body and Blood of Christ for the first time. As good shepherds, you parents brought them to the waters of baptism seven or eight years ago, promising that you would be the best of teachers in the practice of the faith. You parents are good shepherds in so many ways, laying down your lives and putting their needs ahead of your own. You give them so many good gifts. Now you give them the best of gifts, modeling the example of the Good Shepherd and bringing your children to be transformed by their participation in the Eucharist. In bringing them to this Sacrament of Initiation, you can trust the transforming power of the Eucharist, just as Peter had done. Peter was changed from a fearful coward denying that he knew Jesus in the courtyard of the Sanhedrin to a bold witness to the truth of the risen Lord in that same courtyard.

Boys and girls, your parents carried you to the waters of Baptism when you were babies. Today, you walk down the aisle on your own two feet to renew the promises made for you by your parents. Then you will bring forward the gifts of bread and wine, which will be transformed by the power of the Holy Spirit into the Body and Blood of Christ. Then, you will be fed by the Lord's Body and Blood for the first time. You are definitely God's children now! As you grow up and continue to be fed by the Eucharist, what you shall later become is still to be revealed. But one thing is certain, you will become more and more like Jesus Christ, as members of the Church, the Body of Christ.

54.5   April 26, 2015

As we continue to reflect on the transforming power of the resurrection of Jesus Christ and apply that Mystery to our lives, our Scripture readings offer us two interesting images today. Saint Peter gives the first in his speech to the members of the Sanhedrin. Peter is clearly changed by the power of the resurrection and the gift of the Holy Spirit. When the Sanhedrin had interrogated Jesus on Holy Thursday, Peter was so filled with fear that he denied knowing him. This time, he stands without fear before that same hostile group. He defends his healing of a crippled man, asking why anyone would condemn him for performing an act of kindness.

Then he explains how this healing occurred. He insists that the miracle was not a result of his own power. Rather, he boldly proclaims the truth that Jesus the Nazorean is the promised Christ, whom they had condemned to death. He quotes Psalm 118, the psalm we pray today as the Responsorial Psalm, and uses the image of Jesus being the stone rejected by the builders. That stone, Peter argues, has been raised from the dead by the Father and has become the cornerstone of a new structure being built of living stones.

That image takes on new meaning for our parish. Last weekend, Bishop Rhoades led us in the groundbreaking of our new church. He blessed the cornerstone, the most important part of that structure. You can check it out after Mass – the stone weighing two hundred pounds in the back of church. That cornerstone reminds us of the centrality of Jesus Christ in our lives and in our parish. Our new church may be very beautiful and more spacious. As we watch the new church being built and put up with the inconveniences caused by construction, we connect that emerging structure to the living members of our parish. Just as that cornerstone will be the most significant stone in that structure, the risen Christ remains the most important part of ours, inviting us to be transformed through the power of the resurrection, as Peter was transformed.

The second image comes from the Gospel, and our children receiving their First Holy Communion can tell you all about it. Jesus says that he is the Good Shepherd. He addresses this image to the religious leaders who are more concerned about their own welfare than the welfare of those entrusted to their care. As the man born blind comes to see the truth about him, they close their eyes to the truth. Jesus uses this image to help us understand that he knows us each of us by name. He recognizes our voice. He invites us to recognize him speaking to us in the Word. He invites us to renew our faith in his life-giving death and resurrection. He has laid down his life for us on the cross to rescue us from the wolves of death and sinfulness. He has laid down his life so that we can share in the transforming power of the resurrection.

That is why this First Communion Mass is so important. These children have been preparing anxiously to be fed by their Good Shepherd, who knows each of them by name, and who feeds them as the Lamb of God under the form of bread and wine. Boys and girls, we pledge our support to you as you take this important step in faith. In a moment, you will walk back to the Baptismal Font to renew your Baptismal Promises. It was at the font that you were incorporated into the risen Christ through the waters of Baptism. You were clothed with a white garment to indicate that you had put on Christ. As you renew those promises, we promise to support you and your families as you continue to listen to the voice of the Good Shepherd speaking to you every Sunday. We promise to walk with you as you approach this Sacrament, trusting its power to conform you slowly and gradually into the Body of Christ, of which you are an important member.

54.6 April 22, 2018

Throughout the Gospel of Saint John, Jesus often uses the words "I am" to identify himself with his divine nature. In the Old Testament, God used those words "Yahweh," or "I am who am" to identify himself to Moses. In most instances, Jesus speaks of himself as the bread of life, or the light of the world, or the resurrection and the life to indicate what he, as the Son of God, has to offer us. Today, he identifies himself in a human role when he says that "I am the good shepherd." To a culture which understood the role of good shepherds with their flocks, he speaks of his own costly freedom, as well as his mutual relationship with the Father and with us, his followers. The people of that culture knew the devotion of good shepherds to their sheep. They also knew the examples of shepherd leaders who cared more for themselves and their own comfort than for the common good of the people they were supposed to be leading.

Jesus speaks this parable to the religious leaders of his day. He had just given sight to the man born blind. As that man gradually came to see Jesus as the Christ who is the light of the world, the religious leaders refuse to acknowledge the truth standing before them. They are the hired hands who are much more interested in the prestige and perks of their office than serving the needs of their people. They will become the wolves who bring death to the good shepherd, because he threatens their authority and influence. The good shepherd will willingly accept that painful and humiliating death and lay down his life for us, his flock.

The image of the good shepherd is familiar to our parish. At the entrance to the Parish Education Center is a copy of the most ancient statue of the Good Shepherd: a young shepherd, without a beard, dressed in a short tunic, and with a pouch around his neck. On his shoulders he carries a lamb. The other image is on our triumphal arch: the Good Shepherd seated on his heavenly throne, drawing the sheep to himself from Bethlehem (on the left) and from Jerusalem (on the right). Beneath that image on both sides are images of two religious leaders who have served as shepherds. On the left is Saint Peter, who has been transformed from denying Jesus on the night he was betrayed to boldly proclaiming the resurrection in the first reading from the Acts of the Apostles. On the right is Pope Saint Pius X, a successor to Saint Peter, who decided to admit children to the Eucharist when they reached the age of reason.

That is why you are here, boy and girls. You became children of God when you passed through the waters of baptism. The Good Shepherd knows each of you by name and has laid down his life for you. He has become the Lamb of God (portrayed in the mosaic on the front of the Altar) who now feeds you for the first time with his Body and Blood. When you were baptized, your parents, who are your shepherds, carried you to the font and made the baptismal promises for you. When you emerged from the waters of Baptism, you were clothed with a white garment, indicating that you put on

Christ. Your parents were told to keep that garment unstained, so that you could go out to meet the Lord. Now you will walk on your own two feet to renew those promises and bring up gifts of bread and wine.

Celebrating First Communion at this Mass is very important, because we are reminded of the important role of this parish community in supporting you parents in training your children in the ways of faith. Parents, you are good shepherds when you sacrifice everything for the good of your children. Just as you sacrifice for their material needs, be sure to sacrifice for their spiritual needs. The first Letter of Saint John assures us that children of God can be transformed by contact with the risen Lord, just as Peter had been. Trust the power of the Eucharist to transform your family and your children in our shared pilgrimage to the new and eternal Jerusalem.

55. 5th Sunday of Easter

Readings
Acts 9:26–31
1 John 3:18–24
John 15:1–8

55.1 May 21, 2000

In 1965, Harvey Cox wrote a best-selling book, *The Secular City*. In it, he describes the process of secularization. Secularization means that humans have turned their attention from the world above and beyond and concentrated instead on this world and this present age. To describe the shape of the secular city, Cox chose one special characteristic of modern society – *mobility*. He wrote:

> [Modern] man is on the go . . . [H] e can be pictured as a driver in a cloverleaf intersection. Other images of the [secular] city include the airport control tower, high-speed elevators, and perpetually moving escalators in department stores and offices. The modern metropolis is a system of roads – thruways, subways, air ways – linking the city to others and parts of the city to each other . . . Urban man is certain in motion, and we can expect the pace and scope of mobility to increase as time goes on.

Thirty-five years later, we know that Harvey Cox could not have been more accurate!

In marked contrast to these images, Jesus proposes a more agricultural image. In comparing his relationship with us in terms of being branches grafted onto a vine, he invites us to participate not in a *secular* city, but a *spiritual* city. As members of a city where we have dual citizenship, we are invited to **remain**. Today's Scripture readings urge us not to flit around from one popular fad to another. They invite us to **remain** – to settle down with, to become rooted and stable – with the true vine, Jesus.

We can learn a great lesson from Saul of Tarsus. Luke tells us in the Acts of the Apostles that Paul was completely ineffective on his own, even after his life was changed so dramatically on the road to Damascus. Only after he was grafted onto the true vine of the fellowship with the Apostles did he begin to bear fruit. Once Paul made his decision to remain with this community, his efforts began to build up the church.

Making the decision to **remain** in Christ always has its consequences. When we choose to remain with Christ on a personal level, we must face our own passions and the tragedies of life with trust and hope. When we choose to remain with a family, we must struggle with doing what is best for the common good of the household. When we choose to remain with this parish, we must face our conflicts with each other, our struggles to make good decisions, and those inevitable misunderstandings that come from being part of a community. At each of these levels, we are invited to recognize the hand of Jesus pruning us, cutting us back to become more fruitful. When we are willing to remain, that pruning hand will ultimately make us stronger members of Christ's Body.

During the last few weeks, we have seen what happens when winds blow huge limbs of trees onto our streets. We watch as these separated branches wither up and die. And so it is with us. If we separate ourselves from the life-giving vine that is Christ – in our personal lives, in the family units in which we live, and in this parish – we too will wither and become ineffective. If we **remain** and participate weekly in these Eucharistic Mysteries, we will be pruned by life's sharp edges. But the life-giving Blood of Christ also flows from the vine to us, who are the branches. Therein lies our life and energy.

55.2   May 18, 2003

Two congregations were struggling financially. Located two blocks apart, they thought it would be better to merge and become one united body, larger and more effective than two separate groups. But, the merger failed after months of negotiations. Each group had its own tradition of praying the Lord's Prayer. One congregation preferred "forgive us our trespasses," while the other demanded, "forgive us our debts." After the merger fell through, a local newspaper reported that one church went back to its trespasses, while the other returned to its debts.

Arguments like these have been part of our Christian history from the beginning. In the Acts of the Apostles, Luke tells us that the leaders of the Church in Jerusalem had to get Paul out of town to save his life. The Jewish people saw him as a traitor, while those who followed Jesus Christ found it difficult to believe that anyone could have made such a dramatic conversion.

As far as I know, no parishioner at Saint Pius has been driven out of Granger, fearful of being shot. But, we have lots of differences here. Some are old and wish for a return to the day when this was a small country church, while others are excited out our growth and the challenges facing us. Some want us to build a school here, while others think it is a bad idea. Many of you welcome more time and reverence in the liturgy, while others want to get out as quickly as possible. Some of you like to sing, and others want the liturgy to be silent. There are differences about the types of music people like, as well as a wide range of political views. And you may have detected that Father Dan and I aren't exactly clones of each other. We are as different as Paul and Barnabas. Paul was the one constantly speaking his mind and causing turmoil, while Barnabas tended to make peace. (Although I would not want to make comparisons, Paul once gave a homily that was so long that it lasted all night!)

Remarkably, Father Dan and I get along very well. In fact, our differences serve this parish better. That same dynamic is true of our parish, as long as we remember what holds us together. Like the different branches in a vineyard, we are connected to the true vine, which is Christ. We maintain that connection when we gather here to celebrate the Eucharist, the source and summit of our life together. We continue to explore a common Catholic Tradition that helps us understand how to stay connected to the life-giving vine.

Several years ago, a severe springtime windstorm tore through the parish where I was serving. As I walked around the neighborhood immediately after the storm, it was impossible to distinguish the leaves on the downed limbs from the leaves that were still connected to the trees. But, within a day, the difference was striking. The leaves on the downed limbs began wilting and losing their bright green color, indicating that they were receiving no life from the tree. In a similar way, we will continue to grow and bear fruit, to the extent to which we stay connected to the true vine. People will notice whether or not we bear fruit by the way we act – by the way we show respect to each other in our differences and the way we reach out to the poor. As we continue to plan for the future, that will be our ultimate test. If we do not remain connected as branches to the vine, we will not succeed. If we do, then we will bear fruit that will endure.

55.3   May 14, 2006

If anyone understood Jesus' image of the vine and the branches, it would be Saul of Tarsus. As a faithful Jew, he knew that the prophets and psalmists compared Israel to a vineyard when they wanted to speak of their relationship to God. He could not have missed the huge golden emblem of the vine and grapes that was emblazoned above the entrance of the Temple in Jerusalem. He would have seen that same image on every coin he used to make a purchase in the Temple. He even knew about pruning. Passing through the many vineyards on the terraced hills north of Jerusalem, he knew that radical pruning of branches was the best way to make sure that the grapes would be the very best quality. He saw God carefully tending his vineyard, the people of Israel.

When Saul encountered the risen Christ on the road to Damascus, he understood that the true vine was no longer Israel, but Jesus Christ, crucified and raised from the dead. Through the waters of Baptism, Paul was grafted as a branch onto the one vine that is Christ. Through the Eucharist, Paul was nourished with the wine crushed from the grapes and transformed into the Blood of Christ. Through his ministry, Paul also knew the pain of being pruned, in being cut back. In Damascus, he had freely spoken about the vine that gave life to the branches and was nearly killed. When he escaped to Jerusalem, he faced the pruning distrust of Christians who could not believe that person could change so radically, as well as the hatred of the Jews who knew that change. That pattern would be played out often in his ministry. For speaking plainly and fearlessly about the Vine that is Christ, Paul would be pruned everywhere he took the Good News. His last pruning at the end of his life must have been the most difficult. He wrote from his prison cell in Rome that everyone had abandoned him, and that he waited alone for his execution, his final pruning for the faith. But he also wrote that the Vine had never abandoned him, one of the branches. In this final pruning, Paul may not have seen the fruits of his labors. But, as a branch firmly rooted on the true vine, the fruits of his labors became clearer throughout the Mediterranean world, and into our own.

We too have been grafted as branches through the waters of Baptism onto the one true Vine, who is Christ. We too are nourished by the grapes crushed into wine and transformed into the Blood of Christ. We too have been pruned by life's difficulties as we struggle to live as branches on the one vine. No one knows this more than mothers, whom we honor today. Mothers can speak of all the times they have been pruned, especially in their disappointment at the behavior of their children. Mothers face the same challenge of Paul. Paul invites you to renew your trust in your efforts to love, even if you do not see immediate results.

I thought of my mother when her grandson, Adam, was baptized at the Easter Vigil. Although she only knew him as a boy before her death, she was that he had never been baptized. She was concerned that his father, my brother, no longer practiced his faith. My mother insisted that I celebrate Mass at her home every Christmas evening – no matter how many Masses I had already celebrated – so that Ed would get to Mass at least once a year. The fruits of her love were clear to me at the Easter Vigil. Those fruits were a direct result of her connection with the vine that is Christ. We wish a happy Mother's Day to all of you mothers. Don't get discouraged. Trust your connection with the Vine that is Christ!

55.4 May 10, 2009

The followers of Jesus would be familiar with his image of the vine and the branches for two reasons. First, they knew from their own experience what a vineyard looks like. As the vine matures, it becomes hard and twisted and exhibits remarkable strength and endurance. From that vine, each branch begins as a delicate, slender, pale green tendril that reaches out to attach itself to a wall or a trellis. Within just a short time, that tendril can be pulled from its place of mooring only with great difficulty. It has taken hold and begins to resemble the gnarled vine that gives it life. As it grows, it fastens itself to other tendrils that have also grown into branches. These form a living network of life and strength that will eventually produce much good fruit.

Second, they would know that the prophets compared ancient Israel to a vineyard. Isaiah in particular argued that God had transplanted the branches of his people from Egypt to the Promised Land. Isaiah warned that Israel would wither and die if they would separate themselves from the living vine of God, who was the source of their life.

Jesus clearly states that he is the vine. He is the source of our life, and we have been grafted as branches on the true vine through the waters of Baptism. As we continue to reflect on his resurrection, he invites us to consider the importance of the Church, of this assembled community, in living our Easter faith. We gain strength, not only from the Vine that is the source of our life, but also from the intertwining of all the tendrils that represent our lives lived together as members of this community, as branches that become stronger as they grow together and hold on to one another for support. When we do this, we can produce much good fruit.

Saul of Tarsus understood this image. After his conversion on the road to Damascus, he returned to the Christian community in Jerusalem, even though they were afraid of him, fearing that no one could undergo such a genuine, radical conversion. With the help of Barnabas, who became his "sponsor," Paul endured the pruning that Jesus describes as necessary for growth as branches of the true vine.

The Greek word for pruning, or cutting back, is the root word for our English word, catharsis. Paul could easily have become bitter at the treatment he received from the Christian community. Instead, he saw that painful process as cleansing, or purifying, as he became one of the intertwined branches connected to the vine (Christ). The same thing happens to us as Church. If you are involved in the parish, you know that it is not always easy to get along with strong personalities or to work with people who do not always agree. As a Church, might regard the painful and difficult conflict at Notre Dame as a form of pruning. The risen Lord is present even in the midst of conflict and division, inviting us to trust that this conflict can be a time of cleansing and purifying, affording us hope that something good can come from what is going on.

If anyone can speak of pruning, it would be the mothers in our assembly. You mothers are essential branches in your individual families, which we regard as the domestic church. You know what it feels like to be pruned, or cut back as you pour your hearts out to be the best mothers for your children. As you reflect on the connection you have as branches with your family and with this parish family, be sure to recognize the source of that connection in the true Vine who is Jesus Christ, raised from the dead. As you endure the painful parts of your vocation, consider the pain you endure as pruning, as cathartic, and as cleansing. The risen Lord invites you to remain hopeful in those times when you are being pruned, because he is present in your efforts to bear great fruit.

55.5   May 6, 2012

It is easy to understand the hesitancy of the early Church to accept Saul of Tarsus as one of their own. He had participated in the murder of Stephen, the first martyr. He was on his way to Damascus to punish the early followers of Jesus Christ. He had been a committed Pharisee, devoted to the very laws that Pharisees had accused Jesus of breaking during his public ministry. The early Church remembered the warning of Jesus to look for wolves in sheep's clothing. Was Saul one of those wolves? It is the same question raised by the example of the Trojan horse. It is the same question we ask when we receive an e-mail from a friend with the subject line, "YOU HAVE TO SEE THIS; OPEN AT ONCE." We may find that opening the attachment may invite a virus in our computer that will wreak havoc to our hard drive.

In the case of the early Church, there was a definite risk in welcoming the stranger known as Saul, as there is always risk in healing the sick, in visiting the prisoner, and in extending forgiveness. But the Church took that risk, and Saul the persecutor became Paul the Apostle, spreading the Good News of Jesus Christ to the Gentiles.

We have a lot to learn from this episode in the early Church. The first lesson is that no one can live the Christian life alone. Saul may have had a powerful religious experience in encountering the risen Christ on the road to Damascus. But he needed to be part of a believing community to allow that experience to continue his continuing conversion, or turning toward, the Lord. He needed to remain connected as one branch to the vine which is Christ, connected with all the other branches of those who belonged to the early Church. The same is true for us. We need to be part of the Church. Otherwise, the glowing embers of our faith can become cold. If we try to live our faith in isolation, our faith can become vulnerable, warped, or broken. We need each other.

We learn a second lesson about the power and grace of advocacy. Barnabas sponsored Saul before the Church. Barnabas (whose name means "son of encouragement") was well known and trusted in the community for his generosity in providing for the poor out of his own means. Now, he uses his generosity to introduce Saul, to tell the community that they could put trust in him. With his advocacy, the more timid and fearful members of the community could embrace Saul more quickly and trust him.

Odds are pretty good that someone has been an advocate for each of us at one time or another. Perhaps someone may have spoken on our behalf at one time, vouching for our integrity as we moved to a new job or come to a new parish. Perhaps someone vouched for the reality of our conversion and trusted us after we had made a terrible mistake. The example of Barnabas can help us to be advocates in the same way. Like him, we can extend an open hand to someone trying to enter into our circle of friends. School-aged students can make room at the lunchroom table for the new kid. Or long-time members of this parish might notice someone new to Saint Pius and invite them to sit with them.

As individual branches, we have been grafted onto the true vine of Christ when we were baptized. Through the Sacramental life of the Church, we are connected with one another and with Christ in such a way that we truly can bear fruit. In his letter to the Galatians,

Saint Paul lists nine different fruits: love, peace, patience, kindness, generosity, faithfulness, gentleness, and self-control. May these fruits of the Spirit characterize our parish community, as we strive to love not in word or speech, but in deed and truth.

55.6   May 3, 2015

When this community gathered for Mass on Palm Sunday, we prayed the beginning verses of Psalm 22. Those verses spoke of God's servant being mocked, abandoned, and murdered. Today, we prayed the later verses of that same Psalm, telling us that God vindicated his servant. The earliest followers of Jesus Christ connected the first part of the Psalm with the passion of Christ and these later verses with the Mystery of his Resurrection. Today's reading from the Acts of the Apostles gives us insights into how they lived that Mystery. Filled with the Holy Spirit, those early believers boldly proclaimed their faith that Jesus had been raised from the dead. That bold proclamation brought death to Stephen and scattered the community. It infuriated Saul of Tarsus, who dedicated himself to eliminating this new movement. Having encountered the risen Christ on the road to Damascus, Paul was equally bold in proclaiming the truth from his encounter with the risen Christ, causing fear in the Christian community and so much anger that the Hellenists tried to kill him. His friend, Barnabas, had to take him back to Tarsus to save his life. And yet, in the midst of all of this chaos and conflict, Saint Luke tells us that the Church continued to be built up and was at peace!

This peace that Saint Luke describes is obviously not an absence of conflict or problems. Rather, that peace is the result of the indwelling of the risen Christ. Those earliest believers knew that Christ was keeping his promise and that he remained in them. They understood the image presented by Jesus in today's Gospel. They saw themselves as branches that had been grafted onto the true vine of Christ when they were baptized. They were being fed by his Body and Blood when they gathered to break bread. They realized that their efforts to keep the commandments to love God and neighbor were connected with their faith that Christ was remaining in them. They also believed that God was using the conflicts and difficulties to prune them, to cause them to bear more fruit by the ways in which they were keeping his commands.

As we continue to reflect on the implications of the resurrection in our own time, our first communicants remind us that we too have been grafted onto the life-giving vine of Jesus Christ through the waters of Baptism. As they march to the Baptismal Font clothed in the white garments that speak of their putting on Christ at their baptisms, we join them in renewing our efforts to resist the temptations of the Evil One and to live the faith we profess by making new efforts to love God and neighbor. As they come forward for the first time to be fed by the Body and Blood of Christ, they remind us of the Sacrament we can take for granted. They remind us that we need to come to Mass on a regular basis, not because of some arbitrary law, but because we need to be nourished as branches on that true vine.

When most members of the Christian community were afraid of Paul of Tarsus, Barnabas stepped forward and vouched for him. Barnabas (his name means "Son of Encouragement") was able to see the surprising ways in which God works in the conversion of his strong headed friend. He encouraged the earliest believers to trust Paul and to protect him from those who wanted to do him harm. Boys and girls, you are "Barnabas" to us. Your uncomplicated faith and obvious joy on this day encourage us as we renew our Baptismal Promises with you. You remind us that Christ wants to remain in us. You remind us that the indwelling of God in our lives will continue to give us that incredible gift of peace. With that gift of peace, we can take another look at the conflicts and difficulties that we face in our daily lives, and even at the ways in which we fail to keep the commandments. That peace remains, even when God uses these difficulties to prune us and help us to produce more fruit.

55.7   April 29, 2018

Being close to the vineyards of southwestern Michigan helps us to understand the images which Jesus presents in today's Gospel. Once the workers in the vineyard plant the first vines, they have to wait several years for the first grapes. Rooted in the earth, their tendrils reach out and travel under the earth, forming long rows. Close to the earth, the tendrils are brown, thick, and woody. However, nearer to the branches, they are green, pliant, and flexible. Not only do the vines have to be propped up to keep them above the ground, but they also have to be pruned continually. The pruning enables the water and nutrients to be directed toward the grapes, and away from the woody stalks. Once a healthy vineyard has been given a few years, those branches begin producing tasty grapes every year. Riding through the vineyards on my bicycle around Labor Day is great, because I can smell the sweet aroma of grapes ready to be harvested.

We are those branches, and we have been grafted to the vine when we passed through the waters of Baptism. To use the words of the First Letter of John, we are the Beloved of God. As branches connected to the vine, we grow in God's love when we keep the commandments to love God and one another. We can bear much fruit, and we can make our world smell much better by the way we treat one another. Jesus makes it very clear that we can bear fruit, only if we remain connected with him, the vine.

At this Mass, our second graders are receiving the Lord in the Eucharist for the first time. After the homily, they will walk to the Baptismal Font, where they were first grafted as branches onto Jesus, the vine. They will renew the promises made for them as babies and bless themselves with water. Clothed with the white garments reminding them of the white garments put on them at Baptism, signifying their union with Christ, they will bring up the gifts of bread, wine, and the sacrificial tithe and will receive the Lord in the Eucharist for the first time.

They will receive bread baked from wheat that has been harvested and ground up and transformed into the Body of Christ. They will drink wine that comes from fermented grapes and which has been transformed into the Blood of Christ. Boys and girls, the Lord promises that he will strengthen you every time you receive Holy Communion, just as he strengthened the Apostle Paul as he boldly proclaimed the risen Lord to people who wanted to do him harm. Every time you come to Mass and receive the Body and Blood of Christ, he will strengthen you to keep the commandments to love God and neighbor and remain with you.

In the Gospel of John, Jesus uses the word "to remain" 67 times. He promises to dwell with us, to abide with us, to stay with us, to remain with us. These children remind us of that promise today. They remind us that we are the branches, grafted solidly on the vine that is Christ. Just as the tendrils of vineyards connect with each other under the earth, we are connected to one another through the Eucharist as members of the Body of Christ. We promise to support you as you bring your children to the Eucharist every Sunday. We promise to be with you, even when you and your children might be pruned by difficult events in your lives.

Today, we prayed Psalm 22 as our Responsorial Psalm. The last time we prayed this Psalm was on Palm Sunday, when we prayed the first stanzas to reflect on the death of Jesus, the Suffering Servant. Today we pray the later stanzas of this Psalm, reflecting on the Servant's vindication in the resurrection. He will remain with us in our suffering and even in our dying. He promises to remain with in a very real ay as we continue to be fed with his body and blood, especially when difficult situations in life will prune us. He will keep his promise to remain with us forever, as we share in his dying and trust in his rising.

56. 6th Sunday of Easter

Readings
Acts 10:25–26, 34–35, 44–48
1 John 4:7–10
John 15:9–17

56.1 May 28, 2000

Three years ago, a television series called *Nothing Sacre*⟩ was cancelled near the end of its first season. You may have seen some of the episodes about the lives of priests, religious, and people in an urban parish. Various reasons have been given for the failure of the series. Some members of the Catholic League for Religious and Civil Rights accused it of being anti-Catholic. Others said its content was too sophisticated. But most likely, the series did not make it because it was aired at the same time as the immensely popular sitcom *Frien*⟩s. I only saw one episode of "Nothing Sacred" and only a couple of episodes of *Frien*⟩s. But it strikes me as ironic that a series about six urban yuppies facing trivial problems has very little to do with real friendship. For any of its limitations, *Nothing Sacre*⟩ was about the kind of friendship Jesus describes in today's Gospel – mutual affection, crossing barriers, and putting one's life at the service of others.

Jesus does not suggest this kind of friendship with one another. Neither does he recommend or ask us to consider it. He **commands** us! And, the Gospel of John makes it very clear that this command is based on a prior experience of grace. "Love one another **as** I have loved you." In giving this command, he shows us how to be friends – by washing the feet of his disciples and by giving his life on the cross. His gift of love comes first. That gift teaches us how to friends with one another.

In the ancient world, there was an unbridgeable gap between those who formed the family unit and the slaves who served them. In fact, the word *free* meant *not enslave*. Jesus wants us to be free of sin and death. That is why he assumed the role of a slave in washing feet. That is why he emptied himself of all freedom of movement to be nailed on a cross. Through the Scripture readings from the Acts of the Apostles, we have seen examples of how the early church learned to be friends. It was not easy for Peter to embrace Cornelius and his family. All his life, Peter had been faithful to keeping Jewish dietary laws and avoiding anyone who ignored them. But we see him baptizing one of those pagans today. Cornelius probably did not know the difference between Abraham and Moses. And Mrs. Cornelius probably served ham sandwiches at the party following the baptism! But Peter knew the prior love of Jesus. Under the power of the Spirit, he freely allowed that love to create a bond of friendship with Cornelius.

We have been celebrating that incredible mystery of Jesus' self-emptying love for five weeks now. We are preparing to celebrate the feasts of Ascension and Pentecost. Now is a perfect time to reflect on our own ability to go forth and bear fruit. We may have our divisions in our parish family and in our human families. We may never agree on certain issues. We may even dislike some of the members of both families. We may have been terribly hurt in trying to find true friendship with each other. But we know the example of the one who gave his life for us. That example empowers us to do the same!

56.2 May 25, 2003

A couple of weeks ago, a man stopped by to see our church. I showed him around and answered his questions. He complimented us on the way we decorated the church – a big candle standing near the Ambo, the live flowers around the Altar, and the banners hanging from the ceiling. When I responded that the church was decorated for Easter, he snorted, "Easter was over a month ago!"

Yes, Easter Sunday was six weeks ago. But, we continue to celebrate Easter as a fifty-day season, because it takes at least that long for us to reflect on the implications of our greatest Mystery. We spent forty days to consider the Lord's suffering and death, realities that do not require faith. Every one of us knows the pain of suffering, and the scourge of death has stung us. It takes faith to believe that life is stronger than death, and our Scripture readings for this Season have consistently proposed ways for us to explore that belief. With two weeks left in the Season, today's Scriptures explore God's love, as we look for signs of the risen Jesus in our daily lives.

The first implication involves the Father's love for Jesus, his only begotten Son. That love ultimately raised him from the dead and transformed him in resurrection. But, it did not protect him from pain, rejection, betrayal, or death. The Father loves us no more or no less than he loves the Son. As a result, we open our eyes to signs of the resurrection in our own lives, even in the midst of our own pain, suffering, and rejections. When those things happen, we can be assured that the Father has not abandoned us, just as he did not abandon Jesus on the Cross. With that constant love, he promises that those who die with Christ will rise with him.

The second implication can be seen in the way Jesus manifests his Father's love in loving other people. Jesus loved all people, even when they rejected his teaching, spat in his face, and murdered him. He laid down his life for everyone, even for those who brought about his death. It is this type of sacrificial love that he demands of those who follow him. Just as Peter laid aside an entire lifetime of observing the Jewish law to reach out to Cornelius and the hated Romans he represented, so we are called to love by laying down our lives to serve other people.

On this Memorial Day weekend, we honor the memory of those who have laid down their lives for our freedom. It is fitting to remember them. But, the actual business of laying down our lives occurs in very ordinary and less than heroic ways.

Let me give you an example. Last year, many of you indicated on the survey that you wanted a Sunday evening Mass. As a result, that Mass will begin in September. It is easy to take a pencil and say, "Yes, I want that Mass." It is more difficult to say, "I am willing to lay down some of my precious time and talent to make it happen." That is what we need. If the Sunday evening Mass is to happen, more of you need to make a commitment to serve as a Eucharistic Minister, Lector, Server, Usher, or Music Minister – especially if you have never made such a commitment before. Your commitment will make a statement that the parish genuinely needs this Mass, instead of offering it merely to make Mass more convenient. Someone wrote on the sign=up sheet at the back table – "How about a Youth Mass?" There is no doubt that we need more of our young people taking part in all of the ministries. In fact, we are hoping that the Mass will attract more of our young people and connect them with our Sunday evening Youth Ministry programs

Jesus chose us to be witnesses of the resurrection. That means more than simply decorating the church for fifty days. It means that we will remain in his love and make that love evident by the way we live our lives. Laying down our lives means moving beyond what is convenient and offering ourselves in service of others. But, it is in the day-to-day process of loving in this way that will convince other people that the final answer is not death, but life in the Lord Jesus!

56.3   May 21, 2006

We are no strangers to the love of God described in today's Gospel. We have been celebrating that love since the First Sunday of Advent. We celebrated the love of God at Christmas, when we marveled that the God who created us emptied himself to become one of us. We celebrated his self-emptying love as we began the Triduum on Holy Thursday, when we reflected on the humbling love of Jesus in washing the feet of his Apostles. We stood in awe on Good Friday as we recalled that Jesus emptied himself totally – giving his entire life for love of us. Ever the Easter Vigil on Holy Saturday, we have been celebrating the triumph of that love in the Resurrection.

When Jesus tells us to love as God has loved us, he is not talking about some fluffy concept that fills people with warm and fuzzy feelings of passing contentment. He is talking about giving to others the great gift of love that has been given to us. That is what Peter does in the Acts of the Apostles. Peter has been raised as a good Jew, having been circumcised on the eighth day of his birth, having avoided those foods forbidden by kosher laws, and having carefully stayed away from any place contaminated by anyone who was not Jewish. Here he is today, emptying himself of all of that and going to the home of a gentile – Cornelius – who is also a member of the occupying pagan Roman forces. He not only baptizes this man who does not know the difference between Abraham and Moses, but he also goes to his baptism party and eats in his house. I wonder if he ate his first ham sandwich, which more than likely caused him tremendous revulsion. But he did all this, because he learned how to empty himself in acts of love as Jesus Christ had loved him.

And so it is with us. The basic commandment that Jesus gives us is to love as he has loved us. That is a tough and difficult love, because it involves emptying ourselves and dying to ourselves. But once we accept that love and make it a part of our lives, then all the other commandments make more sense. We may not find it convenient to drag our families here every Sunday when there are so many other demands on our time. But, we do it, because we understand our participation here as a way of loving as God has loved us. It may be difficult for children to keep the fourth commandment, especially when your parents seem to be unreasonable in their demands. But you do it, because it is specific way of loving as God has loved you. It may be tough for us to follow the teachings of the Church on laws regarding the sanctity of human life, especially when it comes to the use of modern technology. But we struggle to be faithful to the wisdom of the Church in these matters, because it is a specific way of loving as God has loved us.

Keeping the specific commandments only makes sense within the context of the way in which God has loved us. But keeping these commandments is not a way of enslaving us, any more than Jesus became a slave when he washed the feet of his Apostles. These commands free us to be friends of God. During these last few weeks, as we have heard from the great Discourse of Jesus at the Last Supper, he has been using the words, "remain with me." That is what it means to be friends – to remain, to abide, to stay with him. When that happens, the love of God dwells in us permanently.

56.4   May 17, 2009

Last Sunday, we reflected on the image of the vine and the branches, taken from the verses immediately preceding today's Gospel. This image is critical to our continuing reflection on the Mystery of the Resurrection, because it applies directly to us as the Church, as God's people. The risen Christ is our vine, our source of life. We, the branches, draw our life from him. We are connected, not only with him through the vine, but also with one another as branches that continue to grow together and provide strength. The image reminds us that we are in a much better position to recognize the risen Christ in our midst and bear much fruit not as isolated individuals, but as a community of the Church.

This week, Jesus tells us that we bear fruit when we love as he does. In the Gospel of John, the word "love" is not associated with warm feelings about someone else. In the ancient world, being loved meant "being attached" to a specific group. Using that definition, Saint John says that God the Father was so attached to human beings that he sent his own Son to be attached to us. Jesus Christ expresses his attachment to us in the Paschal Mystery, in giving his entire life. We will bear fruit, if we imitate this style of loving, by giving ourselves to each other.

There are many ways of participating in this mystery by giving ourselves to each other. Parents do that with their children, and brothers and sisters do that with each other, when they are not fighting. That way of loving happens in this, because so many of you give yourselves in service, strengthening your attachment to this community and bearing much fruit.

Today, the risen Christ invites us to reflect on the ways in which we love, on the ways in which we give ourselves in humble service to the parish. Giving our time and talent is an important component of stewardship, and we could not offer the programs and opportunities we do without them. Later this week, you will receive a form inviting you to make a commitment, change your commitment, or make a new one for a year. Please pray over your decision and return the form. As a way of helping us to reflect, Mary Jo Kocovski has agreed to tell her story of stewardship of service. Please listen carefully to her story, as we pray over our own decisions.

56.5   May 13, 2012

Very few of the contemporaries of Cornelius and Peter would have regarded them as "friends." Cornelius was a Roman Centurion, in charge of a large group of Roman soldiers stuck in an unpopular assignment on fringes of the Roman Empire. He was charged with keeping an unruly group of religious fanatics in line. Peter was one of those "religious fanatics," a common fisherman saddled with the oppressive rule of foreign occupiers. As an observant Jew, he would never have defiled himself by entering into the home of a pagan Gentile.

And yet, Cornelius and Peter became friends, because each laid down his life to fulfill the Lord's command. Cornelius experienced the presence of the risen Christ and humbled himself by falling at the feet on the Jewish fisherman who had become the head of the community of Christian believers. Peter listened to the promptings of the Holy Spirit and entered into the house of Cornelius, explaining to him that it was the risen Lord had worked wonders for Cornelius and his family, and not himself. Peter not only had Cornelius and his family baptized, but he also welcomed them into the bond of friendship with those who chose to remain in Christ's love. Both of these two characters became friends and bore much fruit. Saint Luke does not tell us what happened to Cornelius. This incident is the beginning of the growth of the Church from its Jewish roots to include the Gentiles. But, we know that Peter literally laid down his life on another cross, after showing the love of Jesus in countless ways throughout his ministry to the community founded by the Paschal Mystery.

Today is the day when we honor our mothers and grandmothers. Hallmark is making a killing on the cards we have bought, and florists are reaping the results of our affection. Jesus' words about love could easily be reprinted on countless Mother's Day cards in flowery and sentimental terms. However, most cards would eliminate words like "keeping my commandments," or "laying down one's life for one's friends." But these words contain the essence of the love which Jesus commands of us. They also show the essence of the vocation of being a mother. Moms do not just talk about the affection they have for their children. Moms keep the Lord's command to love every time they put the needs of their children ahead of their own. Moms bear much fruit when they teach their children the sacrificial love of Jesus Christ, even when their children do not understand and become angry with them. Moms give us an insight into the command of Jesus to love one another.

This command of Jesus is rooted in his own example. He gave everything – his entire life out of love for us. The cross which hangs above the Altar is a powerful sign of that love. During this Easter Season, we celebrate the triumph of that love and reinforce our own efforts to love in the same way, creating friendships that we could never imagine. And we honor our mothers and grandmothers for showing us what that love looks like.

56.6 May 10, 2015

People often speak of taking a journey to find God in their lives. People sometimes do crazy things like biking from Canterbury to Rome to search for God. While there are many good things to be said about making efforts to find God in our lives, the First Letter of Saint John gives us a very different perspective. He says just the opposite. He tells us that God wants to find us. God is love. Because God IS love, and not just a God who has one of the attributes of love, God wants to give that love to us. We do not earn it. We do not deserve it. It is a gift, and God invites us to accept the gift and give it to others.

Saint Peter understands that truth well. The Son of God had found him and invited him to follow him. Peter had responded and listened to Jesus teach the essentials of God's love. Peter would certainly remember the words of Jesus in today's Gospel spoken at the Last Supper. He knows that he has become a friend of Jesus and understands the command to love others as the Lord had loved him. Peter witnessed the ultimate expression of that love when Jesus had washed his feet, given his life in expiation for Peter's sins, and then forgiven him when he was raised from the dead. Peter realizes that love is not some overpowering emotion that makes him feel good. Rather, love is seen in action, in making sacrifices out of love for other people.

As Peter continues to reflect on this incredible love, he comes to understand that the risen Lord has not chosen to love a select few of his best friends. Through the Holy Spirit, the risen Lord was finding pagans, people outside Peter's comfort zone, and calling them to be included in the circle of friends. The pagan soldier, Cornelius, is one of them. As a faithful Jew who had never have entered the home of a pagan, Peter has the courage to walk into the home of Cornelius and welcome him to the community of believers. He does not make Cornelius wait in line until everyone else had been chosen (as I had to wait until everyone else had been chosen as a kid to be part of a team!). Instead, Peter listens to the promptings of the Holy Spirit and welcomes Cornelius and his family into the community of believers.

To use the image of Jesus from last Sunday's Gospel, Cornelius and his family are now branches connected to the true vine of Christ through the waters of Baptism. As disciples, they too are given a command, a mission: go out and bear fruit; go out and love others as I have loved you. Those of you who have the vocation of being a mother understand what Jesus is talking about. You have responded to the Lord's call to love your children as the risen Lord has loved you. So many times, the many sacrifices you make for your children are taken for granted. Children simply presume that their needs are taken care of. They presume that they will have clothes to wear, food to eat, and tender loving care when things go badly. They can even become resentful and rebellious when mothers try to teach them lessons that they do not want to learn. Today, within the context of the truths we hear about the love of God, we get a chance to thank our mothers for showing us so many ways in which they make visible the love that our Scripture readings describe.

At the end of Mass, we are told to go in peace. Our English words, Go, the Mass is ended, translate the Latin command, Ite, Missa est! In other words, get out of here and continue the mission of spreading the sacrificial love made present in the Eucharist. We are sent to bear much fruit, to continue to show that the way we behave reflects the Mystery of the death and resurrection of Jesus Christ. Our response is appropriate, Deo gratias, or thanks be to God. We do not imply that we are glad that the Mass is over. Instead, we are glad to get another chance to show the world that the risen Lord has chosen us to love as we have been loved.

56.7   May 6, 2018

As we continue to reflect on the Lord's Resurrection during this Easter Season, both the first Letter of John and the Gospel of John make a critical point about the love of God. Not only is God love, but God has loved us first. God loved us in the Mystery of the Incarnation when Jesus took on human flesh. Jesus Christ demonstrates his incredible love by giving his entire life on the cross for us. We know the love of God as he remains in us. We imitate the love of God when we lay down our lives. In that action, we understand the intimate friendship which we share with the risen Lord and with each other as members of his Body at this Eucharist.

You parents know this kind of sacrificial love when you lay down your lives for your children. There are countless examples when each of us has responded to the love of God by laying down our lives for another.

Please consider another way of laying down your life for others. God has given each of us gifts and talents. Be sure to take some time to reflect to thank God for your talents. Please consider sacrificing some time to give them in humble service to our parish. Under the guidance of the Holy Spirit, our parish is active and alive, because so many parishioners are grateful for their gifts and are willing to use those gifts to meet the needs of our parish. Please pick up your family packet in the Parish Life Center and pray over your decision.

You would expect me to say these things. I have come to believe the truth of the Gospel message. I also have a vested interest in making sure that our parish remains alive and well. For that reason, Cindy Hestad will tell her story of how she came to participate in the Stewardship of Service at Saint Pius.

57. Ascension of the Lord

Readings
Acts 1:1–11
Ephesians 4:1–13
Mark 16:15–20

57.1 June 4, 2000

A worker was concentrating on his work at a construction site. Without warning, a beam slipped out of the grasp of a crane operator and fell on the man. It took him six months to recover from his wounds. When he finally returned to work, he made up his mind that he would never allow an accident like that to happen again. So he constantly kept his eyes on the sky above him. But in watching for dangers from above, he stepped into an 18-inch hole on the ground and broke his leg.

When Jesus ascended to the right hand of his Father, that's what the apostles did. As they looked up at the sky, two messengers clothed in white asked them what they were doing. In polite Biblical language, the angels said that it was time to stop admiring the beauty and grandeur of God. It was time to get back to Galilee and do what Jesus commissioned them to do – spread the Good News they had experienced in his teachings, his works of healing, and his passion, death and resurrection. Instead of gazing upward, they were to keep their eyes on the ground and nurture the Gospel of love, compassion, forgiveness and peace given them by the Risen One.

And that is what the Word of God tells us! "Men and women of Fort Wayne, why are you standing there looking up at the sky?" In other words, that ninety-day time of reflecting on the mysteries of the Lord's dying and rising is about to end. We have fasted for forty days. We spent three days celebrating those mysteries. We have spent a little over forty days feasting on the Lord's resurrection. In ending this season on Pentecost next Sunday, we prepare to move back into ordinary time. Jesus tells us what he told his disciples at the end of Mark's Gospel: "Go into the whole world and proclaim the gospel to every creature."

The style of proclaiming the gospel varies with each of us. Not many of you go on and on with words like I do. Most of us speak with our actions – in our schools, in our homes, in the places where we work, in the places where we take our summer vacations. Our job is to share with others the mysteries we have been celebrating. Perhaps we will not see demons leaving possessed people in Hollywood style. But our faithfulness to the Lord's dying and rising just might drive out demons of greed and jealousy. We may not master French or Spanish. But we know the language of love and compassion. We may not bring poisonous snakes into this church. But we can handle the slithering passions of envy and criticism. We may not drink poison. But we can take the risk of confronting smoldering anger and prejudice. We may not arrange for cripples to throw away their crutches, but we can minister to the homebound and elderly in our parish.

This business of proclaiming the gospel is a serious one. But we are not alone. The promised Holy Spirit impels us and urges us on. And we cooperate best when we keep our eyes to the ground, instead of sitting around and gazing up at the sky!

57.2 June 1, 2003

On Friday, I received an interesting card from some friends. On the front is a picture of their two-year-old – seated at his high chair, tippy cup spilled on the tray, with his head looking to the sky, and his right hand pointing up. The caption under the photo reads, "Men of Galilee, why are you standing there looking at the sky?" In the inside reads the greeting, "Happy Ascension Feast Day." Odds are good that not many of you received an Ascension Feast Day card this week. I would be willing to wager my salary this month that you will not find such a card in a Hallmark Store.

No matter how little attention most of our society pays to this Feast, the Ascension is an integral part of the Paschal Mystery that we have been celebrating for almost ninety days. (In fact, some would argue that the Bishops moved it to Sunday, so that more people would participate.) For forty days, we were invited to carry our crosses with Jesus and to face our death with him. For the past forty days, our Scriptures have invited us to catch glimpses of the power of Christ's resurrection, and the ways life triumphs over death. In explaining that Mystery to the Ephesians, Paul quotes Psalm 68, which uses the imagery of a triumphant warrior returning home with the prisoners he has captured. But Paul turns that imagery around and insists that Christ returns home to the Father, having triumphed over sin and death. Instead of enslaving us, he gives the gift of complete freedom to us, taking us with him to free us forever from whatever binds us.

The two angels dressed in white give us another insight into this Mystery, when they ask the men of Galilee why they stand there looking up at the sky. They may have been disappointed that Jesus had not restored the kingdom of Israel, and they may have been longing to be taken up with him at that moment. The angels tell them that the way to follow Jesus into eternity is to walk down the Mount of Olives and return to Jerusalem, and – with the power of the Holy Spirit – spread the Good News to the ends of the earth.

The Mystery of the Ascension gives us the same path into eternity. The risen Jesus may not be present to us physically. But, through the power of the Holy Spirit, the risen Jesus is more present to us than he ever was to the disciples during the three years of his public ministry. We can confidently proclaim to the entire world – or at least to Granger – the Mysteries we have been celebrating. We proclaim these truths best by the way we live the Gospel, and we will also see signs accompanying us. A more confident faith can truly drive out the demons of fear that hold us back. Our new language will use the words of love, mercy, and forgiveness. We can handle all kinds of slippery serpents – like the vexing questions of trying to discern in what direction this parish should go. We can drink the deadly poisons of criticism and negativity. And we truly can attend to those who are sick in any way in our community, because the risen Christ is with us.

Next Sunday, with the Feast of Pentecost, we will end our 90-day springtime of the Spirit. With those being confirmed today, we can confidently ask the Holy Spirit to guide us and give us courage. The Lord has ascended to the right hand of the Father. Where he goes, we hope to follow. And we follow best by believing the Good News we have heard and celebrated – and sharing it to the ends of the earth!

57.3 May 28, 2006

When we Christians speak of Mystery, we are not talking about the occult, nor of some muddy obscurity, nor a play or gesture that does not fulfill its claims. We speak of Mystery as a reality that can only be revealed by God. It takes time to open ourselves to the Mystery that God reveals. That is why we spent 40 days in the desert of Lent preparing to celebrate the central Mystery of our faith – the Paschal Mystery. It took us three days of the Triduum to make present that Mystery, beginning on Holy Thursday, with the Last Supper and Jesus washing his disciples' feet and the giving of the Eucharist. We continued on Good Friday, with the dying, death, and burial of Christ. Since the Easter Vigil on Holy Saturday, we have been celebrating the Mystery of his Resurrection, reflecting on what it means to rise with Christ.

Traditionally, the Church has celebrated the next dimension of the Paschal Mystery, the Feast of the Ascension, on the Fortieth Day of Easter. But our Bishops worried that too many people did not take the Fortieth Day seriously enough, and they transferred the Ascension to this Sunday. They were correct about its importance. This Feast is integral to the Paschal Mystery, because it involves letting go of Jesus Christ, who let go of the right hand of the Father to empty himself to become one of us.

The disciples knew the pain of letting go of Jesus on Good Friday. On that day, Jesus died a failure, and all their hopes in him seemed to have been a mistake. Today's departure has something triumphal, something assuring about it. Jesus departs this time, not to go to a horrible death, but to enter life. The risen Lord is not a failure. God the Father has vindicated him. Even though the disciples might have suffered when they lost his physical presence, they returned to Jerusalem filled with great joy.

Their great joy in the face of their loss is the key to understanding the Ascension. The martyrs understood that joy as they faced their own deaths for the sake of their own faith in the Paschal Mystery. We are told that Maximilian Kolbe sang as the Nazis were starving him to death, because the risen Christ gave him strength to dispel the demons of fear. The English martyrs spoke more eloquently with their death than they ever had with the words of their mouths. Stephen rejoiced and did not allow the deadly poison of hatred to keep him from being the first martyr in the Christian Tradition. These people could never explain that joy totally. But they trusted in the Paschal Mystery – in the Death, Resurrection, and Ascension of Jesus Christ to the right hand of the Father.

In celebrating the Ascension today, we are invited to embrace that same joy, even in the midst of our own losses. We remember the words of those two men dressed in white garments: "Men of Galilee, why are you standing there looking up at the sky? This Jesus who has been taken up from you into heaven will return in the same way as you have seen him going into heaven." They say something similar to us: Men and women and children of Granger, don't stand there looking up to the sky. Continue to celebrate the Paschal

Mystery by putting your noses to the ground and proclaiming the Kingdom of God. You are the Body of Christ, waiting to celebrate the completion of this Paschal Mystery next Sunday with the Feast of the Sending of the Spirit. You proclaim the Kingdom by making this Mystery a part of your daily lives. You are the Body of Christ, and you can walk with joy to your own death. The risen Lord will never abandon you, even in the worst of times.

57.4 May 24, 2009

In reflecting on the Paschal Mystery at this season, we have seen Jesus taking leave of his disciples more than once. At the Last Supper, he tells them that he is going away from them and returning to the Father. At the time, they do not understand what he is saying. In the Garden of Gethsemane, he is physically taken away from them, bringing great fear and causing them to scatter. When he dies on the cross and is laid in the tomb, they finally understand what he is talking about, leading them to deep grief, despair, and darkness. When he is raised from the dead, they begin to make sense of his taking leave of them. With them, we have been meditating on the implications of his risen presence during these past forty days or so, allowing the Easter Season to open our eyes to the risen Christ in our midst.

When Jesus takes his leave of them in ascending to the right hand of the Father, the disciples seem to be better prepared. We can sense a note of sadness that they watch him disappear from their sight, no longer present to them in the flesh. But we can also sense a certain confidence. As Luke tells us, they obey his command to wait in Jerusalem for the coming of the Holy Spirit. As Mark tells us, they seem to trust the assurance of Jesus that they will be able to handle difficult situations, even without his physical presence. In proclaiming the Gospel, they can confront the demons that threaten their mission. They can speak a new language – one of love and unity. They will be able to handle conflicts as slippery as serpents. Even the poison of opposition and hatred will not harm them. They will develop ministries to heal the sick and comfort those in great need.

It is with this sense of confidence that we celebrate the Ascension of the Lord. During this Easter Season, the Word of God has opened our hearts to recognize the Lord's risen presence, primarily in the Breaking of Bread, but also in our daily lives. The Lord may not be present in the flesh. But he is present in us, his Body, the Church. He continues to send us forth to proclaim the Gospel every time we are dismissed from Mass. That is why the Mystery of the Ascension is so important. The risen Christ is more present to us than he could have been in the flesh. The risen Christ has not abandoned us, but has gone before us to show us the way to the Father, to the complete indwelling with the Trinity which we call "heaven."

Even with their confidence in the Lord taking leave of them in the Ascension, the disciples still do not fully understand the implications of the Kingdom of God. Their last question to Jesus reveals that they still cling to the hope that Jesus would restore the Kingdom to Israel. Instead of lecturing them, Jesus promises that the Holy Spirit will guide them, so they will recognize him when he comes again at the end of time.

Like them, we too do not always understand fully the implications of the Kingdom of God in our midst. We want to hold onto our own ideas of what God's Kingdom should look like. We like to cling to the illusion that faith in the risen Christ involves warm feelings about others, or that faith in the risen Christ will help us avoid any controversy or pain when we choose to serve the parish. That is why we spend this next week in prayer, waiting for a new outpouring of the Holy Spirit upon us. The Holy Spirit will guide us, even when we do not fully understand what the Kingdom of God looks like, just as the Holy Spirit guided those disciples looking up to heaven. With them, we listen to the words of the two men dressed in white garments: Men and women of Saint Pius, why are you standing there looking up at the sky? Once dismissed from this Mass, go out to all of Granger to continue our mission as Christ's Body and proclaim the Gospel by the way we live the presence of the risen Christ.

57.5 May 20, 2012

At Christmas, we celebrated the Mystery of the Incarnation – the Lord's coming down from Heaven to take on our human nature. At the Triduum, we celebrated the Mystery of the Lord's suffering, death, and resurrection. In these last forty days, we have been reflecting on his victory over death and sin, along with his promise that those who die with him will rise with him. Our reflections have focused on the Apostles' encounters with the transformed body of the risen Lord, granting them peace and joy. Today, we celebrate the Mystery of the Lord's Ascension. He has returned to where the Mystery of our redemption began – at the right hand of the Father. His Ascension has created a new reality, because he has paved the way for us to follow and given the Holy Spirit to guide us on that way.

We do not experience the risen Lord in the same way that the earliest Apostles did. But, do experience him in the sacramental life of the Church. We have become one with him in Baptism. We have been sealed with the Holy Spirit in Confirmation. We are fed with his Body and Blood in the Eucharist. The Sacraments of healing and commitment continue his work.

Just as the Lord sent the original Apostles into the world to proclaim the Kingdom, so he sends us, his Body, to do the same thing. We do that primarily through our stewardship of service. Our parish is known for its vitality and its many services. In a society which tends to tell people to put their own needs first, those who serve the needs of the parish do just the opposite, putting the needs of the community ahead of their own.

Today, we invite you to take a step in faith and make a one year commitment of service to the parish, to be part of our effort to obey the risen Lord's command. If you have never had a chance to do so, take a first step today. If you are already involved, renew your commitment, or change it to another ministry. Please read the information which you received in the Stewardship of Service packet. But, for now, please listen to Aaron Wall's story of how he took his steps in faith. Through the new language of encouragement from his wife, he has learned that giving of his time and talents to the parish has not caused some deadly poison to harm him. Instead, handling the slippery serpents of service has enriched his life.

57.6   May 17, 2015

Saint Luke tells us that Jesus was **taken up** into heaven. This taking up of Jesus is an essential part of the Paschal Mystery. Jesus showed incredible trust in his Father during his earthly ministry. He trusted that his Father knew what he was doing when he carried his cross to Calvary. He could trust, because he had learned detachment. In being removed from his physical existence in this world, he trusts his disciples to carry on his mission, even though he knows they are clueless. He trusts them even when they ask a really dumb question about when he would kick out the Romans and restore the Kingdom of Israel.

As Jesus is taken up, two men dressed in white tell the disciples to **take a journey within**. In taking a long, sobering look within their own souls, they begin the process of learning to be detached. They are like young parents who are holding their first newborn child in their arms. Filled with joy, they suddenly ask themselves, "What now?" As the reality of a new child sinks in, they will eventually learn how to detach themselves from so many things they had considered important to focus on the needs of their child.

That is why the two men dressed in white garments tell the disciples that they now need to **take the journey out**. Saint Mark tells us that they went forth and preached everywhere. Filled with the Holy Spirit, they could speak the language of love, which drove out demons, allowed them to handle slippery situations, bring the healing power of Jesus to people, and not be afraid to swallow insults from others.

As we reflect on the Mystery of the Ascension, the Lord invites us to respond to the trust he has given us. He has been taken up. We respond by taking a journey within. In taking that long and sobering look at our souls, we will discover the gifts and talents God has given us. Then the Lord sends us on the journey outside ourselves. He wants us to trust him and learn detachment, so that we can be free to proclaim the Kingdom of God through our service to our families and to our parish.

That is why the message of stewardship is so important. Stewardship gives us a structure way of responding in faith to the Mystery of the Ascension. During Lent, we renewed our stewardship of prayer. Today, we are invited to renew our stewardship of service. Please read the materials in your stewardship of service packet. Please consider renewing your commitment or making a new one. As you take this journey within and pray over how you can move out, please listen to Phil Hayes. Phil has been a faithful catechist in our CCD program for many years. As he speaks of his humble service, listen to the Holy Spirit nudging you to take a step in faith and allow the Lord to work through you, as he worked through those first disciples.

57.7   May 13, 2018

Several years ago, the Bishops moved the Solemnity of the Ascension from the fortieth day of Easter to this Sunday. Their concern was that too many Catholics were not present on a Thursday, and that many more would be present on Sunday. The Ascension is an integral part of the Paschal Mystery. However, the move wreaked havoc with the number forty. In the Acts of the Apostles, Saint Luke says that Jesus spent forty days with his disciples after he rose from the dead, presenting many proofs after he had suffered and speaking of the kingdom of God.

The number forty indicates that we are dealing with a Mystery when we reflect on the Ascension. In the Book of Genesis, it rained forty days and forty nights to create the flood. The Israelites spent forty years in the desert learning how to act like free people. The prophet Elijah walked forty days to reconnect the Covenant at Mount Horeb. Jesus spent forty days in the desert to prepare for his public ministry. We spent forty days during Lent in praying, fasting, and giving alms to prepare to celebrate the Paschal Mysteries. Saint Luke uses this symbolic number to indicate that the risen Christ had spent sufficient time with his disciples to prepare those who had witnessed the resurrection for the mission of the Church.

That is the challenge for us as we celebrate the Solemnity of the Ascension. We have reflected on the presence of the Risen Lord in the Sacramental life of the Church for over forty days during this Easter Season. The Scriptures have invited us to recognize his risen presence in our daily lives. In doing so, we are like those original disciples in many ways. Even though Jesus had clearly taught about the kingdom of God, they still wanted the kingdom to conform to their ideas. As Jesus departs, they want to see God's kingdom freeing them from the domination of the Romans. Despite hearing the Word of God every Sunday, we still cling to our own ideas of what God's kingdom should look like in our world. They stand there looking up at the sky, paralyzed with fear. We tend to do the same; fearful about taking new steps to put ourselves in humbles service of others. They are told to wait for the Holy Spirit. We are invited to wait and pray for a new outpouring of the Holy Spirit at Pentecost.

In today's Gospel, Jesus gives his disciples a commission. They are to go into the whole world and proclaim the gospel to every creature. He gives the same commission to us, his disciples today. Like those earliest disciples, we are sent to drive out the demons of hate and division with words and actions of respect. We are given the new language of love at Pentecost. Unlike Adam and Eve, we can handle the serpent, whose real power was destroyed by the death and resurrection of Jesus Christ. That is why people stomp on the image of the serpent when they enter into the main door of our church. As much as there are so many poisonous elements of our culture, they cannot harm us. We can extend the healing hand of Jesus Christ to those who are sick through our pastoral care for them.

Saint Paul reminds us in his letter to the Ephesians that God has given each of us gifts to build up the unity of the Church, centered in Jesus Christ. We go into the world and proclaim the gospel to every creature not only with our words, but with humble service. It is ironic that we celebrate the Mystery of the Ascension on Mother's Day. If we want to serve with humility, gentleness, and patience, bearing with one another through love, we look to our mothers and grandmothers. They teach us the paradox of the Ascension. The risen Christ is more present to us now than he could have been in his earthly ministry, located in one geographical place. Through the power of the Holy Spirit, he encourages us to continue his ministry in our own time. To all mothers, thank you for showing us the face of Christ.

58. Pentecost Sunday

Readings

Acts 2:1-11
1 Corinthians 12:3b–7, 12–13 or Galatians 5:16–25
John 15:16–27; 16:12–15 or John 20:19–23

58.1 June 11, 2000

For a variety of reasons, I am always hot in this church. Maybe it is my normal body temperature. Perhaps it is my age. Maybe it is the vestments we wear. In the summer, it always seems that the air conditioning is not working properly, because I cannot see or feel the air moving. Before calling for repairs, I always check with Kevin. "Are you hot?" If he isn't, then the system must be working. However, the decorations on the ceiling during the Easter Season provide a better clue. We may not see or feel the air moving, but we see the results of the moving air in the material that moves.

In the Gospel of John, Jesus gives the Holy Spirit to his apostles by breathing on them. Like the air moving our material, they did not see the Spirit. But they saw the results of the Spirit's presence when they opened the locked doors and extended God's mercy and forgiveness to everyone. Saint Luke describes the giving of the Spirit on Pentecost in terms of a strong driving wind. Like the people of Florida who see the power of a hurricane in the destruction of trees and property, the people in Jerusalem saw the power of the Spirit when an unlikely group of people emerged from their hiding place and spoke a common language of love and enthusiasm.

Like breath or like wind, the Holy Spirit is always moving and is always present. The Feast of Pentecost invites us to look for the fruits – the results – of the Spirit moving through us and through our community. For young people, coming to Mass here on Sunday may seem like a boring burden. But the Spirit has ways of revealing to you how important you are to this community and how much we need you. We wonder at times how a parish community with so many differences can possibly accomplish anything. And yet, we can see the results of the Spirit moving, as we did yesterday at the Festival or in our response to a family who has suffered a tragedy. At times we feel so discouraged and so disheartened that we wonder whether we can keep going in a commitment or in our work. And yet, somehow, we pick ourselves up try again. That is the Spirit giving strength we did not know we had.

At the end of the fourth century, Saint John Chrysostom described those who believe in Jesus in this way: "You are not only free, but also holy; not only holy, but also just; not only just but also children; not only children but also heirs; not only heirs, but also brothers (and sisters) of Christ; not only brothers (and sisters), but also joint heirs; not only joint heirs, but also members; not only members, but also the temple; not only the temple, but also the instruments of the spirit." We are instruments of the Spirit. If we are open to that Spirit, then people will definitely see the fruits, the results of the Spirit's presence here.

58.2 June 8, 2003

A fireman in a small midwestern town was being honored for his courage in rescuing two small children from their burning home. He had heard their cries for help and risked his life to bring them to safety. But, he was uncomfortable with the title "hero", because he was simply doing his job. In fact, he had been afraid during the entire ordeal. "Maybe courage is not about not being afraid," he said. "Maybe courage is knowing you are more afraid than anyone else, but not letting fear keep you from doing the right thing."

The disciples of the risen and ascended Lord were also afraid, hiding in a room in Jerusalem behind locked doors. They should have been out celebrating with the rest of the people, because it was the feast of Pentecost. This Feast occurred 50 days after the Passover Feast of liberation from slavery in Egypt, and it attracted Jews from around the world to come to Jerusalem to celebrate the gift of the Law given at Mount Sinai. That Law enabled them to continue living as God's free people.

The disciples had experienced Passover that year in a new and unexpected way. Their Master had passed from death into new life, and he had returned to the right hand of the Father. Raised from the dead, Jesus had promised that he would not abandon them. But, they were afraid that what happened to their master would happen to them. So, they kept that Good News to themselves. On Pentecost, the Holy Spirit rushed upon them to give them the courage to do what they had been afraid to do – to publicly proclaim the Good News in clear terms that everyone could understand.

Our Feast of Pentecost, the fiftieth day of Easter, invites us to trust the same Holy Spirit. Luke tells the story of the Holy Spirit coming upon the disciples as tongues of fire, not as a history lesson, but as a way of helping us believe that this same Holy Spirit gives us courage to proclaim in clear terms what we have been celebrating for ninety days – that the Lord Jesus suffered, died, rose from the dead, ascended to the right hand of the Father, and invites us to walk that same path.

Perhaps we can best appreciate the work of the Spirit among us when we admit our own fears. What do you fear most? Do you fear for the future of our parish as we work for a strategic plan? Do you fear that your personal hopes and dreams will be dashed? Do you fear speaking the truth to those who might reject you? My time on retreat last week provided an unexpected opportunity to face one of my deepest fears. I was one of the youngest priests on that retreat, bringing the average age down to 85! I gazed upon what I fear most – losing my hearing or eyesight; not being able to walk on my own; being confused about which way is the dining room. Looking at what I fear most gave me courage. Listening to these men tell stories of what they did in their prime gave me more confidence. Through them, the Holy Spirit whispered that it is possible to face the future with courage, no matter what the aging process may bring.

A good friend told me one time that what we fear most will most likely happen to us. He should know. He had been harboring a terrible secret for many years, and he feared that it would be revealed. When it finally was revealed, he was stripped of everything that was important to him – his job, his dignity, and his reputation. But, the Holy Spirit graced him with the courage to face the truth. Today, he lives a peaceful life he had never considered. In a similar way, the Apostles stayed behind locked doors, because they were afraid the authorities would execute them, as they had executed their master. By the power of the Holy Spirit, they faced their fears. All of them, except for John, were murdered for their faith, and John was banished to a tiny island for the rest of his life. By the power of the Holy Spirit, they became the foundation of the Church, born on that first Pentecost. By the power of the Holy Spirit, we remain essential stones in that structure today, graced to face our fears and trust in God's promise.

58.3 June 4, 2006

The Book of Genesis tells us that when God created the heavens and the earth, the earth was a formless void, and darkness covered the face of the deep, while a wind from God swept over the face of the waters. That wind, the Spirit of God, brought light and life out of chaos and darkness. That wind, the Spirit of God, brought tongues of fire on the Apostles locked in that upper room. The Holy Spirit literally blew them out of that room and opened their tongues to speak of the power of the resurrection. In this new creation of the Church, light and life emerged from chaos and darkness.

That same Holy Spirit is given to us. The Holy Spirit continues to move through the Church today. Like breath or wind, we cannot see the Holy Spirit. But we can see the fruits – the results – of the Spirit moving. An analogy might be the air conditioning of our church. Because I am always hot, I wonder many times if the system is working. But, before I panic and incur unnecessary service charges to the parish, I look for some evidence that the air is indeed moving in here. During the Easter Season, I have relied on the Easter Candle. If the flame is flickering, then the system is working fine. If not, it's time to shell out more money to repair the system.

The Feast of Pentecost invites us to renew our trust in the ways the Holy Spirit moves in our midst and to identify the fruits, the results, of his presence. We see those fruits when parishioners believe the words of Paul and identify the specific gifts God has given them. The Spirit moves them to offer these gifts not for their own benefit, but to build up the Body of Christ. We see the fruits of the Holy Spirit when people are willing to let go of their angers or hurt feelings to be reconcile with one another. We see the fruits of the Holy Spirit when so our parishioners give up their time to assist our sister parishes either in Mississippi or Saint Adalbert's.

We have especially seen the fruits of the Holy Spirit when we have witnessed so many people have received the Easter Sacraments. Our Easter Candle does more than tell the pastor not to call the repairman. It describes the ways in which God has created light and life through water. Beginning at the top, we see Noah and his family saved from the waters of the great flood. We see Moses and his people escaping slavery through the waters of the Red Sea. We see Namaan the Syrian healed of his leprosy through the waters of the Jordan. We see Jesus healing the paralytic at the Pool of Bethesda and telling him to carry his mat away. We recognize the Paschal Mystery in the cross bearing the Greek words alpha and omega, along with the incense imbedded into the nails. Even though we celebrate his Resurrection in time, in 2006, the candle is complete with the ultimate victory of the Lamb who was slain and who reigns in heaven, with the waters of salvation flowing to wash all of creation.

Whether we have been baptized this Easter Season or 50 Easter Seasons ago, we have been incorporated into the Body of Christ through the saving waters of Baptism. The Holy Spirit given to us moves freely in our midst and pushes us away from any fear that could paralyze us. Pentecost celebrates our birth – the birth of the Church. The Holy Spirit moves us out of this church to do what those who first received the Spirit did – to renew the face of the earth.

58.4   May 31, 2009

Some ninety days ago, we gathered in this church on Ash Wednesday to begin the "Lenten Springtime of the Spirit," even though there was very little evidence of spring. The trees were barren. The ground was frozen. The weather was nasty. But, we did not allow the many evidences of winter to stop us. We embarked on a thorough spring cleaning of our souls, preparing ourselves to enter more deeply into the Paschal Mystery. We celebrated that Paschal Mystery with great solemnity during the Triduum, when we commemorated the Lord's Last Supper, his suffering, death, and resurrection. We entered into the fifty days of Easter to reflect on the implications of his resurrection in lives. Last Sunday, we celebrated his Ascension to the right hand of the Father. Today, we conclude the Easter Season by celebrating Pentecost, the sending of the Holy Spirit and the birth of the Church. Today, we also rejoice in the abundant evidence of springtime in the natural world.

The disciples experienced this Mystery first hand. As they remained locked in their safe place after Jesus had been crucified, they reflected on his risen presence and pondered what it meant for him to ascend to the right hand of the Father. On this day, the Holy Spirit came upon them as wind. The wind reminded them of the breath of God blowing over the chaos before God created the world. That same wind blew over the Red Sea to clear the way for the people of Israel to escape from slavery to freedom. That wind blew over Mount Sinai as Moses received the Law. That same breath of God inspired the prophets to speak the truth, even in the face of terrible opposition. As wind, the Holy Spirit blew the earliest disciples out of their safe haven into a world which was stunned by their boldness.

On this day, the Holy Spirit also came as tongues of fire on those gathered in that upper room. The fire reminded them of God speaking to Moses from the burning bush and from lightning on Mount Sinai. They remembered that Elijah had called down fire from heaven to consume the sacrifice at Mount Carmel and was taken up to heaven in a fiery chariot. As fire, the Holy Spirit purified the faith of the disciples and heated their conviction that the Lord Jesus had intended his message to reach the ends of the earth.

That same Holy Spirit comes to us today, as we gather in this safe place to conclude the Easter Season and our reflection on the Paschal Mystery. The Sequence describes well the power of the Holy Spirit. The Holy Spirit shines with grace in our most secret places. The Holy Spirit provides pleasant coolness in the heat of our woes. The Holy Spirit cleanses our soiled hearts of sin and heals the many wounds in our lives. The Holy Spirit bends stubborn hearts and wills and melts what is frozen or chilled within us. The Holy Spirit gives the gifts we need to guide us home.

The Holy Spirit pushes us out of this safe place at the end of the Easter Season and at the end of this Mass with the force of a mighty wind. The Holy Spirit fires us with a passion to live our faith in a way that we too will speak a new language. We speak the language of faith, which expresses our confidence that the risen Christ lives in our midst. We speak the language of hope, which says that life will come from death, just as surely as spring has come from winter. We speak the language of love, which mirrors the Mystery we have been celebrating for ninety days.

58.5   May 27, 2012

The Book of Genesis tells us that a mighty wind swept over the chaos before the world was created. In the second story of creation, God took some clay and breathed into it, forming from the earth Adam, our first parent. In his account of the first Easter Sunday, Saint John tells us that the risen Christ broke through locked doors and breathed on his disciples huddled together. By breathing the Holy Spirit upon them, he created a community of disciples from a group of frightened people. In telling the story of Pentecost, Saint Luke tell us that the Holy Spirit blew into the upper room like a strong driving wind and drove the disciples out of that upper room to speak the new language of the Paschal Mystery to the entire world. The Church did not drop like a meteor from heaven. The Church was created from the human beings of God's creation with the breath of the Holy Spirit.

The same is true of vocations to the priesthood. Priests do not drop, ready to serve, from Heaven. God calls priests from the community formed by the Paschal Mystery of the Lord's Death, Resurrection, Ascension, and Sending of the Holy Spirit. Father Jacob Meyer was formed by the love of his parents, Curt and Julie. He grew up with his brother, Ryan, and his sister, Ellen. That family formed his faith, with help from the parishes of Holy Cross and

Saint Pius. At Saint Pius, we have had the privilege of being part
of his formation, as the Spirit has guided him in these last six years.
Through the light of the Holy Spirit, he began to figure out that the
Lord might be calling him to the priesthood. Much to his mother's
chagrin, he has lived with us at the rectory, providing him rest from
his labor, coolness in the heat, and solace in the midst of his seminary woes. We have seen the Holy Spirit heal his wounds and renew his strength. We have also been amused as we watched the
Holy Spirit try to bend his stubborn heart and will. (The Holy Spirit
had to work overtime on this one!) The Holy Spirit has guided his
steps when he has gone astray. Yesterday, through the laying on
of hands, Bishop Rhoades ordained him to the priesthood of Jesus
Christ. Words cannot express our joy and gratitude that Father
Jacob has responded to the promptings of the breath of the Holy
Spirit.

Many centuries ago, Saint Augustine reflected on the experience of the Holy Spirit in the Church. He offered three particular insights about the Holy Spirit as the bond of unity within the Blessed
Trinity. Saint Augustine argues that for those who are open to the
Holy Spirit, that unity is experienced as communion, abiding love,
and giving and gift. Father Jacob, you will bring that gift of communion to the parishes you serve. You understand that living in communion goes much deeper than tastes in vestments and cassocks.
You know that communion involves a deep need for God and one
another. You will work to build up that communion. You will be
in the position of helping people understand the experience of the
Holy Spirit as abiding love. Through your ministry, parishioners
will learn to trust the abiding love of God which dispels uncertainty,
which overcomes the fear of betrayal, which carries eternity within.
Finally, in giving the gift of yourself, your parishioners will see that
the Holy Spirit will push them also out of the upper rooms of their
comfort zones to give of themselves in humble, loving service.

Saint August knew what he was talking about. Like you, Father
Jacob, he followed the promptings of the Holy Spirit and allowed
God to form him from a very human family. Like you, he allowed
the Holy Spirit to form him continually in his priestly and Episcopal ministry to his people. May his example and intercession guide
you as you begin your priestly ministry! May unifying love be your
measure! May abiding love be your challenge! May self-giving love
be your mission!

58.6 May 20, 2018

When Jesus ascended into heaven, he told his disciples to wait for
the coming of the Holy Spirit. Odds are pretty good that they had
no idea of what they were waiting for. That is why Saint Luke indi-

cates in the Acts of the Apostles that the coming of the Holy Spirit is
very sudden. He connects this encounter with the Divine with the
encounter with God in the First Covenant at Mount Sinai. Then,
the mountain shook. At Pentecost, the entire house shakes with
the outpouring of the Holy Spirit. Just as there was fire at Mount
Sinai, tongues as of fire come to rest on those gathered in the upper
room. In contrast to the Tower of Babel, when arrogance and pride
prevented people from communicating with one another, the outpouring of the Holy Spirit enables everyone to understand what the
disciples say. The Holy Spirit transforms a timid group of disciples
who had experienced the Paschal Mystery into a bold band sharing
that experience with everyone. With this outpouring of the Holy
Spirit, the Church is born.

Today, we celebrate the birth of the Church and trust that this
same Holy Spirit is given to us, who have been reflecting on the
Paschal Mystery for the last fifty days. The Holy Spirit can transform us from a timid group of disciples into a bold band of disciples
eager to share the Mystery of the death and resurrection of Jesus
Christ with everyone. But, in order for the Holy Spirit to work in
us, we must heed Saint Paul's advice to the Galatians and live by the
Spirit.

Saint Paul contrasts two very different ways of living – either
in the flesh or in the Spirit. When he talks about the flesh, he does
not imply that our gift of sexuality is bad or that we can be holy
only if we separate ourselves from the body. Rather, by living in
the flesh, he means a way of living that is centered on satisfying
our selfish desires. If we live in the flesh, we use our sexuality for
self-gratification instead of giving ourselves totally in love to a committed spouse. The easy access to pornography emphasizes living
in the flesh. Living in the flesh erodes our trust in God's providence
and encourages us to hate those who are not like us, making them
rivals. Living in the flesh causes jealousy, dissensions, factions, and
drinking bouts. In other words, living in the flesh is destructive of
healthy relationships within the community.

Living in the Spirit produces very different effects, or as Saint
Paul calls, them: fruits. The first fruit is love, the greatest gift. Love
is not merely a feeling, but a sincere desire to want what is best
for the other. When we learn to love, then we will experience joy,
peace, patience, kindness, generosity, faithfulness, gentleness, and
self-control.

We pray today for a new outpouring of the Holy Spirit on our
community. In truth, we live in both worlds. There are aspects of
living in the flesh and living in the Spirit in all of our lives. Because
we entered into the Mystery of the dying and rising of Christ when

we entered the waters of Baptism, Saint Paul insists that we nail those aspects of the flesh to the cross of Christ and learn to live in the Spirit.

Jesus promises at the Last Supper that the Holy Spirit, the Advocate, will guide us to all truth. He makes this same promise to us, who are gathered here to celebrate this Memorial of the Last Supper. As a parish, we have a unique opportunity to trust his promise and to take steps in faith to become that bold band of disciples who can proclaim with one voice the Good News to our local community. As we complete the final phase of our construction project during this year, we are embarking on a five-year strategic plan to guide us in the future. We will invite the entire parish to give input and guidance. As we nail our ways of living in the flesh to the cross of Jesus Christ, we trust the Lord's promise and ask the Holy Spirit to guide us, just as the Holy Spirit guided those disciples on the first Pentecost.

VII

Feasts & Solemnities

59. Conversion of St. Paul

Readings

Acts 22:3–16 or Acts 9:1–22
Mark 16:15–18

59.1 January 25, 2009

Saul of Tarsus began his life as a strict follower of Gamaliel, a prominent teacher in the ways of the Pharisees. As a Pharisee, Saul was convinced that people were saved by careful and meticulous observance of the Law of Moses. As a Pharisee, Saul was alarmed by the new movement among his people who claimed that the carpenter's son, Jesus of Nazareth, was the promised Messiah. He was so convinced of the harm that could be done by this new movement that he traveled to Damascus to do what he could to eliminate those who advocated this new Way. On the road to Damascus, he encountered the One he was opposing and underwent one of the most dramatic conversions in history. As Paul the Apostle, he lived the rest of his life spreading the Good News about the One who changed him, doing more than any other single person to convince others that they could be saved, not by the Law, but by the death and resurrection of Jesus Christ.

Not many of us have experienced such a dramatic conversion in our lives. But in celebrating this Feast of the Conversion of Saint Paul, we can learn something from the intensity of his words to the Corinthians. Writing to them soon after the destruction of Jerusalem, he knows that many feared that the end was near. Drawing on his deep conviction that all of life is rooted in Jesus Christ, he urges the Corinthians to take another look at their priorities, making sure that they live each day as if it were their last. Now is the time to let go of whatever does not last and replace those things with Christ.

He gives us the same message. We sometimes speak of conversion to describe a dramatic change in our lives. Like Paul, dramatic changes do happen. But, more often, conversion is a gradual and lifelong process. The two Latin words that form the English word "conversion" are "con" and "verso," meaning "to turn toward." Conversion means a turning toward the Lord. As we celebrate Paul's conversion, we can reflect on what needs to change in our lives, so that Christ can be at the center. Young people can always look at what distracts you from seeing Christ in your parents or teachers or classmates. Parents can make adjustments, so that your children truly can become your first priority, seeing your children as gifts from God. All of us can identify those realities in our lives that absorb our time and energy and ask ourselves if they are blocking the abundant flow of God's saving Grace.

Paul took to heart the instructions given to the eleven by Jesus at the end of the Gospel of Saint Mark as he sends them out to proclaim the Gospel. Armed with the Gospel, Paul cast out the demons of fear as many opposed him in violent ways. He spoke the new language of the Lord's saving death and resurrection. He handled the slippery serpents of those enemies who tried to adjust his message to suit their own purposes, and he drank plenty of poisonous venom of those who accused him of selling out. When our conversion (our gradual turning toward the Lord) gets tough, we can look to Paul. Through his intercession, we too can cast out our own demons. We can speak the language of love coming from the Lord's death and resurrection. We need not fear those serpents that try to draw us away from Christ. We can even drink the poison of opposition when others make fun of our faith. Paul sets the tone for turning toward the Lord, and we can embrace it.

60. Presentation of the Lord

Readings
Malachi 3:1–4
Hebrews 2:14–18
Luke 2:22–40

60.1 February 2, 2003

Forty days ago, we gathered in this Church to celebrate the birth of a child. Our celebration was filled with joy and hope, because we acknowledged that this newborn child is the Son of God. We gather again today to further reflect on that birth. With the burning candles held in our hands, our celebration continues to radiate joy and hope. But, today, we also become aware that the same fire that warms us will also burn us!

Simeon uses the image of a sword. He tells Mary, the Mother of the Child, that her heart will be pierced with a sword. The old man foretells that her Son will be rejected and brutally murdered. The sword will separate her from the life of her son. But, as she will find out, her faith and acceptance of the Will of God will eventually bind her to a more intimate and permanent union with her Son than she ever could have imagined.

We call Mary our Mother and the Mother of the Church, because her experience of the Mystery of faith is ours. With her, we share the joy of her Son's birth, in the Good News he proclaims as an adult, and in the miracles he works. But there is no such reality as faith without the sword. We feel the sword in questions that have no answers, in grief that seems to have no consolation. We know the sword of leave taking and being betrayed by those we thought we could trust. We eventually know the sword of sickness, death, and isolation. Faith does not protect us from the sword. But, like Mary, faith opens us to being bound more intimately and permanently with the Mystery of her Son, as she has experienced.

That is why we are pushing this Lenten Program, Disciples In Mission so strongly. Disciples In Mission invites everyone in the parish to make a commitment to meet in a small group with 7 to 9 other people once a week for six weeks of Lent, and then one time during the Easter Season. It is a program that gives us an opportunity to look carefully at the Word of God assigned to the following Sunday and make it a part of our daily life experience. When you come to Mass, you will already have made the Scripture Readings for that Sunday a part of your flesh and blood. Father Dan and I are a little nervous about the entire congregation, sitting there with your hands folded across your chests, challenging us to say something about those Scriptures that you have not already considered. You have already reflected on the ways the Word of God has comforted you, and how it has pierced your heart. Talk about intimidation!

And that is not all. Something very powerful happens when people begin meeting in small groups. It is easy to get lost in this parish, because it is so large. Disciples In Mission has the potential of breaking our size down into manageable proportions. It gives us a chance to connect with other people on a very human and deep level. With better connections and with a deeper sense of sharing our common bonds, our faith can be stronger when that sword pierces us, because we have support from others who share our bond of faith at a very deep level.

When the swords of life pierce our hearts, the pain can certainly open us to the mystery of the healing and caring and mercy of God. That is what happened to Mary. But we have a better chance of entering into that mystery when we understand more fully the Word of God and have the real support of others who share a common baptism.

61. Most Holy Trinity

Readings
Deuteronomy 4:32–34, 39–40
Romans 8:14–17
Matthew 28:16–20

61.1 June 18, 2000

Some time ago, a teacher worried that her students would not be able to answer the Bishop's questions when he came for the Sacrament of Confirmation. So, she devised a system using the Nicene Creed – the Creed we pray at Mass on Sundays and Holy Days – as a way of preparing the candidates for Confirmation. But she worked backwards. She started with the section "We believe in the Holy Spirit" and asked questions. Next, she moved her questioning upwards to the part that speaks of Jesus Christ. Then, she went to the section about God the Father, posing more questions. If there was time, she reviewed the last part of the Creed – the part that talks about the church.

Her decision to move backwards says something about how the Trinity works. The Holy Spirit is the power of the church in all our teaching, all our ministering, and all our praying. Through the Holy Spirit working, we come to know Jesus Christ, the one who acts in everything that the church says and does. In coming to know Jesus, all glory and praise are given to his Father, who is also our Father. Without the Spirit, we could never have faith in Jesus. Without the Son, we could never know the Father.

In just a few minutes, we will recite that ancient Creed together. Notice its Trinitarian structure. And once we recite that Creed, we prepare the Altar and gifts in order to pray the Eucharistic Prayer – the greatest public profession of faith in Father, Son, and Holy Spirit.

Listen carefully to the words of that prayer today, and notice its Trinitarian structure. We give praise and thanks for God's action in our world, and specifically for the salvation won for us in Christ. We ask the Father to send the Holy Spirit to change gifts of bread and wine into the Body and Blood of Christ. Through the power of the Spirit, God's saving work is made present to us now, as we remember. God's gift to us in Jesus becomes the gift we offer to God. And remembering what God has already done for us in Jesus, we ask God to show great care for our pope and bishop, for the clergy, and for all God's people, living and dead. Finally, the doxology "through him, with him, in him . . ." is like a sacred toast to God the Father for the salvation which Jesus won for us and which unites us in the Holy Spirit.

When we respond "Amen" to that prayer, we express our faith that our God is a God of three distinct Persons gathered in a perfect unity of love. In the fourth century, Saint Jerome wrote that the great Amen echoed like thunder throughout the churches in his day. May our "Amen" today be our thunder of assent to the God who draws us with all our differences into the unity of the Trinity. May our "Amen" support our own Candidates for Confirmation as we send them to contribute their own thunder at the regional Confirmation Mass (tomorrow) later today.

61.2   June 15, 2003

By their very definition, Mysteries can never be fully understood. That is certainly true of the Mystery of the Trinity – one God in three distinct Persons. However, we might gain some insights into what we can never fully grasp when we reflect on our own human lives, which reflect the divine image. We come to know the nature of God as we grow older and live life completely.

It is part of the divine logic that the Second Person of the Blessed Trinity reveals himself to us as a baby. Infants are completely dependent on their parents for everything, and Jesus demonstrates that utter trust in his Father as he grows to maturity and begins his public ministry. Jesus maintained that trust in his Father even in the face of death. We learn that same lesson as we continue to pray to the Lord's Prayer, when we let go of the temptations to rely simply on our own talents and interests. We learn how to trust from children.

On this Father's Day, we learn something of the First Person of the Trinity, the Father, when we thank our human fathers and reflect on their roles in our lives. I have found that it helps to be middle-aged to understand the demands of what it means to be a father. By its nature, authentic fatherhood involves a total gift of self for the common good. The prodigal son was not able to appreciate the gifts of his father until he lost them through his own stupidity – and then received them back through his father's mercy. We learn how to empty ourselves for the good of others from parents, and on this weekend, from fathers.

Older people have the advantage of identifying with the Holy Spirit, the Third Person of the Trinity. Once the body begins to go, it becomes a little easier to imagine what it is like to be a Person without a Body. As we lose some of our former physical abilities, we realize that our very identity does not depend on strength, or agility, or even what our culture defines as beautiful. We begin to make priorities in life, yearning more for the spiritual. Saint Cyril of Alexandria said this about the Holy Spirit: "The Holy Spirit changes those in whom he comes to dwell and alters the whole pattern of their lives. With the Spirit within them it is quite natural for people who have been absorbed by the things of this world to become entire other worldly in outlook, and for cowards to become people of great courage." We learn how to be courageous from the elderly, who always remind us that old age is not for the faint hearted!

It is within the context of a community that we begin to appreciate the divine nature. In this particular community of Saint Pius X, we have all these age groups – children who teach us what it means to trust; fathers and mothers who teach us how to give of themselves for the common good; and the elderly who help us to put life into a better perspective. We not only learn something about the nature of our Trinitarian God as we listen to each other and learn to respect each other. We catch a glimpse now of what is ultimately our destiny through the transforming power of God's grace – complete unity with God, one and three!

61.3 June 11, 2006

The word "Trinity" does not exist in the Bible. However, the reality we celebrate today is at the heart of all the Scriptures. In the readings proclaimed today, we hear of the Father, who revealed himself to Moses and his people as a faithful God who kept the Covenant, even when they did not. We hear of the Holy Spirit, who was given to us at Pentecost and makes us children of God. We hear of Jesus, the only begotten Son, who died and rose for us and sends us to proclaim the Good News until the end of the age.

It took the Church three hundred years to reflect on this reality. During much of that time, the earliest Bishops argued over the ways in which this Mystery should be expressed. Finally, they agreed on a series of careful philosophical distinctions and precise terminology in 325, when they wrote the Creed at the Council of Nicea – the Creed we pray together every Sunday.

On this Sunday, we might wonder how the Mystery of the Trinity affects our daily lives. We might think that the theological formulations are beyond us, and that is probably true. It is impossible to grasp the utter Mystery of one God and three distinct Persons and to understand their relationship with each other. But, we are wrong if we think that this Mystery has nothing to do with our daily lives. At our level of being, we celebrate the absolute triumph of love at the highest level of being. Through the Paschal Mystery, we are invited to imitate that love in the best way we can at our level.

Last week, the priests of our Diocese went on our annual retreat. As the retreat went on, I found myself getting depressed, as I do every year. Usually, I handle that depression by riding my bike or playing racquetball or tennis to distract myself. This year, I still rode my bike a lot. But, in riding all over the place, I began to reflect on what I was feeling and began connecting it with my life. I came to two conclusions.

The first is that the average age of our priests on retreat had to be 80 – even with Father Dan bringing the average down. It occurred to me that it would not be too long before I would hobble into the chapel on my walker and keep taking my hearing aid out, for everyone to hear it screeching. It would not be too long before a younger priest would have to carry my tray of food to me in the dining room. Part of my depression was a result of a real encounter with my own immortality.

The second came when the Franciscan priest giving the retreat spoke of his vows of poverty, chastity, and obedience. As a vowed religious member of the Franciscan Order, hi first commitment is to his brothers in that community. That is not true of the commitment of the Diocesan priest. We promise obedience to our Bishop, and we promise that we will never marry. We are expected to live as simply as possible. But, as I was looking around, it was clear that my commitment was not to the men in that room. It may be my duty to get to know them better and treat them with respect. But, my commitment is to this local church, and in my present assignment, to Saint Pius X. It is in this parish, and not in the company of the priests of this Diocese, that I must first build bonds of community, to learn how to live together in peace, and to learn how to forgive and let go of those things that harm or break apart the bonds of our unity. I was with them temporarily. My place is here on a permanent basis.

That is the message of Trinity Sunday. It is within the context of this parish that we are called to learn to live the unity of the Trinity within the diversity of many members. It is within the context of those family units that form this parish where you learn those same lessons and bring the successes to this Eucharist to celebrate, or your failures to the Sacrament of Reconciliation for healing. Saved by the Son and driven by the Spirit, we are called to continue our journey in faith as we walk together to full union with the Father. We may not be able to explain that Mystery. But, we can do our level best to try to live it in this parish and in our families.

61.4 June 7, 2009

When we celebrate this Solemnity of the Most Holy Trinity, we are tempted to regard the Mystery as a complicated dogma that belongs to professional theologians who can discuss it in learned journals. However, by celebrating this Mystery as a Solemnity on the Sunday following Pentecost, we become aware that the Mystery of the Trinity is an integral part of our faith experience. We bless ourselves with holy water every time we enter this church as a reminder that we were incorporated into this Mystery when we passed through the waters of baptism. We begin Mass with the sign of the cross. Every prayer at Mass is addressed to the Father, through the Son, and in the Holy Spirit.

When we reflect on these words, it becomes clear that God wants a life with us. Unlike the ancient pagans, who fashioned their gods into their image and their behavioral patterns and enslaved themselves to those gods, the God of ancient Israel became involved in the life of his people and revealed himself to them as the creator of the world who made a Covenant with them at Mount Sinai. Those disciples who experienced the risen Christ came to understand the words of the Gospel of John that Jesus and the Father are one. In their encounter with the Son, they encountered the Father. Through the power of the Holy Spirit given to them at Pentecost, they fearlessly spoke about their experience of the Father through Jesus and in the Spirit, inviting those who responded to enter into this life themselves through the waters of Baptism.

The central prayer we pray at Mass is the Eucharistic Prayer, which gives thanks to the Father for the sacrifice of Jesus made present by the power of the Holy Spirit through our liturgical remembering. We conclude each Eucharistic Prayer with the words: "Through him, with him, in him, in the unity of the Holy Spirit, all honor and glory are yours, Almighty Father, forever and ever. Amen." As these words are prayed, we are all too conscious of the differences that divide us. We have differences in personalities, in the gifts given to us, and in our different perspectives of how these mysteries affect our lives. And yet we trust that the Eucharist gradually forms us into God's Trinitarian image: three different persons united as one God in a radical union of love. In being drawn into that radical union of love, we are invited to see our conflicts and divisions not as obstacles. Instead, we can see them as Paul does – participating in the sufferings of Christ that lead us to be glorified with him.

Saint Matthew tells us about the great commission. On that mountain in Galilee where Peter, James, and John caught a glimpse of Christ's glory in the transfiguration, he commissions them to proclaim the Good News of salvation to all the nations. Like the Magi at the beginning of Matthew's Gospel, they worship him and recognize him as the Christ. Like Peter, who sank into the waters of the Sea of Galilee when he left the safety of the boat to walk toward Jesus, they have their share of doubts. Jesus repeats the promise we heard in Advent at the beginning of Matthew's Gospel that he is Emmanuel, "I am with you always until the end of time."

With the Easter Season behind us, we too worship him as the Christ. We too bring our share of doubts and difficulties to this Mass with us. If the eleven had their share of doubts even when they saw the risen Lord in the flesh, then we too can bring our doubts and the ways into which we sink into the waters to this Mass and to this assembly. We can continue to walk together on the shaky waters of our world, because Jesus is Emmanuel, he is with us until the end of the age. Through this Eucharist we celebrate on this Solemnity, he is drawing us through him and to the Father and in the Holy Spirit.

61.5 June 3, 2012

It took the Church almost three centuries to come up with language to express the Mystery of the Trinity, and we use that language at Mass when we recite the Nicene Creed. The Catechism of the Catholic Church reminds us that the Trinity is "the mystery of one God in three Persons... The mystery of the Trinity in itself is inaccessible to the human mind and is the object of faith only because it was revealed by Jesus Christ, the divine Son of the eternal Father."

We know that this statement is true. That is why we do not celebrate Trinity Sunday to have theological discussions about defining the mystery of the Trinity in exact terms. Rather, we celebrate this Sunday to reflect on our experience of the Trinity. Like Moses, we have encountered the presence of God in our lives. Like Paul, we know that we have become adopted children through the power of the Holy Spirit. Like the disciples on that mountain, we have encountered the risen Christ in the Easter Season and in Word and Sacrament.

If we reflect on the mystery of the Trinity, we begin to understand that at the very highest level of being, there is one God and three distinct persons. At the very highest level of being, there is perfect community in the midst of perfect diversity. When we understand this portion of the mystery of the Trinity, we realize that God calls us to live in community. Even though faith can be very personal, and even though we express our faith in very private ways, our faith is radically communal. The eleven disciples on that mountain certainly did not form a perfect community. They even doubted when they experienced the risen Lord. But, like us, they nurtured their faith together and worked on their differences.

Because we live our faith together in this community, we are called to mission. Just as those eleven disciples were sent out to spread the Gospel, so are we. We spread the Gospel when we take our faith into the community beyond the walls of this church and try to live it in our homes, places of business, schools, and all those places where we meet our local culture. Programs like *Catholics Come Home* may have their benefits. But the best way to attract inactive Catholics to come home is to allow them to see us trying to practice our faith.

When we live our faith, we are not alone. At the very beginning of the Gospel of Matthew, the angel announced to Joseph that Jesus would be called "Immanuel," which means "God with us." At the very end of the Gospel, Jesus tells the eleven that he will be with them always, to the end of the age. He makes that same promise to us. No matter what happens when we honestly practice our faith, he will be Immanuel – God with us – until the very end.

In the twelfth century, which many call the "Dark Ages," a Benedictine abbess named Hildegard of Bingen shared a vision which she hoped would brighten the lives of the believers of her time. She wrote, the flame of a fire has three qualities ... **light** that it may shine, **red power** that it may endure, and **fiery heat** that it may burn So, there is one God in three persons ... by the brilliant light, understand the Father who with paternal love opens his brightness to the faithful. By the red power which is in the flame that it may be strong, understand the Son who took on a body ... in which his divine powers were shown. By the fiery heat understand the Holy Spirit who burns ardently in the minds of the faithful.

As we reflect on God's presence in this community of faith, we give thanks to the light that shines in the darkness, for the red power that strengthens us in adversity, and for the fiery heat that burns in our hearts. May we go forth from this community to spread the Good News of the Gospel in the name of the Father, and of the Son, and of the Holy Spirit.

61.6   May 27, 2018

The late Cardinal Richard Cushing told of an incident that happened when he was a young priest in Boston. He was summoned to give last rites to a man who had collapsed in a store. Cushing knelt beside the man and began with the traditional question: "Do you believe in God the Father, God the Son, and God the Holy Spirit?" The man opened one eye and said, "Here I am dying, and he asks me a riddle."

The Doctrine of the Trinity is not a riddle. But, it is a Mystery. It took three centuries for the early Church to define this Mystery with precise terminology. Throughout the history of the Church, theologians and scholars have developed very technical theological language to explore this Mystery of one God and three distinct persons. We may not be trained theologians or experts in Trinitarian theology, but we have participated in the Mystery for the last ninety days in the Liturgical life of the Church. We have spent forty days during Lent reflecting on the suffering and death of Jesus Christ. We focused on the essence of the Paschal Mystery when we celebrated the three days of the Triduum. We have spent the final fifty days of Easter renewing our faith in the resurrection of Jesus Christ.

In celebrating this one Solemnity centered on a Doctrine, we know that we will never fully understand how there is one God and three distinct persons. However, we participate in that Mystery in our lives of faith. We were baptized in the name of the Father and of the Son and of the Holy Spirit. We bless ourselves with water in the name of the Trinity every time we enter this church. We begin all of our prayers with that same Trinitarian sign of the cross. In our prayers at Mass, we pray to the Father through the Son and in the Holy Spirit. We pray in this way, not to solve a riddle, but to allow the love of Father, Son, and Holy Spirit to guide us as we walk together in our pilgrimage of faith. At the highest level of being in the Trinity, there is perfect love, perfect unity, and perfect diversity. A famous icon by the Russian painter Andrei Rublev pictures the three persons of the Trinity seated around a table in a circle. There is an empty space on the viewer's side of that table, and all who gaze on this icon are invited to complete the circle. The table is spread, the door is open. We are invited to join them.

This invitation is best expressed in today's Gospel, which is the conclusion of the Gospel of Saint Matthew. The beginning of the Gospel announces that the words of the Prophet Isaiah have been fulfilled with the coming of Jesus, whom he calls Emmanuel ("God with us"). Even though Saint Matthew wrote his Gospel for Jewish Christian readers, the pagan Magi were the first to worship the newborn child. Throughout his Gospel, Saint Matthew outlines the many ways that Jesus remained absolutely faithful to the will of his Father, beginning with his ministry in Galilee. Back in Galilee after the resurrection, the eleven worship him and receive his great commission. He tells them to go, not just to their Jewish brothers and sisters, but to all nations and to make disciples of them, baptizing them in the name of the Father, and of the Son, and of the Holy Spirit. He promises that he will be with them always. He will continue to be Emmanuel ("God with us") through the power of the Holy Spirit.

We are gathered here to worship, as did the first disciples. We have our share of doubts, as they did. The risen Christ gives us the same commission. During the last three pontificates, our Popes have spoken of the "new evangelization." They are calling us to make disciples, not just by teaching the Mysteries we celebrate here, but more so by making those Mysteries more evident by the way we live our lives. There is a place at the table in the heavenly Jerusalem. The Holy Spirit is guiding us to that table, and he wants us to bring lots of people with us.

62. Corpus Christi

Readings
Exodus 24:3–8
Hebrews 9:11–15
Mark 14:12–16, 22–26

62.1 June 25, 2000

People at Saint Jude sometimes get upset when I soak them with holy water at the beginning of each Mass during the Easter Season. If you feel that way, then you should be glad that you were not present when Moses sealed the Covenant at Mount Sinai. He sprinkled the blood of animals on the altar, signifying the people's sacred relationship with God. Then he sprinkled it on those assembled, signifying their close relationship with one another as a result of God's Covenant with them.

When Jesus took bread and wine, blessed the Father, broke and poured, and gave to his Apostles at the Last Supper, he anticipated the sealing of the new covenant. His body was broken on the cross. His blood was poured out for our salvation. At this Mass, we do exactly what he told us to do: we take bread and wine, bless the Father for the sacrifice of Jesus made present as we remember, and we give. In this Eucharistic action, we are formed a bit more into his body, the church.

Over the centuries, we Catholics have developed a tradition of reserving some of the consecrated bread from this Eucharistic action. We reserve the Eucharistic species, so we can take it to those who are dying. We also reserve it, so we – the Body of Christ – can pray in the presence of the Blessed Sacrament.

At Saint Jude, we are blessed with a Perpetual Exposition Chapel. The term "exposition" is more technically correct than "adoration," because the Blessed Sacrament is exposed 24 hours a day. Our Chapel is open only with the express permission of the Bishop, and only on the condition that two people are present in prayer at every moment.

Mickie Tanesky is a member of the Perpetual Exposition Committee. She has spent many hours there. She will share her story with you, hoping that more people might be moved to spend some time in prayer in the presence of the Blessed Sacrament.

62.2 June 25, 2000 (Devotions)

The pastor asked her if she would consider becoming a Eucharistic minister. After a lot of fretting and a great deal of hedging, she finally said yes. She was a nervous wreck that first Sunday! After the great Amen, she walked to the altar, her heart pounding. "What if I forget what to do? What if I mess up? What if – horror of horrors – I drop the cup or the host?" She took one of the chalices and went to her station. Her hand shook as she presented the cup to each parishioner with the simple words, "the blood of Christ." But before long, her nervousness was changed. It was transformed into awe at the profound love of God, who gives each of us such a wonderful sacrament.

Later that week, she was called to help at the soup kitchen downtown. This she could handle! She had volunteered many nights and weekends at the soup kitchen. As she carefully ladled soup into a bowl and handed it to a poor, elderly woman, she found herself holding the bowl with the same reverence as the chalice. She looked at the poor woman with the same love and concern as she did at the communicants on the previous Sunday. She felt the same awe and wonder and love at the soup kitchen as she did at the altar. She had experienced the Eucharist again!

The gift of the Eucharist comes with an important string attached to the real presence. It must be shared! In the first century, a Eucharistic instruction known as the *Di·ache* made the following observation. "As grain once scattered on the hillsides was, in this broken bread made one, so from all lands let your Church be gathered into your kingdom by Christ your Son." Every time we gather to celebrate the action of the Eucharist – every time we take, bless, break, and give – we not only share the Body of Christ. We *become* the Body of Christ. We become what we receive, and we receive what we are. What we consume should now consume us. If we partake of the one bread and the one cup, then we must be willing to become Eucharist for others. We must be willing to make the love of God real for all.

Being part of Christ's Body in our lives is not an easy task. Like the woman who recognized Christ in the poor woman at the soup kitchen, it takes faith to experience the Eucharist outside these walls. It takes faith to listen attentively to an elderly neighbor who is telling the same story for the fourth time that day. It takes faith for a parent to deal firmly yet lovingly with a child who must learn the lessons of taking responsibility for his or her actions. It takes faith to recognize in the dirty hands of a beggar downtown the hands of Christ reaching out for help. But when we see through those eyes of faith, we are behaving as Christ's Body, formed by the Eucharistic food and drink.

As we find ourselves in the presence of Christ, really and truly present in this Sacrament on our Altar, it is critically important to remember the importance of the action of the Eucharist in forming us to be Christ's Body in our world. We believe that what stands on that altar is not bread. It is not a symbol. It does not remind us of something else. What stands on that altar is the real presence of Jesus Christ. It is the fruit – the result – of the action of the Eucharist celebrated earlier this morning at 11:00. As we adore and show reverence to Christ's real presence here, we do so as the Body of Christ. As we adore and show reverence, we are led back to the Eucharistic action, to confess those times when we did not act like Christ's Body and to be fed once again. Then we are sent out to look a little more like the body of Christ in our lives.

There is tremendous value to prayer before the Blessed Sacrament. That presence is real, and the quiet and peace of the chapel or this church can provide a much-needed refuge from the noise and chaos of our daily lives. But in a mysterious sense, we are never alone when we pray before the Blessed Sacrament. Through the power of the Holy Spirit and the prayer of the church – God's people who are the Body of Christ – we enjoy a solidarity that cannot be put into words. We open ourselves to the depths of God's peace when we open ourselves in such a vulnerable way.

As members of Christ's Body, we know that we are not without our wounds and our brokenness. Like the bones of our physical bodies that sometimes get broken, we experience our own fractures and breaks as the church, the body of Christ. Sometimes, people lose faith in the church precisely because of these fractures. The Eucharist plays an important role in healing those wounds.

Medical experts say that broken bones in our bodies are actually stronger at the point of the healed break. And the same can be true of us as the Body of Christ. The difficulties, tragedies, and storms of our lives can help us become stronger men and women of faith. Or, they can destroy us in hatred, despair, and anger. The

Blessed Sacrament provides us with the grace of the risen Jesus to
have the wisdom, the patience, and the courage to realize the presence of God amid the storms of tension, fear, anxiety, and injustice.
The grace of the risen Christ enables us to discern the presence of
God amid the roar of anger and mistrust. The grace of the Risen
Christ enables us to recognize the light of God in the darkness of
selfishness and prejudice.

The Lord did not institute the Eucharist to be an end in itself.
He gave us this Sacrament to build us up. Thank God for this greatest of gifts! Thank God for what it can do in our lives!

62.3 June 18, 2006

When we celebrate this Solemnity of the Most Holy Body and
Blood of Christ, we celebrate our Holy Communion. It is a
Mystery we have been celebrating for three weeks. On Pentecost,
we celebrated the Holy Communion we share as a result of the
sending of the Holy Spirit. With the presence of the Holy Spirit,
our Church today is a Holy Communion, a fellowship established
through the waters of Baptism. On the Solemnity of the Holy
Trinity, we celebrated the Holy Communion of one God in three
Persons, a Communion that invites us to imitate their union in
the midst of diversity here on earth and to share that Communion
with God and all the saints in eternity.

Today, we celebrate the Holy Communion that is the real presence of Jesus Christ given to us under the form of bread and wine.
Whenever we gather here to take gifts of bread and wine, to praise
the Father for the Sacrifice of Jesus made present here as we remember, to break the bread, and to give it, we are truly in Communion
with the Lord and with one another. This Holy Communion is a
result of the total gift of Jesus, the sacrifice of himself out of love
for us. Unlike the sacrifice of animals and the pouring out of their
blood upon the Altar and the people, Jesus himself became the sacrifice. Out of love for us, he poured out his blood – his entire self –
for our salvation.

It is ironic that we celebrate this Feast of our Holy Communion
on the same day when we honor our fathers. At the very heart of
being a father is the notion of sacrificial love. Fathers lay down
their lives for their families; they pour out their blood; they make
sacrifices to build the communion that we call a family. On this day,
I remember the sacrifices my Dad made for our family. To provide
for our needs, he sacrificed the security of the places he knew to
make better provisions for us. From the time I was in the seventh
grade, we moved every four years as he adapted his own dreams
and hopes for the good of the family.

Fathers have the responsibility of making sure that the communion of the family runs as smoothly as possible. My brothers and sisters and I remember the very clear rules our father sat down. He insisted that we eat meals together, and he did not highly regard any complaints we may have had about Mom's food. He knew it was important that we got lots of sleep, and we had to go to bed at ungodly hours (I think bed time for us was 5:00!). Even now, Father Dan can tell you how he suffers when I don't get enough sleep. We may not have liked his rules. As the oldest, I led the way in rebelling against them. But, looking back, we understand. The same dynamic applies to this parish family. As we return to the Sundays of Ordinary Time, we continue to share the Holy Communion that makes the Sacrifice of Jesus present. Once we move away from these specific feasts of Holy Communion, the danger is that this Mystery too becomes too ordinary. For that reason, I offer these reminders of ways in which our behavior reflects what we believe:

- Genuflecting to the Real Presence in the Tabernacle in the Chapel.
- Bowing to the Altar, the anointed symbol of Christ in our midst.
- Paying attention to the praying of the Eucharistic Prayer, the central blessing prayer of the Mass.
- Not chewing gum.
- Joining in the singing of the hymn during the Communion procession – celebrating our Holy Communion with the Lord and with one another.
- Bowing (not genuflecting) before receiving the Eucharist, both the Host and the Cup.
- Avoiding the action of intinction.
- Taking the time of silence after Communion.
- Remaining until the end of Mass.
- Dressing for Mass – no dress code here, but making conscious decisions about dress when coming to Mass.

We spend most of the year celebrating the Sundays of Ordinary Time. They are "Ordinary," in the sense that they are numbered. Next Sunday is the 13th Sunday in Ordinary Time. Even though our participation here becomes routine, and in a sense "ordinary," there is nothing ordinary about the Holy Communion we share. Paying more attention to these details can help immensely.

62.4   June 14, 2009

The ceremony described in the reading from the Book of Exodus might strike us as bizarre. After Moses read the Covenant to the people, he built an altar made of twelve stones and slaughtered young bulls. Moses sprinkled half of the blood of the bulls on the altar, and the other half on the people (and you get upset during the Easter Season when we sprinkle water at the beginning of Mass!). What appears bizarre to us was a common way of worshipping for ancient people. The sacrifice of animals represented a sincere desire to be in union with God. Blood was a symbol of life. Sprinkling blood on the altar spoke of sharing God's life through the Covenant. Sprinkling blood on the people reminded them that they were blood brothers and sisters – their lives connected through God's life.

That is why the author of the letter to the Hebrews describes the death of Jesus Christ in sacrificial terms. Unlike a bull or a lamb dragged to the sacrifice, Jesus gave himself willingly out of love for us. In Jesus Christ, the priest offering the sacrifice became the victim himself. He poured out his blood (his life) for us and sealed the New Covenant with the Father. Through his sacrifice, he has reconciled us with the Father and brought us new life.

The sacrifice of Jesus culminated in death, which spoke of his offering of himself during the course of his public ministry. His sacrifice happened only once. But, drawing on Mark's account of the Last Supper, we believe that his sacrifice is made present to us every time we do what he commanded us to do at that meal. Every time we praise and thank the Father for the sacrifice of Jesus at Mass, his sacrifice is made present to us through the power of the Holy Spirit in our liturgical remembering. In this sacrificial meal, the Lord Jesus truly gives himself as bread and wine to feed us, as we bring our own sacrifices to this altar.

We no longer bring bulls or lambs to be slaughtered as part of our worship. That is not exactly part of our culture. However, every time we come to Mass, we bring all the sacrifices we made out of love during this past week. You who are parents bring all those sacrifices you made for the welfare of your children and place them in front of this altar. You children bring those hours when you wanted to do something else but spent paying attention to your younger brothers and sisters and do the same. Those of you who have given yourselves in humble service to the parish bring your sacrifice of time and talent. We join our sacrifices to the sacrificial tithe and the bread and wine brought forward for the Eucharist, and we offer them with Christ's sacrifice when the priest invites us to "pray, brothers and sisters, that our sacrifice will be acceptable to God, the

Father Almighty." We respond, trusting that the Father will accept our sacrifice.

This sacrificial aspect of the Eucharist is extremely important, because many times we fear that all those sacrifices we do out of love do not make a difference. We are also painfully aware that our sacrifices are not perfect, and that we have mixed motives for the sacrifices we make. That is why we join our sacrifices to the Sacrifice of Christ, which was perfect and which was acceptable to the Father. When we become more aware of the sacrifice of Jesus, we can come forward to be fed by the Body and Blood of Christ with a deep sense of humility and gratitude. Many centuries ago, Saint Augustine expressed the Mystery we share. "Through bread and wine, the Lord gives us his body and blood. If you receive them well, you are that which you receive; you become what you eat. That is the call of God to all of us."

62.5 June 10 2012

When Moses announced the Covenant initiated by God with his people at Mount Sinai, he celebrated the relationship in a way that might seem very strange to us today. He built an altar with twelve pillars, representing the twelve tribes of Israel. He sent young men out to slaughter young bulls. Then he offered the bulls as a sacrifice, sprinkling some of the blood on the altar and some of the blood on the people. The bulls were external signs of an internal desire to be in union with God. The blood was a sign of life, the life binding God with his people.

Once we understand this ritual and all rituals involving animal sacrifice in the Jerusalem Temple, we can understand the meaning of the Letter to the Hebrews. This letter argues that there is no longer a need for the temple or for animals sacrificed on altars. Jesus Christ has become both the priest and the sacrificial offering. By shedding his blood (pouring out his life) for us, his sacrifice has accomplished what all other sacrifices had hoped for – complete union with the Father. Priests no longer need to offer animal sacrifices over and over again, because this one sacrifice has mediated a new covenant of love. That new covenant opens the doors for us to enter into the Temple of the new and eternal Jerusalem.

We have been initiated into this New Covenant, not by having blood sprinkled on us, but by passing through the waters of Baptism. Every time we celebrate the Eucharist, this memorial of the Last Supper, the sacrifice of Jesus Christ, which occurred only once in history, is made present through our liturgical remembering.

When we celebrate this Solemnity of the Most Holy Body and Blood of Christ, we become more aware of the great gift which we have received in the Eucharist. Today, we walk in procession with the Blessed Sacrament in our neighborhood. This custom took on new meaning for me last year when we joined the Corpus Christi Procession in Rome. Our group of six pilgrims had biked the Italian portion of the ancient pilgrimage route from Canterbury to Rome, with the support of two other pilgrims who drove a support van. We became aware of the fact that we formed a small portion of the Body of Christ as we traveled 700 miles, celebrating the Eucharist, joining in prayer, and sharing meals. On the way of our pilgrimage, we had experienced our shares of ups and downs, as all of us do in our pilgrimage through life. Now, we walked in procession with the Blessed Sacrament and Pope Benedict XVI from his Cathedral Church of Saint John Lateran, to the Basilica of Saint Mary Major, where he celebrated Benediction. The procession reminded us that we are all pilgrims, making our way through life with the nourishment that comes from the Lord's real presence in the Body and Blood of Christ.

Whether we are part of a procession today or not, today reminds us of the centrality of the Eucharist in our lives. The Eucharist literally provides food for our pilgrimage as we journey together to the New and Eternal Jerusalem. We can appreciate this sacred food if we pay attention to the careful preparations and specific instructions Jesus made for the Last Supper. As we prepare to celebrate this memorial of the Last Supper, we can take some time to read the Scriptures before coming to Mass. We can reflect on all the sacrifices we have made during the past week, knowing that authentic love always involves making a sacrifice. We bring those sacrifices to be joined with the perfect sacrifice of Jesus Christ at this Altar. We can be more careful about the hour fast. We can approach the Eucharist with more reverence, making the bow with our heads and making our hands a throne for the King of Heaven. This is no ordinary meal that we share. This is food for the journey. This is the Supper of the Lamb, sacrificed for our salvation.

62.6 June 7, 2015

On the Sundays during the Easter Season, our liturgy expressed the truth that we are members of the New Covenant through our Baptisms. We began every Mass by sprinkling the congregation with Holy Water. It is my favorite time of the year, watching people remove their glasses and shielding their heads from the dousing of the water that they know is coming.

If you are glad to see the Easter Season gone because you are tired of being doused with water, you can be glad that you were not part of the congregation when Moses sealed the First Covenant at Mount Sinai. During that liturgy, Moses took the blood of two young bulls and sprinkled part of the blood on the Altar, and the other part on the congregation. That is much worse than being doused with water at Saint Pius! Blood signified life. The blood of sacrificed animals symbolized the life that God has now shared with his people through the Covenant.

The Letter to the Hebrews uses the image of this First Covenant Liturgy to help us understand what Jesus Christ has done. By shedding his blood on the cross, Jesus gave his entire life for us. He established a New Covenant, sealed in his blood, which promises eternal life for those who participate. That perfect Sacrifice is made present every time we gather to celebrate the Eucharist. On this Feast of the Body and Blood of Christ, we rejoice that we have been formed into the Body of Christ and nourished by the Body and Blood of Christ at every Mass.

This is also a perfect day for a new priest to celebrate his First Mass. Father Bill, as a priest configured in a unique way to the person of Jesus Christ, you now have the task of pouring out your very life in the service of the people to whom you are assigned. As you pour out your life, the celebration of the Eucharist will be central to everything you do. It will be your greatest joy. It will be your greatest comfort. It will be your greatest strength as you learn to live the implications of pouring out your life in humble service.

We, the people of Saint Pius X, cannot tell you how happy we are that you have been assigned to us. You are no stranger to us. We know your wonderful strengths and talents, and we love to make fun of those character quirks that you so prominently display. We will have to figure out how to distinguish two Father Bills. "Father Bill the Greater, and Father Bill the Lesser!" "Father Bill the senile and Father Bill the young one!" We'll see!

But that great joy of ours is balanced by the real sadness of losing Father Terry. He has been a much beloved priest here for four years, and we will miss him. This mixture of joy and sadness will be an integral part of your priestly ministry. You will help a family mourn the tragic and unexpected loss of a young person at a Funeral Mass on one day. On the next, you will share the joy of two families coming together to celebrate the wedding of their children. A couple will come to you for help, because their marriage is falling apart. Within an hour, another couple will approach you with the good news that they are expecting a child. Fourteen people will come to you after Mass to congratulate you on the great homily you just gave. One person will criticize you, and you will freak out for weeks!

In your priestly ministry, trust the power of this Eucharistic Sacrifice. As you pour out your very lifeblood for your people, the death and resurrection of the Lord will be made present to you in the Eucharist. You will identify with the dying of the Lord in the tough situations. You will rejoice with the rising of the Lord in the joyous times. It is that Mystery which defines the New Covenant sealed by the Blood of Jesus Christ. It is that Mystery which you will proclaim in so many ways. May God bless you and keep you as you begin this great ministry. May God bring to completion the good work in you that he is beginning today!

62.7   June 3, 2018

Blood was a very powerful sign for the people of ancient Israel. They regarded blood as sacred. When God entered the Covenant at Mount Sinai with the people he had freed from slavery, Moses used the blood of bulls to seal the Covenant. He took half of the blood and poured it over the Altar, signifying that his people were now blood relatives with God. Then he took the other half of the blood and sprinkled it on the people, signifying that they were blood relatives with one another as God's chosen people. This sprinkling of blood is very strange to our modern sensibilities. As I watched people recoil from the sprinkling of holy water at the beginning of all the Masses during the Easter Season, the prospect of Deacon Lou gleefully showering everyone with the blood of bulls would be preposterous.

We need to consider the important symbolism of blood to understand what Jesus is doing at the Last Supper. Jesus is clearly in charge as he gathers the disciples to eat the final Passover Meal with him. He sends two of them to find the place where they will celebrate the meal, giving as a sign the man carrying a water jar. They could not miss a sign like this, because carrying water jars is something women do. Once they gather at table, they immediately recognize the ancient rituals of the Passover Meal. Although Saint Mark does not mention the exact foods, Jesus would have shared the symbolic foods and reminded them of God's saving action in freeing his people from slavery in Egypt. But then, Jesus makes a radical departure from the traditional Passover meal. He takes bread, says the blessing, breaks it, and gives it to them. Then he takes an extra cup, gives thanks, gives it to them, and they all drink from it.

He shifts their attention from the Covenant sealed with the blood of bulls at Mount Sinai to the new Covenant that will be sealed with his blood on Mount Calvary. He takes the old symbols and applies new meaning to them. He will become the Passover Lamb. His blood will be poured out to free the people of the New Covenant from sin and death. As the Letter to the Hebrews reminds us, the tabernacle made of stones on Mount Zion in Jerusalem has been replaced with the tabernacle of the Body of

Christ. The one sacrifice of Jesus Christ is made present every time we celebrate the Eucharist in his memory.

That is exactly what we do at this Mass and every Mass. At this Mass, we will take gifts of bread and wine at the Preparation of the Altar and Gifts. The celebrant will lead the assembly in blessing (praising) the Father in the Eucharistic Prayer for the sacrifice of Jesus made present as we remember. As we chant the "Lamb of God," we break the consecrated Host and give the Body and Blood of Christ to all who walk in procession to the Altar.

Many centuries ago, Saint Augustine taught about the Eucharist when he offered these time-honored insights: "So now, if you want to understand the body of Christ, listen to the Apostle Paul speaking … 'You are the body of Christ, member for member' (1 Cor. 12:27) … You are saying 'Amen' to what you are: your response is a personal signature, affirming your faith. … Be a member of Christ's body, then, so that your 'Amen' may ring true!"

With Saint Augustine's words in our heads, we approach the Holy Eucharist admitting that we are not worthy for the Lord to enter under our roof. In saying "Amen", we affirm our conviction that we are receiving the Body and Blood of the Lord under the form of bread and wine. We also affirm our conviction that every Eucharist received in an open-hearted, mindful, humble, and prayerful way forms us just a little more into our true identity: members of the Body of Christ, washed clean by his blood.

63. Nativity of John the Baptist

Readings

Isaiah 49:1–6
Acts 13:22–26
Luke 1:57–66, 80

63.1 June 24, 2012

The prophet Isaiah reflects on his prophetic ministry and admits that he sees himself as a failure. Even though God had called him to be a prophet from the time when he was in his mother's womb, he does not see much success in his ministry. God may have made him a sharp-edged sword. But, God had concealed him in the shadow of his arm. God may have made him a polished arrow. But, God had hidden him in his quiver. As he admits that he had often seen himself as a failure, he has come to understand that God is the judge of whether or not he had succeeded. In God's eyes, he had been successful. Because of his humility and sense of his own sign, God has made him a light to the nations. He is content knowing that God was with him.

John the Baptist must have felt the same way. He had spent most of his life living on the fringes of society in the desert near the Dead Sea. He had experienced some success in calling people to change their hearts and administering a baptism of repentance. But, after he had baptized Jesus in the Jordan River, he began to decrease as Jesus began to increase. For telling Herod that it was wrong to live with his brother's wife, he was thrown into prison and beheaded. But God has clearly judged his ministry successful, precisely because he had found his voice and paved the way for the Messiah to be recognized as the Lamb of God.

We celebrate his birth today, because it is easy for us to fall into the same trap of thinking that we are not successful in what we are trying to accomplish as followers of Jesus Christ. Young people are tempted to think that they do not have a voice, because they are too young. Middle aged people can sometimes think that they are on the wrong track, because life is not turning out as they had expected. Those of us who are older look back on our lives and wonder exactly what we have accomplished. In celebrating the birth of the Baptist, we are reminded that God is the judge of what is successful in our lives, just as he had been the judge in the life of Isaiah the prophet and John the Baptist. People heard their voices, and that made a difference.

John the Baptist's father lost his voice when he doubted that God could provide a child when his wife and he were so old. But, he regained that voice to name the child, because he finally realized that God's ways were not his ways. God could accomplish anything, even in his doubts. And the same is true for us. God has given each of us a voice when we passed through the waters of Baptism, and he encourages us to use that voice to build up the Kingdom of God.

The Bishops of our country have asked us to join our voices with theirs in what they are calling the "Fortnight for Freedom." As they work to protect the freedom of Catholic Institutions to refuse services contrary to our moral teachings, they are asking us to raise our voices in prayer and support. We do that at each Mass during these fourteen days. We will do that as a parish when we enter into the Fifty Hours of Prayer for the Fifty States.

Last week when we were on retreat, Bishop Rhoades reminded us priests that we are engaged in an effort to protect our basic freedom as Catholics. He urged us not to turn this Fortnight into a campaign to push our particular political agendas. Instead, we raise our voices to protect basic freedoms guaranteed by the First Amendment. Once Zechariah had recovered his voice and proclaimed the Lord's working in his life, he set the course for his son to do the same. We ask the Baptist for his intercession as we allow God to be the judge of what should be regarded as success or failure in our lives. We ask his intercession as we join our voices with his to point out the Lamb of God who takes away the sins of the world.

63.2 June 24, 2018

John the Baptist was born into a family associated with priesthood. Elizabeth, his mother, was a descendent of Aaron, the first priest. Zechariah, his father, was a priest associated with worship in the Temple. Zechariah had been chosen by lot to enter the sanctuary of the Lord to burn incense. As he was performing his priestly duties, the angel of the Lord announced that he and his wife would give birth to a son. Zechariah refused to believe that he and his wife could conceive, because they were really old. Rendered speechless for his unbelief, Zechariah must have reflected on his experience during his wife's pregnancy.

Because of the family connection with priesthood and temple worship, his neighbors presume that John would follow in his parents' footsteps and be named after his father. But, Elizabeth objects. She insists that he be named "John," which means "the Lord has shown favor." To echo what he had heard from the angel, Zechariah takes a tablet and writes, "John is his name." His tongue is loosened as he proclaims the greatness of God. That Canticle of Zechariah is omitted in today's Gospel reading. But we pray it at Morning Prayer, and we will sing it as the hymn of thanksgiving at this Mass. His neighbors quickly understand that there has been some kind of divine intervention. They are amazed, yet fearful: common human responses to an encounter with God. They gossip among themselves about what role this child will have.

Saint Luke says that the child grew and became strong in spirit. As an adult, John does not go to the Temple in Jerusalem. King Herod is in the process of rebuilding that Temple on a grand scale, bringing with the reconstruction a host of abuses and corrupt practices. Instead, John goes to the desert, that wilderness long associated with the liberation of his ancestors from slavery in Egypt. The desert had been for his ancestors a place of protection and testing. It was in the desert that they encountered God at Mount Sinai. It was in the desert that death could come quickly if people were not careful.

In the desert, on the banks of the Jordan River, John the Baptist would invite people to undergo a baptism of repentance, expressing their desire to change their ways. In the desert, John the Baptist would point to Jesus, the Lamb of God, who would give his life in sacrifice, not on the Altar in the Temple, but on a hill of execution outside the city. In the waters of the Jordan, John would baptize his cousin and witness the voice from the heavens announcing that this is God's beloved Son, in whom the Father is well pleased. In the desert, John the Baptist would condemn Herod for marrying the wife of his brother Philip. In response, Herod locked him up and eventually beheaded him.

In the liturgical calendar of the Church, we normally celebrate the feast of a Saint on the day that the Saint died and was reborn into eternity. That is not true with John the Baptist. We also celebrate his birth, his nativity. The only two other nativities that we celebrate are the birth of Mary, the Mother of God, on September 8, and the birth of Jesus Christ on December 25. We celebrate the Baptist's birth soon after the Summer Solstice, the longest day of the year in the northern hemisphere. We celebrate the Savior's birth soon after the Winter Solstice, the shortest day of the year in the northern hemisphere. The placement of these feasts reminds us of the role of John the Baptist. He must decrease, so Christ can increase.

That is our role also. Our lives of faith must point away from ourselves toward Jesus Christ. Jesus Christ is present in the good times and the bad times of our lives. When things go badly, we depend on the Lord to walk with us. If things go well and we are successful, it is because of the presence of Christ. In decreasing ourselves, Christ can increase.

64. Saints Peter and Paul

Readings

Acts 12:1–11
2 Timothy 4:6–8, 17–18
Matthew 16:13–19

64.1 June 29, 2003

Our culture elevates athletic stars as heroes and role models. Of course, there are some positive results of this practice. From the super athletes, our young people learn the value of hard work, the benefits of cooperating as teammates, and the results of healthy competition. But, in placing the super athletes on a pedestal, our young people run the risk of ignoring how wealth and fame can destroy personal relationships. Perhaps more dangerously, young people ignore the truth that very few athletes in this country can ever join their heroes, no matter how talented they are. Superstardom is for the very few.

We interrupt the normal rhythm of Ordinary Time this Sunday to consider two super heroes in the Christian Tradition. We honor Peter and Paul, because they poured became two very significant foundation stones, of which we remain as living stones. Peter and Paul are superstars, because each one helped the Church grow in his own way. Peter became the rock that guided the Church through its earliest days, giving all his successors a glimpse of the proper use of the keys of the Kingdom. Paul became the Church's first missionary and spread the Good News of Jesus Christ throughout the Mediterranean world, allowing the Church to expand from its Jewish base. Both had their own unique talents and temperaments.

Each respected the other's differences and worked together to bring the Church to Rome, the center of the Empire.

In providing these super heroes as models in faith, the Scriptures do not hide their faults and sins. Peter may have correctly identified Jesus as the Messiah. But he also tempted Jesus to consider being Messiah in a way that did not involve suffering. Peter denied Jesus three times at his darkest hour, and he was constantly putting his foot in his mouth. Paul was a zealot whose tunnel vision allowed him to stand by as Stephen, the first martyr, was murdered. Peter was thrown into prison because of people like Paul. In his writings, Paul admitted that God had given him a thorn in the flesh. Yet, both trusted the Lord's mercy that went beyond "three strikes and you are out!" Both knew that God's love could shine best even in their faults and failings.

Best of all, Peter and Paul invite us to join them as superstars. Through baptism, every single one of us is called to invest our own talents and follow the Lord Jesus into his Kingdom. Becoming a saint is not restricted to those with the most unusual talents or the best agents. Becoming a saint is possible for every one of us, with all our weaknesses, faults, and sins.

From his prison cell in Rome, Paul urges Timothy to keep steadfast in faith. Interestingly enough, he uses athletic imagery. Just as libations were poured out before the beginning of the ancient Olympics, Paul says that he has poured out his life in service of the Master. He argues that he has followed the rules and run the good race. He looks to the finish line and to the rewards of winning. He knows that God has been with him all the way, and that his victory is assured in the death and resurrection of the Master he has served. We need to take Paul's words to heart. We are invited to pour ourselves out in service, to follow the rules established by Christ, and to keep our eyes on the finish line. Christ prepares for us the same eternal life he has shared with Peter and Paul.

65. Transfiguration of the Lord

Readings

Daniel 7:9–10, 13–14
2 Peter 1:16–19
Mark 9:2–10

65.1 August 6, 2006

We can hardly blame Peter for wanting to build three tents for Jesus, Moses, and Elijah. Ever since he had left everything to follow Jesus, Peter knew the ups and downs of being a disciple. He may have marveled at the words and miracles coming from his Master. But he must have been puzzled at being chosen to be the Rock of the new Community formed around Jesus. He tried to keep Jesus from speaking of his upcoming suffering and death, only to be reprimanded harshly. On the top of that mountain, it was beautiful. They had caught a glimpse of the true nature of Jesus, and everything finally was making sense.

Most of us have had transfiguring experiences. It may have been your marriage day or the first birth of a child. For others, it may have been a triumph in school or time away spent with friends. Those women of the parish participating in the *Christ Renews His Parish* Retreat this weekend have opened themselves to a transfiguring moment. One of those moments happened to me last year when we began our Jubilee Year. As we processed from Saint Joseph Farm with a huge crowd in perfect weather, the feelings ran strong. It was almost impossible to put into words when we reached Saint Pius and greeted Bishop D'Arcy with so many other parishioners waiting for us. The Mass in the tent was one of the most moving I can remember. And the picnic following was truly one of the best ever. On that day, many of us caught a glimpse of the essence of a parish – God's People knowing themselves to be the Body of Christ in this world.

As much as we would have wanted that day to never end, we had to take things down and clean everything up. We had to pay the bills and face the challenges of a new school year. We had to struggle with the scope and delays of our building project. Like Peter, James, and John, we had to come down from that wonderful mountaintop where everything seemed to be so clear and continue walking our way with him through the other demands of being his disciples. In much the same way, the women will walk away from their retreat this afternoon and return to their families all fired up, with the rest of the family trying to figure out what happened to Mom.

That is why the Feast of the Transfiguration replaces the normal Sunday this year. In reflecting on the experience of Peter, James, and John, we are invited to recall those transfiguring moments in our lives when following Christ made so much sense. Those moments remind us of the glory that awaits us, if we too are willing to walk the way of the Cross with Christ, who was not just transfigured after his death, but raised to permanent glory and life that nothing can destroy.

In forty days, the Church will celebrate the Triumph of the Cross, the next major feast in our Liturgical Calendar. In choosing to follow Christ, we do not choose which feast we would prefer to celebrate. We celebrate both, because both are part of our journey of faith. However, it is through our sharing in the Cross and in the death of Jesus Christ that we too will be transfigured, changed permanently into that vision of eternity described by Daniel in the First Reading. Supported by the memories of those transfiguring experiences, we walk more confidently through the valleys we all must cross on our way to the Mount of Crucifixion, knowing that the death of the Lord makes it possible to transform those moments into eternity.

66. Exaltation of the Holy Cross

Readings

Numbers 21:4b–9
Philippians 2:6–11
John 3:13–17

66.1 September 14, 2003

Imagine our emotional reaction if we would come into this Church today to see a huge banner of an electric chair – or a noose hanging from the rafters – or a firing squad – or a needle connected with a lethal injection. Then imagine our reaction if a sign would proclaim that this cruel instrument of death is exalted – the source of our hope.

In a sense, that is exactly what this cross – that hangs above the Altar represents! The Romans reserved crucifixion as their most cruel and extreme form of execution. Crucified people not only suffered horrific deaths. But their horrible and public deaths were intended to deter others from repeating the same crime. In fact, Christians refrained from portraying the crucified Christ in art for almost two centuries, because the instrument of his execution was an unbearable symbol.

However, we venerate this cross today, because we acknowledge the utter mystery of how it expresses God's incredible love for us. In today's second reading, Saint Paul uses a Greek word to describe this love – kenosis – or a self-emptying. Though Jesus was in the form of God, Paul says, he did not deem equality with God something to be grasped at. Rather, he emptied himself, and took on human flesh, descending to our level out of love. At the very bottom of that descent we find the cross on which he was murdered. It is that cross which begins his ascent back to the Father. Nicodemus had to sneak away in the middle of the night to learn the power of this mystery. We hear it plainly in daylight as we celebrate this feast.

That self-emptying love of Jesus Christ, accompanied by his lifting up to heaven as a result of embracing the Cross, has tremendous implications for us today. Because of the Cross of Jesus Christ, those crosses that seem to have the power to destroy us can save us and give us tremendous hope. Because of the power of the Cross of Jesus, you young people who bear the cross of being unpopular and on the fringe can see in your cross the hope of being healed. Because of the power of the Cross of Jesus, those of you who have suffered economic setbacks, career losses, or terrible embarrassments can share the hope of triumphing in ways you could never imagine. Because of the power of the Cross of Jesus, those of you who have chronic or terminal illnesses will be raised up.

Those promises seem counter intuitive. So did the promises Moses gave to his people, bitten by snakes in the desert. He told them to look upon what was killing them. Modern vaccinations are also counter-intuitive. Doctors inject germs into our system that we want to avoid. By celebrating the Feast of the Exaltation of the Holy Cross, we are invited to trust the ultimate Mystery of counter-intuitiveness. God truly does love us so much that he emptied himself, took the form of a slave, and died on a Cross. We are invited to imitate that love, to embrace the crosses that come as a result in loving in this fashion, and to see in those crosses the promise of being raised up with Jesus Christ.

67. All Saints

Readings

Revelation 7:2–4, 9–14
1 John 3:1–3
Matthew 5:1–12a

67.1 November 1, 2009

When Jesus climbs this mountain, he takes with him those disciples whom he has just called: Peter and Andrew, James and John. As faithful sons of Abraham, they understand the significance of this mountain. They can see that Jesus is the new Moses. Seated in the position of that great teacher, Jesus gives them what one Scripture scholar called their "ordination charge". He describes how they are to behave as he sends them out to their tasks.

He calls them "blessed," or "fortunate," or "happy" when they carry on their tasks with some specific attitudes that are counter cultural. They will be happiest when they put their entire faith in God instead of wealth; when they can express true human sorrow at those realities in life which break their hearts; when they moderate their passions; when they hunger and thirst for God as starving people hunger for food or parched people thirst for drink; when they can walk in other people's shoes and understand their reasons for acting; when they do the right things for the right reasons; and when they speak the truth even in the face of hatred and persecution. Jesus tells them that these attitudes will be the hallmarks of pilgrims, walking together in the midst of God's Kingdom toward the ultimate fullness of God's Kingdom.

We too are his disciples, and we too hear these words as Jesus encourages us to embrace the attitudes characteristic of pilgrims on our journey. More often than not, we fail to make these attitudes our own. More often than not, we get discouraged and lose our way as God's pilgrim people. For that reason, the Book of Revelation provides a wonderful vision of those who now share the perfection of these attitudes. Saint John speaks of the men and women surrounding the Throne of God in Heaven. He numbers the Communion of Saints as 144,000 – 12 squared, signifying the 12 tribes of Israel as God's Chosen People and the 12 Apostles upon whom Christ builds his new Chosen People of God, times 1,000, a number of perfection in the Book of Revelation. He tells us that these saints are interceding for us. They may have reached perfection. But, they also know the difficulties and failures in their own lives. They have literally walked in our shoes.

We know the names of some of these saints, because they have been officially canonized by the Church. Odds are good that some of them are our parents, or our grandparents, or those who have been close to us. But there are countless others whose names we will never know. As we celebrate this great Communion of Saints today, we can walk along our pilgrim path a little more confidently. Their white robes have been washed in the blood of the Lamb. And so have ours. We received our white robes when we were baptized, and the Blood of the Lamb continues to purify us. They remind us that living our baptismal promises can transform us into the image of Jesus Christ. They remind us that faith is much more than just a relationship between God and me. It is an invitation to be part of a great communion. As we pilgrims walk together in this Communion, the saints are hooting and hollering and rooting for us today.

67.2 November 1, 2015

When Jesus chooses eight different groups of people to be called "blessed," or "happy," or "holy," we might scratch our heads. What are you telling us, Lord? In order to be truly holy, do we have to be dirt poor, or go around with sorrowful faces all the time, or allow bullies to kick us around, or make ourselves so obnoxious that other people will automatically hate us? Is that what constitutes true holiness?

The answer, of course, is NO! The world already has too many grumpy, obnoxious people! Instead, we need to look at the beatitudes from the perspective of the second reading. Saint John says that God is love. Four of the eight beatitudes reflect God's love. If we hunger and thirst for righteousness, we imitate the right judgment of God and behave according to God's will. If we are merciful, we mirror the great mercy of God that will be the theme of the coming Year of Mercy. If we are clean of heart, we have a single-minded focus on Jesus and his teachings that reveal God's face to us. If we act as peacemakers, we radiate the peace that comes from God's abiding presence in our lives. Because the essence of love is to seek the good of the other, living these four beatitudes will free us to love others as God has loved us. We are truly blessed. We know authentic happiness and holiness.

The other four beatitudes warn of dangers that distract us from the love of God. If we are addicted to material goods, we will give all our attention to those things that ultimately cannot last. If we are addicted to pleasure, we will do whatever we can to protect ourselves from the pain and sorrow that are part of life. If we are addicted to power, we will never learn how to depend on God's providence. If we are addicted to honor, we will not have the courage to speak the truth, especially when it makes us unpopular. If we find ourselves making ends of any of these means, then we will be less likely to love others as God has loved us.

Saint John tells us that we have become children of God through the waters of Baptism, allowing the grace of the Sacrament to guide us in living the Gospel beatitudes. The Book of Revelation gives us an image of what we shall be. Because the essence of heaven is beyond our human experience, Saint John uses symbolic language to convey what heaven is like. To give a sense of how many people are saved, he comes up with the symbolic number 144,000, using 12 squared to speak of the 12 tribes of Israel and the Church built on the foundation of the 12 Apostles. The number 1,000 symbolizes perfection. Clothed in the robes of salvation made white through the Blood of the Lamb, this immense throng comes from every nation, race, people, and tongue. And the best thing of all is that they are interceding for us. They know from their own experience that they have failed in living the beatitudes. They know from their own experience that they needed God's mercy. Most importantly, they know from their own experience how difficult it is to share in Christ's dying in order to share in his rising.

Becoming a saint is not reserved for those who are spiritual giants or for those whom the Church officially recognizes as saints by canonizing them. We celebrate their feast days throughout the Liturgical Year. Today, we remember all those people who have learned to embrace the middle four of the beatitudes, and who have learned to see the dangers of being addicted to material goods, or pleasure, or power, or honor. We know them, because they have been members of our families and loved ones. Having fully died in the Lord, they want us to join them and to trust that our sharing in the fullness of the Lord's dying will not destroy us. We are God's children now. Even if the world does not always know us, God knows what we can be. We can be saints! There is a great crowd cheering us on!

68. All Souls

Readings
Wisdom 3:1–9
Romans 5:5–11 or Romans 6:3–9
John 6:37–40

68.1 November 2, 2003

Yesterday, on the Feast of All Saints, we received some wonderful news. Around the Throne of God are countless men and women – the saints who are interceding for us to join them. Today, on the Feat of All Souls, we receive the bad news. Those people – the ones canonized by the Church and the ones we have known in our families, in this parish, and in our neighborhoods – have gotten there only because they died! Not only did they experience that final death which all of us dread, but they also trusted the promise made by Jesus Christ that those who would die with him will rise with him. Having learned completely how to die, they share fully in the glory of the resurrection.

Learning how to die is never easy. Those of you who sit down to do your homework must die to your desire to be outside doing anything else, before you can rise to the task of paying attention to your work. Those of you who are married had to die to an old independence in order to rise to a new way of living together. Those of us who are celibate priests have to learn how to die to an old assignment, before we can possibly rise to accept a new one. I have been here at Saint Pius long enough to admit that dying to my old parish was extremely painful. I had to die to a whole web of relationships, an accustomed way of doing things, and all kinds of comfortable habits. To the extent to which I held on to my last parish, I found it impossible to open myself to the new life this parish has offered. It has taken two years, but I can honestly say that the dying is complete. In letting go of the past, I am able to embrace the present, with all its possibilities and all kinds of new relationships and ways of doing things here.

The same thing happens to us at death. At the moment of our physical death, odds are very good that very few of us have learned how to die to those things that hinder our relationships with God. None of us see clearly, in the way God sees things. As long as we have not completely turned our back on the Lord, he takes us exactly as we are at the moment of death. Because God loves each of us so much, God continues to teach us how to die, even after we have passed through the moment of our physical death. We call God's school of dying "purgatory," from the Latin word *purgare*, meaning to purify. In mysterious ways that we can only picture in images, God teaches people how to die to those lies they tried to believe about themselves, so others would accept them. God teaches people how to let go of titles and pretensions and egocentric behaviors that held him at arm's length during their lives.

That is why we pray for those who have gone before us in faith – for those on whose shoulders we stand today. Just as our prayers support those who are learning the lessons of dying here on this earth, so our prayers help those who continue to learn how to die after their physical death. John tells us that the Father will not lose anything of what he has given to the Son. He has given to the Son those he has claimed in baptism. God will not give up on us. God tries to teach us, the living, how to die in order to begin sharing the resurrection of his Son now. God continues to teach those who have passed through physical death how to die in such a way that they will live completely. This "school of God's love", known as Purgatory, has a definite and positive goal. When our beloved have completely died to all those things that hinder them from being completely one with God, then they share the fullness of Christ's resurrection and join the saints in glory.

69. Dedication of St. John Lateran

Readings

Ezekiel 47:1–2, 8–9, 12
1 Corinthians 3:9–11, 16–17
John 2:13–22

69.1 November 9, 2003

If you have ever had the good fortune of visiting Rome, you probably visited the Basilica of Saint John Lateran. One of the four major basilicas, it contains some striking features. The mosaics in the apse portray images from the two patrons of the church – John the Baptist preaching the need for repentance, and John the Evangelist offering streams of life giving water. It was built in the fourth century on land donated by the Laterani family. Pope Sylvester I dedicated it on this day in 324.

You might be asking yourself: why on earth does the Feast of the Dedication of a church thousands of miles from Granger replace the ordinary Sunday this year? Unfortunately, most of you have never been to Rome and probably will not get the chance. However, there are two reasons why this we celebrate this Feast – one particular to our parish, and the other particular to how we understand ourselves as Church.

One of the most remarkable features of the Lateran Church is its baptismal font. The enormous font reveals the engineering brilliance of the ancient Romans. Like our font, it allows for the full immersion of both adults and infants. Inscribed on the ceiling is a wonderful meditation on baptism written by Pope Saint Leo the Great, who was the Bishop of Rome (Pope) from 440 to 461. That same inscription is written (in Latin) on the floor around our baptismal font. If you have never paid attention to it, go to the font after Mass and read those words. If your Latin is not so good, there is an English translation posted on the wall. We use Leo's words as part of our preparation sessions for infant baptisms.

A second connection to Saint John Lateran appears on another inscription in Latin placed above the entrance to the church: mother and head of all the churches of Rome and the world. As the Cathedral Church of the Diocese of Rome, it contains the chair (cathedra in Greek) of the Bishop of Rome, who is the Pope, the successor of Saint Peter. This Feast is important for us in the church of Saint Pius X in Granger, because it celebrates the connection between our church (the Church of Fort Wayne - South Bend) and our bishop (John D'Arcy) with the Church of Rome, and its bishop (John Paul II). In recognizing the primacy of the Bishop of Rome, we celebrate his ministry to the entire Church and celebrate our identity as Roman Catholics.

Saint Paul puts all of this into proper perspective in his letter to the Corinthians. As important as sacred buildings may be, including the ancient temple of Jerusalem, the Church of Saint John Lateran in Rome, and the Church of Saint Pius X in Granger, their purpose is to serve the Church – God's holy people. The Church is composed of living stones – you and I, who are being formed into a human temple, built on the foundation of Jesus Christ. Jesus made it clear in today's Gospel that his body was the fullest dwelling of God, and that through the power of his death and resurrection, that real presence dwells in us today; living stones being formed into the structure of the Body of Christ.

Saint John Lateran in Rome stands where it does today, because a specific family who believed in the death and resurrection of Jesus Christ gave the land to the Church. The Church of Saint Pius X stands where it does today, because a number of families shared that same faith and celebrated their connection with the churches throughout the world through the Chair of Peter. Our celebration today is really about the church that exists in every one of the families of our parish. We call each of your homes a "domestic Church," and the vitality of the Church as a whole depends on the strength of your faith, as you continue to live it in your families. As you bring your children to this font to be joined to this structure, you continue a work in progress over many centuries. You are building what can never be destroyed – even by death!

70. Solemnity of Christ the King

Readings
Daniel 7:13–14
Revelation 1:5–8
John 18:33b–37

70.1 November 26, 2000

Our long human history has not often had positive experiences of kings and their kingdoms. Our American revolution began as a revolt against the English King George. More often than not, kings have put themselves and their own interests before the needs of their people. What we heard from the Book of Daniel is part of a vision outlining the suffering of the Israelite people at the hands of foreign conquering kings. At the time the Book of Revelation was written, the Emperor Dormitian had proclaimed himself as "our lord and god," killing those who refused to worship him. He banished the author of the Book of Revelation to the Island of Patmos in the Aegean Sea. Pontius Pilate was a backwater governor sent to protect the interests of Caesar. Neither truth nor justice prevailed when he heard the case of Jesus of Nazareth!

That is why it is so ironic that we end the Liturgical Year by speaking of Jesus Christ as "King." Unlike so many kings, presidents, or dictators, Jesus lived a simple life with no royal trappings. Instead of protecting his own comfort, he gave totally of himself in service. Unlike most monarchs who were crowned, enthroned, and then reigned until they died, Jesus established his reign at the moment he died. His crown was made of thorns, his throne became the cruel instrument of the cross, and his reign is eternal. Even though he waged outright war against sin and death, he never led an army. His victory continues to be shared by grateful sinners. And his kingdom has no physical boundaries. It exists wherever truth and justice, righteousness and peace triumph!

Throughout this past liturgical year, our scripture readings have presented aspects of that kingdom for our prayer and reflection. We have also been nourished at the Banquet of the Kingdom when we share the Lord's Body and Blood. By ending this liturgical year with this Feast of Christ the King, we are reminded of the truth that eluded Pilate when he condemned Jesus to death. History would have been different if Pilate had been less fearful; or if Peter would have been more honest; or if Judas had been more faithful; or if men and women down through the ages had made better choices. In the face of all the evil accumulated through human history, Jesus has won the victory over sin and death once and for all. The outcome of human history has already been decided in that victory.

That truth sustains us and guides us as we are confronted with difficult decisions and tough choices. That truth opens our hearts to God's mercy when we make bad choices and embrace the illusion of sin. The reign of Jesus is something we can attain in our daily lives, and it extends to God's Holy City when we die. The invitation is clear – to make choices consistent with those of the King!

70.2   November 23, 2003

We Americans have not been comfortable with kings and their kingdoms. History has taught us that too many kings were more concerned with their own comfort and welfare than with the common good of their people. Our nation began as a revolt against the taxation policies of King George of England. Even today, news about the royal family evokes a mixed reaction in us.

Given that history, what does it mean for us to honor Jesus as king? Unlike most kings, he did not live in comfortable settings. Instead, he lived simply and depended on the hospitality of others. Unlike most kings who ruled until their deaths, the Kingdom of Jesus was established with his death and resurrection. Unlike most kings who wore regal attire, Jesus wore a crown of thorns and was stripped of his garments.

Perhaps the most enduring quality of the kingship of Jesus Christ emerges in his exchange with Pontius Pilate in today's Gospel. While Pilate holds tightly to his own version of reality, Jesus calmly offers him the truth. Those Jewish leaders who bring Jesus to trial are not at all concerned about the rule of Pilate's boss, Caesar. The truth is that they were telling lies to get Jesus condemned. Pilate thinks that he exercises power over this Jewish peasant. The truth is that the man standing in front of him was present at the creation of the world. For a variety of reasons, Pilate chooses to ignore Jesus' invitation to belong to the truth. He washes his hands and walked away. Ironically, the world knows the name of this administrator in a backwater Roman province only because of his encounter with the King who gave his live in service of his people.

We live in a very similar world in which we are being pulled between one version of reality and the truth offered by Jesus, the King. On this last Sunday of the liturgical year, Jesus invites us to face the truth about ourselves and become part of his kingdom. He invites us to apply our Catholic principles to the public debates that are currently raging about what is true and best for our society. More than anything else, he invites us today to face the truth about ourselves.

A current novel (*The DaVinci Co*e, by Dan Brown) has become popular. Its plot is based on the premise that the bloodline of Jesus was carried on when he married Mary Magdalene and had children with her. The novel claims that a secretive group known as the Priory protected his royal bloodline. The enemy in the novel becomes the official Catholic Church, fearful that this secret would undermine our teaching. Of course, this novel is a work of pure fiction. But, that did not stop ABC from running a special program on it, as if there was any credibility to its premise. In truth, there is no secret to the royal bloodline of Jesus Christ, the King. You and I have been made part of that line through the waters of baptism, when we became priests, before Pontius Pilate. He invites us to change whatever strands in the way of being part of his Kingdom. He looks into the eyes of young people and invites you to take another look at those little lies you tell your parents, so that you can get your own way. He invites us to closely examine those illusions about ourselves that we love to project to others, even though we know they are not part of who we really are. He invites us to face those destructive patterns or habits of our lives that tend to erode the truth.

We do not belong to some secret organization that protects the blood descendants of Jesus of Nazareth. We belong to a very public Church in which Jesus, the King, feeds us with his own Body and Blood. Nourished by that real bloodline today, we must make our choice. Will we be like Pilate and hold tightly to what we want to believe and wash our hands of the King? Or will we accept his invitation and become more closely united with him in truth, and in his Kingdom?

70.3 November 26, 2006

Of all the thousands of governors and administrators who ran things for the Roman Empire during the 500 years they were the world's super power, only one name is remembered through the centuries. Pontius Pilate is mentioned in all 4 Gospels, and we mention his name every time we recite either the Apostles' Creed ("he suffered under Pontius Pilate") or the Nicene Creed ("he was crucified under Pontius Pilate"). We continue to mention the name of that Roman governor, not to blame him for the death of Christ, but to put the entire Christ event into a historical context.

Even though Pontius Pilate was a relatively unimportant government official who would never approach the status of the Caesars, he understood what it took to get ahead in Caesar's Kingdom. Getting ahead in Caesar's kingdom involved domination, privilege, power, and prestige. Living in that kingdom, he was curious about the qualities of this man accused of making himself a king. In saying that his kingdom does not belong to "this world," Jesus is not denouncing the created world given to us as a gift. Rather, Saint John constantly uses the term "this world" to describe those people who have rejected the light shining into the world and have preferred darkness, or the qualities needed to get ahead in Pilate's world. The kingdom of Jesus Christ involves love, justice, and service. Through Pilate's judgment, Jesus is about to offer the ultimate service – the sacrifice of his own life, for the sake of the Kingdom of God.

Throughout the Gospel of John, Jesus seldom uses the word "kingdom," as he does in the other three Gospels. Instead, he invites his followers to trust in the truth. In John's Gospel, the word for truth is a Semitic term that forms the basis of the Hebrew word, "Amen." It means to be reliable, constant, secure, permanent, and honest. In inviting us to give ourselves to the truth, he invites us to align ourselves with a Kingdom that is reliable, constant, secure, permanent, and honest. That is why we continue to use that Hebrew word, amen, to respond to the conclusion of the Eucharistic Prayer at every Mass and to respond to the Body and Blood of Christ when it is offered us. The Lord has given his own body and blood to secure a position in that Kingdom which cannot be ended by death, won by his death on Pilate's cross.

When we reflect on the differences between Pilate's kingdom and the Kingdom offered by Jesus Christ, we must be honest that we are more comfortable in the kingdom of Pontius Pilate. Like Pilate, we understand that getting ahead often means learning how to dominate the competition, whether that competition comes from classmates at school or fellow workers at the office. We too yearn for privilege, so that we can enjoy the comforts that come with positions. We understand how power works, and we find it difficult to resist the temptation to be prestigious whenever we get a chance. It is more difficult to understand love, justice, and service.

That is why we celebrate the Feast of Christ the King on the Final Sunday of the Liturgical Year. Christ, our King, invites us to be honest about all of those ties we have to Pilate's kingdom and to move a little more to the bonds of God's Kingdom. We do not have to reject all that is good about our world, including our families or the many bonds that bind us together. But, we must move closer to the values of the King betrayed by those who hated him and who appeared before a petty Roman governor for judgment. Next Sunday, we begin another liturgical year, when we again move through the Mysteries of the King who gave his life for us. We have a choice. We can choose Pilate's kingdom, which came to an end. Or, we can choose the Kingdom of the one who was crucified under Pontius Pilate – a Kingdom that continues in our midst and which never ends.

70.4 November 22, 2009

When Jesus stands before Pontius Pilate, Saint John clearly shows us the irony of the situation. Pilate is a Roman official assigned to one of the least desirable outposts of the empire. He sees himself as being in charge and presides over a trial of a Jewish peasant accused by his own people of being an insurgent against Roman rule. But he cannot see the truth. Jesus is the Incarnate Word of God, present at the creation of the world. He knows the truth about himself, about Pilate, and about the hearts of those who dragged him here. He knows that Pilate's judgment will be part of his Father's plan to reconcile the creatures he created and loves.

Jesus tells Pilate that his kingdom does not belong to this world. **This world** is not the world created by God and pronounced very good in Genesis. **This world** is not the one that God so loved that he sent his only Son to save, as John tells us in the Prologue of his Gospel. Rather, the world in which his kingdom does not belong is the world of Pontius Pilate. In Pilate's world, people work to dominate one another. In Pilate's world, governors like him do their best to attract the emperor's attention and get moved to a better position closer to Rome. In Pilate's world, privilege and prestige are very important. (I would suspect that Pilate always wanted to be a Monsignor!) In Pilate's world, power is the most important virtue, and he does not hesitate to use violent means of asserting his power and bolstering his control.

The world of Jesus' Kingdom is very different. In this Kingdom, importance is not measured by the best seats or fancy titles, but by sharing in the suffering of the One who came to give his life out of love. In this Kingdom, those who are the first put themselves last and give themselves in humble service. In this Kingdom, justice for the oppressed and healing for the poor are much more important than exercising power over someone else. In this Kingdom, children lead the way, and mercy abounds for all.

During this Liturgical Year, we have gathered as disciples to hear the words of Christ our King. Mostly through the Gospel of Mark, Jesus has been gradually helping us to understand the presence of this Kingdom and the qualities we need to be part of that Kingdom. On this last Sunday of this Liturgical Year, Christ the King challenges us to make a decision. Which Kingdom will we choose? Will we choose the world of Pilate – the world of domination, privilege, power, and prestige? Or will we choose the Kingdom of Christ the King – the world of love, justice, mercy, and service?

We live in the world created and loved by God. There are many good qualities about this world in which we live, and we can grow in true holiness in the midst of this world. But the world of Pontius Pilate is still very much with us. When we consumed by ambition, power, prestige, and titles, we can be just as blind as Pontius Pilate and not be able to see the truth standing right in front of us. Jesus Christ the King invites us to choose his world, which he loved so much that he redeemed it through his death and resurrection and introduced his Kingdom.

Both Pilate's world and our world will end, sooner or later. But the Kingdom of God will not end. For that reason, we will begin a new liturgical year next Sunday, and Jesus will teach us again about belonging to his Kingdom through the Gospel of Luke. As we begin again, we can learn an important lesson from Pilate. There were thousands of officials who governed during the time of the Roman Empire. We do not know any of their names. We know the name of Pontius Pilate, only because of his connection with Jesus Christ the King. When it is time for us to leave the kingdom of this world, the same will be true of us. The Father will recognize us, only through our connection with Jesus Christ, the King, and whether we chose to see his truth.

70.5 November 25, 2012

This passage from the Gospel of John gives us two very different visions of what a kingdom looks like. Pilate's Kingdom is one which we readily recognize. He relies on his power and domination, even though he senses that this man is completely innocent. He fears for his position if he does not give in to the wrath of those who want this man crucified. As a friend of Caesar's, he understands the value of privilege, and he yearns for the prestige of his office. Pilate is a second-rate governor in a second-rate province far from Rome, and he knows what he has to do to keep his position and further his career.

Jesus offers a very different understanding of what a kingdom looks like. Jesus is handed over to this governor by his own people. Throughout the course of this liturgical year, Saint Mark has told us stories of Jesus announcing the Kingdom of God. But, he has not imposed his Kingdom on anyone. During the course of this liturgical year, we have heard Mark's stories of Jesus manifesting the Father's love, establishing justice, and putting himself at the humble service of those who accepted his invitation to his Kingdom.

The Book of Revelation makes it very clear whose Kingdom will last. The kingdom of the Roman Empire has passed into history many centuries ago. We know the name of Pontius Pilate, only because he is the one who condemned Jesus to death. The Book of Revelation assures us that Christ's Kingdom will last forever. This passage from the Book of Revelation says that Jesus Christ loves us now. Unlike the goat sacrificed every year on the Day of Atonement, Jesus has suffered death on the cross and has atoned for our sins. He has reconciled us to the Father. The Book of Revelation assures us that this redemption has been accomplished for all time, and that this ultimate act of love has established a community that continues the priestly and kingly functions of Jesus Christ. At baptism, we were anointed as priests, prophets, and kings. We end this current Liturgical Year as the Lord wants us to end our lives: not in fear and trembling, but in hope and confidence in the love manifested by our King, Jesus Christ.

The Hebrew word "amen" comes from a Semitic word for truth, which means "reliable, faithful, constant, certain, permanent, and honest." Pilate could not recognize the truth spoken by this man crowned with thorns and rejected by his own people. He could not break through the constraints of his kingdom to recognize these values in the Kingdom of God. But the Book of Revelation recognizes these values and gives a hearty "amen" to the King recognized by everyone at the end of time. When we say "Amen" in this Liturgy, we attest to the constancy and faithfulness of the Kingdom of God.

In affirming the Kingdom of God at this Mass, we realize that we must continue to live and operate in this world, which is created and loved by God. We need to participate in the society in which we live, in this world given to us by God. But we also need to be aware that the kingdom claimed by Pontius Pilate is not the Kingdom proclaimed by Christ and the Book of Revelation. As citizens of this country and this world, we need to be aware of the pitfalls of Pilate's kingdom. When we are aware of these pitfalls, we avoid temptations to dominate, to use our power to control people, to embrace privilege as ways of rewarding ourselves, to regard prestige as a way of being recognized. We stand with Jesus Christ, crowned with thorns and accepting the cross, to recognize the Kingdom of God already firmly planted in our midst. That Kingdom has nothing to do with power, domination, privilege, or prestige. It has everything to do with love, justice, and humble service.

70.6   November 22, 2015

When Pilate asks Jesus if he is a king, he speaks from the perspective of his kingdom. In Pilate's kingdom, privilege, comfort, and prestige are very important. Pilate enjoys all of these perks, because he has been appointed by Caesar to exercise power and domination over the people under his thumb. If Jesus answers "yes," Pilate can have him executed, as a threat to Caesar. If Jesus answers "no," Pilate can let him go.

But the kingdom of Jesus is very different from that of Pilate. Jesus does not answer Pilate's question. Instead, he asks a question: "Do you say this on your own or have others told you about me?" When Pilate responds that he is not a Jew and that Jesus' own people have handed him over, he wants to know what Jesus has done. Jesus then explains to Pilate what Saint John had told us at the very beginning of the Gospel. Jesus has come into the world to testify to God's truth. God's truth establishes a kingdom marked by love, justice, and humble service; not dominion, privilege, power, or prestige.

Because Pilate is so immersed in the values of his kingdom, he cannot see the truth standing right before him. Instead, he sees a bloodied, beaten peasant. Even though Pilate knows the truth that this man is innocent, he will condemn him to a humiliating and painful death. From the comfort of his governor's palace, Pilate will move on to other matters of state in his kingdom. Pilate does not know that God will transform this dark death into the bright light of the resurrection, revealing the truth of God's incredible love.

Throughout this Liturgical Year, the Scripture readings have invited us to reflect on the truth of Jesus Christ. They have revealed him as the Way, the Truth, and the Light. On this final Sunday, the Book of Revelation reminds us that Jesus Christ loves us now. Saint John had originally written these words to Christians facing death and persecution by a kingdom which Pontius Pilate would recognize immediately. He has atoned for our sins by his death on the cross. He has redeemed us through the mystery of the resurrection.

That kingdom is still alive and well in our world. The recent scourge of terrorist attacks reminds us that there are still ruthless individuals who will use any means for power and domination. The fear generated by these violent acts can cloud our vision of the truth of the victory already won for us by Jesus Christ, our King. That same fear can also cause us to abandon our care and concern for vulnerable people who need our help. As we enter the "holiday season," the materialism of our culture can prevent us from seeing the truth about Jesus. Instead of focusing on the Lord's presence in our families gathered for Thanksgiving, we might be drawn instead to the good deals of Black Friday. Instead of recognizing the truth of seeing the Lord in the people we might serve, we can think only of our own comfort and security.

Next Sunday, we begin a new Liturgical Year and enter into the Season of Advent, to begin again our annual preparation to look for the ways in which our Lord comes to us in truth. Just as these years come and go, so will the kingdom of Pontius Pilate. His particular kingdom ended a long time ago, and the values of that kingdom will end for us also. Jesus Christ is the Alpha and the Omega, the beginning and the end of all existence. When we were baptized, we were incorporated into his Body as priests, prophets, and kings. Sharing the kingship of Jesus Christ, we can renew our efforts to see the truth standing right before our eyes. It is that truth which enables us to separate those things that pass away from those things that last. It is that truth which enables us to live in a dangerous and violent world without fear.

70.7 November 25, 2018

When Jesus rode on a donkey into Jerusalem on Palm Sunday, the crowds welcomed him with great joy, waved palm branches, laid their cloaks on the ground, and hailed him as king of Israel. In giving him that title, they expressed their belief that he was the Messiah promised to Israel. They had remembered the victories won by King David, when he defeated their enemies and established Jerusalem as the city of peace. In calling Jesus the king of Israel, they voiced their hopes that this son of David would save them from the Romans, the current foreign occupiers of the land given originally to Abraham.

A few days later, Jesus stands before the Roman governor, Pontius Pilate. Pilate does not ask him if he is king of Israel. Instead, he asks him if he is king of the Jews. He asks this question, because Jesus had threatened the religious authorities with his preaching, teaching, and miracles. So, they bring him to Pilate and accuse him of trying to become a king to challenge the authority of Caesar, and his puppet King Herod. Pilate has no understanding of the religious questions of the people he is oppressing in Caesar's name. All he cares about is keeping them from rebelling. Jesus becomes a threat, if he truly wants to be the king of the Jews.

Jesus does not answer Pilate's question. However, their conversation reveals that Jesus Christ and Pontius Pilate inhabit very different kingdoms. Pilate's kingdom revolves around power, prestige, and wealth. Pilate is interested in keeping this portion of the Roman Empire under Caesar's control. He is willing to use any means, including military force and execution, to maintain the status quo. He is even willing to ignore the truth that this Galilean peasant is innocent of the charges brought against him.

The kingdom of Jesus Christ revolves around love. He knows the truth that this governor stands before the Son of God who was present at the creation of the world. With true humility, he has emptied himself of the privileges of divinity and has spent the last three years revealing the truth about his nature. His mission is not to defeat the power of the Romans at that time in history, but to defeat the power of the evil one for all ages.

Because of his cowardice and fear, Pontius Pilate condemns Jesus to die a painful death on the cross. He mocks Jesus by placing above his cross the Latin words: Jesus of Nazareth, king of the Jews. Saint Catherine of Siena points out that as King, Jesus behaves like a true knight who perseveres in battle until his enemies are defeated. His breastplate is made of Mary's flesh that will bear the blows to make up for our wickedness. The helmet on his head becomes the painful crown of thorns, driven into his brain. The sword at his side will be the wound caused by the soldier's lance, revealing the incredible love that he has for us. The gloves on his hands and the spurs on his feet will be the scarlet wounds of his blood poured out for us.

Today is the last Sunday of this Liturgical Year. Throughout this year we have reflected on the incredible love that the Word made flesh expressed by his miracles, the truth that he preached with his mouth, and the compassion and mercy shown to the suffering. Now he will give himself totally out of love on the cross. From his wounded side will flow the water of baptism and the blood representing the Eucharist. Through baptism, we have become his Body, the Church. Raised from the dead, he has fed us with the Eucharist. Today, he stands before us and challenges us to make a choice. As we begin another Liturgical Year next Sunday, which kingdom will we choose? Will we choose the kingdom of Pontius Pilate and pursue privilege, wealth, power, and control? Or will we choose the kingdom of Jesus Christ to live our baptismal promises to die to ourselves and trust that we will rise with Christ when he comes again in glory?

VIII Index

Index

T

W

Made in the USA
Monee, IL
26 August 2020